DRUGS, SOCIETY, AND BEHAVIOR 91/92

Sixth Edition

Annual Editions

A Library of Information from the Public Press

Editor

Erich Goode
State University of New York at Stony Brook

Erich Goode received his undergraduate degree from Oberlin College and his Ph.D. in sociology from Columbia University. He is currently professor of sociology at the State University of New York at Stony Brook; he has also taught courses at Columbia, New York University, Florida Atlantic University, and the University of North Carolina, Chapel Hill. He is the author of a number of books, articles, and chapters on drug use and abuse, including *The Marijuana Smokers* (Basic Books, 1970), *The Drug Phenomenon* (Bobbs-Merrill, 1973), and *Drugs in American Society* (3rd edition, McGraw-Hill, 1989). Professor Goode has taught several courses on alcoholism and drug abuse.

Cover illustration by Mike Eagle

D1314399

The Dushkin Publishing Group, Inc.
Sluice Dock, Guilford, Connecticut 06437

The Annual Editions Series

Annual Editions is a series of over fifty volumes designed to provide the reader with convenient, low-cost access to a wide range of current, carefully selected articles from some of the most important magazines, newspapers, and journals published today. Annual Editions are updated on an annual basis through a continuous monitoring of over 200 periodical sources. All Annual Editions have a number of features designed to make them particularly useful, including topic guides, annotated tables of contents, unit overviews, and indexes. For the teacher using Annual Editions in the classroom, an Instructor's Resource Guide with test questions is available for each volume.

VOLUMES AVAILABLE

Africa
Aging
American Government
American History, Pre-Civil War
American History, Post-Civil War
Anthropology
Biology
Business and Management
Business Ethics
Canadian Politics
China
Comparative Politics
Computers in Education
Computers in Business
Computers in Society
Criminal Justice
Drugs, Society, and Behavior
Early Childhood Education
Economics
Educating Exceptional Children
Education
Educational Psychology
Environment
Geography
Global Issues
Health
Human Development
Human Resources
Human Sexuality

Latin America
Macroeconomics
Management
Marketing
Marriage and Family
Microeconomics
Middle East and the Islamic World
Money and Banking
Nutrition
Personal Growth and Behavior
Psychology
Public Administration
Race and Ethnic Relations
Social Problems
Sociology
Soviet Union and Eastern Europe
State and Local Government
Third World
Urban Society
Violence and Terrorism
Western Civilization,
   Pre-Reformation
Western Civilization,
   Post-Reformation
Western Europe
World History, Pre-Modern
World History, Modern
World Politics

Library of Congress Cataloging in Publication Data
Main entry under title: Annual Editions: Drugs, Society, and Behavior. 1991/92.
   1. Drugs—Addresses, essays, lectures—Periodicals. 2. Drug abuse—United States—Addresses, essays, lectures—Periodicals. 3. Alcohol—Addresses, essays, lectures—Periodicals. 4. Drunk driving—Addresses, essays, lectures—Periodicals. I. Goode, Erich, comp. II. Title: Drugs, Society, and Behavior.
ISBN 1–56134–017–0   362.2′92′0973′05

Sixth Edition

Manufactured by The Banta Company, Harrisonburg, Virginia 22801

Editors/Advisory Board

To The Reader

In publishing ANNUAL EDITIONS we recognize the enormous role played by the magazines, newspapers, and journals of the *public press* in providing current, first-rate educational information in a broad spectrum of interest areas. Within the articles, the best scientists, practitioners, researchers, and commentators draw issues into new perspective as accepted theories and viewpoints are called into account by new events, recent discoveries change old facts, and fresh debate breaks out over important controversies.

Many of the articles resulting from this enormous editorial effort are appropriate for students, researchers, and professionals seeking accurate, current material to help bridge the gap between principles and theories and the real world. These articles, however, become more useful for study when those of lasting value are carefully *collected, organized, indexed,* and *reproduced* in a *low-cost format*, which provides easy and permanent access when the material is needed. That is the role played by *Annual Editions.* Under the direction of each volume's *Editor,* who is an expert in the subject area, and with the guidance of an *Advisory Board,* we seek each year to provide in each *ANNUAL EDITION* a current, well-balanced, carefully selected collection of the best of the public press for your study and enjoyment. We think you'll find this volume useful, and we hope you'll take a moment to let us know what you think.

Interest in and concern about drug use is cyclical. In some decades, there is relatively little concern about the issue; people rarely talk about drugs, few articles are written about their use in newspapers and magazines, and hardly anyone considers drug abuse the most important social problem facing the country. In other decades, drug use emerges as a central social issue; it provides a major topic of conversation, the newspapers and magazines are filled with news and commentary on the subject, and a substantial proportion of the population regards drug abuse the number one problem the country faces.

In the mid-1980s, public concern over drug abuse fairly exploded, and it has remained high—with some competition from the Mideast crisis—to this day. Our society is saturated with this public concern. In some quarters, this concern is so intense it is fair to refer to it as a kind of hysteria or panic. Is this panic justified? Are drugs as central a problem as much of the public believes? What are drugs in the first place? What short-term effects do they have? How do they affect the individual and the society over the long run? How should we deal with drugs and drug abuse? The articles included in *Annual Editions: Drugs, Society, and Behavior 91/92* represent a sampling of current thinking on the subject of drug use. The selections are intended to be thought-provoking and informative. I hope that reading them will help the student meet the challenge that drug use poses and permit him or her to reach reasonable, well-informed conclusions on this troubling issue.

Unit 1 is designed to provide the student with a general framework toward drugs; it makes four basic points. First, our society tolerates certain (legal) drugs, and is concerned about users of other (that is, illegal) drugs. Second, drug use has a long history, both around the world generally and in this society specifically. Third, illegal drug use generates a worldwide structure or network of sellers that makes use extremely difficult to eradicate, but it is the consumer, ultimately, on which this enterprise is based. And fourth, all drug use is a sociological or anthropological phenomenon that has to be understood before the problem can be attacked. Unit 2 emphasizes the fact that drug use and abuse—or physical dependence—form a continuum or spectrum. Too often, many of us assume that if someone is a user of a given (usually illegal) drug, he or she is chemically dependent, indeed, high nearly all the time. Unit 2 shows that users come in all degrees of involvement, from experimenters to heavy, chronic, dependent abusers. Unit 3 explores a variety of explanations for drug use: Why do people use and abuse drugs? Why do *some* people use certain drugs—while the rest of us do not? In short, *why drugs*? Unit 4 demonstrates that drug use is highly patterned and variable over time and according to social characteristics. Who uses? Who does not? What are some basic recent *trends* in drug use?

Unit 5 emphasizes the fact that drugs are not unitary phenomena, but can be classified according to type. Too often we refer to drugs—illegal drugs, that is—in a generic fashion, as if they all had identical or extremely similar effects. This is false; in fact, certain drugs do certain things to us, others do very different things. Unit 6 looks at the impact of drugs on the society over the long run. Unit 7 focuses on an extremely crucial aspect of drug use: buying and selling. Drug consumption is an economic enterprise, and that fact influences many features of the drug scene. Why? How? In what specific ways? Unit 8 looks at how our society is attacking the problem of drug abuse, what is wrong with what we are doing, and what should be done about it? Is legalization a viable option? Several observers support this option, while others do not. And finally, Unit 9 deals with how drug abusers, and the people they hurt, can be treated, and what educational programs are effective in convincing young people to avoid becoming involved in the first place.

Erich Goode
Editor

Contents

Unit 1

Thinking About Drugs

Seven articles in this section examine how drugs are defined today. The history of drugs in our culture is also discussed.

The concepts in bold italics are developed in the article. For further expansion please refer to the Topic Guide, the Index, and the Glossary.

Unit 2

Use, Addiction, and Dependence

Eight selections in this section discuss what is meant by drug addiction. Topics examined include physical dependency and drugs such as crack, alcohol, and nicotine.

The concepts in bold italics are developed in the article. For further expansion please refer to the Topic Guide, the Index, and the Glossary.

Unit 3

Why Drugs?

Six articles in this section discuss how and why individuals get "hooked" on drugs.

Unit 4

Patterns and Trends in Drug Use

Five articles in this section discuss the divergent patterns in the use of drugs as they lose and gain popularity.

The concepts in bold italics are developed in the article. For further expansion please refer to the Topic Guide, the Index, and the Glossary.

Unit 5

The Major Drugs of Use and Abuse

Eight articles in this section examine some of the major drugs in use today. The drugs discussed include cocaine, crack, methamphetamine (speed, crank, or "ice"), MDMA or "ecstasy," marijuana, prescription drugs, alcohol, and heroin.

The concepts in bold italics are developed in the article. For further expansion please refer to the Topic Guide, the Index, and the Glossary.

Unit 6

The Impact of Drug Use on Society

Five selections in this section discuss how drugs have devastated some portions of our society.

Unit 7

The Economy of Drug Use

Five selections in this section discuss the enormous driving economic force behind the marketing of both legal and illegal drugs.

The concepts in bold italics are developed in the article. For further expansion please refer to the Topic Guide, the Index, and the Glossary.

Unit 8

Fighting the Drug War

Five articles in this section examine the current state of the war on drug usage. Topics include today's drug scene, new programs to combat drugs, and drug legalization.

The concepts in bold italics are developed in the article. For further expansion please refer to the Topic Guide, the Index, and the Glossary.

Unit 9

Drug Prevention and Treatment

Six selections in this section discuss drug dependence and treatment. Topics covered include educational programs, live-in therapeutic communities, and integrating former drug abusers back into the community.

The concepts in bold italics are developed in the article. For further expansion please refer to the Topic Guide, the Index, and the Glossary.

Topic Guide

This topic guide suggests how the selections in this book relate to topics of traditional concern to students and professionals involved with the study of drugs, society, and behavior. It can be very useful in locating articles which relate to each other for reading and research. The guide is arranged alphabetically according to topic. Articles may, of course, treat topics that do not appear in the topic guide. In turn, entries in the topic guide do not necessarily constitute a comprehensive listing of all the contents of each selection.

Thinking About Drugs

Everything that exists can be looked at or thought about in a variety of ways, through the lens of different perspectives. Although each perspective tells us something different about what we are looking at, some are more relevant and insightful than others. The phenomena of drug use and abuse follow this rule. Some perspectives toward drugs tell us a great deal about their reality; others tell us little beyond the biases of the observers using them.

How should we think about drug use? What perspectives tell us about the reality of drugs? The first thing we should know about drugs is that they encompass an extremely wide range of substances. Ask the man and woman in the street what "drugs" are and, in all likelihood, most of the answers you get will include illegal substances—crack, cocaine, heroin, perhaps LSD, marijuana, and PCP or "angel dust." Answers you will be less likely to receive will be the legal drugs—alcohol, tobacco, our morning cup of coffee, prescription drugs, and routinely available over-the-counter (OTC) medications, such as aspirin. But in at least two respects, legal substances such as alcohol, Valium, and aspirin are drugs in the same way as illegal substance such as LSD, heroin, and crack are: First, all but the OTC drugs are *psychoactive*, that is, mind-active; they influence the workings of the human mind—how we think, feel, and even act; and even the over-the-counter drugs are active in some other way—at the very least, they influence the workings of the human body. A second parallel is that both legal and illegal drugs are often overused, misused, and abused, thereby causing a great deal of damage to human life and to society generally. In fact, legal drugs—cigarettes and alcohol specifically—kill 20 to 30 times as many people as illegal drugs. Clearly, the distinction between legal and illegal drugs is an artificial, humanly-created one, not extremely crucial in most respects to the student of drug use. "Drugs 'R' Us" emphasizes the fuzziness of the line between legal and illegal drugs and the damage that the use and abuse of legal drugs cause to our society.

The second lesson any meaningful approach imparts to us is that there is a great deal of widely disseminated misinformation about drug use; much of what most of the public believes about the subject is wrong. We tend to exaggerate the dangers of illegal drug use and minimize the dangers of legal drug use. In "Getting Real About Getting High," physician and author Andrew Weil argues that drugs per se are not the problem—it is the way in which they are used. Drugs should be taken responsibly, in their natural forms, in moderation, for the purpose of conscious expansion. Regardless of whether or not you agree with this thesis, it is provocative and controversial.

The third important conclusion we have to draw from a careful look at the phenomenon is that drug use and abuse are not confined to the twentieth century. Drug abuse is an ancient problem; humans have been ingesting psychoactive substances since the Stone Age—and possibly longer—over 10,000 or 12,000 years ago, when alcohol was first discovered. In the United States, alcohol was consumed in vastly greater quantities in the late 1700s and early 1800s than it is today, and in the second half of the nineteenth century, addiction to narcotics, such as morphine and opium, was far more common, on a per-population basis, than heroin addiction is today. Problems associated with drug abuse and abuse have always, and, in all likelihood, will always, be with us. "Grandma Was a Junkie" provides a detailed discussion of late nineteenth century and early twentieth century drug use—quite a different picture most of us carry around in our heads. "Illicit Price of Cocaine in Two Eras: 1908–14 and 1982–89" emphasizes the long history of drug use and abuse this country has experienced. And, "Cycles of Craving" stresses the up-and-down, fad-and-fashion cycles different drugs undergo at different times.

The fourth lesson we learn from looking at drugs is that illegal drug use generates an immense network of social relations that exert a powerful influence worldwide. The base on which this network rests is the purchase and use of illegal substances by the consumer. The drug problem will not go away until people stop using drugs; it is futile to denounce drug dealers when the demand—and the profits—are so huge. "Drugs: The World Picture" discusses the size, appeal, and the impact of the global drug trade.

The fifth lesson any meaningful approach imparts to us is that drug use is a sociological, psychological, and even anthropological phenomenon; that is, it is generated and sustained by the people interacting in a specific setting and their customs and social networks. While drug use may be universal, or nearly so, the specific qualities it

possesses in a particular community or society are dependent on the characteristics of the users themselves, that community, and that society. Too often, drug use and abuse are looked upon as a simple pathology—a sickness—in need of removal. Given this limited perspective, we will never be able to understand what sustains them, what they grow from. When we begin asking who uses drugs and in what social situations and contexts, we begin to understand why they are so difficult to eradicate and what part they play to users and abusers. In "Interview With James Schaefer," this sociological and anthropological side of the use of one drug, alcohol, is stressed.

Looking Ahead: Challenge Questions

What is a drug? How are psychoactive drugs different from drugs that only influence the workings of the human body? From the point of view of a drug's effects, is it meaningful to distinguish between legal and illegal drugs? Why are certain legal psychoactive substances not widely regarded as drugs?

Why is a study of drug use and law enforcement in the past important? Does it tell us something important about the current drug scene? Why have the lessons of history been lost on the present generation?

How would you go about studying drug use? What issues and questions are important to you?

Why do drugs, drug use, and drug sales make such a powerful impact on our society?

Is it possible to use drugs reasonably and sensibly, in moderation, as Dr. Weil suggests?

DRUGS 'R' US

Daniel Lazare

Judging from what one hears in Washington these days, there are two theories as to why people use drugs. One is the Republican theory, advanced most vehemently by drug czar William Bennett, that people indulge in heroin, cocaine and the like because law and order has broken down, and families, churches and schools are disintegrating. The other is the Democratic theory, which holds that people do drugs because they're poor, downtrodden and longing for escape. "Up with hope, down with dope," says Jesse Jackson, appearing to imply that once social conditions are ameliorated, the drug problem will vanish like a puff of smoke.

But rarely are things so simple. While racism and poverty help explain why some Americans resort to ultra-potent substances like crack, they're hardly the whole story. Throughout history people have resorted to various mind-altering substances, from beer to peyote, for reasons that are as varied as human experience itself. They've taken drugs to get closer to God or to heighten their experiences here on Earth; to sharpen their senses or anesthetize their brains; to blend in with the crowd or to distinguish themselves from the pack.

During the '20s, middle-class kids drank bathtub gin to show their contempt for the repressive, puritanical America of Calvin Coolidge. Forty years later, they demonstrated revulsion for American consumerism by turning their nose up at booze and puffing away happily on pot. In the '70s, yuppies snorted coke because it seemed to go with the quickening pace on Wall Street, while, more recently, aspiring arbitrageurs have downed gallons of black coffee in imitation of caffeine-junkie Ivan Boesky.

Thus, the question of intoxication turns out to be as complex as sex, death, money or other fundamental aspects of the human condition. One generation's meat quite frequently turns out to be another's poison. The only constant is that most people do something to alter their conscious state. While Mormons eschew all mind-altering substances right down to coffee, tea and chocolate, they and people like them are a distinct minority.

What's your drug? In fact, all of us may be hooked in one way or another, teetotalers included, whether we know it or not. Since the '70s, medical researchers have zeroed in on a group of internally generated mood-control agents known as endogenous morphines, or endorphins, that are believed to play a key role in determining whether we're anxious or relaxed, unable to concentrate or immersed in thought.

Ironically, endorphins are chemically related to forbidden exogenous opiates such as opium, morphine and heroin, and produce a similar psychological state—a sense of bliss, floating and transcendence of ego.

For centuries, people who have spoken of "losing" themselves in their work, of shutting out the world while they concentrate on an intellectual problem, may actually have describing a heightened mental state brought on by an internally generated drug. They may not be so much devoted to their profession as devoted to a chemical high that scientists now believe may be brought on by hard work or vigorous physical exercise.

Committed joggers, of course, are so devoted to their daily "runner's high" that many injure themselves through over-training. When ordered by a doctor to stop, they may often display such classic symptoms of withdrawal as irritability, nervousness and loss of concentration.

When doctors speak of being addicted to their work, according to *Messengers of Paradise: Opiates and the Brain,* an interesting new book by Charles F. Levinthal, they may mean it quite literally. One surgeon interviewed as part of a 1975 study said operating was "like taking narcotics." Another compared it to heroin. A third confessed that he never felt under more stress than when he was vacationing with his family in the Bahamas. A fourth said he was so nervous after two days of sight-seeing in Mexico—the first vacation for him and his wife in years—that he volunteered his services to a local hospital and spent the rest of his vacation in surgery.

Surgeons are not the only ones who describe work in such terms. A world-class chess master quoted by Levinthal said that whenever he sits down to a game, "Time passes a hundred times faster . . . it resembles a dream state. A whole story can unfold in seconds, it seems." In his 1934 novel, *The Search,* C. P. Snow described the ecstasy of scientific discovery in terms bordering on the hallucinatory: "It was as though I had looked for a truth outside myself, and finding it had become for a moment a part of the truth I sought; as though all the world, the atoms and the stars, were wonderfully clear and close to me, and I to them. . . ." This may have been literary hyperbole—or an accurate description of a scientist who has made the breakthrough of a lifetime and is soaring on opiates as a result.

Whatever their political or moral value, hard work and self-discipline may also be routes to self-medication. Similarly, those dependent on outside sources to satisfy their

From *In These Times,* October 18-24, 1989, pp. 12-13. Reprinted by permission of *In These Times,* a weekly newspaper based in Chicago.

opiate craving may never have learned to generate their own. Conventional solutions to the "problem" of addiction frequently make it worse. By throwing exogenous-opiate junkies in jail or depriving them of employment—one goal of militant organizations like Partnership for a Drug-Free America—they likely will remain locked in their exogenous addiction and will never be able to produce their own drugs in ways that society deems legitimate.

Alcohol—the legal high: If opiates, internal or external, are the most common mind-altering substances, then alcohol is a close second. We celebrate anniversaries with champagne, the end of the work day with beer and a good meal with wine. In 1954, the French government estimated that a third of the electorate derived all or part of its income from the production or sale of alcoholic beverages, while in Italy a few years later an estimated 10 percent of arable land was said to be given over to viticulture.

According to archaeologists, beer-making is as old as agriculture; in neolithic times, it was probably the only method of preserving the nutritive value of grain. Since then, alcohol has been brewed from just about every conceivable fruit or vegetable—mead from honey, sake from rice, wine from palm, mezcal and Central American pulque from agave and cactus. North American Indians even made a liquor from maple syrup, while South American Indians made one from various jungle fruits.

According to the Book of Genesis, grape wine was discovered by Noah, who promptly got drunk and threw off all his clothes, presumably in celebration. Approximately 1,000 years later, the Book of Proverbs advised: "Give strong drink to him who is perishing, and wine to those in bitter distress; let them drink and forget their poverty, and remember their misery no more"—a reminder that seeking escape from oppressive social conditions through intoxication is not necessarily a cardinal sin.

Why is alcohol so popular? For one thing, users have learned to savor the taste of beer, wine, cognac, eau de vie and so on that goes with inebriation. For another, it is a source of nutrients, goes well with food and, as a common agricultural byproduct, is all but unavoidable in a wide range of cultures. It is also a highly sociable drug that a vast range of societies have used to bring people together to laugh, talk, sing, dance and worship (e.g. the Passover seder, in which inebriation is a *mitzvah* or commandment).

Finally, alcohol has the advantage of being highly modulatory. Whether at a party or dinner, experienced users know how much to drink in order to attain an appropriate level of intoxication. They may happily gulp down one and another, but then wait until their mind has settled a bit before venturing on to a third. At a business gathering, they may decide not to drink at all.

Of course, alcohol has its dark side—18 million problem drinkers in the U.S. alone, 23,000 alcohol-related traffic deaths per year, tens of thousands of work-related injuries— but it also has benefits that are frequently overlooked. While everyone knows of marriages destroyed by alcohol, how about the marriages it helps save? Who speaks up for the worker who, after a hard day, fortifies him or herself with a drink or two before facing up to the rigors at home?

Whereas feudal peasants worked to exhaustion and then, on feast days, drank to collapse, industrial man uses alcohol in smaller amounts to fine-tune the means of production— himself. After working eight hours, he uses it as a reward and relaxant. Would the same worker be more productive if he didn't settle himself down with a beer, but instead fidgeted nervously in front of the TV or yelled at the kids? Perhaps. But considering that periods of peak economic growth have sometimes coincided with periods of peak alcohol consumption (e.g. the U.S. in the '50s), the answer, very possibly, is that productivity would not be enhanced.

By the same token, despite a pronounced shift since the '70s from hard liquor to white wine, low-alcohol beer and the ubiquitous Perrier-with-a-twist, industrial productivity has been stagnant. Americans are drinking less, but not working better as a result.

Dying for a smoke: Then there is nicotine, a mood-control agent whose popularity worldwide is only slightly less than that of alcohol. Beginning in 1493, when Columbus returned from the New World with an interesting new plant called tobacco, nicotine's progress has, until recent years, been unchecked. Users were executed in 17th-Century Russia, while Bavaria, Saxony and Zurich decreed bans. Whenever Sultan Murad IV traveled around the Ottoman Empire during this period, he delighted in executing his subjects for the heinous offense of lighting up. "Even on the battlefield . . . he would punish them by beheading, hanging, quartering or crushing their hands or feet," according to one account.

Nevertheless, the popular will has prevailed. When the director general of New Amsterdam tried to impose a smoking ban in 1639, virtually the entire male population camped outside his office in protest. While fond of wine, Thomas Jefferson inveighed against tobacco (which he called "productive of infinite wretchedness"), yet after the revolution it emerged as a major cash crop.

Besides being useful as a fumigant, nicotine has a mild calming effect that can be used to promote sociability, which is why it quickly became a fixture in coffee houses and taverns. Rip Van Winkle, everybody's favorite peaceful layabout, was, according to his creator, Washington Irving, never to be seen without his hunting rifle, his dog and his pipe. Gen. Douglas MacArthur smoked a corncob pipe, a homely touch that was immediately picked up by the press, while college men in the '50s favored briars because it gave them the firm-jawed look appropriate to the American Century.

Since then, however, nicotine in general, and cigarettes in particular, have been under sustained assault. Smokers nowadays are segregated in restaurants, barred from lighting up on airplanes, shunned by co-workers and harassed by friends. Yuppies pollute the air with their BMWs, but nonetheless are aghast at the thought of soiling their lungs with so much as a whiff of someone else's "sidestream" smoke. Yet, in a certain roundabout sense, we owe a debt of

For centuries, people who have spoken of losing themselves in their work or shutting out the world may have been describing an elevated state brought on by an internally generated drug.

gratitude to nicotine for helping to show how to run a proper anti-drug campaign. Smokers are encouraged by an array of government subsidies, but millions of nicotine addicts have been persuaded to quit through means that stop somewhat short of driving them into the arms of Uzi-toting drug dealers.

Rather than driving users underground, the anti-smoking forces have mounted a nonstop propaganda campaign that has proved devastatingly effective simply because it is true. Outside the tobacco lobby, few people doubt that cigarettes cause lung cancer and are a prime contributor to heart and respiratory diseases causing hundreds of thousands of deaths in the U.S. each year. The credible campaign appeals to people's self-interest, rather than bludgeoning them into obedience.

Meanwhile, amid all the hysteria over crack, no one seems to notice the growing amount of tobacco advertising pitched directly at the inner-urban market. Faced with declining sales, cigarette manufacturers have tried to recoup by appealing to blacks and Hispanics, a strategy as devastating in terms of health and mortality as the efforts of the Medellin and Cali cartels. Yet, if affluence and education rise, it seems reasonable to presume that nicotine addiction will decline in these areas as well.

Reefer madness: On the other hand, probably no drug has been the subject of more lies than marijuana. The 1936 propaganda film *Reefer Madness* is valuable both as a camp classic and a window onto the obsessions of a middle-class society then terrified of sex, jazz and "letting go." Although American society seemed to be coming to its senses in the '70s, when marijuana came within a hair's breadth of decriminalization, it has since beaten a hasty retreat behind a curtain of disinformation and lies.

Due to the war on drugs, marijuana is back as an official "gateway" drug leading inexorably, according to official dogma, to cocaine, heroin and a lifetime of addiction. Yet millions of students have used marijuana since the '60s with no noticeable ill-effect. Millions of adults with kids, jobs and mortgages relax occasionally with a joint without winding up in the gutter. But simple facts like these mean little to a Republican-Democratic establishment hopelessly hooked on rhetoric and revenge.

The curious thing about marijuana, though, is that just as its evils have been vastly inflated by the government, its virtues have probably been exaggerated by supporters as well. In Holland, where marijuana is decriminalized, surveys indicate that a smaller percentage of people smoke than in the U.S. In India and the Caribbean, where marijuana is

ubiquitous, those with the economic means prefer booze. Steve Hagar, editor of *High Times* magazine, the pot-smoker's bible, tells of an American traveler who, when offered palm wine in an African village, asked for some potent local herb instead. The villagers were puzzled: why would anyone prefer something as lowly as marijuana to a delicacy like palm wine?

Why indeed? If drug prohibition were lifted, marijuana would undoubtedly find a niche in American society, but probably not much more. Laborers, taxi drivers and construction workers might find it useful in relieving boredom, but others might find that its hypnotic quality makes them feel groggy. Some might prefer it on weekends, while others might find that its effects are not very sociable. It makes many people quiet and withdrawn, which is why the noise level at a party usually drops whenever joints begin circulating. People opposed to noisy parties on principle might appreciate marijuana for precisely that reason. But judging from the experience in Holland, where marijuana is neither stigmatized by the government nor glamorized by the underground, a majority, arguably, would not.

Just say yes: Given the multiplicity of drugs and uses, what is one to make of a slogan like "Just Say No," endorsed by nearly the entire political spectrum, from Jesse Jackson to Jesse Helms? What's most apparent about the slogan is its arbitrariness. It does not ask Americans to forgo all mind-altering substances, obviously, since drugs like caffeine, nicotine or highly addictive Valium are still freely available.

It does not ask them to steer clear of only the most dangerous since, in terms of sheer bodies, alcohol and nicotine kill approximately 150 Americans for every one who succumbs to the effects of heroin, coke or other prohibited substances. (According to the National Council on Alcoholism, alcohol and tobacco were implicated in more than half a million deaths in 1985, while illicit substances were found to be factors in only 3,562.) Banning one without the other is like banning deer rifles while permitting sales of automatic weapons to go forward unimpeded.

Rather, the purpose of the "Just Say No" campaign is to shore up political authority. Using the circular logic favored by authoritarian governments, the campaign asks Americans to forgo those substances that have been prohibited not for reasons of health but for reasons of custom and politics. It urges them to just say no for no other reason than that their leaders have just said no.

The results may be unreasonable, but that's exactly the point. Right-wing authoritarianism is, in the final analysis, irrationality by decree. Those on top seek to limit debate not because it's disruptive but because it may lead to something more intelligent and democratic, and thereby upset their rule. Similarly, if drug czar William Bennett succeeds in enforcing unthinking drug obedience, he and other conservative hardliners no doubt will try to achieve it in other areas as well, such as abortion rights, collective bargaining, race relations and foreign policy.

The goal is mass cerebral anesthetization, more complete than that achieved by any drug.

GETTING REAL ABOUT GETTING HIGH

An Interview with Andrew Weil, M.D.

BY RICHARD GOLDSTEIN

The current war on drugs is taking its toll on knowledge about drugs. There has been no debate about the assumptions that underlie our laws, or about the reasons so many people—young and old, rich and poor—choose to break them. If anything, the antidrug crusade has had, as its aim, the elimination of discussion and dissent.

In 1983, Andrew Weil, a drug researcher, and Winifred Rosen, a writer of books for young people, published *Chocolate to Morphine: Understanding Mind-Active Drugs* (Houghton Mifflin). It is a remarkably revealing book, even for adults; but its language and contention that "drugs are here to stay" are clearly aimed at teenagers. Teaching adolescents who want to use drugs how to do so with the least damage to self and society is controversial in liberal times, but in the current climate, that idea seems, to some, impermissible.

Paula Hawkins (Republican, Florida), who faces a tough battle for her Senate seat, recently read selections from Weil's book into the Congressional Record. "With drug abuse running rampant," she proclaimed, "we may well ask ourselves why it is that our children are being exposed to such garbage. . . . I would recommend that all curricula be redirected to teach our children to say no to drugs. No more teaching about responsible use." As a result of Hawkins's objections, the Tampa school board voted to remove *From Chocolate to Morphine* from school library shelves. Does the senator support that decision? "Her statement speaks to the point," an aide replied—and declined to say more.

Andrew Weil is a lecturer at the University of Arizona College of Medicine. He has written several books on drugs and consciousness, including *The Natural Mind* (Houghton Mifflin). "The truth about drugs cannot do harm," Weil writes. "It may offend sensibilities and disturb those who do not want to hear it, but it cannot hurt people. On the other hand, false information can and does lead people to hurt themselves and others. . . . People make decisions on the basis of the information available to them. The more accurate the information, the better their decisions will be."

What's going on now?

Well, I think there's a politically motivated drug panic which is more severe than anything I've seen in the 20 years I've been involved in this issue. Some of it is because the elections are approaching. Some of it is to divert people's attention from issues that are more serious. Some of it is generated by the news media, which have learned that fearmongering sells programs and papers.

But the media are always titillating, and there are always serious problems that people are trying to hide. Why didn't this happen 10 years ago?

It *was* happening 10 years ago, but not in as extreme a form. I think it is the same stuff that's gone on for most of the century. There was an anti-opium paranoia in this culture 80 years ago, a lot of it motivated by racial prejudice against the Chinese. There was an anticocaine hysteria around the time of the First World War, which was motivated by racial prejudice against blacks. There was marijuana stuff going on in the '20s and '30s, and all the '60s stuff around psychedelics, which produced tremendous polarization of society. Whenever a new intoxicant comes into a culture, it invokes this kind of response. Usually, the people who take up a new intoxicant are going to be the deviants—the subcultures and ethnic minorities and outsiders; they're perceived with suspicion already and their drug use is colored by that. There was an antitobacco hysteria in Europe and Asia in the 16th and 17th centuries, when some countries tried to prohibit its use by the death penalty. That didn't work; in fact, if anything, it hastened the spread of it.

Are drugs more prevalent in America today?

Well, no, I think we've always been a drug-ridden society. There probably were as many psychoactive drugs in use 100 years ago. But there was no crime associated with drugs. There was no use of these things by very young children. There was no use of them to drop out of society or act out anger or aggression against authority. I think all of those features of the drug problem are creations of our policies. The more we create stiffer penalities and so forth, the more we produce the very thing we want to change. As I say, the policies that we've followed have created the phenomena that we're afraid of. The reason we have kids using crack today is because of the approach we've taken in trying to deal with this through criminal law. It has made drugs attractive and it has made worse forms of drugs come into existence.

Do you anticipate that the result of this hysteria will be that drugs become more prevalent?

Yeah, I think that they will continue to be prevalent and to be used in worse and worse ways. By more and more people. Wars on drugs never work. The end result of them is to stimulate interest and curiosity on the part of people who other-

From *The Village Voice*, September 30, 1986, pp. 21-22, 24. Reprinted by permission of the author and *The Village Voice*.

wise wouldn't be interested in them. It also, I think, encourages the drug taking in negative ways: To act out anger and resentment against authority. Especially when information is presented in a hypocritical manner as this society is now doing. In other words, we have this bill called the Drug Free America Act, but there's no intention to include alcohol and tobacco. The government continues to subsidize tobacco addiction, and cigarettes are the worst form of drug abuse in this culture, the greatest public health problem that we have, and the most flagrant example of drug pushing, since most of it is pushed on teenagers, who are lured by advertising into thinking it's cool to smoke. If you want to talk about death penalties for drug pushers start with the executives of tobacco companies.

But the argument against illegal drugs is that they produce violent, antisocial behavior.

Look, maybe there's, at the outside, something like 300 deaths from crack a year. That's not good, but how many deaths are there from cigarettes a year? Something like 300,000. How many instances are there where somebody on crack has committed an act of violence? I don't know. But compared to the number of acts of violence committed under the influence of alcohol, it's insignificant.

Are you suggesting that consumption of alcohol is more dangerous than consumption of crack?

In terms of its pharmacological power, the behavior it produces, and the numbers of people involved in its use.

Would that be true of angel dust?

It's true of all of them. I think there is no illegal drug that comes near alcohol in dangerousness. All you have to do is ask law enforcement agencies about the association of alcohol and violent crime.

What is the pharmacology of crack? How dangerous is it?

I think its dangers are exaggerated. I don't think it's a good drug; I don't think it's wise to smoke cocaine, first of all. If you want to explore its effects, you should chew coca leaves; I think that's a safe way to do it. It's not good to take cocaine out of coca leaves and it's especially not good to put it into your brain by smoking.

Why is it relatively safe to take coca leaves?

Because the content of cocaine is very low, so you're taking it in a highly dilute form, combined with other substances that moderate its effects, and when you chew coca leaves the cocaine that's there

gets into your bloodstream and brain very slowly. So it's not just what the drug is, or the dose, but the manner in which you introduce it into the body. There's an enormous difference between chewing a coca leaf and letting a small amount of cocaine diffuse slowly into the bloodstream, and smoking cocaine and having it rapidly rise in concentration and enter into the brain. That's why tobacco—cigarettes—is the most addictive drug known: Because nicotine is a very strong drug, stronger than cocaine in terms of its effects. And that manner of introducing it into the brain enhances addictiveness. So when you smoke cocaine, that's the most extreme way to experience its pharmacological effects; that's a stupid way to take it. But our policies have made coca leaves disappear from the market, because they're bulky and nobody wants to smuggle them, and we have created a situation in which it's profitable to smuggle this isolated, refined drug. And also to find ways of using a drug to get the maximum pharmacological power out of it.

What you're suggesting is that if there were a more open environment for drug use, people would, as a consequence of having more choice, choose substances that are better for them?

Might. Especially if they were educated. I'm not just arguing for a more open situation; I think it has to go hand in hand with real drug education. What passes for that today seems like thinly disguised attempts to steer people away from the drugs we don't like by exaggerating their dangers, while not paying attention to the drugs that we do like. And I think that leaves our culture very uneducated about the benefits and risks of psychoactive substances.

So let's talk about an alternative way of educating young people about drugs.

I think the alternative is first of all to be objective about all drugs. I mean, there's nothing that sets alcohol, tobacco, and caffeine apart from crack, marijuana, and PCP. I think grade school students should start to learn about the nature of addiction. It's not just a drug problem: people get addicted to sex, food, athletics. Most people get caught up in addictive behavior. And you need teaching about that as well. I think there are two basic strategies: one is to teach people to satisfy their needs without using drugs at all. I'm very much in favor of that, and it's something I try to practice in my own life. But realistically a lot of people are going to use drugs because they take you where you want to go with no work. And I think it is important to encourage those people to use drugs sensibly. And that's the issue that just drives these Reaganites up the wall. You're talking about responsible drug use.

Why is there such a consensus on this issue, as opposed to, say, pornography—another form of pleasure-taking that's said to produce antisocial behavior.

All I can say is that if you look around the world at different societies, you see the need to divide behavior in this area into good and evil. In every society you see the same pattern: A small number of drugs are encouraged and defined as being good, and the rest are banned as being evil.

What is it about drugs that distinguish them from other forms of pleasure? Is it their capacity to alter consciousness?

I think that's the root of it, and I think it's that they are so powerful.

Does what's really going on have to do with the desire to regulate consciousness?

That's possible. I have written in other books that nondrug methods of altering consciousness often bring on the same kind of response.

There seems to be a desire to track transcendence toward the religious passions. Even toward militaristic ones. And there are more and more ceremonies that have to do with patriotism, sports—ceremonies of muscularity—but these are public highs. Maybe there's a connection between this tendency and the repression of drugs, which are, in this society anyway, a private and individual experience.

That is possible.

How does it feel to be singled out by a U.S. senator? Are you apprehensive about articulating your ideas in public now?

Well, I think that the hysterical mood that I've seen, this kind of legislative-feeding frenzy, and the fact that I don't see people standing up to be counted on the other side, makes me feel that this is really not the time to debate the Reaganites in public. I just don't want to draw that kind of heat.

Are you in a tenured position?

No, I'm not, and obviously, life can be made difficult in that area. The thing is that this is all past work of mine. My current work is in alternative medicine; I have a medical practice, my research on medicinal plants. I'm not actively doing this drug stuff any more.

So you're tempted to retreat.

Yeah, but I've put it all out there. Over the past few weeks, when I've been asked to be on TV and radio shows, I've turned them down and told them that they can go read the book.

How do you know that your information about the effects of drugs is accurate? You yourself talk about the highly subjective nature of these substances.

I know it both, first of all, from my own experience with them and, secondly, from having studied them from many different perspectives. I've studied drugs from the point of view of botany and medicine and psychology and psychiatry and sociology and politics, as well as having worked and lived in many different countries around the world, looking at these same issues. So I think that, more than most people, I don't adhere to any one frame of reference.

Let's define the terms *set* and *setting*.

Set is expectation of what a drug will do, both conscious and unconscious, and *setting* is the environment in which the drug is used, both the physical environment and cultural environment. And those factors are major determinants of drug effect, at least as important as pharmacology. So I don't see anything intrinsic about, say, PCP that makes people violent. I think it is likely to do that in certain sets and settings. The majority of people who use PCP are prone to violence and often take that drug out of anger and frustration—to get messed up. In that context, it's very likely to cause violent behavior.

Let's design a curriculum for high school students that would be realistic about drugs. How would you approach that?

First, so that people have a sense of how set and setting modify the effects of drugs. And then you could talk about problem sets and settings: The idea of taking drugs to get out of bad moods, for example, or taking drugs when you're bored, as opposed to using them for positive reasons. For example, many people use drugs as an excuse for social interaction, as we do with coffee. Many people have used drugs for religious experience. I would look at traditional people who use hallucinogenic plants in that way. And I would try to encourage people to find nondrug methods of satisfying their needs. I think that's very legitimate.

In your book you talk about forming a relationship with a drug. How would you define a bad relationship?

Addiction is one example. Unconscious use of a drug—that is, not knowing what

I don't think it's wise to smoke cocaine. If you want to explore its effects, you should chew coca leaves.

it is or not knowing that you're using a drug. Using it so frequently that you're impairing your health or your social or economic functioning. Using it so frequently that it's lost a desired effect.

So, for example, you would encourage people to use marijuana less frequently because being sparing about it enhances the effect.

Right. And losing the effect is a step on the way to using it addictively.

To enhance the effects of drugs, what general suggestions do you have?

I think, first, a very important one: that less is more.

What would be a good relationship with heroin, if it's possible?

I think probably it would be best to use it in the form of opium and to take opium by mouth rather than to smoke it or inject one of its derivatives.

What would you teach a teenager about heroin?

That the addictive potential of it is very great, that the physical harmfulness is not, that the addictive potential of it is increased by putting it into the body in very direct ways, that the consequences of addiction to heroin are not terrific in terms of limitation of freedom—and that's a serious issue—and that all addicts think they can avoid addiction at the beginning.

Is it true, though, that heroin is not more addictive than cigarettes?

I think cigarettes are more addictive than heroin.

So in effect when you teach young people about cigarettes you would be very severe.

I would say that you should never smoke a cigarette. I think if you want to experiment with tobacco, you should put some in your mouth and chew it to see what its effects are and then you can decide if you want to use it or not; but it is not reasonable to smoke a cigarette to see if you like it or not, because the risk of addiction is too great.

What about coffee?

The thing to emphasize is that it's a very strong drug, with addictive potential and also the potential to alter behavior significantly and affect the body. It should not be thought of as a beverage, and it should be used only occasionally, not regularly.

How would you reduce the incidence of drug-related crime?

If drugs were legalized there would be no drug-related crime.

How do you know that?

Most of the crime associated with drugs has to do with their enormously inflated price, which is a direct consequence of their illegalization, so that people have to get the money to afford them, which often involves committing crimes. But the pharmacological effects of many drugs are against violence— that's certainly true with heroin, and probably with marijuana.

One thing we haven't talked about is the demographics of drug use. If you were looking at this from the perspective of a black woman living in Bed-Stuy who was in great danger of being mugged by almost exclusively male drug users, wouldn't you feel differently?

Probably.

You see these faces at the anticrack rallies, a lot of them are poor people who are just fed up with living in fear.

Right.

What would you say to those people?

That governmental policies—not crack or heroin or any other substance—have put you in danger. And that, as result of these policies, everything associated with this problem has gotten bigger and worse.

Research: Robert Marchant

GRANDMA WAS A JUNKIE

A century ago, narcotics were cheap and available without prescription, and granny ran the risk of being hooked by the family doctor.

Richard T. Griffin

I never knew Great-Great-Grandmother Mary Mac-Guillicuddy Morgan—she died in 1900—but there are two stories my family tells about her. One is that in the middle of the nineteenth century young Mary and two brothers fled from starving Ireland in a small boat that they fearlessly sailed across the Atlantic to the United States, where they lived out their lives.

The other story, skipping to late in the last century, is that old Mary, by then the widow of a Harvard-educated physician, spent her final years as a narcotics addict in Chicago. She was hooked on laudanum—opium doused in alcohol—and she visited druggists in the neighborhood to buy it by the pint. Her children and grandchildren, disgusted by her "evil habit," called on the druggists to beg them not to sell any more narcotics to the old lady. But driven by her terrible compulsion, old Mary trudged about town and rode the horse trolley to other neighborhoods where druggists and grocers who didn't know her would provide the irresistible deadly drug.

Occasionally, she might order the laudanum from her Sears Roebuck catalogue, which at the turn of the century offered a two-ounce bottle for eighteen cents, or two dollars for one and a half pints. (The catalogue also sold turpentine "for internal or external use," opium, and paregoric, another dangerous opiate. They were described as "Special Family Remedies, a necessary article in every house . . . . They often relieve severe pain and sometimes save life.")

On the other side of the family was Grandfather Johnny Griffin. I never knew him, either. He died in 1931, a year before I was born. Half a century earlier, about 1880, Johnny also endured a nightmare of narcotics when he discovered to his horror that his young bride, Amelia, was a "dope fiend," as addicts were called in those days even in the scientific literature. An 1881 Chicago newspaper put it this way: "She was an habitual morphine eater, taking as high as three bottles

a week. She started using opium and morphine powders to allay pain from some head trouble."

Trying to help free Amelia from her private hell, Johnny arranged to have her hospitalized for three and a half months in order to cure her.

There were three primary "cures" in those days. The first, which probably was worse than addiction, was called the "perturbative" method. Today we'd call it "cold turkey," meaning the victim was cut off instantly from drugs. This was a violent procedure that drove some sufferers to suicide and visited upon all the psychic horrors and unspeakable pain that comes with sudden withdrawal.

The second was the "reductionary" method, in which the daily dosage of narcotics was gradually reduced.

The popular third method was substitution, in which an addict was "cured" of one addiction by substituting another. Doctors cured opium addicts by hooking them on morphine and morphine addicts on codeine or cocaine.

Whatever it was that the hospital tried on poor Amelia, however terrifying the eternal nights that chilled her frightened bones, regardless of the mad carnival of grotesque visitors from hell that danced before her eyes—all was in vain. Within weeks after her release she was fully addicted again, and Johnny was at his wits' end trying to scratch out a living by renovating used feathers and living in a smelly room over a public stable with a wife who seemed to be growing insane from drugs. Finally, he tried to take them away from her and Amelia, remembering the horror of withdrawal in the hospital, seized a hatchet and swung it violently at Johnny's head. He dodged the blow from the blade and knocked her down, pinning her to the floor until her rage subsided.

"She is insane," he was certain now, and decided she must be committed to the county asylum, not realizing how the system worked even then in Chicago. The assistant county medical officer examined her, demanded two dollars from Johnny for the efforts that were supposed to be administered free of charge, and only then agreed to sign the court petition for Amelia's insanity hearing.

Then he told Johnny: "For another ten dollars, I'll testify she's insane." Johnny, to whom money did not come easily then or ever, protested. The doctor responded that if Johnny didn't pay it, he'd testify Amelia was sane. And that's exactly what the county's doctor did. The judge freed poor Amelia and seven days later she swallowed thirty grains of morphine powder, slipped into a coma, and died.

A family's horrors. A coincidence, was it, that nearly a century ago two of our women, from separate branches of the family, were narcotics addicts? A family's disgrace, to be whispered behind closed doors, an "unutterably disgusting habit" (in the words of one nineteenth-century doctor) confined to "degenerates and moral imbeciles with weak willpower" (in the words of another)?

On the contrary, poor old Mary MacGuillicuddy Morgan and young Amelia Armstrong Griffin were typical victims of their times. The United States had more drug addicts in the second half of the nineteenth century than it does today, some historians say, even though the population then was much smaller. Early in the twentieth century, according to a U.S. Treasury study, the United States was consuming ten times as much opium per capita as the largest opium-using country in Europe. Americans were seized by addiction—not hooked on drugs by vile criminals slinking in the shadows, but by their family doctors. They were lured into lifetime bondage by advertisements for drug-soaked patent medicines in the nation's most respected newspapers and magazines. Novelists and essayists sang the siren song of opium, morphine, and laudanum. Narcotics were all but forced upon Americans in the last third of the nineteenth century in drugstores, grocery stores, and other outlets, cheap in price and as freely available without prescription as aspirin and cold tablets are today.

Many soft drinks were loaded with cocaine, and thousands of Americans were addicted to such drinks as Koca Nola, Celery Cola, Café Cola, Koke, and other popular beverages of the day.

Physicians, in keeping with the best medical opinions of the time, prescribed opium and other narcotics for almost every ailment. Many doctors then acted as their own druggists by filling prescriptions from their own supplies.

"Much as we may loathe the drug," one physician said, echoing the attitude of most, "it is undeniable that it destroys the germs of seven-tenths of the diseases of mankind. If I were limited by law to the use of a single drug in my practice . . . I should not hesitate to name that toxic remedy. There are special diseases that can be reached by no other known agencies."

Special diseases? In fact, opium and its deadly offspring were prescribed in virtually every situation known to medicine. They were used (and still are, with devastating effectiveness) as painkillers and agents for controlling the diarrhea that was chronic in post–Civil War urban America. But encouraged by medical textbooks, doctors also used opiates for everything from asthma to tuberculosis, including diabetes, cancer, insanity, "excessive brain work," itching, and "nerve pain."

There even was some hope for narcotics as sexual stimulants. One respected medical writer in 1871 called hashish "a powerful aphrodisiac, ranking second after [get this!] arsenic." A physician announced to the American Philosophical Society that a young man of his acquaintance had swallowed a dose of hashish and alcohol, resulting in a sexual erection "which did not relax short of three days." An important medical journal reported on the case of a thirty-year-old man "of prodigious development of the sexual organs and a proportionate exaltation of function amounting to an impetuous and uncontrollable salacity." It attributed his extraordinary size and appetite to his habitual use of opiates from the age of four. A medical writer, commenting on the case, said similar cases of uncontrollable appetite for sexual adventure could be "neutralized by the free use of lemon juice." He didn't say whether one should drink it or soak in it.

Many responsible authorities were convinced that narcotics were no more dangerous or habit-forming than any of the other "vices" of the day, and far less vile than drunkenness. They ranked the use of narcotics with drinking tea (a mild aphrodisiac, they said) and coffee (a drink that "increases intellectual powers") and smoking tobacco (which they thought caused blindness, gray hair, memory loss, and an unstable mind).

In 1860 an indignant physician named Oliver Wendell Holmes had this to say about the state of medicine: "If the whole *materia medica*, as now used, could be sunk to the bottom of the sea, it would be all the better for mankind—and all the worse for the fishes."

But the famed poet and dean of the Harvard Medical School made an exception for opium, "which the Creator himself seems to prescribe, for we often see the scarlet poppy growing in cornfields, as if it were foreseen that wherever there is hunger to be fed there must also be pain to be soothed."

As late as 1894 a London physician, Patrick Hehir, wrote a massive book defending the use of opium. Dr. Hehir said it's untrue that opium smokers and opium eaters require larger and larger doses and it's also untrue that they can't quit at the snap of their fingers if they decided to.

Warming up to his extraordinary theme, Dr. Hehir

told the world that coffee, tea, tobacco, and alcohol are "far more harmful" than opium when used in moderation.

"Excessive use of opium . . . is not worse than excess of alcohol, beef, etc.," he insisted, advising that the drug also prevents cholera and helps keep you warm in cold weather. Besides, he added in what might have been the central point, the opium trade was worth ten million pounds a year to the Indian exchequer.

Dr. Hehir's wishful thinking was typical of the medical profession's attitude towards narcotics in the nineteenth century. Physicians sought to cure puzzling diseases even though little more knowledge was at their disposal in those years than was possessed by medical men in the dark days of the Middle Ages.

Doctors treated symptoms, such as pain, diarrhea, and coughing, instead of the ailments themselves because they didn't know the causes of most illnesses. There was a hopelessness about disease, and when cholera epidemics and other diseases swept the nation's filthy cities, doctors and druggists were among those who fled to the countryside for safety, leaving the poor citizenry alone to face the vicious killers that couldn't be seen or heard.

One treatment for cholera required the patient to put his feet in hot ashes and water, swallow a dose of opium and calomel, and then cover up in a bed filled with heated bricks and boiled ears of corn.

Each time a new discovery was made in the drug field in the nineteenth century, it was heralded as mankind's savior. About 1805, a young, self-taught German chemist named Frederick Serturner discovered a new substance in opium. He called it *morphium,* for the god of sleep; but after several experiments that nearly put some of his neighbors to sleep for good he warned: "I consider it my duty to attract attention to the terrible effect of this new substance in order that calamity may be averted."

Nobody listened to young Serturner, and physicians and scientists throughout Europe and the United States acclaimed morphine a marvelous drug with the curative powers of opium but without its terrible habit-forming attribute. Decades passed before they discovered they had never been more wrong.

In 1844 cocaine was isolated from coca leaves and it was seized upon by the medical profession. Years later a young Viennese doctor named Sigmund Freud discovered it for himself. Calling it "a magical drug," he said cocaine was superb for depression and indigestion and enduring hunger, pain, and fatigue. He swore it was nonaddictive "even after repeated taking," used the narcotic himself, and pushed it on patients, friends, colleagues, and even his sisters.

In 1854 a Scottish physician perfected the first practical syringe and the technique to use it; his wife became the world's first known morphine addict hooked by

syringe and also the first person to die from an overdose administered by syringe.

But the medical profession was ecstatic about the development of the syringe, which offered a faster and more direct way to administer medicine than orally or through an incision made in the skin. According to one important source: "It is very doubtful if any painful condition to which the human is heir escaped the list of those for which [the hypodermic use of morphine] was recommended."

More wishful thinking: the best authorities were convinced for many years that narcotics could be injected without leading to addiction, and as late as 1900 medical texts carried no word of warning about the terrible dangers of hypodermic application of morphine.

In 1899 Heinrich Dreser, of Germany's famed Bayer Works, gave the world what became its most widely used painkiller, aspirin. But a year earlier Dreser had made a different sort of discovery. He produced a chemical, diacetylmorphine hydrochloride, which he proudly described to a meeting of the Congress of German Naturalists and Physicians as a wonder drug ten times as effective as codeine in slowing respiration but only one-tenth as toxic. It would find widespread use, Dreser predicted. He was right. He had discovered heroin.

Wishful thinking at its worst: medical men on both sides of the Atlantic supported Dreser's claims and added new ones, telling the world that the first non-habit-forming narcotic finally was available to mankind. They said they found heroin useful in treating tuberculosis, bronchitis, asthma, insomnia, coughs, chest pains, peritonitis, heart disease, and pelvic problems. One physician in 1902 even advised his peers to use heroin to cure morphine and codeine addiction, and the medical profession continued to debate how heroin might be used as a medicine as late as the 1920's.

As one might guess, there were many bronchitis sufferers, insomniacs, and others in the early 1900's who suddenly discovered that they had a new and far worse problem—heroin addiction. In fact, a leading medical historian believes that the epidemic of drug addiction in the United States would have been ended or at least sharply diminished early in the twentieth century but for Heinrich Dreser's unfortunate discovery.

But an epidemic it was, and it has never quite ended. However, the nineteenth century's addicts were far different persons from today's. Women outnumbered men by nearly three to one, many of these women were middle-aged, and most were white. The addicts were "the noblest and the best" among womanhood, mourned one observer.

An Iowa health official wrote in 1885 that narcotics' "helpless victims . . . have not come from the ranks of reckless men and fallen women, but the majority of them are to be found among the educated and most honored and useful members of society. . . . The habit in a vast majority of cases is first formed by the unpardonable carelessness of physicians, who are often too fond of using a little syringe, or relieving every ache and pain by the administration of an opiate."

Another authority described the type of person that he thought was most prone to addiction: "A delicate female, having light blue eyes and flaxen hair, possesses, according to my observations, the maximum susceptibility."

Women of that time used opium and morphine on the advice of their doctors for "female complaints," both real and imaginary; they also dosed themselves with a variety of patent medicines widely advertised as cure-alls, women's friends, consumption cures, and pain-killers—many of which were loaded with narcotics.

Young mothers gave their fretful and restless infants such universally patent medicines as Mistress Winslow's Soothing Syrup, Mother Bailey's Quieting Syrup, and Kopp's Baby's Friend—all of them loaded with opium and virtually certain to addict their tiny users.

Wives secretly dumped opium and morphine powders into their husbands' coffee or tea, following the directions on the label that said taking doses of these narcotics would cure alcoholism.

Doctors consumed it—and probably constituted the greatest group of narcotics addicts in the nation after women: they used it to calm themselves and increase their stamina. At least one country doctor kept his faithful horse as doped as himself to endure the endless hard days and nights of work.

One Missouri doctor so overworked himself during a malaria epidemic that he suffered terribly from insomnia. Finally, he gave himself an injection of one-fifth of a grain of morphine, and twenty minutes later—feeling no reaction—took another shot of one-third of a grain. Almost instantly after the second dose of the Judas drug ("it kisses, then it betrays," wrote one frightened addict), the doctor passed into what he described as "a rested and delightful frame of mind." He said he soon saw ecstatic visions of "marble palaces, stately dames dancing minuets, lovely girls flitting about hilariously to sensuous music, the cathedrals of Milan and Cologne, whirling along in cabs across the continent of Europe and sailed over oceans, at all times accompanied by agreeable companions who talked delightfully on the most entertaining subjects."

But when the delirium ended, he said, "the awakening was terrible. My mouth was parched, my lips dry, my head ached violently, and I cursed morphine as the very devil among drugs. Yet, think of the folly and the weakness of man! Within two months I was bound hand and foot by the demon and he held me fast for fourteen years."

Whole families were hooked by the deadly drugs. For many years after the hypodermic syringe came into widespread use during the Civil War, many doctors taught patients or members of the family to use it so they wouldn't have to make a personal appearance each time a patient was scheduled for an injection. Artistically decorated syringe kits were available for home use.

One family of four—mother, father, son, and daughter—was addicted by a physician who left a syringe with them. The same doctor is said to have led at least two hundred of his patients into the hell of narcotics addiction.

Wives of a few addicts voluntarily addicted themselves so they could share their husbands' agonies and try to make the horror easier to endure. But cases of addicts luring others into the habit were virtually unknown in the nineteenth century, when drugs were cheap and legal and addicts didn't have to raise huge sums of money to support the habit, as they must today.

One Ohio doctor, however, himself an addict and weary of the incessant reproaches of his wife, laced her tea with morphine three times a day until she was hooked. It still didn't shut her up.

Merchants took narcotics to steel their nerves against the pressures of business; many preferred it to liquor because there was no telltale odor on their breath and because addiction under normal circumstances is difficult to detect, even for a spouse.

Students used narcotics because they were overworked, and soldiers because they were underworked. Preachers, temperance lecturers, writers, and lawyers depended on drugs to quicken their minds and waiters to quicken their memories. Clerks, vendors, and teamsters used them, as did overworked and underpaid factory workers.

In high society drugs were used for two reasons, a writer of the day said: For the men, "society's whirl demands late hours—a little punch, perhaps salad; sleep must be immediate or the man of business will not get any." He got his sleep, thanks to an injection or a powder. And then there was "the lady of *haut ton*, idly lolling upon her velvet fauteuil and vainly trying to cheat the lagging hours that intervene ere the clockwork tintinnabulum shall sound the hour for opera or whist."

Workers in the fisheries of Alaska were given morphine to make them work faster, at the end of each season many were confirmed addicts. In the South, overseers put cocaine in the rations of black field hands to get more work out of them. Construction, mill, and mining workers were offered or fed narcotics with their rations.

Every pioneer family going West carried a medicine chest with their favorite patent medicines and bottles of opium and morphine. Frontier doctors, what few there were, depended on opiates as the only sure painkiller in a place where pain was an everyday occurrence.

Disease, accidents, and gunshot wounds were so common that frontier men and women surely were the unhealthiest Americans in history, and among the most doped up.

One mountaineer with a toothache, which drove him almost out of his mind with pain, traded all his furs for one bottle of laudanum at a frontier town. A Texas doctor gave every patient a dose of opium, regardless of complaint. He might have been the reincarnation of a celebrated European physician of two centuries earlier, who used opium so promiscuously that he was called Dr. Opiatus.

The epidemic embraced the nation. A physician-historian wrote in 1871: "Corroborative accounts come in from New Jersey and Indiana, from Boston at one extreme and from St. Louis at another, and from the impoverished South as well. In the Mississippi Valley particularly the use of stimuli of every name is fearfully on the increase."

It was to get far worse, until the greatest mass of opiate addicts in history were walking the earth, horrified by their plight but too terrified to end it.

Opium has been used medicinally for thousands of years. The Egyptian, Persian, and Greek civilizations were familiar with it. Homer mentions it in the *Iliad* and Hippocrates recommended it. Virgil remarked on it in the *Aeneid*. It became so popular in the Roman Empire that shopkeepers and wandering quacks were hawking it to the plebeians. The drug continued in widespread use through the Middle Ages and when Cardinal Richelieu was ill in 1642, his French doctors gave him horse dung in white wine. Next they gave him a dose of laudanum. Next he died. In 1700 a London textbook on opium called it "a safe and noble Panacea."

Opium was popular in colonial America and was commonly used by military surgeons in the Revolution.

In 1822 Thomas De Quincey, one of several English writers addicted to opium, published his dismaying masterpiece, *Confessions of an English Opium-Eater*. It made addiction fashionable and continued to lure many new victims to the treacherous drug for a century or more after it was published.

Patent medicines, many heavily laced with opiates, were imported from England in the 1700's until our own charlatans began pushing homemade nostrums after the Revolution. But it wasn't until the middle of the nineteenth century that patent medicines came into their own. There were several reasons for this: doctors were distrusted, often for good cause, and the people tended to try to cure themselves; giveaway postal rates were authorized by Congress; it became economical to publish cheap newspapers, thanks to free delivery by the Post Office in the county of publication; and, because rising numbers of people learned to read, the American masses could now be scared out of their skins by quack medical advertisements in newspapers, magazines, almanacs, farm journals, and on roadside signs, sidewalk sandwich boards, and even handbills delivered door to door—in short, virtually everywhere a person turned.

The nostrum makers terrified millions into using their usually worthless and often dangerous products by describing horrible diseases—many of them invented by advertising agents—waiting to destroy mankind. Revolting intestinal worms, growing as long as sixty feet, were described so often in advertisements that they must have been especially effective salesmen for the quacks. After terrifying the reader, they reassured him or her by guaranteeing—absolutely guaranteeing!—that there was a single miraculous product that would cure this malady and many others as well. Many of the nostrums were described as cures for a wide range of problems. One claimed to cure twenty-five ailments, from headaches to sore feet. Another laid claim to fifty-five disorders, and said it also was good for what ails horses, cows, and sheep. There was no law against lying in ads; outrageous claims were considered to be just good salesmanship.

When the guns at Fort Sumter called Americans from North and South to war, the young soldiers from city and farm brought with them bottles and tins of their favorite patent remedies. Their military surgeons treated them with the same nostrums and made liberal use of opium, which the Union army's surgeon-general later called "an invaluable remedy." The wounded were usually given an opium pill or a shot of morphine automatically "because they expected it," the surgeon-general said. For each of the North's four hundred thousand wounded, fifteen more were felled by sickness. The average soldier was sick enough to need medical help more than twice a year during the war. Most often he suffered cruelly from diarrhea, dysentery, and malaria. Opiates were used against these and other illnesses, plus as a painkiller and sleeping powder, and so many soldiers marched home after the war with a monkey on their backs that addiction came to be known as the "army disease." Soldiers shared with their families their terrors from the war and the pain from their injuries and ailments that sometimes lasted a lifetime. Quite often their wives and their children became addicts, too.

The "Westerling" movement added illnesses and hardship to the American fabric, and patent-medicine makers, unshackled by laws, lured increasing numbers to their dangerous wares after the war ended. Doctors, ignorant of the causes of many diseases, treated the ailing with their favorite narcotics.

Opium, morphine, laudanum, paregoric, and patent medicines containing these drugs were available throughout the country, without a doctor's prescription. An 1878 Michigan state health department report said "it would not be difficult for a lunatic or a child" to get all the opium he wanted, "provided he told a plausible story and had the money to pay for it." Every drugstore carried it, and some doctors, frightened by the spreading addiction, took to carrying a notice on their prescription blanks "respectfully requesting" druggists not to refill an opiate prescription without first obtaining the doctor's permission.

Many pharmacists insisted that misuse of narcotics was the customer's problem, not the pharmacist's. Also, they said, poor people couldn't afford to pay for both the writing of a prescription and the medicine itself, and they clearly needed the medicine more than the prescription.

Drugstores weren't the only place narcotics and hypodermics were sold. Grocers carried them. So did bookstores, tobacco shops, and department stores. Country stores kept farm families supplied with opiates.

And, of course, the mail-order houses offered wide selections of opium products, syringe kits with instructions on how to use them, and all the important patent medicines. (Experts estimate that there were between 50,000 and 65,000 different nostrums readily available around the turn of the century.)

The public didn't approve of narcotics addiction, but neither did it consider the habit monstrous. Addicts were viewed more with pity than loathing, although many persons considered addiction as immoral as dancing and theatergoing. Unlike today, addicts didn't expect to be fired if their bosses discovered their habit, and husbands and wives didn't divorce their hooked spouses.

The addicts lived normal lives in their communities—addicted men worked regularly, addicted women managed their households, and addicted children attended school without interruption.

Many authorities believed drug addiction was far better than being a drunkard ("opium soothes, alcohol maddens," it was said), and there was a movement to convert alcoholics to the syringe.

One Cincinnati physician bragged about converting a number of his hard-drinking patients and said if all drunks in America were switched to narcotics, "the mayors and police courts would almost languish for lack of business; the criminal dockets, with their attendant legal functionaries, would have much less to do than they now have." He insisted that he could prove "the law-abiding quality of opium-eating peoples" and said it's obvious to anyone who "carefully watches and reflects on the quiet, introspective gaze of the morphine habitué and compares it with the riotous, devil-may-care of the drunkard."

Nor would drug addiction send the addict's family to the poorhouse. Narcotics were far cheaper than liquor in those days. A doctor estimated in 1889 that an addict could stay doped up for about two and a half cents a day, but that it could cost as much as twenty-five cents a day to stay boozed up.

Poor blacks in the South favored cocaine because it was the cheapest high they could find. Furthermore, many persons, both black and white, believed that cocaine imparted protection against bullets, and this led police in several Southern towns to raise the caliber of their pistols from .32 to .38.

If most people pitied "opium-eaters," there was one class that despised them: opium smokers.

Chinese immigrants brought the smoking habit to this country, and after the Civil War it spread eastward from San Francisco. By 1880, opium-smoking dens were reported to be operating in almost every town and city in the United States. (A den in downtown Chicago was charging "pipe hitters" twenty-five cents a pipeful in 1877.) Rich actresses, businessmen, and doctors in New York City were reported in 1914 to have elaborate rooms set aside in their homes for smoking opium with jeweled pipes.

Cowboys said that as late as 1910 they could ride anywhere in the West and find a smoking den wherever they stopped, without having to carry along a supply of opium and a pipe.

Smokers despised addicts who swallowed or injected the drug because they correctly considered those habits more difficult to break. When a smoker in a New York opium den discovered a man giving himself a hypodermic injection in the bathroom, the smoker stormed angrily into the manager's office and complained to him loudly: "There's a goddamn dope fiend in the can!" The troublemaker was immediately thrown out.

This feeling of contempt was returned tenfold by opium-eaters and the general public. A reformed opium-eater, who felt compassion and pity for most users, had this to say in 1895 about smokers: "Let there be full understanding. The opium-smoking habit comes of association with unholy persons. . . . The surroundings are always repulsive and the inmates of these resorts are criminals or petty offenders against police regulations. They are ignorant, illiterate, vulgar, brutal, and wicked. An insistence that a virtuous and good person could be led thither by any sort of influence . . . is a suggestion of absurdity. . . . The more depraved wretches of the sinful-female class resort to the pipe and their exit from this world is along a fast road that has no way stations."

Many Americans, once hooked on narcotics, were horrified at their plight and spent the rest of their lives trying to warn others away.

1. THINKING ABOUT DRUGS

"Better death or invalidism than the contraction of a habit that degrades, demoralizes, and finally kills," warned one despairing addict.

Nevertheless, frustrated medical men and addicts themselves tried everything to cure the habit that enslaved so many. Sober medical journals recommended cold baths, hot baths, and steambaths; frequent, vigorous shampoos of the addict's hair; administering electric shocks; drinking jugs of coffee and beef broth; giving addicts hypodermic injections of coffee, caffeine, cocaine, and codeine; and substituting claret for laudanum and brandy for morphine.

It was concern for the plight of the Chinese, who were imprisoned by an addiction foisted on them by India and England, that brought the first great international pressure for controls on narcotics in the early years of this century. American missionaries in China, appalled at what they saw, bombarded the American public and politicians with letters, articles, and speeches describing the condition of the people of China and demanding action. President Theodore Roosevelt swung his weight behind the movement and many in Congress followed him. As the international campaign developed, America slowly discovered that it had an enormous narcotics problem of its own, probably the worst in the Western world.

The first important step was passage of the Pure Food and Drug Act in 1906, which required labeling of patent medicines for the first time. No longer could a nostrum contain opiates, alcohol, or other dangerous ingredients without saying so on the label. The act stunned the charlatans.

A 1909 federal act prohibited importation of smoking-type opium.

In 1914, the Harrison Narcotics Act, the nation's basic narcotics law, was signed by Woodrow Wilson. It brought all opiates under strict federal control.

The *New York Times* reported in April 1915 that the police department's seventeen-man "dope squad" had dried up street sales of heroin and cocaine and that many addicts were appearing at police stations across the country begging to be supplied with narcotics or cured. Many despondent addicts had committed suicide, the *Times* said, and several others died after consuming other dangerous drugs and chemicals in a vain effort to head off the dreaded symptoms of withdrawal from narcotics.

Meanwhile, diplomats from the United States and other powers throughout the world were weaving a tapestry of agreements between 1909 and 1914 that they believed would lead to international control on the movement of opiates. "The great purpose" had been accomplished, announced a happy Secretary of State, William Jennings Bryan.

Illicit Price of Cocaine in Two Eras: 1908-14 and 1982-89

DAVID F. MUSTO, M.A., M.D.

DAVID F. MUSTO, M.A., M.D., Professor of Psychiatry, Child Study Center; Professor, History of Medicine, Yale University School of Medicine, New Haven.

Reprint requests to: P.O. Box 3333, New Haven, CT 06510 (Dr. Musto).

Introduction

THE legal status of cocaine in the United States passed through three stages: it could be legally obtained by anyone from the time of its introduction in 1884 until about 1900; then, a movement at both state and local levels restricted its availability to a physician's judgment; and lastly, after 1914, severe constraints on access to cocaine were enacted by the federal government. During the middle stage, responsibility for licit cocaine availability was increasingly assigned to physicians and pharmacists. This action during our first wave of cocaine use is similar to recent proposals to turn the cocaine problem over to health professionals and their clinical judgment. The following is a report on licit and illicit prices of cocaine during that middle or "medical stage."

When cocaine became commercially available in the United States in 1984, its purveyors were allowed an open market. Until the early 20th century, regulation of medical and pharmaceutical practice was reserved to the police powers of the states and was not an appropriate arena for federal legislation. As a result, the first legal controls on the distribution of cocaine occurred at the local and state level.

One reason there was no initial restriction on cocaine availability is that it was considered by prominent authorities to be a harmless tonic without any untoward side effects or after effects, if "used in moderation." As demand soared, pharmaceutical manufacturers rapidly increased production.[1] The initial wholesale price for cocaine hydrochloride was $15 per gram, but dropped within two years to a much lower figure, about $0.25, and thereafter generally followed the rate of inflation.

The early approval of cocaine gradually changed to concern and eventually to fear of its side effects on the mind and behavior of users. Medical journals and newspapers increasingly reported on persons whose careers and lives had been distorted and damaged by inordinate use of cocaine. In Connecticut, for example, a newspaper report of 1896 stated that cocaine was in more common use than tobacco in a local textile mill.[2] During this rising public concern, the Connecticut State Medical Society established an *ad hoc* committee in 1896 to consider the problem of cocaine. The committee concluded that the problem of excessive and uncontrolled use arose from self-administration by patients, but that when applied by a physician in low concentration at the time of a surgical procedure, the drug was safe.[3] In 1905 Connecticut enacted a statute restricting cocaine to a physician's prescription but without limitation as to amount or purpose.[4]

New York State legislators also turned to the wisdom of health professionals as a defense against the cocaine problem. In 1907 Alfred E. Smith, then a member of the assembly, led a legislative attack on cocaine.[5] The subsequent Smith anticocaine law restricted cocaine availability to a physician's prescription and required record-keeping. The law placed no restriction on the amount or purpose of the prescriptions.[6]

These steps, however, did not bring cocaine under control to a degree satisfactory to the public or legislature. Some physicians and pharmacists provided cocaine without the professional restraint anticipated by law-makers. In spite of this liberality, cocaine was still being sold on the streets of New York. One loophole regarding possession without a prescription was addressed by an amendment in 1910.[7] Then, in 1913, after continued frustration over the the easy access to cocaine, an even stricter anticocaine law was passed with support from Smith, now speaker of the New York Assembly. This act imposed severe restrictions on the health professions as well as penalties for any "patient" having cocaine without a certificate of authorization provided by a pharmacist or physician.[8]

The final stage of control, limiting the freedom of the health professions in dispensing cocaine and ending any latitude in its possession, had been reached to the extent feasible in New York State. The following year, the federal Harrison Act would bring an unprecedented restriction of cocaine's availability to the entire nation. More than alcohol, even during a national campaign which would lead to Prohibition in 1920, cocaine stood out as a fearful substance almost universally condemned.

In 1906 the Pure Food and Drug act had required that the existence and amount of cocaine in over-the-counter remedies be revealed on the label, although the amount was unregulated.[9] Then, on 1 March 1915 the Harrison Narcotic Act came into force. It required that records be kept of all opiates and cocaine from the importer or manufacturer down to the patient's prescription. Unlike the Pure Food and Drug Act, it also limited the amount of opiates — while prohibiting any cocaine — in non-prescription remedies. The Act required that physicians prescribe these drugs only "in the course of professional practice" and "in good faith."[10] Coupled with state anti-cocaine laws, the high water mark of restrictions on cocaine in the first wave of cocaine use had been reached.

Eventually cocaine use faded in the United States. The gap between the beginning of the current wave of cocaine use, about 1970, and the waning years of previous use, the 1930s, was so long that the earlier experience has been, for all practical purposes, forgotten.

The current resurgence of cocaine led to calls for legalization in the 1970s on the basis of its apparent harmlessness, while in recent years legalization proposals have stressed the economic argument to reduce the profits from illegal cocaine sales. Legal cocaine, according to this reasoning, would undercut costs, eliminate turf-wars between rival drug sellers and reduce the economic motivation for enlisting new cocaine users. Some have suggested turning cocaine distribution over to health professionals, an idea that has echoes of the Al Smith law of 1907.

Methods

The object of this study is to estimate the illicit price of cocaine during what might be called the "medical" phase of cocaine control, in New York City, from 1907 through 1914 and to compare that price with illicit cocaine prices in the 1980s.

As a comparison for purchasing power, the average industrial hourly wage was chosen. This information was obtained from Department of Commerce records (see Sources).

To establish the lowest wholesale price of a gram of cocaine, information on wholesale prices of an ounce of cocaine hydrochloride was obtained from pharmaceutical journals and price catalogs of various manufacturing chemists (see Sources).

It has been difficult to discover examples of retail cost to consumers of a gram of cocaine purchased from pharmacists in New York City. No record of a retail sale was located and none was present at the Archives of the American Institute of the History of Pharmacy. Of course, there was no standard retail price for the multitude of independent pharmacies.

To estimate the illicit street price of cocaine, the New York *Times, Tribune,* and *Herald* for the period 1906 through 1915 were searched. The amounts given in grains were converted to grams. The cocaine, usually described as mixed with an adulterant, was sold routinely on the streets in envelopes or paper packets for 25 cents each.

Data for the range of cocaine prices during the period 1982-1989 were obtained from the Drug Enforcement Administration. The street prices are for a gram offered to the user as cocaine (see Sources). The figures for 1989 are for July-September.

Results

1908-1914:

The wholesale price of cocaine in the earliest period, after a rapid fall from 1884 to 1886, settled down at a fairly steady level. Interestingly, the cost per gram at the wholesale level stayed close to the average hourly wage for industrial workers (Table 1). Also, the price, 25 cents, of the illicit street unit, or "deck," from 1908 until 1914 approximated the hourly wage.

Table 1

Price of Cocaine per Gram in NYC compared to Nat'l Industrial Wage/Hour

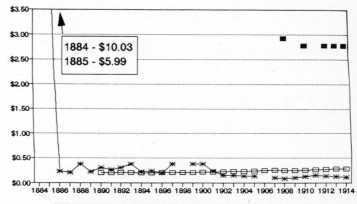

1884 - $10.03
1885 - $5.99

New York City street market prices for cocaine during the period before 1908 have not been located. Following passage of the Smith anticocaine law, prices began to be reported in the newspapers as arrests were made. The street or illicit price of a "deck" appears to have remained steady over the seven years between the Smith law and the coming into force of the Harrison Act, 1 March 1915.

That the typical street unit was a deck for 25 cents is concluded from newspaper accounts. In one of the early arrests under the Smith act it was reported in the New York *Times* that a seller provided cocaine at the rate of 26 (sic) cents a package to "any one — man, woman or boy" (3 August 1908). The State Department report of 1910 also gave 25 cents as the typical package. The New York *Tribune* (2 December 1912) reported in detail the process of making "decks" to sell for 25 cents. The following year (10 November 1913) the *Tribune* reported more street sales at the rate of 25 cents each. In 1914 the *Tribune* reported the arrest of a cocaine dealer while weighing out 25 cent "decks" of cocaine (1 July 1914).

The amount of cocaine in a deck is estimated in the following way. In the federal government's report, "Opium Problem," submitted to Congress in February 1910, the amount of cocaine in an envelope is estimated to be "one to two grains" (65 to 130 mgms). The New York *Tribune* account of 2 December 1912 estimated the amount of cocaine in a "deck" to be 1.3 grains (85 mgms). This amount has been taken as a reasonable estimate of cocaine in the illicit street unit. The above references are used to estimate the cost of cocaine on the street market from 1908 through 1914 in Tables 1, 2, and 4.

The rate for a gram of cocaine on the street market would be about $2.75, eleven times the unit price and, for the period under analysis, about 10 times the average hourly industrial wage (Table 2).

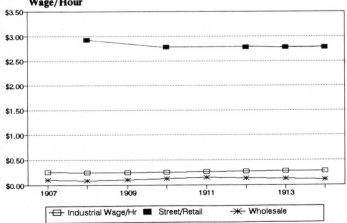

Table 2

Price of Cocaine per Gram in NYC compared to Nat'l Industrial Wage/Hour

According to newspaper reports, a well-established illicit pricing scheme as well as profiteering organizations existed during the "medical" phase of control.[11]

1982-1989:

In 1982 the DEA began compiling statistics based on the sale of cocaine at the street level and also providing estimates of cocaine costs at higher levels of the drug trade.

The prices of bulk and street cocaine have been drifting down since the early 1980s. By now the street unit cost of cocaine — often stated to be between five and 15 dollars — approximates the average industrial hourly wage. The cost per gram on the street has declined from about 10 times to (if we take the lowest price reported by the DEA for 1989) about four times the wage level. The wholesale price of a gram of cocaine has levelled off during the last three years to near the average hourly industrial wage (Table 3).

The street costs of a gram of cocaine can be compared between the two time periods by dividing the hourly wage into the price. Table 4 shows that there is a striking similarity between the two eras with the exception that the cost of cocaine at the street level is now lower, in buying power, than it was on the streets of New York City prior to the Harrison Act and while the legal control of cocaine was vested in the judgment of health professionals.

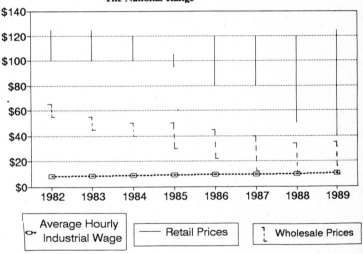

Table 3

Cocaine Prices in the US

The National Range

Discussion

Stable Illicit Market before 1914

Whether there was an illicit market for cocaine prior to the earliest state laws has not been determined. The prices in New York City found for the period 1907-14 were reported as a result of police arrests of illegal distributors, but prior to 1907 there were accounts of voluntary restrictions by local pharmacists and physicians.[12] Furthur research may clarify the question as to when an illicit market could be sustained because of the creation of voluntary restriction and the beginning of popular condemnation.

1. THINKING ABOUT DRUGS

Table 4
Ratio Cocaine Street Price/Hourly Wage

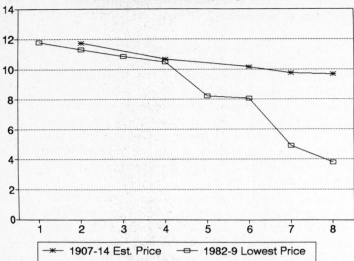

- -✳- 1907-14 Est. Price   - -▫- 1982-9 Lowest Price

The question of a previous "street market" for cocaine is significant because, if the assumptions about the cost and content of a "deck" are valid, there does not seem to have been a period of adjustment to market demand after the 1907 Smith law. The post-law market apparently maintained a fairly steady price for a "deck" of cocaine for nearly eight years.

The existence of this illicit market while the regulation of cocaine was turned over to the judgment of physicians and pharmacists suggests that this measure did not affect the supply or the availability of cocaine outside professional distribution. A gram of cocaine continued to cost on the street about ten times the average industrial hourly wage, a multiple as high or higher than cocaine has cost on the street since 1982. In this regard, it is not unreasonable to conclude that syndicates which provided illicit cocaine before the Harrison Act had profit margins comparable to our own day.

One of the most interesting comparisons between the pre-World War I unit price on the street, 25 cents, and the more recent street unit prices, five to 15 dollars, is their coincidental similarity to the hourly wage. Perhaps the wages for an hour's work is a natural market rate for the street unit. Until the Harrison Act, the United States had no national uniform law for the legal distribution of cocaine. That the street price in New York City could be maintained at such a high level before the Harrison Act is further evidence that reliance on health professions failed to eliminate an illicit market.

The reasons for this failure are several. Visits to a physician were assumed to keep access to cocaine under the watchful eye of a professional who could, if needed, treat a patient's cocaine problem. This requirement, however, would add the cost of a physician's visit to the cost of cocaine from a pharmacist. Also, drug users may have had a disinclination to become involved with formal and offical suppliers then as now. Whatever reasons one might want to assign, the hurdle presented by professional contact and record-keeping was apparently sufficient to maintain a stable illicit market in cocaine. Signif-

icantly, this illicit market was sustained in the face of some health professionals who prescribed and dispensed liberally, literally selling prescriptions to all comers.

There is evidence that the price of cocaine after World War I was much higher, even taking inflation into account, than in the era before the Harrison Act.[13] An important component of this rise in price and gradual decline in demand is the prolonged length of time required for the shift in consumption pattern. If we assume the time required now for a change in popular demand for cocaine may be roughly similar to the time taken for the previous episode, the curve in the cocaine price has been the opposite in each era. The shape of the price curve over the earlier wave of cocaine use resembled the shape of a "J" (extending the price curve into the apparent rise after World War I), and, while the current price curve is incomplete, we know that the recent curve has been the very reverse of that before 1915, starting high in the early 1970s and going lower. It will be interesting to see whether we are in a trough which will begin to rise and form a "U" shape, or whether the decline of cocaine prices will continue. If the condemnation and reaction against cocaine continues, it is possible the price will rise as a reflection of domestic restrictions, both social and legal, as it did after the anticocaine consensus established 70 to 80 years ago.

The Timing of Anticocaine Laws

Unlike our current cocaine episode which began about 1970, laws were not in place during the earlier "epidemic" until the public and legislators demanded controls. Escalating legal severity after 1907 in New York State and the rest of the nation paralleled popular opinion. A report that President Taft transmitted to Congress in 1910 described cocaine as "more appalling in its effects than any other habit-forming drug used in the United States."[14] A further reflection of fear of cocaine is that the section of the Harrison Act of 1914 that permitted some opiates, even heroin, in over-the-counter remedies, allowed no cocaine.

The contrast between attempts to control cocaine in the two waves of use is striking. Even after the substantial decline of cocaine use by World Wae II, increasingly harsh penalties for cocaine use were placed on the statute books.[15] These laws created a dramatic disparity between the fairly relaxed attitude toward cocaine in the mid-1970s and the severe penalties. The conflict between severe laws and widespread toleration of cocaine use meant that we experienced about 15 years of additional controversy over cocaine and controls until a consensus was once again established against the use of cocaine in the mid-1980s.

In this second cocaine era we have had anticocaine laws from the beginning of its renewed popularity and availability, whereas cocaine use during last century began in the absence of laws restricting it. After 1884, only as cocaine use continued and its damage was seen, did laws against the drug begin to be enacted and gradually strengthened. Since 1970, in contrast, the extended controversy over controls on cocaine — the prolonged disharmony between anticocaine laws on the books and more tolerant public attitudes — may be reflected in the frustration that has led to calls for drastic measures on opposite sides: those who propose legalizing cocaine believe it is time we all admitted to 20 years of failure in controlling it, while others call for draconian penalties which aim sharply and quickly to curtail drug use through punishment. The quest for a simple answer to the drug problem does not take into account the gradual fall in demand for cocaine that, at least in the past, followed the establishment of a popular anticocaine attitude. The decline phase may last 15 to 20 years. Reasonable policies might not appear effective as quickly as the public wishes, but impatiently rejecting these measures for extreme criminal justice measures will flood courts and jails, sponsor extravagant interdiction methods, and lead to a psychology of scapegoating foreign nations and domestic groups, such as the inhabitants of the inner cities — all without substantially affecting the rate of decline in cocaine use.

On the other hand, this study suggests that anything less than open access to cocaine, even the apparently liberal public health position of turning over responsibility to the flexible judgment of physicians and pharmacists, will support an illicit market with prices comparable to those in our own day.

The Cocaine Quandary

The public faces the quandary of fearing cocaine too much to allow open access, but being outraged by the corruption and profits that are products of the illicit trade in drugs. In the previous wave of drug use this cocaine impasse was resolved by an almost total elimination of the demand for cocaine through public experience with the drug and its users. In spite of profiteering in the illicit market, cocaine eventually faded away in the United States. This awareness of cocaine's danger was not effectively passed on to later generations — although severe penalties did persist — and by 1970 cocaine reappeared in the United States as fresh and exciting, an apparently useful tonic, stimulant, or ideal recreational substance.

The period of cocaine's availability after the mid-1880s and before action began to be taken against it, about 20 years, and the stage of increasing control, about 10 more years, followed finally by about two more decades while the problem subsided, suggests that cocaine use is not quickly corrected by simple, dramatic actions. Neither reverting to free access, the very condition that brought demands for control, nor a simple reliance on punishment offers hope for a speedy solution.

Sources

I. Cocaine Prices in the US:

1884: the price quoted represents the average of the prices reported in the *Druggist Circular* of December 1884, p. 177 ($.50-$.80 per grain).

The Medical Record 22 November 1884, p 578: price of cocaine up to $.50/grain.

1885: the price quoted represents the average of the prices reported in the *Chemist and Druggist* of 15 April 1885, p. 221 ($.30-$.50 per grain).

1886-1887: the price quoted represents the average of the prices reported in the *Proceedings of the American Pharmaceutical Association* 35:397 (1887).

1889: price is quoted from the Annual Catalogue (1889-90) of the Meyer Brothers Drug Company of St. Louis (Collection of Mr. William Helfand, New York, NY).

1891-1915: except for 1886, 1898, and 1906, are quoted from the following issues of *Merck's (Monthly) Report* (courtesy of Mr. Jeffrey Sturchio, corporate archivist, Merck & Co., Rahway, NJ): December issue of 1891, June issues of 1892-1894, April issue of 1895, June issues of 1896-1915. The quotation for 1896 is from the catalogue of the Cooke, Everette and Pennell company of Portland, Maine (collection of Mr. William Helfand).

1888, 1890, 1893, 1897, 1899, 1900 — these quotations are taken from the catalogue of Peter Van Schaak & Sons, Chicago (courtesy Dr. Gregory J. Higby, The American Institute of the History of Pharmacy, Madison, WI).

1901 — from the catalogue of McKesson and Robbins, New York (American Institute of the History of Pharmacy).

Prices for 1898 and 1906 have not been located.

II. 1982-1989: *The Illicit Drug Wholesale and Retail Price Report*. United States Department of Justice, Drug Enforcement Administration, Strategic Intelligence Section of the Office of Intelligence. The data in these reports derive from DEA case studies, DEA Quarterly Progress Reports or Field Management Reports and "street studies" supported by the DEA and the National Institute on Drug Abuse or "liaison with Field Intelligence Groups." Prices reported from all areas are used to determine the national average, but selected cities are also available to represent the price range. "Wholesale" prices are those paid by both high and mid-level dealers, while "retail" refers to the price at which a street dealer sold the drug.

III. Average Industrial Hourly Wages:

1890-1926: these figures are quoted from *Historical Statistics of the United States: Colonial Times to 1975*, p. 168, Series D 766.

1965-1987: these figures are quoted from the *Statistical Abstracts of the United States* published in the following years:

1968, p. 231: n. 332 ("manufacturing," "total," "current prices" for 1966 and 1967).

1975, p. 366: no. 594 (Manufacturing)
1977, p. 413: no. 668   ″
1980, p. 421: no. 699   ″
1982-83, p. 401: no. 665   ″
1985, p. 417: no. 694   ″
1988, p. 392: no. 646   ″   Preliminary
1989, p. 404: no. 661   ″   Preliminary

1. THINKING ABOUT DRUGS

REFERENCES

1. For a review, see: Musto DF: America's first cocaine epidemic. *Wilson Quarterly* 1989;13:59-64; and Musto DF: *The American Disease,* expanded edition, New York, N.Y., Oxford University Press; 1987; p. 3ff and 251-77.

2. Ansonia *Sentinel*, 29 December 1896.

3. Report of the Committee on Matters of Professional Interest in the State. I. Cocaine. *Proceedings of the Connecticut Medical Society. 1896;253-64.*

4. Connecticut Public Acts, 1905, Chapter 127, "An Act concerning the Sale of Certain Narcotic Drugs."

5. *New York Times,* 21 February 1907, p. 4, col.4.

6. Laws of New York, 1907, Chapter 424, "An Act to amend the penal code, in relation to the sale of certain drugs."

7. Laws of New York, 1910, Chapter 131, "An Act to amend the penal law, in relation to the sale of cocaine and eucaine."

8. Laws of New York, 1913, Chapter 470, "An Act to amend the penal law, in relation to the sale or possession of cocaine or eucaine."

9. Pure Food and Drug Act (1906), Chapter 3915, Section 8. see also: Young JH: *The Medical Messiahs* Princeton, N.J.; Princeton University Press; 1967:35ff.

10. Musto: *American Disease,* p. 121ff.

11. For example, "Police Blind to Cocaine Selling" p. 1, and "Gangs of Gunmen Protect Sellers from Competition" p.2, New York *Tribune* 2 December 1912.

12. Musto, op cit, p. 14ff and Ansonia *Sentinel,* loc. cit.

13. For example, New York *Tribune*, 28 July 1921 ($1.50/deck) and New York *Times*, 4 January 1923 ($2.00/deck).

14. Opium Problem, Message from the President of the United States: Senate Document No. 377, 61st Congress, 2nd Session, Washington, DC, Government Printing Office; 1910: p. 48.

15. Musto, op cit p. 230ff.

Cycles of Craving

Society's drugs of choice appear to come in waves: LSD and marijuana, cocaine, now crack. But cutting across the gradual shifts in drug-use patterns and the severe crisis in many of our cities is a growing disenchantment with it all.

Dan Hurley

Dan Hurley is a contributing editor of Psychology Today.

Lenard Hebert is an expert of sorts on America's patterns of drug abuse over the past 25 years. He hasn't studied them; he's lived them.

"I did each drug of the decade," says Hebert, a 40-year-old man now glad to be recovering in New York City's Phoenix House, one of the largest residential drug treatment centers in the world. Sitting in a lounge at the center, dressed neatly in white shirt and tie, he recalls his time as a Marine in Vietnam in 1967: "We'd wear peace signs on our helmets and love beads around our necks. Drugs were another way to get in touch with home. And LSD was definitely the most popular drug at the time."

When he returned home in the early '70s, Hebert became a black militant, bought a beret and, as he says, "did strictly reefer. A good militant did natural, herbal things. Then I went disco. I snorted cocaine for 10 years. It was chic because it was so expensive."

Along came crack, the smokable, highly addictive form of cocaine with its five-minute high. Hebert stopped dealing cocaine and turned his middle-class high-rise apartment into a crack den. Before he made it to Phoenix House, he was sleeping in abandoned cars and shelters for the homeless.

Spotting National Trends

The cycles of drug abuse that nearly ruined Hebert's life represent fairly well the way that different drugs sweep across our country in waves. "It's as if we've been conducting a huge social experiment since the early 1960s," said the late Norman E. Zinberg, a psychiatrist at Harvard who, since 1963, had been studying national drug abuse patterns. (He died in April.) In his view, the nation has gone through four major waves of drug use, beginning with LSD in the early 1960s, marijuana in the mid- to late-'60s, heroin from 1969 to 1971 (Hebert escaped this heroin wave somehow) and cocaine in the late '70s and '80s.

Zinberg believed shifting patterns in drug abuse are signs of the times, reflections of the country's shifting zeitgeist. "Cocaine became the drug of the '80s because it's a stimulant," he said. "People were looking for action. It fit the mood, just like psychedelics fit the mood of the early '60s."

For years, experts have been trying to spot large trends in drug abuse with the hope that they might better prepare and adapt treatment, prevention and law enforcement efforts, according to David E. Smith, a specialist in addiction medicine who opened the Haight Ashbury Free Clinic in 1967 and has been monitoring drug-use patterns ever since. Although we have become increasingly sophisticated in identifying patterns, several factors muddy tidy calendars of drug usage such as Zinberg's. Most notably, researchers have found that: 1. Drug use varies tremendously from region to region, even city to city; 2. Drugs of choice move with some predictability through the social class structure; and 3. Rather than a simple succession of drugs in use, one drug often will piggyback on another, complicating efforts at prevention.

The East-West Transfer

In 1976 the National Institute on Drug Abuse (NIDA) took the first step toward monitoring regional trends when it formed the Community Epidemiology Work Group, an assembly of drug-abuse experts from 20 cities around the country who meet biannually to exchange data. "Drug-abuse problems sometimes develop very quickly at the local level," says Nicholas J. Kozel, chief of NIDA's statistical and epidemiologic analysis branch and chairman of the group.

"Up until about a year and a half ago, there wasn't much of a crack problem in Washington, DC," Kozel explains. "Then all of a sudden we had more violence and murder than we'd ever seen, most of it associated with drugs, especially crack. Drug abuse is different from Boston to Buffalo to Washington. It pops up this month and recedes the next. That's why we need local surveillance. It keeps you on the edge of your seat, trying to stay alert to these changes and their impact on the health of our nation."

Class Distinctions

Compounding these regional variations is the movement of particular drugs through social classes. In a fairly predictable pattern, drug epidemics seem to begin among a small, elite group, then filter down into the broad middle class and finally permeate the ghetto. In 1983, half of the callers to 1-800-COCAINE, the national cocaine-abuse hot line, were college-educated, 52% had family incomes of at least $25,000 and only 16% were unemployed. By 1987, only 16% of the callers were college-educated, a mere 20% had incomes of $25,000 and fully 54% were among the unemployed.

"Cocaine use is going down among the people who work and can't afford not to show up for their jobs," says psychiatrist David F. Musto, a Yale medical historian and author of *The American Disease: Origins of Narcotic Control.* "The first people to go on a drug are the avant-garde and the wealthy, and they're the first to go off it, too. But in the inner city, drugs become a source of status and money, at least for the dealers."

Demand for illegal drugs has been dropping in the middle class for 10 years, according to two national surveys sponsored by NIDA. The most recent National Household Survey on Drug Abuse showed that drug use among 18- to 25-year-olds leveled off between 1979 and 1985. The first substantial decline in cocaine consumption among American high-school seniors, college students and young adults showed up in a 1987 survey conducted by the University of Michigan's Institute for Social Research. The most recent available poll shows that the decline continued in 1988.

Drugs that Travel Together

Despite regional variations, there do appear to be predictable patterns of abuse once a drug arrives on the scene. For instance, heavy abusers of cocaine or speed often use heroin simultaneously, usually at the end of a binge to ease themselves down. It shouldn't be surprising, then, that in 27 cities across the country the number of deaths associated with both heroin and cocaine leapt between 1984 and 1988. From 1987 to 1988 alone, domestic heroin seizures by the Drug Enforcement Agency more than doubled, jumping from 382.4 kilograms to 793.9 kilograms.

"It's predictable that we've had an increase in heroin abuse," says Smith. "Anytime you see a stimulant upswing, you see an opiate upswing. The stimulant epidemic was the door for the opiate epidemic."

And Smith is now worried by a disturbing new trend—a simultaneous increase in the use of *both* speed and cocaine. "Normally the trends go in different directions," he says. "The speed curve went up and the cocaine curve went down. But since the advent of crack, it's the first time I've ever seen both the speed curve and the cocaine curve go up. The current stimulant epidemic is without a doubt the worst I've seen since 1967—and in fact it's worse than 1967."

What Shapes the Patterns?

Experts have found the patterns of drug abuse are formed not only by vague national moods and fashions but also by the ordinary stuff of any business: packaging, marketing, distribution, research and development. "Crack has grown because of new marketing techniques," says Jim Hall, executive director of Up Front, a national drug-information center based in Miami. "When the yuppies were buying cocaine, they bought it in somebody's apartment, usually at prices of at least $50. The crack user

buys it on the street or at a crack den in a vial that costs $10. This less-expensive alternative is what has brought cocaine to a whole new user group in the poverty pockets." It's not unlike the single-serving marketing strategy that has been successfully adopted by the food industry.

Arguably the strongest regulator of drug use is the public's perception of a drug's safety. America's first epidemic of cocaine abuse a century ago began when doctors had only good things to say about it. In 1884, Sigmund Freud wrote in *Uber Coca* that "The psychic effect of cocaine consists of exhilaration and lasting euphoria which does not differ from normal euphoria of a healthy person . . . . Absolutely no craving for further use of cocaine appears after the first or repeated taking of the drug." Thirty years later, the U.S. Congress passed the Harrison Act, designed to restrict severely traffic in opiates and cocaine, which by then had come to be considered serious public health hazards.

Cocaine's perceived risks have followed much the same trajectory in its second epidemic. As recently as 1985, psychiatrist Lester Grinspoon and lawyer James B. Bakalar wrote in a chapter of *The Comprehensive Textbook of Psychiatry* that "High price still restricts consumption for all but the very rich, and those involved in trafficking. . . . If used moderately and occasionally, cocaine creates no serious problems." In that same year, the University of Michigan's annual survey of high-school students and young adults found that only 34% believed that trying cocaine once or twice was a "great risk." By 1987 amidst thundering anti-drug news in the national media, that proportion had jumped to 47.9%, and by 1988 more than half of those polled thought that even experimenting with cocaine was very risky. "The perceived risks have shifted enough that they could fully account for the shifts in use," says Jerald G. Bachman, one of the survey researchers.

Drugs for the '90s

Even now, as the uproar of negative publicity about crack's debilitating effects has checked its spread among middle-class users, another stimulant—a smokable, fast-acting form of methamphetamine—has entered the drug scene in the West and, according to some experts, has begun moving eastward. Police officers in various areas have been seizing unprecedented numbers of clandestine methamphetamine laboratories, and there has been a sharp rise in both hospital emergency-room reports and deaths related to use of the stimulant.

In contrast to crack, which gained its foothold in the East and then began moving westward, methamphetamine seems to be a West Coast phenomenon. It also differs from crack in that "methamphetamine use tends to be highest among white, blue-collar types," says Smith. "The clandestine labs tend to be controlled by the white biker gangs, while crack tends to be controlled more by inner-city blacks."

The growth of methamphetamine seems to stem from the ease with which it is manufactured in secret labs. A drug that can be made here at home avoids the problem of smuggling across our increasingly patrolled borders. In addition, its effects are advertised as similar to those of cocaine, without the reputation for deadliness. Hall, of Up

Front, says that the spread of methamphetamine "looms as a potential national drug crisis of the 1990s."

The Empathy Drug

A case study in the progression of a new drug trend can be seen in the recent emergence of MDMA, better known as Ecstasy. First produced in 1914 but forgotten for years, the drug attracted the attention of psychotherapists in the '70s because, besides its stimulant and mildly psychedelic qualities, it could also increase patients' insight and empathy. "There's very little question in my mind that it can facilitate insight-oriented psychotherapy," says psychiatrist Lester Grinspoon.

By 1985, however, Ecstasy had become a recreational drug associated with a distinct type of music and dancing called "acid house" that originated on the Spanish island of Ibiza where wealthy people vacation. It served as a sort of new, improved brand of cocaine: It was exclusive, it provided the energy for dancing until dawn, it was allegedly "harmless," and—perhaps most attractive—it made people not only want to talk—as most stimulants do—but also to listen.

Researchers quickly found, however, that Ecstasy can damage brain cells in animals, even in low doses that correspond to the dosages people use for recreation, and the DEA outlawed it for most purposes in 1985. Recently made illegal in most of Europe, it drew the kind of sensational headlines there last summer that crack had garnered in America. Yet that publicity failed to cross the Atlantic, and Ecstasy continues to enjoy a safe and exclusive image here.

"It's a very white, very middle-class drug," says Bill Brusca, general manager of The Tunnel, a popular Manhattan nightclub. "It's not the kind of drug you're going to hear a lot about, because it's not habit-forming."

But positive accounts such as these, says Nicholas Kozel of NIDA, "are similar to what was said about cocaine in the early '80s. They're looking for the safe drug, and we're realizing that there isn't any." Even so, Kozel isn't prepared to predict that Ecstasy abuse will reach epidemic proportions. "Forecasting is difficult," he says, "and MDMA is an especially difficult drug to track."

What Does the Future Hold?

Despite the advances in trend analysis for drug abuse, nobody seems prepared to forecast the future. Some—including, most notably, psychiatrist Jerome Jaffe, the country's first "drug czar" under President Richard Nixon and the current head of federal addiction research efforts—are skeptical about our ability to make accurate predictions at all. Although he concedes that, without question, drug abuse follows a "trendy, fashionable popularity cycle," he doesn't believe we know enough about those cycles to predict what will happen next.

Historian Musto thinks that the most important trend is the decreased use of illegal drugs by the middle class that has cut through all of the various cycles since 1979. "We're 10 years into a phase of growing intolerance toward drugs," says Musto. "If history is a guide, it will take 20 to 30 more years for drug use to hit the nadir." History

is indeed a guide to Musto, who investigated long-forgotten documents on America's first drug epidemic at the turn of the century for *The American Disease*. To him, the year-to-year shifts in drug use are all-but-imperceptible "blips" in our declining interest in illicit drugs.

According to Musto, "Crack seemed to be the ultimate drug problem, one so frightening that it crystallized our intolerance toward all drugs. It has created a consensus in society against drugs and ended the ambivalence that had been prevalent for decades."

Musto fears that America's turn against drugs could have serious social repercussions. "My concern is that as demand goes down in the middle class, instead of channelling efforts into long-term plans to help, people will get angrier and angrier at those in the inner city who still use drugs," he explains. "If we triple the amount of money we spend to battle the drug problem and if we pass a death-penalty measure expecting to solve the problem in a year, we'll only become frustrated by the results. The decline in drug use will be a long, gradual process. We're going down a road, and we've still got a long way to go."

A drug epidemic takes on a different character when it reaches the ghetto: There are more deaths—including the killing of innocent standers-by—and other tragedies such as addiction in newborns. Failure to recognize these people as victims, Musto says, and consequent failure to pursue aggressive public education and jobs programs, will only exacerbate an already difficult social problem.

Breaking the Cycle

Once this, America's second drug epidemic, bottoms out, will we begin cycling inexorably into a third? Musto is willing to make one prediction: A society that forgets its history of abuse is doomed to repeat it. Unfortunately, says Musto, when America's first cocaine epidemic began fading in the '20s, "it became policy in the federal government to mention drugs as little as possible, and if they did mention them, to give descriptions so exaggerated and disgusting that no one would try them even once." Many adults are familiar with the 1936 propaganda film *Reefer Madness* that was circulated in the late 1950s and became a cult favorite in the '60s and '70s. When the young people who experimented with drugs in the '60s discovered that the exaggerations couldn't be trusted, they discarded all cautions to explore the reality of drugs in earnest.

Tragically, America's ahistorical attitude toward drug abuse continues to this day. "The Department of Education in California recently came up with a new syllabus of American history," Musto says. "There's no mention of the history of drug abuse. And in one place it lists drug abuse among the unacceptable topics for history electives. The largest education system in America gives no space on its syllabus for the important history of drug abuse in the United States."

In Musto's opinion, "The history of drugs and alcohol should be integrated into American history. If people had had a vivid knowledge of the first cocaine epidemic, the second epidemic might have taken a different route."

As we live with the fallout of America's second great drug-abuse epidemic in decline, a national commitment to remember the toll it has taken may be the only way to avoid a third.

Drugs: The World Picture

Mary Ellen Sullivan

The lure of drugs is strong. For dealers, money motivates. For users, the desire for pleasure or escape usually prompts the entry into drugs. The quest to repeat the experience drives addiction.

Unwittingly, each user fuels an international drug economy that is built on violence, greed, and a callous disregard for human life.

The drug business is an ugly one, full of exploitation, wrecked health, and wasted lives. It also is a big business, the biggest in the world, with an annual volume exceeding $300 billion (some estimates go as high as $500 billion). But it is a big business that law enforcement agencies, national governments, and many small but powerful local initiatives are working to destroy. What are the chances of their doing this in the '90s?

There are more than 40 million illegal drug users throughout the world—more than half of them in the United States alone. In fact, the United States is the single biggest market for the illegal drug trade.

Once thought of as merely a health or a social problem for drug users and their families, drug abuse in the United States during the last five to 10 years has created a set of problems so destructive and far-reaching that solving them has become one of our country's top priorities. Why? Consider:

• Chief Justice William Rehnquist of the U.S. Supreme Court reports that the number of drug-related cases in the federal courts has risen 85 percent in the last four years.

• The U.S. Department of Justice says that half of all men arrested for serious crimes are drug users.

• Between 1986 and 1988, there was an 1,100 percent increase in the number of semi-automatic weapons (the weapons favored by drug dealers and also the weapons involved in several mass murders at school playgrounds in recent years).

• In urban areas, entire neighborhoods are taken over by drug gangs, making them unsafe for residents.

> *"All of us agree that the gravest domestic threat facing our nation today is drugs. Drugs have strained our faith in our system of justice. Our courts, our prisons, our legal system are stretched to the breaking point. The social costs of drugs are mounting. In short, drugs are sapping our strength as a nation . . . . Who's responsible? Let me tell you straight out. Everyone who uses drugs. Everyone who sells drugs. And everyone who looks the other way."*
>
> —President George Bush, in a speech last September setting out his plans for a national drug control strategy.

From *Current Health 2,* February 1990, pp. 4-10. Special permission granted by *Current Health* Magazine, published by Field Publications. Copyright © 1990 by Field Publications.

Also, in these neighborhoods innocent children are often killed in the crossfire of warring drug gangs.
• The spread of the deadly disease AIDS currently is highest among intravenous drug users.
• Approximately one in 10 babies in the United States is born with illegal substances in his or her system.

A Global Issue

Although the United States' drug problem right now seems uncontrollable, we're not the only ones with problems. Drugs have become a global issue. Use has dramatically increased in Europe and even in such previously untouched areas as the Soviet Union. Violence is a way of life—and a fact of life—for the international drug traffickers, where informants are routinely tortured and killed, and opponents are murdered by hired killers for as little as $10. And some Third-World countries' entire economy is based on the illegal drug trade.

Take, for instance, Colombia, so much in the news in recent months. Cocaine is this country's major export, bringing in more than $4 billion a year and supplying about 80 percent of the world's cocaine. Entire villages in the Andes mountains depend on the coca leaf crop, from which cocaine is extracted, for their existence, not to mention the cities that have come alive from the conspicuous spending of the high-level drug traffickers. Medellin, the home of the country's biggest drug cartels, or organizations, has million-dollar high-rise apartments equipped with huge satellite dishes for picking up American TV shows, expensive clothing and jewelry stores, imported cars, and other luxuries. Accompanying this opulence, however, is a staggering level of violence: Medellin has the highest murder rate of any city in the world not at war.

"Plomo o plata"

In addition, in many Latin American and Caribbean countries, the drug organizations have corruption

The Great Crack Attack

Nightmare: That's what crack has caused since its explosive debut in 1985. This smokable derivative of cocaine has transformed the drug scene virtually single-handedly.

The drug is easy to make and highly profitable. Its cheap street price—$10 to $15 a vial—and the almost instant high it delivers, make it attractive to the urban poor (who comprise the majority of its users). And its highly addictive quality—crack and its parent cocaine are among the most addictive substances known to modern science—guarantees steady customers. Crack users reportedly can become addicted after as little as one hit. Because the high only lasts a few minutes, crack addicts develop an almost insatiable hunger for the drug.

For the last several years, the crack problem has been at its most nightmarish in large U.S. cities, namely Detroit, Los Angeles, Miami, New York, and Washington, D.C., although it can now be found in mid- and small-size towns as well. In the urban areas, however, crack dealers have turned neighborhoods into war zones. They openly deal on the street or set up shop in abandoned buildings called crack houses, where people can purchase the drug and then use it on the premises.

Big-time crack dealing is almost entirely the province of the street gangs who, once only concerned with skirmishes over turf, now engage in deadly battles over profits. Some crack gangs run as efficiently and coolly as many businesses, using databases to keep track of customers and inventory, and car phones and electronic pagers to keep in touch with employees. But there's a big difference between them and conventional businesses: Crack gangs are run by young men often armed with military style semi-automatic weapons, ready to kill for as little as a $10 debt.

Crime as a By-product

Crime has become one of the worst by-products of crack. Not only do dealers and warring gangs murder each other, but addicts resort to crime to support their habit. They will steal on a daily basis, sell their body, neglect their children, kill. In Detroit, 53 percent of felony suspects tested positive for crack or cocaine.

The crack problem may be at its most severe in Detroit. In 1988, a Little League team folded because the players were too busy selling crack to play baseball. Beepers and pagers—tools of the trade of drug dealers—were banned in high schools. So were certain status symbols flaunted by them, such as warm-up outfits and leather jackets. Detroit's Wayne County medical examiner reports a 525 percent increase in cocaine-related deaths. And in their "war on cocaine," Detroit police arrested almost 5,000 people in a two-month period in 1988.

In New York City, crack has more than tripled the number of cocaine users since 1986, as well as, according to the *New York Times,* "multiplied the cases of child abuse and neglect and caused a surge of prisoners." The paper also reports that the crack scourge has become "more pervasive, more violent and more insidious, especially in poor areas...." It estimates that drugs were involved in at least 38 percent of all murders in that city in 1988, compared with 20 percent for many years.

on their side. With the drug traffickers' policy called "plomo o plata" (which literally means lead or silver, or a bullet or a bribe), they have managed to buy off and scare people ranging from local police officers to a country's highest leaders. In Colombia, this policy reigns supreme: Last August, a leading presidential candidate and anti-drug campaigner was shot down at an open-air political rally. More than 50 judges and two cabinet members were assassinated in the last two years after trying to crack down on the drug cartels. Making law enforcement even more difficult is the fact that in Colombia and neighboring countries, some elected officials are known drug dealers.

In Burma, the Southeast Asian country that is the world's largest producer of heroin, the drug warlords have private armies to protect their businesses. There are no restrictions for crossing the border into neighboring Thailand. And the laws are such that dealers can only be arrested if they have possession of the drug—and they make it a policy never to touch it.

Clearly, the drug problem is complex and destructive. Here's a closer look at this world issue.

The Big Three—And Where They Come From

Supply and demand. That's what rules the drug trade. It's classic Keynesian economics. Says a writer in the Spanish news magazine *Cam-bio 16*, "On the day that a pound of bananas is worth more than a pound of cocaine, there will be no more South American coca farmers."

And, conversely, the day Americans stop craving drugs, the world supply will shrink.

Marijuana, cocaine, and heroin are the drugs with the highest demand worldwide. In the United States, there are 18 million marijuana and hashish users, 700,000 heroin addicts, and an estimated 7 million who regularly use cocaine.

Mexico actually supplies more drugs to the United States than any other country, growing its own marijuana and heroin and serving as an entry point for Colombian cocaine.

Colombia, Peru, and Bolivia produce almost all of the world's cocaine. The coca plant thrives in the mild, high-altitude climate of the Andes mountains.

Most of the heroin that reaches the United States comes from the opium grown in the poppy fields of what's called the "golden triangle," where Burma, Laos, and Thailand converge. Iran, Pakistan, and Afghanistan also ship this drug to our country.

The majority of illegal drugs slip into our country through southern Florida and across the Mexican border—drop-shipped onto high-speed boats, packed into private planes, hidden in imported goods, and concealed on bodies. Customs officials say they've seized drugs in the most improbable places: in coffins, in flower shipments, in diapers, and in beer cans. They've reported heroin-laced shampoo and dog collars containing cocaine.

The Allure of Drugs

Once it gets here, the attraction of the drug world is particularly strong for inner-city kids who can make $200 to $3,000 a day selling crack. Some children start as early as 8 or 9 years old as lookouts for drug dealers, warning them when police enter the neighborhood. Lookouts make about $100 a day. In a few years they can graduate to "runners," transporting drugs from the makeshift factories where drugs are processed to the dealers. Their salaries also graduate—to about $300 a day.

By the time they are teenagers, they can become "king of the street" or dealers. An aggressive crack dealer can rake in more than $15,000 a week. That's more than half a million dollars a year. This money buys them the status symbols that make them neighborhood heroes—Mercedes Benzes, BMWs, Rolex watches, gold chains, designer clothes.

It's no different for the South American peasant. The $1,000 offered by traffickers for every 2.5 acres to plant coca, whose leaf cocaine is made from, often means the difference between eating and starving. Nor is it different for the local *poseros,* or processors, who grind the coca leaf into paste. They fare even better: It's not unusual to

---

The Littlest Victims

Sad: Drugs' saddest casualties are the babies born addicted, primarily to cocaine or crack. William Bennett, head of the Office of National Drug Control Policy, in a June 1989 interview with *USA Today* was asked what surprised him the most in his study of the drug problem. "I didn't know about the babies. Cocaine babies. I didn't know about 375,000 babies born with drugs in their systems...I hadn't heard the details about what their life is like—those who make it," he replied.

According to a New York health professional, an estimated 11 percent of mothers giving birth in urban areas are addicted to drugs, and the number of babies who test positive for controlled substances has more than tripled in the last few years. In Illinois, the number of "cocaine babies" rose 79 percent in 1988 from the previous year.

What does this mean for the babies? The ones who are not permanently damaged spend their first weeks of life "withdrawing" from the drugs. Nurses report that crack babies don't thrive well. They are unusually cranky, jittery. They flail their fists. They don't want to eat. And, neglected in utero, they often face a life of further neglect from an addicted parent.

Drug Facts

• The number of current cocaine users has decreased by half since 1985—from 5.8 million to 2.9 million.
• Drug use among high school seniors has dropped 13.6 percent since 1982.
• Cocaine use in young adults has dropped 20 percent.
• Among the 8 million people who used some form of cocaine in 1988, the proportion of frequent users jumped by 33 percent.

• There are more estimated drug dealers in the United States than dentists.
• Since 1983, hospital emergency rooms report that cocaine-induced overdoses have risen more than 700 percent.
• About 7 percent of the U.S. population are addicted to drugs or alcohol.
• Of the 46,000 reported medical emergencies due to cocaine abuse in 1988, 15,000 related to crack.

see color televisions in their shacks and four-wheel drive vehicles in their dirt driveways. And so it goes all the way up the ladder. The people who chemically process the coca paste, turning it into the powder form it is sold in, make even more. Pilots can earn $5,000 a kilo to transport the drug out of the country. And, of course, the leaders of the cartels are millionaires. *Fortune* magazine estimates Pablo Escobar, one of Colombia's biggest drug barons, is a billionaire.

Big bucks are in the heroin trade, too. Opium from Burma costing $170 can be turned into $2 million on the streets of New York or Europe with minimal processing.

The United States Fights Back

In the fight against the drug trade, the United States is making a full-blown assault. FBI. DEA. CIA. Coast Guard. Customs agents. Local police. Schools. Hospitals. The legal system. Congress. Everyone's getting involved. The federal government budgeted $6 billion for 1989. "Drug Czar" William Bennett wants more. "The bill will be big," he says, "but the bill for not doing something will be bigger: $150 billion to $200 billion."

It seems, however, whatever the United States spends is never enough. The federal government's dollars seem like pennies compared with the millions the drug dealers have to spend. Often they have faster boats, more powerful weapons, and a cold-blooded lack of hesitation in killing anyone who stands in their way.

In addition, our overloaded legal system has difficulty handling the number of cases it has. In some cities, only a small percentage of adults arrested on drug charges actually serve time. Cases where the drug offender is a minor—as is true with the majority of crack offenders—mostly go through the juvenile court system. This involves a series of court supervisions, probations, and foster homes for first-time offenders. Sometimes it takes as many as seven or eight arrests before a juvenile dealer is jailed.

But the United States is making progress. Each year surpasses the last in the number of drug seizures, drug busts, drug related arrests. In Washington, D.C., between 1983 and 1987, drug arrests increased by 45 percent, drug prosecutions by more than 500 percent, and drug convictions by more than 700 percent. One of Colombia's most powerful drug kingpins is currently serving a life sentence in a Florida prison. But our war on drugs is being fought in skirmishes, using guerrilla tactics, under cover of night. It is a war where the enemy is everywhere—and hard to find. Right now we're winning many battles but still losing the war.

For More Information

American Psychiatric Association
Division of Public Affairs
1400 K Street N.W.
Washington, DC 20005
  Booklet: "Substance Abuse," single copy free.

Consumer Information Center
Dept. 510V
Pueblo, CO 81009
  Booklet: "Schools Without Drugs," single copy free.

Wisconsin Clearinghouse
P.O. Box 1468
Madison, WI 53701
  Booklet: "You Asked for It," (Drug Information for Teens), single copy $1.50.

Clearinghouse for Drug and Alcohol Abuse
P.O. Box 2345
Rockville, MD 20852
  Pamphlets: #PHD 507 "What You Can Do About Drugs in America"; #PHD 04 "When Cocaine Affects Someone You Love," single copy of each free.
  Fact Sheets: #CAP 05 "Cocaine Abuse"; #CAP 11 "Heroine"; #CAP 12 "Marijuana"; #CAP 17 "Facts About Teenagers and Drug Abuse," single copy of each free.

*The Indiana Jones of the tavern scene,
this anthropologist studies the
American drinker like a lost tribe of the
Amazon. In documenting the rituals
of the bar, he's discovered how and why
we booze it up the way we do*

INTERVIEW
JAMES SCHAEFER

A. J. S. Rayl

The rain drizzles down on the car windows as Jim Schaefer pulls off the main road and into a packed parking lot. "Most anthropologists spend a lifetime trying to find a tribe that will accept them," Schaefer says as we approach a building pulsing with light and music. Nailed to the door is a big sign that reads: ANYONE WHO IS NOT OF LEGAL AGE WILL BE ARRESTED ON THE SPOT AND ESCORTED FROM THE PREMISES. "But my tribe," he continues, "is here and now. And they accept me." Schaefer is an anthropologist whose tribe is American drinkers. Associated professor and director of the Office of Alcohol and Drug Abuse Prevention at the School of Public Health at the University of Minnesota, he has spent almost 20 years studying American drinkers, the bars they patronize, and the role of alcohol in society.

We enter the Hoggsbreath, a bar on the outskirts of St. Paul. Clearly this is Schaefer's territory. Like some kind of Indiana Jones of the tavern scene, he swashbuckles a path through the mass of humanity to the watering hole and orders drinks. The Hoggsbreath is a theme bar and thus features a different sort of ambience every night. Monday nights the theme is country and west-

ern, and that means there'll be a tight-jeans contest, complete with free shots for the contestants, and all the bumping and grinding it takes to win, "And things," Schaefer warned earlier, "can get down and dirty."

"Hey, there's the professor!" shouts the bar's cowboy DJ. "And he says if you listen to slow country music you're gonna drink more. Whaddya thinka that!" The tribe responds with boos and hisses. Then these urban cowboys break into a chant: "Bullshit! Bullshit! Bullshit!"

Born in Schenectady, New York, in 1942, Schaefer is the son of a General Electric scientist who discovered the principle of cloud seeding. As a young child Schaefer showed an interest in anthropology, archaeology, and hunting for arrowheads and other buried relics in upstate New York. The West always held an allure, and in 1960 Schaefer enrolled in the University of Montana as a forestry major. But with most of his time spent in Missoula's heavy party scene at the local bars, he was on the verge of flunking out. To pick up his grade point average, he was advised to go into anthropology, a subject that had a reputation for being easy at Montana. In those courses Schaefer found direc-

tion, however unintentionally. He earned a degree in anthropology in 1966 and "made it into graduate school" at the State University of New York at Buffalo.

When Schaefer couldn't come up with a topic for his doctoral thesis, his adviser asked what it was that Schaefer felt he knew a lot about. In a moment of unadulterated honesty, he replied, "Drinking." His life's work began that day. Schaefer completed his dissertation, a cross-cultural study of family structures, supernatural belief systems, and drunkenness in 57 tribal societies worldwide. In 1973 he earned his Ph.D. with distinction.

Schaefer returned to the University of Montana as an assistant professor. And with newfound awareness and self-control, he returned to the Missoula bar scene—this time to study the whys and wherefores. He also spent a year as the Fulbright Visiting Lecturer at Sri Venkateswara University in India and a year as a National Institute of Alcohol Abuse and Alcoholism Research Fellow at the Center for Alcohol Studies of the University of North Carolina. But mainly, during the next decade Schaefer, along with research assistants and students, hung out at local bars, investigating patron behavior and environmental influences. Conducting their research in an unobtrusive, participant-observation style, Schaefer and colleagues discovered that the jukebox served as a mood-selection device. He realized further that by studying the impact of music, decor, lighting, and other factors on customers, he could draw up an environmental-risk profile with regard to overindulgence for almost any bar.

And on this particular night at the Hoggsbreath? "It's definitely high-risk," Schaefer says. "The bar is crowded. The dance floor is crowded. People can't really move. They'll get frustrated and start drinking more. And check out the lighting. It's what I call twilight lighting: It's light enough to see but dark enough to cover the faults."

In 1978 Schaefer moved to Minneapolis, to the University of Minnesota, where he has since taken part in several research and development projects. In 1979 he and University of Montana graduate student Paul Bach published a paper on slow country music and drinking. It put Schaefer on the map in many circles, both scientific and lay. In 1985 he was enlisted as a coproject investigator with sociologist Richard Sykes, also of the University of Minnesota, for a long-term study on self-regulation of alcohol abuse among tavern patrons in the Midwest. He is currently participating in an investigation of biological markers for alcohol consumption and a study of environmental influences on gambling and drinking.

Alcohol remains the United States' number one recreational drug. Schaefer has crossed detached scientific lines and become something of an activist in community education, outreach, and intervention programs geared toward reducing alcohol abuse. In 1982 he organized Anthropologists Concerned for Anthropologists, a support group for those professionals struggling with alcohol and drug abuse. The same year he was awarded a grant to head the Grand Rapids, Minnesota, Drinking and Driving Project. It gained nationwide attention when Schaefer replanted old Burma Shave signs along Minnesota highways (IT'S BEST FOR/ ONE WHO HITS/ THE BOTTLE/ TO LET ANOTHER/ USE THE THROTTLE). And in 1988 he was appointed to the science advisory board of the American Council on Alcoholism.

Schaefer is frequently hired as an expert witness for both plaintiffs and defendants in drunk driving cases. He has served as a consultant to major law firms around the country and to the Federal Trade Commission on product liability and fraudulent advertising practices.

Schaefer is also an entrepreneur of sorts. In recent years he has helped design bars and has lent his expertise to the development of Alcosorb, an anti-intoxicant and hangover remedy, for 21st Century Pharmaceuticals.

A.J.S. Rayl spent an extended weekend with Schaefer, barhopping throughout the Twin Cities—from cowboy night at the Hoggsbreath to the upscale Rupert's to small neighborhood bars.

Omni: How did your bar research begin?
Schaefer: I took a job at the University of Montana and while visiting some of the old places ten years after, I thought about applying ideas I'd gleaned from theoretical work. What could I observe in an actual place where people drank? I started hanging out all over again, only this time as an anthropologist.

Sammy Thompson, owner of the Trail's End in Missoula, was by far the best bartender I'd ever seen. A maestro, he orchestrated the scene. One day, about five P.M., the jukebox ran out of plays and suddenly I saw the place die. While people weren't verbalizing it, their eyes were saying, "What's wrong here?" Sammy picked up on it right away and brought out this bean game, a long-necked jug with maybe fifteen beans in it, one of which was red. The one who winds up with the red bean loses and forks out the money to play the jukebox.

As the guy with the red bean headed toward the jukebox, regulars started shouting out the songs people wanted to hear. I suddenly realized that here was a microcosm of bar culture and that the jukebox was a mood-selection device. That was really neat—something I could systematically investigate. My graduate student Paul Bach came up with an ingenious way to measure the relationship between mood, music, environment, and drinking. We'd put a tape recorder on the table in front of the jukebox and tape the ten- to twelve-o'clock set of songs on consecutive Friday nights. We observed patrons drinking in different areas of the bar. We'd also tap our table with a pen or glass every time someone in our sample areas sipped a drink.

Back at the office, Paul converted the music into beats per minute and correlated it with the number of sips per minute. We assumed that as the tempo went up, the drinking would, too, but it didn't turn out that way. Slower songs went with faster sipping.

Next we looked at lyric content and tried to figure out whether country-western [CW] songs tended to portray images of self-controlling the world—internal locus of control—or external. Slower songs tended to be sad—"your lyin' cheatin' heart" or "cryin' in the beer" type songs. Country music is not like the "I Want Your Sex" stuff of modern rock and roll. Country is more of a working-class blues—"I'm sufferin' and hurtin' since you been gone" variety. It's the stuff of the work-hard, play-hard folks who are the hard core of this country, whether they

live in Detroit, Los Angeles, or the Rocky Mountain west. I don't know if you need to put warning labels on CW songs, but the surgeon general might be interested!
Omni: Have you gone into a bar and challenged the norms, say, punched numbers for certain kinds of songs on the jukebox at the wrong time?
Schaefer: Yeah, and do they give you stares! There is a recognition of normative sounds in a bar, and when that norm is being broken or challenged, people will leave or let their preferences be known. At the Trail's End, we did things like playing a sequence of slow songs and took a baseline count of the number of times the cash register rang at twenty-minute intervals. I did that a couple of times, and once the sales quadrupled.
Omni: You also began to establish a risk profile with regard to overdrinking. What did you find?
Schaefer: There's a greater likelihood in a "high-risk" environment. For instance, moderately lit bars with a twilight kind of darkness—bright enough for effective cruising, but dark enough to cover up faults—are high-risk.

Heavy drinking also occurs when the ratio of men to women is high, like five to one. The men get very frustrated because they have a limited capacity for expressing themselves. There's also a premium on being able to get to a table and, you know, "cut out a heifer"—take her out to the dance floor and she's yours. A small, crowded dance floor is high-risk. You can't do your thing. You're bumping into people, so you tend to drink more. I've looked at the artwork, too. High-risk bars often show images of action: In a cowboy bar you'll see a picture of a cowboy bustin' a bull. Or, in other bars, sports pictures: Somebody is about to make a touchdown or is skiing off a cliff. This can be an affirmation of risky or highly competitive behavior and tends to encourage a bragging, storytelling bravado, and there's more drinking.
Omni: What about low-risk drinking environments?
Schaefer: Bright and very dark bars are relatively low-risk. Casino bars, in particular, are on the bright side because the premium is not on drinking but gambling. Darker bars tend to be more of a romantic setting for couples or lonesome singles. In yuppie bars, where you dress up and eat food, there's a premium on not spilling, not getting messy, and that sets a certain decorum for the group. If there's a big dance floor and lots of space to move around, then there's a premium on struttin' your stuff: You're out there swinging, gliding, or stomping—or you're Cotton-Eyed Joe. In bars where there's moderate drinking, I found landscape artwork or just wallpaper. And there are family-type bars, usually restaurants with a sec-

tion where the kids play video games and the women can eat and socialize. These tend to be low-risk because the premium isn't on drinking. These places aren't real common in the United States.

Omni: How does behavior differ in certain types of bars?

Schaefer: Observation—not testing—tells me the drinking in the rock scene—disco, rock, or live-band pop—is more controlled. A slightly different game's being played. In the country-western bar there's more male acting out and rowdy behavior: "Let's get drunk and *be* somebody." In the rock and pop scenes there's a premium on meeting someone, impressing them with your good taste in drink, clothing, and maybe dancing.

Omni: What about the *Cheers* kind of bars, the neighborhood bars?

Schaefer: If we are talking about reinforcing a core value system, a shared system of values that is anchored in a community, then *Cheers* bars act as places where everybody knows your name, there's a place for you to be someone, and they know what you drink. It's a home away from home that provides you with the security of peer group protection. If Norm has a drinking problem, someone will see him about it. If Sam Malone is a teetotaler, they respect it. They'll joke about his fake male prowess, lack of intellect, but they don't joke about his drinking. It might be interesting to see some real intoxication on *Cheers*, see them cut somebody off and perhaps go through treatment. There are possibilities on that show that aren't being explored.

Omni: According to your studies, how often do people who go to bars actually become intoxicated?

Schaefer: The bad news is that more than fifty percent of the people in a bar at a given time in the area we sampled were intoxicated, twelve percent seriously. By intoxication we mean drinking at a rate of three or more drinks an hour and actually consuming three or more drinks an hour. If you drink at that rate for two hours, you're well over the legal limit [.10 milligram] for blood alcohol.

Surprisingly, Richard Sykes's study showed that the vast majority of bar staff are pretty darn accurate in gauging just how intoxicated their patrons are. Our objective observers' estimates of slightly and seriously intoxicated patrons almost perfectly matched the perceptions of the bartenders and cocktail waitresses interviewed. We originally thought that they would substantially underestimate the number of intoxicated people.

But while bartenders are accurate, they frequently are overserving. In most jurisdictions, overserving is against the law, though it's a law that's not enforced. The feds aren't out there trying to monitor that,

6In small-town America, the bar is the gossip center—the center of social activity. Without that corner bar to go to, there would be more homicides, violence, and trouble.9

but overserving makes for drunk driving and is the stuff of alcohol abuse.

Omni: Have you found regional differences in drinking patterns?

Schaefer: Lots. The Southeast generally has very low consumption rates, yet every third generation has serious drinking problems. There is strict adherence to the Bible, and Fundamentalists often teach that one must abstain entirely from alcohol. This is overdone in many households, and as a result, the next generation reject the values and become alcohol abusers. Yet the societal effects [job impairment, drunk driving, familial breakup, and so forth] of problem drinking in the Southeast are the lowest in the country. The vast middle of the United States tends to be the beer-consuming part of the country. In the upper Midwest we have moderate drinking, and that part of the country is also right in the middle in terms of social problems related to drinking. New York City and Washington, DC, are extremely heavy drinking areas. Texas, Nevada, California, Oregon, and Washington—wine states—show heavy drinking and high rates of alcohol abuse. And the indexes of alcohol problems in the New England states are very high. It's thought that where wine is inexpensive, there's a pump-priming effect: Wine consumption leads to consumption of spirits and beer.

Omni: What about gender differences?

Schaefer: Men drink more than women. That hasn't changed. Older men drink earlier in the day. Women drink about half as much as men and tend to drink later in the day, as well as later in the week. Perhaps women feel that later is safer because more people are around. If a lady were to go into a bar alone early in the week, she might be perceived as not meeting the cultural norm. Now Tuesday night is ladies' night, and that's a widespread phenomenon. Women do come out, at least for the first shift, to drink the free champagne. Usually they leave then,

unless they meet someone who's worth staying around for. There's still a stigma against a woman being intoxicated in public. Women pay attention to making sure they don't show signs of it.

Omni: But certainly you've seen women who've had a little too much, and men responding to it with a sort of endeared amusement?

Schaefer: You mean when they become foulmouthed, telling jokes, and being more like a guy? Sure, but when it goes beyond the cultural norms, then she becomes the subject of exploitation. There are a good number of predators looking for women who've had a little too much. They follow an agenda of buying her a good stiff drink to make sure she's over the edge, presumably not caring what happens to her. It works differently in other parts of the world. When I was in India, it was taboo for a woman to drink in public, but alcohol is available everywhere. I saw partying college women who would go up to men and feign drunkenness, feign passing out, so they could have sex. The women wanted it, so they played the same game the other way around.

Omni: Are there racial differences in drinking patterns?

Schaefer: You'd find about the same rate of alcoholism among whites, blacks, Hispanics, Latinos, and Chicanos. There is, however, more excessive drinking among American Indians than any other group. Their unique tribal traditions have now become essentially welfare-state traditions, a culture of poverty. There are some proudly held core traditions, but the majority are losing that core value system. There's tragedy on every reservation. There's no history of moderate drinking among Native Americans, although there's now an attempt to increase a culture of sobriety. Biological or genetic factors may also play against them with regard to metabolizing alcohol.

Some evidence suggests that genetic factors play a role for Orientals as well. But the consequences differ from those for the Native Americans. The vast majority of Japanese and Chinese people have an enzyme system that is slow to break down acetaldehyde, the first metabolite of alcohol, which is probably more intoxicating and damaging to the system than ethanol. This enzyme defect translates to a flushing response, dizziness, pounding of the heart, sweating, and general dysphoria. This unpleasantness may be protective against alcohol abuse. The abuse problem is at a low percentage in first-generation Orientals.

Omni: Is the same metabolic factor present in the American Indian?

Schaefer: Possibly. American Indians are part of the Asiatic gene pool. Although, having migrated millennia ago, they must be considered very diluted Asians. There is a strong theoretical argument, supported by animal studies, that if one persists in drinking heavily in the face of this enzyme defect, that person will quickly become addicted to alcohol. It may be that persistent heavy drinking under those circumstances causes a biological adaptation similar to tolerance buildup in normal people—only much faster. Lab rats with this deficiency that are exposed to alcohol quickly develop another enzyme, THP [tetrahydropapaveraline], a by-product of acetaldehyde. THP seems to enhance the animals' craving for ethanol, and they go after it until they convulse or die. It may be that due to the extreme stress caused by their cultural disenfranchisement, the American Indians continue to drink in spite of the protection conferred by the enzyme defect. So this devastating mechanism of addiction has taken hold.

Omni: What's the role of the local bar?

Schaefer: If any society chose to reject alcohol, it would probably have other, more serious problems. There's the workplace, the homeplace, and this third place, where we talk, drink, and release ourselves from our everyday worries and troubles. A little bit of drinking goes a long way in terms of the health of the community. Without that outlet we'd have more fighting, violence, and civil strife. In Minnesota we recently passed stricter drunk driving laws that upshifted the penalties for drunken driving. Shortly thereafter, when the cops started busting people, domestic violence increased. The heavy drinkers were staying at home. Bar sales went down, but package store sales went up, as did spouse and child abuse.

It's an age-old explanation, but I am more and more convinced that drinking alcohol in a relatively controlled public environment, where professionals are trained to recognize the intoxicated and immature drinkers, is the context in which our society can blow off steam. In small-town America the bar *is* the gossip center, the center of social activity. Without that corner bar to go to, there would be more homicides and violence.

Omni: But can't we learn to release tension without alcohol?

Schaefer: With milk and cookies? It's been tried and it's not nearly as successful as with alcohol.

Omni: So the release lies in the high?

Schaefer: Right. Some psychopharmacologists say altered states may be another human drive. I'm not necessarily buying into that, but there are people who believe that the occasional search for an altered state of consciousness is a healthy way of adjusting to life.

Omni: In your opinion, what is a safe level of alcohol consumption?

Schaefer: If you're downing more than thirty-five drinks a week, or five drinks a day, you're risking chemical dependency and medical consequences like cirrhosis, pancreatitis, cancer, and stroke. A person weighing more than one hundred thirty pounds should stick to about eight to ten drinks a week, with no more than five in one sitting. More than five per sitting could cause long-term problems. For someone weighing less than one hundred thirty pounds, we recommend seven to eight drinks a week, with no more than four at one sitting. We also recommend that people stand when drinking, because people feel their intoxication more rapidly if they only have two-point support. If you know your weight, you should have your blood alcohol chart memorized. God, I can't believe I said that, but it's the truth. Know just how many drinks you can drink. Stick to your limit. If you can't, get help.

Omni: You mentioned that at one time you had a drinking problem.

Schaefer: In the early Sixties a lot of events brought me to that realization. I was really kind of out of control, and a lot of my buddies knew it.

Omni: How did you deal with it?

Schaefer: I never did anything official. I slowed down, got into a relationship with the woman I ended up marrying, and stayed married for a considerable period of time. If I had been living in Minnesota, for example, I would have been confronted and counseled into a treatment program. But back then in Montana—and still in Montana—the value system was one where people took care of their own problems. The opinion of my alcohol-recovering friends to the contrary, I can now drink and then leave it alone. I don't drink the bottle dry. I intersperse nonalcoholic drinks with my alcohol. What I did was mature out of my drinking problem from a hell-raiser to a family man.

Of course, by choosing my career in the alcohol abuse prevention field, I was helping myself. I exposed myself to all the reasons why people drink, biological as well as sociocultural. I continue to be in contact with treatment people and work extensively in developing programs that educate and train people in abuse prevention. I guess my work and life are a kind of therapy. Having been there—literally having gone to skid row and back, getting into fights, getting arrested and thrown in the drunk tank, and then getting bailed out by my favorite bartender at the Trail's End—gives me a unique kind of credibility.

I can now get into the scenes quickly. That's very subjective, and from a scientist's point of view, that subjectivity is often questionable. But the typical anthropological scheme is to use your intuitive and deductive powers by going into a scene, coming back with preliminary data, then systematically replicating them. The original insights usually come from a subjective, involved participant frame of reference. There's trial and error in understanding cultural patterns.

Omni: Why is alcohol abuse the country's number one drug problem?

Schaefer: American society is very immature. We're on this treadmill of "Gotta go! Gotta get the bucks!" It may be endemic in a capitalist system that we tend to overdo in our lives and sometimes burn out. Our self-imposed, highly competitive system puts us all under a great deal of risk for outlets such as excessive drinking or bouts of depression. Our biochemical, neurochemical wiring hasn't been prepared for these kinds of stresses. Self-medicating is a pattern of culturally approved behavior.

Per capita consumption of alcohol is, on average, declining, indicating that by the mid-Seventies, community tolerance for alcohol abuse had reached its peak. A number of things occurred, the most recent being housewife Candy Lightner forming the group Mothers Against Drunk Driving [in 1981]. People resolved that driving while drunk is a totally inappropriate social behavior. But the reality is a lot of people still drink and drive.

You change behavior in a Judeo-Christian society by deglamorization and mild repression. Look at cigarette smoking. That's what our drunk driving laws do. The recognition of alcoholism as a disease was a major step in the direction of helping people with problems. People arrested today have a slightly lower blood alcohol level than they did in the early Eighties. Yet I do foresee alcoholism continuing to be the number one drug problem in the coming millennium.

Omni: What about Alcoholics Anonymous [AA] or the Betty Ford Clinic or the many other treatment centers? How well do they work?

Schaefer: The twelve-step program of AA is a blueprint for living that has helped a huge number of people recover from very serious problems with alcohol. It's a wonderful and effective fellowship. At Betty Ford you enroll full-time as an inpatient for a month, then return on an outpatient basis or, in some cases, not until you relapse. There is a good likelihood of a slip, maybe a full-blown relapse, with any of these treatment programs. Statistics are hard to come by, but I've heard that about one in four slips. And of those, one in four has a full-blown relapse [within four years] and will need to get back into a program.

Omni: Philosopher Herbert Fingarette created a stir two years ago by hypothesizing that alcoholism is really just a bad drinking habit.

1. THINKING ABOUT DRUGS

Schaefer: There have been few governing ideas about alcohol. There's the "Colonial" view: Alcoholism is a moral wrong. That eventually led to Prohibition: demon rum wrapped up in temperance. Then came the idea, surfacing about thirty years ago, that people who become chemically dependent suffer from an illness. The majority position is that of Fingarette's philosophy. Although in the United States its greatest expression has been found in behavioral psychology, it dominates European thinking about drinking. Alcohol, the argument goes, is a beverage that we learn to use. Some people get into trouble; some don't. The problem is behavioral, not genetic.

If you buy into the other, disease model—which, quite frankly, has been primarily conceived as a particular kind of alcoholism—then your only choice in correcting the problem is complete abstinence. Yet I accept the idea that some people change their alcoholiclike behavior and control their intake or spontaneously stop without help. I think Fingarette makes a good case for behavior modification as a possibility for some people with drinking problems. Such programs work best with persons who have a stable social and spiritual framework with which to rebuild their lives.

But I believe that up to twenty-five percent of all alcohol problems may someday be explained by genetic factors. Many families have gone from generation to generation inheriting the biological baggage of addiction. But the legacy doesn't necessarily have to be genetic. It can be passed on through poor family patterning in a disruptive atmosphere, a weakened moral network.

Omni: Will it ever be possible to eradicate alcoholism?

Schaefer: Yes and no. Remember that with alcoholism we're only talking about seven percent of the population. The biggest societal cost is not from alcoholism but *periodic* abuse of alcohol and other drugs. Treating the psychosocial part of alcoholism is our best chance for eradicating the problem in the short run. We can reduce the risk by building a culture with a better sense of individual responsibility about alcohol use. We can also build stronger families, neighborhoods, and communities with more awareness about appropriate use of alcohol among adults. That is what prevention's all about.

Now, the biological part may be more difficult. First we have to elucidate the precise addictive pathways. In the future we may understand the chemical structure of the chromosomes and where the genetic markers for the addictive potential lie. Then with gene therapy, say, we could adjust a person's genetic makeup prior to the reproductive years. That way he would not pass on the addictive genetic material to his children, and then eventually we might be able to eradicate the defect from the gene pool. Maybe we could give the person a choice of having the adjustment done or not. If not, then he could pay a large fine or something. [He laughs.] Alternatively, we could transplant a lot of livers and related body parts in addicts and abusers. Any biological tinkering might be too Draconian for our libertarian tastes. Yet another way of dealing with these problems is to create a novel family of drugs of anti-intoxicants that enable you to experience better living through chemistry, so you could drink, enjoy it, and not suffer the medical consequences.

Omni: Haven't you been consulting on the development of such a product?

Schaefer: I'm a scientific consultant with 21st Century Pharmaceuticals, a company here in Minneapolis. It has a patent on a product called Alcosorb that is much like what I've described. It's not a drug; it's a microversion of the charcoal slurry used in acute poisonings. Alcosorb is an activated carbon caplet that acts as a superfilter in the intestine. After the first stage of clinical tests, it looks promising. It appears to alter dramatically the blood alcohol level. Alcosorb will be controversial because it won't completely block the intoxicating effects of alcohol.

We are talking an *Alice in Wonderland* view now, but I think we can get close to blocking the physical consequences of alcohol abuse with a product that would absorb the toxic substances created by ethanol. It would save your liver and pancreas but still allow you to enjoy the intoxicating effects. It would require, of course, that we develop a whole cultural value system around it.

Omni: But wouldn't that open a Pandora's box of trouble? Without the threat of a hangover, what's to stop a person from getting drunk every night? Doesn't this encourage addiction to alcohol?

Schaefer: Not necessarily. In the short run it causes an ethical dilemma for people promoting the use of such a product. Should people always have to suffer the natural consequences of overconsumption: pounding heart, sweats, waking up in a pool of urine, the foul odor? If this product kept you from receiving those messages, it would not be a good idea. But again, this is a futuristic idea, and we need revolutionary changes in how we deal with the problems of addiction. I envision sophisticated chemistry enabling us to block or reduce some of the effects that are very costly to individuals, communities, and society as a whole.

The dog tests on Alcosorb are under way now in Texas, and they're looking good. We need to test humans at relatively high blood alcohol levels. So our next big hurdle will be the current federal guidelines that prohibit us from taking humans up to very high alcohol levels.

Omni: Tell us about the search for the biological marker of alcohol *consumption*, rather than alcoholism.

Schaefer: We're interested in detecting in simple blood samples whether an individual has been drinking during the prior week, month, three or four months, or year. Based on the ratio of certain blood chemistry structures, we should be able to see a person's drinking history and advise the individual or family about the relative risk of developing problems related to alcohol abuse or potential addiction.

We are not trying to develop a marker for alcoholism per se. There are numerous gross blood-based measurements available, and although perhaps useful for verifying alcoholism in some people who already have a problem, they have what we think are some fatal flaws: They depend on liver damage, for one thing, and that's already looking at the problem after the fact. They don't take into account, nor do they reflect, alcohol intake or dose-related responses, so they put the cart before the horse. We are looking for a marker covering the continuum, from abstinence to heavy abuse. We are investigating people with different levels of consumption: those who don't drink, those who drink moderately, social drinkers who overdo it from time to time, and heavy drinkers who do *not* develop full-blown chemical dependency problems.

The principal investigator, biochemist John Belcher, also at the University of Minnesota, has studied ways of detecting risks in both smokers and people in passive or secondary smoke situations such as airplanes. With alcohol we're looking at two different metabolic pathways. One is the oxidative pathway, where we're following the breakdown of the ethanol molecule into its various metabolites, particularly acetaldehyde.

In the other, nonoxidative pathway we're following the fatty acid ethyl esters and studying disruptions in chemical structure as a result of varying doses of alcohol. Using mass spectrometry and novel gas chromatography techniques, we're analyzing the sequences of certain amino acid chains and long-chain peptides for minute differences. On a preliminary basis we've found remarkable differences between people who drink and those who don't. That was our first clue that we were on to something. Now we're sorting through our data to make sure we are not creating our own monster through various detection methods: fusions, dilutions, saturations, and so forth.

We have examined a couple dozen nondrinkers and about a dozen drinkers and are comparing their blood samples under different doses. My role is recruiting the subjects. I'm out there beating the bushes for drinkers, abstainers, and recovering alcoholics, those who have abstained for five, ten, and seventeen years. We want to see if their hemoglobin structures are any different from people who have never been exposed to alcohol. We'll give some subjects doses of alcohol; then we'll take blood samples over various periods of time. We have them come back the next day, three days, then a week later, and months later. They'll keep a diary, too, of any drinks they have. We hope to correlate blood structures we've analyzed with their self-reports. What got us very excited about this was that we were able to isolate a particular point in a hemoglobin molecule, the first line on the chart we think will eventually be able to delineate the light, moderate, and heavy drinker. And we found it in a place we never thought we'd find it: in the abstainer.

Omni: Grants for alcohol-related studies are plentiful. Have times changed?

Schaefer: Yes. The National Institute of Alcohol Abuse and Alcoholism is now very interested in research on drinking environments. And I've seen a number of proposals for investigating such things as what happens when you deregulate a state with liquor controls or begin to train bar staffs in a specific community. Ten years ago people were skeptical of the relevance of my work. It was pretty lonesome out there. Now there's lots of attention. Richard Sykes and I put in a proposal to recruit a hundred groups of drinkers to essentially go out and drink in bars, wearing body-packed microcassette recorders. We'll transcribe their conversations in time-sync so we can analyze how bar customers make decisions about drinks, reorders, and driving.

Omni: What do you hope to achieve by your work?

Schaefer: I like my idea of the hospitality covenant where a community gets the retail liquor businesses together and they promulgate their own set of voluntary standards. A number of communities are employing my idea. Also, I hope more social scientists will now be willing to get out to do work in the establishments, the grocery and liquor stores, and not rely on proxy studies. Unless you've done your share of hanging out, you can't ask the right questions.

Omni: Do you think the role of alcohol will change in the next few years?

Schaefer: Right now we're headed for a continuation of neo-Prohibition. I think we're going to continue to swing to the right regarding alcohol controls, because the governing image is still of alcoholism as a disease whose spread must be curbed. In the long run, though, there'll be a rebound, and we'll see per capita consumption go back up. But what our children's children will do with alcohol is anybody's guess. I also expect we'll legalize marijuana. All the cigarette companies are patiently waiting. They've already trademarked names.

Omni: Bar owners have consulted you about the design of their establishments.

What ideas do you have for future bars?
Schaefer: I would have exits that mimic the field sobriety tests. The exit itself would resemble a fun house. You'd go into a tunnel with a floor that's not quite level. To get out you'd have to navigate a maze. Maybe the sides would be electronic so if you hit them, there'd be a light show—and then a cab would be waiting for you when you finally made it out. If you did. Or you might automatically be given a breath test. Instead of waiting for the sobriety test from Smokey, why not have the bars provide it?

Omni: Will we always have bars?
Schaefer: In the late Seventies I was giving a paper in Norway on alcohol abuse. On a day off, I headed for a bar, where I met two guys who said they had a film showing at a local film festival. They were George Lucas and Mark Hamill, and they asked me if I wanted to come to their screening. I did, and *Star Wars* came on, and it was fantastic. One scene that bothered me a bit, though, was the cantina scene, with the pulling down of hookahs by all those weird creatures. I asked Lucas, who is anthropologically trained, about it. He said he believed there's always going to be a place where ideas are brokered. And it's more likely going to be in a situation where people can have unlimited access to whatever chemical they want. Although I argued with him on details, Lucas is basically right. There's always going to be a place to go to achieve altered states—the third place. And in the future we'll have much more open minds about the benefits of achieving altered states now and then.

Use, Addiction, and Dependence

Of all approaches to drug use and abuse, perhaps the least fruitful and most fallacious is what might be called the *either-or* perspective, that is, the view that one is either a complete abstainer *or* an addict, that there is no in-between territory; as soon as one "fools around" with drugs, one becomes "hooked for life." The reality is quite otherwise. In fact, drug use is a continuum, not an either-or proposition. Experimentation does not necessarily lead to regular use, and regular use does not necessarily lead to compulsive use or addiction. For every drug, it is possible to find users at every point along the spectrum—from experimentation to occasional use to regular use to outright addiction. There is no inevitable "slide" from less to more involved levels of use.

At the same time, there is a biological and biochemical *basis* for physical dependence, or addiction. Certain drugs possess properties unique to themselves that influence how—and how often—they are used. Most researchers today believe that addiction, or physical dependence, is strongly linked to how *reinforcing* drugs are. Some drugs are highly reinforcing, which means that it is extremely pleasurable to take them; these drugs are more likely to generate a physical dependence in the user. With other drugs, the pleasure is less immediate, more diluted, less sensuous and more of an acquired taste; these drugs are less likely to generate a physical dependence.

Physical dependence can be demonstrated even in laboratory animals in experiments. If certain drugs are self-administered, these animals will take them again and again if they are available, and they will undergo a great deal of pain and deprivation to do so; on the other hand, certain other drugs are difficult for researchers to get animals to self-administer, and animals will discontinue them fairly readily when they can. Drugs that animals will self-administer extremely readily and which, it can be inferred, are highly reinforcing: heroin, amphetamines, and cocaine (including, presumably, crack); drugs that animals have relatively little interest in taking in the laboratory setting and which, it may be inferred, are far less reinforcing: alcohol, marijuana, and the hallucinogens. In biological terms, then, looking at the factor of reinforcement alone, it can be said that heroin, amphetamines, and cocaine possess a high addiction potential, while that of alcohol, marijuana, and the hallucinogens is fairly low.

Another factor has to be emphasized: *route of administration*, that is, *how* a drug is taken. Certain methods of use are highly reinforcing, that is, the drug's effects are immediate and highly sensuous; other methods are less so, that is, the drug's effects are slower, more muted, less immediately sensuous. Intravenous injection and smoking are more immediate, more highly reinforcing methods of use; oral (swallowing a pill, for instance, or drinking alcohol) and nasal (sniffing or "snorting" cocaine or heroin) ingestion are slower, less reinforcing techniques. When a highly reinforcing drug is taken in a highly reinforcing fashion, its addiction potential is large; when a less immediately pleasurable drug is taken in a less reinforcing fashion, its addiction potential is far smaller.

These two factors—the characteristics of the drug and the mechanism of use—help explain why heroin, crack, and injected cocaine are likely to generate a high proportion of drug-dependent users. However, there are many features of the drug scene that are not fully explained by the biological model: Why, for instance, are there so many alcoholics, given that the drug is not especially reinforcing and it is nearly always taken in a non-especially reinforcing fashion? Why does nicotine, a psychoactive chemical found in tobacco, generate so many addicts when laboratory animals avoid taking it altogether? Why is marijuana, taken via a highly reinforcing technique, likely to generate users dependent on the drug? Clearly, sociological and cultural factors come into play here, and determine how, and how often, certain drugs are taken.

Looking Ahead: Challenge Questions

What is the difference between dependence on a legal drug and dependence on an illegal drug?

What is the difference between dependence and addiction?

What is the most addicting drug known?

Is alcohol addicting? Are cigarettes?

Is it possible to use drugs on a recreational, sporadic, once-in-a-while basis?

What is the difference between the user and the addict?

Why is the degree of immediate pleasure generated by different drugs so strongly related to a drug's potential for chemical dependence?

Unit 2

ADDICTION AND DEPENDENCE

Erich Goode

Although it has been known for at least 2,000 years that certain drugs "have the power to enslave men's minds," it was not until the nineteenth century that the nature of physical addiction began to be clearly understood. At that time, a "classic" conception of addiction was formed, based on the opiates—at first, opium and morphine, then, after the turn of the century, heroin as well. Much later, it was recognized that alcohol, sedatives, such as barbiturates, and "minor" tranquilizers also produced most of the symptoms of "classic" addiction.

What is "classic" addiction? If a person takes certain drugs in sufficient quantity over a sufficiently long period of time, and stops taking it abruptly, the user will experience a set of physical symptoms known as *withdrawal*. These symptoms—depending on the dose and the duration—include chills, fever, diarrhea, muscular twitching, nausea, vomiting, cramps, and general bodily aches and pains, especially in the bones and the joints. It does not much matter what one thinks or how one feels about the drug, or even whether one knows one has been taking an addicting drug. (One may not attribute one's discomfort to the drug, but these physical symptoms will occur nonetheless.) These symptoms are not psychological—that is, "all in the mind." They are physiological, and most of them can be replicated in laboratory animals. The withdrawal syndrome is the nervous system's way of "compensating" for the removal of the drug after the body has become acclimatized to its presence and effects.

Although the label "addicting" has been pinned at some time or another on practically every drug ever ingested, it began to be recognized that certain drugs simply do not have physically addicting properties. Regardless of the dose administered or the length of time the drug is ingested, the same sort of withdrawal symptoms exhibited with heroin, alcohol, or the barbiturates cannot be induced in humans or animals taking LSD, marijuana, or cocaine. Users will not become physically sick upon the discontinuation of the use or administration of these drugs. In a word, these substances are not addicting in the "classic" sense of the word. If we mean by "addicting" the appearance of "classic" withdrawal symptoms after prolonged use and abrupt discontinuation, then certain drugs are addicting and others are not.

This bothered a number of officials and experts a great deal. Saying that a drug is not addicting seemed to border perilously close on stating that it is not very dangerous. Something had to be done. Some new concept or terminology had to be devised to make nonaddicting drugs sound as if they were in fact addicting. In the early 1950s, the World Health Organization, in an effort to devise a new terminology that would apply to the "abuse" of all drugs, and not simply those that are physically addicting, adopted the term "drug dependence." As it appeared in its final form in a later statement, drug dependence was defined as:

. . . a state of psychic dependence or physical dependence, or both, on a drug, arising in a person following administration of that drug on a periodic or continued basis. The characteristics of such a state will vary with the agent involved, and these characteristics must always be made clear by designating the particular type of drug dependence in each specific case. . . . All of these drugs have one effect in common: they are capable of creating, in certain individuals, a particular state of mind that is termed "psychic dependence." In this situation, there is a feeling of satisfaction and psychic drive that require periodic or continuous administration of the drug to produce pleasure or to avoid discomfort (Eddy et al., 1965, p. 723).

Under the new terminology, each drug has its own characteristic type of dependence: There is a "drug dependence of the morphine type," a "drug dependence of the cannabis [marijuana] type," a "drug dependence of the alcohol type," and so on. In other words, the new terminology is a definition, or a series of definitions, by enumeration, for it was felt that no single term could possibly cover the diverse actions of the many drugs in use (or "abuse").

The new terminology was extremely imprecise and clearly biased. The intent of the drug experts who devised this terminology was ideological: To make sure that a discrediting label was attached to as many widely used drugs as possible. Under the old terminology of "classic" addiction, it was not possible to label a wide range of drugs as "addicting." It thus became necessary to stigmatize substances such as marijuana and LSD with a new term that resembled "addicting." In other words, the scientists and physicians who devised the new terminology of "dependence" were in effect disseminating propaganda to convince the public that nonaddicting substances were just as "bad" for them, that they could be just as dependent on them as on the truly "addicting" drugs. Medical authorities labeled the continued (or even the sporadic) use of nonaddicting drugs as "dependence" in large part because they were unable to understand why anyone would want to take them in the first place.

Physical dependence is a powerful concept. With a great deal of accuracy, it predicts what will happen physiologically to an organism that takes enough of a certain drug for a long enough period of time. Can psychological dependence be an equally useful concept? Does the fact that it was devised for propagandistic purposes mean that it is automatically meaningless?

During the 1970s and 1980s, researchers began to see some strong parallels between physical and psychological dependence. To put it another way, the fact that one drug is physically addicting and another is not does not seem to predict the patterns of their use very well. Some crucial facts and findings have emerged in the past generation—since the World Health Organization's notion of psychological dependence was formulated—to suggest that perhaps the concept of psychological dependence may not be meaningless.

First, . . . *most* regular users of heroin are not physically addicted in the classic sense. They take wildly varying amounts of heroin on a day-by-day basis, often go a day or two without the drug and do not suffer powerful withdrawal symptoms, take several doses a day for the next several days, and so on (Johnson et al., 1984; Johnson, 1984; Zinberg, 1984). If physical addiction were so crucial in determining use, this pattern would be unlikely, perhaps even impossible.

Second, even the heroin users who are physically addicted and withdraw—whether because of imprisonment, the intervention of a treatment program, or self-imposed withdrawal—usually go back to using heroin; roughly nine addicts in ten who withdraw become readdicted within two years. If physical dependence were the major factor in continued use, we would predict a much lower relapse rate than this. If the physical compulsion or craving is absent, why return to a life of addiction?

Third, many of the drugs that are not physically addicting are often used in much the same way that the addicting drugs are—that is, frequently, compulsively, in large doses, at an enormous personal and physical toll on the user. How could an addicting drug like heroin and a nonaddicting drug like amphetamine or cocaine produce similar use patterns? If addiction—the product of a biochemically induced craving—is the

principal explanation for compulsive use, then how is this possible?

Fourth, and perhaps most crucial, was the hold that cocaine, a supposedly nonaddicting drug, was found to have on laboratory animals. The researchers who conducted these experiments wanted to answer several basic questions: How reinforcing is cocaine? How dependent do animals become on the drug? How much will they go through or put up with to continue receiving it? They discovered that animals will go through practically anything to continue receiving their "coke."

Three key sets of experiments establishing cocaine's dependence potential were conducted. In all three, a catheter was inserted into the vein of a laboratory animal (rats, monkeys, and dogs were used). A mechanism, usually a lever, was rigged up so that animals could self-regulate intravenous (IV) administration of the drug. In one set of experiments, animals were given a choice between cocaine and food; they could have one or the other, but not both. Consistently, laboratory animals chose to continue receiving cocaine instead of food, to the point where they literally died of starvation.

In a second set of experiments, the cocaine was abruptly withdrawn; pressing a bar no longer produced any cocaine. The researchers reasoned that the longer that unreinforced bar-pressing behavior continued, the more dependency-producing a drug is: The more frequently that animals press the bar before they give up—before bar-pressing is "extinguished"—the greater the dependence potential of the drug. Not only did animals that had taken cocaine over a period of time continue to press the bar many times after the drug was withdrawn, but, even more remarkable, they did so far longer than did those animals that had taken heroin—a clearly addicting drug! (A summary of the experiments conducted on the dependence potential of cocaine in animals may be found in Johanson, 1984.)

In a third experiment, one set of laboratory rats was allowed to self-administer cocaine; and a second set, heroin. Both groups could do this continuously and ad libitum—that is, at will, as much or as little as they chose. Those rats that self-administered heroin developed a stable pattern of use, maintained their pretest weight, continued good grooming behavior, and tended to be in good health. Their mortality rate was 36 percent after thirty days. Those self-administering cocaine ad libitum exhibited an extremely erratic pattern of use, with "binges" of heavy use alternating with brief periods of abstinence. They lost 47 percent of their body weight, ceased grooming behavior, and maintained extremely poor physical health. After thirty days, 90 percent were dead (Bozarth and Wise, 1985).

It is absolutely crucial to emphasize that humans are not rats, and experimental conditions are not the same as everyday life. What animals do in the laboratory may not tell us even in a rough way what humans do in real life. At the same time, laboratory experiments give us the framework within which drug effects can be understood. They establish the inherent pharmacological properties of drugs. Just *how* people take them is another matter; for that we have to examine drug use in naturalistic settings. Laboratory experiments give us an important *clue* as to how drugs might be taken in real life; they do not provide the whole story.

The facts and findings that these experiments brought to light point to the inescapable conclusion that the concept of psychological, or psychic, dependence is a meaningful, powerful mechanism. In fact, the results of the many studies conducted on the subject "indicate that psychological dependence might be more important than physical dependence" in much drug use, including narcotic addiction. "Psychological dependence, based on reinforcement is apparently the real driving force behind even narcotic addiction, and tolerance and physical dependence are less important contributors to the problem" (Ray and Ksir, 1987, p. 26). Taking a highly reinforcing or intensely pleasurable drug over a period of time does not necessarily lead to physical addiction, but it does lead to a powerful desire to repeat the experience, and to make enormous sacrifices in order to do so. The more intensely pleasurable or reinforcing the experience is, the more psychologically dependency-producing it is.

But aren't many activities or substances pleasurable? In a letter to the editor of *Trans-action* magazine, one observer (Freidson, 1968, p. 75) commented on the assertion that marijuana produces a "psychic dependence" by saying: "What does this phrase mean? It means that the drug is pleasurable, as is wine, smoked sturgeon, poetry, comfortable chairs, and *Trans-action*. Once people use it, and like it, they will tend to continue to do so *if they can*. But they can get along without it if they must, which is why it cannot be called physically addicting."

Clearly, we run into a conceptual dilemma here. On the one hand, many activities or substances are pleasurable; does it make any sense to dub all of them psychologically dependency-producing? To do so is to be guilty of using a concept that is so broad as to be all but meaningless. On the other hand, certain drugs do produce a syndrome that is clearly distinct from, but as powerful as—indeed, in some ways, even more powerful than—physical dependence. Unlike several of the activities or substances mentioned above, such as comfortable chairs, poetry, and smoked sturgeon, an alarmingly high proportion of users *cannot* get along without certain drugs—cocaine being the outstanding example. We are led to the following inescapable conclusions with respect to drugs and dependence.

First, psychic and physical dependence are two separate and to some degree independent phenomena. That is, someone, or an organism of any species, can be psychologically dependent on a given drug without being physically dependent. Likewise, the reverse is also true: it is possible to be physically dependent on a drug without being psychologically dependent—for instance, as a result of having been administered that drug without realizing it (in an experiment, for instance, or in the form of a medicine or painkiller in a hospital).

Second, substances vary in their potential for causing psychological dependence—with cocaine ranking highest, heroin next, possibly the amphetamines after that, and the other drugs trailing considerably behind these three. It is highly likely that this potential is closely related to how reinforcing each drug is—that is, the intensity of the pleasure that each delivers to the user. The more reinforcing the drug, the higher its potential for psychic dependency.

Third, psychological dependence is a continuum, with gradations between substances, whereas physical dependence is probably more of an all-or-nothing affair. The potential for psychological dependence is a matter of degree. Heroin, barbiturates, and alcohol are clearly dependency-producing drugs; this property can be demonstrated in laboratory animals. Drugs either *are* or *are not* physically addicting. In contrast, drugs can be arranged along a continuum of psychic dependency—with cocaine ranking high on this dimension, and marijuana ranking considerably lower on it.

Fourth, substances vary in their "immediate sensuous appeal" (Lasagna et al., 1955; Grinspoon and Bakalar, 1976, pp. 191–194). This is not quite the same thing as the capacity to generate pleasure. It is, more precisely, *the capacity to generate intense pleasure without the intervention of learning or other cognitive processes*. For the most part, one has to learn to enjoy marijuana (Becker, 1953; Goode, 1970, pp. 132ff.) The same is true of alcohol. It has been asserted for heroin, but it may be less true than has been previously assumed (McAuliffe and Gordon, 1974). Certainly it is true of many pleasurable activities and substances—including eating smoked sturgeon, reading certain books and magazines, and appreciating fine art. Here, the pleasure is great but cultivated. In any case, it is not true of cocaine and, to a lesser degree, amphetamines. Subjects who take these substances without knowing what they are taking tend to enjoy them the very first time and want to take them again. In short, they have an immediate sensuous appeal (Lasagna et al., 1955).

Fifth, different routes of administration are differentially capable of generating intense and immediate pleasure in individuals who take drugs by these means. As we've seen, intravenous injection is one of the fastest ways to deliver a drug to the brain; smoking—especially of cocaine—is also an extremely rapid and efficient means of drug-taking and is therefore highly reinforcing and likely to cause psychological dependence. Injecting and smoking cocaine have been described as being like "a jolt of electricity to the brain." On the other hand, chewing coca leaves, which contain less than 1 percent cocaine, is far less instantly reinforcing and is far less likely to lead to dependency (Weil and Rosen, 1983, p. 46).

And sixth, individuals vary with regard to their degree of susceptibility or vulnerability to becoming psychologically dependent on varying substances or activities. Clearly, the variation from one person to another in this respect is vastly greater than from one animal to another of the same species, or even from representatives of some animal species as compared with those of others.

The term "behavioral dependence" is sometimes used as a synonym for psychological dependence (Ray and Ksir, 1987, p. 25). This is not entirely accurate. Psychological dependence can refer to both a potentiality and an actuality: We can say that cocaine has a high potential for psychological dependence, and we can say that a specific individual, John Doe, is psychologically dependent on cocaine. On the other hand, the concept of behavioral dependence always refers to an actuality. It makes no sense to refer to a drug having a high potential for behavioral dependence; we can only say that John Doe is behaviorally dependent on a particular drug.

Behavioral dependence refers to actual, concrete behavior enacted by an actual, concrete person taking an actual, concrete drug. What has John Doe gone through or given up in order to take or continue taking a specific drug? What is John Doe now going through to do so? What will John Doe go through? To continue taking their drug of choice, some individuals have lost their jobs, destroyed their marriages, given up all their material possessions, gone into enormous debt, ruined their health, threatened their very lives. They exhibit behavioral dependence. While psychological dependence can be inferred from someone's behavior, behavioral dependence is what we see concretely—an actual person sabotaging or giving up concrete values and possessions previously held in esteem to take a specific drug. We recognize behavioral dependence by the sacrifices a particular user makes to get high. Behavioral dependence has been known for some time to be common among alcoholics and heroin addicts. It is now known that cocaine causes similar manifestations in users as well.

In short, although physical dependence (or "classic" addiction) is a very real and very concrete phenomenon, behavioral dependence does not depend on physical addiction alone. In many ways, the distinction between physical dependence and true psychological dependence—for the drugs that are powerfully reinforcing—is largely irrelevant. Chronic users of drugs that produce "only" psychological dependence behave in much the same way (that is, are *behaviorally dependent*) that addicts of physically dependency-producing drugs do. On the other hand, to throw drugs that produce a weak psychological dependence (such as marijuana) into the same category as drugs that produce a powerful one (such as cocaine) is misleading. Many experts "now regret" the distinction they once drew between cocaine as a "psychologically addictive" drug and narcotics like heroin that are "physiologically addictive." Heroin is "addictive" in a different way—it is both physically and psychologically dependency-producing. But both drugs activate pleasure centers in the brain in such a way that users feel impelled to take them again and again. Some users can overcome this message, but it is a factor that all users have to contend with. "We should define addiction in terms of the compulsion to take the drug rather than whether it causes withdrawal," says Michael A. Bozarth, an addiction specialist (Eckholm, 1986a).

REFERENCES

Becker, Howard S. 1953. "Becoming a Marijuana User." *American Journal of Sociology,* 59 (November): 235–242.

Bozarth, Michael A., and Roy A. Wise. 1985. "Toxicity Associated with Long-Term Intravenous Heroin and Cocaine Self-Administration in the Rat." *Journal of the American Medical Association,* 254 (July 5): 81–83.

Eckholm, Erik. 1986a. "Cocaine's Vicious Spirals: Highs, Lows, Desperation." *The New York Times* August 17, p. 2E.

Eddy, Nathan B., H. Halbach, Harris Isbell, and Maurice H. Seevers. 1965. "Drug Dependence: Its Significance and Characteristics." *Bulletin of the World Health Organization,* 32: 721–733.

Freidson, Eliot. 1968. "Ending Campus Drug Incidents." *Transaction,* 5 (July-August): 75, 81.

Goode, Erich. 1970. *The Marijuana Smokers.* New York: Basic Books.

Grinspoon, Lester, and James B. Bakalar. 1976. *Cocaine: A Drug and Social Evolution.* New York: Basic Books.

Johanson, Chris E. 1984. "Assessment of the Abuse Potential of Cocaine in Animals." In John Grabowski (ed.), *Cocaine: Pharmacology, Effects, and Treatment of Abuse.* Rockville, Md.: National Institute on Drug Abuse, pp. 110–119.

Johnson, Bruce D. 1984. "Empirical Patterns of Heroin Consumption Among Selected Street Heroin Users." In G. Serban (ed.), *The Social and Medical Aspects of Drug Abuse.* New York: Spectrum Publications, pp. 101–122.

Johnson, Bruce D., et al. 1985. *Taking Care of Business: The Economics of Crime by Heroin Abusers.* Lexington, Mass.: Lexington Books.

Lasagna, Louis, J. M. von Felsinger, and H. K. Beecher. 1955. "Drug-Induced Changes in Man." *Journal of the American Medical Association,* 157 (March 19): 1006–1020.

McAuliffe, William E., and Robert A. Gordon. 1974. "A Test of Lindesmith's Theory of Addiction: The Frequency of Euphoria Among Long-Term Addicts." *American Journal of Sociology,* 79 (January): 795–840.

Ray, Oakley, and Charles Ksir. 1987. *Drugs, Society, and Human Behavior* (4th ed.). St. Louis: Times-Mirror/Mosby.

Weil, Andrew, and Winifred Rosen. 1983. *Chocolate to Morphine: Understanding Mind-Active Drugs.* Boston: Houghton Mifflin.

Zinberg, Norman E. 1984. *Drug, Set, and Setting: The Basis for Controlled Intoxicant Use.* New Haven, Conn.: Yale University Press.

Drugs of Choice

Drug users who never suffer addiction attract scientific interest

BRUCE BOWER

Nancy Reagan's battle cry in her war on drugs was "Just say no" — a simple phrase that carries the implicit message that once you say "yes" and take a snort of cocaine or a swig of whiskey, or taste any intoxicating substance, you risk falling into dangerous, uncontrolled drug use.

Many recent theories reflect this notion in suggesting that repeated exposure to an addictive substance inevitably saps the human will and segues into unrestrained drug consumption.

But what those theories ignore, and what some people forget amid alarming stories of crack cocaine deaths and other drug-induced tragedies, is that many people "just say yes" to over-the-counter or under-the-table substances and use them moderately without getting hooked.

Although most drug researchers concentrate on abusers, some focus on people who manage to control their ingestion of mood-altering drugs. In fact, some investigators maintain that occasional users may help clarify the nature of drug addiction and present new approaches to preventing or curing it.

"The occasional user of narcotics and other drugs is more common than most people realize," says psychopharmacologist Ronald K. Siegel of the University of California, Los Angeles. "These users are difficult to study because they do not regularly appear in hospitals, clinics, coroners' offices, courts or other places where abusers surface."

On the other hand, researchers cannot point to a typical "addictive personality" or predict who will and who will not become addicted to a particular drug.

One attempt to illuminate the nature of controlled drug use focuses on people who ingest a highly toxic, extremely habit-forming and entirely legal substance — nicotine. Psychologist Saul Shiffman of the University of Pittsburgh and his colleagues study "tobacco chippers" — light smokers who regularly use tobacco without developing symptoms of physical or psychological dependence.

"Chipping" is a street term originally used to describe the occasional use of opiates such as heroin.

Tobacco chippers are not easily found. Federal statistics indicate one-quarter to one-third of U.S. adults smoke cigarettes. Recent studies of smokers find that more than 90 percent experience intense cravings for cigarettes and other withdrawal symptoms typical of nicotine dependence.

Shiffman and his co-workers compared 18 tobacco chippers who regularly smoke five or fewer cigarettes per day with 29 dependent smokers who consume 20 to 40 cigarettes daily.

Chippers differed from dependent smokers in a number of ways, Shiffman reports in the April PSYCHOPHARMACOLOGY. Dependent smokers reported numerous signs of withdrawal, such as irritability and cigarette craving, after an enforced overnight abstinence; chippers appeared unaffected by the deprivation and reported regularly abstaining from smoking for days at a time. Thus, chippers continue to smoke without any of the withdrawal symptoms that reinforce the addiction in other smokers, Shiffman asserts.

Chippers appear psychologically dis-

tinct from dependent smokers, he adds. They report less stress in their daily lives and more effective methods of coping with stress, perhaps lessening their need to smoke.

Tobacco chippers also tend to smoke while drinking a cup of coffee or in response to other external cues, Shiffman says, whereas dependent smokers "basically smoke when they're awake." His research team confirmed this observation with reports from 25 chippers and 25 dependent smokers who carried hand-held computers for several days, on which they recorded their moods and activities just before lighting up a cigarette.

Chippers smoke as often when they are alone as when they are with others who are smoking, Shiffman says, dampening suspicions that occasional smoking is primarily a social behavior.

Further findings suggest tobacco chippers and dependent smokers may differ biologically, he notes. Surprisingly, chippers report fewer uncomfortable reactions to their first cigarette, such as dizziness, coughing and nausea, than do heavy smokers. Also, fewer of the chippers' relatives ever smoked, and more of their smoking relatives successfully gave up cigarettes.

Despite the contrasts between the two groups of smokers, chippers fully inhale tobacco smoke and absorb the same amount of nicotine from each cigarette as do heavy smokers, Shiffman and his co-workers found in a study to appear in the ARCHIVES OF GENERAL PSYCHIATRY. After smoking one cigarette, chippers' blood nicotine levels increase in amounts equal to those of dependent smokers, as do their blood levels of a long-lasting nicotine metabolite.

The researchers also found that heavy smokers who agreed to reduce their consumption to five cigarettes per day compensated by inhaling more deeply and tripling their per-cigarette nicotine intake. Chippers, however, do not compensate for their limited use with deeper inhalation.

"I don't claim to understand how chippers do what they do," Shiffman says. But long-term observations of their smoking behavior and physiological responses will illuminate individual differences in tobacco use and perhaps help clarify the nature of dependent smoking, he contends.

Shiffman's work follows in the footsteps of research on heroin chippers directed by the late Norman E. Zinberg, a psychiatrist at Harvard Medical School in Boston. Zinberg held that three major forces mold a person's use of and experience with heroin or any other substance: the pharmacology of the drug, the personality of the user and the physical and social setting in which use takes place.

Zinberg saw the social setting as an especially powerful influence on heroin use. In 1972, he observed two types of heroin addicts in England, where these users obtained the opiate legally through public clinics. The first type used heroin in a controlled fashion and functioned adequately or even quite successfully, while the second took heroin constantly and lived desperate, self-destructive lives. But the latter group was not a cause of societal unrest, crime or public hysteria, Zinberg writes in *Drug, Set, and Setting* (1984, Yale University Press), because British social and legal sanctions allowed them to live as addicts.

Zinberg then studied small groups of heroin chippers and addicts in the United States. He found that occasional users did not experience the distressing withdrawal symptoms of hard-core addicts and tended to use heroin at specific times when it would not disrupt their jobs or other responsibilities.

The Vietnam War also provided a natural laboratory for studying controlled heroin use. Southeast Asian heroin was cheap, plentiful and delivered in an easy-to-use smokable form. About one out of three U.S. soldiers tried heroin while in Vietnam and half of them became addicted, according to surveys conducted in the early 1970s by psychologist Lee N. Robins of Washington University in St. Louis and her colleagues.

Yet when these veterans came home and left the bleak social setting of the war behind, their craving for heroin largely diminished. In one study, Robins and her co-workers interviewed 617 enlisted men before their return from Vietnam in 1971 and again three years later. Half the veterans addicted in Vietnam had used heroin since their return home, but only 12 percent of those became readdicted.

As early as 1947, heroin chippers were recognized as "joy poppers" who used the drug occasionally without signs of addiction, Siegel points out.

"Even if most heroin addicts had once been chippers," he asks, "why didn't all chippers become addicts? Is there a secret to controlled intoxicant use?"

No one offers a simple answer to this question, but in Siegel's opinion, the drug dose taken by an individual and its frequency are critical.

Consider crack, a smokable form of cocaine produced from cocaine hydrochloride powder through a chemical process known as freebasing. Smoking crack leads to a much faster and more intense intoxication than sniffing cocaine hydrochloride. In the early 1980s, Siegel studied about 200 arthritis sufferers under treatment at a desert clinic in California, where they regularly received Esterene — the pharmaceutical trade name for an experimental form of crack. Not one case of abuse surfaced in Siegel's investigation.

Esterene proved nonaddictive because doses were fixed by physicians and the drug was sniffed through the nostrils and absorbed slowly through the nasal membranes, he contends. Esterene did not cure arthritis, but many patients — who did not know they were using a form of cocaine — reported less pain and greater freedom of movement after the treatments.

Esterene remains nonaddictive when used outside a medical setting, Siegel says. The Esterene program in California is now banned, but Siegel located 175 people in the Los Angeles area who concocted crack at home for a variety of reasons. Some were cocaine users attracted to reports that snorting crack was safer than snorting cocaine hydrochloride powder, while others were elderly people seeking relief from arthritis or depression.

Again, these crack users — including those with a history of cocaine consumption — experienced few problems. They reported more energy and less physical pain but did not experience the rapid and reinforcing euphoria that helps give cocaine its addictive punch. While daily cocaine hydrochloride users snort the white powder around the clock, the 175 people sniffing their homemade crack took the drug infrequently and displayed no physical side effects or signs of dependency.

In contrast, street users of crack repeatedly smoke large doses of the drug, which rapidly enters the brain. Taken in this way, crack produces an almost instantaneous "rush" of intoxication, promoting rapid addiction as well as toxic physiological effects.

Nonetheless, Esterene users, crack addicts and other consumers of both legal and banned drugs share a common motivation, Siegel argues in *Intoxication: Life in Pursuit of Artificial Paradise* (1989, E.P. Dutton). "People use intoxicants to change the way they feel and satisfy their needs for psychological or physical stimulation," he says. "Intoxicating drugs are medications for the human condition."

Siegel, hardly in the mainstream of drug research, draws harsh criticism from those who believe abstinence is essential in the prevention of drug addiction. But his book has been read widely in scientific circles, as well as by at least one official in the White House Office of Drug Control Policy.

The pursuit of substances that alter mood and consciousness has evolved into a "fourth drive," on a par with sex, thirst and hunger, Siegel contends. Not only is intoxicant use a characteristic of people in virtually all societies, but evidence of the fourth drive turns up throughout the animal kingdom, he says. Siegel and his colleagues have observed the self-administration of naturally occurring drugs among mammals, birds, insects, reptiles and fish (SN: 11/5/83, p.300). Bees, for instance, taste the nectar of opium flowers and drop to the ground in a stupor, then go back for more; elephants seek out fermented fruits and proceed to get drunk; and monkeys munch hallucinogenic mushrooms and then assume a reflective pose, sitting with their heads on their hands.

Yet animals do not have significant problems with uncontrolled drug use in the wild, Siegel says. They consume infrequent, relatively small drug doses in the natural plant form, a pattern not likely to produce addiction.

Humans are another story. "We take benign intoxicants out of their natural packages, purify them and turn them into poisons," Siegel says.

Efforts to stem the ravages of addiction by cutting off drug supplies wither before the power of the fourth drive, and legalizing currently outlawed drugs will not make them safe, he argues. Moreover, it seems unrealistic to expect that drug addiction will disappear if people are taught about controlled "chipping" techniques or exposed to educational messages through the media, he says.

2. USE, ADDICTION, AND DEPENDENCE

If society acknowledges both controlled and excessive drug use as efforts to meet the needs of the fourth drive for a change in mental state or mood, the next step is a scientific search for safe intoxicants, or "utopiants," Siegel contends. These designer drugs would balance pleasurable effects with minimal or no toxic consequences, have fixed durations of action and contain built-in chemical antagonists to prevent addiction or overdose.

In one possibility Siegel cites, future molecular chemists may combine Esterene preparations with nitrenidipene — a chemical that reverses cocaine overdoses — to create a controllable form of cocaine.

In the meantime, Siegel supports efforts to prevent and treat drug abuse, including plans by the National Institute on Drug Abuse to spend nearly $100 million annually in search of medications that block the effects of cocaine and other illicit drugs.

But the fight against dangerous drugs must also embrace the scientific pursuit of safe intoxicants, he maintains. "Just saying 'no' often does not work, because the fourth drive is too strong," Siegal says. "This is not moral surrender [in] the war on drugs. The development of safe, man-made intoxicants is an affirmation of one of our most human drives and a challenge for our finest talents."

A Dirty Drug Secret

Hyping instant addiction doesn't help

Larry Martz

How could Marion Barry be on crack?" demanded a skeptical New York editor, debating the Washington mayor's recent arrest in a sting operation. "If you're on that stuff, I thought you go out of your mind. You forget your kids' names, sell your wife, do nothing but smoke crack. So how could he run a city?"

Don't tell the kids, but there's a dirty little secret about crack: as with most other drugs, a lot of people use it without getting addicted. In their zeal to shield young people from the plague of drugs, the media and many drug educators have hyped the very real dangers of crack into a myth of instant and total addiction. It has yet to be proved that Marion Barry was using crack or any other drug, but his semblance of control doesn't prove he wasn't. By the best estimate, at least 2.4 million Americans have tried crack, but contrary to the myth, less than half a million now use it once a month or more. And even among the current users, there are almost surely more occasional smokers than chronic abusers. As children in drug-using communities can see for themselves, the users show a wide range of drug symptoms, from total impairment to almost none.

That doesn't mean it's safe to play with crack, or with most other drugs, legal or illegal. Addiction is a slippery slope. But what worries a growing number of drug experts is that the cry of wolf about instant addiction may backfire. "It's a dangerous myth," says Herbert Kleber, the demand-reduction deputy to federal drug czar William Bennett. "If the kids find out you're lying, they'll think you're lying about other things too." The pattern is an old one. Exaggerated warnings about demon rum at the turn of the century sparked derision; the 1936 scare movie, "Reefer Madness," became a cult film for jeering potheads in the '60s and early '70s. And that in turn, as Kleber says, helped foster the delusion that cocaine itself was safe.

"We're seeing a whole lot of scare tactics," says Sheigla Murphy, codirector of a National Institute on Drug Abuse study of cocaine use among San Francisco-area women. "The truth is bad enough. We don't have to exaggerate it." But the scare tactics have triggered a wider skepticism about the whole drug issue. A New York Times op-ed piece recently denounced "Bennett's Sham Epidemic," accusing him of manipulating figures to create a false sense of emergency. Some experts call for legalizing drugs on grounds that the war is hopeless, the cure worse than the disease. How bad is the truth? Three key questions:

■ **Is there an epidemic?** The latest NIDA study of national drug use found mostly good news: nobody knows precisely why, but people are using fewer drugs. Taken in 1988 and released last summer, the survey found that use of all illicit drugs had fallen by 37 percent since the 1985 study. NIDA officials estimate that the heroin-addict population is steady at 500,000 or more. Marijuana users who said they had smoked in the past month fell from 18 million in 1985 to 11.6 million, a drop of 33 percent. And cocaine use showed the steepest decline of all: monthly users fell by 50 percent, from 5.8 million to 2.9 million.

The big, new problem was crack, a form of cocaine too rare to measure in 1985. The NIDA survey estimated that there were 484,000 regular crack users. And including crack, the survey found an increase in the number using cocaine weekly or oftener, from 647,000 to 862,000. This seemingly precise statistic was projected from just 44 users in the sampling of 8,814 households, but Bennett said it was "terrible proof that our current drug epidemic has far from run its course."

The survey itself is problematical. To begin with, it reaches only households and thus ignores the homeless, prisoners and people in barracks and dormitories. Then, too, it expects honest answers to a question that one researcher neatly mocks: "Hi, I'm from the government. How often do you use illegal drugs?" But whatever its flaws, most researchers accept the survey as a valid indicator of trends. In any case, Bennett argues, the good news proves that defeatists in the drug war are wrong, while the growing crack problem shows that it's not time to ease up.

■ **How addictive is crack?** One answer is another question: compared to what? Among widely used drugs, nicotine is by far the most addictive. According to Jack Henningfield, NIDA's chief clinical pharmacologist, fully 90 percent of casual cigarette smokers escalate to the point of addiction. The nation has 106 million users of alcohol, and one of every eight is a problem drinker. But there are no precise lines separating casual users, abusers and addicts, and in any case addiction differs widely from one drug to another. Stressing that it's a rough estimate, Kleber says that perhaps one cocaine user out of four or five will become a chronic abuser or addict. With crack cocaine, he says, the figure may be one in three.

For at least a few crack smokers, addiction can indeed seem nearly instantaneous. The chemistry of cocaine in the brain seems to be the same in any form, but the drug reaches its target much more efficiently through the lungs than by any other means. The tiny dose of crack provides a fast, intense high, followed by a quick depression encouraging the user to repeat the experience. This can lead to binges lasting for hours or days, sometimes starting with the first pipeful. Some users smoke just a few crack pellets; some spend the weekend smoking and return to their jobs; a few lose all control. But the mothers who sell their babies for crack are a tiny minority.

Any addiction is hard to break, but some users find crack surprisingly easy to drop. In her San Francisco study, Murphy has found at least two women who went cold turkey from full-scale addiction. "They were just sick to death of it," she says, "tired of the high, didn't want it anymore." But people can also walk away from other drugs. Sociologist Lee Robins of Washington University in St. Louis found that 90 percent of a sampling of Vietnam veterans simply gave up drugs including heroin, morphine and amphetamines after coming home in 1971. In general, says neuroscience professor Michael Gazzaniga of Dartmouth Medical School, drug abuse of all kinds dwindles as users grow older: "After 35, it just drops off precipitously."

■ **So it's safe to take drugs?** No. Especially with any form of cocaine, the passage from casual use through abuse to addiction is perilously easy. As UCLA criminologist James Q. Wilson puts it, cocaine is unlike other drugs: tobacco may shorten life, but cocaine debases it. The user feels talkative, affable, brilliant and confident, no matter how far along the slippery slope he or she may be. In reality, however, the high becomes the main goal in life, and the user will rationalize doing almost anything to get the drug. "The loss of control involves the delusion that you are still in control," says Marian Fischman, a biologist at Johns Hopkins Medical School. It may be telling that shortly before his arrest, Mayor Barry was referring to himself as "invincible."

Nevertheless, some experts argue that some or all illicit drugs should be legalized. The key question here is how much added drug use legalization would promote. Some researchers, like Dartmouth's Gazzaniga, maintain that every society has a natural level of substance abuse that won't vary much in any case: as cocaine rises, heroin and alcohol wane. But the evidence for this beguiling theory is thin, and the risks are high. As Wilson argues, it boggles the mind to imagine that making drugs safer and cheaper wouldn't lead to more use. If a legalization experiment fails, he warns, "There is no way to put the genie back in the bottle, and it is not a kindly genie."

That argument will continue: in the end, the war on drugs is a commitment the whole society has to make. But whether we fight or surrender, it's crucial to see the enemy clearly. The truth is bad enough; there's nothing to be gained, and a lot to be lost, by hyping the dangers of drugs.

The Biological Tangle of Drug Addiction

Alcohol and cocaine, a legal and illegal drug, affect the brain in different ways yet both are addicting—the question is why

RESEARCH ON DRUG ADDICTION is booming but hard facts on its biological underpinnings are spotty. For instance, no one can explain the relationship between alcohol's many effects on the brain and its potential to be addictive, and scientists are only beginning to understand this link in cocaine addiction. Researchers are accumulating a great deal of information associating genetic factors with alcohol abuse, but have yet to demonstrate a genetic predisposition for cocaine abuse. No one is discounting the contribution of social and cultural factors to drug addiction.

The way in which many researchers view addiction is changing as they learn more about how drugs alter normal brain function. In particular, they focus on a group of structures in the brain called the reward system. The system is not well defined in humans, but it probably extends from the forebrain through the midbrain and into the hindbrain (see box). Cocaine and alcohol differ in many respects, but the notion that they somehow stimulate a common brain reward system is very seductive, a 1950s concept that enjoys a revival today.

The gist of the theory is that a drug like cocaine stimulates the reward system directly, producing such intense pleasure that one wants to repeat the experience. In this sense, the drug is said to be reinforcing because animals or people will work to take it again. The effects of alcohol are different, however. It is much less clear that alcohol stimulates the brain's reward system, at least directly, and it often takes longer to become dependent on alcohol than on cocaine. Not everyone agrees that stimulating the brain's reward system is the key to addiction, even for cocaine abuse.

"From my point of view there does not seem to be a unifying theory of addiction," says Charles O'Brien of the University of Pennsylvania and the Veteran's Administration Medical Center in Philadelphia. "The diversity of response to a drug at the clinical level is impressive. Even the diversity seen in animal models of addiction is impressive." Monkeys, for example, become addicted to cocaine much more easily than to heroin. It is difficult to get a rat addicted to alcohol, but easy with either heroin or cocaine. Humans, of course, can become addicted to any of the three drugs.

To further complicate the issue, no one is certain what "addiction" really means. The American Psychiatric Association (APA) addresses the issue in terms of psychoactive substance dependence and abuse (24 June, p. 1731). Dependence and abuse do not always go hand in hand, however. For example, cancer patients can become dependent on morphine to relieve pain but not abuse the drug. Correspondingly, a person can abuse a drug without being dependent on it.

The evidence that cocaine stimulates certain structures in the brain reward pathway—the nucleus accumbens or the ventral tegmental area, in particular—comes largely from experiments with animals. Although researchers cannot experiment with people, they think the human brain's initial response to cocaine goes something like this: A person takes cocaine; if it is smoked, the drug reaches the brain within 15 seconds. The person feels high, euphoric. The euphoria probably occurs because cocaine blocks the sites on nerve cell terminals where dopamine is recycled back into the cell. This means that more dopamine than usual is available to stimulate other neurons in the reward pathway, an effect that is pleasurable and reinforcing.

Based on his studies with rats, James Smith of Louisiana State University Medical Center in Shreveport proposes that the initiation of cocaine reinforcement—which includes the brain phenomena that appear to drive repetitive drug-taking behavior—occurs in the prefrontal cortex. George Koob of the Research Institute of the Scripps Clinic in La Jolla, California, thinks that the nucleus accumbens of the rat brain sustains reinforcement. Michael Kuhar of the Addiction Research Center in Baltimore, Maryland, and his co-workers have new data that support both ideas. They report a strong correlation between cocaine's ability to bind to the dopamine reuptake sites in the prefrontal cortex and the nucleus accumbens, and its ability to induce monkeys to self-administer the drug.

Between cocaine binges, the chronic user is anhedonic, a pleasureless state that some researchers attribute to a functional depletion of the brain's supply of dopamine, a point of debate. In these people, the dopamine that normally triggers the brain reward pathway may be so low that they do not feel pleasure. Alternatively, Frank Gawin of Yale University proposes a more discrete mechanism for anhedonia. He thinks that chronic cocaine abuse induces an extreme sensitivity of dopamine receptors on nerve cells that release the transmitter, so that the system by which dopamine normally tunes itself down is working overtime. This would result in less available dopamine, less stimulation of the brain reward pathway, a reduced response to pleasurable stimuli, and a craving for cocaine—all of which typify the chronic abuser.

In addition to its effect on dopamine transport, cocaine also blocks the reuptake of serotonin and noradrenaline into brain neurons. At high concentrations it is a local anesthetic, probably because it blocks the ion channels that allow sodium ions to flow into nerve cells. Cocaine is a powerful constrictor of blood vessels, an effect that may lead to death from a heart attack if the blood supply to the heart is cut off. And new evidence indicates that cocaine may bind to

From *Science*, July 22, 1988, pp. 415–417. Copyright © 1988 by the American Association for the Advancement of Science.

the same site as phencyclidine, also known as angel dust. But none of these actions is linked specifically to its addictive properties.

Unlike cocaine, which acts as a stimulant, alcohol often depresses brain function and can induce sedation. In one area of alcohol research, several groups of investigators are trying to link the addictive effects of the drug to a particular brain pathway or neurotransmitter system. According to Floyd Bloom, also of Scripps, the list of brain neurotransmitters affected by alcohol includes gamma-aminobutyric acid (GABA), serotonin, dopamine, noradrenaline, somatostatin, acetylcholine, and vasopressin. Intoxicating doses of alcohol may affect the metabolism of steroid hormones in the brain. New evidence suggests that alcohol alters the interaction of certain membrane proteins and lipids, which in turn affects intracellular processes regulated by cyclic adenosine monophosphate. And recent data indicate that alcohol may stimulate the brain reward system directly—by triggering dopamine release from the nucleus accumbens.

The overall effect of alcohol on the brain therefore becomes impossible to predict on the basis of its interaction with any one neurotransmitter system. Other complicating factors are that the acute effects of alcohol may differ from its chronic effects and that different doses of alcohol may have different effects. "The basis of the reinforcing action of alcohol is not clear," says Bloom. "It's a lot easier to explain what being intoxicated is than to explain why being intoxicated is reinforcing."

Perhaps the clearest link between the biological actions of alcohol on brain neurons and behavioral responses to the drug involve the inhibitory neurotransmitter, GABA. "It turns out that most of the effects of alcohol—reducing anxiety and causing sedation and motor incoordination—are related to the GABA system in the brain," says Maharaj Ticku of the University of Texas Health Science Center in San Antonio.

Data from several laboratories, including Ticku's, indicate that alcohol enhances the function of the GABA receptor complex, where barbiturates, benzodiazepines such as Valium, and many convulsants also act. Ticku does not know precisely how alcohol works, "but it may act on a lipoprotein domain associated with the chloride ion channel regulated by GABA," he says. It remains to be seen if alcohol has the same effect on human brain neurons as it does on the cultured mouse spinal cord cells that Ticku studies.

A commonly cited difference between cocaine and alcohol addiction is that it often

Drug Reward in the Brain

The human brain has a reward system that is both primitive and powerful. It is so primitive in evolutionary terms that a similar system exists in rats. It is so powerful that an animal will take a drug that stimulates the system until it dies. Exciting the brain reward pathway apparently causes intense feelings of pleasure, leading some to argue that brain hedonism may be the biological basis of addiction.

No one is certain what structures the human reward system consists of, but in rats it probably includes the medial forebrain bundle, a pathway from the frontal cortex to the ventral tegmental area (VTA), says Roy Wise of Concordia University in Montreal, Quebec. Fibers branch off this pathway toward the dorsal and medial raphe nuclei, groups of neurons in the hindbrain that use acetycholine as the primary neurotransmitter. These neurons synapse onto dopamine neurons in other parts of the reward pathway and indirectly increase their activity.

George Koob of the Research Institute of the Scripps Clinic in La Jolla, California, focuses on different structures. He sees the dopamine pathway from the VTA to the nucleus accumbens as most critical for brain reward and says the olfactory tubercles and frontal cortex—parts of the limbic system—are also important. Two closely associated roles of the reward system in rats are to motivate and direct movement, he says. For instance, the neural pathways leading into the nucleus accumbens from the amygdala are associated with emotion and motivation. The circuit leading out of the nucleus accumbens to the ventral pallidum helps control motor behavior.

"The question that gets complicated is where does pleasure come in," says Koob. Rats in which the nucleus accumbens has been removed or dopamine transmission to it cut off will cease to work for cocaine, presumably because they no longer feel pleasure from the drug. Whereas in rats dopamine transmission in the nucleus accumbens and VTA seems to be important for the rewarding properties of cocaine, in humans no one is certain which brain structures are most important for the pleasurable effects of drugs. But the pharmacology of the rat and human brain is similar, and researchers who study the reward pathway think that the process of drug addiction may also be similar.

■ **D.M.B.**

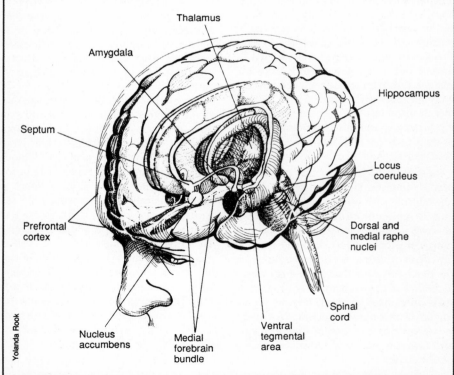

The **brain reward system** is closely associated with structures of the limbic system. [Adapted from F. E. Bloom, Ed., Brain, Mind and Behavior (Freeman, New York, 1988), with special assistance from L. Porrino and E. Palombo]

takes much longer to become addicted to alcohol. One reason for this, says Boris Tabakoff of the National Institute on Alcohol Abuse and Alcoholism (NIAAA) in Bethesda, Maryland, is that people must learn to tolerate the unpleasant effects of alcohol, such as a bad taste, feeling drowsy, or having a hangover after drinking too much, before they develop a habitual drinking pattern.

It is also much more difficult to train a rat to give itself alcohol than cocaine because the animal must also develop tolerance to the drug. "With alcohol it's a long, slow process and a striking contrast to cocaine," says Harold Kalant of the University of Toronto and the Addiction Research Foundation in Toronto. Data from his laboratory and Tabakoff's research group indicate that a serotonin system in the brain, which goes from the medial raphe nucleus in the brainstem to the hippocampus, and the brain's noradrenergic system must be intact for an animal to become tolerant to the unpleasant effects of alcohol. "What all of this means to me is that the reinforcement model projected for addiction to cocaine is not a general reinforcement model that can explain the abuse of all drugs by humans," says Kalant.

A second area of alcohol research is identifying genetic factors that may predispose a person to alcohol abuse. "We are actually inheriting varying capacities to direct our behavior," says Robert Cloninger of Washington University in St. Louis, Missouri. "Some people are more predisposed to anxiety, which alcohol alleviates, so they drink." Cloninger finds that these people often have "passive-dependent" or "anxious" personalities and he terms them type I alcoholics. Type II alcoholics, in contrast, want the stimulating effects of alcohol. They seek novel experiences and apparently drink for different reasons. "These individuals have primarily antisocial personality traits," he says. They often develop a habitual pattern of heavy drinking before the age of 25 and may get into trouble with the law when they drink. Cloninger also contends that certain brain systems and neurotransmitters—norepinephrine, dopamine, and serotonin, in particular—influence behavior and personality.

"The idea that something about the vulnerability to alcoholism is inherited is supported by an overwhelming amount of evidence from studies of population genetics,"

says Enoch Gordis, director of NIAAA. "But the question is, what is inherited—certainly not a gene with alcohol on it." Research to identify what complement of genes may predispose a person toward alcohol abuse is still in the planning stages.

A third area of alcohol research is identifying biological factors that may mark a future alcoholic. Marc Schukit of the University of California School of Medicine and the Veteran's Administration Hospital in San Diego compares the 18- to 25-year-old sons of alcoholic fathers to the sons of nonalcoholic fathers. The sons of alcoholics show smaller "increases in body sway and hormone levels, and changes in electroencephalogram (EEG) patterns," says Schukit. These men also report feeling less sleepy, dizzy, or high than their counterparts when they take either a low dose of alcohol that corresponds roughly to three drinks or a high dose that corresponds to five. Both groups show changes in their responses but the sons of alcoholics show less of a change.

Schukit, Eric Gold, also of UCSD, and their colleagues find no difference between the two groups in "baseline factors" such as personality types, performance on certain cognitive tests, or electrical activity in the brain. A follow-up study of the population, to conclude in 1995, should answer whether diminished responses to alcohol, which occurs in about 40% of the sons of alcoholics, identifies individuals who are more likely to become alcoholics.

In their recent studies, Henri Begleiter and Bernice Porjesz of the State University of New York Health Science Center in Brooklyn also find biological differences in the young sons of alcoholics that may predict future alcohol abuse. The researchers randomly present flashes of light, from a very dim to a very bright intensity to three different groups of boys—controls, sons with a family history of alcoholism that spans at least two generations and in which at least three members are alcoholic, and sons with only fathers who are alcoholic.

"We find that the group with a multigenerational history of alcoholism shows a very large response to intense stimuli that varies considerably from the control group," says Begleiter. Unlike Schukit, Begleiter monitors EEG activity in boys who have never had any alcohol to drink. His data suggest that the problem of alcoholism involves the frontal cortex and limbic system, brain re-

gions also implicated in chronic cocaine abuse.

Experiments with animals lend further support to the notion that alcohol abuse may have a genetic component, and it also constitutes a fourth major area of research. Ting-Kai Li of the Indiana University School of Medicine and the Veteran's Administration Medical Center in Indianapolis and his colleagues select rats that have a high preference for drinking alcohol (given free choice and available food and water) and breed them. Similarly, they breed animals that do not like alcohol. "We get two lines of animals that show different responses to alcohol," says Li. "The alcohol-preferring animals find low to moderate concentrations of alcohol to be rewarding."

To determine why the rats behave so differently, Li, William McBride, and Lawrence Lumeng, also of Indianapolis, study neurochemical differences between the two groups. "The brains of alcohol-preferring rats are about 20% lower in the neurotransmitters serotonin and dopamine," says Li. Cloninger compares the preferring rats to human type II alcoholics who seek novelty and the stimulating effects of the drug. It is this group in which alcoholism seems to be the most heritable, says Cloninger, and he would expect them also to be low in brain serotonin and dopamine levels.

Despite the vast amount of recent information on how cocaine and alcohol alter brain function, no one is willing to say that addiction can be explained on the basis of these effects. "Cocaine can gradually gain control over behavior, but the concept that the drug changes behavior because it induces changes in nerve cells is not clear," says Jerome Jaffe of the Addiction Research Center in Baltimore, Maryland. "Memory may be the real biological basis of drug dependence," he says. "It is a loss of innocence in some respects."

The question of what causes drug addiction will not be answered solely by explanations of how drugs affect the brain. Many researchers emphasize that habitual drug-taking constitutes a powerful form of behavioral conditioning that is very difficult to disrupt in chronic users. They also see social pressures and acceptance of drug use—particularly with alcohol—as contributing to the problem of addiction.

DEBORAH M. BARNES

Recognizing Everyday Addictions

by Susan Perry

Illustrations: Courtesy FDA Consumer

For weeks, Ariana was looking forward to the big camping trip in the mountains planned by her school's outdoors club. But once she was there, an annoying headache got in the way of her fun.

Ariana is a coffee-drinker—two or more cups every morning at breakfast and another cup during morning break. Since no one brought coffee on the trip, Ariana had to skip her usual habit. Her headache was a withdrawal symptom and a tip-off that Ariana was probably *addicted* to caffeine.

While we usually think of addiction as having to do with illegal drugs such as cocaine and heroin, people can also become addicted to everyday, legal substances such as the caffeine in coffee or the nicotine in cigarettes. Addiction is a condition in which people strongly feel they need or want to use a drug on a continuous basis, either to experience its effect or to avoid the discomfort of not using it.

According to former Surgeon General Koop's 1988 report on nicotine addiction, the difference between drug dependence and addiction, and other habits not involving drugs, is that drugs enter the bloodstream and cause mood-altering effects in the brain. When you drink coffee or smoke a cigarette, you are changing the chemistry of your brain. The definition of drug addiction also includes the fact that the mood-altering chemical involved acts as a reinforcer, which means that when a person uses this substance, it makes him or her want to continue using it.

For example, teenagers might begin drinking coffee, smoking, or trying some form of alcohol to feel better or sharper, or to get a "buzz." However, with many drugs, a tolerance is built up, so that they have to use more and more of the drug to feel its pleasurable effects. Often, withdrawal—when they stop using the substance—causes a set of physical symptoms. As Ariana discovered on her camping trip, uncomfortable symptoms can occur when the body is denied its usual dose of a drug, whether alcohol, heroin, or something as ordinary as the caffeine in coffee.

Researchers used to feel they could distinguish clearly between physical and psychological dependence. That is, if a drug caused withdrawal symptoms (such as Ariana's headache) when the person stopped using it, that was considered a physical dependence. If it didn't, but the person craved it anyway, that was considered mainly a psychological dependence. However, research has shown the distinction between physical and psychological dependence to be less definite.

"Withdrawal symptoms are very tangible, demonstrable. You can see tremors and other physiological changes that are occurring," says C. Anderson Johnson, Ph.D., director of the Institute for Health Promotion and Disease Prevention Research at the University of Southern California School of Medicine. "The psychological dependence, which in fact is probably much more important, is just not observable to someone on the outside."

The dangers of being addicted to *illegal* drugs are widely known. Yet, negative consequences also come with addictions to such everyday substances as caffeine, nicotine, non-prescription pills, and alcohol.

All around them and in the media, teenagers see adults using drugs. They drink alcohol to celebrate a special day, or to forget a bad day. They take a pill to ease a headache, relieve the symptoms of a cold, decrease their appetite, or to sleep. The message teenagers get is that feeling good is a goal, and that whatever it takes to make bad feelings go away must be okay.

Yet when people "prescribe" for themselves a legal, everyday drug to make themselves feel good, they are taking a risk. Drugs, even legal ones, are chemical compounds that change your brain in order to change your consciousness, and there are always side effects. Some of these side effects are only unpleasant, while others may be quite harmful.

"I Need My Caffeine"

Among beverages, coffee contains the most caffeine, between 86 milligrams (mg) and 150 mg per cup, depending on whether it is brewed and how strong it is. Tea and cola drinks also contain a significant amount of caffeine (60 mg to 75 mg for tea, 40 mg to 60 mg per glass of cola drink). A number of over-the-counter pain relievers and cold pills also contain caffeine (30 mg to 66 mg per tablet).

Caffeine releases neurotransmitters in the synapses of the brain, which in turn causes more brain activity to happen. This is the stimulating effect that causes most people to become dependent on caffeine. However, it only has this stimulant effect up to a certain blood dose level, after which it may have the opposite effect. Caffeine, like a lot of stimulants, can have a rebound effect. "A lot of people who drink coffee have noticed that they've been drinking it all morning, and then they'll drink a cup in the afternoon, and all of a sudden they find

themselves feeling down," points out Dr. Johnson.

In addition to increasing brain activity, caffeine raises blood pressure and increases cardiac output, by increasing both heart rate and stroke volume, so that each time the heart beats it is putting out more blood.

Using a lot of caffeine actually makes people feel worse. They may get jumpy, or they may feel "down" because of the rebound effect, so they try to use more caffeine, and may end up feeling even more sluggish. Another problem with caffeine is that it can affect the quality and length of a person's sleep, as well as the ability to fall asleep in the first place.

When people take in less than the amount of caffeine they are used to, they may get a headache and will probably feel sluggish. If you think you are addicted to caffeine and want to be less dependent on this drug, it is possible to slowly reduce your intake until your body adjusts to the change. Also, make it a habit to read labels on all soft drinks and medications from the drugstore, so you know if they contain caffeine.

The Nicotine Habit

A University of Southern California study of tobacco use among adolescents found that at around sixth grade, the percentage of teenagers who take at least one puff a week begins to increase sharply. While only 6 percent of seventh graders smoke at least once a week, an additional 3 percent of students pick up the habit each year. Transitions to junior high, high school, and college appear to be particularly high-risk times for increased tobacco use.

According to Steve Sussman, Ph.D., the study's principal investigator, the general pattern is for a teenager to try a cigarette the first time in a group of friends. "Most kids cough or feel nauseated, and a few will feel a buzz. If they recall liking it at their first experience, they're more likely to use it in the future," says Sussman. And even if they do not like it the first time, the discomforts soon pass with increased use.

Depending on the dosage, nicotine has a stimulating effect. What happens over time is that there are nicotine receptor sites that increase in number as well as in their ability to process nicotine. It takes two to four years to become dependent, though it can happen much sooner to daily smokers. Once a person is dependent or addicted, it is difficult to break the habit. Withdrawal symptoms include the urge to smoke, headaches, and feeling bad or irritable.

"Kids don't think they're going to get addicted," says Sussman. "They know that lung disease is out there, but they think they're going to

quit before that point. By the end of high school, 90 percent of them want to quit."

"Stopping smoking when the habit is one, two, three, or even six years old is a million times easier than it will be in one's 20s," says Dee Burton, Ph.D., a psychologist at the University of Illinois School of Public Health. "By 21, the majority of tobacco-users will never quit, no matter how hard they try." Burton advises teenagers to see kicking an addiction as a show of strength. She also points out that once teenagers

are aware of the horrendous health problems that often result from smoking, they are more motivated to quit.

According to the Surgeon General's 1988 report, nicotine affects many organ systems. An increased risk of heart disease, cancer, and gastrointestinal disorders is only one of the long-term health effects of smoking. Even first-time users experience the effects of nicotine, and since tolerance builds quickly, people usually increase their dosage rapidly to unhealthy levels. In fact, the processes of addiction to tobacco are similar to those that determine addiction to drugs such as heroin and cocaine.

Beyond health concerns, the bad side of smoking includes unpleasant breath, holes burned in clothes, and offending other people with the smoke.

According to Sussman, for most people, quitting "cold turkey" seems to be the best and most reliable way to break the addiction to nicotine. Most people have to try again and again, and many have to try numerous things. For many young people, the use of cigarettes is a social habit. When it's done to be accepted by their peers, the most effective way of quitting is to learn to gracefully refuse offers to smoke.

Smokeless tobacco either in the form of chewing tobacco or snuff is not a safe alternative to cigarettes, as it is possible to become addicted even more quickly than to cigarettes. One pinch of snuff ("dipping") is equivalent to three or four cigarettes. The method of transport is different so it takes a longer period of time, perhaps 20 minutes, before a user experiences a buzz, but then the buzz is more sustained. According to recent research, for everyone who is a daily user of smokeless tobacco for 3½ years or more, the likelihood of oral cancer increases significantly.

For information about the effects of smoking and help with quitting, call the National Cancer Institute's Cancer Information Service at 800-

4-CANCER (800-422-6237). They can also refer you to smoking cessation clinics.

An Alcohol Problem

Although alcohol is not a legal substance for teenagers, nearly 90 percent of teens admit to drinking alcohol at least occasionally.

New research indicates that alcohol can do greater damage to many more body parts than we thought. It damages the body because it weakens the basic unit of the body itself—the cell. Some people cannot drink at all without becoming addicted. It only takes a few months to become alcoholic for those people who are genetically predisposed to become alcoholics. Though they think they can control themselves and choose not to overdo it, leading medical experts have found that addiction is more a biological fact.

One in every 15 Americans is now thought to be at a higher genetic risk for becoming an alcoholic, even if the parents do not drink. With some people it takes years to develop, while others are born vulnerable and can develop alcoholism very easily.

Alcohol affects the pleasure centers in the brain, creating temporary feelings of happiness. However, the natural chemistry of the brain is disrupted. When the drug wears off, the positive feelings will be replaced by feelings of withdrawal, aggression, depression, paranoia, and anxiety. The physical effects of drinking alcohol include destruction of brain cells that can never be replaced, disoriented heartbeat, lack of energy, anemia, and damage to the kidneys, liver, heart, lungs, and pancreas.

If you need help with an alcohol problem, check with your school counselor or doctor for referrals to local treatment agencies, or look in the white pages of your local phone directory for an Alcoholics Anonymous listing.

"Everyday" Pills

Some people can become dependent or addicted to over-the-counter diet pills in an attempt to achieve their goal of not gaining or of losing weight. They come to feel the drug is necessary. The safety of such drugs is currently being reviewed by the U.S. Food and Drug Administration (FDA). Some contain stimulants that may cause dizziness, insomnia, and increased heart rate. Even those that contain no stimulants should not be taken in larger doses or for a longer period than recommended on the package.

Sleeping pills are another everyday drug to which people can become addicted. Because of the rebound effect, they actually disrupt rather than promote sleep after a few days use, points out Dr. Johnson. "There is no sleeping pill that's good for chronic use," he adds.

When we first start to use any of these everyday substances, we never expect to become dependent on them just to get through the day comfortably. Yet, it is easy to become addicted—and it can be surprisingly difficult to get free again.

Alcoholism: The mythical disease

HERBERT FINGARETTE/*THE PUBLIC INTEREST*

Herbert Fingarette is a professor of philosophy at the University of California, Santa Barbara. He has served as a consultant on alcoholism and addiction to the World Health Organization.

The idea that alcoholism is a disease is a myth, and a harmful myth at that. This assertion obviously conflicts with the barrage of pronouncements in support of alcoholism's classification as a disease by health professionals and organizations such as the American Medical Association, by the explosively proliferating treatment programs, and by innumerable public-service organizations.

But the public has been profoundly misled, and is still being actively misled. Credulous media articles have featured so many dramatic human-interest anecdotes by "recovering alcoholics," so many "scientific" pronouncements about medical opinion and new discoveries, that it is no wonder the lay public responds with trusting belief. Yet this much is unambiguous and incontrovertible: The public has been kept unaware of a mass of scientific evidence accumulated over the past couple of decades, evidence familiar to researchers in the field, which radically challenges each major belief generally associated with the phrase "alcoholism is a disease."

Why is it important whether alcoholism is a disease? To begin with, "disease" is the word that triggers provision of health-insurance payments, employment benefits such as paid leave and worker's compensa-

The public has been profoundly misled about alcoholism.

tion, and other government benefits. The direct cost of treating alcoholism is rapidly rising, already exceeding a billion dollars annually. Add in all related health costs and other kinds of benefits, and the dollar figure is well into the tens of billions annually.

Alcoholism is, of course, profoundly harmful, both to the drinkers themselves and to others. But if it ceased to be characterized as a disease, all the disease-oriented methods of treatment and resulting expenditures would be threatened; this in turn would threaten the material interests of hundreds of thousands of alcoholics and treatment staffers who receive these billions in funds. The other side of the coin would be many billions in savings for taxpayers and those who pay insurance premiums.

It is not surprising that the disease concept of alcoholism is now vigorously promoted by a vast network of lobbies, national and local, professional and volunteer, ranging from the most prestigious medical associations to the most crassly commercial private providers of treatment. This is big politics and big business.

Use of the word "disease" also shapes the values and attitudes of society. The selling of the disease concept of alcoholism has led courts, legislatures, and the populace generally to view damage caused by heavy drinkers as a product of "the disease and not the drinker." The public remains ambivalent about this, and criminal law continues to resist excusing alcoholics for criminal acts. But the pressure is there, and civil law has largely given in. In regard to alcoholics, civil law now often mandates leniency or complete absolution from the rules, regulations, and moral norms

From *Utne Reader,* November/December 1988, pp. 64-69. Excerpt from *The Public Interest,* Spring 1988. Copyright © 1988 by Herbert Fingarette. For a fuller account of the subject, see the book HEAVY DRINKING: THE MYTH OF ALCOHOLISM AS A DISEASE by Herbert Fingarette, University of California Press, 1988.

to which non-diseased persons are held accountable. Such was the thrust of a recently denied appeal to the U.S. Supreme Court by two veterans, who claimed certain benefits in spite of their having failed to apply for them during the legally specified 10-year period after discharge from the Army. Their excuse: alcoholism, and the claim that their persistent heavy drinking was a disease entitling them to exemption from the regulations.

When the facts are confronted, what seems to be compassion done in the name of "disease" turns out to subvert the drinker's autonomy and will to change, and to exacerbate a serious social problem. This is because the excuses and benefits offered heavy drinkers work psychologically as incentives to continue drinking. The doctrine that the alcoholic is "helpless" delivers the message that he might as well drink, since he lacks the ability to refrain. As for the expensive treatments, they do no real good. Certainly our current disease-oriented policies have not reduced the scale of the problem; in fact, the number of chronic heavy drinkers reported keeps rising. (It is currently somewhere in the range of 10 to 20 million, depending on the definitions one uses.)

The disease concept of alcoholism not only has no basis in current science; it has *never* had a scientific justification.

The understanding of alcoholism as a disease first surfaced in the early 19th century. The growing popularity of materialistic and mechanistic views bolstered the doctrine that drinking problems stemmed from a simple malfunctioning of the bodily machinery. The new idea was popularized by Benjamin Rush, one of the leading medical theorists of the day.

Rush's claim was ideological, not scientific, since neither Rush nor anyone else at that time had the experimental facilities or the biological knowledge to justify it. It seemed plausible because of its compatibility with the crude biological theories of the time, assumptions that we now know to be erroneous. Nevertheless, the idea seized the public imagination, in part because it appealed to the growing mercantile and manufacturing classes, whose demand for a disciplining "work ethic" (especially among the working class) was supported by this new "scientific" indictment of drinking. We should realize that the 19th-century version of the doctrine, as advanced by the politically powerful temperance movement, indicted *all* drinking. Alcohol (like heroin today) was viewed as inherently addictive. The drinker's personal character and situation were considered irrelevant.

The 19th-century temperance movement crested in 1919 with the enactment of the Prohibition Amendment; but by 1933 the idea of a total prohibi-

The disease model of alcoholism is big business.

tion had lost credibility, and the amendment was repealed. For one thing, the public no longer accepted the idea that no one at all could drink alcohol safely. In addition, the costs of prohibition—such as gangsterism and public cynicism about the law—had become too high. Most people wanted to do openly and legally, in a civilized way, what large numbers of people had been doing surreptitiously.

For the temperance impulse to survive, it had to be updated in a way that did not stigmatize all drinking on moral or medical grounds. Any new anti-alcohol movement had to be more selective in its target, by taking into account the desires of drinkers generally, as well as the interests of the now legal (and growing) alcoholic beverage industry.

A new sect arose with just the right formula. Alcoholics Anonymous (AA), founded in 1935, taught that alcohol was not the villain in and of itself, and that most people could drink safely. (In this way the great majority of drinkers and the beverage industry were mollified.) A minority of potential drinkers, however, were said to have a peculiar biological vulnerability; these unfortunates, it was held, are "allergic" to alcohol, so that their drinking activates the disease, which then proceeds insidiously toward addiction.

This contemporary version of the disease theory of alcoholism, along with the subsequent minor variants of the theory, is often referred to now as the "classic" disease concept of alcoholism. Like the temperance doctrine, the new doctrine was not based on any scientific research or discovery. It was created by the two ex-alcoholics who founded AA: William Wilson, a New York stockbroker, and Robert Holbrook Smith, a physician from Akron, Ohio. Their ideas in turn were inspired by the Oxford religious movement, and by the ideas of another physician, William Silkworth. They attracted a small following, and a few sympathetic magazine articles helped the movement grow.

The "alcoholism movement," as it has come to be called among those familiar with the facts, has grown at an accelerating rate. Its growth results from the cumulative effect of the great number of drinkers indoctrinated by AA, people who passionately identify themselves with the AA portrait of "the alcoholic." AA has vigorously supported the idea of "treatment" for alcoholics; in turn, the rapidly proliferating treatment centers for the "disease of alcoholism" have generally supported AA. All this has generated a kind of snowballing effect.

By the 1970s there were powerful alcohol-related lobbying organizations in place at all levels of government. The National Council on Alcoholism (NCA), for example, which has propagated the disease concept of alcoholism, has been a major national umbrella group from the early days of the movement. Until 1982 the NCA was subsidized by the liquor industry, which had several representatives on its board. The alliance was a natural one: At the cost of conceding that a small segment of the population is allergic to alcohol and ought not to drink, the liquor industry gained a freer hand with which to appeal to the majority of people, who are ostensibly not allergic.

Large and powerful health-professional organizations (such as the American Medical Association) now have internal constituencies whose professional power and wealth derive from their role as the authorities responsible for dealing with the "disease" of alcoholism. As usual, these interest groups lobby internally, and the larger organization is persuaded to take an official stand in favor of the disease model of alcoholism.

Judges, legislators, and bureaucrats all have a stake in the doctrine. They can now with clear consciences get the intractable social problems posed by heavy drinkers off their agenda by compelling or persuading these unmanageable people to go elsewhere—that is, to get "treatment." Why should these public officials mistrust—or want to mistrust—this safe-as-motherhood way of getting troublesome problems off their backs while winning popular approval? The ample evidence that treatment programs are ineffective, and waste considerable amounts of money and resources, is ignored.

There is a consensus among scientists that no single cause of alcoholism, biological or otherwise, has ever been scientifically established. There are many causal factors, and they vary from drinking pattern to drinking pattern, from drinker to drinker. We already know many of the predominant influences that evoke or shape patterns of drinking. We know that family environment plays a role, as does age. Ethnic and cultural values are also important. The belief in a unique disease of alcoholism leads many to wonder whether these sorts of influences can make much of a difference when it comes to the supposedly "overwhelming craving" of alcoholics. Once one realizes that there is no distinct group of "diseased" drinkers, however, one is less surprised to learn that no group of drinkers is immune to such influences or is vulnerable only to other influences.

Even if the disease concept of alcoholism lacks a scientific foundation, mightn't it nevertheless be a useful social white lie, since it encourages alcoholics to enter treatment? This common—and plausible—argument is flawed because medical treatment for alcoholism is ineffective. Medical authority has been abused for the purpose of enlisting public faith in a useless treatment for which Americans have paid more than a billion dollars. To understand why the treatment does no good, we should recall that many different kinds of studies of alcoholics have shown substantial rates of so-called "natural" improvement. As a 1986 report concludes, "the vast majority of [addicted] persons who change do so on their own." This natural rate of improvement, which varies according to class, age, socioeconomic status, and certain other psychological and social variables, lends credibility to the claims of success made by programs that "treat" the "disease" of alcoholism.

Many of the clients—and, in the expensive programs, almost all of the clients—are middle-class, middle-aged people who are intensely motivated to change, and whose families and social relationships are still intact. Many, often most, are much improved by the time they complete the program. They are, of course, delighted with the change; they paid money and went through an emotional ordeal, and now receive renewed affection and respect from their family, friends, and co-workers. They had been continually told during treatment that they were helpless, and that only treatment could save them. Many of them fervently believe that they could never have been cured without the treatment.

One of the most fiercely debated issues is whether "controlled drinking" is a legitimate goal.

The sound and the fury signify nothing, however, for the rates of improvement in these disease-oriented treatment programs (which cost between $5,000 and $20,000) do not significantly differ from the natural rates of improvement for comparable but untreated demographic groups.

There is some disagreement about the effectiveness of more modest forms of treatment. Some reports—for example, a major study done for the Congressional Office of Technology Assessment—conclude that no single method of treatment is superior to any other (a judgment made by all the major studies). But according to the study, the data appear to show that "treatment seems better than no treatment." That is, some help-oriented intervention—it doesn't matter what kind—may contribute modestly to improvement.

The more pessimistic reading of the data is that elaborate treatments for alcoholism as a disease have no measurable impact at all. In a review of a number of different long-term studies of treatment programs, George Vaillant states that "there is compelling evidence that the results of our treatment were no better than the natural history of the disease." Reviewing other major treatment programs with long-term follow-ups, he remarks that the best that can be said is that these programs do no harm.

In recent years, early evaluation studies have been re-examined from a non-disease perspective, which has produced interesting results.

The new perspective suggests a different conception of the road to improvement. Instead of hoping for a medical magic bullet that will cure the disease, the goal here is to change the way drinkers live. One should learn from one's mistakes, rather than viewing any one mistake as a proof of failure or a sign of doom.

Also consistent with the newer pluralistic, non-disease approach is the selection of specific strategies and tactics for helping different sorts of drinkers; methods and goals are tailored to the individual in ways that leave the one-disease, one-treatment approach far behind.

Much controversy remains about pluralistic goals. One of the most fiercely debated issues is whether so-called "controlled drinking" is a legitimate therapeutic goal. Some contend that controlled drinking by an alcoholic inevitably leads to uncontrolled drinking. Disease-concept lobbyists, such as the National Council on Alcoholism, have tried to suppress scientific publications reporting success with controlled drinking, and have excoriated them upon publication. Some have argued that publishing such data can "literally kill alcoholics." Even so, hundreds of similar reports presenting favorable results have appeared. One recent study concludes that most formerly heavy drinkers who are now socially adjusted become social drinkers rather than abstainers.

In any case, the goal of total abstinence insisted upon by advocates of the disease concept is not a proven successful alternative, since only a small minority achieves it. If doubt remains as to whether the controversy over controlled drinking is fueled by nonscientific factors, that doubt can be dispelled by realizing that opposition to controlled drinking (like support for the disease concept of alcoholism) is largely confined to the U.S. and to countries dominated by American intellectual influence. Most physicians in Britain, for example, do not adhere to the disease concept of alcoholism. And the goal of controlled drinking—used selectively but extensively—is widely favored in Canada and the United Kingdom. British physicians have little professional or financial incentive to bring problem drinkers into their consulting rooms or hospitals. American physicians, in contrast, defend an enormous growth in institutional power and fee-for-service income. The selling of the term "disease" has been the key to this vast expansion of medical power and wealth in the United States.

What should our attitude be, then, to the long-term heavy drinker? Alcoholics do not knowingly make the wicked choice to be drunkards. Righteous condemnation and punitive moralism are therefore inappropriate. Compassion, not abuse, should be shown toward any human being launched upon a destructive way of life. But compassion must be realistic. It is not compassionate to encourage drinkers to deny their power to change, to excuse them legally and give them special government benefits that foster a refusal to confront the need to change. Alcoholics are not helpless; they can take control of their lives. In the last analysis, alcoholics must *want* to change and *choose* to change. To do so they must make many difficult daily choices. We can help them by offering moral support and good advice, and by assisting them in dealing with their genuine physical ailments and social needs. But we must also make it clear that heavy drinkers must take responsibility for their own lives. Alcoholism is not a disease; the assumption of personal responsibility, however, is a sign of health, while needless submission to spurious medical authority is a pathology.

NICOTINE BECOMES ADDICTIVE

It has taken more than half a century to prove finally and indisputably that the colorless, oily liquid in tobacco hooks smokers just as surely as heroin does junkies.

ROBERT KANIGEL

Robert Kanigel, author of Apprentice to Genius, *is working on a biography of the Indian math prodigy Ramanujan.*

1942. British tanks battled Rommel's Panzers in North Africa. The pages of *The Lancet*, Britain's leading medical journal, told of physicians killed in battle and tuberculosis patients denied extra rations at home. Meanwhile, Glasgow physician Lennox Johnston was shooting up with nicotine.

Three or four times a day he'd inject himself with a hypodermic syringe of nicotine, the colorless oily liquid that, on exposure to air, gives tobacco its pungent smell and brownish color. After eighty shots, he found that he liked them better than cigarettes and felt deprived without them. He observed a similar pattern among 35 volunteers to whom he also gave nicotine shots. "Smoking tobacco," he'd assumed from the start, "is essentially a means of administering nicotine, just as smoking opium is a means of administering morphine." And nothing in the course of his study led him to change his mind.

Later, critics objected to Johnston's lack of scientific controls. "And they were right," says Jack Henningfield, a smoking researcher at the Addiction Research Center in Baltimore. "But Johnston was right, too": nicotine was why people smoked—a judgment embodied in the very title of the Surgeon General's latest report on smoking, *Nicotine Addiction*, issued last spring.

The 618-page report drew sneers from the tobacco industry, but no full-dress rebuttal. "We haven't had to," insists Tobacco Institute spokesman Gary Miller, pointing to newspaper editorials that damned the report as the work of zealots and painted its conclusions as ill-founded. "Smokers and non-smokers are just not buying it." But if anything, Surgeon General Everett Koop's report—which summarized the work of hundreds of scientists in thousands of studies, and was itself reviewed by dozens of outside experts—granted scientific legitimacy to folk wisdom and anecdotal evidence of centuries' standing.

The phrase, *tobacco addict*, goes back at least to the eighteenth century, when Samuel Johnson used the expression. *Dope fiend*'s entry into the language during the 1870s was followed by *cigarette fiend* just a few years later; today *nicotine fit* is in common usage. More than half a century before the Surgeon General's report, John L. Dorsey, a Baltimore physician writing in *The Practitioner*, took as a given "that the use of tobacco in its various preparations is a form of drug addiction.... The real addict, the smoker of 20 to 50 cigarettes a day, cannot lay aside the habits of years with an easy nonchalance. He has ahead of him wretched days of withdrawal symptoms which will usually end with surrender to the habit." In the devastated cities of Europe after World War II, people cheated, stole, and prostituted themselves for a smoke, and German prisoners of war on diets of 900 calories a day would sometimes swap food for cigarettes.

Indeed, midst today's climate of inhospitability to smoking, and confronted with a thick, citation-studded government report fairly bursting with proof that smoking is addictive and nicotine is its agent, it can be hard to recall that anyone ever thought otherwise. Yet for all those, like Dr. Dorsey, who deemed tobacco addictive,

> *"The cloud of white smoke*
> *rising before the smoker*
> *is soothing and companionable.*
> *The gradual ascent of the completed rings,*
> *their changing forms*
> *and their picturesque movements*
> *disappearing into thin air*
> *all tend to rouse the imagination."*

others had insisted its hold on the smoker was weak. "Smoking," pharmacologist W.E. Dixon had written in the same journal just a few years before, "does not lead to addiction comparable with that of morphine or cocaine. . . . The loss of one's smokes is an annoyance, but not a tragedy."

Why, then, *did* smokers reach for their cigarettes 20 or 30 or 40 times a day—or as was more common in Dixon's day, their pipes and cigars? "The cloud of white smoke rising before the smoker is soothing and companionable," noted British pharmacologist Sir Robert Armstrong-Jones in the 1920s. "The circular shape of the completed rings are attractive. Their gradual ascent unaided and without apparent effort from the 'gurgling briar,' their changing forms and their picturesque movements disappearing into thin air, all tend to rouse the imagination." Smoking, then, granted pleasure—even, as Armstrong-Jones would have it, aesthetic pleasure. Indulging in it hardly made you a drug addict. Oral gratification, "pulmonary eroticism," and all manner of other psychological explanations were trotted out over the years, too. Was it not these that held the smoker in thrall, and not anything so insidious as an addictive drug?

Until recently, of course, the issue wasn't really thrashed about much. After all, smoking, in the view of most scientists, physicians, and smokers, was harmless. So whether or not it was addictive didn't *matter*.

And then, almost all of a sudden, it did.

First came the early studies, in the 1950s, linking smoking to lung cancer and other health problems. Then, the Surgeon General's landmark 1964 report saying as much. Then, over the next 15 years, the steady drumbeat of data buttressing that conclusion: Smoking *was* dangerous to your health. It gave you lung cancer. It contributed to heart disease. It was responsible, yearly, for 300,000 people dying before their time . . .

Mort Levin, a retired Johns Hopkins School of Medicine epidemiologist who established some of the earliest ties between smoking and lung cancer, still remembers the press conference, at the Hotel de la Paix in Paris in the early 1950s, at which he first presented his findings to the world. Afterwards, some in the audience came up and told him they planned to sell their cigarette company stock. When Levin's evidence became known, they said, people would simply give up smoking and the tobacco companies would go under.

Well, people *didn't* stop smoking. The tobacco companies *didn't* go under. All during the 1950s, the prevalence of smoking among adult males barely budged from its long-steady figure of just over fifty percent. The 1964 report brought it down to the mid-40s, but meanwhile more women were smoking—from less than 20 percent of them in the 1930s to about 30 percent in the 1960s. All told, cigarette sales rose.

Nor was it that people hadn't gotten the message. A 1969 poll found that 81 percent of Americans in their twenties, and 71 percent of all Americans, thought smoking caused cancer. Every magazine ad, every billboard, every cigarette packet carried the word. People apparently wanted to give it up; one recent Gallup Poll, for example, found that 77 percent did. But they didn't, or wouldn't, or couldn't. Why? A question previously accorded scant attention now beginning in the 1960s and then more insistently during the 1970s became one of consuming interest: Was smoking, in some meaningful sense of the word, "addictive"? And if so, was nicotine responsible?

* * *

Of the 4,000 chemical constituents of tobacco, nicotine, which takes its name from Jean Nicot, the sixteenth century French ambassador to Portugal who introduced tobacco to the French court, constitutes 1.5 percent of it by weight and has long been known to have powerful pharmacological effects. Indeed, its use to study transmission of nerve impulses even before 1900 left a whole branch of the cholinergic nervous system forever dubbed "nicotinic."

In his 1931 study, *Phantastica: Narcotic and Stimulating Drugs*, L. Lewin asserted that "the decisive factor in the effects of tobacco, desired or undesired, is nicotine and it matters little whether it passes directly into the organism or is smoked." In 1961, F. S. Larson and two other Medical College of Virginia pharmacologists came out with their classic, encyclopedic survey of the tobacco literature. That nicotine played a role in maintaining tobacco use was to them abundantly clear; but as to how central a role, or whether smoking was a habit, or an addiction, or something else altogether, they reached no consensus. Meanwhile, when it came to hard data, Lennox Johnston's war-time experiment remained largely alone.

And that's how matters stood for a quarter century, until 1967. In that year, B. R. Lucchesi and his colleagues at the University of Michigan Medical School, took another swipe at the question. It was Johnston's work all over again, but this time *with* the controls.

Experimental subjects would arrive at the lab in the morning, having gone without food, drink, or cigarettes since midnight. After blood pressure and heart rate tests, they would enter sound-proofed air-conditioned isolation booths, get hooked up to instruments, and have 23-gauge hypodermic needles inserted in their forearms. To each needle was attached a Y-shaped extension, one arm of which dispensed salt solution, the other nicotine. During some six-hour sessions they got nicotine equivalent to one or two cigarettes an hour. During others they'd get only saline solution. They never knew which. Throughout each session, while kept busy with tests of reaction time, hand steadiness and the like, the volunteers could smoke whenever they wished.

Would they smoke less when they were getting nicotine fed into their veins?

They did. Subject No. 4 consistently smoked about 11 cigarettes per session when he wasn't getting IV nicotine, eight when he did. For Subject No. 2, it was seven and four. Moreover, subjects tended to smoke less of the cigarettes they did consume. "Small but significant," the authors labeled nicotine's effect. There were plainly other factors in their smoking. But just as plainly, the nicotine they got through the needle was nicotine they didn't have to get from their smokes.

*During the 1970s the evidence mounted.
And yet none of it
made smoking an addiction.
Because for many people, even today,
addiction meant only one thing.
It meant morphine or heroin. It meant* bad.

In 1971 came evidence of quite a different sort. Sponsored by the American Cancer Society, William A. Hunt and two colleagues at Loyola University of Chicago compared relapse rates of smokers trying to give up smoking, as reported in dozens of earlier studies, with those of alcoholics trying to give up alcohol and heroin addicts trying to give up heroin. The studies had been performed under vastly different circumstances and so the results of the comparison, the authors apologized, were merely "illustrative."

But *illustrate* they did, in the form of a memorable graph. The horizontal axis represented time since going off heroin, alcohol, or tobacco. Plotted on the vertical axis was the percentage of those still off—100 percent at first, then a fall-off over subsequent weeks and months. And the thing you could never get out of your mind once you'd seen it was that laying the curves for any of the three atop the others, you could scarcely distinguish one from the other: Smokers, the graph said, had as much trouble staying off cigarettes as alcoholics did in staying off drink—and as heroin addicts did in staying off junk.

During the early and mid-1970s, a series of seemingly small, methodological improvements helped give re-searchers a clearer sense of how nicotine exerted its addictive spell. Puff on a cigarette and nicotine reaches its primary site of action, the brain, within seven seconds, being taken up by the circulatory system through capillaries in the lungs. Nicotine levels in the blood, then, give a measure of how much has reached the brain. And now, more reliable methods for measuring blood levels began to be reported in the literature.

When they were applied, the same figure would crop up with uncanny regularity in experiment after experiment. For some smokers it was 20, for others 50, but on average 35 nanograms per milliliter was how much nicotine, in billionths of a gram per milliliter of blood, smokers seemed to "want." When his blood level fell substantially below it, the smoker lit up—whereupon the figure would shoot up to perhaps fifty. Then, over the next half hour or hour, it would decline, to perhaps 20 or 25. Which meant it was time for another cigarette. And so on during the smoker's waking hours. Plot blood concentration over the course of a day and you'd wind up with a saw tooth marching across the paper.

The "titration hypothesis," researchers called it, using lab terminology for the precise adjustment of a chemical's concentration to some particular value. And while the data never made for so tidy a picture as the model implied, a wide variety of evidence supported its general outlines: smokers manipulated their smoking pattern to get the desired blood levels of nicotine, inhaling more or less deeply, or more or less often. When smoking a low-nicotine cigarette, they might cover up the air vents designed to dilute the smoke—and wind up with blood levels far higher than otherwise. It was as if smokers could "read" their own blood. Thirty-five nanograms per milliliter? They were happy. Twenty? They'd want a cigarette, but could manage without one. Five? They were climbing the walls.

During the early and mid-1970s, the evidence mounted. And yet to most lay people, most physicians, and even most smoking researchers, none of it made smoking an addiction, and none of it made nicotine an addictive drug. Because then—and for many people even today—"addiction" meant one thing. It meant addiction to the opium poppy. It mean morphine or heroin. It meant *bad*.

* * *

Before World War I, the line separating "good" drugs from "bad" was hazier than it is today. Anyone could go out and buy McMunn's Elixir of Opium or any of at least 600 such "soothing syrups," "pain killers" and "cough medicines," all containing opiates. According to E. M. Brecher in *Licit and Illicit Drugs*, it wasn't unknown for a prominent physician to take morphine every day for 30 or 40 years and never lose a day of work because of it. Sigmund Freud used cocaine for years.

"An opium den at the beginning of the century was a social club. When you say 'opium den,' think 'bar,' " says Neal Grunberg, a psychologist at the Uniformed Services University of the

Health Sciences in Bethesda, Maryland who helped write some of *Nicotine Addiction's* key sections. Being addicted carried few of the connotations—evil, crazed, criminal—it does now. Etymologically, to be addicted means to be *bound over* against one's will like a prisoner or a slave—whether to a drug or anything else. That older, broader, more innocent sense of the word lingers today in such expressions as being addicted to chocolates, or addicted to love.

By the 1980s, it had become clear that while abstaining from tobacco did not induce a withdrawal syndrome like that seen among heroin users, the symptoms were just as distinct, just as specific, and just as measurable.

Then, in 1914, came the Harrison Narcotics Act which, aimed at regulating the drug trade, came to be interpreted as a ban on narcotics use for all but the most narrowly medical purposes. For the first time, morphine and its opiate cousins were illegal. The nation's estimated 200,000 addicts turned to illicit drug dealers—and became criminals.

During the 1940s, classic studies with narcotics addicts imprisoned at the federal facility in Lexington, Kentucky, began to lay the groundwork for an understanding of addiction. But in the process, addiction began to lose its earlier, broader meaning and to ever more intimately fuse with heroin abusers in the public mind. Between about 1940 and 1965, as Jack Henningfield reckons it, addiction came to *mean* opiate addiction, with all its intimations of back alley drug deals and junk-crazed muggers.

So that when, in 1957, the World Health Organization established its definition of addiction, the opiates model was about the only model around. To be addictive, WHO said, a drug had to cause physical dependence, pronounced changes in behavior, and withdrawal symptoms. Cocaine and amphetamines, both today universally regarded as addictive, were excluded, being classed as merely "habituating."

In 1964, WHO discarded the distinction between habituating and addictive. "It was refuted, disowned, by the very committee that put the old definition together," says Jerome Jaffe, director of the Addiction Research Center. But the change came too late to influence the Surgeon General's landmark study appearing that same year. Applying the old definition, the Surgeon General ruled that nicotine was not addictive. Because, says Jaffe, evidence for withdrawal symptoms and behavioral changes among tobacco users was, at the time, still scanty. Yes, nicotine was so potent that barely one smoker in ten could keep to fewer than five cigarettes a day. Yes, it might be "habituating," to use the discarded WHO definition. Yes, it might be "dependence-producing," to use jargon that came into use later.

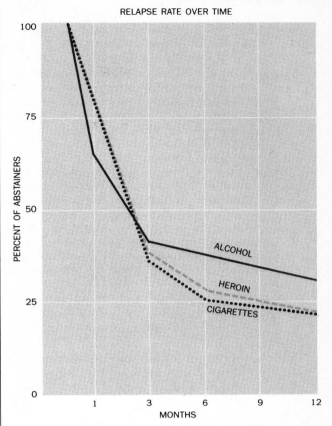

RELAPSE RATE OVER TIME

Smokers trying to give up the weed backslide about as frequently as alcoholics and heroin addicts trying to give up their favorite drugs.

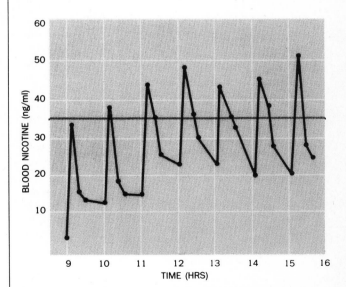

This subject who smoked one cigarette an hour illustrates the titration hypothesis—how smokers manipulate their smoking pattern, inhaling more or less deeply or more or less often, to get the desired blood levels of nicotine—on average 35 nanograms per milliliter.

But no, it wasn't addictive. *Heroin* was addictive.

"We tend not to believe that the things we do routinely and normally are bad," observes Neil Grunberg. So it was with smoking. All through the 1930s, 40s, and 50s cigarette smoking had been advertised as a symbol of success, of healthy sexuality, of the American way of life. It was socially acceptable. It didn't make you crazy. It wasn't heroin. And so, as evidence mounted through the early 1970s that smokers were—to again invoke addiction's etymological roots—*bound over* to the drug, resistance to the idea lingered.

You could see it at a conference, "Smoking As a Dependence Process," held by the National Institute of Drug Abuse in 1978. At it, many of the presentations given were fairly riddled with ambivalence. On the one hand, *of course* smoking was addictive, and *of course* nicotine responsible. On the other hand, there was reluctance, reaching even beyond normal scientific caution, to say so as long as any gaps remained in the scientific record.

M.A.H. Russell of Maudsley Hospital in England, for example, reviewed the evidence for nicotine's role—how it affected behavior and performance in ways that might be reinforcing, how it induced tolerance in animals, and so on—only to add a cautionary note: "If we could prove that nicotine is what smokers seek, we could be confident that the puzzle was virtually completed. Unfortunately this is not the case and we cannot escape the nagging fact that powerful addictive syndromes occur where pharmacological factors clearly play no part." How did we know, in other words, that smoking, with its comforting little rituals, wasn't more like such persistent habits as gambling, say, or nail biting?

Jerome Jaffe, then at Columbia University's College of Physicians and Surgeons, also expressed doubt. In a paper with Maureen Kanzler, he noted that, while nicotine *seemed* responsible for smoking's hold on the smoker, "reliable laboratory evidence that nicotine is a reinforcer of drug-taking behavior has been more difficult to develop than comparable evidence for drugs like morphine, amphetamine or cocaine." It was hard to get animals to give it to themselves. And when they did, they did so less compulsively than they did other drugs.

"We believe that most drinkers of gin and tonic want the gin more than the fizz or the quinine, that people who drink paregoric want the morphine and not the camphor," wrote he and Kanzler. But their personal convictions aside, they weren't *quite* ready to say it was nicotine that smokers craved more than the flare of the match, the lung-filling pull of the inhalation, or the leisurely rise of smoke rings into the air.

* * *

How did we know that smoking, with its comforting little rituals, wasn't more like such persistent habits as gambling, say, or nail biting?

The doubts, though, were soon to be dismissed once and for all. Just as a generation earlier hundreds of millions of dollars had poured out of the National Cancer Institute to pin down smoking's effects on health, now NIDA sank resources into the study of tobacco addiction. "This is a psychoactive drug with effects that fit the most stringent definitions of addiction," Jack Henningfield remembers NIDA director William Polling pronouncing with certainty; now it was time to make the case airtight. "All of a sudden," recalls Henningfield, "this behavior-controlling drug was being studied by people trained to study behavior controlling drugs." And within a few years beginning in the late 1970s, the remaining doors through which nicotine might escape the label of addictive were slammed shut.

One measure of addictive potential can be gained by simply asking human subjects how much they like whatever they're being fed through an intravenous needle, comparing the drug at various dosages to a placebo. Give a small dose of morphine and people like it significantly more, on a standard five-point scale, than a placebo. Up the dose and they prefer it still more. Do the same for a drug like chlorpromazine, known not to encourage compulsive use, and subjects like it no more than a placebo; a higher dose changes matters not at all. Give them nicotine, as Jack Henningfield reported in a key experiment, and the scores climb with higher dosages just the way they do for morphine.

Around this time came a series of studies by the Addiction Research Center's Steven Goldberg and colleagues at Harvard. One anomaly long nagging at the composure of smoking researchers had been nicotine's apparent failure to satisfy the self-administration test. If a drug is addictive, you'd expect people and animals to fairly lap it up—or, the way such experiments are done, to eagerly press a lever that metered it out to them. At the 1978 conference, there'd been reports of self-administration in rats, but at unimpressively low levels. And other researchers had been unable to demonstrate it at all.

What Goldberg and his colleagues did was to mimic human smoking behavior in monkeys. When people smoke, any effects of the nicotine become intimately linked to—and amplified by—environmental cues: *Dinner's over. Time for a smoke.* So with the nicotine they delivered intravenously, the experimenters periodically flashed an amber light. Sure enough, the monkeys would press away, usually about once or twice a second, self-administering the drug. When the nicotine, unbeknownst to the animals, was replaced by saline, lever pressing fell off dramatically. When the monkeys were given mecamylamine, a drug known to block nicotine's pharmacological actions, pressing likewise fell. The results were clear. "In one fell swoop," says Henningfield, "all the equivocal studies were out."

During the same period came key work on nicotine's withdrawal effects. Three hundred years before, following tobacco's introduction to England, King James I observed that smokers "are not able to forebear the same, no more than an old drunkard can abide to be long sober, without falling into an uncurable weakness and evil constitution." But difficulty in giving up smoking is one thing, withdrawal effects quite another. "You feed a vending machine that doesn't deliver, and you start beating on the machine," offers Jerome Jaffe, playing attorney for the defense. His point? "*Any* time you interrupt a habit, you can get irritable. Now if I give up smoking, do I vomit? Do I have seizures? Do I fall down on the floor, have hallucinations?" Junkies and alkies do. Smokers don't. Q.E.D., tobacco was not addictive, Jaffe portrays the skeptics insisting.

But by the early 1980s it had become clear that while abstaining from tobacco did not induce a withdrawal syndrome like that seen among heroin users, the symptoms were just as distinct, just as specific and just as measurable. Retrospective studies consistently showed signs of irritability, restlessness, difficulty concentrating, and weight gain. Now, the same symptoms showed up in more reliable prospective studies. Why, you could give smokers a battery of psychological and cognitive tests, watch their performance deteriorate within eight hours after their last smoke, then watch it return to normal once they started smoking again—or even, for that matter, when you fed them nicotine-laced chewing gum.

There had been other arguments long raised against calling nicotine addictive. Smoking, some said, doesn't exhibit tolerance; you don't require ever-increasing doses to achieve the desired effect. Sure it does, Henningfield points out. You don't *start out* smoking two packs a day. "And there are *no* drugs that people escalate their use of forever."

But wasn't it so, insisted critics like Gary Miller of the Tobacco Institute, that most ex-smokers gave it up on their own without outside help, or drugs, or treatment programs? What kind of an addiction is that? An addiction like any other, says Henningfield. Of alcohol users, for example, only 15 per cent are alcoholics. And nine in ten servicemen addicted to heroin in Vietnam got off once they got home. Because a drug exerts a powerful hold, doesn't mean it exerts an absolute hold.

Proponents of nicotine's central role in keeping smokers smoking don't say, and never said, that nicotine was the whole story. Give nicotine intravenously and smoking drops—but does not stop. Give nicotine chewing gum to would-be quitters and, without counseling and support, their relapse rate is almost as high as if you just let them go cold turkey. As Jerome Jaffe points out, "there's a lot of conditioning that goes with the inhalation of cigarette smoke. You have thousands of couplings" between the pleasure you get from smoking and the rituals surrounding it. To give up smoking means giving up nicotine—but also much more.

Later in the 1980s would come studies holding up whole new areas of nicotine's workings to the scientist's searchlight. Kenneth Kellar and his colleagues at Georgetown Medical Center, for example, discovered binding sites in the brain at which nicotine presumably acts. Other researchers experimented with nicotine gum, introduced in 1984 as a means of supplying smokers with a more benign source of nicotine while weaning them off cigarettes. Still others explored nicotine's role as a mood regulator and its ability to improve scores on cognitive tests through subtle nervous system effects.

But in essence, by the early 1980s, the case was already made; smoking was addictive—not just by the new, 1964 WHO definition but by the earlier, more rigid 1957 one—and nicotine was what made it so. So it was just a matter of time before the full force of the federal government lined up behind that determination.

In 1982, NIDA director William Pollin formally testified before Congress that nicotine was an addictive drug.

Later that year, summarizing Pollin's testimony and bearing the imprint of the U.S. Department of Health and Human Services, appeared a Public Health Service pamphlet, *Why People Smoke*. Placing tobacco right beside heroin, alcohol, and marijuana among drugs of abuse, the pamphlet reckoned it "the most widespread example of drug dependence in our country," one that drew its power and compulsion from nicotine.

In 1987, the American Psychiatric Association, which seven years before had included tobacco dependence within its Diagnostic and Statistical Manual of Mental Disorders, established "nicotine withdrawal" as an organic mental disorder.

Then, finally, on May 16, 1988, Surgeon General Koop stood before the cameras and microphones. . . .

* * *

About ten years earlier, in a hospital in Jaipur, India, a three-year-old Hindu child from a rural family was admitted to the pediatrics ward for malnutrition, anemia, and acute bronchitis. Two days later, the child was given a transfusion. During it, despite two shots of tranquilizer, he could not be stilled. Later, "the child was unable to sleep," the doctors who wrote up the case in *Clinical Pediatrics* reported, "crying and fretting through much of the night, begging for bidis."

A bidi is a crude, indigenous form of cigar popular in India, typically a three inch-long wad of sun-cured tobacco wrapped in Tendu leaf. It turned out that the boy's grandmother had surreptitiously supplied them to him for the past six months, and that he now smoked, inhaling deeply, eight to ten of them daily. When denied the bidis at the time of the transfusion, he became cranky and irritable and could neither eat nor sleep comfortably.

The three Indian physicians had little doubt about what they were seeing. They entitled their case study, "Probable Tobacco Addiction in a Three-Year-Old Child."

Street-Wise Crack Research

Like earlier students of tribal culture, modern ethnographers live and work with "crack families" in the toughest neighborhoods of New York, collecting unique behavioral data

A TYPICAL DAY for Philippe Bourgois, a 33-year-old Stanford-bred anthropologist, begins like that of many homemakers: he drops his 2-year-old son off at a day-care center in the neighborhood and then proceeds on to do errands and chat with neighbors. But around dusk, Bourgois's routine dramatically departs from the norm. That's when he migrates to one or another of numerous youth hangout places—"copping corners"—where kids go looking for drugs. Bourgois, on leave from the University of California at San Francisco, now lives in Spanish Harlem. There, he often completes his day by sitting around in a crack house, watching the action and interviewing the clientele. He gets home around 2 a.m., although sometimes he stays out all night.

Bourgois is a basic researcher—one of a small cadre of individuals known as street ethnographers who immerse their lives in the bewildering and dangerous world of urban crack addicts. Like the anthropologists who act as "participant-observers" in isolated foreign cultures, they are pioneers in uncharted territory. And like basic biologists or physicists, they rely heavily on serendipity to shape the course of their investigations.

But ethnography, like other social sciences, has not been very popular with funding agencies because of the complexity of its subject and nonquantitative orientation. Now that the drug war is a top national priority, however, the street ethnographers are getting a lot of publicity and are being sought after by government officials for inside information on drug use patterns.

Why and how do people get drawn to crack? How is the market structured? How does crack use affect the social and economic life of the community? What is its role in crime and violence? The answers may be crucial to breaking the destructive and seemingly intractable patterns of urban life that aggravate, and are aggravated by, drugs. But they cannot be supplied through traditional surveys.

This puts ethnographers in a key spot, because such matters are likely only to be illuminated by intimate exposure, over time, to the lives of the people affected and the development of trusting relationships.

This personal involvement makes a street ethnographer's task all the more difficult. Some very special characteristics are required—a bottomless interest in people, a high tolerance for seamy surroundings, guts, patience, and a willingness to work nights. As Terry Williams, a black sociologist from the City University of New York, points out, the subject under study is basically a "nocturnal culture."

Bourgois's extra challenge is his inherent visibility. He lives in a crack-ridden East Harlem neighborhood whose residents are about 65% Hispanic, mainly Puerto Rican; the rest are black. As a white man he is noticeable—particularly by police who often question him during sweeps in heavy crack-dealing areas. He acknowledges that his is a dangerous calling—he once was nearly hit by a bullet ricocheting off a curb—but says he is generally well treated and not in any more danger than anyone else who chooses to lurk in drug-ridden areas at night.

Still, the rigors of their existence don't exempt street ethnographers from the standards of the conventional anthropologist or sociologist. They use the participant-observer method, pioneered by anthropologists Bronislav Malinowski and Franz Boas in the early years of the century. Conventional researchers, even those administering questionnaires to addicts on park benches, impose their own structure and interpretations on what's being studied, says sociologist Bruce Johnson of the Manhattan-based Narcotic and Drug Research Inc. (NDRI). But none of the assumptions prevailing in mainstream society are taken for granted in ethnography, where, says Johnson, researchers want instead to find out what meaning the subjects themselves ascribe to the events in their lives.

The roots of ethnographic studies in the United States go back to the years between the wars, particularly at the University of Chicago, when anthropologists and sociologists—in the days before they split off into separate departments—worked together to explore a variety of urban subcultures. By the 1950s, the results of ethnographic research on alcoholism and drug abuse had started to appear.

Crack ethnography has emerged with the rapid spread of the drug that began in 1985. That was when soaring Latin American cocaine production caused prices to drop precipitously and the perilous process of cooking "freebase" was being replaced by the ready-to-use product, crack—little rock-like pellets of cocaine in its most intense form. Cheap—a day's use can now be financed for $10 to $20—and rapidly addictive, and producing an intense high, crack has spawned record levels of crime and violence and has dramatically eroded the social controls and rituals usually attendant on cocaine use. It is drawing an ever-younger clientele, and is particularly attractive to women. This has ravaged the last vestige of stability from one-parent families, filling the newspapers with tales of children living in crack houses, crack-addicted babies, and women whose mothering instincts have been obliterated by drugs.

Ethnographers are first-hand witnesses to the tragedies wrought by crack. Anthropologist Ansley Hamid of the John Jay College of Criminal Justice, for instance, has watched the deterioration of Sonya, a woman he has known since she was a 13-year-old involved in marijuana and alcohol. Now 22, she started experimenting with freebase 5 years ago. She has had two children, one of whom lives with her mother and the other in an orphanage. Now a confirmed crack addict, she lives in a shelter. Hamid has helped her get into several rehabilitation programs, but she always drops out.

A career among such lives sounds depressing. But researchers emphasize that, unlike other drug researchers, they are interested not only in deviance and pathology but also in the normal aspects of the community. Says Bourgois, "People forget that the majority of people living in the neighborhood are healthy people." Williams says, "There are elements that would depress anybody.

But to me it's all about people finding a way to survive. People do get out of it. . .that gives me hope."

Bourgois, who is repeatedly hailed by locals as he walks around the neighborhood, spends much of his time talking with individuals—in small Spanish-owned coffee houses, in apartments, on stoops or park benches. "I spend a lot of time shivering in the winter," he says. He will hold conversations with a person over a period of days, weeks, even months, asking questions about the person's life, jobs, family, health, social relationships, and drug involvement. Contacts often call him to tell him what's been happening.

Sometimes he tape records conversations; sometimes, if contacts are skittish, he stores up as much as he can to add to the several hundred typed pages of notes and about 50 hours of tapes he has accrued. "In the early phases you write up absolutely everything because you're not sure what's important."

Ethnographic researchers do not start out with a particular hypothesis, but rely on inductive methods to coax theories out of their observations. Anthropologist Lambrose Comitas of Columbia University says traditional anthropologists might regard drug ethnography as applied anthropology, since it is focused on a problem rather than a particular culture. But, he says, it also falls in the tradition of "community study" developed by Conrad Arensberg of Columbia University. Arensberg, formerly at the University of Chicago, applied anthropological methods to modern societies, using communities as microcosms of the larger culture. In his case, the community is that of drug users.

Findings from such observations can have direct relevance for public policy, as illustrated by two AIDS-related findings cited by Bourgois. One discovery, in which he participated, is about cracked lips. It seems that sometimes users will inhale the flame when lighting their crack pipes, which leads to burns on the lips. Since oral sex is the preferred mode for hurried and less-than-private sexual transactions, the AIDS virus is probably being transmitted to users through their lip lesions.

The other finding was made by University of Colorado researcher Stephen Koester from sitting in a heroin "shooting gallery" in San Francisco. Needle users were using a common dish of water to rinse their needles and to dilute the drug before shooting it. So, even though they were cleaning their needles with Clorox, they were shooting "pink water" into their veins. Koester says the Centers for Disease Control has been broadcasting this finding and a number of communities have revised their needle exchange programs as a result.

Sociologist Terry Williams says street research also offers a clear message about how authorities should be trying to communicate with inner city minority people. Although TV is ubiquitous, he says it doesn't get through to them. "Who gets respect? Not Oprah. TV is a joke." But they have radios going on all the time, including in crack houses, and they do relate to local disc jockeys—so "radio, not TV, is the medium to reach minority folk" with messages about drugs. Best of all, though, are person-to-person connections. "We are looking at an interactive culture," says Williams.

Street ethnographers like these are the only investigators who see drug use in a holistic context, says Comitas. Some say the dean of drug ethnography was anthropologist Edward Preble, formerly with NDRI.

Past and Present Cocaine Epidemics

In the late 1950s, when Yale University psychiatrist and drug historian David Musto was in medical school, there were only about 50,000 cocaine users in the United States. Musto says his professors would cite cocaine "as an example of a problem we used to have and has now been almost completely eliminated."

The old chestnut by George Santayana—about those who forget history being condemned to repeat it—seems particularly apt with regard to today's cocaine epidemic. Even in the mid-1970s, when cocaine use had begun a sharp climb, the Carter White House took a tolerant view. Jimmy Carter's drug adviser, psychiatrist Peter Bourne, went so far as to write that cocaine "is probably the most benign of illicit drugs currently in widespread use."*

Musto says Bourne and others had forgotten what happened around the country's first cocaine epidemic in the early years of this century. Cocaine (like opiates) used to be completely legal and widely available in a variety of products. But over the years prices fell and the sniffing, swallowing, and injecting of cocaine became widespread.

The year 1910 signalled the peak of the epidemic. In 20 years, says Musto, cocaine had been transformed from "a miracle drug to the most dangerous drug in America." In his annual message to Congress, President William Howard Taft said, "Cocaine is more appalling in its effects than any other habit-forming drug used in the United States."

Public fears eventually found expression in the passage of the first federal antinarcotics law, the Harrison Act of 1915. Although physicians were still allowed to dispense dangerous drugs, this loophole was tightened in Supreme Court rulings.

"Nothing is a better example of forgetting history," says Musto. And the forgetting was "intentional." During the 1930s and '40s, everyone thought the policy was working and mandatory drug education in the schools faded away, so "all the information from the first epidemic was not transmitted."

Despite the heroin epidemic of the late 1960s, the national mood was still one of relative toleration toward illicit drugs, marked by calls for legalization or decriminalization of marijuana, until the advent of the Reagan years.

Since then the tide has turned with a vengeance. Once again calls are being sounded for legalization—but this time against a background of increasing public intolerance of drugs. Musto, who calls legalization "a fad born of frustration," thinks its advocates are also guilty of forgetting history when they try to make analogies with Prohibition. For one thing, a great many Americans have always believed that alcohol is harmless in moderation. A more apt comparison would be to the laws against cocaine, but "you never read an article about how cocaine prohibition didn't work, because it was completely successful."

The reason for its success was the strong public consensus, which is far more crucial than any legal measures, says Musto. He sees a similar consensus building now, catalyzed by crack. But public fervor is a two-edged sword, says Musto, who fears that it could lead people to writing off the problems of inner cities as beyond redemption.

■ **C.H.**

The American Disease: Origins of Narcotic Control by David F. Musto (Oxford Univ. Press, New York, 1987).

Preble, for example, found that heroin users, contrary to the stereotype held in the 1950s, were not a passive, lethargic breed but "active hustling persons," according to Johnson. Similarly, says sociologist Patricia Adler of the University of Colorado, ethnography has debunked the Mafia-based image of the social organization of criminals as being a mirror of legitimate enterprises. But they have their own kinds of organization: For example, members of criminal groups use violence or the threat of it as a way of asserting status and control in the absence of conventional values such as trust and commitment. Thus, violence in the drug trade is not as random as it may be perceived by outsiders.

Researchers living in the neighborhoods they study have no difficulty making initial contacts. "This neighborhood is swarming with crack," says Bourgois. "You can buy it on virtually any street corner." People love to talk about themselves and crack users are no exception. Indeed, when Bourgois took a reporter for a walk on a notorious crack block, there was a man leaning against the hood of a car smoking, who—after being assured the strangers were not police—cordially showed off his crack pipe, a simple glass tube with a screen to hold in the rocks. Across the street was a cluster of people who were obviously lining up to buy crack. One man hollered out an offer to sell a well-known brand of heroin. Bourgois said the police regularly make sweeps of such blocks, rounding up anyone who doesn't have justi-

Flipping the Main Switch in the Central Reward System?

Cocaine, says Michael Kuhar of the government's Addiction Research Center in Baltimore, "is the most powerful reinforcer known."

That's animal researcher talk for the fact that a variety of species from mice to monkeys will learn to self-administer cocaine faster than any other drug and will do it until they die. In human terms it implies what has become self-evident in the inner cities—people get addicted to cocaine faster than they do to opiates, and much faster to crack, which produces a vapor when burned that floods the brain indiscriminately in a matter of seconds. Says psychiatrist Charles O'Brien of the University of Pennsylvania: "The average heroin addict takes 10 years to come in for treatment. We see people with cocaine, especially crack addiction, coming in after 2 or 3 years, sometimes 6 months."

While researchers have not yet found an effective pharmacological treatment for cocaine craving, they have made enormous strides in understanding how cocaine acts once it arrives in the brain. They have identified what appears to be the "cocaine receptor." They are zeroing in on just which brain sites are implicated in cocaine's euphoria-producing action in animals. In humans, they are using new scanning techniques to track the drug as it activates and is metabolized in various brain areas. And they have identified a number of chemicals that may relieve aspects of addiction by blocking the craving for drugs, flattening the high, reducing seizures from chronic use, and blunting post-high agitation and depression.

Cocaine—like amphetamines—produces its "high" by causing the brain to be flooded with the neurotransmitter dopamine. According to Kuhar of the National Institute on Drug Abuse, it blocks the reuptake of dopamine into the cell that releases it, thus making more dopamine available to be taken up by other neurons. Cocaine attaches to and plugs the dopamine transporter, so that it cannot signal for dopamine release to be terminated.

On the molecular level, therefore, says Kuhar, one of the primary aims of research is to further define the dopamine transporter by cloning it. Among those attempting to do this is George Uhl, also at the Addiction Research Center. Uhl is taking RNA from dopamine-containing cells and injecting it into frog eggs where it directs manufacture of the transporter. Uhl says successful cloning would open up a big new field of exploration. It would "give us a first look at the molecular basis for cocaine action." And it might make it possible to identify areas where drugs work selectively at cocaine sites without affecting normal dopamine activity.

There are many areas of the brain rich in dopamine neurons, and they have different functions in different places. Addiction research focuses on certain structures in the limbic system (the emotional brain) where cocaine is reinforcing in animals. A major goal is to characterize the anatomy and chemistry of the dopamine circuit by studying cocaine self-administration in rats.

George F. Koob of the Scripps Clinic research institute looks at how disabling dopamine neurons of selected brain areas affects intravenous self-administration of cocaine. He finds that such "denervation" in the nucleus accumbens results in "dramatic" decreases in cocaine self-administration, which suggests to him that "the nucleus accumbens seems to be the hot spot."

But not everyone agrees. James Smith at Bowman-Grey Medical School of Winston-Salem, North Carolina, has found that when rats self-administer cocaine directly into their brains, the drug is not reinforcing when aimed at the nucleus accumbens. Yet when it goes to the prefrontal cortex, it is reinforcing.

Once this apparent conflict is resolved, says Koob, the next "big question" concerns what long-term changes are effected in the brain by chronic cocaine use. Although prolonged use reduces the amount of dopamine functionally available, researchers have yet to show that dopamine is actually depleted. No gross long-term changes have been identified, says psychiatrist Frank Gawin of Yale University. For this reason people used to think snorting cocaine was "just a psychological addiction." But Gawin has found that the state of anhedonia, or inability to feel pleasure, can last weeks or months in humans after they stop taking the drug, which qualifies as a withdrawal syndrome even though it does not fit into the definition of physiological withdrawal.

fication for being there—but the minute they depart, business resumes as usual. The life of a daily crack user is a very busy one. Since the high from one pipe lasts only about half an hour there is no time to waste in finding the next fix.

Bourgois monitors a half dozen crack houses, but he says there are basically only two types. The safest is the "buy and fly" operation where buyers are not allowed to smoke on the premises. These can range

from a "walk-in" operation to a "hole in the wall" where buyer and seller do not even see each other, to a copping corner where the exchange takes place outdoors. The other type is the "crack bar" where customers buy drugs, rent paraphernalia, and sit around smoking and listening to music. ("Rap music is to crack what reggae is to marijuana," says anthropologist Hamid.) There is usually sexual activity going on in the periphery, behind a curtain, in the bathroom, or in the hall. Crack bars, says Bourgois, are becom-

ing less common, having been hard hit by the drug war.

Williams, now on leave at New York's Russell Sage Foundation, has been tracking the crack culture for the past 3 years by focusing on a particular group—he calls them a "family"— whose existence revolves around seeking, finding, consuming, and trading crack. He soon plans to publish a book, "The Crack House," which is in effect a sequel to his recent book, *The Cocaine Kids*, the fruit of 3 years of hanging out with a

Researchers now suspect that chronic cocaine use does indeed produce a variety of subtle changes in the brain. For one thing, the slightest environmental cue can trigger acute craving in an addict, even after years of abstinence. Gawin says this phenomenon may be based on neuroadaptation, which makes for decreased sensitivity to pleasure-producing substances.

In other ways, scientists say cocaine produces a long-term increase in sensitization, otherwise known as "reverse tolerance." Robert Post of the National Institute of Mental Health says chronic use increases the brain's sensitivity to the non-"euphorogenic" effects of the drug, to the point that very small doses are required to trigger them. This applies to two other functions of a drug that are not related to its high-producing (dopamine-mediated) properties. One is as a psychomotor stimulant which causes the hyperactivity seen in cocaine users. The other is as an anesthetic which, says Post, is responsible for the fact that repeated use produces epilepsy-like seizures in the limbic system. These potentially fatal seizures can be triggered by very low doses in chronic users, the "kindling effect."

Although researchers are keenly interested in learning the specific effects of cocaine, the key to counteracting its effects may lie in the commonalities it shares with other drugs of abuse in activating what is called the "central reward mechanism." Although every drug affects a particular group of brain receptors, some researchers speculate that the results all feed into the same central mechanism. But so far there is no consensus on the degree to which dopamine circuits are involved in other addictions.

Certainly, the commonalities are extensive, as shown by the extent of multiple addictions and cross-addiction (when abuse of one substance automatically creates vul-

nerability to another). Other research, showing that a wide variety of therapeutic drugs can also influence addictive behavior, also suggests a common link among addictions. Gawin warns, however, that even if a drug were found to block the high this would not be sufficient. "Therapies accepted by addicts are those that work on craving."

Some drugs under investigation include:

■ The pain-killer **buprenorphine**, currently the number one candidate. A mixed opiate agonist-antagonist (meaning it both mimics endogenous opioids and blocks their receptors), buprenorphine seems to act like methadone when given to heroin addicts. There is evidence that it also works with cocaine addiction. It has been shown to suppress cocaine self-administration by monkeys in a trial recently reported by a team headed by Nancy K. Mello and Jack H. Mendelson of Harvard Medical School.

■ The antidepressant **desipramine**. This has helped people in a trial at Yale abstain from cocaine significantly longer than those on a placebo or lithium. Sixty percent of the subjects taking desipramine for 6 weeks were able to abstain for at least 3 weeks—compared with about 20% of the two control groups. Researchers at the University of Minnesota have found that another antidepressant, fluoxetine, which affects serotonin rather than dopamine, reduces cocaine self-administration in rats.

■ **Flupenthixol**, an antipsychotic drug used in Europe, acts as an antidepressant when administered in low doses. Gawin says the virtue of this drug is that, unlike tricyclics, it can be administered as a slow-release injection. "The problem with crack abusers is they go 30 steps out of the clinic and run into a seller," he says. "The conditioned cues are overwhelming." But with flupenthixol in their blood, he says addicts in a trial in the Bahamas were able to stay abstinent for an average of 24 weeks—as opposed to 8 weeks at most without it.

■ **Carbamazapine**, an antiseizure drug, may help reduce cocaine craving and stem seizures from chronic use. The Addiction Research Center, in cooperation with O'Brien of the University of Pennsylvania, is planning a double blind clinical trial.

■ **Buspirone**, an antianxiety drug. Bristol-Myers Co. has found that it can help relieve the anxiety and depression attending alcohol withdrawal. The drug, which partially blocks serotonin receptors, is now being tested on cocaine users.

■ **Bromocriptine**, a dopamine antagonist that relieves the effects of Parkinson's disease. This has shown some promise in clinical studies for relieving agitation and the "crash" effects from cocaine. However, Roy Wise of Concordia University says animal studies indicate bromocriptine may itself be addictive.

■ **Mazindol**, a dopamine blocker used to suppress compulsive eating. It may be useful in stemming cocaine craving according to Robert Balster of the Medical School of Virginia. Balster is testing the effect of that and other drugs on monkeys' self-administration of cocaine.

The treatment picture is complicated by the fact that the pure cocaine addict is becoming an increasingly rare bird. Cocaine users develop multiple addictions as they are always experimenting with other drugs to mellow out their highs and alleviate the ensuing jitters and depression.

The insidious and pervasive nature of addiction is such that pharmacological therapies can never be expected to be more than an adjunct to treatment and long-term behavior change. Nonetheless, Gawin, for one, thinks the commonalities among addictions, rather than making the picture hopelessly complex, actually "could mean that there is a potential single pharmaceutical solution for euphoria." "Disordered pleasure systems," he concludes, are "an area with substantial gold to be mined."   ■ C.H.

teen-aged gang of Dominican cocaine dealers. The kids went out of business around 1985 when the scene started getting too rough.

Williams says his core interest lies in the socialization of small groups, rituals, and play. In many ways, he says, the nine members of the crack family he is now following represent a regression to a more primitive society—a hunting-and-gathering "tribe" oriented to nothing more than day-to-day survival. It comprises an unlikely combination of people, most of them females, most teen-aged, and most Dominicans. They float from crack house to crack house, following their leader, a middle-class Jewish man who

used to own property in the area. Because men dominate the crack trade, Williams says the setup gives the girls opportunities to get the drugs without money—usually through sex. Members sometimes get money by acting as runners delivering drugs to middle-class buyers. Taking much of their lexicon from "Star Trek," their lives are centered on the "mission" of finding drugs. "Scottie" refers to the drug; a "beamer" is a smoker; and an "interplanetary mission" is when you go from one crack house to another.

Williams says he is always up front with his subjects about what he is doing. Whenever he went to one of the 38 crack houses he visited for the book, he explained what he

was up to and asked people what name they want to go under in the book. When *The Cocaine Kids* came out, he says the proprietors of one crack house cleaned the place up and held a book party for him.

He never uses a tape recorder and says he learned to memorize situations in detail to write up when he got home in the early morning hours. Sometimes he would spend a week or so using one of the methods he developed himself: ignoring the dialogue and just recording physical gestures, facial expressions, and peculiar behaviors that crack users engage in. One is an activity called "ghostbusting" when a person, after having "chilled out" for 5 or 10 minutes (the

Kleber Offers Expert and Blunt Opinions on Addiction

Yale University psychiatrist Herbert Kleber seems to be made to order for the job of deputy to drug chief William Bennett. Widely respected in his field, he has 25 years of experience in research and the administration of treatment programs. His own pioneering research focused on drugs to block addictive craving. He is also a registered Republican—a rarity for a Yale professor, much less a psychiatrist.

Kleber took an indefinite leave from Yale to be Bennett's "deputy for demand reduction" in the President's drug war, which is much sniped at by other academics for being wrong-headed and underfunded. However, a Yale colleague, psychiatrist David Musto, says Kleber knows "what it takes to make things work."

Kleber is not shy about his accomplishments. "I am considered one of the leading experts on treatment and policy aspects of substance abuse." Like his boss, Kleber has a sizable portfolio of blunt opinions. Of needle exchange programs, he says, "Morality aside, it won't work." He cites data from England showing that only 60% of clients came back after the first visit and 20% after the tenth, indicating "impulsive" addicts are unlikely to comply. As for the supposed futility of criminal punishment, he responds, "Criminologists say deterrence *does* work if applied swiftly and surely," but the present system offers little deterrence because so few suspects end up in jail. On pregnant women addicts, Kleber says those already in trouble with the law could be compelled to stay in a treatment facility for the duration of the pregnancy. The others pose a "much harder" question.

Kleber is unequivocal on the subject of drug legalization. Most advocates of the policy, he says, waffle when asked whether they would permit cocaine sales, which Kleber says would be an unqualified disaster. Government-regulated prices would not drive out drug crime, he argues, because if prices were kept up, illegal trade would continue to flourish, and if they were kept down, cocaine would be put "in the reach of every third grader." He believes crime would become more

widespread and there would be more drug-associated violence because crack, in particular, causes "paranoia, irritability, and the need for action." Furthermore, he thinks legalization would result in rampant cocaine addiction, maybe even approaching alcoholism in scope.

Kleber's job centers on drug abuse treatment, prevention, and research. One of his major tasks will be prodding states to formulate systematic plans. Although many people have called for radical increases in funding for treatment, Kleber says the system is going to have to be improved first. One immediate need, he says, is for more "accountability." Quality reviews may be handled by a new branch of the Alcohol, Drug Abuse and Mental Health Administration, the Office of Treatment Improvement, which will administer demonstration programs and grants to states.

Many think that treatment should be provided for all addicts. But Kleber points out that there are many who don't want help and many others who will fail to benefit even if offered it. Of the 4 million estimated heavy drug users, Kleber thinks about 1 million fall in this category. Another 1 million are sufficiently motivated to stop on their own. The drug strategy is aimed at the remaining 2 million who might benefit from treatment.

Another big issue in treatment is "co-morbidity," the fact that recent studies show a high proportion of drug abusers also suffer from some psychopathology such as depression or schizophrenia. "Most programs don't have the capacity or sophistication" to treat such problems, says Kleber, who thinks treatment centers should be better coordinated with mental health providers.

Furthermore, "most of the treatment money out there now is for heroin," but the big problem now is cocaine, which is being regularly used by close to 3 million people. Despite the special challenges posed by crack addiction, Kleber says the main reason it is so difficult to treat is "because of who's using it." There is not much leverage available for "competing reinforcers"—that is, inner city crack addicts are less likely to have jobs, families, and reputations at stake. ■ C.H.

most intense part of the high), will resort to scrabbling around on the floor looking for nonexistent particles of crack. This state is a mild version of the more serious paranoid psychosis often accompanying crack use.

Williams, says Johnson of NDRI, has laid much of the foundation for current investigations in New York. For one thing, "he has demonstrated he can make connections and affiliations with dealers and get them to cooperate. A lot of people out there don't believe you can study crack dealers."

Ethnographic research often paints a picture that differs from common public perceptions. For example, from where Bourgois sits, the problem of pregnant addicts is even greater than policy-makers believe and is "an absolutely urgent, urgent, urgent avenue for research." While epidemiologists know how to count the crack-addicted babies, Bourgois says ethnographers are needed to identify long-term problems.

Another issue that needs attention is housing. Crack neighborhoods are littered with abandoned buildings that become breeding grounds for crack. Says Bourgois, "The biggest landlord of crack houses in New York is the city of New York." Another aspect of the problem is the shortage of low-income housing, which results in the disruption of hitherto stable neighborhoods as existing residents are pushed out to make room for renovated condos and co-ops. The situation also breeds further suspicion of the law, because the police are regarded as "agents of gentrification."

Hamid of John Jay College is currently getting a street's eye view of the effects of law enforcement efforts. A Trinidadian of East Indian descent, he lives in a West Harlem apartment that looks out on one side to a Jamaican eatery where drugs are sold and on the other to an abandoned building used as a crack house. With funding from the Vera Institute of Criminal Justice, he is currently gathering baseline information on the crack trade in order to gauge the effects of New York's new anti-drug initiatives.

Hamid and many others believe that the heavy involvement of children in the cocaine business is a direct result of the "Rockefeller laws" imposing stern penalties on offenders over age 18. He now contends that police activity is making the problem even worse. He says crack houses are going out of style in favor of mobile and less vulnerable out-

door operations. This, he says, is making the scene more volatile and dangerous, breaking down even the minimal social controls and rituals in crack houses. And "busting established dealers opens doors for anyone to come in and deal."

Street researchers are clearly partisans of the people they study, regarding them as victims rather than perpetrators. But as sociologist Adler points out, the whole point of the research is that it is subjective, representing attempts to get inside the feelings and motivations of the people and see the world as they see it.

But that is part of why it is so hard to get government support. "I couldn't begin to describe how difficult it is to get money for scientific research using qualitative research methods," says Johnson of NDRI. Johnson says the government turned down a proposal he and Williams submitted in 1985, therefore losing a golden opportunity to obtain "major documentation of the crack phenomenon which was just emerging."

Williams now bypasses such hurdles altogether. He gets his money from private foundations and publishes his stark portrayals of the crack culture in journalistic form to get it read fast by as many people as possible.

Bourgois, on the other hand, spent 2 years in bureaucratic hassles before finally obtaining a 6-month $25,000 grant from the National Institute on Drug Abuse (he now has grants from several private foundations). But since drug czar William Bennett began work early this year, his office has been calling researchers such as Bourgois to get the answers to questions only they can answer, like: How much does a regular crack user smoke daily? (Answer: As much as he can get; maybe five to eight pipes daily; much, much more if he is on a binge.)

Most of New York's small cadre of crack researchers collaborate or interact at some point. But Johnson and another colleague, criminologist Jeffrey Fagan of John Jay College, have a somewhat more theoretical orientation than the lone souls who haunt crack locales.

Fagan has recently completed a survey of convicted offenders to explore whether violence is essentially created by the nature of the crack business or whether the business attracts violence-prone individuals. He found that crack offenders tended to be convicted for more serious offenses, which seems to support the latter hypothesis. John-

son says this suggests that when it comes to incarceration, priority should be given to crack offenders even if they have committed fewer crimes than other chronic offenders.

A larger question relates to whether the crack epidemic is a brand new type of phenomenon, different from earlier drug epidemics. It looks different in some ways, such as in the increased violence and the rapidity with which people lose control over their use. In contrast to the relative stability and centralization that characterizes the retail trade in heroin, cocaine, and particularly crack dealing is a dangerous and constantly shifting free-for-all. A crack seller who manages to stay in business for 3 months is a senior crack seller, says Johnson. But in some ways, such as the growing organization and entrenchment of some local dealers, it resembles the usual course of a new drug. If that is the case, the researchers say we can assume that it will level off and stabilize—much the way heroin use has done. If crack does represent a departure from historical patterns, there is no telling what will happen.

In hopes of illuminating this question NDRI has recently obtained $200,000 from NIDA, an unusually large grant, which will be used over the next 2 years to support research on "the natural history of crack" by four or five trained ethnographers. They will be hired to amass information from about 140 subjects on the crack business and individual careers of those involved.

As Johnson points out, the actual role of drugs and the drug trade in the larger picture is difficult to tease out because the crack explosion has occurred at a time when inner city infrastructures are rapidly decaying, crime is growing, AIDS is spreading, minority populations are increasing, education is in crisis, and teen pregnancies and family breakups are on the rise. Micro-social investigations such as are being conducted by these researchers may be the only way society can sort out causes from effects in the relationship of drugs to people, neighborhoods, crime, and the economy.

Whether policy-makers will listen to the answers is another story. In Johnson's opinion, the interpretations of the drug scene that ethnographic researchers come up with don't fit with prevailing policies that are based "primarily on moral rhetoric." Says he: "The reality of what's happening in the inner city rarely gets through to policy-makers." ■ Constance Holden

Why Drugs?

Why do people use and abuse drugs? And why do some people use, abuse, and become dependent on, certain psychoactive substances while others do not? What explanations account for drug use? The medical profession calls explanations that attempt to answer the "why" question, *etiology*; what is the etiology or cause of drug use and abuse? In short, *Why drugs?*

A variety of perspectives attempt to answer the "why" question. In the early 1980s, a federal agency, the National Institute on Drug Abuse, published a nearly 500-page monograph entitled *Theories of Drug Abuse*, which described some 40 different explanations of why people abuse drugs. Clearly, a definitive explanation of drug use and abuse—one on which nearly all informed observers will agree—has not yet been devised. This issue is still fraught with controversy.

Some experts believe that drug use is a universal human need—indeed, an instinct that is characteristic of all, or most, members of the animal kingdom. "High Times in the Wild Kingdom" summarizes this perspective, originally put forth by Andrew Weil in his book, *The Natural Mind* in 1972, and recently expanded by Ronald Siegel in *Intoxication: Life in Pursuit of Artificial Paradise*. Siegel's conclusion is that, since humans have a universal need to get high, and since all currently-known intoxicating substances have dangerous side-effects, scientists ought to search for one that is completely safe. While most experts do not agree with this theory, it is worthy of attention.

The "animal instinct" theory, however, does not address the question of the variability of drug use among humans. After all, instinct or not, some of us are lifetime abstainers, others use drugs (alcohol and coffee, for instance) safely, moderately, and without untoward effect, and still others are compulsive, drug-dependent abusers. How do we account for the difference? For an answer to this type of question, we have to look at explanations that seek differences among individuals.

Some experts believe that there is a genetic basis to dependence and addiction—that, for example, some people are born with a genetic propensity to abuse and become dependent on addictive drugs such as alcohol. What exactly does this "genetic propensity" consist of? With respect to alcohol, some observers believe that an unusual insensitivity to the effects of alcohol causes some people who drink to drink to excess; this insensitivity causes them to feel only slightly drunk when they are very drunk, which influences them to drink more than others do. The same could be true of drugs generally, some argue.

The genetic theory is controversial and is not accepted by all, or even most, drug abuse experts. Some observers argue that there is a syndrome known as the "addictive personality." Those individuals who become chemically dependent do so because they are, to quote Benjamin Stein, author of "The Lure of Drugs," "lonely, sad, frightened people" who have a basic personality flaw for which drugs offer a crutch that "organizes" their lives. Still other experts argue that alcohol and other chemical dependencies are "intoxicating habits," that the chemically dependent have simply learned to do the wrong things with the substances they use and abuse. Just as Pavlov's dogs learned to salivate at the sound of a bell, the stimuli in the addict's environment serve as cues that generate a drug craving. Addicts associate these cues with pleasure because they have been associated with reinforcement in the past; such associations can be unlearned as readily as they were learned. Still other experts point to more natural causes. The brain produces a set of morphine-like chemicals called endorphins (or "endogenous morphines") which, under certain circumstances, give us a "natural high." When endorphins are released, the body feels pleasure and wants to repeat what caused it; Could these endorphins be a clue to the etiology of drug use and abuse?

Sociological perspectives stress the influence of the society, the culture, social contexts or settings, and subcultures within a given society on drug dependence. Certain categories in the population are more likely to use and abuse drugs than others; certain drugs penetrate poorer neighborhoods more readily than more affluent ones; men learn that it is acceptable and normative to drink at higher levels than women do; drinking in some societies takes place in family settings, and tends to be moderate, whereas in other societies, drinking typically takes place among single men in a bar setting, and tends to be more excessive; and so on. In any explanation of drug and alcohol abuse, it is incomplete and misleading to leave sociological factors out of the picture.

Recently, many observers have concluded that several explanations are necessary for a complete understanding of the "why" question. Perhaps, one day, an integrated theory may emerge.

Looking Ahead: Challenge Questions

Why do people use drugs? Why do some people use certain drugs? Why do some people who use drugs abuse and become dependent on them—while others do not? Why do so many drug users not become drug abusers? Where does use end and abuse begin?

Is abuse a chemical, a genetic, a psychological, or a sociological phenomenon? Is it a combination of all of these factors? In what way? Is it a different combination for different individuals?

Is drug abuse rational or irrational behavior? Why?

If drug abuse can be explained by factors beyond the individual's control, are we, therefore, not responsible for our abuse of drugs?

If the supply of a certain drug suddenly dried up, would the users and abusers of that drug simply stop taking drugs altogether—or turn to another chemical substance?

Do we need a different explanation for use than we do for abuse? Abuse than for addiction and dependence? Do we need a different explanation for the abuse of each drug separately?

If alcoholism is genetically caused, how can one member of the same family become an alcoholic, one an abstainer, and the third a moderate drinker? If drug abuse is hereditary, what about other factors?

Why can some people handle alcohol while others cannot?

High Times in the Wild Kingdom

Is drug abuse natural?

One of the surest ways to kill a rat is to let it shoot cocaine. Teach a rat, or a dog or a monkey, to dose itself at will, and it typically becomes just as helpless as any urban junkie. Addicted animals will give up food or companionship, even endure electrical shocks, to get another fix. And they'll continue to dose themselves as their lungs and nervous systems start to fail.

This is in the lab, of course. Such depravity would never occur in nature, right? Wrong, says Ronald Siegel, a psychopharmacologist at UCLA. In a recent book titled "Intoxication: Life in Pursuit of Artificial Paradise,"* Siegel argues that the urge to get high is as basic and universal as the desire for food or sex—and that it has some of the same consequences in the wild as it has in urban America. "The entire animal kingdom is driven by the same pursuit," he says. "It is part of our nature."

Siegel traces the roots of today's drug problem back 135 million years to the Cretaceous Period, when angiosperm plants started manufacturing toxic chemicals as a defense against herbivores. By the time humans discovered the pleasing effects of certain plant toxics, some 5,000 years ago, other animals were already forging "the new chemical bond we call addiction." Humans have recently carried the relationship to new extremes, of course, by extracting and refining the poisons of choice. But modern drug taking remains part of a "long natural tradition." Siegel doesn't always back his assertions with data, and his prose style is a bizarre amalgam of Scientific American and the New York Post. Yet despite its flaws, his treatise offers a refreshing perspective on the drug problem, and it's full of amusing yarns.

Addiction, as Siegel makes clear, is not always a bad thing. Australian koalas spend their lives feeding exclusively on eucalyptus leaves, not just for nutrition but to alter their body temperatures and make themselves unpalatable to parasites and predators. The leaves are bitter medicine: infants have to start out on a predigested pulp excreted by their mothers. But once they learn the habit, there's no giving it up. They die when deprived of eucalyptus, because their addicted bodies have no other way to get nutrients.

Other animals use drugs for sheer pleasure. In the Canadian Rockies, bighorn sheep grind their teeth to the gums nibbling at a narcotic lichen that grows on bare rocks. And various creatures eat the hallucinogenic mescal beans that grow in the Texas desert, even though the beans lack usable nutrients. When Siegel led a group of goats to a patch of shrubs to gauge the veracity of this rumor, several munched themselves into a daylong delirium. So did one of his pack horses (he had to restrain the others). Small wonder that the Wichita Indians, who developed an entire pharmacology by observing animals, became mescal eaters themselves.

Drunk elephants: Psychedelics don't have a broad animal following, but drunkenness seems ubiquitous. It often results from a chance encounter with fermented fruit or grain, yet many creatures actively lust after alcohol. Farm animals are notorious for breaking into vats of moonshine mash. So are elephants. Siegel recounts how a herd of 150 once raided an illegal still in West Bengal, drank liberally, then "rampaged across the land, killing five people, injuring a dozen, demolishing seven concrete buildings and trampling twenty village huts." Baboons can get carried away, too. In "The Descent of Man," Darwin recounts how a troupe in North Africa "held their aching heads with both hands and wore a pitiable expression" a day after gulping down bowls of strong beer. "When beer or wine was offered them, they turned away with disgust."

Luckily, natural forces usually converge to keep animals from wasting their lives, even when they lack a sense of restraint. When flocks of migrating robins arrive in southern California each February, they gorge themselves on ripening firethorn and toyon berries. For a few weeks the birds go utterly berserk, and many die in high-speed flying accidents. But because the berries are seasonal, sobriety prevails the rest of the year. In the Andes, llamas, birds, snails, insects and people all consume cocaine by eating leaves or seeds from the coca plant. But the drug's natural packaging effectively prohibits harmful doses.

Insect anarchy: There are exceptions to this pattern, however—instances in which drug use tears at the fabric of animal society. Ranchers have known since the 19th century that locoweed, a flowering plant native to the American Southwest, can turn cattle and horses into crazed, hopeless junkies. Many addicts die of starvation or thirst, as they give up food and water in favor of the drug. And their offspring tend to perpetuate the cycle of dependency. *Lasius flavus,* or yellow ant, suffers similarly from its appetite for beetle juice. Colonies of yellow ants typically feed and care for *Lomechusa* beetles in exchange for the chance to lick an intoxicating goo from their abdomens. If the worker ants drink too much, they get careless and damage the ant larvae in their care. The workers' addiction also compromises their loyalties: in a crisis, they tend to safeguard the beetles' larvae instead of their own kin's. Entire societies can collapse as a result.

The fact that drug use is natural doesn't mean it's good, then, just that chanting "no" isn't likely to rid us of it anytime soon. The most controversial alternative—to haul off and legalize currently controlled substances—could prove disastrous, given the deadly pharmacopia we've amassed. The obvious solution, in Siegel's view, is to restructure our chemical environment—to fabricate drugs that "balance optimal positive effects, such as stimulation or pleasure, with minimal . . . toxic consequences." If medical science could perform that feat, he reasons, everyone could have a good time and no one would get hurt. It's a fanciful notion, a bit like that of erecting a high-tech global missile shield. The difference is that, in this case, a partial success would represent progress.

Geoffrey Cowley

The Lure of Drugs:

They 'Organize' An Addict's Life

Benjamin Stein

Benjamin Stein, an aide in the Nixon-Ford White Houses, is a lawyer and freelance writer in Los Angeles. His latest book is "Hollywood Days, Hollywood Nights" (Bantam).

AND NOW for a few words about drugs . . . Everyone in America talks on television and at political gatherings about drugs — politicians, preachers, teachers, lawyers, law enforcement officials, even parents. Everyone talks about drugs, that is, except for the one group most directly affected by drugs: drug addicts and users. It might make sense for the nation to listen to what they think.

Now, I am not exactly a drug addict. But I do take a variety of tranquilizing and sleeping pills, and in my past life, when I was a '60s kind of guy, I used my share

of what was hip. That was a while ago, but for whatever reasons since the days of law school, through the days in Washington, in the bureaucracy, in the White House, at a university, and the days in New York, at a great newspaper, and in Los Angeles, around the studios, and the cars and the bars and the flash and the cash and the trash, I have spent much time with drug users. Even now, I am involved in a number of self-help programs for major, heavy-duty drug abusers. These are not people I am studying. These are my friends, and this is a big part of my life.

In a word, I know something about drugs and drug users from the inside out.

I'd like to share a little bit of what I know, and correct a few wrong impressions. Some of these have public

policy implications, and some of them are just interesting in the way learning about any new kind of people is interesting.

First, drug addicts do not become drug addicts by mistake, by accident or because someone lurks on a corner offering reefers. Drug addicts do not get high just because they have nothing else to do and getting high would be a cool way of spitting on the bourgeoisie.

Drug addicts (and by that is meant, without any doubt, alcohol addicts) get that way because drugs have a way of, temporarily, organizing an otherwise disordered life. I have heard hundreds, maybe thousands of drug addicts talk about how they got into drugs so heavily that drugs ruled their lives.

Every single one of them wanted

some outside power to take over his life. Each man or woman felt that his or her life was grossly defective, that he or she was severely lacking the basic equipment needed to cope with existence. "I feel like I was dropped here from another planet without any travel brochure," one particularly articulate young man once said. "I have felt like a lonely, heartbroken child my whole life," said another man, who spoke for every addict I have ever known. "I never felt like I even belonged in my own skin, let alone in my family or in my high school," said another young woman. I defy anyone to find a drug addict who had a happy childhood or who emerged from childhood with a well-integrated personality.

Drugs — and again, this includes alcohol in a big way — made the psychically split feel whole again. "When I first started to use coke, I felt six-feet tall and bulletproof," said one diminutive man. "I used blow (cocaine) in eighth grade, and I wondered where it had been all my life," said another man. "For the first time, I felt like I belonged, like I could talk to people, like I was going somewhere," is a sort of synthesis of hundreds of comments by addicts about how the felt when they got onto drugs. In other words, drugs that are illegal do exactly what prescription psychoactive drugs do.

Drugs are not like going to a dance or having a vacation or getting a great stereo or even like having sex. They are not interludes in otherwise different lives. For the drug addict, the effect of the drug, the knowledge that a drink or a shot or a snort or a pill can change their relation to the universe is the overwhelming fact of their lives for the time they are allowing drugs to organize their lives. They genuinely believe that their lives would be unbearable without drugs.

In other words, you will not stop drug addiction by nuclear bombing Peru. The drug addict will find something legal, something by prescription, something that will organize his life again and take his shattered self and make it real.

That is, drug addiction is not a problem made by smugglers. It is a problem of lonely, sad, frightened people — some of them truly wonderful people — who want something to help, and if they can't get it from Colombia, they will get it from the corner liquor store or from a doctor, and they will be addicts all the same.

The problem in America is not the importation of illegal drugs. The problem is the minds and hearts and

bodies of broken people who need to be made whole by something, and drugs come easily to hand.

Second, and this is crucial, drug addiction in each case is usually self-limiting in either tragic or miraculous ways. The tragic way in which drugs are self-limiting is obvious: People die from them sooner or later.

The miraculous way comes from the fact that drugs simply do not keep on succesfully organizing addicts' lives. Addicts come to know that. At some point, early or late, the drug addict sees that the negative effects of the habit are far more dangerous than whatever life he had before he took up drugs. He finds that sleepless nights, car crashes, nights in jail, loss of family, loss of job, loss of self-respect, loss of home are worse than what he had before. In other words, the drug has lost its ability to put the addict back into one piece again. The drug addiction has made him far more shattered than he ever was before he began to get high.

Drug addicts get saved by having something to organize themselves without drugs. This can be religion, self-help groups, new friends, a new environment, new creative challenges or some combination. Those who felt themselves psychically crippled before they used drugs or alcohol will still feel incomplete when they stop using or drinking. They need something to fill up the empty spaces inside.

To an astonishingly impressive extent, Alcoholics Anonymous (by far the largest active multi-faith non-profit organization in Southern California) gives men and women a reason to live, and organizing principles (their famous and inspiring 12-step program) to glue splintered egos together. (Every drug addict and alcoholic knows of at least one person whose life has been saved by AA, and knows that the opportunity is out there.) I have no doubt that there are religious organizations outside AA that do excellent work as well.

The point is that drug addiction is something that comes from inside

---

> ## 'The point is that drug addiction is something that comes from inside individuals. It will never be stopped by speedboats, helicopters or search dogs.'

---

millions of individuals. It will never be stopped by speedboats and helicopters and search dogs, nor by defoliating marijuana acreage in Humboldt County, California. It will be slowed down (not stopped, because realistically it is never going to be stopped altogether) when millions of individuals realize that there are alternatives to drugs for binding up wounds, alternatives that do not cut still deeper lacerations, alternatives that build lives.

It's a happy sign that the Congress has realized this, in an election year, and has increased funding for drug treatment centers. But the continuing illusion that pouring money into high-tech search gear for border patrols — the path Washington took in earlier legislation — will stop drug abuse when drugs are available freely inside the stores of America is a joke.

The idea that drug addicts will stop booting up because of appeals by movie stars or politicians' wives simply bears no relation to the reality of the problem. Drug addicts need to be brought back to sanity one by one, from the inside out. To the extent that the government can help addicts by helping hospitals, drug treatment centers and self-help groups make their services more widely available, then it can help the addicts I know. (It is deeply instructive to know, however, that AA, which has probably saved more addicts than every other public or private program put together, proudly will not accept any outside contributions, and is entirely self-supporting from the dollars and quarters placed onto plates at the meetings.)

There are more truths that can be learned by listening to the people most directly affected by addiction — the addicts. I have only touched on a few. But it is clear that the huge volume of knowledge of what drug addiction is and how it can be stopped lies mainly in the experience of drug addicts, present and recovering, grateful or still suffering. It might make sense to listen to them.

Intoxicating Habits

Some alcoholism researchers say they are studying a learned behavior, not a disease

BRUCE BOWER

Most alcoholism treatment programs in the United States operate on the assumption that people seeking their help have a disease characterized by physical dependency and a strong genetic predisposition. The goal of treatment, therefore, is total abstinence.

Herbert Fingarette, a philosophy professor at the University of California, Santa Barbara, pored over alcoholism and addiction research and came up with a suggestion for the many proponents of this approach: Forget it.

In a controversial new book (*Heavy Drinking: The Myth of Alcoholism as a Disease*, University of California Press, 1988), Fingarette says alcoholism has no single cause and no medical cure, and is the result of a range of physical, personal and social characteristics that predispose a person to drink excessively.

"Let's view the persistent heavy drinking of the alcoholic not as a sin or disease but as a central activity of the individual's way of life," he contends. Seen in this context, alcoholism treatment must focus not just on the drinking problem, but on developing a satisfying way of life that does not revolve around heavy drinking. Total abstinence — the goal of medical treatment centers as well as Alcoholics Anonymous — is unrealistic for many heavy drinkers, holds Fingarette.

Disputes over the nature of alcoholism have a long and vitriolic history. But Fingarette's arguments reflect a growing field of research, populated mainly by psychologists, in which alcoholism and other addictions — including those that do not involve drugs, such as compulsive gambling — are viewed more as habits than as diseases. Addictive behavior, in this scheme, typically revolves around an immediate gratification followed by delayed, harmful effects. The habitual behavior nevertheless continues and is often experienced by the addict as uncontrollable.

"Addiction occurs in the environment, not in the liver, genes or synapses," says psychologist Timothy B. Baker of the University of Wisconsin in Madison. Biology may, in some cases, increase a person's risk of developing a dependency, but "an individual chooses to take drugs in the world. The likelihood of a person trying a drug or eventually becoming addicted is influenced by his or her friends, marital happiness, the variety and richness of alternatives to drug use and so on," Baker contends.

Expectations and beliefs about alcohol's power to make one feel better shape the choices leading to alcohol addiction, according to one line of investigation. The most notable of these beliefs, says psychologist G. Alan Marlatt of the University of Washington in Seattle, is that alcohol acts as a magical elixir that enhances social and physical pleasure, increases sexual responsiveness and assertiveness, and reduces tension (SN: 10/3/87, p.218).

The initial physical arousal stimulated by low doses of alcohol pumps up positive expectations, explains Marlatt. But higher alcohol doses dampen arousal, sap energy and result in hangovers that, in turn, lead to a craving for alcohol's stimulating effects. As tolerance to the drug develops, a person requires more and more alcohol to get a short-term "lift" and a vicious cycle of abuse picks up speed.

Despite falling into this addictive trap, Marlatt says, some people drastically cut back their drinking or stop imbibing altogether without the help of formal treatment. In these cases, he maintains, external events often conspire to change an individual's attitude toward alcohol. Examples include an alcohol-related injury, the departure of a spouse, financial and legal problems stemming from drinking or the alcohol-related death of another person.

When treatment is sought out, Marlatt advises, the focus should be on teaching ways to handle stress without drinking and developing realistic expectations about alcohol's effects. Marlatt and his co-workers are now developing an "alcohol skills-training program" for college students, described more fully in *Issues in Alcohol Use and Misuse by Young Adults* (G. Howard, editor, Notre Dame University Press, 1988). Preliminary results indicate many students who consume large amounts of alcohol every week cut down considerably after completing the eight-session course. In fact, says Marlatt, children of alcoholics show some of the best responses to the program and are highly motivated to learn how to drink in moderation.

Psychologists teach the students how to set drinking limits and cope with peer pressure at parties and social events. Realistic expectations about alcohol's mood-enhancing powers are developed, and participants learn alternative methods of stress reduction, such as meditation and aerobic exercise.

The program does not promote drinking, says Marlatt, and students showing signs of hard-core alcohol dependency are referred for treatment that stresses abstinence. "But it's inappropriate to insist that all students abusing alcohol are in the early stages of a progressive disease," he contends. "Our approach acknowledges that drinking occurs regularly and gives students more options and choices for safer drinking."

Asimilar approach to helping adult alcoholics has been developed by psychologists W. Miles Cox of the Veterans Administration Medical Center in Indianapolis and Eric Klinger of the University of Minnesota in Morris. Their model, described in the May JOURNAL OF ABNORMAL PSYCHOLOGY, holds that although a number of biological and social factors influence alcohol abuse, the final decision to drink is motivated by conscious or unconscious expectations that alcohol will brighten one's emotional state and wipe away stress. An alcoholic's expected pleasure or relief from a drinking binge, for example, may outweigh fears that it eventually will lead to getting fired or divorced.

Cox and Klinger's technique aims at providing alternative sources of emotional satisfaction. They have developed a questionnaire to assess an alcoholic's major life goals and concerns. A counselor then helps the alcoholic formulate weekly goals based on his or her responses. Counseling also attempts to reduce the tendency to use alcohol as a crutch when faced with frustration. "Alcoholics often have unrealistically high standards and lack the capacity to forgive themselves for not meeting these standards," Cox says.

The focus on an alcoholic's concerns and motivation is intended to complement other treatments, say the researchers. It is consistent, they note, with the efforts of Alcoholics Anonymous to drive home the negative side of drinking and the benefits of not drinking.

The context in which people consume alcohol is another part of the addictive process under study. Any combination of drinking and mildly pleasant activity, such as television viewing, conversation or card games, appears to provide the best protection against anxiety and stress, report psychologists Claude M. Steele and Robert A. Josephs of the University of Michigan's Institute of Social Research in Ann Arbor. Alcohol's ability to draw attention away from stressful thoughts and onto immediate activity may play a key role in its addictive power, they suggest.

Steele and Joseph tested this theory in their laboratory. They gave enough vodka and tonic to adult subjects to induce mild intoxication. Another group expected to receive vodka and tonic, but was given tonic in glasses rubbed with alcohol to create the odor of a real drink. Everyone was told that in 15 minutes they would have to give a speech on "What I dislike about my body and physical appearance." Researchers asked some from each group to sit quietly before making the speech, while others were asked to rate a series of art slides before speaking.

Those subjects who drank alcohol and rated slides reported significantly less anxiety over the speech than the other participants. Viewing the slides when sober had no anxiety-reducing effects.

According to the researchers, this supports the notion that alcohol's reduction of psychological stress has less to do with its direct pharmacological effects than with its knack for shifting attention with the aid of distractions.

On the other hand, being intoxicated and doing nothing before the speech significantly increased subjects' anxiety, note the investigators in the May JOURNAL OF ABNORMAL PSYCHOLOGY. Without any distraction, alcohol appears to narrow attention to the upcoming situation.

Recent investigations also suggest alcohol users are motivated by alcohol's ability to reduce psychological stress among people who are highly self-conscious and constantly evaluating themselves. Steele and Josephs did not, however, evaluate the "self-awareness" of their subjects.

A different approach to unraveling drinking behavior involves the search for cues that set off an alcoholic's craving or irresistible urge to drink. Just as Pavlov's dogs were conditioned to salivate after hearing a bell that previously had preceded the appearance of food, there are internal and external "bells" that provoke craving in many alcoholics, explains psychiatrist Arnold M. Ludwig of the University of Kentucky Medical Center in Lexington.

These cues are often quite specific, he says. For instance, recovered alcoholic and major league baseball pitcher Bob Welch has reported experiencing a craving to drink during airplane flights, after a game of golf and after pitching.

In a survey of 150 abstinent alcoholics reported in the fall 1986 ALCOHOL HEALTH & RESEARCH WORLD, Ludwig finds nearly all of them can identify one or more "bells" that trigger craving. With the exception of "internal tension," mentioned as a cue by more than half the subjects, there was considerable individual difference in reported drinking "bells." These included going to a dance, feeling lonely, having a barbecue, seeing a drink in an advertisement and driving past former drinking hangouts.

Alcoholics Anonymous, notes Ludwig, teaches that four general conditions — hunger, anger, loneliness and tiredness — make recovered alcoholics more vulnerable to drinking urges, an observation supported by research on craving.

Other evidence, Ludwig says, suggests that the more times uncomfortable withdrawal symptoms — shakiness, agitation, hallucinations or confusion — have been relieved by drinking in the past, the greater the likelihood that familiar drinking cues will elicit craving in alcoholics.

Many alcoholics feel helpless and bewildered when craving strikes, seemingly out of the blue. "But craving is not the elusive, mysterious force many believe it to be," says Ludwig. To successfully recover, he contends, alcoholics must become aware of the emotional and situational cues that trigger drinking urges.

The first drink in the right setting, he adds, often whets the appetite for more. Alcoholics should seek out "safe havens" where drinking is discouraged, he suggests, such as workplaces, Alcoholics Anonymous and outdoor activities.

Whereas Ludwig sees drinking cues as stoking the internal embers of craving, other researchers focus solely on external "reinforcers" that affect an alcoholic's drinking behavior. When important reinforcers outside the realm of drinking, such as a job or marriage, are lost, say psychologists Rudy E. Vuchinich and Jalie A. Tucker of Wayne State University in Detroit, a recovered alcoholic becomes more likely to resume drinking.

"The growing consensus from clinical studies [points to] the important role of environmental variables and changes in life circumstances in influencing the drinking behavior of alcoholics," they write in the May JOURNAL OF ABNORMAL PSYCHOLOGY. But the development of appropriate environmental measures to study drinking is still in the early stages, the investigators add.

While research into the psychology of alcohol addiction is beginning to mature, it remains largely ignored by the biologically oriented advocates of alcoholism-as-disease, says Marlatt. The research and clinical communities are especially polarized over suggestions from addiction studies that some alcoholics — about 15 to 20 percent, according to Marlatt — can safely engage in moderate or social drinking.

The characteristics of alcohol abusers who can handle controlled drinking are not clear, but Marlatt and other researchers see milder alcoholics as prime candidates for this treatment approach.

Given that most current alcoholism treatment is based on the disease model of total abstinence, which has been endorsed by the American Medical Association and the American Psychiatric Association for many years, reconciliation between opposing theoretical camps is not imminent.

"But biological and genetic approaches to alcoholism need to be integrated with psychological and social approaches," Marlatt says. "This really hasn't been done yet."

Roots of Addiction

First drugs, now alcohol. Kitty Dukakis stirs the debate over the causes of chemical dependence.

As she has now discovered, whether it comes in a bottle or is a solid, if you are chemically dependent, you are chemically dependent.

—Gov. MICHAEL DUKAKIS,
announcing that his wife had entered an alcohol treatment program

They are often haunted, self-doubting, escapist. Or they are reckless, sensation seeking and antisocial. Some common thread seems to bind them to an addictive way of life, whether the enslaving agent is alcohol or drugs. Frequently it is both: actor Tony Curtis, a former patient at the Betty Ford Center in Rancho Mirage, Calif., used to augment his heavy drinking with cocaine and prescription drugs—"a little of everything." He was trying, he says, to escape "a feeling that something in your life is undone or loaded with bad luck." Kitty Dukakis had overcome a 26-year attachment to amphetamines before it was revealed she had a drinking problem. Her husband said it was the result of a crushing "postelection letdown" following his failed campaign for the presidency. By a friend's description, she felt "sad and empty." And when the governor announced at a somber state-house press conference last week that Kitty was entering a treatment program at the Edgehill Newport center in Rhode Island, the disclosure stirred fresh interest in the question of who gets hooked and why.

Dr. David Musto, a medical historian, calls addiction the "American disease." Other nations surely suffer. But this country appears to have been rendered especially vulnerable to the drug scourge—on one hand, by a careering, fast-lane affluence that denies itself no thrill that can be bought, and on the other, by a racial and economic divisiveness that has made social alienation a way of life in the ghettos. A generation ago heroin took a dreadful toll on the minority poor. Nowadays, high-priced cocaine and its nickel-and-dime derivative, crack, have left their mark at both ends of the social spectrum. And alcohol may be the oldest abused substance of all.

But while chemical dependence casts an outsize shadow across the land, it is true that the majority of Americans don't become substance abusers—indeed, there are millions who have never touched a drug that wasn't prescribed by a doctor. The inescapable question is, why do some people become addicts and not others? Is there such a thing as an addictive personality—something in the makeup of an individual that sets him up for addiction?

For decades, researchers have sought to sketch a portrait of the typical drug abuser in the hope it could provide early warnings of addiction risk. Such a predictive model would have obvious advantages for treatment. But many researchers now believe it

How Do You Know If You're Hooked?

Adapted from the National Council on Alcoholism's self-test, the following questions are designed to point up symptoms of both drug abuse and alcoholism. "Yes" answers suggest that you may need help.

- Do you sometimes binge on alcohol or drugs?
- Do more people seem to be treating you unfairly without good reason?
- Do you try to avoid family or friends while you are drinking or using drugs?
- Are you secretly irritated when family or friends discuss your drinking or drug use?
- Do you sometimes feel guilty about your drinking or drug use?
- Do you often regret things you have done or said when drunk or high?
- Have you often failed to keep the promises you have made to yourself about controlling or cutting down your drinking or drug use?
- Do you eat very little or irregularly when you are drinking or getting high?
- Do you feel low after indulging, and sometimes miss work or appointments?
- Do you use more and more to get drunk or high?

would be misleading to list the "traits" of the addict. "To me," says John Grabowski, a researcher at the University of Texas Health Science Center in Houston, "the notion of an addictive personality is conceptually just not very useful. It presumes all sorts of things about prediction I don't think we are capable of doing."

A more accurate profile, if it could be drawn, would embrace a compendium of characteristics, internal and external, that go into the making of an addict. "Anyone with a healthy, functioning nervous system is vulnerable," says Jack Henningfield of the National Institute on Drug Abuse. "What we see is an interaction of personality, environment, biology and social acceptability. We don't want to be fooled by looking at only one factor."

Researchers are still trying to sort out the welter of influences that come to bear on addiction. They are looking, with growing sophistication, at such clues as the specific needs that different substances seem to satisfy. They are examining more closely than ever the chemical pathways by which drugs work their way into the so-called pleasure centers of the brain. Some of the more recent findings of laboratory research tend to confirm long-suspected genetic links in alcoholism. In several studies, children of alcoholic parents were found to be four times more at risk of becoming alcoholics themselves, even when they were raised by nonalcoholic adoptive parents—a case of nature undermining nurture.

Pitfall persists: Personality links remain less understood. One hazard for scientists seeking definitive factors is that they tend to look for what they *expect* to find. In the 1950s psychiatrists looked at a set of attributes called "preaddictive personality disorder." It included tendencies toward lying and manipulation that, on closer inspection, turned out to be results, rather than causes, of addiction. The pitfall persists in present-day research. Asked what turned them to drugs, addicts are apt to describe unhappy childhoods, embattled family lives, bad marriages. Yet those general conditions do not even predict alcoholism, one of the most prevalent addictions (an estimated 10.5 million victims in the United States). Dr. George Vaillant, director of a developmental study of 600 men, says he has found that psychological instability does not cause alcoholism. The reverse is true: "Alcoholism causes the stress. It puts people out of control of their lives. It makes everything harder."

Not many years ago, addiction was regarded as a social problem, belonging to the realm of immoral or criminal behavior. The present view that it is a lifelong chronic disease emerged only in the 1960s. This so-called medical model now covers a broad spectrum of dependency-forming substances, from caffeine and nicotine, the two most widely available and abused, to alcohol, opiates, amphetamines and barbiturates. By some looser definitions, gambling, sex, shopping, eating and exercise are included among addictive behaviors, if they reach the point of being self-destructive. Some scientists object to the inclusions. Says Dr. Jack Mendelson, a Harvard Medical School professor of psychiatry: "Are we ski addicts if we feel the need to ski? There are some people who can't refrain from behaviors that are not in their own interest. But to label those in the same way as outside things that interact with our brain is really extending the metaphor."

Meanwhile confusion has increased over the definition of addiction. The diagnostic manual of the American Psychiatric Association avoids the term altogether, choosing "dependency" and "abuse" instead. "The addictions field is going through an identity crisis because of this idea of defining," says G. Alan Marlatt, director of the Addictive Behaviors Research Center at the University of Washington. Addictions were once largely defined by the physical response produced by opiates and barbiturates: dependence, tolerance and withdrawal, all easily observed reactions. Heroin, for one, clearly produced each of those.

As researchers began studying other substances, they found the old classifications too limiting. Cocaine, for instance, does not produce the clear physical manifestations of heroin addiction. Only a few years ago, in fact, cocaine was considered a "recreational" drug. Now crack is commonly believed to be the most addictive drug available. What changed was the scientific understanding of cocaine's acute effect on the brain, which makes breaking an addiction to it tremendously difficult. And it was not until last year that Surgeon General C. Everett Koop put forth what he called "overwhelming" evidence that tobacco is "addicting in the same sense as are drugs such as heroin and cocaine."

Mask pain: As the definition of addiction has changed, so has the understanding of who is likely to become an addict. Dr. Robert B. Millman, director of the alcohol-and-drug-abuse service at New York Hospital-Cornell Medical Center, sees two basic models for addiction. The first attributes the compulsive behavior to psychological difficulties, such as a need to mask pain. The second blames it all on chemical dependency. Addicts, according to this chemical model, are no different from the rest of the population until they drink or take drugs. Then they develop a dependency on the substance, which in turn can cause changes in their personality.

To ask which model is right is to ask the wrong question, says Millman. "The truth is in how to fit them together." A percentage of addicts do turn to drugs for psychological reasons, he says, and a percentage become physically "hooked" when they happen on a drug. No one is sure what the percentages are. Millman makes a middle-ground guess that about 40 percent of addicts have underlying psychiatric disorders that led them to drug abuse. Others estimate as many as 70 percent have such problems as major depression and panic disorders, sometimes the result of drug abuse, sometimes the cause.

Some consensus does exist on personality traits in dependent drug users, but the traits mainly seem to describe what the APA diagnostic manual identifies as the "anti-social" syndrome. A 1983 report by the National Research Council, called "Commonalities in Substance Abuse and Habitual Behavior," lists, among others, nonconformity, a sense of social alienation and a general tolerance for deviance; impulsivity and a need for instant gratification. Another predisposing factor is stress. With the deadly pressures of the Vietnam War and the easy access to drugs, for instance, heroin use was common among GI's. But follow-up studies showed that even though 88 percent of addicted Vietnam veterans used heroin occasionally after their return, 90 percent of them avoided becoming readdicted. For most of them the stress had vanished, and so had the problem.

Sheer availability of drugs and the extent of their reinforcing power are two key factors unrelated to personality. The presence of crack on every street corner may override any other factors. A few years ago, for example, a cocaine craze swept through the Yuppie purlieus of Wall Street, and it took a series of mass police roundups to dampen the fad. Dr. Frank Gawin, a cocaine researcher at Yale University's substance-abuse treatment center, argues that in addition to the drug's availability, a balance exists between its "addictive power" and a "predisposition" to addiction. If the drug is sufficiently powerful, other factors become irrelevant. All animals exposed to unlimited amounts of cocaine in laboratory tests, for example, become addicted. "It is a powerful enough addictive force that personality doesn't matter," Gawin says.

One of the more provocative notions about drug use is that it is a subtle form of self-medication, used to cope with emotional conflicts and shortcomings. A leading proponent of the theory is Dr. Edward Khantzian, the principal psychiatrist for substance abuse at Cambridge Hospital in Massachusetts. Over the years Khantzian has begun to suspect that the most frequently cited reasons, pleasure seeking and self-destruction, are not driving forces in drug use. But trying to alleviate problems and emotional pain are. Listening to addicts, he was impressed by the violence and aggression in their background and their descriptions of how mellow and calm—"normal for

'She Clearly Recognizes She Has a Sickness'

During last year's presidential race, Kitty Dukakis often stopped at addiction-treatment centers to talk about her 26-year amphetamine habit (which she kicked in 1982) and to repeat a warning. "You are never recovered," she would say. "You are always recovering." That message took on a special poignancy last week when her husband, Massachusetts Gov. Michael Dukakis, announced at a press conference that she had entered a treatment center for alcohol abuse. Says her former campaign press secretary, Paul Costello: "Obviously she found herself on a slippery slope."

The stresses of the campaign trail are well documented. But in Kitty Dukakis's case, it was the return to a more private life that proved too great a strain. Michael Dukakis reported that his wife's alcohol problems began after he lost the November presidential election; the cause, he said, was "a combination of physical exhaustion, the stress of the campaign effort and the postelection letdown." Although her husband asked family members not to talk to reporters and most of her friends won't be quoted by name, people close to her say that she has been extremely depressed recently. She was at "loose ends," one friend observed. "It's no longer 18-hour days with people totally taking care of you," says Michael Goldman, a Dukakis adviser. "Suddenly you're just a governor's wife—and you're alone."

Michael Dukakis was back in his Beacon Hill office the morning after the election, tackling a severe budget crisis that has occupied him almost full time ever since. The couple didn't get away for a vacation until December, and then could manage only a week. "He went to bed and got up and got on with his life," says Dukakis biographer Richard Gaines. "Kitty was left to do the mourning. She has always had to bear the emotional burden for both of them."

Career irony: Her family had hoped that Kitty would be encouraged by the many opportunities that stemmed from her strong campaign performance. Simon and Schuster reportedly had offered her $175,000 to write a book, and the lecture circuit was promising $10,000 to $15,000 a speech. But Leonard Zakim, a close family friend, says that Kitty may have found it difficult to enjoy her success because it was coupled with her husband's failure. "The irony of her own career taking off," Zakim says, "while her husband had been so thoroughly rejected, wasn't lost on her."

People close to Kitty Dukakis insist that she had no problems with alcohol during the campaign. They say it would have been impossible for her to maintain a rigorous schedule while concealing even the slightest drinking problem. She was, they say, a social drinker, who usually limited herself to a single vodka on the rocks at dinner or at night on the campaign plane.

Michael Dukakis says that after the election, Kitty did not drink constantly, but that "on a limited number of occasions while at home, she has used alcohol in excessive quantities." A longtime smoker who has tried unsuccessfully to stop several times, she apparently was able to control her drinking to some degree. One acquaintance said he and his wife had dinner with the Dukakises a couple of weeks ago and Kitty didn't even take a drink, though everyone else did. Yet the times when Kitty did drink could be characterized as "binges" that wiped her out for a couple of days. Another friend says that Kitty had been increasingly withdrawn lately, sometimes canceling personal engagements; or she'd be "lying down" and unavailable for phone calls—which was not like her.

Another 'episode': Last month Kitty and her younger daughter, Kara, 20, spent a week at Canyon Ranch in Tucson, Ariz., a health-and-fitness resort that does not allow liquor. Kitty reportedly did not drink for the entire week. But after she came home she had another "episode" and decided to seek treatment. She insisted on waiting until after the Feb. 3 birth of her first grandchild, Alexandra, the daughter of her son John and his wife, Lisa. Two days later she entered the 160-bed Edgehill Newport center in Newport, R.I. "She knew she had a problem and told me, 'I've got to catch this early'," her husband said. "Obviously, she's not happy about this, but she clearly recognizes she has a sickness—and it is a sickness—and she had to deal with it."

The facility Kitty chose, on the grounds of a former estate overlooking Narragansett Bay, is the largest in New England. Although she kicked her amphetamine habit at the Hazelden Foundation in Minnesota, she apparently wanted to be closer to home this time. Edgehill Newport is expensive—about $8,600 for the 28-day program—but it is not luxurious. Treatment is rigorous. For example, patients are assigned "therapeutic tasks." One former patient recalls that because he was labeled a "people pleaser," he was assigned the unpleasant task of ripping up people's beds and asking them to make them up again properly.

After she first disclosed her drug addiction in 1987, Kitty Dukakis frequently discussed the problems of recovering from substance abuse. She talked about how she had first started taking diet pills when she was 19, and how she had hidden her habit from her husband and her family. Part of the recovery process, she said, was helping others. Given her reputation for openness, it's likely that eventually she will talk about her difficulties with alcohol as well. Her brother-in-law, Al Peters, a recovering alcoholic himself who works as a substance-abuse counselor, says that Kitty learned some important lessons from her long battle with amphetamines. She knew she had to get help before things got worse. "Kitty's going to be all right," says Peters. "I view her as a very courageous lady."

BARBARA KANTROWITZ *and* MARK STARR *in Boston*

the first time"—they felt following narcotics use. After all, he observes, "What are narcotics but painkillers?"

Preferred drug: From his study of other patients, Khantzian decided their choice of drugs was far from random. Opiate users tended to be aggressive and violent; the opiates muted intense emotions. Alcohol is "disinhibiting"; it seemed the preferred drug of people who had problems showing their feelings.

Stimulants like amphetamines and cocaine fill a very different need, says Khantzian. Their main use is for energizing purposes, and they appeal to people who are feeling either high or low. For those feeling low and depressed, the drugs stoke energy and enthusiasm. Those on the high side are usually already overactive, and cocaine "makes it easier for them to be the way they like to be." (Cocaine, Khantzian believes, is especially insidious because of the wide net it casts, snaring both ends of the social spectrum.) The people who self-medicate, typically, tend to be out of touch with themselves, explains Khantzian. "I believe if you are more or less in touch with your feelings, if you like yourself, if you have varied and reasonable relationships, you are not apt to find the drugs so seductive . . . A lot of people who are reasonably OK just don't find drugs that fantastic."

Beyond seductiveness—the promise of epiphany or nirvana—scientists are exploring what it is about drugs that makes them as entrapping as quicksand. The search for answers now centers on the so-called pleasure centers in the middle reaches of the brain. Normally, when we get a pleasurable stimulus, a neurotransmitter (or chemical messenger) called dopamine is released into the space between two nerves, then taken up again by the transmitting nerve. Drugs like cocaine act to block the uptake system, and the dopamine keeps stimulating the receiver nerve. Eventually the chemical begins to run low, and at the same time, the receiving nerve

nection, they still have much to learn about the action of other drugs. Dopamine is believed to be a central agent in all the pleasure-giving substances, but the basic mechanisms of addiction and withdrawal remain largely mysterious. "What we do know," says Harvard's Mendelson, "is that there are very diverse substances: the alcohol molecule is very different from the cocaine molecule and the morphine molecule. Some

Inherited trait: Other researchers, like Dr. Marc A. Schuckit, are trying to determine what children of alcoholics actually inherit that puts them at greater risk than other children. Schuckit is certain there is no such thing as an alcoholic gene. But evidence from a major study he and his colleagues began in 1978 points to the possibility that one crucial inherited trait is decreased reaction to drinking. "The sons of alcoholics show less response in the three- to five-drink range," Schuckit notes. "It's as if their body is giving them less indication that they've consumed a lot."

The solution to the drug scourge may ultimately come from researchers like Schuckit zeroing in on the addiction process at the molecular level. It can come none too soon. The problem still appears to be growing. The heroin plague of the '60s has been supplanted by an equally pernicious spread of cocaine and the ubiquitous crack. Certainly, one commonality of the abused drugs is that they alter thinking and feeling. "The perception is they are pleasurable, that people feel better and their mood improves," says Dr. Donald Jasinski, director of the Center for Chemical Dependency at Baltimore's Francis Scott Key Medical Center. As long as that perception remains, there seems little hope of heading off new generations of abusers. A 1986 study of 7,000 Alcoholics Anonymous members in the United States and Canada, for example, showed that 3 percent were under 20 and 18 percent were 21 to 30. "Our trend line shows that the average age gets younger with each survey," says an AA spokesman. And at Phoenix House in New York City, the largest private multiservice drug treatment program in the United States, with six centers in New York and four in California, assistant director of public information Arlene Spiller notes that because of crack, "people are coming in much faster than ever before. It takes them less time to fall apart on crack than on other drugs." She adds that crack is also catching more women—about 30 percent of the Phoenix caseload—in its tentacles. "They're losing control of their bodies and children because of crack."

Spiritual solace: For the present, help has to come after the fact of addiction. AA, established in 1935 by an alcoholic stockbroker and a surgeon, has been one of the bulwarks in the treatment field, and it has spawned such spinoffs as Al-Anon, for families of alcoholics, NA (Narcotics Anonymous) and CA (Cocaine Anonymous). Many treatment programs across the country are modeled on AA's by-now-famous 12-step method of spiritual solace and compassionate support in group meetings. The 1986 AA survey found a sobriety rate of 29 percent over five years, 38 percent for one to five years—about as impressive as outcome statistics get in addiction treatment. At Phoenix House, only 20 percent of those who enter

A Consumer's Guide to Highs and Lows

Turn on any radio or television talk show and listen to America confess its addiction to gambling, jogging, shopping, chocolate. But as disruptive as these habits may be, they are in a separate category from true physical addictions.

Alcohol

How it works: Absorbed into the bloodstream, mostly through the small intestine; acts as a depressant on the central nervous system
How it feels: Initial "high," leading to relaxation, loss of inhibitions
How it hurts: Increased depression; long-term abuse linked with nutrition-related diseases; can lead to brain disorders, cirrhosis, birth defects
How to get help: National Council on Alcoholism, 1-800-622-2255.

Cocaine

How it works: Blocks dopamine uptake in brain's neurotransmitters, stimulating "pleasure nerves"
How it feels: Rush of euphoria, energy, confidence, talkativeness, followed by a "low"; suppresses pain and appetite
How it hurts: Increases heartbeat, respiration, depression, paranoia; can induce heart attack, stroke, psychosis, coma
How to get help: Psychiatric Institutes of America, 1-800-COCAINE

Nicotine

How it works: Alters availability of chemicals involved in feelings of reward and well-being; stimulates cardiovascular system
How it feels: Simultaneously arouses and relaxes; induces sense of well-being, calm
How it hurts: Some say not addictive; others say smokers feel increased craving for cigarettes, resulting in emphysema, lung cancer, heart disease
How to get help: American Cancer Society, 1-800-227-2345.

begins to be desensitized to the dopamine. As a result, scientists conclude, the sending nerve has to transmit a heavier dose to produce the same amount of pleasure. This, apparently, is the process that creates increased tolerance in drug users, the critical link in the chain of addiction.

While researchers now understand a great deal about the cocaine-dopamine con-

act as stimulants, some as depressants and some both ways depending on how much is taken. Right now, there's an intense search for commonalities." Some investigators are focusing on substances called G proteins that appear to affect the way nerve cells receive messages. "It is probably at that level that you're going to find common ground," Mendelson says.

stay through the drug-free, residential course of 18 months to two years, although 80 percent of the "graduates" apparently remain drug-free for five years.

One hopeful development is that treatment programs are beginning to be more individually tailored to address emotional problems that may have precipitated drug use. A person who drinks to feel more at ease in group situations, for instance, might benefit from treatment that helped him with social skills. "The addiction field has become less myopic," says Michael Miller, vice president of the U.S. Journal of Drug and Alcohol Dependence. "They are regularly incorporating therapeutic approaches from the mental-health field, marriage and family therapy and behavioral techniques. It's slowly shifting away from a pathology-based model to a healthy functioning model."

But overall, the treatment picture is catch as catch can. For the more affluent there are some free-standing clinics, which may not be covered by medical insurance because they are not in hospital settings. This puts these clinics beyond the reach of the average addict. For the less well-to-do, there are programs like Phoenix House.

For the poor, who make up the largest percentage of the addict population, there are only in-hospital detoxification units and outpatient clinics. In the vital area of after-care, little is available or affordable.

Little tolerance: Health-insurance coverage of addiction treatment can be erratic. Many hospital clinic programs are under pressure to reduce their typical inpatient stay of 28 days and look at more outpatient programs, which are usually less fully covered. According to Mary Lee Zawadski of the Center for Problem Resolution, a treatment center at Sun Coast Hospital in Largo, Fla., some insurers will pay for only five days of treatment. Most show little tolerance for relapses, viewing them as a failure of treatment. "They want it to be like a gallbladder operation—take it out and don't pay for it again," says Zawadski.

In fact, most doctors and therapists agree, recovery from addiction is a lifelong process. AA, operating on the theory that no one is ever completely cured, encourages members to continue attending its meetings for the rest of their lives. Some psychiatrists feel there is more hope of recovery in ongoing support systems than in

substitution of chemicals—methadone for heroin, for example. Actor Tony Curtis has his own fond vision of continuing support: "I see instead of having bars every few blocks, we should have little therapy centers where you can pull your car over and have a chance to talk to somebody."

That idea has a certain poignancy—a view of a friendly, small-town universe, instead of the drug-ridden combat arena millions of Americans inhabit. "Maybe people in these [treatment] groups are in fact re-creating a more natural and normal environment for themselves, literally providing something missing from modern life," muses Dr. Randolph Nesse, a University of Michigan psychiatrist. "It's happening just at the point in society when both the extended family and nuclear family are breaking down." It is an interesting piece of speculation, but small comfort to think that the way to return to a humane, supportive environment is first to become completely estranged from it.

DAVID GELMAN *with* LISA DREW *in New York,*
MARY HAGER *and* MARK MILLER *in Washington,*
DAVID L. GONZALEZ *in Miami and*
JEANNE GORDON *in Los Angeles*

SECOND THOUGHTS ABOUT A GENE FOR ALCOHOLISM

*Claims of a genetic basis for alcoholism, a leading theorist argues,
are not scientifically supportable and ignore the crucial link between personal
values and self-destructive or antisocial behavior*

STANTON PEELE

*Stanton Peele is a psychologist and health-care researcher in
Morris Plains, New Jersey. He is a co-author of* Love and
Addiction *(1975) and the author of* Diseasing of America:
Addiction Treatment Out of Control *(1989).*

Major news stories about discoveries of the genetic sources of emotional and behavioral problems surface every year or so. Since 1987 such reports have appeared on the front page of *The New York Times* in connection with manic-depressive disorder, schizophrenia, and alcoholism. Last year, however, the *Times* published a story titled "Scientists Now Doubt They Found Faulty Gene Linked to Mental Illness." This story received less attention than the announcements of positive findings, for it appeared not on the front page of the newspaper but buried deep inside. The article revealed that both new data and further analysis of the original data "cast serious doubt" on the earlier finding that a defective gene was, in fact, associated with manic-depressive disorder. The article furthermore noted that "the new findings underscore the difficulty of assigning specific causes to such a complex and variable illness," and that problems also plague efforts to identify precisely any sort of genetic role in schizophrenia. One of the authors of the original study said, "We are sort of back to square one."

The Blum-Noble "Alcoholism Gene"

THE STUDY THAT THE *TIMES* REPORTED LINKing alcoholism to a specific gene was published in the *Journal of the American Medical Association* on April 18 of this year, as the journal's lead article. It was accompanied by press releases, a highly publicized news conference in Los Angeles, and video interviews with the study's authors, which the AMA transmitted by satellite in its weekly television news release. The study's chief authors were Kenneth Blum, a pharmacologist at the University of Texas Health Science Center, in San Antonio, and Ernest Noble, a psychiatrist and biochemist at the UCLA Alcohol Research Center and a former director of the National Institute of Alcohol Abuse and Alcoholism.

Unlike the manic-depressive-disorder and schizophrenia studies, which were conducted within individual families or communities, the alcoholism study involved seventy unrelated cadavers, thirty-five of which had been alcoholics and thirty-five of which were controls. According to the researchers, the alcoholic cases were of an extremely "virulent" type—many of the thirty-five people had died of cirrhosis. Genetic material from all seventy brains was analyzed. A genetic marker was found in 69 percent of the alcoholics in the study but in only 20 percent of the nonalcoholics.

Blum and Noble concluded that the A1 "allele," or variant, of the dopamine D2 receptor gene was associated with alcoholism. Dopamine is one of a number of neurotransmitters, or chemicals produced in the body that convey information throughout the nervous system. Neurotransmitters communicate by attaching to receptors on nerve cells which are tailored specifically to them. One important question not answered by the gene discovery is exactly what dopamine receptors, the physiological mechanisms affected by the gene, have to do with alcoholism. Another question is how this discovery fits in with what has previously been established about the heritability of alcoholism.

Theories of the Heritability of Alcoholism

THE DOPAMINE RECEPTOR GENE IS NOT CLEARLY implicated in the major existing genetic theories of human alcoholism. According to these theories, a certain personality type predisposes a minority of male problem drinkers to both crime and alcoholism; an inherited insensitivity to alcohol allows alcoholics to drink more while being less aware of the effects of the alcohol they are consuming; alcoholics are not able to metabolize alcohol normally; and alcoholics have inherited neurological and intellectual dysfunctions. Not only are the originators of some of these theories the sole researchers to have found evidence to support them, but also several of the theories and findings directly contradict the premises or reasoning of others.

The inherited-personality theory has been promoted by a research group at the School of Medicine at Washington University, in St. Louis, under the direction of Robert Cloninger, a psychiatrist. This may be the most popular current notion about how alcoholism is inherited. However, it must face the formidable difficulties involved in associating entire personality syndromes, such as criminality, with particular genes.

The idea that alcoholics inherit an insensitivity to alcohol has been presented by Mark Schuckit, a psychiatrist at the University of California at San Diego Medical School. Another research team (led by Barbara Lex, of Harvard Medical School) has supported Schuckit's hypothesis in a study comparing small numbers of women from alcoholic and nonalcoholic families. But James Wilson and Craig Nagoshi, of the University of Colorado, in a much larger study, found the lessened sensitivity to alcohol to hold for some age-and-sex groups among offspring of alcoholics but not for others.

Schuckit also at one time presented evidence that alcoholism results from an inherited flaw in the way alcoholics metabolize alcohol. According to this theory, alcoholics' bodies do not break down alcohol properly and, as a result, build up abnormal levels of acetaldehyde (one of the products of alcohol's oxidization) when they drink.

The acetaldehyde hypothesis got strong play in the widely read book *Under the Influence*, by James Milam and Katherine Ketcham, which was published in 1981. Milam and Ketcham forcefully argued that acetaldehyde is a primary biological and genetic basis for alcoholism, which they claimed is *completely* biologically determined. However, in recent years researchers have lost enthusiasm for this model, which has been contradicted by subsequent research. For example, several research teams investigating the offspring of alcoholics were unable reliably to identify abnormal acetaldehyde buildups after their subjects consumed alcohol. Schuckit himself no longer focuses on acetaldehyde as the most likely mechanism for the heritability of alcoholism.

According to another alcohol-metabolism model, the oxidized alcohol product, or aldehyde, interacts with neurotransmitters to create tetrahydroisoquinolines, or TIQs, which are thought to create the intense craving for alcohol that alcoholics demonstrate. However, the idea that alcoholics produce abnormal amounts of TIQs has never been demonstrated satisfactorily, and several prominent investigators have abandoned this path of research. Nonetheless, the TIQ model is often taught to alcoholics at treatment centers in the United States. When several TV news shows interviewed alcoholics (attractive middle-class women who would not have been diagnosed as advanced alcoholics, as the cases that Blum and Noble examined had been) in connection with the *JAMA* gene study, the women claimed they had inherited an exaggerated reaction to alcohol that made them drink more. They were likely referring to TIQs, about which they were probably lectured in treatment.

Another set of theories about the heritability of alcoholism concerns abnormal brain waves and other cognitive or neurological impairments that children of alcoholics are said to inherit. The most prominent brain-wave researcher, Henri Begleiter, a psychiatrist at the Downstate Medical Center, in Brooklyn, has found such abnormalities in alcoholics' sons who have never drunk alcohol. However, other factors—such as diet or physical abuse—may explain why many children of alcoholics show abnormal brain activity. Moreover, different research teams have found different abnormalities in the brain-wave patterns of different groups of alcoholics and children of alcoholics. Finally, no link has been shown between the abnormal brain waves and the development of alcoholism, because the children with the suspect brain waves have not been followed up to an age where their rate of alcoholism can be compared with that of children of alcoholics without these specific abnormalities.

Children of alcoholics have also been studied with tests that measure perception, coordination, and intellectual abilities, and are often found deficient in these areas. But Schuckit finds the results of this research inconsistent. Moreover, one of his own studies, using subjects who on average had completed more than three years of college, did not find such impairment, which may be owing to social differences between these subjects and, for example, children of alcoholics identified through the juvenile justice system.

Plainly, the various heritability theories about alcoholism tend in quite different directions. Schuckit has strongly criticized the idea of an inherited "antisocial" personality disposition to alcoholism, which he has not found in a group of college students and staff who are sons of alcoholics. The insensitivity model seems to be the opposite of the TIQ model: according to the former, those likely to become alcoholics drink more and respond less, whereas according to the latter, those predisposed to alcoholism respond more. According to the insensitivity model, those predisposed to alcoholism may drink heavily for extended periods because they cannot detect the physical effects of the alcohol they consume, and consequently become dependent on alcohol. Most of the modern theories about the heritability of alcoholism recognize that no matter what their genetic makeup, people must drink a lot for a long time to become alcoholics. In this sense genetic research in alcoholism actually contradicts stories commonly told at Alcoholics Anonymous meetings and popular treatment myths about people who become alcoholic with their first drink.

How Does the Blum-Noble Gene Fit In?

THE BLUM-NOBLE TEAM PROBED NINE DIFFERent genes, all hypothetically linked to alcoholism, in the DNA of the brains they examined. They found that only the A1 allele of the dopamine D2 receptor gene correlated significantly with the diagnosis of alcoholism in their subjects. Where does this discovery leave other theories of the heritability of alcoholism?

The absence of a statistically significant relationship between any of the eight other genes and the occurrence of alcoholism actually undercuts most of the other theories about the way alcoholism is inherited. Thus this discovery yields more disconfirmation than support for researchers in the field.

On the other hand, if a range of inherited mechanisms leads to alcoholism, how can the dopamine receptor gene alone account for more than two thirds of a group of cases of alcoholism? Commenting in the same issue of *JAMA* in which the alcoholism-gene study appeared, Enoch Gordis, who is the director of the National Institute on Alcohol Abuse and Alcoholism, and three colleagues wrote that the association between the gene and alcoholism was "surprisingly strong" in view of the "presumed heterogeneity of alcoholism and its likely polygenic causes."

Gordis, who has long championed genetic views of alcoholism, noted problems with the Blum-Noble research that make it "possible that the differences between the groups were caused by characteristics of the groups that were unrelated to alcoholism. This type of comparison, although provocative, cannot substitute for . . . complex family studies." The standard practice in gene-mapping research is to identify genes in a range of living related persons. This "family-tree" approach can then trace whether or not various relatives with a specific genetic marker develop a given disease. To disprove a specific genetic link is easier than to prove one: a finding that relatives who do not share the genetic marker in question become alcoholic as frequently as relatives who do share it would be strong evidence against that genetic link.

All sophisticated observers who have commented on the *JAMA* study have cautioned that additional research must be designed to examine the nature of the relationship between the dopamine D2 receptor gene and alcoholism. Blum and Noble are now mapping this gene in a study of living relatives, and their results are awaited eagerly.

Another form of replication would be to compare the incidence of the Blum-Noble marker in a random sample of patients in alcoholism clinics with its incidence in a general population. Would such investigations affirm the results of the original research? Many observers interviewed about the Blum-Noble finding seemed skeptical. Donald Goodwin, the psychiatrist whose research first pointed to the heritability of alcoholism, says that "the history of this kind of work so far has been a failure to replicate."

How Might a Gene Cause Alcoholism?

FOR A THEORY TO BE ACCEPTED SCIENTIFICALLY, not only must the finding or findings that support it be replicated in rigorously designed research, but also the hypothesized connection between a mechanism and an effect must be plausible and consistent with everything else we know. How, exactly, does the dopamine receptor gene influence the alcoholic's biochemistry and behavior? This connection is not at all obvious, since dopamine receptors are not directly affected by alcohol. Indeed, it is not even known how the Blum-Noble marker affects the dopamine receptors. The alcoholism-associated allele might increase or reduce the number of dopamine receptor sites in brain cells, or affect how well dopamine binds at these sites. One theory is that if the allele reduces the number of receptor sites or minimizes binding at them, then the person's brain might be deficient in dopamine activity. Drinking might compensate for this deficiency by increasing the drinker's levels of dopamine.

But does this complex series of links account for the alcoholic's motivation to drink? Some researchers propose that dopamine is related to pleasure-seeking activity. This is a very long way, however, from explaining how people with the A1 allele become alcoholic. Alcoholics often receive negative feedback about their drinking from other people, from their own internal standards, and from physical problems they encounter. Why don't these experiences overcome the presumed pleasurable nature of the dopamine activity and cause the person to curtail drinking? Put in another way, the question is whether a complex behavior can be said to be motivated solely by the pleasure (or comfort or relief) it produces. For example, orgasms are intensely pleasurable and most people can produce them at will, yet relatively few people become compulsive fornicators or masturbators, at least in the long run.

Moreover, dopamine stimulation is simply not so direct or exclusive an effect of drinking that it seems likely to be the root cause of compulsive drinking. Many human activities other than drinking stimulate dopamine release. Some may argue that alcoholics are part of a larger group of people who seek such stimulation, and who therefore experience a higher level of dopamine activity in their brain cells. But why do only some people seek this effect from alcohol?

In an interview about the *JAMA* study Gordis speculated that the gene marker "may not be specific for alcoholism but it might have a more general influence on appetite, personality, and behavior." Noble has concurred: "The good Lord did not make an alcoholic gene, but one that seems to be involved in pleasure-seeking behaviors." These statements seem skeptical about the existence of a link between the gene and alcoholism. The idea that people with the A1 allele may be predisposed to pleasurable stimulation, of which alcoholism may be one example, also falls short of supporting claims that alcoholics have an innate response to alcohol that dooms them to alcoholism once they begin drinking.

Even if Blum and Noble's finding holds up, most people with the A1 allele will not become alcoholics. According to the study, about 25 percent of the population have this form of the gene. Estimates of the proportion of alcoholics in the U.S. population range up to 10 percent. However, the "virulent" type of alcoholism that Blum and Noble talk about probably occurs in less than five percent of the population. Thus if every full-blown alcoholic had this allele, then only a fifth of the 25 percent that have it would be severely alcoholic. Since only 69 percent of the alcoholics in the Blum-Noble study actually had the allele, even fewer than a fifth of those with the marker will conform to the diagnosis of alcoholism used in the study.

How Can This Discovery Be Used?

BLUM AND NOBLE HAVE ANNOUNCED THAT THE identification of a gene that places people at risk for alcoholism should open new treatment and prevention options. The most likely step, given the current cultural climate, would be to tell those with the genetic marker that since they have an elevated risk of alcoholism, they should not drink. But this idea has its problems. In the first place, since less than a fifth of the people with the gene will actually become alcoholics, the warning is unnecessary for most of those with the marker and could make their lives needlessly difficult.

Moreover, unforeseen, and lamentable, consequences might occur. We frequently tell young people not to drink, and they frequently don't listen. But if a person has been told that drinking will lead to alcoholism, the prophecy may ultimately prove to be self-fulfilling. According to Peter Nathan, who was until last year the di-

rector of the Rutgers Center of Alcohol Studies, "It has become increasingly clear that, in many instances, what alcoholics *think* the effects of alcohol are on their behavior influences that behavior as much [as] or more than the pharmacologic effects of the drug." For example, alcoholics have been shown to drink excessively and even behave drunkenly when they are told they are drinking an alcoholic beverage even though the drink does not actually contain alcohol.

In other words, indoctrinating young people with the view that they are likely to become alcoholics *may take them there more quickly than any inherited reaction to alcohol would have.* In fact a majority of children of alcoholics do not become alcoholic themselves, for whatever reason. No epidemiologic study has ever found that as many as half of such children develop a drinking problem of their own, and most research places the figure at 25 percent or less. That many children don't inherit their parents' alcoholism is indicated by the rapid growth of the "adult children of alcoholics" movement, whose typical member is a woman who has never had a drinking problem. Moreover, adolescents and young adults who have drinking problems often overcome them without abstaining, even if they have an alcoholic parent.

Blum and Noble have also suggested that their genetic finding will lead to medical therapies for alcoholism. That is, if the source of alcoholism is biochemical, then a drug therapy might be designed to eliminate the alcoholic's craving for alcohol. If a vitamin stimulated dopamine activity, for example, or if a drug blocked the binding of dopamine to receptors, then alcoholics could be freed from their biological motivation for excessive drinking and might drink moderately.

Yet it is unlikely that treatment centers and AA would recant their commitment to total abstinence for alcoholics. Nonetheless, it is in these quarters that we can expect the most enthusiastic reception for the Blum-Noble research, because genetic causation of alcoholism is seen to support their fundamental assumption that alcoholism is an involuntary disease.

What Now?

THE NEW YORK TIMES AND OTHER MEDIA claimed that the *JAMA* study appeared to offer "strong new evidence" for the heritability of alcoholism (this was, of course, the point of the AMA press release), an issue that has "been widely debated for decades." Actually, enthusiasm for the idea that alcoholism is inherited has prevailed in the United States for some time. AA and most proponents of the disease theory (including most of the people who manage America's 4,600 private alcohol-treatment programs) have for a long time insisted that alcoholism is an inherited disease. For about the past decade the number of researchers investigating the topic has been growing, along with the assumption that alcoholism is at least in part genetically caused. For example, the National Institute on Alcohol Abuse and Alcoholism published a pamphlet in 1985 titled "Alcoholism: An Inherited Disease."

Even many psychologists now assert that the problem drinking of at least some alcoholics has a significant genetic component. Moreover, the public has accepted the idea that alcoholism is inherited. A 1987 Gallup poll found that nearly 90 percent of Americans believe alcoholism is a disease, and more than 60 percent think it may be inherited. Both figures represent a steep rise from earlier ones; even five years previously a solid majority of respondents to the second question had said they didn't believe that alcoholism is inherited. Thus the *JAMA* report did little more than affirm what most Americans—including alcoholics, treatment personnel, and researchers—already believe.

Although the heritability of alcoholism is often presented as a modern discovery, alcoholism (along with sexual promiscuity, intelligence, criminality, and insanity) was widely believed to be an inherited trait in the nineteenth century. That view receded in this century; in 1938 Karl Menninger could state, "The older psychiatrists . . . considered alcoholism to be an hereditary trait. Of course, scarcely any scientist believes so today, although it's still a popular theory. Alcoholism cannot possibly be an hereditary trait. . . ." Today, obviously, the tide has shifted again. As Robin Murray, a British psychiatrist, notes, "Students of alcoholism must continually beware lest they fall victim to the extravagant swings of intellectual fashion that bedevil the field, and nowhere is such vigilance more necessary than in considering the possible etiological role of heredity." Murray's views are particularly interesting because he is Britain's leading investigator of the heritability of alcoholism. Murray and his research team have found that the rates of coincidence of alcoholism are similar for identical and fraternal twins, a result that substantially undermines genetic hypotheses—and one that is almost never cited by American researchers.

Will views on this question swing back? Oddly, the attention attracted by the *JAMA* study may encourage them to, as bold genetic claims draw sophisticated clinical geneticists into the field. (As far as I am aware, the leading current investigators in human studies of the heritability of alcoholism are not trained as genetic researchers.) Paul Billings, the director of the Clinic for Inherited Disease at New England Deaconess Hospital, was interviewed about the *JAMA* study for *The New Republic*. Billings commented, "If this type of genetic analysis was carried out for a disease or a behavior less attractive than alcoholism, it would never get published. It tells you nothing of significance."

What *Does* Cause Alcoholism?

DOUBTS ABOUT GENETIC RESEARCH ASIDE, A large body of findings about alcoholism and its correlates cannot possibly be translated directly into biological and genetic terms. One such area of research concerns drinkers' expectations. Alcoholics have stronger expectations about how alcohol will affect them than other drinkers do. Alcoholics believe that alcohol transforms their personalities, making them more attractive to others, more relaxed, more alert, and more sexually responsive, even though in alcoholics it usually has the opposite effect in all these areas.

Mark Goldman, a psychologist at the University of South Florida, and his colleagues have extended research on expectations to college problem drinkers and even adolescents. Goldman and his colleagues found they could predict the likelihood that adolescents would develop drinking problems on the basis of their expectations about alcohol—*before they had begun drinking*. Furthermore, even elementary school children have distinct beliefs about how alcohol will affect them. Thus when Cathleen Brooks, the president of the National Association for Children of Alcoholics, describes her first drink, at age eleven, in euphoric terms—"I remember the warmth, I remember the well-being"— she is more likely reflecting what she had seen or been taught than what her body inherited.

Expectations about the effects of alcohol relate to parental, peer-group, and cultural influences. The psychiatrist George Vaillant's widely cited 1983 book, *The Natural History of Alcoholism*, examined the drinking histories of more than 600 men over forty years. Vaillant found that Harvard students were a third to a quarter as likely to develop alcoholism as inner-city Boston ethnics, and that Irish-Americans in Boston were *seven times as likely* to become alcoholic as Italian-Americans.

If a researcher were to find a biological marker for alcoholism as strong and reliable as the ethnic and social markers Vaillant identified, he or she would likely win the Nobel Prize. Yet the discrepancy between Irish and Italian alcoholism rates is far from the largest ethnic difference. Two sociologists, Barry Glassner and Bruce Berg, expected to find the legendary moderation of Jewish drinkers much attenuated in an assimilated upstate New York Jewish community. They found instead that none of their eighty-eight Jewish subjects had ever had a drinking problem. The most dire count of the city's Jewish alcoholics implies an alcoholism rate of about 0.1 percent for that Jewish community, or one hundredth the rate reported for Americans at large.

Another sociologist examined police blotters in New York's Chinatown for the period 1933–1949. Among the 17,515 arrest records, *not one* specifically reported violent or disorderly drunkenness. What is most remarkable about Chinese sobriety is that the Chinese, like other Asian groups, show a high incidence of flushing after imbibing alcohol. This visible reddening has been connected to acetaldehyde buildup in the drinker and is inherited genetically. Some researchers have proposed that such flushing makes the Chinese less likely to drink excessively. Working against this hypothesis is the fact that Native Americans and Eskimos, likewise prone to flushing, have the highest incidence of alcoholism among American ethnic and racial groups. The difference in the incidence of alcoholism among Native Americans and Chinese-Americans reflects how poorly or how well the group's indigenous values have fit in with those of the broader American culture.

One of the other cultural (and individual) factors that most clearly elevates alcoholism rates is, paradoxically, the acceptance of conceptions of alcoholism as disease-like. That is, alcoholism-prone groups such as Native Americans and Irish-Americans invest alcohol with tremendous power and readily accept that they cannot control its effects. Groups with a low incidence of alcoholism, such as Chinese-Americans and Jews, do not tolerate "loss of control" as an excuse for problem drinking or antisocial drunkenness. Glassner and Berg discovered that Reform and nonpracticing Jews among their subjects viewed alcoholism as a psychological dependence or weakness—exactly the attitude the modern genetic movement disavows. Yet people from social backgrounds in which antisocial drunkenness is strongly disapproved of and people who believe they *can* and *should* control their drinking are less likely to lose themselves in the experience of intoxication.

Rats can be bred to drink large quantities of alcohol. But rats do not have values and cultures that contravene the urge to drink excessively. While human beings clearly differ in how their bodies process and respond to alco-hol, these differences do not translate into alcoholism independent of individual needs, options, and values. Someone who has a strong reaction to alcohol, or who cannot sense when he or she has had too much to drink, may just as easily choose habitually to stop after one or two drinks as to become intoxicated.

To deny these commonsense insights in the light of putative genetic findings is to deny the connection between human values and self-destructive or antisocial behavior as well as the crucial role that both individuals and social groups have in regulating such behavior. Even a researcher like Robert Cloninger, who espouses genetic theories, recognizes this role. According to Cloninger, "The demonstration of the critical importance of sociocultural influences in most alcoholics suggests that major changes in social attitudes about drinking styles can change dramatically the prevalence of alcohol abuse, regardless of genetic predisposition."

Addictive drinking is one of a range of dependencies that people may acquire in attempting artificially to regulate their sense of themselves and their world. Some people become compulsively enmeshed in destructive drinking as they pursue sensations that they are progressively less able to attain through any other means. And yet we cannot take the power and the seeming inevitability of this self-destructiveness for proof that it is written in the genes.

A Pleasurable Chemistry

Endorphins, the body's natural narcotics, aren't something we have to run after. They're everywhere.

Janet L. Hopson

Janet L. Hopson, who lives in Oakland, California, gets endorphin highs by contributing to Psychology Today.

Welcome aboard the biochemical bandwagon of the 1980s. The magical, morphine-like brain chemicals called endorphins are getting a lot of play. First we heard they were responsible for runner's high and several other cheap thrills. Now we're hearing that they play a role in almost every human experience from birth to death, including much that is pleasurable, painful and lusty along the way.

Consider the following: crying, laughing, thrills from music, acupuncture, placebos, stress, depression, chili peppers, compulsive gambling, aerobics, trauma, masochism, massage, labor and delivery, appetite, immunity, near-death experiences, playing with pets. Each, it is claimed, is somehow involved with endorphins. Serious endorphin researchers pooh-pooh many or most of these claims but, skeptics notwithstanding, the field has clearly sprinted a long way past runner's high.

Endorphin research had its start in the early 1970s with the unexpected discovery of opiate receptors in the brain. If we have these receptors, researchers reasoned, then it is likely that the body produces some sort of opiate- or morphine-like chemicals. And that's exactly what was found, a set of relatively small biochemicals dubbed "opioid peptides" or "endorphins" (short for "endogenous morphines") that plug into the receptors. In other words, these palliative peptides are sloshing around in our brains, spines and bloodstreams, apparently acting just like morphine. In fact, morphine's long list of narcotic effects was used as a treasure map for where scientists might hunt out natural opiates in the body. Morphine slows the pulse and depresses breathing, so they searched in the heart and lungs. Morphine deadens pain, so they looked in the central and peripheral nervous systems. It disturbs digestion and elimination, so they explored the gut. It savages the sex drive, so they probed the reproductive and endocrine systems. It triggers euphoria, so they scrutinized mood.

Nearly everywhere researchers looked, endorphins or their receptors were present. But what were they doing: transmitting nerve impulses, alleviating pain, triggering hormone release, doing several of these things simultaneously or disintegrating at high speed and doing nothing at all? In the past decade, a trickle of scientific papers has become a tidal wave, but still no one seems entirely certain of what, collectively, the endorphins are doing to us or for us at any given time.

Researchers do have modern-day sextants for their search, including drugs such as naloxone and naltrexone. These drugs, known as opiate blockers, pop into the endorphin receptors and block the peptides' normal activity, giving researchers some idea of what their natural roles might be. Whatever endorphins are doing, however, it must be fairly subtle. As one researcher points out, people injected with opiate blockers may feel a little more pain or a little less "high," but no one gasps for breath, suffers a seizure or collapses in a coma.

Subtle or not, endorphins are there, and researchers are beginning to get answers to questions about how they touch our daily lives—pain, exercise, appetite, reproduction and emotions.

•ANSWERS ON ANALGESIA: A man falls off a ladder, takes one look at his right hand—now cantilevered at a sickening angle—and knows he has a broken bone. Surprisingly, he feels little pain or anxiety until hours later, when he's home from the emergency room. This physiological grace period, which closely resembles a sojourn on morphine, is a common survival mechanism in the animal world, and researchers are confident that brain opiates are responsible for such cases of natural pain relief. The question is how do they work and, more to the point, how can we make them work for us?

The answers aren't in, but researchers have located a pain control system in the periaquaductal gray (PAG), a tiny region in the center of the brain, and interestingly, it produces opioid peptides. While no one fully understands how this center operates, physicians can now jolt it with electric current to lessen chronic pain.

One day in 1976, as Navy veteran Dennis Hough was working at a hospital's psychiatric unit, a disturbed patient snapped Hough's back and ruptured three of his vertebral discs. Five years later, after two failed back operations, Hough was bedridden with constant shooting pains in his legs, back and shoulders

From *Psychology Today*, July/August 1988, pp. 29-30, 32-33. Copyright © 1988 by PT Partners, L. P. Reprinted by permission.

and was depressed to the point of suicide. Doctors were just then pioneering a technique of implanting platinum electrodes in the PAG, and Hough soon underwent the skull drilling and emplacement. He remembers it as "the most barbaric thing I've ever experienced, including my tour of duty in Vietnam," but the results were worth the ordeal; For the past seven years, Hough has been able to stimulate his brain's own endorphins four times a day by producing a radio signal from a transmitter on his belt. The procedure is delicate—too much current and his eyes flutter, too little and the pain returns in less than six hours. But it works dependably, and Hough not only holds down an office job now but is engaged to be married.

Researchers would obviously like to find an easier way to stimulate the brain's own painkillers, and while they have yet to find it, workers in many labs are actively developing new drugs and treatments. Some physicians have tried direct spinal injections of endorphins to alleviate postoperative pain. And even the most cynical now seem to agree that acupuncture works its magic by somehow triggering the release of endorphins. There may, however, be an even easier path to pain relief: the power of the mind.

Several years ago, neurobiologist Jon Levine, at the University of California, San Francisco, discovered that the placebo effect (relief) based on no known action other than the patient's belief in a treatment) can itself be blocked by naloxone and must therefore be based on endorphins. Just last year Levine was able to quantify the effects: One shot of placebo can equal the relief of 6 to 8 milligrams of morphine, a low but fairly typical dose.

Another line of research suggests that endorphins may be involved in self-inflicted injury—a surprisingly common veterinary and medical complaint and one that, in many cases, can also be prevented with naloxone. Paul Millard Hardy, a behavioral neurologist at Boston's New England Medical Center, believes that animals may boost endorphin levels through self-inflicted pain and then "get caught in a self-reinforcing positive feedback loop." He thinks something similar may occur in compulsive daredevils and in some cases of deliberate self-injury. One young woman he studied had injected pesticide into her own veins by spraying Raid into an intravenous needle. This appalling act, she told Hardy, "made her feel better, calmer and almost high."

Hardy also thinks endorphin release might explain why some autistic children constantly injure themselves by banging their heads. Because exercise is believed to be an alternate route to endorphin release, Hardy and physician Kiyo Kitahara set up a twice-a-day exercise program for a group of autistic children. He qualifies the evidence as "very anecdotal at this point" but calls the results "phenomenal."

•RUNNER'S HIGH, RUNNER'S CALM: For most people, "endorphins" are synonymous with "runner's high," a feeling of well-being that comes after an aerobic workout. Many people claim to have experienced this "high," and remarkable incidents are legion. Take, for example, San Francisco runner Don Paul, who placed 10th in the 1979 San Francisco Marathon and wound up with his ankle in a cast the next day. Paul had run the 26 miles only vaguely aware of what turned out to be a serious stress fracture. Observers on the sidelines had to tell him he was "listing badly to one side for the last six miles." He now runs 90 miles per week in preparation for the U.S. men's Olympic marathon trial and says that when he trains at the level, he feels "constantly great. Wonderful."

Is runner's high a real phenomenon based on endorphins? And can those brain opiates result in "exercise addiction"? Or, as many skeptics hold, are the effects on mood largely psychological? Most studies with humans have found rising levels of endorphins in the blood during exercise.

However, says exercise physiologist Peter Farrell of Pennsylvania State University, "when we look at animal studies, we don't see a concurrent increase in the brain." Most circulating peptides fail to cross into the brain, he explains, so explaining moods like runner's high based on endorphin levels in the blood is questionable. Adds placebo expert Jon Levine, "Looking for mood changes based on the circulating blood is like putting a voltmeter to the outside of a computer and saying 'Now I know how it works.' " Nevertheless, Farrell exercises religiously: "I'm not going to waste my lifetime sitting around getting sclerotic just because something's not proven yet."

Murray Allen, a physician and kinesiologist at Canada's Simon Fraser University, is far more convinced about the endorphin connection. He recently conducted his own study correlating positive moods and exercise—moods that could be blocked by infusing the runner with naloxone. Allen thinks these moods are "Mother Nature's way of rewarding us for staying fit" but insists that aerobic exercisers don't get "high." Opioid peptides "slow down and inhibit excess activity in the brain," he says. "Many researchers have been chasing after psychedelic, excitable responses." The actual effect, he says, is "runner's calm" and extremes leading to exhaustion usually negate it.

In a very similar experiment last year, a research team at Georgia State University found the mood-endorphin link more elusive. Team member and psychologist Wade Silverman of Atlanta explains that only those people who experience "runner's high" on the track also noticed it in the lab. Older people and those who ran fewer, not more, miles per week were also more likely to show a "high" on the test. "People who run a lot—50 miles per week or more—are often drudges, masochists, running junkies," says Silverman. "They don't really enjoy it. It hurts." For optimum benefits. Silverman recommends running no more than three miles per day four times a week.

Silverman and Lewis Maharam, a sports medicine internist at Manhattan's New York Infirmary/Beekman Downtown Hospital, both agree that powerful psychological factors—including heightened sense of self-esteem and self-discipline—contribute to the "high" in those who exercise moderately. Maharam would still like to isolate and quantify the role of endorphins, however, so he could help patients "harness the high." He would like to give people "proper exercise prescriptions," he says, "to stimulate the greatest enjoyment and benefit from exercise. If we could encourage the 'high' early on, maybe we could get people to want to keep exercising from the start."

The questions surrounding exercise, mood and circulating endorphins remain. But even if opioids released into the bloodstream from, say, the adrenal glands don't enter the brain and give a "high" or a "calm," several studies show that endorphins in the blood do bolster the immune system's activity. One way or the other, regular moderate exercise seems destined to make us happy.

•APPETITE CLOCKS AND BLOCKS: Few things in life are more basic to survival and yet more pleasurable than eating good food—and where survival and pleasure intersect, can the endorphins be far behind? To keep from starving, an animal needs to know when, what and how much to eat, and researchers immediately suspected that opioid peptides might help control appetite and satiety. People, after all, have long claimed that specific foods such as chili peppers or sweets give them a "high." And those unmistakably "high" on morphine or heroin experience constipation, cravings and other gastrointestinal glitches.

Indeed, investigators quickly located opiate receptors in the alimentary tract and found a region of the rat's hypothalamus that—when injected with tiny amounts of beta endorphin—will trigger noshing of particular nutrients. Even a satiated rat will dig heartily into fats, proteins or sweets when injected with the peptide. Neurobiologist Sarah Leibowitz and her colleagues at Rockefeller University produced this result and also found that opiate blockers would prevent the snack attack—strong evidence that endorphins help regulate appetite. The opiates "probably enhance the hedonic, pleasurable, rewarding properties" of fats, proteins and sweets—foods that can help satiate an animal far longer than carbohydrates so it can survive extended periods without eating.

Intriguingly, rats crave carbohydrates at the beginning of their 12-hour activity cycles, but they like fats, proteins or sweets before retiring—a hint that endorphins control not just the nature but the timing of appetites. Leibowitz suspects that endorphins also help control cravings in response to stress and starvation, and that disturbed endorphin systems may, in part, underlie obesity and eating disorders. Obese people given opiate blockers, for example, tend to eat less; bulimics often gorge on fat-rich foods; both bulimics and anorexics often have abnormal levels of endorphins; and in anorexics, food deprivation enhances the release of opiates in the brain. This brain opiate reward, some speculate, may reinforce the anorexic's self-starvation much as self-injury seems to be rewarding to an autistic child.

Researchers such as Leibowitz are hoping to learn enough about the chemistry of appetite to fashion a binge-blocking drug as well as more effective behavioral approaches to over- or undereating. In the meantime, people who try boosting their own endorphins through exercise, mirth or music may notice a vexing increase in their taste for fattening treats.

•PUBERTY, PREGNANCY AND PEPTIDES: Evolution has equipped animals with two great appetites—the hunger for food to prevent short-term disintegration and the hunger for sex and reproduction to prevent longer-term genetic oblivion. While some endorphin researchers were studying opioids and food hunger, others began searching for a sex role—and they found it.

Once again, drug addiction pointed the way: Users of morphine and heroin often complain of impotence and frigidity that fade when they kick their habits. Could natural opioids have some biochemical dampening effect on reproduction? Yes, says Theodore Cicero of Washington University Medical School. Endorphins, he says, "play an integral role—probably the dominant role—in regulating reproductive hormone cycles."

This formerly small corner of endorphin research has "exploded into a huge area of neurobiology," Cicero says, and researchers now think the opioid peptides help fine-tune many—perhaps all—of the nervous and hormonal pathways that together keep the body operating normally.

Cicero and his colleagues have tracked the byzantine biochemical loops through which endorphins, the brain, the body's master gland (the pituitary), the master's master (the hypothalamus) and the gonads exchange signals to ensure that an adult animal can reproduce when times are good but not when the environment is hostile. Cicero's work helped show that beta endorphin rules the hypothalamus and thus, indirectly, the pituitary and gonads.

The Washington University group also sees "a perfect parallel" between the brain's ability to produce endorphins and the onset of puberty: As the opioid system matures, so does the body sexually. A juvenile rat with endorphins blocked by naloxone undergoes puberty earlier; a young rat given opiates matures far later than normal and its offspring can have disturbed hormonal systems. Cicero calls the results "frightening" and adds, "there couldn't possibly be a worse time for a person to take drugs than during late childhood or adolescence."

Endorphins play a critical role in a later reproductive phase, as well: pregnancy and labor. Women in their third trimester sometimes notice that the pain and pressure of, say, a blood pressure cuff, is far less pronounced than before or after pregnancy. Alan Gintzler and his colleagues at the State University of New York Health Science Center in Brooklyn found that opioid peptides produced inside the spinal cord probably muffle pain and perhaps elevate mood to help a woman deal with the increasing physical stress of pregnancy. Endorphin activity builds throughout pregnancy and reaches a peak just before and during labor. Some have speculated that the tenfold drop from peak endorphin levels within 24 hours of delivery may greatly contribute to postpartum depression.

•CHILLS, THRILLS, LAUGHTER AND TEARS: Just as the effects of morphine go beyond the physical, claims for the opioid peptides extend to purely esthetic and emotional, with speculation falling on everything from the pleasure of playing with pets and the transcendence of near-death experiences to shivers over sonatas and the feeling of well-being that comes with a rousing laugh or a good cry.

Avram Goldstein of Stanford University, a pioneer in peptide research, recently collected a group of volunteers who get a spine-tingling thrill from their favorite music and gave them either a placebo or an opiate blocker during a listening session. Their shivers declined with the blocker—tantalizing evidence that endorphins mediate rapture, even though the mechanics are anyone's guess.

Former *Saturday Review* editor Norman Cousins may have spawned a different supposition about endorphins and emotion when he literally laughed himself out of the sometimes fatal disease ankylosing spondylitis. He found that 10 minutes of belly laughing before bed gave him two hours of painfree sleep. Before long, someone credited endorphins with the effect, and by now the claim is commonplace. For example, Matt Weinstein, a humor consultant from Berkeley, California, frequently mentions a possible link between endorphins, laughter and health in his lectures on humor in the workplace. His company's motto: If you take yourself too seriously, there's an excellent chance you may end up seriously ill.

Weinstein agrees with laughter researcher William Fry, a psychiatrist at Stanford's medical school, that evidence is currently circumstantial. Fry tried to confirm the laughter-endorphin link experimentally, but the most accurate way to assess it would be to tap the cerebrospinal fluid. That, Fry says, "is not only a difficult procedure but it's not conducive to laughter" and could result in a fountain of spinal fluid gushing out with the first good guffaw. Confirmation clearly awaits a less ghoulish methodology. But in the meantime, Fry is convinced that mirth and playfulness can diminish fear, anger and depression. At the very least, he says, laughter is a good aerobic exercise that ventilates the lungs and leaves the muscles relaxed. Fry advises patients to take their own humor inventory, then amass a library of books, tapes and gags that dependably trigger hilarity.

Another William Frey, this one at the University of Minnesota, studies the role of tears in emotion, stress and health. "The physiology of the brain when we experience a change in emotional state from sad to angry to happy or vice versa is an absolutely unexplored frontier," Frey says. And emotional tears are a fascinating guidepost because "they are unique to human beings and are our natural excretory response to strong emotion." Since all other bodily fluids are involved in removing something, he reasons, logic dictates that tears wash something away, too. Frey correctly predicted that tears would contain the three biochemicals that build up during stress: leucine-enkephalin, an endorphin, and the hormones prolactin and ACTH. These biochemicals are found in both emotional tears and tears from chopping onions, a different sort of stress.

Frey is uncertain whether tears simply carry off excess endorphins that collect in the stressed brain or whether those peptides have some activity in the tear ducts, eyes, nose or throat. Regardless, he cites evidence that people with ulcers and colitis tend to cry less than the average, and he concludes that a person who feels like crying "should go ahead and do it! I can't think of any other physical excretory process that humans alone can do, so why suppress it and its possibly healthful effects?"

All in all, the accumulated evidence suggests that if you want to use your endorphins, you should live the unfettered natural life. Laugh! Cry! Thrill to music! Reach puberty. Get pregnant. Get aerobic. Get hungry, Eat! Lest this sound like a song from *Fiddler on the Roof*, however, remember that stress or injury may be even quicker ways to pump out home-brew opioids. The bottom line is this: Endorphins are so fundamental to normal physiological functioning that we don't have to seek them out at all. We probably surf life's pleasures and pains on a wave of endorphins already.

Test yourself by imagining the following: the sound of chalk squeaking across a blackboard; a pink rose sparkling with dew; embracing your favorite movie star; chocolate-mocha mousse cake; smashing your thumb with a hammer. If any of these thoughts sent the tiniest tingle down your spine, then you have have just proved the point.

Patterns and Trends in Drug Use

Drug use is socially patterned; different drugs are used in different frequencies by different social categories in the population. In addition, drug use displays a trend: It varies over time. Consequently, in order to understand the phenomenon of drug use, we must examine its pattern and trends. Who uses drugs? How frequently? And how does this change from year to year?

More basically, how do we study drug use? Won't people simply lie about their use which, with respect to illegal drugs, is a criminal act? With the legal drugs, our job is relatively easy. All officially tabulated sales are taxable, which means that there are detailed and precise records on how many purchases of what quantities of which legal drugs available for inspection. Legal drug sales are a matter of public record, so, in order to know how much alcohol, tobacco, prescription drugs, and over-the-counter drugs are used, we look at their official sales.

The matter is not *quite* this easy, of course. There are unofficial sales of legal drugs—moonshine whiskey, cigarettes and cigars smuggled into the United States from abroad, legal drug use by American tourists on vacation in other countries, and so on—that do not get recorded anywhere. And someone may purchase a bottle of liquor, put it on the shelf, and never drink it at all; this represents a sale, but no use. Because of these and other complexities, scientists refer to sales as "apparent" consumption; sales are not *exactly* consumption, but they are very close to it. Sales per year represent a very rough, but fairly accurate, reflection of levels of actual use of legal drugs.

With respect to alcohol specifically, there is another complexity: Different alcoholic beverages contain different percentages of alcohol, which scientists call *ethanol* or ethyl alcohol. In the United States, for distilled beverages, the "proof" of a type of drink designates the percentage of ethanol it contains; to get that percentage, simply divided the proof by a factor of two. So, 100-proof vodka is 50 percent ethanol; 80-proof whiskey is 40 percent alcohol. Each type of drink contains its own specific percentage of ethanol. Beer is 4–5 percent alcohol; wine is 12–13 percent; "fortified" wines, such as sherry and port, are nearly 20 percent; distilled beverages, such as vodka, gin, rum, Scotch, and tequila, are 40–50 percent ethanol. Thus, for the many types of alcoholic drinks it is necessary to apply a "conversion factor": For beer, to determine the consumption of alcohol or ethanol itself, one must divide the total quantity of beer sold by 20 or 25; for wine, one must divide by 8; for whiskey, divide by 2 or 2.5, depending on the proof; and so on. Though these tabulations are complicated, they can be done.

With illegal drugs, the matter is more difficult. Here, we have no official record of sales. How do we know who uses and who does not? Whether use changes over time? Many social scientists believe that, to answer these questions, we can conduct surveys. How do we know about drug use? Simply ask a sample consisting of an accurate cross-section of Americans about their own use, some experts believe. Would people lie about their own drug use? The evidence suggests that most people tell the truth about matters like that—to the best of their ability, of course. It is important that we sample a fairly large number of respondents, and they reflect the composition of the population at large. But study after study has shown that the answers people give in a survey tell us a great deal about their drug use patterns.

What patterns do we see in drug use, judging from the many currently-available surveys on the subject? Many of the findings of these studies are fairly commonsensical. Men tend to use illegal drugs—and alcohol as well—more than women. The young use more than the old, urban residents more than rural dwellers, residents of the East and the West coasts more than those living in the South and the Midwest, high school and college drop-outs more than those who graduate, and—especially very recently—the poor more than the affluent.

With respect to trends, one dramatic change took place in the 1980s that is still ongoing: Drug use, both legal and illegal, is declining significantly and dramatically. The peak for illegal drug use was the late 1970s; not only are Americans using less, they also disapprove of drug use more, they are more likely to believe that it is harmful, and less likely to favor legalization, even of marijuana. Alcohol and, somewhat less so, tobacco use also declined during the 1980s, although far less sharply than was true for the illegal drugs.

But in addition to this downhill overall trend, we also notice a less heartening one. One of the most remarkable changes in the area of drug use and abuse in recent years is the growing *divergence* in drug use patterns between

Unit 4

the poor and the affluent, between middle and lower class Americans. While drug use declined among the members of the middle classes, among the lower and working classes, it increased, remained stable, or declined much more slowly. Thus, the people with the most resources to deal with the problem of drug use are giving it up, while those with the fewest resources are most likely to continue. It is painful paradoxes such as these that we must grapple with in this extremely difficult area of study.

Looking Ahead: Challenge Questions

What changes have taken place in the drug use and abuse patterns in the United States during the past generation or so? Why do certain drugs experience ups and downs in popularity over time? Do you think that these variations are a matter of availability, cultural preference, stresses and strains—or what?

Why are certain categories in the population more likely to use and abuse certain drugs? Why are others less likely to do so?

How accurate are surveys on drug use?

Why do you think that members of the middle and the lower classes are diverging in their drug use patterns over time?

What do you foresee as the "drug of the future"? What will the drug use patterns be in the near future? Will drug use and abuse remain high in the United States a decade from now? Or do you foresee a decline? Why?

Drug Use, Drinking, and Smoking:

National Survey Results from High School, College, and Young Adults Population

Drug use is becoming more unfashionable among the mainstream of young Americans, according to University of Michigan social scientists.

Lloyd D. Johnston, Patrick M. O'Malley and Jerald G. Bachman—reporting on their 15th annual national survey of American high school seniors, and their 10th national survey of American college students—conclude that the longer-term trend away from the use of marijuana, cocaine and other drugs continued in 1989. "In fact," Johnston says, "the likelihood of a young person in high school or college today actively using illicit drugs is only about half of what it was a decade ago."

Among the findings reported from the 1989 survey are the following:

—Marijuana: Current use of marijuana, defined as any use in the prior 30 days, is down from a peak of 37 percent in 1979 to 17 percent in 1989 among high school seniors, and among college students the decline between 1980 (the earliest year for which college data are available) and 1989 was from 34 to 16 percent. The proportional drop in daily marijuana use has been even greater in both populations.

—Cocaine: Cocaine use, which remained at peak levels throughout much of the 80s, began an important decline in 1987 and 1988 that has continued into 1989. Among high school seniors the proportion who are current users of cocaine fell by more than half between 1986 and 1989, from 6.2 percent to 2.8 percent. An even larger proportional drop in current use has been observed among American college students over the same interval—from 7 percent to 2.8 percent.

—Amphetamines: Amphetamines, which also have been widely used throughout the drug epidemic of the past two decades, have shown an even larger and longer-term decline than cocaine. Current amphetamine use (again, defined as any use in the prior 30 days) peaked among high school seniors in 1980 at more than 12 percent, but was down to approximately 4 percent by 1989. For college students current use in 1980 was also about 12 percent, but by 1989 it had fallen to slightly more than 1 percent.

—Tranquilizers, barbiturates and methaqualone: A number of drugs have reached such low levels in the high school

and college populations that they are no longer showing much decline. These include the non-medical use of a number of sedating drugs, including tranquilizers (current use in 1989, for seniors and college students, respectively, of 1.3 percent and 0.8 percent), barbiturates (1.4 percent and 0.2 percent), and methaqualone or quaaludes (0.6 percent and 0.0 percent). All three of these classes of drugs had shown appreciable declines in earlier years. In fact, the decline in use of tranquilizers and barbiturates goes back at least to 1975 when the study began.

"It is still true that a large proportion of young people have tried drugs. In 1989 some 51 percent of the high school seniors and 56 percent of the college students in the survey reported having at least tried an illicit drug use during their lifetime. However, an increasing proportion of users are discontinuing their use," the U-M researchers note.

—Young adults ages 19 to 28: "These conclusions are not confined to high school and college students," the investigators add. "Our panels of high school graduates, covering an age range from 19 to 28, show these same general improvements." The investigators note that the late teens and 20s tend to be the ages of greatest risk for drug abuse in this country.

—Dropouts: "We are quite aware that the segment of the population missing from these samples—namely, those who fail to complete high school—is at higher-than-average risk for drug involvement," Johnston states. "While it is possible that this dropout segment could be trending in ways that are different than those in the 80 percent to 85 percent of the age group that we do cover, our available evidence suggests that this may not be the case. We find at least as great an improvement among the seniors who are most like the dropouts, that is, among those who are frequently truant or have poor grades, as among students who are seldom truant or have excellent grades. This suggests to us that the improvements tend to be very broad." (According to government statistics, the national dropout rate has shown little overall change in the past 15 years.)

—Crack: Crack—the smokable form of cocaine that comes in chunks or rock form—has not shown as large a decline as did powdered cocaine, but the investigators report that the

 Reprinted by permission from *The University of Michigan News and Information Services*, February 9, 1990. pp. 1-6.

movement seems to be in the downward direction. Among high school seniors, the proportion having used any crack in their lifetime fell from 5.4 percent in 1987 to 4.7 percent in 1989, and the proportion using any in the past year fell from 3.9 percent in 1987 to 3.1 percent in 1989. Current use—use in the past 30 days—has remained fairly stable over this interval at 1.3 percent and 1.4 percent, respectively.

Declines in crack use were also observed among the college student sample and the total sample of high school graduates 19 to 28 years old in the 1987–89 interval.

"Two facts are noteworthy in the data on crack use," Johnston observes. "First, compared with a number of the other drugs, relatively small proportions of these populations have ever become involved with crack, no doubt in large part due to the rapid recognition and dissemination of the dangers associated with its use. Second, all three populations have been showing some decline in their use of crack.

"However, we know we are not going to capture many heavy crack users in these surveys," he adds, "and it is clear from other types of information that there are plenty of heavy users out there. What may be most significant here is the fact that crack has not heavily penetrated these mainstream populations of American young people and that the initiation rates among them appear to be on the decline."

—Ice: "Ice," or crystal methamphetamine, is another stimulant drug that can be smoked and which has many of the same euphoric and adverse effects as crack. Because of increasing concern about the spread of this drug, the U-M researchers have begun to ask about its use. "We will have more questions about crystal methamphetamine in the 1990 survey, and we plan to watch this drug carefully," Johnston notes, "but what we have so far suggests rather limited levels of use." Annual prevalence use within the past year—the only usage statistic currently available for this drug—was found to be about 1.2 percent nationally among high school seniors, although it was more than twice that (3 percent) in the West, the region that was expected to be most affected to date. The annual prevalence rates for college students and young adults are about the same as for high school seniors at this point: 1.5 percent of the college students and 1.4 percent of the 19- to 28-year-old sample report any use of ice in the prior year.

"Because ice is probably just as dangerous as crack, we think it important that its hazards become documented and known to the population as quickly as possible," Johnston says. "Over the past decade our research on trends in marijuana, cocaine, and PCP use have led us to the conclusion that concerns about the hazards of a drug play a pivotal role in deterring use. Thus one way of containing threatened epidemics of new substances like ice is to gather good clinical, laboratory and epidemiological evidence fast and to get it out to the relevant populations as quickly and credibly as possible; in other words, to accelerate and reinforce a natural self-correction process that otherwise may take years.

"Another approach may be to teach our youngsters a more general lesson about mood-altering drugs, and that is that all of the ones we know about to date have eventually exacted a high toll on their users. It may take years to show up, as in the case of cocaine, or even decades, as in the case of cigarettes, but eventually there is a price to be paid. That means that whatever next year's new offering may be, it almost surely holds false promise and quite possibly tragic consequences. I hope we can get today's young people to learn from our recent history with drugs, and not to repeat the errors of their predecessors when the next seemingly 'safe' drug comes along."

—Ecstasy: MDMA or "ecstasy" may be one such drug. Like ice, it was included for the first time in the 1989 study in order to assess how widespread its use is among college students and young adults. (Questions about its use were not asked of high school students.) "So far, relatively small proportions of these samples have used ecstasy," Johnston says. Among the 19- to 28-year-olds, 3.3 percent had tried it (4.5 percent of males and 2.3 percent of females) and only 0.4 percent had used it actively in the prior 30 days. Among college students, 3.8 percent had tried it and only 0.3 percent reported use in the prior 30 days.

—Steroids: Finally, a somewhat different type of drug— namely, anabolic steroids—was added to the study for the first time in 1989. "While these drugs are not generally used to alter mood and consciousness, as are all the other drugs we have been studying, they are controlled substances that can be abused by young people and which pose a definite risk to their health," Johnston says. "While the prevalence of use we find among high school seniors is not as high as some other studies led us to expect, it is clear that there is enough use to be the basis of some concern." The lifetime prevalence among seniors in 1989 was 3 percent; however, since these drugs are used largely by males to enhance muscle development and athletic performance, there is a large difference between the sexes in levels of use. Among male seniors, 4.7 percent reported ever using steroids and 1.4 percent reported use in the prior 30 days. Among females, the corresponding numbers are 1.3 percent and 0.3 percent.

—Causes of the Trends: "We think that the forces leading to the continued downward trends in marijuana and cocaine are much the same as they have been in the past," Johnston adds. "That is, a heightened concern about the health and other effects of these drugs. The proportion of seniors and young adults in their 20s concerned about the adverse consequences of cocaine use—particularly experimental and occasional use—continues to increase, as does the proportion concerned about the use of crack cocaine specifically." Of the seniors surveyed, 54 percent now see "great risk" of the user harming himself physically or in other ways even if he uses powder cocaine only once or twice, and 63 percent now feel that way about experimenting with crack.

"Peer norms have tended to move in parallel to perceived risk, with growing proportions saying they disapprove of the use of these drugs," Johnston notes. "We think these norms shift in part because they have come to see the drugs as more dangerous."

4. PATTERNS AND TRENDS IN DRUG USE

Changes in reported availability have not accounted for the downturns, since the proportion saying they could get cocaine or crack "fairly easily" actually has increased, and because very large proportions of these age groups continue to say marijuana is "readily available" to them. In fact, in the 1989 survey there were significant increases in the perceived availability of LSD, PCP and heroin as well as cocaine and crack.

"The broad trends we are seeing are due almost entirely to a change in demand, not supply," Johnston comments. "This reduced demand is attributable largely to the important changes occurring in the attitudes, beliefs, and social norms among our young people."

—PCP: "While most of the story from the 1989 survey is positive, there are several troublesome findings. One is that the use of PCP animal tranquilizer used for its hallucinogenic effects increased slightly in 1989, with current prevalence among high school seniors rising from 0.3 percent to 1.4 percent. While the present rates of use are far below what they were in the late 1970s, any increase in the use of this particularly damaging drug should be the basis for some concern," Johnston says. An increase was observed in all four regions of the country.

—Inhalants: "Another troublesome finding is that the use of inhalant drugs (glues, aerosols, nitrous oxide, etc.), although not particularly high, has resisted the more general decline in drug use in recent years (despite the decline in use of the component class of inhalants—the amyl and butyl nitrites ['snappers' and 'poppers'])." The overall proportion of students reporting use of this class of drugs has remained fairly stable through most of the 1980s. Approximately 7 percent of high school seniors indicate using some inhalant drug during the prior year. The comparable figure for college students is 4 percent, and for the 19- to 28-year-old sample, 2 percent.

—Cigarette smoking: "By far the most disappointing part of the story," Johnston concludes, "is the fact that over most of the decade there has been practically no improvement in smoking rates among American high school seniors. In 1989, 29 percent of them were current smokers, which is the same proportion as in the class of 1981." (Based on other research it is known that a much higher proportion of the dropouts smoke.)

"The implications for their generation, in terms of unnecessary death and disease, are enormous," Johnston argues. Asked what can be done, he points to advertising. "Anybody who thinks that two and one-half billion dollars a year in the advertising and promotion of cigarettes doesn't contribute to the smoking rates among our children and adolescents simply hasn't given very much thought to the subject."

—Alcohol use: A more encouraging picture emerges for alcohol use. "While clearly a large proportion of American teen-agers drink, and, indeed, many drink to the point of inebriation with some regularity, these statistics have been moving in a constructive direction of late," the investigators conclude. The proportion of seniors indicating that they had consumed any alcoholic beverage during the prior 30 days has fallen by one-sixth, from the peak level of 72 percent in 1980 to 60 percent in 1989 (including a 4 percent decline in 1989). The proportion of seniors reporting recent occasions of heavy drinking (that is, having five or more drinks in a row during the prior two weeks) also has declined, from a high of 41 percent in 1983 to a low of 33 percent in 1989.

"While the numbers are certainly still too high, particularly since purchasing alcohol is illegal for all high school students, they are at least moving in a constructive direction," Johnston concludes. Among college students and young adults in their 20s, however, declines in alcohol use have been much more modest.

The study, titled "Monitoring the Future," is also widely known as the National High School Senior Survey. It has been conducted under a series of research grants from the National Institute on Drug Abuse to the U-M Institute for Social Research. Surveys of American high school seniors have been carried out each year since 1975, and of American college students each year since 1980.

The annual senior samples are comprised of roughly 17,000 seniors in 135 public and private high schools nationwide, selected to be representative of all high school seniors in the continental United States. They complete self-administered questionnaires given to them in their classrooms by U-M researchers.

The annual college samples are part of the follow-up studies of previous participating graduating classes, all of whom are resurveyed by mail. College students are defined as high school graduates one to four years past high school enrolled full time in a two-year or four-year college or university. Each year the national sample of college students numbers about 1,200 cases, while the sample of high school graduates, one to 10 years past high school, numbers about 6,600.

TABLE 1
Trends in Lifetime Prevalence of Eighteen Types of Drugs

Percent ever used

	Class of 1975	Class of 1976	Class of 1977	Class of 1978	Class of 1979	Class of 1980	Class of 1981	Class of 1982	Class of 1983	Class of 1984	Class of 1985	Class of 1986	Class of 1987	Class of 1988	Class of 1989	'88–'89 change
Approx. N =	(9400)	(15400)	(17100)	(17800)	(15500)	(15900)	(17500)	(17700)	(16300)	(15900)	(16000)	(15200)	(16300)	(16300)	(16700)	
Any Illicit Drug Use[a]	55.2	58.3	61.6	64.1	65.1	65.4	65.6	65.8	64.1	61.6	60.6	57.6	56.6	53.9	50.9	−3.0ss
Adjusted Version[b]	—	—	—	—	—	—	—	*64.4*	*62.9*	—	—	—	—	—	—	
Any Illicit Drug Other Than Marijuana[c]	36.2	35.4	35.8	36.5	37.4	38.7	42.8	45.0	44.4	40.3	39.7	37.7	35.8	32.5	31.4	−1.1
Adjusted Version[b]	—	—	—	—	—	—	—	*41.1*	*40.4*	—	—	—	—	—	—	
Marijuana/Hashish	47.3	52.8	56.4	59.2	60.4	60.3	59.5	58.7	57.0	54.9	54.2	50.9	50.2	47.2	43.7	−3.5ss
Inhalants[d]	NA	10.3	11.1	12.0	12.7	11.9	12.3	12.8	13.6	14.4	15.4	15.9	17.0	16.7	17.6	+0.9
Inhalants Adjusted[e]	*NA*	*NA*	*NA*	*NA*	*18.2*	*17.3*	*17.2*	*17.7*	*18.2*	*18.0*	*18.1*	*20.1*	*18.6*	*17.5*	*18.6*	*+1.1*
Amyl & Butyl Nitrites[f,g]	NA	NA	NA	NA	11.1	11.1	10.1	9.8	8.4	8.1	7.9	8.6	4.7	3.2	3.3	+0.1
Hallucinogens	16.3	15.1	13.9	14.3	14.1	13.3	13.3	12.5	11.9	10.7	10.3	9.7	10.3	8.9	9.4	+0.5
Hallucinogens Adjusted[h]	*NA*	*NA*	*NA*	*NA*	*17.7*	*15.6*	*15.3*	*14.3*	*13.6*	*12.3*	*12.1*	*11.9*	*10.6*	*9.2*	*9.9*	*+0.7*
LSD	11.3	11.0	9.8	9.7	9.5	9.3	9.8	9.6	8.9	8.0	7.5	7.2	8.4	7.7	8.3	+0.6
PCP[f,g]	*NA*	*NA*	*NA*	*NA*	*12.8*	*9.6*	*7.8*	*6.0*	*5.6*	*5.0*	*4.9*	*4.8*	*3.0*	*2.9*	*3.9*	*+1.0*
Cocaine	9.0	9.7	10.8	12.9	15.4	15.7	16.5	16.0	16.2	16.1	17.3	16.9	15.2	12.1	10.3	−1.8ss
"Crack"[f]	NA	NA	NA	NA	NA	NA	NA	NA	NA	NA	NA	NA	5.4	4.8	4.7	−0.1
Other cocaine[f]	*NA*	*NA*	*NA*	*NA*	*NA*	*NA*	*NA*	*NA*	*NA*	*NA*	*NA*	*NA*	*14.0*	*12.1*	*8.5*	*−3.6sss*
Heroin	2.2	1.8	1.8	1.6	1.1	1.1	1.1	1.2	1.2	1.3	1.2	1.1	1.2	1.1	1.3	+0.2
Other opiates[j]	9.0	9.6	10.3	9.9	10.1	9.8	10.1	9.6	9.4	9.7	10.2	9.0	9.2	8.6	8.3	−0.3
Stimulants[j]	22.3	22.6	23.0	22.9	24.2	26.4	32.2	35.6	35.4	NA	NA	NA	NA	NA	NA	NA
Stimulants Adjusted[b,j]	*NA*	*NA*	*NA*	*NA*	*NA*	*NA*	*NA*	*27.9*	*26.9*	*27.9*	*26.2*	*23.4*	*21.6*	*19.8*	*19.1*	*−0.7*
Sedatives[j]	18.2	17.7	17.4	16.0	14.6	14.9	16.0	15.2	14.4	13.3	11.8	10.4	8.7	7.8	7.4	−0.4
Barbiturates[j]	16.9	16.2	15.6	13.7	11.8	11.0	11.3	10.3	9.9	9.9	9.2	8.4	7.4	6.7	6.5	−0.2
Methaqualone[j]	*8.1*	*7.8*	*8.5*	*7.9*	*8.3*	*9.5*	*10.6*	*10.7*	*10.1*	*8.3*	*6.7*	*5.2*	*4.0*	*3.3*	*2.7*	*−0.6*
Tranquilizers[j]	17.0	16.8	18.0	17.0	16.3	15.2	14.7	14.0	13.3	12.4	11.9	10.9	10.9	9.4	7.6	−1.8ss
Alcohol	90.4	91.9	92.5	93.1	93.0	93.2	92.6	92.8	92.6	92.6	92.2	91.3	92.2	92.0	90.7	−1.3
Cigarettes	73.6	75.4	75.7	75.3	74.0	71.0	71.0	70.1	70.6	69.7	68.8	67.6	67.2	66.4	65.7	−0.7

NOTES: Level of significance of difference between the two most recent classes: s = .05, ss = .01, sss = .001. NA indicates data not available.
[a] Use of "any illicit drugs" includes any use of marijuana, hallucinogens, cocaine, and heroin, or any use of other opiates, stimulants, sedatives, or tranquilizers not under a doctor's orders.
[b] Based on the data from the revised question, which attempts to exclude the inappropriate reporting of non-prescription stimulants.
[c] Use of "other illicit drugs" includes any use of hallucinogens, cocaine, and heroin, or any use of other opiates, stimulants, sedatives, or tranquilizers not under a doctor's orders.
[d] Data based on four questionnaire forms in 1976–1988; N is four-fifths of N indicated. Data based on five questionnaire forms in 1989; N is five-sixths of N indicated.
[e] Adjusted for underreporting of amyl and butyl nitrites. See text for details.
[f] Data based on a single questionnaire form; N is one-fifth of N indicated in 1979–1988 and one-sixth of N indicated in 1989.
[g] Question text changed slightly in 1987.
[h] Adjusted for underreporting of PCP. See text for details.
[i] Data based on two questionnaire forms; N is two-fifths of N indicated in 1987–1988 and two-sixths of N indicated in 1989.
[j] Only drug use which was not under a doctor's orders is included here.

TABLE 2
Trends in Annual Prevalence of Eighteen Types of Drugs

Percent who used in last twelve months

	Class of 1975	Class of 1976	Class of 1977	Class of 1978	Class of 1979	Class of 1980	Class of 1981	Class of 1982	Class of 1983	Class of 1984	Class of 1985	Class of 1986	Class of 1987	Class of 1988	Class of 1989	'88–'89 change
Approx. N =	(9400)	(15400)	(17100)	(17800)	(15500)	(15900)	(17500)	(17700)	(16300)	(15900)	(16000)	(15200)	(16300)	(16300)	(16700)	
Any Illicit Drug Use^a	45.0	48.1	51.1	53.8	54.2	53.1	52.1	50.8	49.1	45.8	46.3	44.3	41.7	38.5	35.4	
Adjusted Version^b	–	–	–	–	–	–	–	*49.4*	*47.4*							*–3.1sss*
Any Illicit Drug Other Than Marijuana^c	26.2	25.4	26.0	27.1	28.2	30.4	34.0	33.8	32.5	28.0	27.4	25.9	24.1	21.1	20.0	
Adjusted Version^b	–	–	–	–	–	–	–	*30.1*	*28.4*							*–1.1*
Marijuana/Hashish	40.0	44.5	47.6	50.2	50.8	48.8	46.1	44.3	42.3	40.0	40.6	38.8	36.3	33.1	29.6	–3.5ss
Inhalants^d	NA	3.0	3.7	4.1	5.4	4.6	4.1	4.5	4.3	5.1	5.7	6.1	6.9	6.5	5.9	–0.6
Inhalants Adjusted^e	*NA*	*NA*	*NA*	*NA*	*8.9*	*7.9*	*6.1*	*6.6*	*6.2*	*7.2*	*7.5*	*8.9*	*8.1*	*7.1*	*6.9*	*–0.2*
Amyl & Butyl Nitrites^f,g	NA	NA	NA	NA	6.5	5.7	3.7	3.6	3.6	4.0	4.0	4.7	2.6	1.7	1.7	0.0
Hallucinogens	11.2	8.4	8.8	9.6	9.9	9.3	9.0	8.1	7.3	6.5	6.3	6.0	6.4	5.5	5.8	+0.1
Hallucinogens Adjusted^h	*NA*	*NA*	*NA*	*NA*	*11.8*	*10.4*	*10.1*	*9.0*	*8.3*	*7.3*	*7.6*	*7.6*	*6.7*	*5.8*	*6.2*	*+0.4*
LSD	7.2	6.4	5.5	6.3	6.6	6.5	6.5	6.1	5.4	4.7	4.4	4.5	5.2	4.8	4.9	+0.1
PCP^f,g	NA	NA	NA	NA	7.0	4.4	3.2	2.2	2.6	2.3	2.9	2.4	1.3	1.2	2.4	+1.2ss
Cocaine	5.6	6.0	7.2	9.0	12.0	12.3	12.4	11.5	11.4	11.6	13.1	12.7	10.3	7.9	6.5	–1.4ss
"Crack"^i	NA	NA	NA	NA	NA	NA	NA	NA	NA	NA	NA	4.1	3.9	3.1	3.1	0.0
Other cocaine^f	NA	NA	NA	NA	NA	NA	NA	NA	NA	NA	NA	NA	9.8	7.4	5.2	–2.2ss
Heroin	1.0	0.8	0.8	0.8	0.5	0.5	0.5	0.6	0.6	0.5	0.6	0.5	0.5	0.5	0.6	+0.1
Other opiates^j	5.7	5.7	6.4	6.0	6.2	6.3	5.9	5.3	5.1	5.2	5.9	5.2	5.3	4.6	4.4	–0.2
Stimulants^j	16.2	15.8	16.3	17.1	18.3	20.8	26.0	26.1	24.6	NA	NA	NA	NA	NA	NA	NA
Stimulants Adjusted^b,j	*NA*	*NA*	*NA*	*NA*	*NA*	*NA*	*NA*	*20.3*	*17.9*	*17.7*	*15.8*	*13.4*	*12.2*	*10.9*	*10.8*	*–0.1*
Sedatives^j	11.7	10.7	10.8	9.9	9.9	10.3	10.5	9.1	7.9	6.6	5.8	5.2	4.1	3.7	3.7	0.0
Barbiturates^j	10.7	9.6	9.3	8.1	7.5	6.8	6.6	5.5	5.2	4.9	4.6	4.2	3.6	3.2	3.3	+0.1
Methaqualone^j	5.1	4.7	5.2	4.9	5.9	7.2	7.6	6.8	5.4	3.8	2.8	2.1	1.5	1.3	1.3	0.0
Tranquilizers^j	10.6	10.3	10.8	9.9	9.6	8.7	8.0	7.0	6.9	6.1	6.1	5.8	5.5	4.8	3.8	–1.0ss
Alcohol	84.8	85.7	87.0	87.7	88.1	87.9	87.0	86.8	87.3	86.0	85.6	84.5	85.7	85.3	82.7	–2.6ss
Cigarettes	NA	NA	NA	NA	NA	NA	NA	NA	NA	NA	NA	NA	NA	NA	NA	NA

NOTES: Level of significance of difference between the two most recent classes: s = .05, ss = .01, sss = .001. NA indicates data not available.
^a Use of "any illicit drugs" includes any use of marijuana, hallucinogens, cocaine, and heroin, or any use of other opiates, stimulants, sedatives, or tranquilizers not under a doctor's orders.
^b Based on the data from the revised question, which attempts to exclude the inappropriate reporting of non-prescription stimulants.
^c Use of "other illicit drugs" includes any use of hallucinogens, cocaine, and heroin, or any use of other opiates, stimulants, sedatives, or tranquilizers not under a doctor's orders. Data based on five questionnaire forms in 1989; N is five-sixths of N indicated. See text for details.
^d Data based on four questionnaire forms in 1976–1988; N is four-fifths of N indicated. See text for details.
^e Adjusted for underreporting of amyl and butyl nitrites.
^f Data based on a single questionnaire form; N is one-fifth of N indicated in 1979–1988 and one-sixth of N indicated in 1989.
^g Question text changed slightly in 1987.
^h Adjusted for underreporting of PCP. See text for details.
^i Data based on a single questionnaire form in 1986; N is one-fifth of N indicated. Data based on two questionnaire forms in 1987–1989; N is two-fifths of N indicated in 1987–1988 and two-sixths of N indicated in 1989.
^j Only drug use which was not under a doctor's orders is included here.

TABLE 3
Trends in Thirty-Day Prevalence of Eighteen Types of Drugs

Percent who used in last thirty days

	Class of 1975	Class of 1976	Class of 1977	Class of 1978	Class of 1979	Class of 1980	Class of 1981	Class of 1982	Class of 1983	Class of 1984	Class of 1985	Class of 1986	Class of 1987	Class of 1988	Class of 1989	'88–'89 change
Approx. N =	(9400)	(15400)	(17100)	(17800)	(15500)	(15900)	(17500)	(17700)	(16300)	(15900)	(16000)	(15200)	(16300)	(16300)	(16700)	
Any Illicit Drug Use[a]	30.7	34.2	37.6	38.9	38.9	37.2	36.9	33.5	32.4	29.2	29.7	27.1	24.7	21.3	19.7	–1.6s
Adjusted Version[b]	—	—	—	—	—	—	—	32.5	30.5	—	—	—	—	—	—	
Any Illicit Drug Other Than Marijuana[c]	15.4	13.9	15.2	15.1	16.8	18.4	21.7	19.2	18.4	15.1	14.9	13.2	11.6	10.0	9.1	–0.9
Adjusted Version[b]	—	—	—	—	—	—	—	17.0	15.4	—	—	—	—	—	—	
Marijuana/Hashish	27.1	32.2	35.4	37.1	36.5	33.7	31.6	28.5	27.0	25.2	25.7	23.4	21.0	18.0	16.7	–1.3
Inhalants[d]	NA	0.9	1.3	1.5	1.7	1.4	1.5	1.5	1.7	1.9	2.2	2.5	2.8	2.6	2.3	–0.3
Inhalants Adjusted[e]	NA	NA	NA	NA	3.2	2.7	2.5	2.5	2.5	2.6	3.0	3.2	3.5	3.0	2.7	–0.3
Amyl & Butyl Nitrites[f,g]	NA	NA	NA	NA	2.4	1.8	1.4	1.1	1.4	1.4	1.6	1.3	1.3	0.6	0.6	0.0
Hallucinogens	4.7	3.4	4.1	3.9	4.0	3.7	3.7	3.4	2.8	2.6	2.5	2.5	2.5	2.2	2.2	0.0
Hallucinogens Adjusted[h]	NA	NA	NA	NA	5.3	4.4	4.5	4.1	3.5	3.2	3.8	3.5	2.8	2.3	2.9	+0.6
LSD	2.3	1.9	2.1	2.1	2.4	2.3	2.5	2.4	1.9	1.5	1.6	1.7	1.8	1.8	1.8	0.0
PCP[f,g]	NA	NA	NA	NA	2.4	1.4	1.4	1.0	1.3	1.0	1.6	1.3	0.6	0.3	1.4	+1.1sss
Cocaine	1.9	2.0	2.9	3.9	5.7	5.2	5.8	5.0	4.9	5.8	6.7	6.2	4.3	3.4	2.8	–0.6s
"Crack"[f,i]	NA	NA	NA	NA	NA	NA	NA	NA	NA	NA	NA	NA	1.3	1.6	1.4	–0.2
Other cocaine[f]	NA	NA	NA	NA	NA	NA	NA	NA	NA	NA	NA	NA	4.1	3.2	1.9	–1.3s
Heroin	0.4	0.2	0.3	0.3	0.2	0.2	0.2	0.2	0.2	0.3	0.3	0.2	0.2	0.2	0.3	+0.1
Other opiates[j]	2.1	2.0	2.8	2.1	2.4	2.4	2.1	1.8	1.8	1.8	2.3	2.0	1.8	1.6	1.6	0.0
Stimulants[j]	8.5	7.7	8.8	8.7	9.9	12.1	15.8	13.7	12.4	NA	NA	NA	NA	NA	NA	NA
Stimulants Adjusted[b,j]	NA	NA	NA	NA	NA	NA	NA	10.7	8.9	8.3	6.8	5.5	5.2	4.6	4.2	–0.4
Sedatives[j]	5.4	4.5	5.1	4.2	4.4	4.8	4.6	3.4	3.0	2.3	2.4	2.2	1.7	1.4	1.6	+0.2
Barbiturates[j]	4.7	3.9	4.3	3.2	3.2	2.9	2.6	2.0	2.1	1.7	2.0	1.8	1.4	1.2	1.4	+0.2
Methaqualone[j]	2.1	1.6	2.3	1.9	2.3	3.3	3.1	2.4	1.8	1.1	1.0	0.8	0.6	0.5	0.6	+0.1
Tranquilizers[j]	4.1	4.0	4.6	3.4	3.7	3.1	2.7	2.4	2.5	2.1	2.1	2.1	2.0	1.5	1.3	–0.2
Alcohol	68.2	68.3	71.2	72.1	71.8	72.0	70.7	69.7	69.4	67.2	65.9	65.3	66.4	63.9	60.0	–3.9ss
Cigarettes	36.7	38.8	38.4	36.7	34.4	30.5	29.4	30.0	30.3	29.3	30.1	29.6	29.4	28.7	28.6	–0.1

NOTES: Level of significance of difference between the two most recent classes: s = .05, ss = .01, sss = .001. NA indicates data not available.

[a] Use of "any illicit drugs" includes any use of marijuana, hallucinogens, cocaine, and heroin, or any use of other opiates, stimulants, sedatives, or tranquilizers not under a doctor's orders.

[b] Based on the data from the revised question, which attempts to exclude the inappropriate reporting of non-prescription stimulants.

[c] Use of "other illicit drugs" includes any use of hallucinogens, cocaine, and heroin, or any use of other opiates, stimulants, sedatives, or tranquilizers not under a doctor's orders.

[d] Data based on four questionnaire forms in 1976–1988; N is four-fifths of N indicated. Data based on five questionnaire forms in 1989; N is five-sixths of N indicated.

[e] Adjusted for underreporting of amyl and butyl nitrites. See text for details.

[f] Data based on a single questionnaire form; N is one-fifth of N indicated in 1979–1988 and one-sixth of N indicated in 1989.

[g] Question text changed slightly in 1987.

[h] Adjusted for underreporting of PCP. See text for details.

[i] Data based on two questionnaire forms; N is two-fifths of N indicated in 1987–1988 and two-sixths of N indicated in 1989.

[j] Only drug use which was not under a doctor's orders is included here.

TABLE 4

Trends in Thirty-Day Prevalence of Daily Use of Eighteen Types of Drugs

Percent who used daily in last thirty days

	Class of 1975	Class of 1976	Class of 1977	Class of 1978	Class of 1979	Class of 1980	Class of 1981	Class of 1982	Class of 1983	Class of 1984	Class of 1985	Class of 1986	Class of 1987	Class of 1988	Class of 1989	'88–'89 change
Approx. N =	(9400)	(15400)	(17100)	(17800)	(15500)	(15900)	(17500)	(17700)	(16300)	(15900)	(16000)	(15200)	(16300)	(16300)	(16700)	
Marijuana/Hashish	6.0	8.2	9.1	10.7	10.3	9.1	7.0	6.3	5.5	5.0	4.9	4.0	3.3	2.7	2.9	+0.2
Inhalants[a]	NA	0.0	0.0	0.1	0.0	0.1	0.1	0.1	0.1	0.1	0.2	0.2	0.1	0.2	0.2	0.0
Inhalants Adjusted[b]	*NA*	*NA*	*NA*	*NA*	*0.1*	*0.2*	*0.2*	*0.2*	*0.2*	*0.2*	*0.4*	*0.4*	*0.4*	*0.3*	*0.3*	*0.0*
Amyl & Butyl Nitrites[c,d]	NA	NA	NA	NA	0.0	0.1	0.1	0.0	0.2	0.1	0.3	0.5	0.3	0.1	0.3	+0.2
Hallucinogens	0.1	0.1	0.1	0.1	0.1	0.1	0.1	0.1	0.1	0.1	0.1	0.1	0.1	0.0	0.1	0.0
Hallucinogens Adjusted[e]	*NA*	*NA*	*NA*	*NA*	*0.2*	*0.2*	*0.1*	*0.2*	*0.2*	*0.2*	*0.3*	*0.3*	*0.2*	*0.0*	*0.3*	*+0.2ss*
LSD	0.0	0.0	0.0	0.0	0.0	0.0	0.1	0.0	0.1	0.1	0.1	0.0	0.1	0.0	0.0	0.0
PCP[c,d]	*NA*	*NA*	*NA*	*NA*	*0.1*	*0.1*	*0.1*	*0.1*	*0.1*	*0.1*	*0.3*	*0.2*	*0.3*	*0.1*	*0.2*	*+0.1*
Cocaine	0.1	0.1	0.1	0.1	0.2	0.2	0.3	0.2	0.2	0.2	0.4	0.4	0.3	0.2	0.3	+0.1
"Crack"[f]	NA	NA	NA	NA	NA	NA	NA	NA	NA	NA	NA	NA	0.1	0.1	0.2	+0.1
Other cocaine[c]	*NA*	*NA*	*NA*	*NA*	*NA*	*NA*	*NA*	*NA*	*NA*	*NA*	*NA*	*NA*	*0.2*	*0.2*	*0.1*	*−0.1*
Heroin	0.1	0.0	0.0	0.0	0.0	0.0	0.0	0.0	0.1	0.0	0.0	0.0	0.0	0.0	0.1	+0.1
Other opiates[g]	0.1	0.1	0.2	0.1	0.0	0.1	0.1	0.1	0.1	0.1	0.1	0.1	0.1	0.1	0.2	0.0
Stimulants[g]	0.5	0.4	0.5	0.5	0.6	0.7	1.2	1.1	1.1	NA	NA	NA	NA	NA	NA	NA
Stimulants Adjusted[g,h]	*NA*	*NA*	*NA*	*NA*	*NA*	*NA*	*NA*	*0.7*	*0.8*	*0.6*	*0.4*	*0.3*	*0.3*	*0.3*	*0.3*	*0.0*
Sedatives[g]	0.3	0.2	0.2	0.2	0.1	0.2	0.2	0.2	0.2	0.1	0.1	0.1	0.1	0.1	0.1	+0.1
Barbiturates[g]	0.1	0.1	0.2	0.1	0.0	0.1	0.1	0.1	0.1	0.0	0.1	0.1	0.1	0.0	0.1	0.0
Methaqualones	0.0	0.0	0.0	0.0	0.0	0.1	0.1	0.1	0.0	0.0	0.0	0.0	0.0	0.1	0.0	0.0
Tranquilizers[g]	0.1	0.2	0.3	0.1	0.1	0.1	0.1	0.1	0.1	0.1	0.0	0.0	0.1	0.0	0.1	0.0
Alcohol																
Daily	5.7	5.6	6.1	5.7	6.9	6.0	6.0	5.7	5.5	4.8	5.0	4.8	4.8	4.2	4.2	0.0
5 + drinks in a row/ last 2 weeks	36.8	37.1	39.4	40.3	41.2	41.2	41.4	40.5	40.8	38.7	36.7	36.8	37.5	34.7	33.0	−1.7
Cigarettes																
Daily	26.9	28.8	28.8	27.5	25.4	21.3	20.3	21.1	21.2	18.7	19.5	18.7	18.7	18.1	18.9	+0.8
Half-pack or more per day	17.9	19.2	19.4	18.8	16.5	14.3	13.5	14.2	13.8	12.3	12.5	11.4	11.4	10.6	11.2	+0.6

NOTES Level of significance of difference between the two most recent classes: s = .05, ss = .01, sss = .001. NA indicated data not available.
[a]Data based on four questionnaire forms in 1976–1988; N is four-fifths of N indicated. See text for details.
[b]Adjusted for underreporting of amyl and butyl nitrites.
[c]Data based on a single questionnaire form; N is one-fifth of N indicated in 1979–1988 and one-sixth of N indicated in 1989.
[d]Question text changed slightly in 1987.
[e]Adjusted for underreporting of PCP. See text for details.
[f]Data based on two questionnaire forms; N is two-fifths of N indicated in 1987–1988 and two-sixths of N indicated in 1989.
[g]Only drug use which was not under a doctor's orders is included here.
[h]Based on the data from the revised quesiton, which attempts to exclude the inappropriate reporting of non-prescription stimulants.
[i]Any apparent inconsistency between the change estimate and the prevalence estimates for the two most recent classes is due to rounding error.

Epidemiology of Alcohol Consumption

Introduction

During the 1980s we have seen a gradual but consistent downturn in per capita alcohol consumption in the United States after two decades of steady increases. The change could simply represent a temporary plateau in the long upswing that characterized consumption during the 1960s and 1970s. However, parallel declines have been noted in many other countries, particularly in the industrialized West, and there have been slight decreases in some indicators of alcohol abuse such as mortality from liver cirrhosis and from alcoholism. Further, population surveys indicate increases in abstention, especially among men, and decreases in alcohol consumption among adolescents. These changes may lend support to the view that the drop in alcohol consumption over the past few years may presage a "drier" era. On the other hand, there is evidence of an increasing proportion of heavy drinkers among young people in their twenties and a small increase in the prevalence of dependence problems—findings that underline the importance of continued surveillance.

With a view toward further examination of patterns and trends in alcohol use and abuse, this chapter describes recent findings related to alcohol consumption, alcohol-related morbidity and mortality, and adverse social consequences of alcohol use and abuse, both in the general population and in several population subgroups: women, adolescents and young adults, older adults, the homeless, and racial and ethnic minorities.

Consumption
Per Capita Consumption

The amount of alcohol consumed in the United States is estimated on the basis of alcohol sales in each State as determined from tax receipts, sales in State-controlled stores, and/or reports from beverage industry sources. These overall statistics do not include estimates of home production, illegal production, breakage, or untaxed alcohol brought in by tourists. Apparent per capita consumption is determined by dividing total alcohol, derived from sales, by the total population aged 14 or older. The term "apparent" is used because these estimates artificially attribute average consumption to all persons in this population, regardless of their actual consumption.

Per capita consumption is expressed in gallons of pure alcohol calculated by multiplying total gallons of each beverage type by a conversion factor (0.045 for beer, 0.129 for wine, and 0.411 for spirits). In 1987, apparent per capita consumption of alcohol was 2.54 gallons of pure alcohol, the

From *Alcohol and Health*, January 1990, pp. 13-20. *Alcohol and Health*, from the Secretary of Health and Human Services, U.S. Department of Health and Human Services.

lowest level since 1970 (NIAAA 1989). Nevertheless, alcohol is used by more Americans than any other drug, including cigarette tobacco. In a U.S. household survey of persons aged 12 and over, 73.4 percent reported drinking alcohol in the past year; 36.2 percent reported smoking cigarettes (NIDA 1988). Figure 1, illustrating the pattern of per capita consumption from 1977 through 1987, shows the peaking of total alcohol consumption in 1980 and 1981 with the subsequent continuing decline.

The major component of the decrease was the large decline in consumption of spirits, which dropped to 0.83 gallons of pure alcohol per capita in 1987—the lowest consumption level for spirits since 1958. Beer consumption remained at the 1986 level of 1.34 gallons per capita, the lowest level of beer consumption since 1978 and 4 percent lower than the 1981 peak level of 1.39 gallons (see fig. 2). For the first time in more than 10 years, wine consumption did not increase.

One suggested reason for the steady decline in alcohol consumption since 1981 is an increase in public awareness of the risks associated with alcohol use and abuse. Changing demographics may be another reason, as the proportion of the population that is over age 60 continues to increase; alcohol consumption in this age group is relatively low. The increasingly conservative cultural climate that has prevailed during the 1980s, with associated decreases in the social acceptability of heavy drinking, could be another factor. Tastes appear to have turned away from distilled spirits and toward beverages with lower alcohol content. For example, wine coolers, which did not exist in 1982, accounted for one-fourth of total wine consumption in 1986 (NIAAA 1988b). Decreases in alcohol consumption may also be re-

lated to increasing concern with overall health and fitness as exemplified by current trends toward reductions in smoking and increased emphasis on nutrition and exercise.

Although estimates of consumption levels for other countries are somewhat variable (Horgan et al. 1986; PGD 1987), apparent per capita consumption began to level off in most industrialized countries except the United States in the mid-1970s, and by the mid-1980s many were experiencing declines. Of 25 countries surveyed between 1979 and 1984, nearly two-thirds experienced declines or stability in consumption (Horgan et al. 1986) (see fig. 3). Only four of the nine countries where consumption increased had rates of increase greater than 1 percent. In contrast, consumption in some of the developing countries has continued to increase (Hilton and Johnstone 1988).

Geographic Differences

Table 1 lists the total apparent per capita alcohol consumption for the 50 States and the District of Columbia in 1977 and 1986 and ranks them by 1986 decile. These figures should be interpreted with caution because they do not necessarily reflect true consumption levels of State residents. For example, consumption in the District of Columbia is affected both by a high level of tourism and by the fact that residents of nearby Virginia and Maryland take advantage of the District's lower alcohol taxes. A high proportion of Nevada's 1 million residents are Mormons and are therefore more likely to be abstainers; however, as a center for conventions and tourism, the State is visited by approximately 26 million people per year.

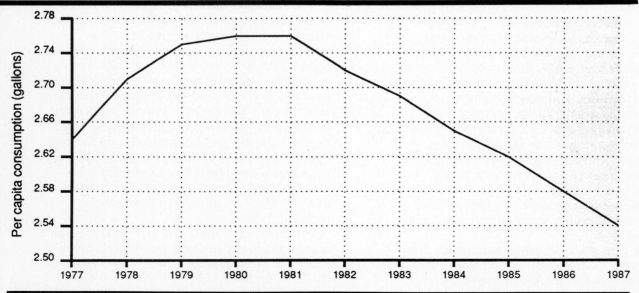

FIGURE 1. Apparent U.S. per capita consumption of pure alcohol, 1977–1987.
SOURCE: NIAAA 1989.

The State decile rankings remained fairly consistent between 1977 and 1986. Although many States have experienced substantial increases or decreases in apparent per capita consumption, there has been little change in their relative rankings. Changes in per capita consumption in the 50 States and the District of Columbia between 1977 and 1986 are illustrated in figure 4, which shows the greatest decreases in the District of Columbia, Hawaii, Montana, Nevada, New Hampshire, West Virginia, and Wyoming, and the greatest increase in Virginia.

When the States are grouped by U.S. census region as shown in table 2, it is apparent that both per capita consumption and numbers of abstainers differentiate the regions in terms of relative "wetness" or "dryness" (Hilton 1988b). Per capita consumption is highest in the wetter Pacific and New England States. However, if consumption is calculated for drinkers only (excluding abstainers), the highest consumption per drinker is found in the drier Mountain and southern regions. Although there are fewer drinkers in these drier States, it appears that they consume more alcohol per capita than drinkers in the other regions. However, it is possible that some drinkers in the drier regions may report themselves to be abstainers because of prevailing social attitudes toward drinking.

Although there were few important indications of regional differences in the prevalence of heavy drinking, men in the drier regions experienced significantly more alcohol-related problems, particularly in the areas of belliger-ence, accidents, problems with police, and problems with friends or spouse (Hilton 1988b). Again, this difference could be a consequence of the less tolerant attitudes prevalent in a relatively abstinent social milieu.

Patterns of Consumption

Drinking patterns and consumption levels are estimated on the basis of individual responses to questions in general population surveys. These surveys may differ in the wording of questions, and thus the information elicited concerning drinking quantity and frequency may not always be comparable. However, these studies do provide valuable information on overall drinking patterns and on changes and trends in these patterns.

Probably the most important differences between surveys are in the construction of typologies of drinking behavior (Room in press). One system of classifying drinkers is based on the average daily quantity of alcohol consumed (Hilton 1988d; Malin et al. 1986; Williams et al. 1986; S. Wilsnack 1987). Another system combines quantity consumed per occasion with drinking frequency (Cahalan et al. 1969). A variation of this system, designated "volmax," combines volume of monthly intake with maximum amount consumed per occasion (Hilton and Clark 1987). Knupfer (1987a) combines frequency of drinking (daily, weekly, or less than weekly) with the frequency of consuming specific amounts (from 1 or 2 drinks up to 12 or more).

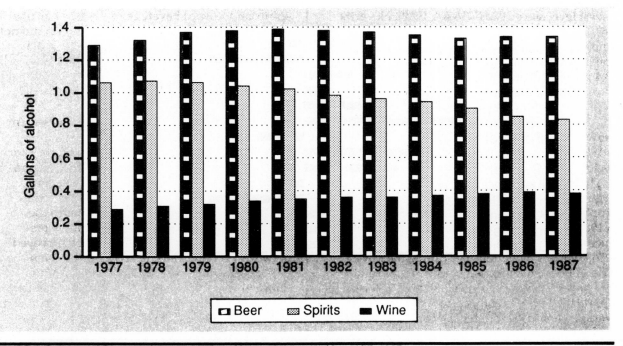

FIGURE 2. Apparent U.S. per capita consumption of beer, wine, and spirits, 1977–1987.
SOURCE: NIAAA 1989.

4. PATTERNS AND TRENDS IN DRUG USE

This system permits the evaluation of quantity and frequency both separately and in combination. A category for the frequency of getting drunk may also be included (Hilton 1988a; Knupfer 1984, 1987a,b).

Two surveys that included identically worded questions, and thus provided a basis for valid comparison, examined drinking patterns and drinking problems over a 17-year span from 1967 to 1984 (Hilton and Clark 1987). The study found few significant changes in reported consumption patterns during this 17-year period, except for a small increase in the proportion of abstainers (from 29 percent to 32 percent). Among men, the increase in abstention rates was statistically significant.

A comparison of results from 11 different surveys conducted during the 20 years from 1964 to 1984 provided a greater number of data points but at the cost of diminished comparability (Hilton 1988d). This study also showed stability in overall drinking patterns, consistent with findings of Hilton and Clark (1987). The 1988 study (Hilton 1988d) used higher cutpoints to define heavy drinking than those used in the Hilton and Clark study, with the result that changes at the higher end of the drinking spectrum were revealed. For example, compared with Hilton and Clark (1987), Hilton (1988d) defined heavy drinking in terms of a higher number of drinks consumed per month, a greater frequency of consuming five or more drinks per occasion, and getting drunk at least once a week (a measure that was not considered in the 1964 survey). Using these criteria, Hilton (1988d) found increases in heavy drinking among men, particularly those aged 21 to 34, and also among women in the same age group. As guides for future research, these findings highlight the importance, stressed by Knupfer (1987b), of using cutpoints that are high enough both to differentiate the heaviest drinking levels and to detect patterns and changes at these levels.

Men are more likely than women to be drinkers and to be heavier drinkers. The hypothesis has often been advanced that drinking and heavy drinking have been increasing among women, resulting in a convergence of drinking

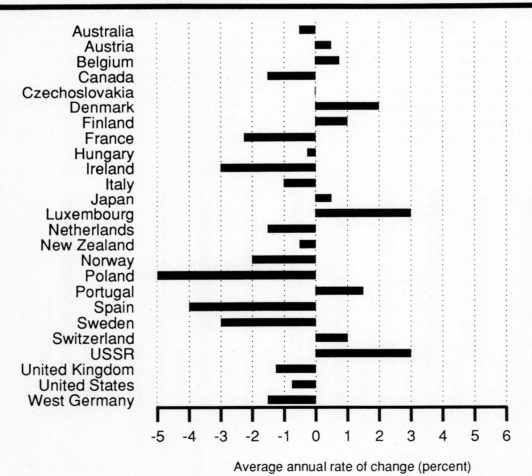

FIGURE 3. Average annual rate of change (percent) in per capita alcohol consumption for 25 countries, 1979–1984.
SOURCE: Horgan et al. 1986.

TABLE 1. Apparent per capita alcohol consumption for the 50 States and the District of Columbia, 1977 and 1986, with decile rankings for 1986

State	Per capita consumption (gallons)		Decile
	1977	1986	(1986)
Alabama	1.96	1.91	9
Alaska	3.31	3.52	1
Arizona	3.10	3.15	2
Arkansas	1.65	1.64	10
California	3.25	3.12	2
Colorado	3.01	2.88	3
Connecticut	2.61	2.80	3
Delaware	2.91	3.13	2
District of Columbia	5.53	5.67	1
Florida	3.13	2.97	2
Georgia	2.47	2.44	6
Hawaii	3.23	2.89	3
Idaho	2.52	2.33	7
Illinois	2.87	2.68	4
Indiana	2.05	2.15	8
Iowa	2.17	2.05	9
Kansas	1.88	1.89	9
Kentucky	2.03	1.85	10
Louisiana	2.57	2.43	7
Maine	2.64	2.56	5
Maryland	3.05	2.76	4
Massachusetts	2.95	2.97	2
Michigan	2.71	2.57	5
Minnesota	2.65	2.56	5
Mississippi	2.05	2.05	9
Missouri	2.25	2.37	7
Montana	3.12	2.74	4
Nebraska	2.53	2.28	7
Nevada	6.84	5.07	1
New Hampshire	5.32	4.52	1
New Jersey	2.69	2.78	3
New Mexico	2.93	2.70	4
New York	2.74	2.55	6
North Carolina	2.05	2.16	8
North Dakota	2.62	2.40	7
Ohio	2.04	2.18	8
Oklahoma	1.98	1.81	10
Oregon	2.74	2.54	6
Pennsylvania	2.29	2.23	8
Rhode Island	2.93	2.87	3
South Carolina	2.49	2.50	6

patterns between men and women. Fillmore (1984), addressing this question in a cohort analysis, found overall consistency in women's drinking patterns for 1964, 1967, and 1979, with the exception of a shift toward more frequent heavy drinking in the younger cohorts. Women in their twenties in 1979, particularly those who were employed, had a higher rate of frequent

TABLE 1. (continued)

State	Per capita consumption (gallons)		Decile (1986)
	1977	1986	
South Dakota	2.38	2.24	8
Tennessee	1.91	1.96	9
Texas	2.58	2.63	5
Utah	1.70	1.58	10
Vermont	3.44	3.18	1
Virginia	2.30	2.53	6
Washington	2.89	2.66	4
West Virginia	1.85	1.84	10
Wisconsin	3.31	3.16	2
Wyoming	3.31	2.64	5

SOURCE: NIAAA 1988b.

NOTE: Placement in the first decile indicates that a State ranks among the top 10 percent in total per capita consumption, placement in the second decile indicates the top 20 percent, and so on.

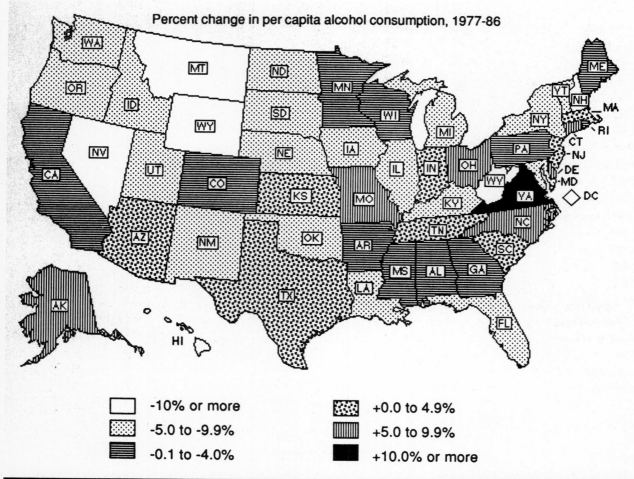

FIGURE 4. Trends in alcohol consumption: percent change in apparent per capita consumption of alcohol (gallons), United States, 1977–1986.
SOURCE: NIAAA 1988b.

heavy drinking than did earlier cohorts measured at the same age. These findings suggest the possibility that changes may be taking place cur-

rently among younger cohorts. Followup surveys are needed to trace the drinking patterns of these women as they age. Findings of this analysis are

TABLE 2. Distribution of apparent per capita alcohol consumption (in gallons of pure alcohol), percentage of abstainers, and apparent per-drinker consumption in the nine U.S. census regions, 1964, 1979, and 1984

Region	Apparent per capita consumption (gallons)			Abstainers (percent)			Apparent per-drinker consumption (gallons)		
	1964	1979	1984	1964	1979	1984	1964	1979	1984
Wetter regions									
New England	2.48	3.14	3.08	21	18	28	3.14	3.78	4.28
Mid-Atlantic	2.41	2.67	2.57	17	25	18	2.92	3.53	3.13
East North Central	2.26	2.67	2.57	25	29	27	3.04	3.75	3.52
West North Central	1.82	2.45	2.32	34	38	20	2.77	3.95	2.90
Pacific	2.55	3.38	3.09	27	16	26	3.47	3.99	4.18
Mean	2.30	2.86	2.73	25	25	24	3.07	3.80	3.60
Drier Regions									
South Atlantic	1.89	2.81	2.68	42	50	38	3.27	5.44	4.32
East South Central	1.01	1.95	1.93	65	66	56	2.87	5.48	4.39
West South Central	1.71	2.62	2.58	38	38	42	2.76	4.21	4.45
Mountain	2.08	3.29	2.96	42	38	38	3.58	5.31	4.77
Mean	1.67	2.67	2.54	47	48	44	3.12	5.11	4.48

SOURCE: Hilton 1988b.

consistent with those of Hilton (1987b, 1988d), who also found stability in women's drinking patterns, with the exception of a similar increase in the proportion of heavy drinkers among younger women.

Temple (1987) analyzed surveys of college students in 1979, 1981, and 1984 and found that alcohol consumption decreased somewhat among both males and females during this time, but differences in drinking levels between males and females remained the same. Thus there had been no convergence in patterns of alcohol use between college-age men and women.

Results of a 1981 survey of women's drinking indicated that younger women were most likely to report frequent heavy drinking and repeated intoxication (R. Wilsnack et al. 1984). However, comparison of this survey with results of several earlier surveys showed that when only drinkers were compared, the greatest increase in the proportion of heavier drinkers was in the 35-to-49 age group. Overall, the 1981 survey results showed that although there is no evidence of any major increase in women's drinking, indications are that some of those who do drink may be drinking more heavily. The result could be future increases in alcohol-related problems among women.

As S. Wilsnack (1987) pointed out, perceptions that drinking patterns of men and women are converging, despite the lack of empirical evidence, may reflect in part a delayed social reaction to earlier changes in women's drinking (i.e., between World War II and the early 1970s). Another possible explanation for this perception of increased drinking by women may be the increased visibility of women's alcohol problems as more women seek treatment. . . .

References

Cahalan, D., I. H. Cisin, and H. M. Crossley. 1969. *American Drinking Practices: A National Study of Drinking Behavior and Attitudes.* New Brunswick, N.J.: Rutgers Center of Alcohol Studies.

Fillmore, K. M. 1984. "When Angels Fall":

Women's Drinking as Cultural Preoccupation and as Reality. In S. C. Wilsnack and L. J. Beckman (eds.), *Alcohol Problems in Women.* New York: Guilford Press.

Hilton, M. E. 1988a. Demographic Distribution of Drinking Patterns in 1984. *Drug and Alcohol Dependence,* 22 (1): 37–47.

Hilton, M. E. 1988b. Regional Diversity in United States Drinking Practices, *British Journal of Addiction,* 85: 519–532.

Hilton, M. E. 1988d. Trends in U.S. Drinking Patterns: Further Evidence from the Past 20 Years. *British Journal of Addiction,* 83: 269–278.

Hilton, M. E., and W. B. Clark. 1987. Changes in American Drinking Patterns and Problems, 1967–1984. *Journal of Studies in Alcohol,* 48: 515–522.

Horgan, M. M., M. D. Sparrow, and R. Brazeau. 1986. *Alcoholic Beverage Taxation and Control Policies* (6th ed.). Ottawa: Brewers Association of Canada.

Knupfer, G. 1984. The Risks of Drunkenness (or, *ebrietas resurrecta*): A Comparison of Frequent Intoxication Indices and of Population Subgroups as to Problem Risks. *British Journal of Addiction,* 29: 185–196.

Knupfer, G. 1987a. Drinking For Health: The Daily Light Drinker Fiction. *British Journal of Addiction,* 82: 547–555.

Knupfer, G. 1987b. New Directions for Survey Research in the Study of Alcoholic Beverage Consumption. *British Journal of Addiction,* 82: 583–585.

Malin, H., et al. 1986. Health Practices Supplement. Epidemiologic Bulletin No. 10. *Alcohol Health and Research World,* 10 (2): 48–50.

NIAAA (National Institute on Alcohol Abuse and Alcoholism). 1988b. *Apparent Per Capita Alcohol Consumption: National, State, and Regional Trends, 1977–1986,* by R. A. Stefens et al. Surveillance Report No. 10. Rockville, Md.: NIAAA.

NIAAA (National Institute on Alcohol Abuse and Alcoholism). 1989. *Apparent Per Capita Alcohol Consumption: National, State, and Regional Trends, 1977–1987.* Surveillance Report No. 13. Rockville, Md.: NIAAA.

NIDA (National Institute on Drug Abuse). 1988. *Highlights from the 1987 National Drug and Alcoholism Treatment Unit Survey (NDATUS).* Rockville, Md.: NIDA.

Room, R. In press. Measuring Alcohol Consumption in the U.S.: Methods and Rationales. In *Research Advances in Alcohol and Drug Problems.* New York: Plenum Press.

Temple, M. T. 1987. Alcohol Use Among Male and Female College Students: Has There Been a Convergence? *Youth and Society,* 19: 44–72.

Williams, G. D., M. Dufour, and D. Bertolucci, 1986. Drinking Levels, Knowledge, and Associated Characteristics, 1985 NHIS Findings. *Public Health Reports,* 101: 593–598.

Wilsnack, R. W., S. C. Wilsnack, and A. Klassen, 1984. Women's Drinking and Drinking Problems: Patterns From a 1981 National Survey. *American Journal of Public Health,* 74: 1231–1238.

Wilsnack, S. C. 1987. Drinking and Drinking Problems in Women: A U.S. Longitudinal Survey and Some Implications for Prevention. In T. Loberg et al. (eds.), *Addictive Behaviors: Prevention and Early Intervention.* Amsterdam, Netherlands: Swets & Zeitlinger, pp. 1–39.

A Penchant for Prohibition?

Smoking Becomes 'Deviant Behavior'

Laura Mansnerus

It was cause for a libel award when a Chicago television commentator said in 1981 that the Brown & Williamson Tobacco Corporation was trying to snare teen-agers with advertisements relating smoking to drugs, alcohol and sex. The idea, the commentator had said, was to present cigarettes as "an illicit pleasure."

Whether the industry meant to send the message or not, illicit is what cigarettes have become.

"Smoking is quickly becoming a deviant behavior," said Barry Glassner, a sociology professor at Hunter College and Syracuse University. "It's not just seen as something that's unhealthy or irrational."

The recent pace of regulation has surprised even the antismoking organizations.

According to Action on Smoking and Health, an advocacy group, 23 states restrict smoking in restaurants, up from 14 a year ago, and 15 have regulations for private workplaces, up from 10 a year ago. More than half of American companies restrict smoking on the job. There are hundreds of municipal ordinances. New York's, which took effect April 6, is fairly typical of the new ones; it bans smoking in most enclosed public places and segregates smokers in restaurants and workplaces. As of yesterday, the Federal Aviation Administration prohibits smoking on flights of two hours or less, and Northwest Airlines forbids smoking on all its North American flights.

There are less official signs of disapproval, too. Corporate annual reports never picture the executives with cigarettes anymore, one consultant noted. The cover of this month's Reader's Digest asks, "Is Smoking Ruining Your Sex Life?"

"In the last two years we've made

1936 magazine advertisement.

more progress than in the previous 30," said Robert A. Rosner, executive director of the Smoking Policy Institute in Seattle, a nonprofit group that advises employers. The reason given most frequently for the change is new data on passive smoking, described in the 1986 Surgeon General's report and in another 1986 report by the National Research Council, which estimated that ambient smoke might cause 2,400 lung cancer deaths annually among nonsmokers.

"The one humongous issue is that the average person can justify harming themselves, but can't justify harming somebody else," Mr. Rosner said.

Some sociologists see something more complicated at work. Professor Glassner, the author of a forthcoming book on attitudes about fitness and health, finds a "craving for control" reflected in all kinds of worries about the body.

"There are so many dangers that are large scale and that we feel we have no control over, particularly in the environment, that this is a way to gain control," he said.

Peter L. Berger, a Boston University sociologist, calls the New York ordinance a "viable democratic compromise" but casts the controversy in terms of class. "It's not surprising that the upper-middle-class agenda has been successful," he said, adding that the wave of regulation is a "delightfully close rerun of Prohibition."

While hesitating to judge the evidence on passive smoking, he said it appeared to be "much, much weaker" than that on active smoking. "The reason it's become so important," he said, "is not because of the weight of the evidence but because of the ideological usefulness of the idea."

"Most people are not in a position to evaluate this evidence. What people believe comes from placing faith in a certain authority. People say, 'The Surgeon General said so.' Well, who's the Surgeon General?"

Professor Glassner, who noted that he "hates" smoke, said, "There is a cost involved in smoking bans. You're taking away a group's prerogatives. This is a country in which we value individual freedoms, and we ought to be extremely careful about which ones we take away."

A libertarian strain persists even among nonsmokers. Dave Brenton, president of the Smoker's Rights Alliance of Mesa, Ariz., said about 20 percent of the group's 700 to 800 members are nonsmokers. "They understand that it's an individual rights issue," he said. "Who knows what they'll take away tomorrow?"

But Mr. Rosner said most restrictions do not keep smokers from maintaining their habit. "My term for this is '80's-style temperance," he said. "Smoke all

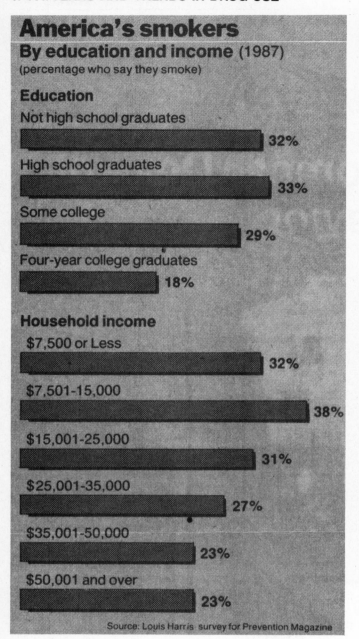

America's smokers
By education and income (1987)
(percentage who say they smoke)

Education

Not high school graduates
32%

High school graduates
33%

Some college
29%

Four-year college graduates
18%

Household income

$7,500 or Less
32%

$7,501-15,000
38%

$15,001-25,000
31%

$25,001-35,000
27%

$35,001-50,000
23%

$50,001 and over
23%

Source: Louis Harris survey for Prevention Magazine

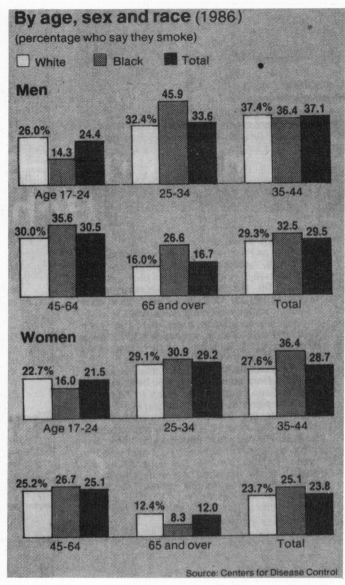

By age, sex and race (1986)
(percentage who say they smoke)

□ White   ▨ Black   ■ Total

Men

Age 17-24: White 26.0%, Black 14.3, Total 24.4
25-34: White 32.4%, Black 45.9, Total 33.6
35-44: White 37.4%, Black 36.4, Total 37.1

45-64: White 30.0%, Black 35.6, Total 30.5
65 and over: White 16.0%, Black 26.6, Total 16.7
Total: White 29.3%, Black 32.5, Total 29.5

Women

Age 17-24: White 22.7%, Black 16.0, Total 21.5
25-34: White 29.1%, Black 30.9, Total 29.2
35-44: White 27.6%, Black 36.4, Total 28.7

45-64: White 25.2%, Black 26.7, Total 25.1
65 and over: White 12.4%, Black 8.3, Total 12.0
Total: White 23.7%, Black 25.1, Total 23.8

Source: Centers for Disease Control

you want—just don't do it in public places."

Indeed, anti-tobacco forces have known fiercer days. In early New England, blue laws penalized public smoking. Prohibition revived the sentiment; between 1920 and 1930, even as per capita consumption doubled, several states prohibited the sale of tobacco.

Respectability came with World War II, when cigarettes were included with K-rations, and it was not until the mid-1960's—the first Surgeon General's report on smoking was issued in 1964—that the decline began. In 1966, according to the Federal Centers for Disease Control, 42.4 percent of the American population smoked; in 1986, 26.5 percent did.

After the 1964 report, popular images of smoking changed, too. Cigarette ads were purged from the airwaves, "Thank You for Not Smoking" signs appeared, and Humphrey Bogart and John Wayne died of lung cancer.

EDUCATION AND INCOME

Clearly, the message has had the greatest effect among the upper-middle class. There is a strong negative correlation between smoking and income and education, though not much difference by race: According to the Centers for Disease Control, 28.4 percent of blacks and 26.4 percent of whites are smokers.

In the current climate, smokers have

been generally compliant. John M. Pinney, executive director of the Institute for the Study of Smoking Behavior and Policy at Harvard University, said its surveys of attitudes about the Cambridge, Mass., ordinance showed very little desire for confrontation.

"We're a very individual-minded nation in many ways," he said, "but we also tend to seek permission for the things we want to do."

Most experts do not predict the eradication of smoking, not even in public places, but expect it to become less and less acceptable. "If this pattern continues," said Professor Glassner, "we'll have a homogenized population in which everybody will be within the recommended weight ranges, and nobody will smoke anymore, and nobody will drink, and everybody will work out."

"As I say this," he added, "I realize some people think this would be an ideal society."

Rich vs. Poor: Drug Patterns Are Diverging

Peter Kerr

Americans generally appear to be turning away from the use of illegal drugs, but, at the same time, the poor face mounting deaths and an ever bleaker future as a result of drug abuse, according to Government statistics and interviews with drug experts around the country.

What may be emerging, some experts believe, is a tale of two drug problems: one in middle-class America, which may be over the worst of a 20-year mass experiment with illegal drugs, the other in the America of the poor, where, amid hopelessness and lack of education, people will suffer the worst consequences of cocaine, heroin and AIDS.

"We are dealing with two different worlds here," said Dr. David F. Musto, a professor of psychiatry and history of medicine at Yale University who has written extensively on the history of drug-use epidemics.

Incentives to Stop

"The question we must be asking now is not why people take drugs, but why do people stop," Dr. Musto said. "In the inner city, the factors that counterbalance drug use—family, employment, status within the community—often are not there. It is harder for people with nothing to say no to drugs."

In recent years, the focus of greatest concern among drug experts has been cocaine, for while the use of other drugs was dropping or remaining stable, cocaine grew widely in popularity throughout the nation in the late 1970's and early 1980's.

Findings from two major Federal studies on drug use in America show that in the last few years, better-educated young people have been reducing their use of cocaine and other drugs.

Meanwhile, the least-educated have increasingly used cocaine.

Experts caution that their conclusions are tentative and that the rise of a new drug or the appearance of other unpredictable factors could easily upset current trends. And, whatever the trends, they say, drug use is so widespread that it will remain a problem in all sectors of society for years to come.

A Mixed Message

However, they point to a newly emerging picture of drug use in America that, they say, carries a mixed message of hope for the well-off and despair for the poor. Among their major conclusions are these:

• With the exception of heroin and crack among the poor, the use of illegal drugs in the nation appears to have peaked, including snorting powdered cocaine.

• Federally financed studies show that the people turning away from drugs are the most educated and affluent. The poorest and least-educated have continued or have increased their drug use.

• Crack, a smokable form of cocaine, has largely remained a poor people's drug. Its rise in the past two years has had devastating effects on poor neighborhoods, but it has failed to make the same inroads into the middle class.

• The most deadly impact of illegal drug use is probably yet to come, as tens of thousands of intravenous drug users, their sexual partners and their children contract acquired immune deficiency syndrome. Most of those people will be poor.

Several drug treatment experts voiced concern that as the casualties of drug abuse shift increasingly into the ghetto, the drug issue may become less visible to many Americans and receive less attention from government.

Putting Pressure on Legislators

"In the heroin crisis of the late 1960's and again with crack in recent years it was the threat to the middle- and upper-middle-class kids that put pressure on legislatures and Congress," said Dr. Mitchell S. Rosenthal, the president of Phoenix House, the operator of drug treatment centers in New York and California. "There is a danger that if they feel less of a threat, the resources won't stay with the problem."

Some scholars say societies experience widespread drug use in historic cycles. From 1885 to 1920, the United States experienced an epidemic of narcotics and cocaine use. Dr. Musto argues that a similar epidemic began in about 1965, but that it took years for casualties to mount and for society to react against drugs.

Statistics indicate that outside of the poorest neighborhoods, the nation's 20-year affair with illegal drugs is on the decline.

According to the National Institute on Drug Abuse, marijuana use peaked in 1978, and by 1985, 7 out of 10 high school seniors believed marijuana use to be harmful. Young people's use of hallucinogens, like LSD, and PCP, or "angel dust," has fallen since 1979 as well.

In 1985, a national household survey conducted by the University of Kentucky for the National Institute on Drug Abuse asked 18- to 25-year-olds if they had smoked marijuana in the last month. It found that people who never graduated from high school were most likely to be using the drug. The better educated the young people were, the survey found, the less they were using marijuana.

Among an earlier generation of smokers—people over 35 who probably developed their attitudes toward marijuana in the late 60's and early 70's—the findings were just the reverse. It was the college-educated who were most likely to be smoking marijuana.

Another study found similar results. The survey, conducted for the National Institute on Drug Abuse by the University of Michigan Institute for Social Research asked high-school seniors what drugs other than marijuana they had used in the previous month.

The survey found that in 1986, seniors of all economic backgrounds were using drugs less than seniors were in 1981. But the greatest change took place among students whose parents had some graduate education: a drop of 13 percentage points, from 36.7 percent to 23.7 percent. The least change took place among students whose parents had never been to high school: a drop of 2.7 percentage points, from 25.4 percent to 22.7 percent.

Flooding Across the Border

What confused the situation last year was cocaine, which had been rising in use since the late 70's. By last year, the white powder was flooding across the nation's southern border and was suddenly appearing in urban areas in the new smokable form of crack; from 1982 to 1986, the number of deaths and emergency room reports involving cocaine quadrupled.

For a time, experts feared that the pellet form of cocaine, which is much more quickly addicting than cocaine powder, would spread to all segments of society, including the middle-class and affluent, who were using powdered cocaine. But it now appears that the growth of crack has leveled off in New York and many other cities around the country, law-enforcement and treatment officials say.

"In general we believe that cocaine has reached its peak," said David L. LeRoy, the chief of domestic intelligence with the cocaine desk of the Federal Drug Administration. "It is going to take a few months to have the numbers to prove it, but we feel fairly optimistic about it."

Drugs and the Influence of Education

Percentage of high school seniors from a nationwide survey who said they used an illegal drug other than marijuana in the last year. Listed according to the education level of parents.

PARENTS' EDUCATION: ☐ 1981   ▨ 1986

Less than high school
25.4%
22.7%

Some high school
32.7%
26.4%

High school graduates
33.3%
26.2%

Some college
34.7%
26.6%

College graduates
34.8%
24.9%

Some graduate school
36.7%
23.7%

Source: University of Michigan

Tracing the Growth in Appetite

The amount of cocaine entering the country could still be rising, Mr. LeRoy said, but the number of users appears to have leveled off or may be dropping. In other words, he said, the growth in America's cocaine appetite can be traced to its most severe addicts, many of them inner-city crack addicts.

According to the household survey of 18- to 25-year-olds, the people most likely to have used cocaine in the previous month in 1982 were those who graduated from college. The least likely to have used cocaine were those who never finished high school. Among college graduates, 11 percent said they had used cocaine in the past month, while among those without high school diplomas, only 4 percent had used cocaine.

But by 1985, the situation was just the opposite. Only 3 percent of college graduates said they used cocaine in the last month. But 10 percent of people who never finished high school said they used the drug. Since the survey did not include people without homes, it may have understated drug use among the poorest and least-educated, according to Prof. Harwin Voss of the University of Kentucky, who helped direct the study.

There is still evidence of middle-class crack use with severe consequences for those who have become addicted. In addition, treatment experts say "freebasing," or smoking of powdered cocaine, which has the same effect as smoking crack, is popular in some circles of middle-class and affluent drug users.

Nonetheless, the New York State Division of Substance Abuse Services and the Los Angeles County Office of Drug Abuse report that most crack users appearing at hospitals and treatment centers are poor members of minority groups.

Such observations about crack and the poor are echoed by other drug treatment experts around the nation.

"Crack seems to have become entrenched in the inner-city areas," said James Hall, the director of Up Front, a drug research foundation based in Miami. "With cocaine we are going to see a shrinking number of users who are going to be at greater risk from the drug. They are the poorest, the least educated, who have the least access to information."

But perhaps the most dire vision of the future concerns the intravenous users of heroin, a drug that has remained predominantly the preserve of the inner-city poor.

While the number of addicts around the nation has remained relatively stable, there has been an alarming rise in the proportion of addicts exposed to the AIDS virus from the sharing of needles.

While only a comparatively small fraction of heroin addicts died from overdoses each year between 20 and 100 percent of those exposed to AIDS are expected to die from the disease.

Among heroin addicts entering drug treatment in New York, more than 60 percent are now testing positive for ex-posure to the virus, said Dr. Beny J. Primm, the executive director of the Addiction Research and Treatment Corporation, a drug treatment program in New York.

Dr. Primm described his vision of the future for the poorest black neighborhoods in New York, where homelessness and family disintegration are already rife.

"Five years from now, those people who are alive then, will find their ranks devastated by AIDS, and there will be a type of hopelessness that is hard to imagine now," Dr. Primm said. "I am hearing people already say 'I am infected with the virus, I might just as well shoot up drugs.' People will be turning more and more to drugs for solace."

The streets are filled with coke

Recent U.S. surveys understate the size of the nation's cocaine problem by a wide margin. The mistake: They don't count most criminals

Trick question time for taxpayers seeking to judge the progress of the war on drugs:

According to national surveys conducted for the federal government, which of the following is true about cocaine and crack use in the U.S.?

a. *The number of current cocaine users (those who used cocaine within the last month) fell by 50 percent from 1985 to 1988*

b. *The annual use of crack among high-school seniors fell sharply in the nation's 12 largest cities from 1986 to 1989*

c. *Cocaine use among blacks dropped from 1985 to 1988. In fact, only 2 percent of all blacks are current users of cocaine*

d. *All of the above are true*

e. *All of the above are true—and also misleading.*

As the correct answer (e) illustrates, the tale of cocaine use in America is a little like the fable of the six blind men and the elephant. The first blind man falls against the elephant's sturdy side and concludes the elephant is nothing but a wall; the second feels the animal's tusk and concludes the elephant is like a spear, and so on for the rest of the blind men. In much the same fashion, policymakers have sometimes misconstrued the full picture of cocaine abuse in the U.S. by relying on one-dimensional data from government-sponsored surveys of drug use in American households and among high-school seniors. Drug czar William Bennett, as well as those in Congress, now routinely uses the survey results to gauge progress in the drug war. Just this month, Bennett claimed the national data showed cocaine use was "down in urban America, black America . . . and poor America."

The problem with such contentions, however, is that the numbers that Bennett and others cite invariably reflect an undercount of the very populations most likely to regularly use cocaine—the homeless, heroin addicts, school dropouts and prisoners. Those omissions, it now appears, are not minor. In fact, a forthcoming study obtained by *U.S. News* suggests that gaps in the government's surveys may have led to a massive undercount of cocaine abusers in America. The study, by Eric Wish, a visiting fellow at the National Institute of Justice, could well prompt federal and local officials to re-examine where they will concentrate their antidrug efforts, who will be tested and what kind of drug treatment will evolve for criminal addicts.

According to Wish's analysis, which is scheduled to appear in *The International Journal of the Addictions* this summer, there may be nearly twice as many frequent cocaine users in the U.S. as show up in national surveys. He projects from urinalysis test results of arrestees that as many as 1.3 million Americans arrested in 1988 in the nation's 61 largest cities used crack or cocaine on a weekly basis—well above the official 862,000 weekly user figure projected by the National Institute on Drug Abuse (NIDA) for all U.S. households. Wish's estimates, however rough at this point, show a vast number, perhaps the majority of regular crack and cocaine users in the U.S., may not be counted in the government's regular drug surveys. The consequence, he says, is that federal and local officials must now begin to "concentrate far more attention on testing and treating the criminal cocaine user."

In part, the discrepancy between Wish's numbers and those in household surveys conducted for NIDA reflects the inevitable limitations of polls on drug use. Senator Joseph Biden (D-Del.), chairman of the Senate Judiciary Committee, asserts that "the NIDA surveys present the most optimistic picture you can find out there—and I think they especially grossly underestimate the number of hard-core cocaine users." The agency's household survey, for instance, purportedly covers 98 percent of the U.S. population, but its limited sample size sometimes requires officials to make heroic extrapolations from tiny subsamples. In the 1988 household survey, only 65 of the 8,814 individuals randomly polled acknowledged using cocaine or crack weekly, yet NIDA projected from that small group that roughly 862,000 Americans were weekly cocaine users. Moreover, as cocaine and crack have lost the luster of a glamour drug, some criminologists now contend that users are less and less willing to acknowledge cocaine use. "A lot of people," says Prof. Mark Kleiman of Harvard's Kennedy School of Government, "just won't tell the nice man from the government that they smoked crack recently."

In contrast to the NIDA polling approach, Wish's numbers are drawn from a 21-city Justice Department pilot program (known as the Drug Use Forecasting System or "DUF") that tracks actual cocaine use through urinalysis tests. DUF tests of more than 10,000 male arrestees show that, while cocaine consumption may have plummeted in recent years in middle and working-class households, crack use has exploded among the inner-city criminal class. On average, almost 50 percent of male arrestees in DUF cities have cocaine-positive urinalyses (which can detect cocaine and crack use within the previous two to three days). In the 21 DUF cities alone, Wish projects that law-enforcement officials arrested some 800,000 frequent cocaine users in 1988, roughly the same number that NIDA officials say existed in the entire U.S. household population that year. And unlike the national survey data, urinalysis tests have not shown a significant downward trend for cocaine use during the last year in DUF cities (with the exception of Washington, D.C., where demand for crack may have reached a saturation point). Perhaps the best that can be said about cocaine and crack use among the inner-city "underclass" is that it is not growing in major urban areas as rapidly as in the past.

A two-front war. In a fashion, Wish's numbers underscore the notion that the nation, as Bennett put it several months ago, is "now fighting two [drug] wars, not just one." The first battle—against casual drug use among middle and working-class Americans, black and white—has generally gone well. But the second, far more intractable struggle against inner-city crack addiction is foundering. Get-tough measures aimed at casual users, such as fining those caught with small amounts of drugs or revoking the student loans and driver licenses of drug offenders, have so far had little impact in the ghetto. As Yale Medical School Prof. David Musto puts it: "Cocaine and crack users in the inner city aren't the folks who will pay attention to an ad campaign. Now you're confronting the users who are least likely to be affected by educational initiatives and changing attitudes."

Nowhere, Wish suggests, is the disparity between the two fronts of the drug war broader than in the area of drug testing. In some cities today, a policeman or fireman is more likely to be tested for drug use than a criminal. Unlike offender-testing programs, urinalyses of private and public-sector employes have typically registered very low rates of cocaine use. When the Department of Transportation recently randomly tested some 22,000 employes over a two-year period, fewer than 50 employes, or 0.3 percent of those tested, were cocaine-positive, a rate roughly 150 times below that of DUF arrestees.

Yet while millions of employes and job applicants now face drug tests in the workplace, only a small proportion of arrestees, prisoners, parolees, or those out on bail are required to submit to urinalyses or prove they are drug-free as a condition of their release. Currently, just five metropolitan areas (Washington, Tucson, Phoenix, Milwaukee and Portland, Oreg.) and one county (Prince George's County, Md.) routinely test substantial numbers of adult arrestees. And only two cities, Washington and Phoenix, randomly test juvenile arrestees, who might be easier to reach with drug treatment. Last year, President Bush proposed legislation that would have required states to adopt offender drug-testing programs as a condition of receiving federal criminal-justice funds. His bill, though, died in Congress following complaints it was costly and cumbersome to administer.

Treatment backlog. Of course, in the bifurcated drug war of the 1990s, an insensate crackdown on inner-city cocaine users could be as ineffective as the current policy—a kind of benign neglect of drug abusers following their arrest. Requiring parolees and those on bail to be drug-free is eminently sensible, yet it is also unworkable. Inevitably, offender testing is expensive and creates added burdens for law-enforcement officials. Urinalysis tracking involves repeated follow-up tests, and identifying a cocaine abuser is of limited value if there are no treatment slots available. In 1989, the District of Columbia alone spent nearly a million dollars on lab services and personnel costs for some 50,000 clients, including costs for monitoring arrestees, referring them for treatment and supervising those out on bail. Most cities, however, are unprepared to make a similar investment, and urban areas around the country report they already have thousands of cocaine addicts awaiting treatment.

To his credit, drug czar Bennett helped boost federal funding for treatment last year by 51 percent (although he has not increased treatment moneys nearly as much as some critics would like). He also has stressed the need to get more-accurate numbers on cocaine and crack use among high-risk populations in the inner city. His current drug-control plan calls for doubling the sample size of the household poll, conducting extensive surveys of drug use in urban areas, and targeting spot surveys on groups like the homeless. But the results of the new studies will generally not be available until next year. Until that time, the best litmus test for judging the extent of America's cocaine and crack problem may be Bennett's own response to a recent query about the world supply of cocaine. "Nobody," he replied, "gains anything from underestimating the size of the problem."

by David Whitman with Dorian Friedman

The new battle to break the link between assault guns and drugs

Drugs and guns go together. That is a dicey problem for Americans because they want to win the drug war but they are ambivalent about reining in the guns that go with it. Now, the Bush administration and Congress are being dragged into another debate over assault guns. As in the past, neither side is likely to come out of the debate happy.

Two developments are driving the renewed interest in cracking down on these weapons: The insistence of Colombian President Virgilio Barco that the U.S. end the export of assault guns that arm the drug cartels and Congress's consideration of tough new restrictions as part of a major anticrime bill in the next few weeks. For Bush, the issue is trouble. He was deluged with protests by pro-gun groups last year when he permanently banned the import of 43 types of semiautomatic assault rifles after five children were murdered in a California schoolyard. At the same time, gun-control advocates denounced the President for not going further and banning the sale or manufacture of domestically produced models, which account for three fourths of America's assault-weapon supply. Bush shied away from the issue after the tempest, but he could not avoid it when Barco bitterly protested that "we can no longer wait while this deadly trade continues." The National Rifle Association believes the point is moot, since high-powered weapons are available from a variety of international sources, but investigation by U.S. authorities leaves little doubt that, at the moment, many of the drug lords' guns are U.S.-made AR-15s, MAC-10s and TEC-9s, many originating in Florida or California.

At the Andean summit, Bush signed agreements pledging to do more in stemming the flow of U.S. guns. That won't be easy, though. Many of these guns are smuggled out in small batches of two or three, hidden in scuba tanks or sewing machines. Administration officials say they'll work harder with recipient countries on overseeing legal weapons exports, since some of the cartel guns are diverted from originally legal deals. Yet coordination in the drug war is never easy. The U.S. Bureau of Alcohol, Tobacco, and Firearms has for months tried to get State Department approval to station a permanent cadre of agents in Colombia, but sources claim State has been sitting on the request. A State Department official counters that there is an expansion of embassy operations in Colombia that needs careful preparations because of the danger involved in sending Americans there.

On the political front, the fight will be bitter. Gun-control opponents probably can kill a proposal to ban the manufacture of popular domestically produced assault weapons—proving that the NRA is still very potent and that the debate will continue far into the future.

by Gordon Witkin

The Major Drugs of Use and Abuse

Perhaps the most important lesson we can learn in any realistic study of drug use is that different drugs have different effects. Smoking marijuana does not feel the same, or do the same things to the human mind and body, as injecting heroin; snorting cocaine is very different in most respects from swallowing a tab of LSD or drinking a gin and tonic. In order to know what drugs do—and are—it is absolutely essential to examine each drug or drug type individually.

Pharmacologists—scientists who study the effect that drugs have on humans and animals—classify drugs into categories. To begin with, some drugs are *psychoactive*, that is, they influence the workings of the mind; others are strictly medicinal, they influence the body but not the mind. Although some drugs that are not psychoactive, such as certain over-the-counter medications, are improperly used, psychoactive drugs are far more likely to be misused, abused, and over-used; clearly, they are more interesting to us here.

Psychoactive drugs are generally classified into the following types:

General depressants depress, inhibit, or slow down a wide range of organs and functions of the body and retard signals passing through the central nervous system, that is, the brain and spinal cord—in most cases, they slow down, relax us, make us drowsier, less alert, less anxious. In most cases, they facilitate sleep. Examples include alcohol, tranquilizers, and sedatives. In sufficiently large doses, depressants can produce intoxication and, if taken over a long enough period of time, physical dependence. If too large a dose is taken at one time, it is possible to die of an overdose of a depressant drug—alcohol included.

Narcotics, or *narcotic analgesics* dull the perception of pain, produce an intense "high" upon administration—and are highly addicting. They include heroin, morphine, opium, cocaine, and the synthetic narcotics. Like general depressants, overdosing is a strong possibility with a large dose of a narcotic drug. There are some other analgesics or pain-killers that are not as effective as the narcotics that do not produce an intoxication (such as aspirin).

Stimulants speed up signals passing through the central nervous system; they inhibit fatigue, and produce arousal, alertness, even excitation. Animals—and hu-

mans—find stimulants extremely reinforcing, that is, they will repeat self-administered doses, even when it interferes with other things they want, such as food, water, and sex. Cocaine and the cocaine derivative, crack, are the most well-known of the stimulants; they also include the amphetamines, or "speed" and an amphetamine cousin, methamphetamine ("crank" or "ice"), as well as caffeine and nicotine.

Hallucinogens, or "psychadelics," produce extreme mood, sensory, and perceptual changes; examples include LSD, mescaline, and psilocybin. The term "hallucinogen" implies that users always or typically experience hallucinations when they take drugs of this type; that is, in fact, rarely the case. Most of the time when users under the influence "see" things that do not concretely exist, they are aware that it is the drug and not the real world that is causing the vision. The term "psychedelic," a word taken from the ancient Greek, implies that the mind is "made manifest"—that is, it works best—under the influence, another extremely misleading notion. In some classifications, PCP or "angel dust," originally an animal tranquilizer, is regarded as an hallucinogen. In addition, "ecstasy," or MDMA, chemically related to the amphetamines, is also thought of as an hallucinogen. Marijuana, once thought to be an example of a hallucinogen, doesn't quite fit into this category, and must be regarded as a separate type of drug altogether.

Over-the-counter (OTC) medications are not psychoactive and do not produce a high or intoxication; in order to become dependent on one or another OTC remedy, or overdose on one, it is necessary to take extremely large doses. They are not entirely "safe"—no drug is—but relative to the psychoactive drugs, they are relatively so. Aspirin and other analgesics or pain-killers cause hundreds of deaths by overdose (nearly all of them suicides) each year in the United States, an indication that there is some measure of danger in any substance that causes bodily changes.

As we saw in the introduction to the section on Use, Addiction, and Dependence, in addition to the impact of the specific drugs or drug type used, there is the factor of *route of administration*—that is, *how* a drug is used. Some drugs, used via certain routes or methods of use, generate an immediate, powerful, sensuous sensation; other

routes of administration produce a slower, less intense, less immediate or "mellower" feeling. Smoking and intravenous (IV) administration produce the quickest and most intense high; oral (swallowing) and intranasal (sniffing or "snorting") ingestion produce a slower, less intense high. Of course, some drugs cannot be taken certain ways; marijuana is not water-soluable, and therefore, cannot be injected, and does not get absorbed by the nasal membranes, and cannot be snorted. Alcohol—obviously—cannot be smoked. Still, for a number of drugs, what a drug can do to the human mind and body is partly dependent on the way it is taken.

Looking Ahead: Challenge Questions

Which of the major drugs of use is most dangerous? What is it about each drug or drug type that some users find appealing? How can two drugs with very different effects become equally popular in a given society at a given time? Why are some drugs more popular during one decade and a very different one at another time?

Given the fact that cocaine, and its derivative, crack, is so pleasurable and reinforcing, how is it possible to stop its spread?

What is it that drug users and abusers are seeking when they take certain drugs? What is the appeal of each one? Reading over the accounts on heroin use, why did these women take a drug that caused them such pain? Why did they both eventually discontinue their use of heroin? What is so bad about certain drugs—marijuana and "ecstasy," for instance—if used in moderation?

Why should users take a drug that is clearly dangerous to their health and their very lives?

The How and Why of a Cocaine High

Advancing methods for treating addiction

William Booth
Washington Post Staff Writer

BALTIMORE—No one knows exactly what a squirrel monkey feels when it does cocaine. But government scientists at the Addiction Research Center here know this: A monkey will flip a switch for hours just to get another dose of cocaine. And just as some humans will go on a reckless binge of abuse, so too will a monkey hit the switch for more and more cocaine until researchers stop the experiment.

But scientists caution that just because they can get a monkey to feed its addiction so voraciously, it does not necessarily support the popular belief that cocaine is the most addictive of abused drugs.

Indeed, they say, the reason the animal keeps hitting the lever may just be because cocaine makes the monkey superalert and hyperactive.

A monkey might be just as addicted to alcohol, but after a few drinks, in contrast to cocaine's effect, the monkey might stop hitting the lever because it feels sleepy or dazed.

In the last few years, drug researchers have learned an enormous amount about cocaine. Not only do they know more about its true addictive properties, they now at last have a rough idea of how cocaine produces its high.

Addiction scientists have learned, for example, that the drug stimulates a still-mysterious pathway in the brain that is involved in feelings of pleasure and reward.

Indeed, some scientists think they now know at least one region of the brain where cocaine does its work, a structure called the nucleus accumbens, which is responsible for helping humans orient and move toward things they find pleasurable, whether the object of their desire is a member of the opposite sex, a fine wine or a rock of crack cocaine.

In addition, researchers know the exact molecular site in the nucleus accumbens where the cocaine molecule binds to its special receptor.

This in turn has led to a better understanding of how cocaine acts to overstimulate certain nerve cells in the brain, a phenomenon that makes users feel good.

Armed with this knowledge, new drugs are being developed to treat the worst symptoms of withdrawal, to suppress cocaine craving and to reduce cocaine-associated depression.

When a user smokes crack in a pipe, researchers believe, he is employing one of the most efficient drug delivery systems known.

In both animals and humans, scientists say, smoked cocaine reaches the brain so quickly that it is almost impossible to distinguish a dose delivered by intravenous injection from a dose delivered by a glass pipe.

"How fast does it get to the brain? We're not sure. It's too fast to measure in the lab," says Jonathan Katz, a behavioral pharmacologist at the Addiction Research Center, a branch of the National Institute on Drug Abuse.

Katz says he assumes crack cocaine reaches the brain in seconds.

Unlike snorting cocaine powder, a relatively slow and inefficient route, smoking crack delivers the drug directly to the lungs, where it is readily absorbed by the blood, pumped once through the heart and then up to the brain.

One researcher compared smoking crack to driving a nail of cocaine directly into one's forehead.

A "single significant dose" of cocaine—in other words, enough to get a person with a history of cocaine use high—increases breathing, boosts blood pressure and may double heart rate. Hunger, fatigue and depression fade. A subject feels vigorous, happy, hypersexual, friendly and alert. Some scientists describe this collection of sensations as euphoria.

Although a full explanation of how cocaine produces euphoria remains elusive, researchers do know that the drug appears to affect the limbic system, the part of the brain involved in the powerful emotional responses, of which the best-known are those important to human survival, such as the primal urges to feed, fight, flee and reproduce.

From *The Washington Post National Weekly Edition*, March 26-April 1, 1990, p. 38. Copyright © 1990 by The Washington Post. Reprinted with permission.

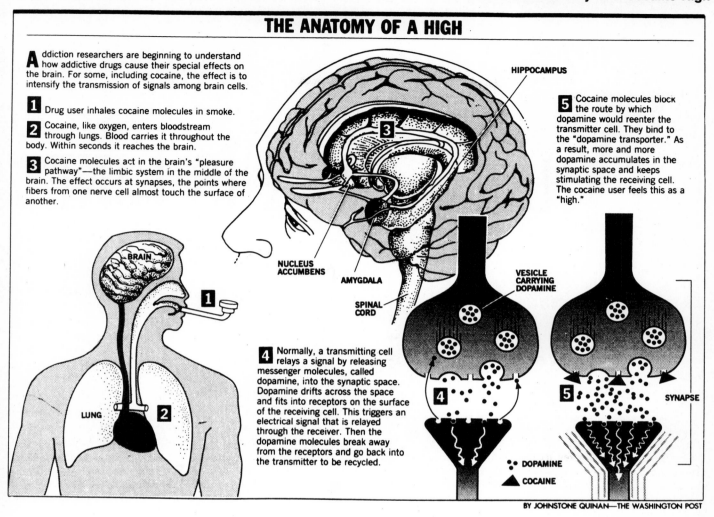

THE ANATOMY OF A HIGH

Addiction researchers are beginning to understand how addictive drugs cause their special effects on the brain. For some, including cocaine, the effect is to intensify the transmission of signals among brain cells.

1 Drug user inhales cocaine molecules in smoke.

2 Cocaine, like oxygen, enters bloodstream through lungs. Blood carries it throughout the body. Within seconds it reaches the brain.

3 Cocaine molecules act in the brain's "pleasure pathway"—the limbic system in the middle of the brain. The effect occurs at synapses, the points where fibers from one nerve cell almost touch the surface of another.

HIPPOCAMPUS

5 Cocaine molecules block the route by which dopamine would reenter the transmitter cell. They bind to the "dopamine transporter." As a result, more and more dopamine accumulates in the synaptic space and keeps stimulating the receiving cell. The cocaine user feels this as a "high."

NUCLEUS ACCUMBENS

AMYGDALA

SPINAL CORD

VESICLE CARRYING DOPAMINE

4 Normally, a transmitting cell relays a signal by releasing messenger molecules, called dopamine, into the synaptic space. Dopamine drifts across the space and fits into receptors on the surface of the receiving cell. This triggers an electrical signal that is relayed through the receiver. Then the dopamine molecules break away from the receptors and go back into the transmitter to be recycled.

BRAIN

LUNG

SYNAPSE

•• DOPAMINE

▲ COCAINE

BY JOHNSTONE QUINAN—THE WASHINGTON POST

Although several components of the limbic system are under study, the one area that appears to get the most action is the nucleus accumbens. The nucleus accumbens is uniquely situated to communicate between the limbic system and the part of the brain called the motor cortex, which directs movement.

"When you see a pretty girl and alert to her presence and orient toward her, or when you smell a good bordeaux wine sauce and move toward the smell, it is the nucleus accumbens that is helping you orient and move toward those things you perceive as pleasurable," says George Koob, a psychopharmacologist at the Research Institute of the Scripps Clinic in San Diego.

Scientists believe that cocaine stimulates the nucleus accumbens by meddling with a special chemical messenger called dopamine. In the nucleus accumbens, cocaine enters the tiny space where one nerve cell almost touches another, a sort of no man's

land called the synaptic space.

For one nerve cell to transmit a signal to another, it must make the signal cross the synaptic space. To do this a neuron releases a load of dopamine molecules. Each dopamine molecule travels across the space, briefly attaches itself to a receptor on the receiving cell and then heads back into the neuron from which it was released.

Cocaine, however, stops the dopamine from returning to the neuron that released it, according to Michael Kuhar of the Addiction Research Center. It forces the dopamine to remain in the synaptic space, where it keeps stimulating the receiving neuron over and over again.

In a sense, it is not the cocaine that makes a user high, it is the dopamine that lingers in the synaptic space, overstimulating the nucleus accumbens.

"It jazzes it up," says Koob.

In a normal person, Koob says, the nucleus accumbens may be activated from time to time. But under the influence of cocaine a person is feeling full-blown pleasure almost non-stop, wallowing in a kind of "brain hedonism."

In fact, a common complaint among former cocaine addicts is that they have difficulty getting enjoyment from life's simple, undrugged pleasures, such as sex and eating.

Indeed, Koob believes that one reason cocaine may be so addictive is that it not only makes users feel good, but it also makes them more active, enabling them and motivating them to take more and more of the drug—just like the laboratory animal in the experimental chamber that keeps hitting the lever for more cocaine—until overdose and death overtake them.

"That's what makes cocaine so powerful," says Koob.

WHAT CRACK IS LIKE

It's great, unfortunately.

Jefferson Morley

JEFFERSON MORLEY, is National Political Correspondent for Spin Magazine.

"Using it even once can make a person crave cocaine for as long as they live." —Peter Jennings, "ABC World News Tonight," September 8

When it comes to crack, politicians and pundits literally do not know what they are talking about. Most of the journalists covering the so-called "war on drugs" have at least tried marijuana. So have many of the rugged young officials now in charge of said hostilities. Both pencil pushers and paper pushers have been known to snort the occasional mound of cocaine. Virtually all came of age before the dawn of zero tolerance. Even heroin is not utterly unknown to the opinion and policy classes.

But crack is something else. Probably no one making our government's drug policy has ever smoked a rock of crack cocaine. Nor has anyone who regularly reports or comments in the media on the ravages of crack capitalism. Now, I wouldn't argue that you have to smoke crack to understand the war on drugs—any more than you have to kill someone to understand the war in Vietnam. And I certainly wouldn't argue that crack isn't hazardous or that anyone should try it. Having been through the experience, though, may facilitate a certain realism about the conflict in question.

Crack is a pleasure both powerful and elusive. Smoke a rock and, for the next 20 minutes, you will likely appreciate sensuous phenomena ranging from MTV to neon lights to oral sex with renewed urgency. After your 20 minutes is up, you will have a chemical aftertaste in your mouth and, in all likelihood, the sneaking desire to smoke another rock—to see what that was really all about. Just one more.

You'll want to pick up a $25 rock, which can be split into four or five smaller rocks. (If you want to know where to buy crack, just tune in to shows like "Geraldo" or "City Under Siege"—Washington's nightly local TV report on the drug crisis—for detailed instructions.)

As you smoke your second rock, it may strike you that the crack high combines the best aspects of marijuana and cocaine. The pleasure of pot is not just a high, but a buzz; smoke a joint and space out. Cocaine, in contrast, is a clear high, a stimulant to sociality; do a line and get into some serious play or some pleasurable work. Crack is both spacey and intense. It has the head rush of marijuana or amyl nitrate with the clarity induced by a noseful of powder cocaine.

On the third rock, you may notice that your world looks just fine, as do various of the women (or men) in it. Reality isn't real and all that was formerly a possibility is now on the verge of actuality. You'll want to turn up the music and maybe your sexual aggression quotient. You'll gain new insight into why crack is so popular among women.

You may find yourself in the company of experienced crackheads as you smoke your fourth rock. You may start to notice other aspects of the crack experience. An individualistic drug, crack is often enjoyed in silence. The silence ends when that last sliver of rock is gone and you want to go out and find another $25 rock. When you're back outside prowling the lunar landscape of post-Reagan urban America at two in the morning with your high fading and your heartbeat racing, you'll begin to learn that crack is a both a mental and a material phenomenon. You want your next rock, you want to get off, get out of this world—or at least transform it for a few minutes. You can be a moral tourist in the land of crack and still get a sense of how the drug can make sick sense to demoralized people. If all you have in life is bad choices, crack may not be the most unpleasant of them.

Even at two in the morning, you can find a guy who's got a rock. But he won't sell to you because he thinks a white guy must be a cop. Or he wants you to give him your money and he'll go get the rock from his friend over there. (Yeah, right.) So he finally gets you a rock but chips off a little for himself. You get high and before you know it you're coming down again, thinking maybe crack combines the worst of other drugs. Like weed, it's stupefying; like coke, it's conducive to paranoia.

After my night of crack, I went home and fell into a light sleep with the lights on. I feared that an air conditioner was going to fall on my head. I woke up tired, alert, still a little buzzed, filled with an urgent desire to get to work to make up for the night's decadence.

I took an unsatisfactory shower. I mused about the weird apparatchiks who wage war on drugs and who claim vindication in the fact that drug use is declining among the middle class. They are the ones, I thought melodramatically, who should—who must!—smoke crack. Before it is too late, I muttered, dragging a comb through my hair.

What if there were a drug (I inquired of the mirror) that could chemically induce feelings of upper-middle-classness. It would be attractive to the poor, and wildly popular among those who had no prayer of ever achieving that comfortable station in life. And it would be despised by people who had worked long, hard years to obtain that same mental state without resorting to the drug. It would be popular, cheap, and the cause of anti-social behavior. It would be a lot like crack.

I put on my clothes and thought, for obscure reasons, of a yuppie acquaintance. I am sure she has never tried crack. "I just bought a CD player," this young woman announced proudly to her sister one day when it was still morning in America, "Do you know of any music I should listen to?" Yuppies are just the crackheads of consumerism, I thought, their CDs just so many rocks of consumptive, sensuous pleasure. My mood was improving already. Crack was a parody of Reaganism, I concluded, a brief high with a bad aftertaste and untold bodily damage.

I flushed the toilet and straightened my tie. Had Bill Bennett ever smoked crack, I wondered? Probably not. I was no longer high, just daydreaming. I remembered meeting a University of Texas alum, and her bemused expression when I asked her if she thought Bill Bennett had smoked marijuana at UT in the late 1960s. "Well, obviously not enough," she said.

The crack had worn off entirely, and I sat down to write an article about the drug problem.

The Fire of 'Ice'

A devastating drug from Asia has triggered a crisis in Hawaii and now threatens the mainland

MICHAEL A. LERNER

Twenty years old and fresh out of college, Tad Yamaguchi saw a good future for himself at an air-freight company in Honolulu. So when one of his superiors offered him a puff from the small glass pipe—a little something to help him get through the grueling 20-hour shift—Yamaguchi felt he couldn't refuse. He says he was instantly hooked. "I felt alert, in control. It didn't seem to have a downside," recalls Yamaguchi. No wonder so many people in his office were using it. Four months later Yamaguchi, who had never done drugs before, was smoking every day. "I'd smoke as much as I could. I started buying large quantities to sell so I could support my habit," he says. Soon Yamaguchi, who kicked the habit a year ago, had lost 35 pounds and was smoking four days at a time, then "crashing" in a comatose sleep that lasted up to 36 hours. Next, paranoia and hallucinations set in.

The Japanese call it *shabu,* to Koreans it's *hiroppon.* To American addicts just discovering its intense highs and hellish lows, the drug is simply "ice," after the clear crystal form it takes in the manufacturing process. As addictive as crack cocaine but far more pernicious, ice—a type of methamphetamine, or speed—is a drug that seems culled from the pages of science fiction. In contrast to the fleeting 20-minute high of crack, an ice buzz lasts anywhere from eight to 24 hours. Unlike cocaine, which comes from a plant indigenous to the Andes, ice can be cooked up in a laboratory using easily obtained chemicals—a drug for the scientific age.

Methamphetamine's side effects are devastating. Prolonged use can cause fatal lung and kidney disorders as well as long-lasting psychological damage. "We're seeing people with dysfunctions two and a half years after they've stopped using. That's scary," says Earlene Piko, director of substance abuse at the Wai'anae Community Mental Health Center in Hawaii,

Highs and Lows: Counting Costs in the Drug Market

Ice
Cost: $50 per "paper" (less than 1 gram)
Duration: 8 to 24 hours
Effects: Immediate, intense euphoria; increased alertness
Side effects: Aggressive behavior, hallucinations, paranoia, fatal kidney failure

Crank
Cost: $50 to $120 a gram
Duration: 2 to 4 hours
Effects: Wakefulness, excitability, mood elevation
Side effects: Irritability, insomnia, palpitations, severe anxiety

Crack
Cost:: $3 to $20 a vial (less than 1 gram)
Duration: 20 to 30 minutes
Effects: Immediate, intense exhilaration, sense of well-being
Side effects: Anxiety, depression, stroke, heart attack, seizure

Heroin
Cost: $10 for a "dime bag"; $70 to $200 a "bundle" (less than 1 gram)
Duration: 4 hours per dose
Effects: Relaxation
Side effects: Drowsiness, nausea, heart and skin infections

the first American state to be afflicted by ice. The drug also tends to make users violent. The Honolulu Police Department estimates that ice was a factor in 70 percent of spouse-abuse cases the force handled last month.

Ice is not a new drug, but a more powerful form of a substance that has been popular in Western states for several years. Purer and more crystalline than the "meth" or "crank" manufactured in cities like San Diego, ice comes from Asia. So far, the spread to the United States has been largely confined to the Hawaiian Islands. But the quickness with which it has overtaken that state is startling. In just over four years, ice has surpassed marijuana and cocaine as Hawaii's No. 1 drug problem.

Korean connection: Now law-enforcement officials fear Hawaii may be a beachhead for the drug's spread to the rest of the United States. Congresswoman Patricia Saiki of Honolulu has started lobbying drug czar William Bennett to declare her city a "high-intensity drug-trafficking area" so it would qualify for more federal anti-drug money. "[Bennett needs to act now] to quell this plague before it gets to the mainland," she says. It may already be too late. In recent months, federal drug and customs agents have made several ice busts in the continental United States.

Hawaii's ice trail goes back to South Korea, which—along with Taiwan—leads the world in the manufacture and export of the drug. The Koreans learned about methamphetamine from the Japanese, who invented the stimulant in 1893. During World War II, Japan's military leaders supplied it in liquid form to weary soldiers and munitions-plant workers, leading to the addiction of hundreds of thousands of Japanese to the then legal drug. Japan banned shabu in the '50s, but many labs that produced it simply relocated to South Korea and smuggled the drug back across the Sea of Japan. In recent years use has leveled off—though Japan remains the drug's largest market. At the same time, Korea's once negligible domestic consumption has boomed, spreading from prostitutes and entertainers to students, housewives and businessmen; 130,000 Koreans are addicted to ice, medical experts believe. A common factor among some users: jobs with high stress and long hours. "It's a very suitable drug for workaholics," says journalist Cho Gab Je, author of "Korean Connection," a book about the hiroppon trade.

The link between Korea and Hawaii was forged in the early 1980s through Paciano (Sonny) Guerrero, a Hawaiian of Filipino origins who last month was sentenced in Hawaii's federal court to 25 years in prison without parole for the sale and distribution of ice. Known as the King of Batu (the word for rock in the Filipino language of Ilocano), Guerrero established the first ice-distribution network on Hawaii, using mostly local Filipino gangs to distribute it. Authorities estimate that Guerrero sold $7.3 million worth of the drug in 1987 and 1988 alone. "Sonny was selling mainly to Filipinos and Koreans, but it quickly spread. And it's spreading still—right into middle-class high schools," says a Drug Enforcement Administration agent in Honolulu.

Gang members: Korean drug organizations are trying to expand the ice market to mainland America. NEWSWEEK has learned that federal authorities are currently pursuing a Korean drug ring that is distributing ice in the United States. Last August U.S. Customs agents in Portland, Ore., seized about five ounces of ice sent by mail from Korea. Last month Honolulu police arrested five suspected members of a violent New York-based Korean gang called K.P. (Korea Power) that allegedly arrived in Honolulu with 17 other gang members to set up an ice pipeline to the East Coast. Police seized $72,000 in cash along with guns and ammunition.

At first puff, ice seems irresistible. Cheap and long lasting, the drug provides users with a sense of well-being. A penny-size plastic bag called a paper costs $50 and, when smoked, can keep a novice high for up to a week. Addicts call the sensation from smoking ice "amping" for the amplified euphoria it gives them. Odorless and hard to detect, ice is used as much for recreation as for staying alert on the job. "On the front end, it doesn't seem so bad. You stay awake, focused on what you're doing. And you feel good about yourself," says Dr. Joseph Giannasio, director of Castle Medical Center Alcoholism and Addictions program in Oahu. "Where it gets scary is at the tail end."

If Hawaii is any indication, a surge in ice use in America could be as destructive as the current crack crisis. Last month Honolulu Police Chief Douglas Gibb told Congress that the number of drug-exposed newborns reported to welfare officials has jumped from two a week to six a week in the past year. Ice largely accounts for the dramatic increase, say health experts, and the fallout is straining Hawaii's social services. "It's totally overwhelming. We're in a crisis," says Dr. Jane Stump, a psychiatry professor at the University of Hawaii and a member of the Child Protective Services medical team. "This ice, it's like a great tidal wave."

No bonding: The little that is known about ice's effects on newborns is alarming. "If you thought cocaine dependency was bad, that's in the minor leagues compared to this drug," says Earlene Piko. As with cocaine babies, ice babies tend to be asocial and incapable of bonding. Some have tremors and cry for 24 hours without stopping. They have to be swaddled to be held. "We know children who didn't bond are likely to be sociopaths," says Daniel Bent, U.S. attorney in Hawaii. "We're now producing 200,000 cocaine babies a year, and nurses tell us ice babies are worse in that area."

Rehabilitation clinics in Hawaii report there are now as many ice addicts as cocaine addicts seeking treatment. Doctors believe it's just the beginning. "You have to build up a large base of users before you start seeing people come in for help," says Giannasio. Most clinics are treating ice addiction as they would cocaine addiction. But ice is proving more difficult to kick. "Some people get hospitalized, start on psychotropic drugs to stop the hallucinations and after a month they're OK. But we have others who after two years haven't improved," says Piko. Honolulu police are preparing a number of public-service announcements to warn the population about the hazards of the drug. "We were ready for crack. We had commercials on TV, we learned how to bust the dealers and prosecute them," says Major David Benson of the Honolulu police. "But in its place, whammo, we got nailed with crystal meth." Federal authorities hope the continental United States won't face the same fate.

with DAVID BANK *and* PETER LEYDEN *in Seoul and* BRADLEY MARTIN *in Tokyo*

THE NEW DRUG THEY CALL 'ECSTASY'

IS IT TOO MUCH TO SWALLOW?

JOE KLEIN

'"THIS IS VERY EMBARRASSING," THE MAN SAID. "I never imagined that I would be a spokesman for a *drug*." He is a respected administrator in the field of medical research and health care, about 50, soft-spoken, conservatively dressed, thoughtful, intelligent. He is actually blushing.

"I get sheepish just thinking about the words I'd use to describe the experience," he said. "I don't want to sound foolish. You have to understand I'm not a big drug taker. I've never taken cocaine or LSD; I smoked marijuana once or twice, but that's it. Anyway, a friend—a very well known writer, a man I respect enormously—told me he had something I might like to try, a new drug. He didn't give it a name, but I later learned it was MDMA—'Ecstasy.' He just said it was interesting and safe, so far as he knew. He said I wouldn't hallucinate or lose track of reality. We discussed it briefly—it's amazing, in retrospect, how little I knew. But I did try it and . . ."

And?

"Well, this is going to sound ridiculous. What happens is, the drug takes away all your neuroses. It takes away the fear response. There is an overwhelming feeling of peace; you're at peace with the world. You feel open, clear, loving. I can't imagine anyone being angry under its influence, or feeling selfish or mean or even defensive. You have a lot of insights into yourself, *real* insights that stay with you after the experience is over. It doesn't give you anything that isn't already there. It's not a trip. You don't lose touch with the world. You could pick up the phone, call your mother, and she'd never know."

He paused then, somewhat nonplussed by his own enthusiasm. He searched for caveats. It wasn't a panacea, he said. Just a useful therapeutic tool. And yes, it probably could be abused—any drug could be abused—although it would be hard to imagine just *how* this one might be, since the level of insight diminishes with frequent use. And no, he didn't think it was an aphrodisiac. "Although it *is* an easy drug to fall in love on. You feel close to whomever you're with, and more at one with the world. There is a feeling of transcendence, a sense of being part of something larger than yourself, at least there was for me.

"It is," he said, "the opposite of paranoia."

There are those who would argue that the opposite of paranoia is gullibility. Certainly, nothing could be as good as Ecstasy sounds. Surely, skepticism is the only reasonable response. After a quarter century of chemical nightmares, we're far too sophisticated to be seduced by a little-known synthetic variation of oil of nutmeg. And any drug with a name this long—3,4 methylenedioxymethamphetamine—just *has* to have disaster lurking amid its molecules. Right?

So why all the excitement? And why are holistic, ecological "New Age" sorts—the very last people you'd expect to be ingesting something *unnatural*—the most ardent proponents of MDMA? And why has this drug aroused more curiosity, won more glowing endorsements, and received more positive media coverage in the past month than any drug since . . . well, since LSD?

For one thing, the marketing has been brilliant: MDMA promises adventure without weirdness, transcendence without alienation—a yuppie way of knowledge, as it were. For another, it is legal—temporarily, no doubt. And finally, within certain limits and under proper supervision, it just may work. A small but determined group of psychotherapists across the country swear by it.

"It is a valuable tool—not an answer but a *catalyst*," says Dr. Rick Ingrasci, who claims to have treated more than 200 patients in the Boston area with MDMA. "It enables people to look at the past without fear. This isn't always an ecstatic experience. It isn't always without pain, especially in the days after the session, as the insights gained through MDMA are integrated. But I can honestly say that there are very few negative reactions. It can speed up the therapeutic process enormously. It facilitates healing."

Of course, the history of drug ingestion is riddled with giddy testimonials from responsible sorts. William James, the noted American psychologist and sibling, wrote of "the tremendously exciting sense of an intense metaphysical illumination" that accompanied the use of nitrous oxide. Sigmund Freud used the word "euphoric" a bit too often to be entirely credible when describing cocaine. Aldous Huxley touted mescaline as the way to bring about a religious revival—in a 1958 article in the *Saturday Evening Post,* of all places. No doubt, when Dr. Timothy Leary began to investigate mind-altering drugs at Harvard 25 years ago, he seemed every bit as reasonable and conservative as the health administrator cited above. From nitrous oxide to Ecstasy, the promise has remained the same: insight without effort.

"My reaction is, 'Here we go again,' " says Dr. Ronald Siegel of the UCLA School of Medicine. "Every few years you get one of these miracle drugs that's going to save the world and make everyone feel good. My favorite was PCP. Remember what they used to call that? The *Peace* Pill. At low doses, people were reporting serene, tranquil, peaceful experiences. Then it hit the street and the name changed—it became angel dust—and dosages increased, and it was cut with God knows what, and you began to get all the reports of bizarre, violent behavior. So now we have Ecstasy. If you take it, you might become a self-actualized, empathetic, caring person, or you might become a nauseated person, or you might have a severe psychotic reaction. Among street users, we're seeing all the above."

The comparison with angel dust isn't quite fair. The history of MDMA is not that of another trippy chemical rushed mindlessly from the laboratories into the street—quite the contrary, in fact. For the past decade, the drug's proponents have been fighting to keep it under wraps, to control its use, to prevent the sort of public reaction that brought LSD research to a screeching halt in the 1960s. It was a battle they were destined to lose, of course. About five years ago, the drug began seeping into college campuses, into gay bars and discos. Inevitably, it came to the attention of the Drug Enforcement Administration (DEA), which announced last summer that it intended to have MDMA "scheduled" as a controlled substance: to make it illegal, in other words.

The announcement brought forth an immediate—and rather surprising—reaction. An array of MDMA proponents emerged from the shadows, hired a law firm, and began to lobby for something less than a total ban.

"That's new, I must admit," says Siegel. "To my knowledge, this is the first psychedelic drug to have a law firm."

To a great extent, the recent media barrage about MDMA—*Newsweek,* all three networks, and Phil Donahue have "done" it in the past month—has been a natural consequence of the drug researchers' decision to challenge the DEA. But it also is the result of a lobbying campaign almost single-handedly orchestrated, promoted, and financed by a 31-year-old University of South Florida undergraduate named Rick Doblin.

I T IS DIFFICULT TO TELL WHETHER RICK DOBLIN IS A vestige of the 1960s or a harbinger of the New Age. He glows, he burbles with psychedelic illumination and good humor. "I don't like to call the drug Ecstasy," he says. "It's false advertising. I call it 'Adam,' which works on several levels: It's a variation on MDMA, it's calmer than Ecstasy, and it connects with the Garden of Eden."

Doblin is an unabashed proselytizer, a psychedelic cheerleader in the tradition of Dr. Timothy Leary, though without

Leary's academic credentials or rebellious spirit. He doesn't see himself at war against the powers that be; indeed, he wants to cooperate with the government on MDMA research. He'd rather embrace the opposition than taunt it. "Last week," he says, "I took a low dose, about 30 milligrams, and went to hear Jerry Falwell speak—just so I could understand him better, to see if we had common ground. This is something I've done before, for Alexander Haig, the Dalai Lama, Robert Muller of the United Nations. Adam is a great drug for listening to lectures."

Such reckless candor has alienated Doblin from most of the more sober, therapeutic sorts promoting MDMA—including his two co-officers of the Earth Metabolic Design Foundation, a nonprofit group researching the drug. "Rick is a good kid, but he may be single-handedly responsible for the emergency scheduling of MDMA by the government," says a foundation source. "If there's any more media coverage, we stand a good chance of losing this thing, which would be a shame because a lot of people have invested years of work on MDMA. It should be made clear that, unlike Rick, the foundation opposes the recreational use of this compound. We're not opposed to having MDMA regulated, but not as strictly as the government is proposing."

"It's a disagreement over strategy," Doblin acknowledges. "The other two officers are friends of mine. I brought them into this, but now they think we should have a low profile until the DEA hearing. I think if people are going to do stories, they might as well have the right information. I might have to start my own foundation."

A PPARENTLY, DOBLIN HAS ENOUGH MONEY—INherited from his grandfather, a Chicago industrialist—to do whatever he wants. He has spent much of his adult life wandering about in quest of illumination, intermittently attending college, building solar houses, and receiving informal instruction in psychedelics—a late-twentieth-century version of the grand tour. He first heard of MDMA in 1982, while taking a monthlong class called "The Mystical Quest," with the noted psychedelic researcher Dr. Stanislav Grof, at the Esalen Institute—another sixties vestige—in California. "A friend gave some to me," Doblin recalls. "She said it made you feel good. That didn't seem very significant, so I didn't take it right away—in fact, I waited until I got home to Florida. I took it with my girlfriend, and it was incredible. We just opened up to each other. I remember saying, 'There's no drug. It's just us.' "

It would be physiologically inaccurate to say that Rick Doblin was hooked after that first experience, but he *was* very interested. He decided to learn all he could about MDMA, a process that led him back to Grof at Esalen.

Experimentation with psychedelic drugs had slowed down after the uproar in the 1960s, but it hadn't stopped. "Grof was one of several people who were at the center of it," Doblin says. "Some of the others don't want their names used. But Grof later taught Rick Ingrasci and George Greer and many of the other therapists who are now using Adam."

Another name that pops up often is Alexander Shulgin, a respected Bay Area chemist and drug designer. Shulgin—who refuses to speak publicly but is cooperating with those who retained the law firm to defend MDMA—didn't invent the drug, but he certainly helped to popularize it. Before he began publishing research papers on MDMA in 1975, it had languished in almost total obscurity since being patented in 1914 by Merck & Company, Inc., as a possible appetite suppressant. About the only other early reference to it was as one of eight psychedelics tested secretly by the army in 1953; MDMA was found to be more toxic than LSD or mescaline—in large doses, it killed animals—but it is not known whether it was tested on humans. In fact, its precise effect on humans is still a mystery.

Shulgin has said that the drug was already in use when it was brought to his attention in the early 1970s. He had been experimenting with members of the same pharmacological family: synthetic derivatives of oil of sassafras and nutmeg that are structurally similar to mescaline and amphetamines. Other members of the family—MMDA, MDA—had enjoyed vogues as mild hallucinogens. But Shulgin soon came to believe that MDMA was something quite different, a step forward. Its active ingredient was the opposite isomer (an isomer is one half of a molecule of any compound) from the one active in the hallucinogenic members of the family. "The effect was much different from MDA," recalls Dr. Claudio Naranjo, who worked closely with Shulgin. "MDMA was not hallucinogenic. It seemed, too, less toxic than MDA. When administered in small doses, there were few, if any, side effects: a slight tightening of the jaw, some nausea, and those would pass in the first half-hour. And the psychological effect—it was completely different from any other drug. It was like a brief, fleeting moment of sanity."

(It should also be noted that MDMA often has amphetamine-like side effects—increased blood pressure and pulse rate—and certainly shouldn't be used by people with cardiovascular problems. Some people find it difficult to sleep after taking the drug, and feel "hung over" the next day.)

Shulgin, Naranjo, and the other early researchers were struck by how *predictable* the effects of MDMA were—at least in a therapeutic setting. "It has proven to be remarkably consistent in chronology (the duration of action is about an hour)," Shulgin wrote in 1983, "and dosage requirements (the effective dosage is 100–150 mgs. orally). In most aspects, it is deceptively simple in action, leading to a sensory and verbal disinhibition, a state of mutual trust and confidence between subject and therapist, but without the distractions of visual distortion or compelling introspection."

The first time Bob Littlehale took MDMA under Dr. Rick Ingrasci's supervision, he experienced an epiphany. "I realized I loved my wife. It was an enormous feeling, it just filled my chest," says Littlehale, a prominent Massachusetts physician. "I had to pick up the phone and call her. She was at work. It didn't matter. That feeling has stayed with me, too. This stuff won't let you forget."

"He sounded totally joyful," Marie Littlehale recalls. "He didn't sound spaced or dulled or buzzed. It was pretty embarrassing."

Though they have taken the drug together since Bob's epiphany, the Littlehales are quick to point out that MDMA hasn't saved their marriage; after 24 years of sporadic warfare, it may not be salvageable. "But it *has* made us a lot more aware of the issues at stake," Marie says. "It's really helped us along in our process of figuring out what we want to do."

"It's not a panacea," says Ingrasci. "It won't save an unhappy marriage. But I've found it to be incredibly useful."

Before he learned about MDMA from friends, Ingrasci had built a successful practice based on holistic principles, emphasizing the connection between mental and physical health. He was especially well known for his work with people who suffered from serious illnesses. In fact, Marie Littlehale first visited Ingrasci because she believed she was in the early stages of multiple sclerosis. The Littlehales spent about a year in therapy, individually and as a couple, before Ingrasci suggested MDMA as a possibility.

"I took the drug myself before I ever gave it to a patient," Ingrasci says, "and I experienced an enormous sense of well-being. I don't recommend it for everyone. Usually, I'll simply suggest that mind-altering drugs are one of several possible therapeutic strategies. If the patient decides that's what he or she wants, I'll set a two-hour appointment for them and tell them to come an hour early to take the drug."

Ingrasci gets his MDMA from a local chemist. He administers it either in capsules or as powder mixed in fruit juice. "About half the people have a mild physical reaction—tightened jaw, nausea, some anxiety—that passes pretty quickly," he says. "Usually, people will just begin to talk, but sometimes I have to take a more active role. With couples, especially, sometimes they'll want to just sit there hugging or rocking back and forth, and I'll have to say, 'Listen, folks, let's get down to the business at hand.' "

Although the experience is pleasant for most, there *have* been some difficult moments. "There was one woman who had been sexually abused by her cousin and was very angry. She said she didn't love her husband. She talked about becoming a lesbian, of how men's bodies disgusted her. Her husband was a rather constricted, professorial type. When they took the drug, he just melted. He was totally there. He took her hand and told her how much he loved her—it was amazing, he'd never said it before. Her reaction was panic. She just couldn't handle it. She became really angry with me for 'forcing' her to take the drug. It was a pretty bad scene. Several days later it hit her: She was terrified of being loved. So, ultimately, the drug worked for her—as a catalyst. Certainly, Ecstasy had nothing to do with it."

There are those who say MDMA might ultimately have other therapeutic uses, and should be tried—as LSD was, inconclusively (the government crackdown occurred before enough results were in)—on criminals, drug abusers, and the terminally ill. "I'd be interested in trying this on heavy cocaine users," says a New York therapist who specializes in drug-abuse treatment and has tried MDMA. "The interesting thing about coke and Ecstasy is that they both access the same thing: fearlessness. With coke, it's an aggressive sort of fearlessness—'I can do anything.' With MDMA, it's more passive—'Anything harmful will pass right through me.' "

The psychic effect of cocaine in doses of .05 to .1 gram consists of exhilaration and lasting euphoria, which does not differ in any way from the normal euphoria of a healthy person.... One senses an increase of self-control and feels more vigorous and more capable of work; on the other hand, if one works, one misses that heightening of mental powers which alcohol, tea or coffee induce. One is simply normal, and soon finds it difficult to believe that one is under the influence of any drug at all.

—Sigmund Freud
"Über Coca," 1884

Cocaine made a fool of Dr. Ronald Siegel of UCLA too. "Ten years ago, you could have gotten a great many researchers to say that cocaine was a safe, recreational drug, including me," he says. "I was actually in favor of reclassification. The point is, you can't be cavalier about these things. There are doctors who are swearing by Ecstasy, but they are only offering anecdotal evidence. To my knowledge, there hasn't been a single supervised, double-blind clinical study to appear in a peer-reviewed, refereed scientific journal. I think it's downright irresponsible to go around touting this drug without adequate research, especially since the things we're seeing on the street are so much at variance with the claims the MDMA lobby is making."

On the street, Ecstasy—which can be manufactured easily and costs only about $10 per dose—seems quite a different drug from the one being used by the therapists. Working with continuing surveys of street users, Siegel estimates that use has increased nationally from 10,000 doses in all of 1976 to a current 30,000 per month. The effects of the drug, he says, seem very similar to those of mescaline. "They're from the same pharmacological family," he says. "You know, the molecular twists and turns that the chemists are playing with—MDA, MMDA,

MDMA—raise nice, interesting academic questions, but out on the street, the experience is the same: hallucinations, disorientation, psychotic episodes."

It is possible that because of the milder, more subtle effects of MDMA, inexperienced users are doubling and tripling the dose. It's also probable that after the recent media coverage, enterprising drug dealers are calling everything from speed to powdered sugar Ecstasy. "We're getting people who claimed to have taken this drug who are disoriented for days on end," says Siegel. "We've had people locked in fetal positions for as long as 72 hours. We had a psychotherapist who took it, disappeared, and turned up a week later directing traffic."

Ecstasy seems to be less popular in New York than in California. "It's been around for a while," says a gay-health expert. "You see people taking it at clubs all the time. But I haven't seen any evidence of either psychosis or nirvana. It's just a great drug for dancing."

It's also nothing new on college campuses. Several students who've tried it say that it's a very "talky" drug, and sensual—touching feels good—but not particularly sexual and certainly not the aphrodisiac some claim it to be.

Given that Ecstasy isn't much of an aphrodisiac and doesn't pack the wallop of any number of other party drugs, it seems possible that it will be little more than a passing fad among "recreational" users—an ultimately disappointing street drug, something tried once because of all the hype and then discarded. Still, Dr. Jeffrey Rosecan, the director of the Cocaine Abuse Treatment and Research Program at Columbia Presbyterian Medical Center, thinks it could turn out to be a very serious problem. "This could be potentially as devastating as cocaine, or worse—it's longer-lasting, it's cheaper, and it's being hyped in the media as *the* new drug."

Rosecan has already treated two college students who had prolonged psychotic reactions to what they claimed was MDMA. One became convinced that his friends wanted to kill him and locked himself in his dorm room for two weeks. "The other was a local-college student who was brought in by his sister," Rosecan says. "He was hallucinating and was convinced that people were trying to kill him. He spent four weeks in the hospital, and never really recovered. He's now in a group home in Pennsylvania."

There were mitigating circumstances in both cases: A family history of nervous breakdowns in the first, a serious family crisis in the second. But that's hardly the point. And even the more responsible advocates of MDMA acknowledge that there are potential dangers. "I have no doubt that this drug can be abused on the street," says Ingrasci. "*Any* drug can be abused. If you take enough aspirin, you can have a real psychedelic experience. No one is saying that MDMA shouldn't be controlled. The question is whether it should be banned, placed in such a restrictive schedule—as LSD was—that research of any kind becomes nearly impossible." That decision will be made in early 1986, after public hearings in Kansas City, Los Angeles, and Washington, D.C., this summer.

EVEN BEFORE THE FEDERAL GOVERNMENT ENTERED the picture, Rick Doblin sensed that MDMA would become a political issue. "Compassion has political implications. Empathy has political implications," he says. Doblin decided to contact various government agencies, to show good faith by *telling* them all about MDMA and asking for guidance.

He contacted Carlton Turner, who is Ronald Reagan's top drug-policy adviser. He contacted Nancy Reagan's anti-drug group, the National Federation of Parents for Drug Free Youth. He contacted the Food and Drug Administration and the National Institute on Drug Abuse and the United Nations. He proposed cooperation. He proposed joint research into MDMA. He proposed to the United Nations that MDMA be used in a project called "Shaping a Global Spirituality While Living in the Nuclear Age."

Both the U.S. government and the World Health Organization proposed that MDMA be made illegal.

"I think," Doblin says, "they were moving in that direction before I contacted them."

In any case, last July 27, the Drug Enforcement Administration announced plans to include MDMA in Schedule I, the most stringent category of the federal Controlled Substances Act, reserved for drugs with high abuse potential and no accepted medical use. Heroin and LSD are Schedule I drugs. (Cocaine is listed in Schedule II: high abuse potential, but some medical use.)

On September 12, Richard Cotton, an attorney with the law firm of Dewey, Ballantine, Bushby, Palmer and Wood, sent a letter to the DEA announcing that he had been retained by a group of MDMA researchers and therapists. They wanted to challenge the proposed scheduling on the grounds (a) that the drug had only a low or moderate abuse potential and (b) that it had great therapeutic possibilities. Informally, Ingrasci and several of the other therapists working with MDMA say they hope it will be put in Schedule III, with prescription drugs like Doriden. The Earth Metabolic Design Foundation takes a similar position.

Apparently, the MDMA lobby took the DEA by surprise. "We had no idea it was being used by therapists," says Frank Sapienza of the DEA's Drug Control Section, quickly adding that it doesn't make much difference: "It's being made in clandestine labs. It's being sold on the street. People are getting intoxicated from it. If it does have medical use, where are the animal studies and pre-clinical trials that prove it? If they ever want it to be accepted, it's going to have to go through the same rigid and rigorous scientific process that every drug goes through."

Traditionally, the only drugs that make it through the "rigid and rigorous" scientific process are the ones sponsored and patented by the major drug companies; it usually takes millions of dollars' worth of research to get a drug approved by the Food and Drug Administration.

And it's unlikely that any drug company would make such a commitment to MDMA for two reasons: The drug already was patented by Merck in 1914, which means that no one can have exclusive rights to it, and—perhaps more to the point—mind-altering drugs are still considered pretty weird by most doctors.

In late summer, Rick Doblin joined with two California researchers to resuscitate the Earth Metabolic Design Foundation, Inc., a nonprofit corporation founded by Buckminster Fuller that had been lying fallow for years. The idea was to raise money for research into MDMA and to begin animal-toxicity and clinical studies. The foundation also sponsored several conferences at Esalen about MDMA, including one, from March 10 to 15 of this year, that brought together researchers, therapists, enthusiasts, and a few opponents (including a representative sent by the president's drug-policy adviser) from around the country.

"This was a very serious meeting," says one of those who attended. "There were a few younger people who see the drug as the key to world peace and that sort of thing, but they were soon quieted down by the tone of the meeting. Most of the people there were over 40, therapists, pharmacologists, academics. We spent several days trading stories, with a special emphasis on bad experiences with MDMA. There weren't very many."

On the fourth day of the meeting, half of those attending took the drug while the other half monitored the experience. That evening, at dinner, they shared their reactions, which ranged from indifference . . . to the claim by a prominent psychiatrist from Los Angeles that he had spent six hours talking to Jesus.

ALL OF WHICH WAS INTERESTING—AND RATHER reminiscent of the 1960s—but, in the end, only served to emphasize how little is known about MDMA. Even the drug's most devoted advocates acknowledge that there has been absolutely no research done into long-term effects. No one knows if it causes cancer or diabetes or brain damage (or, indeed, if it cures any of the above).

"Let's say it works," says Siegel of UCLA, who was invited to the Esalen meeting but didn't attend. "For the sake of argument, let's say these guys are right and it really does have enormous therapeutic potential—that's all the more reason for it to be thoroughly tested and proved and refined. If they're right, this is too important a breakthrough to be cavalier about. Why not take the time and do it right?"

"Why not take the time?" asks a New York therapist. "I'll tell you why—because we see people walking into our offices every day who are in enormous, debilitating pain. I just saw this family—they were convinced the daughter was doing coke. She wasn't. I'm sure she wasn't. Anyway, they walked in here carrying such garbage and anger and repression and wrongheaded responsibilities on their backs . . . I wish I could've given them the drug and eased their pain, given them real peace with each other for just a few hours, probably for the first time in their lives. Given that, you'll pardon me if I say, 'Who *cares* about the long-term effects?'"

The Drug Enforcement Administration cares, and so does the Food and Drug Administration, and for that reason it seems quite probable that they will put MDMA in Schedule I as soon as the hearings are over.

"It's a shame," says Dr. David Nichols, professor of medicinal chemistry at Purdue University. "That will make it virtually impossible to continue research into MDMA, which is a real tragedy, because I think we've come across something new and important here, something we've never seen before. Even if MDMA isn't the answer, second- or third-generation versions of it might be, and this ruling is going to make finding those drugs more difficult. It will reinforce the damper on research into this field that has existed since the 1960s."

But even though psychedelics have been roundly discredited for the past fifteen years, research *has* continued. Progress apparently has been made. Synthetics like MDMA are far more subtle than sledgehammer drugs like LSD. No doubt, research will continue no matter what the DEA decides, and still more subtle drugs will be developed as time goes on.

"The real question—the one that won't be addressed by the DEA—is how we use drugs in this society," says Ingrasci. "A tacit decision has been made that it's okay to use drugs to ease pain. It's okay to take aspirin or Valium, both of which may well be more dangerous than MDMA. But it's not okay to use drugs to gain insight.

"My hope is that MDMA will force us to reevaluate our attitude about that."

It's an issue that certainly isn't going to go away. "Say they throw MDMA in the wastebasket, as they probably will," Ingrasci continues. "What happens then? Well, there are maybe 50 other molecules sitting on the shelf, waiting to be used. Before you blink an eye, MDMA will be replaced by another drug that will do essentially the same thing. In fact, the drug already exists. It's called MDE."

MARIJUANA

Is there new reason to worry?

Winifred Gallagher *is a Senior Editor of* American Health.

America just can't decide what to do about marijuana. Some people equate smoking pot with sipping wine, others with abusing hard drugs. Most rank it somewhere in between. The confusion is awkward but understandable: Marijuana is the nation's most popular but perhaps least understood illegal psychoactive substance.

So far, studies of pot's health effects suggest what many who've smoked it would predict: For most people, occasional use probably isn't particularly harmful. Heavy use over long periods is likelier to be dangerous, although the kind of expensive, long-term studies that proved the destructive effects of tobacco and alcohol remain to be done. At present, those who seem most at risk include young people, pregnant and nursing women, heart patients and the emotionally unstable. Harvard psychiatrist and drug researcher Norman Zinberg summarizes the inadequate and conflicting data this way: "Nothing's been proved, but there's reason to worry."

There's a pressing reason to learn more about marijuana's effects: The pot on the street has increased in strength and potential harmfulness. Thousands of professional growers, many of them in Northern California, have transformed American homegrown from a cottage industry into a multibillion-dollar-a-year agribusiness. These knowledgeable farmers use sophisticated technologies like hydroponics to cultivate pot powerful enough to command astronomical prices—more than $100 an ounce in big cities.

Recent studies show there are plenty of customers, though not quite as many as there used to be. Pot smoking peaked in 1978, and has declined since, especially among teenagers. The number of high-school seniors who smoke it daily fell by over half from 1978 to 1986. However, the drug remains enormously popular: Some 62 million Americans have tried it, and 18 million smoke it regularly. Many of today's smokers are the babyboomers who first lit up in the '60s and '70s. But some have found that the drug that mellowed them as hippies can make them uptight as yuppies.

One reason that pot smoking makes many graying members of the Woodstock generation anxious these days is that even occasional use can jeopardize their livelihoods; Many face tests to detect traces of the drug in their urine as a condition of employment. Even long-ago indulgence can damage reputations, as Judge Douglas Ginsburg learned when he was forced to withdraw himself from consideration for the U.S. Supreme Court.

The uncertainty over almost every aspect of marijuana has created confusing, contradictory policies. At the same time that the practice of urine testing spreads, laws in many states increasingly treat users with leniency. Although smokers can still be jailed in some states, they are now merely fined in others where the drug has been "decriminalized." In Alaska they can even legally grow their own. Smoking marijuana continues to become more socially acceptable, but the question remains: Is it safe?

What Pot Is, How It Works

Marijuana is not a simple—or even a single—drug. Its wide range of effects on body and mind is caused by the more than 400 chemicals of the Cannabis sativa plant especially the 60 or so that are unique to it—the cannabinoids (see "Medical Benefits?"). Some of these may contribute only minimally to the "high," but THC (delta-9-tetrahydrocannabinol) produces most of the psychoactive effects. While the potency of street

Signs of Trouble

"There are no simple signs that a person has a serious problem with marijuana, but there are some common patterns," says Dr. Robert Millman, of the New York Hospital-Payne Whitney Clinic. "An interaction of the drug, the person and the environment is usually involved." According to the American Psychiatric Association, 4% of adults in this country suffer from "cannabis dependence" at some time in their lives.

Doctors stress that it can be very difficult to distinguish whether a pot problem is a symptom or a cause. The problem is that users in trouble often have pre-existing personality or mood disorders, which are aggravated by the drug. However, indications of a dependence on marijuana include:

■ A pattern of daily or almost daily use, usually developed over a long period. Chronic heavy users generally increase the frequency of smoking over time, rather than the dose. But they also find, with long-term use, that they eventually get less pleasure from smoking.

■ Impaired ability to function socially or on the job.

■ Use of other drugs together with marijuana.

■ Lethargy.

■ Anhedonia—the inability to feel pleasure.

■ Attention and memory problems.

Pot mellowed the hippies, but can make yuppies uptight.

drugs varies greatly, the average concentration of THC by weight has increased from about 1% or less in the '60s and '70s to anywhere from 4% to 10% in the '80s.

When marijuana is smoked, THC enters the lungs, passes into the blood stream and is carried to the brain in minutes. Both THC and its chemical by-products dissolve in fatty tissue—such as the brain, the adrenals, the gonads and the placenta—and remain there for three or more days. (These chemicals can be detected in the urine of frequent smokers for four weeks or more.) It's worrisome that these compounds linger in the body and accumulate with repeated smoking, but there's no evidence yet that they cause harm.

In the brain itself, according to Dr. Billy Martin, a professor of pharmacology at the Medical College of Virginia in Richmond, THC seems to turn on a number of biochemical systems. In low concentrations it may cause two or three changes; in stronger doses, 10 or 12. Says Martin: "The high is probably a combination of effects—sedation, euphoria and perceptual alterations—each caused by a separate mechanism." He thinks that molecules of THC produce their effects by fitting into special receptor cells in the brain, like keys in locks. If Martin and his colleagues could prove the existence of the receptors, their discovery would suggest that a THC-like biochemical occurs naturally—the body's own version of marijuana. "Such a substance could serve in the maintenance of mental health," Martin says, "perhaps by helping the individual to calm down or protect himself against stress."

High Anxiety

During the marijuana high, which lasts for two to four hours after smoking, users often experience relaxation and altered perception of sights, sounds and tastes. One of pot's commonest side effects is the "munchies"—a craving for snacks, especially sugary ones. Participants in a study at Johns Hopkins ate more snacks—and consumed more calories per day—while they had access to marijuana in a social situation.

The high can be subtle and somewhat controllable, and intoxicated users can seem sober to themselves and others. But this *feeling* of sobriety is one of pot's greatest risks to well-being. Hours after the sensation of being stoned is over, the drug can still impair psychomotor performance.

The user's coordination, visual perceptions, reaction time and vigilance are reduced, which can make it dangerous to drive, fly or operate machinery. In a study done at Stanford University, simulated tests of pilots' skills showed they were affected for up to 24 hours after smoking, although they felt sober and competent. Another California study showed that a third of the drivers in fatal car crashes had been smoking marijuana. Driving under the influence of pot may be especially dangerous, because the driver may not know when his ability to function is askew.

Short-term memory and learning ability are also curtailed for hours after smoking. This delayed effect could be a serious problem for students, especially frequent smokers. Because the duration and extent of marijuana's psychomotor effects are not known for sure, the practice of testing urine to determine workers' competence is very controversial. "For the first two to four hours, say, on a Saturday night, the drug decreases one's ability to think, drive and work," says Dr. Reese Jones, a drug researcher and professor of psychiatry at the University of California, San Francisco. "But it's yet to be determined if those effects are still present on Monday morning."

Dr. Robert Millman, director of the alcohol and drug abuse service of the New York Hospital-Payne Whitney Clinic, agrees. "Most of the urine screenings that test positive for drugs

Medical Benefits?

Marijuana can be a useful medicine, but it's no wonder drug. People have used it for 5,000 years to assuage a variety of complaints, most recently in the effort to help treat glaucoma, asthma, spasticity, seizures and certain other nervous system irregularities, as well as the nausea that accompanies chemotherapy. In fact, doctors can now legally prescribe THC, pot's most active ingredient—usually in a capsule marketed as Marinol—for chemo patients.

However, marijuana has not proved itself to be superior to other drugs for most patients. So far, it's just an alternative that may work better for certain people. Many scientists doubt it will ever be a truly significant addition to the pharmacopeia. Its action is neither potent nor focused enough to produce the predictable, clear, isolated effects of first-class drugs. Moreover, the intoxication it causes often makes THC medication undesirable.

On the other hand, marijuana does have limited but documented medical potential. With further research, its components could be teased apart. Those that produce the desired effects—say, the suppression of vomiting or relaxation of muscles—could be isolated, and the rest, causing euphoria and sedation, could be eliminated. Its remedial action is sometimes different from that of standard drugs, which could point pharmacologists to new research directions—one reason scientists are dismayed over the reduction of research funds.

Marijuana may have some medical uses, but it's no wonder drug.

man Zinberg, author of *Drug, Set, and Setting* (Yale University Press, $10.95), studied a group of marijuana smokers, he concluded that "essentially, marijuana doesn't cause psychological problems for the occasional user." Many of his colleagues agree. Most of Zinberg's subjects described the drug as not particularly deleterious to normal functioning, and difficult (though not impossible) to abuse; they tended to restrict smoking to leisure time and special occasions, often planned around food.

Deadheads & Other Potheads

The researchers' consensus on long-term heavy marijuana smokers is bleaker, although hard data are more elusive than those on the drug's acute effects. For the vast majority of users, pot isn't physically addictive. It ranks far below drugs such as cocaine and heroin—or alcohol and tobacco—in inviting compulsive use. Nonetheless, a significant number of smokers use the drug frequently, often daily. Such regular use is one of the most obvious signs of a serious marijuana problem; heavy daily smokers are usually at least a bit out of it (see "Signs of Trouble").

Being out of it is less noticeable in the countries where the three large field studies of chronic users were conducted than in the fast-paced United States. Marijuana is widely accepted in Jamaica and Costa Rica, and within certain subcultures in Greece. These studies found that pot smokers were by and large as healthy—and functioned as well—as nonsmokers. However, although these surveys didn't prove any major, permanent health consequences of long-term pot use, that doesn't mean there aren't any. Researchers caution that the subjects of these studies were mostly poorly educated, working-class adults who have lower standards for produc-

pick up signs of pot—a very widely used drug," he says. "Companies are confused about what to do—should they fire everybody?"

Evaluating marijuana's impact on mental ability is difficult, but gauging its effects on emotional health is even more so. Responses are subjective and unpredictable. Marijuana is often associated with a feeling of mellowness, but it causes anxiety as well. It might make one user drowsy, and another—or the same user on a different occasion—hyperactive. One smoker becomes chatty, another withdrawn.

The strength of the drug, frequency of use, and physiological differences among users—for example, in body size and neural sensitivity to the drug—help account for the wide range of reactions. "About a third of people who smoke it feel no effects, a third feel ill and a third feel high," says Dr. Renaud Trouvé, a drug researcher and assistant professor of anesthesiology at Columbia-Presbyterian Medical School in New York.

What Timothy Leary and others called "set and setting"—the mental state of the user and the environment in which the drug is taken—also plays a part in emotional reactions to marijuana. According to Millman, many people now in middle age found smoking pot relaxing as youths within the laid-back '60s counterculture. As they've increased in age, power and responsibility, they've tuned out, turned off and dropped in.

"There's a natural history to marijuana use," he says. "The baby boomers have acquired a sense of their vulnerability and of the finiteness of time—'This is my life we're talking about!'" he says. "Feeling lethargic and giving up control make them anxious now."

That fear of losing control, or even one's mind, can induce paranoia and anxiety—pot's commonest unpleasant side effects—in people who would not have had these problems if they hadn't taken the drug, according to Millman. Moreover, he says, "marijuana can open a door to psychosis in predisposed persons similar to the action of many hallucinogens like LSD." Many doctors suspect that in these rare instances of users losing touch with reality, the drug has simply activated a latent psychiatric problem. Because of marijuana's potential for stirring up the psyche, psychiatrists say those with pre-existing disorders should stay away from it.

However, after Harvard's Dr. Nor-

tivity and health than middle-class Americans. And it took decades, not years, to determine the serious risks now known to be associated with alcohol and tobacco.

For those who look on pot as a buffer against stress, so-called "self-medication" can be dangerous: The person who smokes in an effort to "treat" his depression, anxiety or personality quirks may only add to his trouble. The psychological problem most often associated with chronic marijuana smoking is the "amotivational syndrome." Those thought to have it—many of them teens and young adults—show diminished goal-orientation, passivity and an inability to master new problems. However, the syndrome poses a chicken-or-egg question: Does heavy pot use cause poor motivation, or vice versa?

New York Hospital's Millman prefers the term "aberrant motivation" to describe the inert attitude of some heavy smokers. "When parents arrive at my office with a son in a ponytail and a tie-dyed shirt, they don't have to say a word. The kid is abusing drugs and doing badly in school and at home—but somehow he can get himself to a Grateful Dead concert in Ohio with $7 in his pocket. He doesn't lack motivation, he's just focusing it in the wrong direction."

Millman, who thinks such flawed motivation is caused by the combination of pot and pre-existing psychological problems, has found that some adolescents smoke grass not only to escape from their troubles, but to explain them. Such self-handicapping protects their egos against feelings of failure. "Many of the kids I see have made pot smoking the rationalization for psychopathology—they and their peers can say they act weird because of dope, rather than because they have an untreated learning disability or an emotional disorder," he says.

Some teens smoke to give themselves an excuse for failure.

Children and teenagers are endangered by any drug, because their bodies and minds—especially their judgment—are immature. A study of middle-class adolescents dependent on marijuana, reported in the May 1987 issue of the journal *Clinical Pediatrics*, helped identify those who may be at highest risk from the drug. Many were learning-disabled, had family histories of alcoholism, and personal and academic problems. Their parents and in some cases therapists hadn't suspected their pot smoking for a year after they started, perhaps because other problems may have disguised the drug use.

The connection between pot, poor motivation and learning disabilities is particularly troubling in an era when 28% of students drop out of high school. The sedation, skewed psychomotor functioning and involvement with other drugs and drug-abusing peers associated with marijuana make any use by teens unwise. A kid who tries pot also has an estimated 10% risk of becoming a daily smoker—and frequent use, at this age, can become truly disastrous.

Revving Up the Heart

Proof of the physical risks of marijuana is as elusive as proof of its dangers to the mind. The lack of comprehensive long-term human studies and the limits of animal research frustrate scientists like Renaud Trouvé. He's convinced that marijuana stresses the heart, lungs and immune and endocrine systems, particularly when it's used frequently. "As for the short-term physiological effects of marijuana, one can believe what is written," he says. "As for the long-term effects, we just don't know."

For example, it seems reasonable that pot smoking would be bad for the lungs. Marijuana contains more tar and carcinogens than tobacco and is inhaled longer and harder. But while heavy users do show a measurable airway obstruction and seem more prone to bronchitis and sinusitis, no links to serious lung diseases like cancer or emphysema have been established. In

Marijuana has more carcinogens than tobacco does.

fact, perhaps the worst threat to the lungs of pot smokers is the herbicide paraquat, which was sprayed widely on marijuana fields, especially in Mexico. The use of the chemical, which can cause severe lung damage, has been discontinued, although it's being considered as a way to deter growers in California and Hawaii.

The effects of marijuana on the reproductive system also seem ominous, but remain unproved. The drug temporarily lowers the level of the sex hormone testosterone in men, and decreases the number, quality and motility of sperm, but the impact on fertility is unknown. However, testosterone also helps govern puberty's changes in boys. Some researchers think that low levels of the hormone could impair adolescent development.

Women who smoke heavily may experience menstrual irregularities, including a failure to ovulate. When pregnant monkeys, rats or mice are exposed to heavy doses of pot, their offspring are more likely to have a low birth weight or to be stillborn. There's no clear proof that marijuana causes birth defects, but doctors urge pregnant and nursing women to treat pot with the same caution they give to alcohol and tobacco.

Similarly grim but inconclusive observations suggest that marijuana use can adversely affect other organs and systems in the body. Some researchers have found that marijuana can cause microscopic brain-cell damage in monkeys—but human brain damage hasn't been shown. Some studies suggest that marijuana can suppress immune function to some extent, but scientists don't yet know whether that degree of dysfunction affects health. What's more, marijuana increases the heart rate by as much as 90 beats per minute. This added workload could be very dangerous for those with cardiovascular disorders such as angina, but

> *Pot can change sex hormone levels, for men and for women both.*

there's no evidence that it causes any permanent harm to healthy hearts.

Toward a Sound Pot Policy

What state-of-the-art marijuana research tells experts is that we need to know more. In 1982, the Institute of Medicine published "Marijuana and Health," a 188-page report based on solid research and compiled by a committee of 21 scientists. Its conclusion, echoed by many marijuana researchers today: "Marijuana has a broad range of psychological and biological effects, some of which, at least under certain conditions, are harmful to human health. Unfortunately, the available information does not tell us how serious this risk may be."

The uncertainty that surrounds marijuana use is compounded when it's compared to the nation's other drugs—both legal and illegal. Despite increasing decriminalization and public tolerance of pot, half of all drug arrests made by local police in 1985—almost 500,000—involved marijuana, according to *The New York Times*. Many citizens consider this police enforcement an inappropriate use of resources that could be used to fight the greater menace of deadly drugs like heroin and cocaine—or, for that matter, tobacco and alcohol, which cause hundreds of thousands of deaths each year.

It's unlikely that either of these two legal, lethal drugs would be lawful if they were discovered today. "The light use of marijuana is certainly not as bad for you physically as alcohol or tobacco," says Harvard's Zinberg. "Our drug policy is based on morals, not on health considerations. The person with a drink in his hand says to himself, 'I'm bad enough, but that guy smoking pot over there is worse.'"

Zinberg says the best approach toward a sound policy on marijuana would be continued decriminalization accompanied by 15 years of serious long-term research. By then, the public would have enough information to make personal choices and public policy decisions. Reese Jones believes

> *We need more money for basic research, not for drug testing.*

that, regardless of policy changes, marijuana's popularity may gradually die out as the group of heavy users ages.

The one point on which all those concerned with marijuana agree is that having so little knowledge of the drug is a dangerous thing. Despite its prevalence and the unanswered questions about its use, federal support for marijuana research, still in its infancy, has decreased— diverted to less-used but "hotter" drugs like cocaine. "I'm a researcher with conservative views on drug use who hasn't found the hard data on the health effects of marijuana," says Jones. "There's a lot of uncertainty about it—you can't say it's unsafe, but there's no proof it's benign, either. We should be studying it to find out, but all the research money is going to help figure out how to detect it in people's urine instead."

How could you become addicted to medicine that doesn't even require a prescription? Very easily, found the author, who recounts her experience with nose sprays and warns of laxatives, eye drops and other drugs to watch out for.

Hooked
on Over-the-Counter Drugs

JEANIE WILSON

I never expected to become addicted to any drug, much less an over-the-counter medication I picked up at the supermarket along with my groceries. Yet it happened, innocently enough, after a foot operation I had at the height of the allergy season. Afraid that taking my usual allergy pills on top of the prescribed pain medicine might sedate me into a coma, I decided to use a nasal-decongestant spray instead. Two weeks later, when I tried to stop using the spray, I discovered I was hooked, desperate for my "fixes." Without them, I could no longer breathe through my nose.

Not that I was an addict in the sense of getting *high* on the drug. But because I'd used the spray longer than the package recommended, I had become physically addicted to it. "Addiction is defined by what we call an 'abstinence syndrome,' " explains pharmacologist Joe Graedon, author of a series of *People's Pharmacy* books (Bantam/St. Martin's Press). "If you experience physical or psychological withdrawal symptoms after you stop using a substance, then you are addicted."

It's possible for people to become *psychologically* dependent on practically anything, even aspirin, says Graedon. But when most of us think of medications that can be *physically* habit-forming, prescription and illicit drugs come to mind. Anything that is available off the shelf must be fairly harmless, right?

Wrong. Not only can many OTC drugs hurt you if taken incorrectly, but several can lead to physical dependency if overused. The problems you get when you abuse these drugs can prove far more debilitating than the ailment you took them for.

Here are the ones to watch out for:

Nasal Sprays

Physicians suspect that thousands of people have inadvertently become dependent on topical nasal decongestants, many to a greater degree than I was. After several months, I needed six times the recommended dosage during the day, plus a dose around 3 A.M. But there are hard-core users of 20 years and longer who consume several bottles of spray every day.

It doesn't take long to get hooked. The package directions states that nasal sprays shouldn't be used for longer than three days—a warning I ignored. After that time, and even sooner for some especially sensitive individuals, you can run the risk of ever-worsening congestion, constant sneezing and a perpetually runny nose.

The reason for all this misery, explains Atlanta allergist/immunologist Dr. Donald C. McLean, is a reaction known as rebound phenomenon. Nasal sprays work by shrinking blood vessels in the nose. If the spray is used too often, though, or for too many days in a row, those blood vessels become fatigued and can no longer shrink. They dilate instead, and the surrounding nasal tissues swell with fluid, causing more con-

---

Using Without Abusing

● Always read the label on a new bottle or package, even if you've taken the drug before. Manufacturers are continually updating ingredients, warnings and other instructions.

● Limit use to the dosage and amount of time specified on the label. "Occasionally you may use a drug longer than the package recommends if you're under a physician's supervision," says Gerald Rachanow of the FDA. "But for self-medication, follow package guidelines."

● If you don't understand any of the instructions, or if you're concerned about mixing medications, ask your pharmacist for advice.

● If you suspect you're taking too much of an OTC drug, make it harder to get to. Store it on a top shelf; don't carry a supply in your purse. If you've ever had a dependency problem with an OTC drug, don't keep that drug around the house.

● Finding it hard to quit? Ask your doctor for help. Don't be embarrassed. You won't be the first case he or she has seen!

From *Woman's Day,* January 19, 1988, pp. 52, 54-56. Reprinted by permission of Don Congdon Associates, Inc. Copyright © 1988 by Jeanie Wilson.

gestion than ever. You *can* make the vessels shrink again, but it takes more spray more often to do it, says the doctor. The end result isn't just discomfort: You can suffer permanent damage to nasal membranes, excessive bleeding, infected sinuses, even partial or complete loss of smell.

Fortunately, my case hadn't progressed that far. When I finally consulted my allergist, I was given a shot of cortisone to reduce inflammation and ease withdrawal. Occasionally, the cortisone is injected directly into the nose, but I got my shot in the rear.

For one hideous day my nose and what seemed like half my throat were completely stopped up, but then the cortisone began to work. I wasn't back to normal for several weeks, though.

Instead of an injection physicians sometimes use a cortisone nasal spray or another prescription spray containing cromolyn sodium, reports Dr. McLean. In cases less extreme than mine, oral antihistamines may be sufficient.

If the dependency isn't longstanding, these home remedies might work:
● Wean yourself from the spray by using decreasing concentrations, recommends Dr. C. Edwin Webb, pharmacist and clinical affairs associate of the American Pharmaceutical Association. Switch from long-lasting, 12-hour brands to short-acting forms, and then to children's formula.
● Use the spray in just one nostril, suggests Graedon. That way you can keep breathing through one side while the other gradually clears.
● Try using a salt solution to help heal sinuses irritated by too much spray. Ask your pharmacist about premixed ones or make your own. Max Leber, pharmacist and author of *The Corner Drugstore* (Warner Books), gives these directions: Dissolve ½ teaspoonful of baking soda and 1 teaspoon of salt in a quart of cool water. Fill an empty spray bottle half full of the solution and spray nostrils several times daily until inflammation subsides.

See a doctor if the problem persists.

Laxatives

Even with a clear warning on the package stating that "frequent or continued use may result in dependency," experts estimate that millions of people still become "laxative junkies." A few do so intentionally in misguided attempts to lose weight. But most abusers have a false concept that normal bowel function means one movement a day, says Dr. Marvin M. Schuster, gastroenterologist at Johns Hopkins School of Medicine. "What is normal can vary from three a day to three a week," he explains, "but we have a hard time convincing people of that."

The most habit-forming laxatives contain *phenolphthalein*. They work by irritating the lining of the intestines, which in turn irritates the nerves that cause intestinal muscles to contract. "Eventually, these nerve cells can permanently degenerate," warns Dr. Schuster. "The intestine actually becomes partially paralyzed, making constipation worse than it was before you took laxatives."

People who use laxatives too often soon discover they must take more and more to get the same effect. Yet the more they take, the more constipated they become. Little wonder they eventually become convinced they can't have a normal movement without the drug.

Most laxative abusers aren't even aware of their dependency, says Dr. Schuster. "Instead, they complain about increasing trouble treating what they see as their constipation problem."

Kicking the laxative habit usually involves tapering off very gradually over a period of weeks, says Dr. Schuster, perhaps substituting a bulk-type laxative, which works more naturally, for the stimulant type. Adhering to a high-fiber, low-fat diet with plenty of fluids and getting regular, moderate exercise is crucial. Retraining the bowel also helps—that is, making a habit of at least attempting to have a movement at the same time every day.

People with eating disorders who purposely abuse laxatives require psychological counseling as well as medical treatment, says internist Dr. Stephanie Zavitsanos of the Renfrew Center for anorectics and bulimics, in Philadelphia. "The ironic part," she adds, "is that although they *think* they're losing weight by taking laxatives, studies show only a minimal amount of calories is actually lost. What they're losing is mostly fluid, not fat."

Eye Drops

Designed to "get the red out," these drops can take you for a long trip on the Red-Eye Express if you aren't careful. Like nasal sprays, they contain vasoconstrictors that constrict the blood vessels in the eyes, making them smaller so the eyes look whiter. If you use them too often—say, several times daily over a period of weeks—rebound phenomenon can occur.

"It's the same action, the same increase to tolerance and the same addiction," explains Atlanta ophthalmologist Ken Kindy. "Using the drops occasionally is all right. But if you abuse them, you may find you're having to use the drops every few hours to get rid of redness, and when you try to stop, your eyes get redder than they were before you started."

The treatment: Stop cold turkey. "It may take two weeks to a month, sometimes even longer, for the eyes to get back to normal," says Dr. Kindy. "It's tough having to walk around with red eyes all that time. You tend to want to use just a little, but that starts the problem all over again."

If you're concerned about chronic eye redness, see an ophthalmologist. The cause could be allergies, sensitivity to makeup or even an underlying systemic illness. "Then again," says Dr. Kindy, "some people just have naturally redder eyes than others because their blood vessels are larger."

Stay-Awake Pills

These OTC stimulants contain nothing but caffeine, and whether in a beverage or stay-awake pill, caffeine can be an addictive drug, says pharmacologist Graedon. "When you're used to having large doses and stop abruptly, a number of well-documented withdrawal symptoms can occur, the most common being a rather severe frontal headache."

The amount of caffeine in an individual tablet is small—usually 100 or 200 milligrams, equivalent to one or two cups of coffee. But Dr. Webb of the pharmaceutical association says, "There are people who use a bottle a week. That does amount to fairly substantial quantities."

What's more, adds psychologist Dr. Stephen Levy, author of *Managing the Drugs in Your Life* (McGraw-Hill), the body develops a tolerance for caffeine, requiring more and more to get the same stimulating effect. The more you take, the more likely you are to experience negative side effects, such as increased heart rate, headache and irritability. "People suffering from severe caffeineism often look like textbook anxiety neurotics," says Levy. "They could be in psychotherapy the rest of their lives and never get the right treatment, which is to cut down on caffeine."

How to quit? Gradually, if you want to avoid the withdrawal symptoms, cautions Dr. Levy. "Just have a little less caffeine each day."

Sleeping Pills

Over-the-counter sleep aids are approved by the FDA "for occasional use only." Using them for longer periods of time "is probably safe," says Gerald Rachanow, deputy director of the FDA's Division of Over-the-Counter Drugs, "but you could get into a dependency problem."

Most of these pills are actually antihistamines, an allergy medicine which has sleepiness as a side effect. People can come to depend on that side effect—psychologically, at least—to get to sleep. Allergy sufferers sometimes get to the point where they can't sleep without an allergy pill, whether or not their allergies are bothering them. Similarly, OTC sleep aids can become a habit for some individuals. "A lot of people don't know when insomnia will strike," explains Joe Graedon, "so they take a sleeping pill 'just in case.' The problem with taking sleeping pills on a nightly basis—even over-the-counter pills—is that discontinuing the practice can have an adverse effect on your sleep."

When you stop, you may have a few nights when you outlast David Letterman. But since antihistamines also have other side effects, such as dry mouth and heart palpitations, it's best to use them only occasionally. Rely instead on other anti-insomnia measures, like getting enough exercise and forgoing naps and caffeine.

Codeine Cough Syrups

Lots of people, including many health professionals and even some doctors, are unaware that it's perfectly legal in many places to get cough syrups that contain the narcotic codeine, an effective cough suppressant, simply by asking the pharmacist for it and then signing a register.

According to Jacob Miller, pharmacist and manager of professional relations at A.H. Robins Company, signing for codeine compounds is legal in about two thirds of the states. You are allowed to buy only 4 ounces in a 48-hour period, however, and the formulas themselves contain no more than a grain of codeine per ounce. "Codeine is a relatively safe drug," explains Miller. "People don't become addicted to it very easily, and if they do take a lot, they're likely to become nauseous and constipated." Nonetheless, he says, some people "can develop a tolerance to these side effects and also develop an addiction."

Those who manage to get hooked "can get very sick, just like a street junkie, when they try to withdraw," adds Dr. Levy. Addicts have been known to go to one drugstore after another, frantic for more codeine cough syrup. One pharmacist, now with the FDA, remembers when a neighboring community changed its laws to require a prescription for the drug. "The first day, so many abusers came across the county line to my store to stock up that we finally had to put the cough medicine away and tell everyone we were out." The treatment for codeine addiction is a step-down schedule of detoxification under a physician's care, says Dr. Levy.

The message from all this is clear: OTC drugs *aren't* harmless. They're strong medicine, helpful only when taken strictly according to package directions. If we lose control over OTC drugs, they may take control of *us*.

Understanding Alcohol There's more to this than just saying no.

Susan Goodman

Our society comes down hard on drugs like cocaine, heroin, and pot. Now it's highly unlikely that you will ever see the mayor of your town, a local fireman, or your grandfather smoking marijuana. But you might well see any one of them having a beer at a picnic or a glass of wine at the dinner table.

Unlike drugs that are illegal, alcohol is everywhere—in the grocery store, on TV commercials, and, quite possibly, in your refrigerator at home.

For you as a teen, alcohol can carry a mixed message. You may be exposed to it in a thoroughly acceptable way—by seeing people you trust and care for having an occasional drink. Or you may have seen its darkest side—as the cause of addiction, illness, and tragedy.

At some point in your life, you will make some choices about alcohol. Chances are, you may have already.

The Choices

The pressure to experiment with it may have come from friends, who tell you that drinking is a cool thing to do. A drink may seem like an easy way to feel loose at a party. Or, you have gotten the idea that drinking is one way to blot out a problem that seems too big to handle.

Our society tells teens that it's against the law for them to drink, but it also broadcasts the idea that drinking is something good. Beer commercials suggest that when you drink a certain brew, you'll have great fun. Movies show beautiful, happy people holding drinks. These messages make you say to yourself, "It's OK for me to drink."

As much pressure as you might feel from these sources, commercials can't place a beer into your hand. Your friends can. Have your friends ever tried to get you to drink by telling you that one drink won't hurt you? Or, have you ever thought that a drink might make you feel older: Or, do you picture yourself feeling cool or being more popular with your hand wrapped around a beer can? Have you been tempted to drink just because you want to fit in?

Like most things, there's nothing wrong with alcohol—under the right conditions. Adults who can drink responsibly can enjoy alcohol without serious consequences. They might relax with a drink after work or on a night out with friends, or have a glass of wine with dinner. They may toast a special occasion with a glass of champagne. They do not, however, endanger their lives or the lives of others by getting behind a steering wheel after they've had too much alcohol to drive safely. Nor do adults who drink responsibly become alcoholics—a disease that afflicts one person out of ten.

The Responsibility

Studies show that a little bit of alcohol may actually be good for adults. It helps them relax from some of the stress of daily life. A moderate amount of alcohol—no more than one or two ounces a day—can cut down on strokes and heart attacks, according to some recent studies. Of course, once people try to drown out the stress with too much alcohol, the positive effects are drowned as well. Although these people may drink to avoid problems with their family or with friends, they end up creating new ones by abusing alcohol.

As soon as you take a sip of alcohol, it begins a race through your system. Part of that sip immediately enters the bloodstream and moves on to the brain. The rest travels down your throat to the stomach, small intestine, and liver, all the while sending more alcohol to your brain via your bloodstream. The liver, recognizing it has a high priority job to do, immediately starts to filter out the alcohol. Once processed by the liver, it will leave the body as sweat or urine.

Alcohol's Quick Trip

That one sip of alcohol travels through your bodily systems at lightning speed. It goes from the mouth throughout the whole body in less than five minutes. In fact, even if it just stayed in your mouth without being swallowed, it would still reach your bloodstream in measurable amounts in less than 60 seconds. Although a shot of hard liquor has the same effect as a bottle of beer or glass of wine, research shows that the more concentrated the form of alcohol the more quickly it is absorbed by the body.

The Brain Slows Down

Your bloodstream carries the alcohol to every cell of your body. None of them are more affected, however, than those of the brain. Simply put, alcohol slows down the brain. It acts as a sedative, blocking certain chemical reactions and nerve endings. Communication between brain cells slows or shuts down so the brain can't do its job properly.

Since the brain is your body's control center, alcohol also slows the control of your nerves, muscles, and senses. It affects your coordination, depth perception, and reflex actions. When you've had a certain amount of alcohol, for instance, your body can no longer quickly sense the difference between hot and cold. If you were drunk enough, you might get burned by a stove or candle before you even noticed your hand was there.

Losing Focus

Another important sense affected by

alcohol is your vision. Normally if you are in a dark room and someone flashes a light in your eyes and then turns it off, your eyes will be blinded for a few seconds, then adjust. Drinking, however, slows your ability to focus your eyes and adapt to light. This loss of ability may pose no problem in a dark room, but what about on a highway at night when headlights flash . . . accident.

Since your senses don't work well with too much alcohol in the bloodstream, the decisions you make based on their information aren't always the best, either. These decisions may be as simple as how to put the key in the lock of your front door. They may, unfortunately, have much more serious consequences, like the decision of when to put your foot on the brake of your car.

Since alcohol affects all parts of the brain, your emotional behavior changes as well. The first part of the brain slowed by alcohol is the one that controls your reason and judgment. So, with just a little alcohol in your system, you may notice a lowering of inhibitions. You may find yourself saying things that you might ordinarily think, but would never say out loud. You might do things that your everyday self would never do.

You're Not Yourself

As the amount of alcohol in your system increases, it can cause mood changes. You may start laughing hilariously at things that aren't really funny. You could sob because a friend didn't say hello. You might shed your usual intelligent behavior and throw a punch at a good buddy.

If you continued to drink, your body would slow down even more. The alcohol would depress the activity of your lungs and heart, which would in turn slow your breathing and circulation. Next, you would most likely pass out or get very sick. The term "dead drunk" has some basis in truth; with enough in your body, alcohol can paralyze breathing completely and cause death.

A Hangover—and Worse

After drinking, many people experience a hangover with a lot of miserable symptoms including a furry mouth, headache, fatigue, and the feeling of being very, very dry. A hangover is really the process the body undergoes to rid itself of alcohol. If someone is a moderate drinker, the body has little trouble reversing the damage caused by alcohol. If someone abuses alcohol for a long enough time, however, it will cause permanent health problems from nerve and brain damage to heart dam-

age. Since the liver breaks down alcohol, it is frequently alcohol's worst victim. Cirrhosis of the liver (most commonly, though not exclusively, caused by alcoholism) is among the 10 leading causes of death by disease in the United States.

Yet disease isn't the only damage caused by this drug. Consider the following facts: Alcohol is involved in half of our country's crimes. Almost 75 percent of all murders are committed by individuals who have been drinking. And that's also true of one-third of all suicides and two-thirds of all suicide attempts. Every year, 25,000 people are killed in alcohol-related automobile accidents. And, six out of every 10 teenage highway fatalities involve alcohol.

"The Drink Takes the Man"

There are a lot of reasons why someone's drinking can get out of control. You may be drinking to be a part of the crowd or to keep from feeling lonely. You may get smashed on weekends to get your parents' attention and to see their reaction. You might even drink in the morning before school because you think that's the best way to get through the long day.

The Chinese have a proverb: "The man takes a drink, the drink takes a drink, then the drink takes the man." Whatever the reason for beginning, drinkers can quickly get physically and psychologically addicted to alcohol. They might have initially found drinking exciting or fun, but they eventually start to feel that they cannot function without alcohol. Even if the drinkers think they want to stop, they feel as if their drinking controls them, instead of the other way around.

Not everybody who drinks will become an alcoholic. In fact, not everyone

who drinks heavily will have this problem. Some people drink too much alcohol to cope with the stress of a specific problem in their lives. A man might frequently drink to the point of drunkenness, for example, after the death of his wife. A year later, he may hardly drink at all.

Family Problems

When heavy drinking, however, does lead to alcoholism in a family, it creates a very painful set of problems. You may never know, for example, if your dad is going to come home drunk and yell at you for nothing at all. Or, your mother may embarrass you in front of your friends.

Your mom might fall asleep with her face on the table or be moody or unpredictable. Your dad may hug you a lot when he's drunk and be grouchy when he's sober. You might stick up for the alcoholic in your family, which makes your brother or sister mad. Or, your older sister might feel that she must replace your mother (since your mom is always drunk), and you don't like it.

Life with an alcoholic parent also affects how your nonalcoholic parent acts. Your nonalcoholic parent can confide his or her bad feelings about your alcoholic parent and make you feel in the middle. You may hate to see your nonalcoholic parent lie and make excuses for his or her partner. Tempers may be short, and you may not be getting the attention and love you require.

Feelings to Sort Out

If you or someone you love has problems with alcohol, you will have some feelings to sort out. You need to find someone you trust and can talk with

---

Signposts of Alcoholism

Sometimes it's difficult to determine who is or will be an alcoholic. Here are some questions you can ask yourself or people you know to determine if there is a problem:

1. Do you think the most important and fun part of a party is drinking?
2. Do you have to drink a lot to feel happy?
3. Do you drink when you feel you have problems?
4. Do you ever have blackouts?
5. Do you have any problems that come from your drinking?
6. Has anyone ever suggested that you are an alcoholic?
7. Have you ever tried to sneak alcohol when you're alone?
8. Do you drink and drive?
9. Do you consider yourself to be an alcoholic?

One "yes" answer doesn't mean that you or anyone else is an alcoholic. But if you do answer yes to any of these questions, you should think about the role alcohol plays in your life. If you answered yes several times, you'd better think very hard and perhaps talk to someone about it.

about what's wrong. It may be a friend or relative or a teacher or counselor at school.

There are also organizations that help people with this specific problem. Alcoholics Anonymous (AA) has meetings for teenage alcoholics. Al-Anon and Alateen are programs, for example, for people who live with alcoholics. They can help you feel less alone and get ideas on how to cope with your particular situation. If you need information on such programs, ask an adult to help you or look in the Yellow Pages under "Alcoholism Information."

There is a vast difference between taking a first drink and becoming an alcoholic. Appreciating a fine wine or enjoying a foamy beer on a hot summer day can add spice to life. On the other hand, a person who chooses not to drink is not missing out on something essential. Learning to understand alcohol—and make responsible decisions about drinking it—is a hard, high-powered lesson.

For More Information

The National Clearinghouse for Alcohol and Drug Information
P.O. Box 2345
Rockville, MD 20852
Pamphlets: #MS229 "Alcohol Problems and Youths: Reading List," #MS270 "For Teenagers Only: How to Say 'No' to a Drink." #PH226 "Think—You Don't Have to Drink," #PH233 "Be Smart! Don't Start!—Just Say No!" single copies free.
Alcoholics Anonymous
Room 408
205 W. Wacker Drive
Chicago, IL 60606

Pamphlets: #P4 "Young People and A.A.," 20¢; #P24 "A Newcomer Asks," 10¢; #P37 "Too Young?" 25¢, send check or money order.
Wisconsin Clearinghouse
P.O. Box 1468
Madison, WI 53701

Pamphlets: #133 "Who's Sending You Signals?" 50¢; #182 "You Asked for It: Information on Alcohol, Other Drugs, and Teenagers," $1.75.
Al-Anon Family Group Headquarters, Inc.
Dept. PI/C
P.O. Box 862
Midtown Station
New York, NY 10018-0862

Pamphlets: "Youth and the Alcoholic Parent," "Alateen, Is It For You?" send self-addressed, stamped envelope. For additional pamphlets and information about a local group, call toll free 1-800-356-9996. New York and Canada residents, call (212) 245-3151.

Using Heroin: Two Accounts Drugs in American Society

Erich Goode

The contributor of this account is 29 years old; she works for a market-research firm. She used heroin for about six years. Although she was never literally physically addicted, she used it almost daily, and had what is called a "chippy" habit. She has remained drug-free (except for cigarettes and an occasional drink) for about five years.

ACCOUNT: USING HEROIN

I started on drugs when I was 16. That's when I was introduced to marijuana. A lot of things were involved with my starting. My brother was having problems, and there was a lot of tension at home, my parents were very upset, and this bothered me, and then I started having my own problems. My older brother was experimenting with various drugs, LSD and things like that, and he started going into therapy, and his shrink told him that his mind had been destroyed by drugs. This is not something you tell somebody who is supposed to be a patient. So he left school, and he stayed home, in his room, all the time. It was pretty bad. Plus, with me, I began having problems with my parents and with my friends. I was raised to believe that everyone is supposed to be treated equally. Only my parents really did not mean that, literally. So I happened to make some friends who were Black, and then it wasn't OK any more. When it came to bringing them home, it was another story—they disapproved. And I was really dong nothing wrong, I wasn't into drugs then or anything, so I became very rebellious about that, because I felt I was right and my parents were wrong. Also, I had my group of friends, and when I started having Black friends, my group of friends did not approve. So I ended up losing all of my previous friends, and it narrowed down to one girlfriend who I had a great friendship with—and she moved away. So there was this, on top of everything else. I was in pretty bad shape. So I started blocking everything out. I couldn't deal with it. People who use drugs don't like pain. They like to take the easy way

out of everything. So I started getting high pretty frequently.

It was marijuana at first. What happened was that people who were using marijuana that I knew, a good number of them, were also using other drugs, like ups and downs. A guy I met in my therapy group, ironically, said, why don't I go to a party with him. And this was a party where they were doing acid. That's when I started using that. I met a lot of people that I ended up hanging out with, and I started tripping. And I started coming home all hours of the night, and my parents could tell something in my eyes, my face, that I was high. I never saw it myself—you never do—but people who know you very well and who love you can detect a change. I became very belligerent and short-tempered. I had been a very good student up until high school. When I started using drugs, I really didn't care very much about school. It didn't matter to me any more. And my grades went down. When I came home at 5 in the morning and I was high, my parents were rather upset. A lot of crying, a lot of screaming and yelling. And trying to get me to go for help, and they went for counseling, and we went for counseling together. It really took its toll on our family. It was very upsetting for us. I couldn't deal with it. So I wanted to be on my own, and be able to do what I wanted.

So my goal in life at that time was to move out of my house when I graduated from high school. That was the most important thing to me then. I didn't want to go to college. So I moved out and got a job driving a taxi. And while I was driving a taxi, one of the people I worked with was dealing heroin, and we developed a relationship. One day, he asked me to take a ride with him to the city to cop. I was 18 or 19 years old. So I went and I snorted some heroin. I thought I'd just try it. And I liked it. And since I had this relationship, and he was selling drugs, I was able to get drugs. And heroin was like a warmth that envelops you. It's an automatic warmth that encompasses your whole being as soon as it enters your body. It softened all of my problems, where they didn't bother me as much. I guess it must be like being in the womb. You feel warm and safe and protected. It makes you feel calm. It made me feel like I loved the whole world.

I started using heroin pretty often, maybe every day. And it wasn't long, maybe a few months, until I started shooting, because everyone tells you that it's much better, much quicker, and you need less. And it was true. When I got into shooting it, the first few times, I got sick. But after the sickness passed, the feeling of euphoria came over me. I never thought, in my wildest dreams—I mean, I'm a stereotype, I'm white, Jewish, middle-class, I live in the suburbs, and when I was younger, I used to yell at my mother for smoking cigarettes, I used to preach against drugs—I never in my wildest dreams thought I'd be sticking a needle in my arm. A lot of people think, oh, I could never do that. But it's *amazing* what you can do. And I ended up doing it just about every day. And I did things that I would not have done if I wasn't under the influence. I became very free with my body. If I hadn't been under the influence, I wouldn't have been as free as I was. When you're high, you are not completely yourself. Because all drugs alter the way you think. You do things you wouldn't ordinarily do. So what happens is, after using whatever drugs, you lose touch with yourself—how bad it is, what it really does to you.

The way I began to live my life was, I'd wake up—there were many times I'd be awakened by somebody who would come to my house because I had a car and the other people I was hanging around with didn't have cars, and they would want to go either to cop, or go hit one of the stores and get some money from there. So maybe we'd go and hit a few stores, try and steal something, and then try and get the money for it by selling the merchandise. And this all takes a while. Then, if nobody in town had any drugs or anything that was good, we'd go to the city to a shooting gallery, which are not very nice places. Sometimes, in the shooting galleries, you could cop right away. Other times, you might be there for hours, waiting. It's probably one of the dirtiest places in existence. You can purchase hypodermic equipment there, which also isn't that sanitary. Of course, we'd try and copy locally before going to the city. There was an area nearby—there still is—where people would hang out on the street and we'd cop, if dope was in town. Most of the time, though, we'd cop in somebody's house. There were a few times when I tried dealing, but I wasn't very good at it, because I liked heroin too much, and I also was generous to other people, so I didn't do very well with that. If we copped someplace and brought it back, sometimes we would pull over on the side of the road on the way back, and stop somewhere to shoot up right in the car. One or two times I cam close to having accidents because I started nodding out while I was driving. We'd come home, shoot some more, use

just about all we could until we had a nice high, and then maybe I would have sex, listen to music, hang out on the street—and that was really about the whole day.

I was never physically addicted. I had what they called a "chippy" habit, where I had the sniffles if I stopped—that was the extent of what I had. I had more of a *mental* addiction, which is just as bad as a physical one. I tried methadone for a while. When I got the methadone, I wasn't serious about kicking. It was just a free high. That's why a lot of people go to the methadone clinics. This one nearby, they're paid by the federal government for each person they have on the program, and it seems, from my experience there, that they actually try and keep people on the program. First, I went into a live-in program for a couple months. And then I left. You're supposed to "graduate" from these places, but I didn't graduate. I just left and ended up getting high again. Then I thought I would try to help myself. I thought at least, with methadone, I wouldn't be involved in copping and the needles and all the illegal aspects of it. And so I tried that for a while. What I did was, before I went to the clinic, I shot a lot of heroin and I went there, and I had a blood test or a urine test they take to see what's in your system, and they found what I had put into my system, and I lied to them about my habit—and that was it. They let me in. They gave me a very high dosage in the beginning, which sometimes put me into a kind of daze, it was so strong. And the funny thing is, withdrawal from methadone is worse than with heroin. When they were cutting me down and I stopped, I felt achy in my bones. I was on the methadone program for two or three months—not all that long. I went on a detox program. They offered me, if I wanted to go on maintenance, and I didn't, I chose detox. Because through all my experiences, I never made a good dope fiend. Through it all, my goals in life came through. Being a dope fiend wasn't enough for me, it wasn't the kind of life I wanted to live. Luckily, I came through it.

The way I was supporting myself during these years was several things. At one point, I was on welfare, which I got on very easily. Also, I had a few friends, one or two, who were very generous with both money and dope, which is unusual to find in dope fiends. And I was working part of the time during this period. But I never lasted at a job, because I always wanted to get high. I used to shoot up at work in the bathroom sometimes. I also resorted to stealing. I had a few friends and we used to go to the store and steal things and bring the merchandise back in and get a refund. I wasn't very good at that either, but I managed to do it a number of times. And maybe I would turn a trick sometimes. I sold myself to men. I rationalized it in my own mind that it wasn't really prostitution because I knew these people somewhat, and it was that we were doing each other a favor. That's how I looked at it. So I did that a few times.

You think that the people you're dealing with are your friends, but they're not. They really couldn't give a damn about you. I didn't find this out until I stopped getting high. I was arrested because I was set up by two of these so-called friends. It was a federal offense—forging a money order or a check or something. I signed the check and went into a bank and my friends took off in my car when they saw the police, and I got busted, my second arrest. I was threatened by these people about saying anything about their involvement in it, but I ratted them out anyway, because they did the same thing to me. After I was arrested and taken to the police station, I wanted to call home. I wanted to tell my parents that I'd be late—I was between apartments and living at home—that I was delayed somewhere. I didn't want them to know what had happened. So the police officer who was questioning me picked up the phone and dialed my parents' house, and my mother answered and he said, hello, this is officer so-and-so, your daughter is under arrest, and he handed me the phone. Which they're really not supposed to do. It's good that he did it, because my parents came down to the police station. When I was there by myself, I was being very rebellious and hardheaded and stupid. Because my parents came there, I ended up telling them everything that had happened. And because my mother went to court with me, and I didn't have a previous record, and I was white, and middle-class—all that had to have something to do with it, I feel—and I wasn't belligerent in court, and I really did want help, they gave me probation.

I got a very easy probation officer. When I was on probation, I was getting high again. And it finally got to the point where she told me, I'd have to do something, because she couldn't keep allowing me to go on like this. So I didn't want to, but I went into a second live-in program, a therapeutic community, like Phoenix House, one of those. They helped me a lot. They also hurt me. Because the therapy that they give there is *very* harsh. I didn't graduate from there, either. I was there nine months, and then I left. I committed an infraction—someone told me about a staff member who had marijuana on his breath, and I didn't report it right away. I was given some kind of therapeutic action—it's not punishment, exactly, it's what they call a "work contract." I wasn't allowed to go to group sessions. There were various other reprisals. I became PO'ed at what they did to them. I felt it was not justified and I got angry. So I left. I was there nine months, and when I came out, I had to try heroin again.

I went to this local bar. I really didn't know where I was going or what I was doing. I wanted to get high, but I didn't know anybody. And someone from this bar, one of the locals, ended up taking me to the city to cop some heroin. And I ended up staying with him that night and going to bed with him. It wasn't that good an experience. The morning after, he was getting a little forceful with me, and I didn't care for it. Plus, the dope we got wasn't that good, either. I had been in the program for nine months, and it was not easy shooting up, after all the therapy I had gone through, and so it wasn't a good experience. So I was depressed, and I was lonely and I needed the caring of the people in the program for me. I was still screwed up. I wanted to go back because that was my family and my home. I was down and out and I needed them. When I went back into the program they cut off all my hair. And these two residents made me stand there and they called me all kinds of names—that I was a whore, that I was trash, that I was trying to kill myself by taking heroin again. I stayed on work contract maybe for two more weeks. I felt, well, I've built up such walls in my life, that it was to the point where they're yelling at me and everything, and I was starting to just block that out and it wasn't doing anything. So I felt that I wasn't going to get any more help there. I had gotten what I could and I was just wasting my time at that point. So I left. That was five years ago. I haven't touched heroin since.

I knew a lot of people who got high with me who had a lot of potential and their lives were ruined by dope. They're never going to go anywhere. I'm 29 years old. I wish that, by now, my career was all settled for me. That I had friends. You don't learn how to be a friend or what a relationship is when you're just getting high. And when you stop getting high, it's like being a baby and starting all over again from the beginning. When you're high, it's like being a robot. It's euphoric, but you could be anybody. All the people that are out there using drugs, the faces change, but they're all the same, they're all nobodies, because they're never going anywhere, they're never going to make anything of themselves.

My veins will never be the same again. From constantly shooting heroin in the same vein, it gets calloused and it collapses. And I guess that's what happened to my veins. And that's something that will never come back. I also have scars on my hands and a few on my feet from shooting in those places. I also got hepatitis. That means that I can never donate blood. The main thing that bothers me is that the years that I lost while I was taking dope I will never get back. And you lose a lot of self-pride because of the things you end up doing, and it takes a long time to get that back. What I should have been doing all that time in my life was going to college, pursuing a career, and going out and doing the so-called normal things. What I was doing was hanging out on the street corner and getting high. And that was my whole life. You don't see a lot of things when you get high. I had various relationships during that time which were all worth nothing. They were mostly physical, and when that's all over, it doesn't leave you feeling too good about yourself. Also, I was almost raped twice by my supposed friends because of the kind of people I used to hang out with. All of this takes its toll. If I hadn't gotten involved with drugs, maybe I would have had a career. Maybe I would have had more confidence in myself at this point in my life, because I don't have it now. I'd have some friends today, which I don't have now because after all those years, I really didn't have any friends left. Maybe I would have been married. That's another thing. I have a record, a past. So that will always be there. And if I do fall in love with somebody, this part of my life, my past, it's not something that I can just forget about and pretend it never happened. It's something that some people won't be able to accept.

I'm able to function in the world now. I have more confidence and pride in myself than I used to. It's not a hell of a lot, but at least it's more than I had. I'm still afraid of people, I really am. There are times I think about getting high. Not as often as I used to—it's less and less now. But I don't feel I could do it again, because if I did, I could never live with myself. I'd have to really go downhill to do that, and I wouldn't be able to deal with that. I'm still trying to learn how to get in touch with my feelings so that I can have relationships with people, and to build up my confidence. Because after everything I've been through, I guess I still think pretty lowly of myself. I'll be 30 soon, and it'll take a while before I can get my act together. [From the author's files.]

I KICKED HEROIN

Susan

Susan is a recent graduate of the State University at Stony Brook and, until recently, a heavy heroin user. The man to whom she related her story is a professional sociologist and a nationally recognized expert on drug use and abuse, Prof. Erich Goode of Stony Brook.

Prof. Goode writes this introduction to Susan's story: "When she talked to me about her experiences, she was a 22-year-old from a comfortable middle-class Long Island family. She was an excellent student, and she went to graduate school. She was bright, articulate, extremely attractive and a weekend heroin user. She shot up heroin two or three times a week for about two years. Incredibly enough, she never became addicted. When I taped this interview, she had moved away from her boyfriend, with whom she had been living, and had not used heroin for two months." Here is the transcript of Susan's story, as transcribed by Prof. Goode:

I didn't even think twice about the dangers or morality of turing on to heroin. As for the immediate cause . . . I did it because my boyfriend did it. He did it because his two closest friends did it.

At the time, all of us were deeply involved in the underground post high school drug subculture in an affluent community on Nassau's north shore. Most of the . . . group were in college, and ranged in age from 18 to around 21 years. As I suspect is the case with almost everyone who passes through the stage (some never leave it) of total and continuous drug saturation within a supportive social context, there was in our group an unofficial competition . . . concerning who could [take] the most drugs. During most of that summer we smoked grass every day and took LSD quite often. Anyway, around the beginning of July, I took my hash-filled body away on a trip with my family, returning three weeks later.

When I got back, my boyfriend . . . had a surprise for me. He said that he had shot heroin. Suddenly, all of the conventional stereotypes were forgotten. Heroin was not only accepted, it was cool. I was more mad about not being there when the first shots were fired than about anything else. Instantly, I said I wanted to try it, too. I was taken over to the house of a friend who had recently dived head-first into heroin without a backward glance. . . . I went to his house and he cooked up shots for my boyfriend, himself and me. . . . We were either very brave or very foolish to put ourselves into his hands like that . . . and I know it wasn't bravery. My boyfriend got his shot first. His previous experience had been very pleasant, a mild, warm feeling, and probably a pretty weak shot. This one was not so weak. The rush was so powerful that he almost fell down. He turned white and began to sweat profusely, saying "I'm afraid I took too much." Of course our friend said, "No, don't worry," and gave me my shot.

The needle went in quickly, with one light tap and no pain. That boy gave me a better injection than I've had from doctors! I watched, fascinated, as he squeezed the clear solution out of the dropper and then gave me a "boot"—letting blood run back into the dropper and then shooting it back into my arm. I, too, began to sweat and tremble. If anyone had seen . . . us coming out of the house, he would have called an ambulance. Our friend was fine, just his drooping eyelids, and thick, slow speech betraying his condition. My boyfriend and I were another story. We could barely walk. For some insane reason, we had decided to drive back to my boyfriend's house immediately after shooting up. . . . We had two cars, each of us driving one. . . . I had to keep pulling over to throw up on the side of the road. I don't know how I made it. I am surprised that we both didn't die that first night. I was more physically miserable than I had ever been. The whole night was spent vomiting.

The thing that surprises me the most is that we didn't forget about heroin right then and there. It was horrible! . . . We later agreed that our dear friend had given us too much. So I decided to give it another chance. Try and explain the logic of *that* decision to some straight person. But my friends were all doing it, and it had become a question of prestige.

And so it began. . . . The second shot, and most from then on, were *good*. I can't describe the rush to you. . . . When I shot up, I felt so superior, so wicked, so unique. I was proud of being the only girl in our scene. I thought I had found the ultimate rebellion, the most deviant act possible. I was drawn to it because it set us apart from, and above, everyone—even the other drug users, the "soft" drug users. . . .

Soon, heroin became the only thing to look forward to. The weekend became synonymous with "getting off." My boyfriend was living with me at the time, and his psychological need for the escape and deadening of pain which heroin provided was the major reason for our continued use. . . . I was simply following his lead. The winter was long and cold, he was depressed, only occasionally holding a job. Heroin was the only warm spot in the week.

We were careful to avoid shooting up more than four days in a row because we knew that addiction would destroy all of the great "therapeutic" value which we attributed to heroin. Also, we just couldn't afford it. I was working at school and got a second job as a waitress for a while. My father was paying the rent, so after I bought food, the rest went for dope. . . . Somehow, I passed my courses in school and we survived that long, cold winter.

We continued shooting up for about a year without getting a habit. We always . . . marked an X on the calendar for each shot. . . . We turned to heroin whenever we were depressed, or when we wanted to reward ourselves. Because of its capacity for alleviating tension and depression, because it enabled us both to overcome our anxiety . . . and because it seemed to fill up the holes in our empty lives (something we couldn't do for each other), heroin acquired a great deal of power. . . . It took a near-fatal overdose for my boyfriend (and three days of waiting to hear if he was dead or alive for me) to make us finally realize where we were at. Death was a price we were not willing to pay, even for all the benefits we thought we had been receiving. We went completely straight—not even smoking grass—for three months.

The problem with kicking heroin, even if you don't have an actual habit, is that all of your friends aren't kicking at the same time. . . . The three months' abstention was accomplished by almost total isolation from friends in the drug world. . . . The power that heroin had over us, however, did not dissipate. . . . We returned from a camping trip late in the summer and experienced a massive post-vacation letdown. . . . School didn't start for another month, and the same for my boyfriends' new job. . . . There wasn't enough time to get a job, really (I told myself). Boredom set in. To make matters worse, our friends had developed

real, honest-to-goodness, habits over the summer and now when we went to see them . . . all they were interested in was heroin. . . . I guess it was inevitable, wasn't it? The brush with death had been so long ago, and if we just did a little bit . . . and we'll only do it till school and the job start . . . and we *deserve* some fun before getting back into the rat race . . . and GOD am I bored. . . .

We began to shoot more dope than ever before. This time no X marks went on the calendar, though we still tried to control it and avoid getting hooked. We did, but it was harder now because everyone else was hooked. We shot up in the basement of my family's house quite often, and even though I was still rebelling, still irresistibly attracted to and *proud* of the deviance and "anti-sociability" of the act, I would nevertheless go to great lengths to keep my family from finding out. I knew they . . . would *never* understand, or even believe, what I was doing. They would say I had everything, I was throwing my life away, I was sick. How could I tell them, "Hey, I'm just looking for kicks, I need to do it because it's illegal and dangerous, and besides, it's such a groovy head." They would have thought I had a split personality to be so different from the daughter they thought they knew. . . . I tend to think that the primary target of my striving for deviance (which has manifested itself in other ways than shooting heroin) is possibly the sterility and blandness of the life I had always been exposed to and told to want for myself. . . . Out of a desire to give me a life of security and "happiness," my parents—and our whole American socialization process—gave me instead a life of real, deep feeling. I wanted to feel! I wanted to play in the dirt. I wanted to transgress those lily-white norms, break those rules designed to make me a good little Doris Day. And when the first transgression was followed not by the wrath of God . . . but by a feeling of being alive, and free, and different, that I had never known before, then I guessed after that, *all* rules and norms lost their meaning and power over me. The "badness" of shooting heroin was precisely why I did not hesitate to do it. . . .

I was shooting several times a week, sometimes daily for four or five days, waiting for school to begin. . . . I still wasn't addicted, not physically anyway, but something else began to happen. I began to get nauseous after I shot up, not immediately as I had on the first shot, but much later.

But it got to the point where I wasn't even enjoying my shots that much because I would already be feeling nauseous before the needle was in my arm. The rush coming on top of that just made me feel worse. . . . We were spending $5, $6, for a bag of dope and then getting sick.

Finally, just a day or two before school was to start, my boyfriend and I reached the turning point. I usually let him have the larger portion of whatever dope we had, but this night I decided to treat myself to a really big one. . . . I got what I wanted: a super rush. But then it went beyond my control and I fell back on the bed in the basement, my eyes wide open. My boyfriend was slapping me . . . but I couldn't move, my mouth was hanging open, eyes staring, hearing him and not being able to answer. I couldn't believe what was happening to me. . . . My boyfriend just kept shaking me until at last I became able to speak. We were both really scared—we had never been that stoned before and we thought we might die. I had always prided myself on being able to control myself on drugs. . . . But not that night. It was even worse than that first shot. No one was home, thank God, and we went outside and staggered up and down the driveway retching and hanging onto one another like couple of drunks. We put ice cubes on our faces and wrists, to keep ourselves from passing out. . . .

Somehow, we came out of it. . . . My boyfriend said he would leave me if I ever got dope again. As for me, my larger shot was manifesting itself as the dry heaves; I had long since emptied my stomach. My acute physical wretchedness was heightened by the psychological anguish I was experiencing as I realized that . . . many of my proud illusions about myself were false. I continued to retch my insides out halfway through the next day (I told my parents I had the flu) in a state of total self-disgust. I never wanted to see another needle. That afternoon, I called up the mental health clinic and asked for help.

So, you say to yourself, after all *that*, she finally got off drugs. Well, yes . . . for another three months, again requiring a complete retreat from the mad drug scene on the home front. . . . We didn't see our friends for months. A very insecure peace reigned. Then my boyfriend lost his job . . . and there we were again. It was winter again. . . . We made holiday visits to our friends, and what were they doing? You know.

I'll never forget one guy, actually the one who was responsible for turning us all on initially . . . as he sat there praising my boyfriend for being the only one who had managed to avoid getting a habit, telling him to "keep it up." My boyfriend said something like, "we couldn't shoot up if we wanted to, we haven't got a spike." Immediately this guy gets a brand new needle and says as he hands it to my boyfriend, "I hate to think I'm knocking down one of the barriers that keeps you away from dope." He then proceeded to offer my boyfriend a free shot.

We got on the merry-go-round again, only the music wasn't quite the way we remembered it. . . . Luckily, it was no longer feeling good enough to make it worthwhile. . . . Even worse, we discovered that when a person becomes a junkie, he often ceases to be a person. There was so much ugliness, lying, cheating and stealing, even among guys who were supposed to be the best of friends, that we finally reached the decision that it wasn't worth it. At least the power of the peer group was broken, but what about the power of the dope? It drove us to the city, where we found a better connection.

It almost turned out to be my boyfriend's connection to the Great Beyond, because after shooting only a small amount of heroin, *it happened again*. A friend and I managed to bring him out of the coma without sending him to the hospital, but it was many minutes before he could breathe on his own. All the poor guy wanted was just a little relief, a little time out from misery. I knew it was the end of heroin for him, because he wouldn't come back the third time. He knew it too, and was glad it had happened.

And what about me? As soon as I got my boyfriend home and in bed, I shot one of the two remaining bags we had. Insane? Probably, but I could tell from the rush I got (weak) and the time I stayed high (short) that heroin has lost its immense power over me, too. I shot the last bag the next day, with the same results. It simply wasn't worth it. The hassle to get it, the money it costs, the risk of dying. . . . It's all not worth some weak sensation in your head and a 10-minute high.

The Impact of Drug Use on Society

Illegal drug users will often argue that society has no right to concern itself with their drug taking. "I'm only harming myself," they will insist, "society has no right to interfere with my private life." Legal and moral arguments aside, the fact is, users do more than increase the likelihood of harming themselves when they take drugs. They can harm others as well, both directly and indirectly—directly, by upping the odds of accidents, crime, and violence, and indirectly, as a result of increasing the cost of caring for them and their offspring, lowering productivity, and stimulating the underground economy, thereby undermining the viability of certain neighborhoods. In short, drugs can have a number of undesirable long-term consequences.

Of all drugs, experts agree, cigarettes cause the greatest loss of life over the long run. The surgeon general of the United States estimates that between 300,000 and 400,000 Americans die prematurely every year as a consequence of cigarette smoking. The increased cost of medical care for those who have contracted diseases as a consequence of smoking is incalculable, running at the very least into the tens of billions of dollars per year—considerably more than the government earns in taxes from tobacco products. Smokers have three times the chance of dying before the age of 65 as nonsmokers, and twice the change of dying before the age of 75; a non-smoker has about the same chance of living to the age of 75 as a smoker does of living to 65! Smokers of more than 2 packs a day have 23 times the chance of dying of lung cancer as nonsmokers. But since tobacco is legal, and the deaths it causes are slow and long-term and likely to strike only the middle-aged and the elderly, most of us do not become overly distressed about its use.

Alcohol causes some 150,000 premature deaths a year, perhaps half from the increased likelihood of accident and violence and the other half from the various diseases the drug causes. One estimate links 3 out of every 100 deaths directly to the consumption of alcohol—and admits that this is probably a gross underestimation. Estimates of the dollar cost of alcohol consumption to American society, which include medical care and loss of productivity, range between $100 and $200 billion per year. Just the deaths from the increased likelihood of automobile crashes—over 20,000 per year—far outweigh the number of premature deaths caused by all the illegal drugs combined. Of all the long-term impacts of heavy alcohol consumption, perhaps the most poignant and painful is that on the family of the heavy drinker. The children of the alcoholics are victims who have to spend their entire adulthood struggling with the pain of the childhood they spent with an alcohol-dependent parent.

Illegal drug use has a serious impact on the user and on society generally, but it is likely to be very different from that of the legal drugs. Most users of heroin and cocaine die not of the chronic, long-term effects of their drugs of choice, but from overdoses. The federal government only collects and complies overdose data for the large cities of the country, which make up roughly one-third of the population. In these cities, in 1988, of all drug overdose deaths, cocaine was found in over 3,000 dead bodies; the same was true of heroin in 2,500 deaths. Only alcohol was mentioned as often in drug overdoses. No other drug came even remotely close to these three. Clearly, death by overdose is a very real possibility when taking at least two illegal drugs—heroin (and the other narcotics) and cocaine (including crack). The major difference between the medical impact of the legal drugs—cigarettes and alcohol—and that of the illegal drugs such as heroin and cocaine is that the legal drugs are more likely to kill the old and the illegal drugs are more likely to kill the young.

The children born to mothers dependent on crack are themselves physically dependent. Such newborns are more likely to suffer from a variety of medical problems, and to become behavioral problems when they grow older. Again, society foots the bill in paying for their care. Entire neighborhoods have been undermined by the sale and use of illegal drugs, most recently, crack, tearing families apart, skyrocketing the homicide rate, alienating children from school, and generating a climate of fear and paranoia. It is difficult to imagine that such an impact would not generate widespread concern and efforts to deal with these problems. But are they a consequence of drug abuse itself, or do they occur because society has criminalized certain drugs? We will find out in a later section, "Fighting the Drug War."

Looking Ahead: Challenge Questions

Is the overall impact on society of the legal drugs—tobacco, alcohol, prescription and over-the-counter

One cancer
you can give
yourself.

Horrible
isn't it?

AMERICAN CANCER SOCIETY

drugs—more positive or negative? Are the troublesome effects of the legal drugs (including medical problems and violence) simply the price we have to pay for tolerating substances whose use is too firmly entrenched to eliminate? If the impact of tobacco and alcohol has been as disastrous as experts claim in the societies in which they are used, why is their use tolerated?

Does drug abuse contribute to the "downfall of civilizations," as some observers have argued?

If legal drugs contribute to far more premature deaths than illegal drugs, why do the latter receive so much more media attention than the former? Why are most people so much more interested in the use of cocaine, crack, and heroin than in cigarettes and alcohol?

If alcohol abuse causes such pain to those the alcoholic loves most, why can't he or she simply given up drinking?

Faced with overwhelming evidence that cigarettes kill, why do some people continue to smoke? How can cigarette companies continue to claim, as they do, that no conclusive proof exists that cigarettes cause disease or death?

If a pregnant woman becomes a crack addict, and endangers the life of her child, should she be criminally liable for her behavior? Is she committing a crime?

What can neighborhoods do to protect themselves against the impact the abuse of a drug has on them?

Can a common household beverage such as coffee really be as harmful as some experts claim?

Alcohol and the Family

The children of problem drinkers are coming to grips with their feelings of fear, guilt and rage

Believe it or not, there are still people who think that the worst thing about drinking is a hangover.

Oh, yeah, on New Year's Day I had a hangover that . . .

No. Forget hangovers.

Huh? So what should we talk about? Cirrhosis?

If you wish, but the liver, with its amazing powers of regeneration, usually lasts longer than the spouse, who tends to fall apart relatively early in the drinker's decline.

You're making it hard for a man to drink in peace.

Sorry, but even if spouses do not abuse alcohol, they can come to resemble drunks, since their anger and fear are enormous: way beyond what you'd find in a truly sober person.

I know, I know, it's terrible what goes on behind closed doors.

You make it sound like there are no witnesses. You're forgetting the children. They grow up watching one out-of-control person trying to control another, and they don't know what "normal" is.

I suppose it's hard for the kids, until they move out.

They may move out, but they never leave their parents behind.

Hmm. Listen, can we talk?

We already are. A lot of people already are.

We are, just now, learning more about heavy drinking, and, simultaneously, putting behind us the notion that what alcoholism amounts to is just odd intervals of strange, and sometimes comic, behavior: W. C. Fields, Dean Martin, Foster Brooks. Since 1935 the members of Alcoholics Anonymous have been telling us, with awesome simplicity, that drinking made their lives unmanageable; Al-Anon brought us the news that relatives and friends of drinkers can suffer in harmony; and then came Alateen and even Alatot, where one picture of a stick person holding a beer can is worth a thousand slurred words. The Children of Alcoholics (COAs)—loosely organized but rapidly growing throughout the United States—reaffirm all of the previous grass-roots movements and bring us new insight into alcoholism's effects on the more than 28 million Americans who have seen at least one parent in the throes of the affliction. The bad news from COAs: alcohol is even more insidious than previously thought.

The good news: with the right kind of help, the terrible damage it does to nonalcoholics need not be permanent.

Imagine a child who lives in a chaotic house, rides around with a drunk driver and has no one to talk to about the terror. Don't think it doesn't happen: more than 10 million people in the United States are addicted to alcohol, and most of them have children. "I grew up in a little Vietnam," says one child of an alcoholic. "I didn't know why I was there; I didn't know who the enemy was." Decades after their parents die, children of alcoholics can find it difficult to have intimate relationships ("You learn to trust no one") or experience joy ("I hid in the closet"). They are haunted—sometimes despite worldwide acclaim, as in the case of

There's a Problem in the House

In "Adult Children of Alcoholics," Janet Geringer Woititz discusses 13 traits that most children from alcoholic households experience to some degree. These symptoms, she says, can pose lifelong problems.

Adult children of alcoholics . . .

- guess what normal behavior is.
- have difficulty following a project from beginning to end.
- lie when it would be just as easy to tell the truth.
- judge themselves without mercy.
- have difficulty having fun.
- take themselves very seriously.
- have difficulty with intimate relationships.
- overreact to changes over which they have no control.

- constantly seek approval and affirmation.
- feel that they are different from other people.
- are super-responsible or super-irresponsible.
- are extremely loyal, even in the face of evidence that the loyalty is undeserved.
- tend to lock themselves into a course of action without giving consideration to consequences.

artist Eric Fischl—by a sense of failure for not having saved Mommy or Daddy from drink. And they are prone to marry alcoholics or other severely troubled people because, for one reason, they're willing to accept unacceptable behavior. Many, indeed, have become addicted to domestic turmoil.

'Hurting so bad': Children of alcoholics are people who've been robbed of their childhood—"I've seen five-year-olds running entire families," says Janet Geringer Woititz, one of the movement's founding mothers. Nevertheless, the children of alcoholics often display a kind of childish loyalty even when such loyalty is clearly undeserved. They have a nagging feeling that they are different from other people, Woititz points out, and that may be because, as some recent scientific studies show, they are. Brain scans done by Dr. Henri Begleiter of the State University of New York College of Medicine in Brooklyn reveal that COAs often have deficiencies in the areas of the brain associated with emotion and memory. In this sense and in several other ways—their often obsessive personalities, their tendency to have a poor self-image—the children of alcoholics closely resemble alcoholics. In fact, one in four becomes an alcoholic, as compared with one in 10 out of the general population.

The anger of a COA cannot be seen by brain scans. But at a therapy session at Caron Family Services in Wernersville, Pa., Ken Gill, a 49-year-old IBM salesman, recently took a padded bat and walloped a couch cushion hard enough to wake up sleeping demons. "I came because I was hurting so bad and I didn't know why," he says. "A lot of things were going wrong. I was a workaholic, and I neglected my family." It took Gill only a few hours of exposure to the idea that he might be an "adult child," he says, to realize that his failings as a parent may be if not excused, then at least explained. Like a lot of kids who grew up in an alcoholic household, Gill, who is also a recovering alcoholic, never got what even rats and monkeys get: exposure, at an impressionable age, to the sight and sound of functioning parents. Suzanne Somers, the actress and singer, spent years working out her anger in the form of a just published book called "Keeping Secrets." "I decided that this disease took the first half of my life, and goddam it," she says, "it wasn't going to take the second half of it."

'Control freak': Not every COA has all of the 13 traits (see chart) ascribed to them by Woititz in her landmark work, "Adult Children of Alcoholics" (*1983. Health Communications, Inc.*), and not all have been scarred. (President Reagan, who has written of sometimes finding his father passed out drunk on the front porch, does not appear, from his famous management style, to suffer from any tendency to be a "control freak," a

■ A nine-year-old's nightmare: Living in denial

most common COA complaint.) Some children of alcoholics are grossly overweight from compulsive eating while others are as dressed for success as, well, Somers. A few COAs are immobilized by depression. Another runs TV's "Old Time Gospel Hour." What these people *do* have in common is a basic agreement with George Vaillant, a Dartmouth Medical School professor who says that it is important to think of alcoholism not as an illness that affects bodily organs but as "an illness that affects families. Perhaps the worst single feature of alcoholism," Vaillant adds, "is that it causes people to be unreasonably angry at the people that they most love."

The movement is only about six years old, but expanding so rapidly that figures, could they be gathered for such a basically unstructured and anonymous group, would be outdated as soon as they appeared. We do know, though, that five years ago there were 21 people in an organization called the National Association for Children of Alcoholics; today there are more than 7,000. The 14 Al-Anon-affiliated children-of-alcoholics groups meeting in the early '80s have increased to 1,100. With only word-of-mouth advertising, Woititz's book has sold about a million copies; indeed, "Adult Children of Alcoholics" reached the number-three spot on The New York Times paperback best-seller list long before it was available in any bookstore—at a time, in other words, when getting a copy meant

collaring a clerk to put in an order and *saying the title out loud.*

"We turned on the phones in 1982," says Migs Woodside, founder and president of the Children of Alcoholics Foundation in New York, "and the calls are still coming in 24 hours a day." The COAs Foundation sponsors a traveling art show that features the work of young and adult COAs; often, says Woodside, an attendee will stand mesmerized before a crude depiction of domestic violence or parental apathy ("Mom at noon," it says beneath the picture of someone huddling beneath the bedcovers)—and will then go directly to a pay phone to find help. "The newcomers all tend to say the same thing," says Woodside. "'Wait a minute—that's my story, that's *me!*'"

"It's private pain transformed into a public statement," says James Garbarino, president of the Erikson Institute for Advanced Study in Child Development, in Chicago, "a fascinating movement." But when you consider that denial is the primary symptom of alcoholism and that COAs tend by nature to take on more than their share of blame for whatever mess they happen to find themselves in, the rapid growth of the COAs movement seems just short of miraculous—something akin to a drunken stockbroker named Bill Wilson cofounding AA, now *the* model for a vast majority of self-help programs throughout the United States. After all, who would want to spill the family's darkest secret after years of telling teachers, employers and friends that everything was fine? ("A child of an alcoholic will always say 'Fine'," says Ro-kelle Lerner, a counselor who specializes in young COAs. "They get punished if they say otherwise.") Who would voluntarily identify themselves with a group whose female members, according to some reports, have an above-average number of gynecological problems, possibly due to stress—and whose men are prone to frequent surgery for problems, doctors say, that may be basically psychosomatic?

The answer is, only someone who had, in some sense, bottomed out, just the way a drinker does before he turns to AA.

The concept of codependency is at the center of the COAs movement. Eleanor Williams, who works with COAs at the Charter Peachford Hospital in Atlanta, defines codependency as "unconscious addiction to another person's dysfunctional behavior." Woititz, in a recent Changes magazine interview, referred to it more simply as a tendency to "put other people's needs before my own." A codependent family member may suspect that he has driven the alcoholic to drink (though that is impossible, according to virtually all experts in the field); he almost certainly thinks that he can cure or at least control the drinker's troublesome behavior. "I actually thought that I could make a difference by cooking my husband better meals and by taking the kids out for drives on weekends [so he could rest]," says Ella S., a Westchester, N.Y., woman. "For all I know, it's a deeply ingrained psychological, and possibly genetic, disease, and here I am going at it with a lamb chop."

Mental movies: Obsessed with her husband's increasingly self-destructive behavior, Ella's next step, in typical codependent fashion, was to hide Bob's six-packs, which made him, to put it mildly, angry. Soon they were fighting almost daily and Ella was running mental movies of their scenes from a marriage all night long. "I was wasting a lot of time and energy trying to change the past, while he kept getting worse," she says. "There was a kind of awkward violence between him and me all the time; our hearts weren't really in it, but it wasn't until he had an affair with an alcoholism counselor *that I got him to* that I left." If you're wondering about children, Ella has a seven-year-old daughter, Ann. Her omission is significant. If life were a horse race, then Ann has been, as they say on the past performance charts, "shuffled back" among the also-rans.

What COAs—all people affected by alcohol—need to learn is that the race is fixed: when there is no program of recovery—either through the support of a group or the self-imposed abstinence of an individual—the abused substance will always win, handily, no matter what the competition. The first step of AA begins, "We admitted we were powerless . . ." But what will become of Ann, who is codependent on *two*

■ The fighting never stops: Living with fear

people? Perhaps, sensing that she is not exactly the center of attention, she will reach adulthood with a need for constant approval, a common COA symptom. Or maybe she will, even as a child, react to the chaos by trying to keep everything in her life under control, and thus give the impression that she is, despite everything, quite a trouper, a golden child.

"[Some] don't fall apart until they're in their 20s or 30s," says Woititz, and in some cases, especially those marked by violence or incest and sexual abuse (three times more common in alcoholic households than in the general population), that's the wonder of it all. One eight-year-old patient at Woititz's Verona, N.J., counseling center

woke up in the middle of the night to see her alcoholic mother shoot herself in the head. "The child called the 911 emergency number, got her mother to the hospital and basically saved her mother's life," says Woititz. "When I saw her she was having nightmares—that she wouldn't wake up and witness this suicide attempt. This is not a normal nightmare. The child had become mother to her own mother."

Each unhappy family, as Tolstoy said, is unhappy in its own way. Artist Eric Fischl, 39, in a short videotape he made for the COAs Foundation called "Trying to Find Normal," speaks of stepping over his passed-out mother, in their comfortable-looking (from the outside) Port Washing-

■ Out of control: Remembering hurts

Heredity and Drinking: How Strong Is the Link?

Research on the genetics of alcoholism took a curious turn a few weeks ago when Lawrence Lumeng analyzed his DNA to demonstrate why he can't tolerate liquor. Lumeng, a biochemist at the Indiana University School of Medicine, is among the 30 to 45 percent of Asians whose response to spirited beverages is a reddened face, headaches or nausea. This "Oriental flush," past studies have shown, arises in those who have an inefficient version of a liver enzyme that is crucial to the body's breakdown of alcohol; this "lazy" enzyme allows the buildup of an alcohol product, acetaldehyde, which is sickening and leads many Asians to shun alcohol. Working with biochemist Ting-Kai Li, Lumeng says that he pinpointed the gene that instructs cells to make the odd enzyme. The experiment offers dramatic evidence that a bodily response to alcohol is genetically dictated—and is thus inherited as surely as eye color.

There is no evidence for the opposite proposition: that a specific gene makes a person *crave* alcohol. Considering the wide variety of reasons why people consume the stuff, it seems unlikely that a "drinking gene" exists. But researchers have firmly established that, compared with other children, an alcoholic's offspring are around four times more likely to develop the problem, even if they were raised by other, nonalcoholic parents. In families with a history of alcoholism, explains C. Robert Cloninger, a psychiatrist and geneticist at Washington University in St. Louis, "what is inherited is not the fact that you are destined to become an alcoholic but varying degrees of susceptibility" to the disorder. So real is the predisposition that many researchers advise adult children of alcoholics (COAs) to drink no alcohol whatsoever.

Even the brains of COAs show faint signs of unusual activity, according to controversial studies by psychiatrist Henri Begleiter of the State University of New York in Brooklyn. Begleiter has found that young boys who have never consumed alcohol produce the slightly distorted brainwave patterns typical of their alcoholic fathers. Such signature brain waves, he says, may mark the son of an alcoholic as likely to develop a drinking problem and perhaps alert him to the risk. However, it remains to be seen whether such brain scans are sufficiently reliable and informative to distinguish potential social drinkers from future alcoholics. The technique, comments psychologist Robert Pandina, scientific director of the Center of Alcohol Studies at Rutgers University, is "at this time not any more valuable" as a predictor of future drinking behavior "than collecting a good family history on an individual."

Other studies show that many COAs respond uniquely to booze. Marc Schuckit, a psychiatrist at the Veterans Administration Hospital in San Diego, has found that college-age sons of alcoholics often react less to a few drinks than other college men; in his studies, the drinkers' sons were generally not as euphoric or tipsy after three to five cocktails. Schuckit believes that this lower sensitivity makes it harder for the alcoholics' sons to know when to stop drinking, starting them down the road to alcohol problems. Preliminary experiments by Barbara Lex of McLean Hospital in Belmont, Mass., confirm that daughters of alcoholics respond similarly. Women from families with a history of alcohol abuse tend to keep their balance better on a wobbly platform after having a drink. Apparently women, too, can inherit traits that might predispose them to addiction, although there are far fewer female than male alcoholics.

Half a beer: The key unresolved issue, of course, is why some individuals from alcohol-scarred families succumb to alcoholism while others don't. Genes play some role in the development, most notably in abstinence. "People say that whether you drink or not has to do only with willpower," explains Indiana's Lumeng, "but the reason I can drink only half a beer is biological."

Yet heredity alone obviously isn't to blame for alcoholism's appalling toll. In fact, about 60 percent of the nation's alcohol abusers are from families with *no* history of the disorder. How much people drink is influenced by factors as prosaic as cost; partly to curb consumption, the National Council on Alcoholism is lobbying to raise federal excise taxes on beer and wine, which haven't changed since 1951. Social influences like cost and peer pressure "are just as important as genes," says Dartmouth psychiatrist George Vaillant. "All the genes do is make it easier for you to become an alcoholic." For now, the value of genetic studies is to warn COAs that they may well have a real handicap in the struggle against the family trouble.

TERENCE MONMANEY *with* KAREN SPRINGEN *in New York and* MARY HAGER *in Washington*

ton, N.Y., home and seeing her "lying in her own piss." His work, which has been the subject of a one-man show at the Whitney Museum in New York, is not autobiographical, he says, and yet "the tone [of it] has everything to do with my childhood." His painting "Time for Bed" "relates to my memory of all hell breaking loose," he says. "I guess you could say the boy is me and his shame, embarrassment and sadness is mine as well. The little boy's Superman pajamas are on backwards, so it's like looking in a mirror. I painted the woman standing on a glass table with spiked heels on to give it a sense of fragility and danger. The man only has one arm because I wanted a sense of impotence."

Alcohol leaves every alcoholic and codependent who does not admit his powerlessness over the substance in a constant state of longing. Fischl didn't realize how sad he'd been until his mother died, in an alcohol-related car accident, in 1970. "The thing about having a sick parent is that you think it's your problem," he says. "You feel like a failure because you can't save her." Even when there is no incest, there is seduction. Fischl's mother kept "signaling," he says, "that if you could just come a little bit further with me in this, you can save me."

Some of the other things that alcohol ruins, before it gets to the liver: family meals ("Alcohol fills you up. My father was never interested in eating with us"); gloriously run-of-the-mill evenings around the hearth ("Alcohol makes you tired. My father was in bed most nights at 8"). When enough C_2H_5HO is added to a home, vases may start to fly across the room and crash into walls. All kinds of paper—court-issued Orders of Protection, divorce decrees, bounced checks—come fluttering down. The lights go on and off. Does that mean Daddy's forgotten to pay the bill again, or that the second act is starting?

Every alcoholic household is, in fact, a pathetic little play in which each of the members takes on a role. This is not an idea that arrived with the COAs movement; a 17-page booklet called "Alcoholism: A Merry-Go-Round Named Denial" has been distributed free of charge by Al-Anon for almost 20 years. Written by the Rev. Joseph L. Kellerman, the former director of the Charlotte, N.C., Council of Alcoholism, "Merry-Go-Round" takes note of the uncanny consistency with which certain characters appear in alcoholic situations. These include the Enabler ("a 'helpful' Mr. Clean . . .[who] conditions [the drinker] to believe there will always be a protector who will come to his rescue"); the Victim ("the person who is responsible for getting the work done if the alcoholic is absent") and the Provoker (usually the spouse or parent of the alcoholic, this is "the key person . . . who is hurt and upset by repeated drinking episodes, but she holds the family together . . . In turn, she feeds back into the marriage her bitterness, resentment, fear and hurt . . . She controls, she tries to force the changes she wants; she sacrifices, adjusts, never gives up, never gives in, but never forgets").

Some of the earliest books in the COAs movement explored the drama metaphor more deeply and defined the roles that children play. Sharon Wegscheider-Cruse, in her 1981 book, "Another Chance" (*Science and Behavior Books, Inc. Palo Alto, Calif.*), wrote about the Family Hero, who is usually the firstborn. A high achiever in school, the Hero always does what's right, often discounting himself by putting others first. The Lost Child, meanwhile, is withdrawn, a loner on his way to a joyless adulthood, and thus, in some ways, very different from the Scapegoat, who appears hostile and defiant but inside feels hurt and angry. (It is the Scapegoat, says Wegscheider-Cruse, who gets attention through "negative behavior" and is likely to be involved in alcohol or other drugs later.) Last and least—in his own mind—is the Mascot, fragile and immature yet charming: the family clown.

'Good-looking' kids: Virtually no one was publishing those kinds of thoughts when Claudia Black, a Laguna Beach, Calif., therapist, began searching for literature on the subject of the alcohol-affected family in the late '70s. "Half of my adult [alcoholic] patients had kids my age and older," she remembers, "but all I found was stuff on fetal alcohol syndrome and kids prone to juvenile delinquency." One thing that fascinated her about young COAs, she says, was that despite their developmental problems "they were all 'good-looking' kids"—presentable and responsible albeit not terribly verbal. "They had friends but weren't honest with them. Everything was 'fine and dandy'."

The title of Black's important 1981 book, "It Will Never Happen to Me" (*M.A.C.*

■ Trauma: Parental neglect

COURTESY CHILDREN OF ALCOHOLICS FOUNDATION

Denver, Colo.), reflects the typical codependent's mix of denial and false bravado. In it, she makes the point that the children in an alcoholic household never have an environment that is consistent and structured, two of the things they need most—and she, too, talks of such stock juvenile "roles" as the Responsible One and the Adjuster. Her unique

warning was that children who survive a parent's alcoholism by displaying unusual coping behavior often experience "emotional and psychological deficits" later on. They are also likely to become alcoholics, says Black, because "alcohol helps these persons become less rigid, loosen up and relax. When they drink they aren't quite so serious." Though those things happen to almost everyone who imbibes, Black says that "for those who are stuck in unhealthy patterns, alcohol may be the *only* thing that can provide relief."

Well, she guessed wrong there: a movement, manifested by often joyous meetings, has come along in the interim. At hundreds of COAs gatherings around the country tonight, people will talk and listen to each other's stories, to cry, to laugh and generally, as Ken Gill says, "recharge their batteries." "This program kept me from being an alcoholic myself," said a woman named Heather at a gathering in an affluent section of San Francisco last week. "Because I was the oldest, everything was always my fault. It's like when you make your parents breakfast and you bring them one scrambled egg and one fried egg—in my house I always scrambled the wrong egg." Heads bobbed in agreement. Who else but COAs could identify with a story about what happens when kids cook for their own mother and father?

Discovering self-esteem: Talking and listening: this is the way we've learned to

■ Physical abuse: An adult remembers

COURTESY CHILDREN OF ALCOHOLICS FOUNDATION

deal with problem drinking. And though it sounds wimpy, don't knock it; it's the surest way to alleviate not just the imbibing but the whole range of symptoms we call alcoholism. A woman named Nina stood up at a meeting in Boston last week, practically glossed over the fact that both her parents were alcoholics—and proceeded to speak about how well she was feeling and doing. COAs meetings and literature, she said, had allowed her to discover self-esteem. At another meeting, Carolyn told a story of complaining to her doctor about depression—and hearing the doctor shoot back a question about whether one of her parents was an alcoholic. "I was shocked," she said, and well she might be. Doctors, as a group, have yet to play a major role in helping mitigate the effects of alcohol, perhaps because the average medical-school student spends a grand total of between zero and 10 hours studying the affliction that kills 100,000 people annually.

An avalanche of information is coming, nevertheless, from another kind of M.D.—call them the Masters of Disaster, the people who've lived with alcoholism or worked with alcoholics so closely that they might as well be their kin. Robert Ackerman, a professor of sociology at Indiana University of Pennsylvania, has been studying the children of alcoholics for an exceedingly long time by the standards of the movement—since the early '70s. In his recent book "Let Go and Grow" *(Health Communications, Inc.),* he reports on a survey he took to test the validity of Woititz's 13 generalizations about COAs, as well as seven more observations of his own. What he found was that "adult children of alcoholics identified about 20 percent more with these characteristics" than did the general population. Other professionals are reporting success with therapies involving hugging, acting out unresolved scenes from long ago and even playing one of several board games for children of alcoholics called Family Happenings and Sobriety. Cathleen Brooks, executive director of a program called Next Step in San Diego, reports that her clients often make life-changing strides after six to 18 months of primary treatment and make the decision never to drink or take drugs.

The 7 million COAs who are under the age of 18 are harder to help, if only because their parents' denial tends to keep them out of treatment. For these children who never know what to expect when they come home from school each day, life, says Woititz, "is a state of constant anxiety."

Some pediatricians think there is a link between such anxiety and childhood ulcers, chronic nausea, sleeping problems, eating disorders and dermatitis. Migs Woodside, from the COAs Foundation, says that the trained teacher can pick the child of an alcoholic out of a crowded classroom. "Sometimes you can tell by the way they are dressed or by the fact that they never have their lunch money," she says. "Sometimes you can tell by the way they suddenly pay attention when the teacher talks about drinking, and sometimes you can tell by their pictures."

Someday, 20 or 30 years from now, those children may feel a vague sense of failure or depression and be hard pressed to explain why. In the meantime, it's their Crayolas that are hard pressed. Beer cans—and not liquor or wine bottles—form a leitmotif in the work of young children of alcoholics. Occasionally, Woodside says, looking a little sad, the big stick figures can be seen tipping the cans into the mouths of the little stick figures.

Charles Leerhsen *with* Tessa Namuth
and bureau reports

How Smoking Kills You

Any way you look at it, lighting up is hazardous to your health.

Maureen Callahan

Maureen Callahan is a Boston-based free-lance writer specializing in health and nutrition.

"SURGEON GENERAL'S WARNING: Smoking Causes Lung Cancer, Heart Disease, Emphysema, And May Complicate Pregnancy." These familiar words appear on cigarette advertisements and cigarette packages around the country. Yet, nearly a third of the American adult population still continues the habit, which, says the American Lung Association, prematurely claims more lives than illicit drugs, alcohol abuse, homicide, suicide, and automobile accidents combined.

Why don't people stop? One reason is that cigarettes, or more specifically the nicotine they contain, are addictive. Ninety percent of smokers start smoking before the age of nineteen, and that makes the habit both physically and psychologically hard to shake. In addition, millions of smokers still do not realize (or perhaps don't accept the fact) that smoking is hazardous to health. Even worse, new studies indicate that smokers may be injuring more than themselves when they light up. According to a recent report from the surgeon general of the United States, "involuntary" smoking (inhaling smoke secondhand) may cause disease, such as lung cancer, in healthy nonsmokers.

For people who like to smoke.

Pack-a-day cigarette smokers shave five years off their life expectancy. Heavy smokers, those who smoke two or more packs per day, cut their lives short by as many as eight years. The grim reality, then, is that the health costs of lighting up far outweigh the short-lived euphoric feeling a cigarette provides. Cigarette smoke, with its dozens of toxic gases—including carbon monoxide—and small particles of tar and nicotine, is lethal to the lungs, to the heart, and to the body as a whole. The length of time a person smokes and the degree to which he inhales determine how much toxic gas and how many toxic particles the lungs and body are exposed to. But, in general, smokers are five times more likely to develop chronic bronchitis than nonsmokers because of this exposure to the toxins from cigarettes. Moreover, smoking can cause more serious lung disease in the form of emphysema—a disease in which the natural elasticity of the air sacs in the lungs is lost, causing difficulty in exhaling—and lung cancer. Estimates are that 85 to 90 percent of lung cancer deaths are caused by smoking.

Smoking also increases your risks of developing heart disease and suffering a stroke. Women under the age of 50 who smoke about one and a half packs of cigarettes each day run at least a fivefold greater risk of having a heart attack than their nonsmoking counterparts. The National Heart, Lung and Blood Institute lists smoking among the top major risk factors for heart disease, along with high blood pressure and high levels of blood cholesterol. Giving up cigarettes can reduce the risk for heart disease and, as one study shows, may cut the risk for stroke by more than half. Researchers involved in the Honolulu Heart Program, a major clinical project that studied the risks for stroke among nearly 8,000 men, conclude that smokers have two to three times the risk of stroke as nonsmokers. But when they quit, that risk is cut dramatically.

Who's come a long way, baby?

For women, the risks attached to smoking are much greater than for men. A woman who smokes not only will be more likely to fall victim to heart disease, lung cancer, emphysema, and chronic bronchitis but also puts herself at risk for a multitude of typically female problems ranging from osteoporosis to early menopause. At last count, 28 percent of American women smoke.

Especially alarming is the fact that smoking among teenage girls seems to be on the rise. In the last ten years, the number of female smokers aged twelve to eighteen has doubled. Twenty-one percent of teenage girls in their senior year of high school smoke daily, an amount that exceeds the numbers of their male counterparts who smoke. If the pace keeps up, the future may see women outsmoking men. That's quite a turnaround when you consider that before World War II, smoking was almost exclusively a male habit.

Thirty-two percent of women between the ages of 20 and 34 smoke. These women, in their childbearing years, are the most susceptible to the hazards of cigarette smoke. For one thing, women who smoke will find it much more difficult to conceive than women who don't smoke. Estimates are that fertility is 25 percent lower in smokers, meaning that on the average it will take much longer to become pregnant. Once pregnant, a woman who continues to smoke has a risk of miscarriage that is three to seven times higher than that of nonsmokers. Her baby runs the risk of being of low birthweight—a condition that has many attendant problems, ranging from mental retardation to chronic infection, all of which can last well into adulthood. A study by Richard Naeye, M.D., chairman of the department of pathology at The Pennsylvania State University College of Medicine, found that babies born to smokers had a 50 percent higher risk of developing Sudden Infant Death Syndrome (SIDS).

At the other end of a woman's reproductive years are some different problems. According to a review study by Donald Mattison, M.D., associate professor of obstetrics and gynecology at the University of Arkansas College of Medicine, women who smoke half a pack a day can bring on early menopause—one to two years ahead of the biological time clock. In addition, women who smoke may actually make themselves more susceptible to the crippling bone disease of old age—osteoporosis. Smoking lowers levels of the female hormone estrogen, a hormone that plays a critical role in keeping bones strong.

Finally, women who take oral contraceptives and smoke put themselves at even greater risk. These women are ten times more likely to suffer myocardial infarction than someone who neither smokes nor takes birth-control

pills, according to Gregory Morosco, Ph.D., of the National Heart, Lung and Blood Institute.

Secondhand risks.

When the smoke clears, the evidence may be overwhelming that nonsmokers are at risk from the toxic hazards of cigarettes. A number of recent studies have suggested that nonsmoking wives who have husbands who smoke are much more likely to fall victim to lung cancer and heart disease than those whose husbands don't smoke. Indeed, some researchers have suggested that there is as much as twice the risk for lung cancer in the wives of smokers and three times the risk for heart attack.

The tobacco industry holds the opinion that the hazardous effects of environmental smoke, and even smoking itself, have not been clearly demonstrated. Granted the evidence is still preliminary in many cases, and there are a few studies that have not been able to find a strong connection between secondhand smoke and lung cancer, but most experts agree that passive smoking can be dangerous. The surgeon general, in fact, issued a report last year that called the scientific case proving the dangers of involuntary smoking "more than sufficient." He added that action should be taken in order to protect the nonsmoker from "environmental tobacco smoke," particularly in the workplace.

" . . . Parents may be swayed into kicking the habit when they realize that smoking can lead to problems for their children. . . ."

Companies, government agencies, and restaurateurs have been tightening restrictions on smoking—some are even banning smoking entirely—since the report. Some bans are successful, such as the one that began in 1985 at Pacific Northwest Bell Telephone Company. Others are not. Restaurant owners in Beverly Hills, for example, found they lost customers after the Beverly Hills City Council initiated a total ban on smoking in eating estab-

lishments and in retail stores. The laws were changed after four months because of the restaurant claims of declining sales, and now smoking is allowed only in certain areas of the restaurant that are equipped with special ventilation equipment that meets established health standards.

Parents may be swayed into kicking the habit when they realize that their smoking can lead to problems for their children. Children who have parents that smoke, according to recent research, are more likely to suffer from respiratory infections—colds, bronchitis, pneumonia—than children of nonsmokers. Furthermore, these problems increase as the exposure to smoke increases. For example, the child whose parents both smoke will have more infections than the child with only one parent who smokes. A recent report in the medical journal *Pediatrics* suggests that children exposed to cigarette smoke may experience stunted lung growth. If lungs do not grow to full capacity, these children may be set up for problems with lung disease, including pulmonary failure later in their lives.

Calling it quits.

To date 41 million Americans have kicked the smoking habit. And these numbers may continue to grow. Indeed, one out of every three smokers tries to quit each year. Quitting, in fact, is big business. Last year, Americans spent about $100 million on aids to stop smoking. What do these businesses provide? Help of all different kinds, it appears.

Smokers can choose between programs that focus on hypnosis, acupuncture, or group therapy, or they can simply quit cold turkey. For a more gradual approach, there are chewing gums laced with nicotine and plastic cigarettes with a boost of nicotine but with none of the harmful toxic gases and particles of tar that are found in a regular cigarette. Although these aids may wean people away for the dependency on nicotine, there is a psychological side to cigarette smoking for which many find no substitute. One ex-smoker, Lois Mack, puts it this way: "There isn't a day goes by that I don't want a cigarette, but I won't take one." After 29 years of smoking, the addiction, she says, is still very much there. But it is controlled.

For many ex-smokers, developing this discipline is the difficult part. The battle to stay smoke-free is a hard one. One of the surest routes to success, according to Tom Ferguson, M.D., author of *The Smokers Book of Health* (G. P. Putman's Sons), is to learn to cope with the urge to smoke. Situations may come up that trigger the desire for a cigarette, but individuals need to find a way to short-circuit that desire. Distractions in the way of a hobby or activity might help. Or it might be wise to avoid situations that make you feel like lighting up. Whatever you do, it must be something that you can stick with. After all, quitting, whether it's cold turkey or gradual, is meant to be a permanent arrangement.

Be smart, don't start.

Still, the best advice is not to start smoking. Not only does smoking speed up the body's metabolic rate 10 percent (which is why many smokers may tend to gain weight once they quit), but it causes a host of serious illnesses ranging from lung cancer to heart disease. Cigarettes, it seems, have nothing to offer but problems. But you can't tell that from the advertisements. Each year, tobacco companies spend $2 billion on advertising that tends to downplay the hazards. Health organizations like the American Medical Association and the American Cancer Society hope to persuade the government to ban the glossy cigarette advertisements. But even if advertisements were banned, here would still be a big task ahead for health professionals. People need to understand fully the dangers of smoking. Until potential smokers realize the risk of their habit, smokers' ranks will continue to swell.

The Crack Children

Their troubles don't end in infancy. As cocaine babies grow up, health and social workers are discovering a whole new set of drug-related problems.

Arthur was already 3 days old when his aunt found him in the Houston garage where his crack-addicted mother had abandoned him. Arthur's aunt adopted him, but at 13 months, he was so wild that his aunt called him "possessed." She brought him to a special program for infants sponsored by Houston's Mental Health and Mental Retardation Authority. There, he would not let his teacher, Geynille Agee, come closer than eight feet before he began hurling toys at her. Two years later Agee thinks she has made a little progress with the boy; he can now walk calmly down the hall holding his aunt's hand—something he could never do before.

Christina, another 3-year-old in the Houston program, does not like to be touched. Her teacher tried gently rubbing the child's skin with soft toys. Most made Christina shrink away. Finally, Christina became interested in puzzles, but rather than pick up the pieces herself, she would gingerly hold her teacher's wrist while the woman put the pieces together.

Arthur and Christina (not their real names) are among the oldest of a generation of children across the country who share a terrible heritage—their mothers all smoked crack while they were pregnant. A few years ago crack-exposed babies made headlines when they began showing up in intensive-care nurseries. Then, the struggle was just to get them out of the hospital. Now, experts say, their problems appear to be long term—and far more difficult to solve.

The first wave of crack babies is just approaching school age, and educators are frustrated and bewildered by their behavior. "They operate only on an instinctual level," says Agee of her students. "They eat and sleep, eat and sleep. Something has been left out." Sometimes withdrawn, these children may have trouble playing or even talking with other kids. Some have tremors or periods when they seem to tune out the world. No one yet knows how to undo the damage caused by a pregnant woman's drug use. Some teachers predict that special-education programs like the one in Houston will soon be swamped with crack children. "We need experts to deal with them immediately," says a spokesperson for the city's mental-health authority. "But who will be the experts? We are all having to learn about this one together."

There's no question that the need is tremendous. According to a major national study of the problem, about 11 percent of all newborns—375,000 babies annually—have been exposed to drugs in utero. Crack cocaine is the primary addiction of pregnant women, although many use other drugs as well. The doctor who conducted that 1988 study, Ira Chasnoff, president of the National Association for Perinatal Addiction Research and Education, thinks his results probably understate the problem because a mother's drug use can be hard to detect. Drug screening is not routine in many hospitals, and even with testing, crack use is not always obvious.

Without reliable testing, doctors must look for other clues. For example, pregnant crack addicts may not visit a doctor until they actually go into labor and are ready to deliver—and sometimes not even then. "When a patient comes in with no history of prenatal care, we automatically start wondering if there's been drug abuse," says Dr. Ezra Davidson of King-Drew Medical

---

Damage Done

■ At least 375,000 babies are born annually to mothers who use drugs.

■ One survey estimates that the number of drug-exposed infants has more than tripled since 1985.

■ Cocaine cuts the flow of nutrients and oxygen to the fetus, causing deformities and growth impairment.

■ Drug-exposed 2-year-olds have trouble concentrating, interacting with groups and coping with structured environments.

Center in Los Angeles. Davidson, who is also president of the American College of Obstetricians and Gynecologists, estimates that a quarter of the babies coming into his hospital's intensive-care nursery have drug-related problems.

Many of these babies start their lives with serious handicaps. They are likely to be born prematurely, says Dr. Gordon B. Avery of Children's National Medical Center in Washington, D.C., and may weigh as little as two pounds. "They get hit with everything other premature babies do—*plus*," Avery says. Compared with other preemies, they're more likely to have hydrocephaly (water on the brain), poor brain growth, kidney problems and apnea (when babies suddenly stop breathing). They are also more likely to have suffered an infarct of the brain—similar to a stroke.

Birth defects: And that's only the beginning. Doctors who have followed the progress of crack babies now believe their drug-related birth defects may contribute to major developmental difficulties. Dr. Judy Howard of the UCLA School of Medicine, who has studied hundreds of crack children, says that they are hard to care for almost from the moment of birth. They may be either extremely irritable or very lethargic, have poor sucking abilities that hamper feeding and irregular sleep patterns. As they grow older, they may be hyperactive, slow in learning to talk and have trouble relating to other people—just like Arthur and Christina, the youngsters in the Houston program.

As part of her research, Dr. Howard compared preemies born to crack users with other (noncrack) preemies. Even at the age of 18 months, after receiving good medical care and educational therapy, the crack kids were in bad shape. They tended to hit their toys or throw them around the room, without apparent motive or provocation. "Their facial expressions appeared flat and joyless and their body language did not demonstrate enthusiasm," says Howard, who points out that children who can't or won't play with toys are missing an important avenue of development. "The kids have an impairment that makes them disorganized in everything they do," she says. Doctors haven't been able to pinpoint the exact reason for these problems, but they suspect neurological damage. Howard says it's as if the part of the brain that "makes us human beings, capable of discussion or reflection," has been "wiped out."

Early intervention: So far, there are only a handful of programs dedicated to helping crack children. At the Salvin Special Education School in Los Angeles, teacher Carol Cole says her two-year-old program is still experimental; every day she and her colleagues try to figure out new ways to help the kids. Early intervention and individual attention seem to be crucial. There are no more than eight 3- and 4-year-olds in each class with as many as three teachers. Much of the day is taken up with regular preschool activities—songs, games, art projects. But the school also has a pediatrician, psychologists, social workers and speech and language specialists. They're all ready to help with the problems caused not only by the mothers' crack use, but also by the youngsters' often chaotic home lives. In some of their families, drug use is still a factor. That puts these kids at high risk for abuse and neglect. Doctors also suspect that the children may be seriously injured just by breathing the crack-filled smoke in their homes. Cole says that the continuity and routine at school help the kids feel secure. They also get lots of opportunities to talk about things that may be bothering them. "We acknowledge what exists," says Cole. "We talk about the specifics of their lives. And they feel safe when they know we know."

Lost generation: As America's crack problem worsens, health and social workers are left with only two options: get mothers into treatment programs in time to protect their babies, or prepare to deal with a steady stream of troubled children.

Unfortunately, many drug facilities exclude pregnant women; in one recent study of programs in New York City, 54 percent wouldn't let these mothers in. And once children are born to crack mothers, the problems become even more daunting. "We simply can't take all these babies away from their mothers," says Dr. Loretta Finnegan of Jefferson Medical College in Philadelphia, who has worked with pregnant addicts for many years. "Where are we going to put them?" In addition to stepping up—and paying for—drug enforcement and drug treatment, the country now must confront a whole new facet of the crack epidemic: an entire generation that may never be free of the scourge.

BARBARA KANTROWITZ *with* PAT WINGERT *in Washington,* NONNY DE LA PENA *in Houston,* JEANNE GORDON *in Los Angeles and* TIM PADGETT *in Chicago*

In Cities, Poor Families Are Dying of Crack

Gina Kolata

Crack is rapidly accelerating the destruction of families in poor urban neighborhoods where mothers are becoming increasingly addicted and children are selling the drug in greater numbers than ever before.

Though drugs have always brought misery to families affected by their use, crack has greatly intensified that misery in recent months in inner cities throughout the nation.

New, Violent Gangs

But perhaps nowhere can this be seen more readily than in the doorways and abandoned buildings in New York City's poor neighborhoods. These are among the observed elements of family breakdown:

• Children are taking over as heads of their families, largely because of their incomes from selling crack.

• Young pregnant mothers are endangering their lives to get the drug, and in many cases, people describe mothers or brothers procuring sex for the young women in their families to raise money to buy it.

• Teen-age girls are abandoning their families and forming what social scientists say are new and violent gangs to sell or buy crack.

• And in some neighborhoods female users outnumber male users for the first time. For years, it had been the women, more often than not, who held poor families together. Yet almost worse than the breakdown of the family are the isolation and sad acceptance expressed by so many people in the affected communities—as if crack has become a final plague they cannot overcome.

The overall picture of the unraveling family emerges in scores of conversations and interviews with members of families hit by crack and with treatment experts and social scientists studying the matter. What emerges as well is the perception that very little community structure is in place to cope with or to stop what is happening. For the most part, there are not enough treatment centers, social workers or law-enforcement officers to give the extensive help that is needed.

On streets where drugs have long been sold, most sellers are much younger than their predecessors. "The kids are taking over," said Dr. Ansley Hamid, an anthropologist at the John Jay College of Criminal Justice in Manhattan.

On a quiet summer day recently, a 12-year-old boy sat on an upturned milk crate at the corner of Regent Place and East 21st Street in the Flatbush section of Brooklyn, selling crack. His mother stood beside him, drinking from a bottle of beer and patting his head.

Crack to Go

Other boys waited for customers in nearby doorways. Outside, children as young as 7, 8 and 9, waited almost nonchalantly, They were the "layaways," who were holding most of the drugs to be sold. They would help protect the sellers from being caught with drugs in their possession. A teen-age boy called the layaways "dumb and young," and said they were paid only $25 to $50 a week. Still, he said, "That's a lot of money for a kid."

In West Harlem, at 132d Street and Frederick Douglass Boulevard, a boy was on a public telephone with a customer. He signaled to two other youths who were double-parked nearby in a 1989 white Chrysler New Yorker. The boys in the car were to make the delivery. Crack to go.

At 140th Street between Adam Clayton Powell Jr. and Frederick Douglass Boulevards, the once-grand brownstones are crumbling backdrops for crack selling. But they are far from vacant. As night draws near, the "vampires come out," as one resident puts it. In nearly every doorway, clusters of teen-age lookouts scrutinize customers. The lookouts — boys as young as 14 or 15 — are very polite as they keep the crowds moving to avoid attracting the police. "Move on, please," one says as three people congregate. Mothers escaping their hot apartments watch from stoops nearby, holding babies sucking on pacifiers.

Inside virtually every building on the block are young guards with guns. Their age and their inexperience with the weapons are two reasons for the sharp increase in the shootings and in other violence in those neighborhoods,

Larry Brown, a former addict now in a treatment program, said.

Gold Teeth Set With Diamonds

A buyer passed the guards and slipped money through a slot in a door. A dealer waited on the other side. The crack, a smokable derivative of cocaine, was passed back through. Again, many of the dealers were teen-agers. "This has not been true before," said Dr. Phillipe Bourgois, an anthropologist at San Francisco State University, who is doing research in East Harlem.

Some teen-agers who work these streets, some with grins that reveal gold teeth with diamonds set along the edges, said they could earn as much as several thousand dollars a week, depending on how high they climbed in the drug network. The most successful are careful not to become addicted themselves.

Dr. Hamid said the higher-level distributors like to employ adolescents because they are often more willing to take risks and because their youthful sense of invulnerability makes them less wary of the violence that stalks a crack seller.

The Parents

Big Rewards For Blind Eyes

The intensive crack activity of these young people — selling it or using it, or both — dominates what home life they have.

Michael H., a skinny 17-year-old who is now in a drug-treatment program, said he paid his mother for the use of her apartment to sell heroin, which is becoming popular among crack addicts because it brings them down from the high of crack. Heroin acts biochemically as a sedative; crack a stimulant.

"I gave her $200 a day," Michael said. "I used to open at 7:30. Went to school at 8. I'd get the workers, get the lookout, and tell my sister to take care of the place until I got home from school." He said he earned $500 a day. "By 10:30 at night, the shop was closed."

Parents of boys like Michael often turn a blind eye to drug dealing by their teen-agers because they want drug money for themselves.

Balance of Power Shifts

"The parents definitely know what's

going on," Dr. Richard Curtis, an anthropologist at John Jay College of Criminal Justice, said. Dr. Terry Williams, an anthropologist at City University of New York who lives and works in East Harlem, agreed, adding: "The kids start bringing in money, buying gifts for Mom and clothes for little brother. The child in essence becomes the parent. Then you can't tell them what to do. The balance of power has been shifted. Suddenly, as a parent, you turn the other way. You are reaping the benefits of the drug trade. This is altering the whole structure of the family."

Dr. Peter Pinto, a clinical psychologist who specializes in drug treatment at Samaritan Village in Queens, said even actions that a teen-ager might think are benign can leave psychological scars. When a boy like Michael supports his family through drug selling, family members get "very, very confused," Dr. Pinto said.

"Every boy wants to please his mother," he said. "Every kid wants Mom's approval. The dad can never make that much money so in a sense it's emotional incest. The kid becomes the husband."

Stealing From Mother

The damage becomes especially acute in relationships between mothers and pregnant daughters. Sonya H., lean, lanky and pregnant with her second child, showed up at the door of her mother's Flatbush apartment recently, her lips swollen and a front tooth knocked out. She said she had been beaten by a dealer who thought she had stolen some of his crack. Sonya, who is 22, admitted that she paid for the crack through prostitution and stealing and that she stole from her mother.

At first glance the mother's apartment looked sparse. The living room had two battered sofas, a low scratched table and a television set, turned on. Sonya's 3-year-old daughter and her younger sister's 2-year-old son watched a game show.

But the back bedroom, where Sonya's mother slept, was crammed with the family's belongings. Clothes, furniture, books and mementos were stacked halfway to the ceiling. On a table next to the bed was a Bible, and fronds collected on Palm Sunday hung on the wall. The mother said she locked everything of value in that back bedroom, to prevent Sonya or her associates from stealing it.

Sonya's mother and sister were afraid that Sonya would not live to 30. She has suffered seizures, the most recent on a subway. And if the crack does not kill her, there is another threat — the recurring beatings she suffers from men from whom she tries to steal. She has scars on her neck, which she says were gotten when a crazed dealer tried to cut off her head.

Recurrent Nightmares

Sonya has entered many treatment programs but usually leaves after a short time and returns to crack. Dr. Pinto said that among teen-agers who sought help at Samaritan Village, the drug-related experiences were so devastating that 44 percent suffered from post-traumatic stress syndrome similar to that of Vietnam veterans. He said 70 percent had recurrent nightmares.

In any event, Sonya's mother felt powerless to control her. She has locked her daughter out of the apartment many times but always weakens and takes her back. So now instead of locking Sonya out, she locks herself in, behind her bedroom door.

Parents in similar situations give up any hope, and particularly in cases like that of Michael H., also give up dignity and authority. If the parents are using drugs themselves, a kind of child-as-parent syndrome develops. "The child is taking on more of the role of an adult," Dr. Pinto said. "On the surface, the child has an exhilarating feeling of power. But inside, the little adult is an angry deprived, lonely child who is hungry for parental nurturance."

Prostituting Children

Family members addicted to crack have gone to extremes to get it, in many reported cases prostituting their own children or siblings. Dr. Pinto said he counseled a 17-year-old girl from Jamaica, Queens, who said her two older brothers kept her a prisoner in a crack house and forced her to prostitute herself so that the brothers could get crack.

Sonya H. said she and a 17-year-old friend were out one night recently. The friend's mother had told her daughter that "she better bring her back something," Sonya said. Later, the mother called down from her window for the girl to come up. She had a man lined up for her daughter. Sonya said her friend went upstairs and performed sex in exchange for crack for her mother.

Keith S., a tall shy, gentle-looking 17-year-old, said he and his mother used crack. Keith also sold the drug, as did most teen-agers he grew up with. He said his mother's increasingly severe addiction concerned him greatly, so much so that he tried to cut off her supply. "I had a couple of conferences with my friends, you know, and that's when I had a certain type of beef with them."

But despite his pleas, the friends continued to sell to his mother. Still, Keith did not cut off his friends or their crack network. Bit by bit, his mother's apartment became a hangout, where crack was bought and sold and used. She lost the apartment, Keith S. said. He said that he does not know where she is living and that he drifts among the homes of friends and relatives.

Trading Crack for Grades

Family members may be alerted to a child's drug use when his schoolwork begins to suffer and his grades drop dramatically.

But in one instance involving crack, a change in grade performance indicated yet another aspect of an adult-child relationship turned upside down. Jon W., who is undergoing treatment at Samaritan Village, said he raised his grades in one class at a Long Island

Lured by their children's profits, parents ignore their drug deals.

high school by selling crack to his teacher. "My parents kept wondering why I kept getting A's in this class," he said. "They wanted to know because I was bringing home C's and D's in my other classes."

"Most of the adults," he said, sneering, "they know you've got something they want, they'll do anything for you."

The Women

Their Strength Crumbles

The loss of women to crack is clearly a powerful element in the breakup of poor families.

And there are indications that in New York City and several other urban areas in the United States more women than men now use crack. The Justice Department reported recently, for example, that for the first time crack-related arrests of women were exceeding those of men in New York, Washington, Kansas City, Mo., and Portland, Ore.

Larry Brown, the former addict who lives in West Harlem, said he sees more women than men using crack in his neighborhood.

A young woman sat on her bed in a small, unbearably hot city-owned apartment in Harlem watching television. She wore her hair in braids, like a child, though she was 22. She was pregnant for the third time. And she knew that the city would make her give up her baby at birth, because this baby, like the other two, was going to test positive for cocaine.

But she was unwilling or unable to stop using crack.

High Is Too Intense

Another young Harlem mother, of a 1-year-old girl, was flying high. She bounced as she talked nonstop on a sidewalk. Her eyes darted and she spoke in bursts. Presently, she grabbed the wrist of an old man on West 140th Street and led him off. Others who watched said he would give her more crack in return for sex.

One woman, a mother in her late 20's, strode nervously up and down another treeless street lined with abandoned buildings. She was leery of speaking to a reporter because she was selling crack.

Still, she could not resist stopping to bemoan the fact that crack was now being used by children as young as 9, who sprinkle it on marijuana cigarettes to dilute its high, which, she said, is too intense for their young brains.

While she talked about the children, she ceased selling. And when two men and two women, in their 30's and 40's, approached to try to buy crack, she shooed them away.

But before long she was back at it again.

Still another woman, now in a treatment program, told of how completely the crack habit had shattered her life and kept her from functioning at any level. Her head was shaved, and her once-beautiful face badly scarred. When she smoked crack she was beset with visions of insects crawling on her. She would tear at her face, trying to get rid of the bugs, and she shaved her head because of the illusion that she had lice.

The Girls

New Gangs Hit the Streets

Although the sale of crack is still essentially controlled by men, some teenage girls are forming gangs to sell it, or to buy it. "This is a new phenomenon in American history," said Dr. William Kornblum, director of the Center for Social Research at the City University of New York Graduate School. Many more women and girls are selling drugs, and they are more organized, he said.

Dr. Bourgois, the San Francisco anthropologist who is doing research in East Harlem, said the new gangs, or posses as they call themselves, have come about as more girls move out of their homes and into the streets. Just as girls are hanging out on basketball courts, practicing their shots, so are they hanging out on the streets, selling drugs, Dr. Bourgois said. Girls "used to not be allowed to participate in street culture," he explained. But now they say, "I'm going to get mine."

Many girls leave home permanently and live on the streets or in crack houses. Some carry razor blades for protection.

Less Likely to Be Searched

Lyvia H., an innocent-looking 16-year-old from Jamaica, Queens, who is in a treatment program at Samaritan Village, said there were five girls in her posse. Aided by two lookouts and two helpers, she was the seller, dressed up "in my church clothes" so that the police would not suspect her.

A male dealer gave her $500 worth of crack at a time, which she said she could sell in a half-hour on a weekend night. She would work twice a week, for 12 hours at a stretch. For every $500 worth of crack she sold, she could keep $25, she said. Lyvia said she sold about $12,000 worth of crack each night, earning a weekly income of about $1,200, most of which she spent on drugs for herself.

Dr. Williams said higher-level drug dealers are willing to use girls as sellers because they are less likely than men to be searched by undercover police officers. Only policewomen search girls, and most undercover officers are men.

In the Greenpoint section of Brooklyn recently, two teen-age girls were on a "mission," as they called it, looking for money to buy crack. The termi-

nology was from the popular television series "Star Trek." They called crack "Scotty," and getting high was "beaming up." On the mission, the girls said, they would hunt for a wallet to steal or would have quick sex for as little as 50 cents.

Searching for Family Ties

In his research on life in crack houses, Dr. Williams sees young girls, known on the street as "TQ's" for teen queens, who have run away from home and who stay in crack houses. The girls, about 14 or 15, "are highly desirable to the older men," Dr. Williams said.

"They are fresh, new," he said.

At the crack houses, which are usually decrepit rooms in abandoned buildings, they go on binges that typically last for two or three days, he said. The girls often perform oral sex in exchange for a smoke. Between binges they sleep in alleyways or abandoned buildings.

Adults at the crack houses become the only family the girls have. They often call the older women Ma and the older men Poppy.

Rays of hope do exist amid the suffering and misery. Some treatment centers have clearly helped addicts to survive.

But Larry Brown said that the despair felt by Sonya H.'s mother and sister, for example, was evident throughout New York's poor neighborhoods, where after a few years most addicts are struck down by shooting or other violence, by the AIDS virus that spreads through crack houses, or by illnesses caused by malnutrition.

Mr. Brown told of a saying repeated often by residents of those neighborhoods, "There are no old crackheads."

Is Coffee Harmful?

What science says now about caffeine and decaffeination

Corby Kummer

YOU CAN LEARN what fine coffee is and brew it far better than you ever did before. You can really like the taste of the stuff. But the reason most people drink coffee, of course, is the caffeine. Caffeine may do a wonderful job of fortifying you to face the day. You may think you couldn't live without it. But is it bad for you?

Frank evaluation of its hazards is not easy. There is a vast literature on the effects of caffeine on the body, and for every study reaching one conclusion, seemingly there is another that contradicts it. Although most major health risks have been ruled out, research continues at a steady clip. I'll summarize here the work done recently.

The first indictment of caffeine in recent years came in 1972, when a Boston group found an association between heavy coffee drinking (more than six cups a day) and elevated risk of heart attack. The association was never confirmed by other studies, however, and the first studies were shown to have been flawed. In 1974 a twelve-year review by the Framingham Heart Study concluded that there was no association between coffee consumption and heart attacks, coronary heart disease, angina pectoris, or sudden death.

Today the possible link between caffeine and heart disease is still controversial, and remains the most widely studied aspect of caffeine; recent studies have separated out other risk factors, chiefly smoking, that misled researchers in the past. They have so far come up pretty much undecided. Because very high doses of caffeine can provoke arrhythmia (irregular heartbeat), the danger to people who already suffered from arrhythmia was for a while widely researched, but a study reported last year in the *Archives of Internal Medicine* concluded that moderate doses of caffeine did not pose a danger even to people with life-threatening arrhythmia. Last fall a widely publicized study suggested that people who drink decaffeinated coffee experience a rise in serum cholesterol, but the medical community has largely dismissed the study as preliminary and inconclusive, and no supporting studies have appeared. A recent study in the Netherlands, reported last winter in the *New England Journal of Medicine*, found a significant increase in serum cholesterol among drinkers of boiled coffee, still popular there but made very little here; filtered coffee, which is what most Americans drink, had no effect.

A famous health scare associating caffeine with pancreatic cancer turned out to be another case of the missing link: cigarette smoking was the important risk factor, and five years after publication of the study its authors reversed their original findings. Studies associating coffee with bladder, urinary-tract, and kidney cancer have also been inconsistent and inconclusive.

No link to breast cancer has been proved, although whether a link exists between coffee drinking and benign breast disease, or fibrocystic disease, is still controversial. Large and well-controlled studies have virtually ruled out any link between caffeine consumption and the development of fibrocystic disease, but abstaining from caffeine as a way of treating the disease has been less thoroughly studied. Although the studies conducted so far suggest that no significant lessening of fibrocystic disease occurs when women give up caffeine, many women believe that doing so is an effective treatment.

Pregnant women were told in 1980 by the Food and Drug Administration that they should avoid caffeine, on the basis of an FDA experiment in which pregnant rats were force-fed the equivalent of 56 to 87 cups of strong coffee at a time through a stomach tube, and gave birth to offspring with missing toes or parts of toes. A later study giving rats the same exaggerated doses, but orally, in drinking water and at a steadier rate over a day, resulted in none of the birth defects. No later studies on human beings have linked coffee-drinking to any birth defects.

The subject for further study seems to be the connection between heavy consumption—more than six or seven cups a day—and low birth weight or birth defects. The average half-life of caffeine in the body, meaning the time it takes the body to get rid of half the caffeine consumed, is three to six hours. Women in the second and third trimesters of pregnancy clear it half as fast, and caffeine, which passes easily through the placenta, can remain in an unborn child for as long as a hundred hours. (Heavy smokers, in contrast, clear caffeine twice as fast.) Although no dangers to infants have been found when pregnant women or nursing mothers drink moderate amounts of coffee, many doctors recommend on principle that pregnant and nursing women avoid caffeine.

HOW CAFFEINE WORKS is still incompletely understood, and the prevailing theory took shape only in the early seventies. The theory holds that caffeine acts less by starting than by stopping something, the something being the depressant effects of adenosine, one of the chemicals the body makes to control neural activity. Caffeine blocks the adenosine receptor sites in cells. This theory is not perfect, for reasons including that there are different types of adenosine receptors, but it is widely accepted.

Proponents of caffeine emphasize its ability to increase alertness and enhance performance on various tasks. Its effects are most pronounced, however, on performance levels that are low because of fatigue or boredom. Also, caffeine seems to affect people to a degree that varies according to personality type. For example, it appears to help extroverts keep performing tasks requiring vigilance more than it helps introverts, who are evidently able to plow through such tasks unassisted. Despite the generations of writers who have assumed that coffee helps them think more clearly, caffeine seems to increase only intellectual speed, not intellectual power. Subjects in experiments do things like read and complete crossword puzzles faster but not more accurately.

Some studies reveal a curious fact. One recent study found that people who were given doses of caffeine varying from none to high and at the same time allowed to drink their normal amount of coffee each day had no idea how much caffeine they were consuming overall or whether they were consuming any additional caffeine. Even at the highest additional doses people who ordinarily drank small amounts of coffee reported no irritability, nervousness, or tremors. Numerous other studies reinforce the idea that people respond to caffeine more in relation to how much they think they have consumed than to how much they actually have.

This is not to say that the effects of caffeine are imaginary. Many studies confirm what most people know—coffee keeps you awake. It also often decreases total sleep time and increases the number of times you wake in the night, depending on how much you drink and on how sensitive you are. Variation among people is great. Everyone knows someone like the woman I met in Brazil who told me, "If I'm sleepy, I take a coffee. If I wake up at night, I take a coffee to go back to sleep." Although caffeine does interfere with some phases of sleep, it has in many studies been shown not to decrease rapid-eye-movement sleep, as alcohol and barbiturates do. The sleep disturbance it causes seems to be more severe in older people, which may be one reason why consumption of decaffeinated coffee increases with age.

That caffeine interferes with sleep doesn't mean that it reliably makes you snap to. It doesn't sober you up, black or with milk—your motor functions are just as badly impaired by alcohol as they were before you drank two cups of black coffee, and even if you feel more awake you're just as dangerous a driver. Similarly, caffeine does not counteract phenobarbital or other barbiturates. But it does help reverse the impairment of cognitive activity caused by diazepam, the chemical that is the basis of Valium and many other tranquilizers.

Caffeine speeds up the metabolism and makes you burn calories faster, although not significantly for purposes of weight loss, as amphetamine does. The body metabolizes caffeine almost completely, and it appears in all tissue fluids about five minutes after ingestion, reaching its highest levels after twenty to thirty minutes. Caffeine is a diuretic and thus dehydrating, so don't think that drinking coffee will slake your thirst. Coffee, both regular and decaffeinated, has a laxative effect.

And coffee can cause stomach pain and heartburn. The exact roles played by caffeine and other substances in coffee in stimulating the secretion of gastric acids remains in question, because there has been proof that both caffeinated and decaffeinated coffee can affect the gastrointestinal tract. One study found that regular and decaffeinated coffee each had twice as much effect on the gastrointestinal tract as caffeine alone. Although coffee, with or without caffeine, and caffeine itself are not thought to cause ulcers, their role has been little studied, and both are known to make ulcers worse.

A source of confusion for anyone trying to learn how much caffeine he consumes is the conflicting estimates that appear in studies. Most say that a five-ounce cup of coffee contains from 80 to 100 milligrams of caffeine, although in fact the variation can be much greater, depending on the strength of the coffee. The same amount of tea, brewed for five minutes, has from 20 to 50 milligrams of caffeine; a cup of tea usually contains less caffeine than a cup of coffee because less tea is used per cup. A twelve-ounce serving of cola generally contains 38 (for Pepsi) to 45 (for Coke) milligrams of caffeine. Some studies say that for caffeine to have its effects the minimum oral dose is 85 milligrams, but this too depends on individual sensitivity.

THE QUESTION OF addiction is similarly thorny. According to a review of the literature on caffeine and the central nervous system by Kenneth Hirsh, in *Methylxanthine Beverages and Foods*, recent data show that tolerance to caffeine develops in the central nervous system and in many organ systems. Tolerance has been better studied than its ugly corollary, withdrawal. In sleep studies researchers noticed that heavy coffee drinkers were less disturbed than light or moderate coffee drinkers by drinking coffee before going to sleep and, if they had had no coffee the night before, felt more in need of a cup in the morning. Those little accustomed to caffeine suffer "caffeinism," or coffee nerves, when they have a high dose. Those accustomed to but deprived of it report, and experiments confirm, irritability, inability to work well, nervousness, restlessness, and lethargy.

Worst, and most common, is the headache that comes with giving up caffeine. The headache can be severe and often lasts for one or two days. The adenosine-receptor theory holds that long-term caffeine consumption creates more adenosine receptor sites, and thus sudden abstention from caffeine means unusual sensitivity to adenosine. This could explain withdrawal headache: overreactivity to adenosine in blood vessels in the scalp and cranium can dilate them, and cause a headache. One very effective way to treat the headache, unsurprisingly, is with caffeine, which constricts the blood vessels in the brain; this effect is why caffeine has long been used to treat migraines. (In contrast, caffeine dilates coronary arteries.) The reason so many over-the-counter headache remedies include caffeine, though, is that it is thought to enhance the effects of the other drugs in them—something that has never been proved. Kenneth Hirsh optimistically thinks that because the body is more sensitive to adenosine after caffeine withdrawal, it will compensate by reducing the number of adenosine receptors to the number that existed before caffeine tolerance developed.

If caffeine is so painful to give up, can caffeine tolerance be compared to addiction to other drugs? Hirsh, like many other scientists, wants to avoid the comparison. "All definitions of addiction . . . eventually boil down to compulsion with and for a drug," he writes. Caffeine, he concludes, just doesn't result in addictive behavior. He points to rat and baboon studies in which animals regularly gave themselves doses of morphine, cocaine, and amphetamine but gave themselves caffeine no more often than saline placebos. Some animals in the experiment seemed more eager for caffeine than others, which supports the idea that individual variation is important. Hirsh, it must be noted, worked for General Foods when he wrote his study, but he is not alone in his conclusions.

However fine one draws the distinction, caffeine use does fit several standards of drug addiction, which include compulsion to continue use, tolerance for the drug, and withdrawal. It is silly to invoke the argument, as caffeine apologists often do, that truly addictive drugs impel their users to commit any act, however violent, to obtain them. You don't have to mug someone in a park at night to get money for a cup of coffee. You can stand on a corner and ask for it.

Whether or not caffeine is hazardous or truly addictive, becoming habituated to it and suffering coffee nerves or caffeine withdrawal is no fun, and many people have chosen to drink decaffeinated coffee instead. In 1962, the peak year for American coffee consumption, decaffeinated coffee made up only three percent of coffee sales; today it accounts for more than 20 percent. It's a shame that most decaffeinated coffee is so terrible, because it doesn't have to be. Traditionally, the inferior robusta species of bean has been decaffeinated, not only because it is cheaper but also because it yields more caffeine,

which can be sold to soft-drink and patent-medicine companies, and because it has more body and so can better withstand decaffeination processes. Arabica beans, which are of higher quality, are now being decaffeinated. But the public buys the vastly inferior water-process decaf, because it suffers from an unwarranted fear of chemical decaffeination.

Decaffeination has been practiced since the turn of the century, mostly using chemicals. Every process starts with steaming the beans, to loosen the bond of caffeine to the coffee bean. Then, in the "direct" process, a chemical solvent is circulated through the beans. The beans are again steamed to remove any residual solvent, and dried; the solvent is mixed with water and the caffeine extracted. In the water process, after beans are first steamed they soak in water, which removes not only caffeine but all the other solids that flavor a cup of coffee. Caffeine is removed from the solution, which is reduced to a slurry that is returned to soak with the still-wet beans and give them back some of the lost solids.

The problems of water-process decaffeination are obvious. The water strips out most of the body and the flavoring compounds. What goes back is sometimes from the previous batch of beans, and it won't all go back anyway. Jacobs Suchard, a large Swiss company, has made improvements in the water process that keep more solids intact in the beans. It has mounted a new campaign to promote the Swiss process, in which caffeine is extracted from the water-solids solution with carbon filters rather than with the chemicals that are sometimes used. Specialty coffee decaffeinated at Jacobs Suchard's new factory in Vancouver has made strong showings in taste tests. But most water-process decaffeinated coffee is still a shadow of its former self and must be overroasted, to give the false impression that it has body and flavor.

The most efficient chemical solvent, methylene chloride, is what people think they should avoid. Methylene chloride has been banned for use in hair sprays since it was shown in animal studies to be dangerous when inhaled. But mice fed methylene chloride in drinking water at doses equivalent to 4.4 million cups of decaf a day showed none of the toxicological or carcinogenic response that had occurred when

mice had inhaled it in much smaller quantities. In 1985 the FDA said that the risk from using methylene chloride in decaffeination is so low "as to be essentially non-existent." Methylene chloride evaporates at 100° to 120°F. Beans are usually roasted at a temperature of 350° to 425°, coffee brewed at 190° to 212°. The amount of methylene chloride left in brewed coffee, then, must be measured in parts per billion—comparable to what is in the air of many cities. Even Michael Jacobson, the crusading leader of the consumer-advocacy group Center for Science in the Public Interest, says that caffeine is more dangerous than any chemical residues in decaffeinated coffee. Coffee decaffeinated with methylene chloride certainly tastes better.

A new process, using "supercritical" carbon dioxide, shows great promise. The supercritical fluid, in a state between liquid and gas, is produced under extremely high pressure. It can pass through steamed coffee beans and remove the caffeine without removing other solids, vaporizing when its work is done and leaving not a trace. So far General Foods is the only company using the process, and its production capacity allows it to decaffeinate only its Sanka brand (not its Maxwell House decaf) and Private Collection, a smaller GF venture into specialty coffee. A new processing plant is being built independently in northern California, and when completed (in about two years) it will decaffeinate beans from specialty roasters using supercritical carbon dioxide, which Marc Sims, a consultant in Berkeley, California, who is involved with the plant, prefers to call "natural effervescence."

"Regular, decaf—it's all caf," a woman said dismissively when I recently offered her a choice of coffees after dinner. She was not entirely wrong. Advertisements for coffee that is "97 percent caffeine-free" might as well describe any coffee, since the caffeine content of coffee beans varies from 1.1 to 2.6 percent. It would be better to say "decaffeinated," since the FDA requires that 97 percent of caffeine be removed from unroasted beans. (It has no requirements for brewed coffee.) Coffee decaffeinated by careful firms like Jacobs Suchard and KVW, near Hamburg, which uses methylene chloride, yields 0.03 percent or less caffeine in unroasted beans. Brewed decaf can thus have one to five milligrams of caffeine per cup, and however little that sounds compared with the supposed minimum 85-milligram dose, it can keep some people—me, for instance—going.

You can rate the processes for yourself. The Coffee Connection (800-284-5282) will send you Jacobs Suchard water decaf. Starbucks, an excellent roaster in Seattle (800-445-3428), and Thanksgiving (800-648-6491) will send you that or KVW chemical decaf. Any of these beans will prove that you don't have to give up what you love about coffee if you give up caffeine.

Not only are people turning away from caffeine, they're turning away from coffee, and in more significant numbers. Since 1962 per capita coffee consumption has fallen by more than a third, from 3.12 to 1.75 cups a day. At the same time, per capita consumption of soft drinks has nearly tripled. The decline can't accurately be attributed to fears about caffeine, because two thirds of it oc-curred before the first health scare about caffeine, in 1972. The culprit is soft drinks, whose manufacturers spend much more on promotion than coffee companies do. Young people drink cola to wake themselves up, and so do many former coffee drinkers. Pepsi recently test-marketed Pepsi A.M., a cola with more than the usual amount of caffeine.

The coffee trade has naturally been alarmed by this trend, but no one quite knows what to do about it. The big fear is that coffee will go the way of tea—now considered (when served hot, at any rate) to be an old person's drink. Big companies have tried to compete with specialty roasters, as General Foods did when it started its Private Collection line of whole-bean and ground coffee, because the specialty-coffee market has been growing by 15 to 20 percent a year while the mass coffee market has been shrinking.

A recent article in *Tea & Coffee Trade Journal* suggested various ways to combat the decrease: trying to break the coffee-caffeine association, both con-ceptual and aural, by using brand names to refer to coffee, as with soft drinks; trying to give coffee a youthful image in advertisements, rather than relying on a logo to sell the product; promoting coffee at colleges; dyeing plain old styrofoam cups so they'll look zippy, like soda cans. The Coffee Development Group, an organization dedicated to increasing the consumption of coffee by improving its quality, thinks that one answer is in promoting iced coffee and sweetened coffee drinks, to compete directly with soda. In fact, the fastest-growing part of the specialty-coffee market is coffee mixed with bits of nuts and dried fruit and stirred with flavoring extracts, making really awful combinations that roasters disdain but stock—"those yucky flavors that sell," in the words of Dan Cox, of Green Mountain Coffee, in Vermont, who is the current chairman of the Coffee Development Group.

Yucky they are. Better to drink straight coffee, with or without caffeine, that tastes good.

The Economy of Drug Use

Drugs are not simply used; they are also bought and sold. They are the foundation for a major economic enterprise—or, to be more precise, a number of major economic enterprises. The alcoholic beverage industry earns $50 billion at the retail level in the United States each year; some $40 billion is spent on tobacco products, and $40 billion for pharmaceuticals; and $7 billion is spent for over-the-counter medications. The size of the illegal drug industry is more difficult to determine because, as we saw, its sales are not taxed and, therefore, not officially recorded anywhere. Estimates range from $50 to $300 billion; if we average the various estimates, this would make the illegal drug trade—if combined into a single industry—the most profitable business in the country, with a dollar volume larger than that of General Motors. Several journalists claim that more money is spent on illegal drugs than for any other existing product or service—more than on food, housing, education, or medical care. This is probably an exaggeration, but no one doubts that the drug trade is huge and extremely profitable.

Each drug is bought and sold in a somewhat different way, by a somewhat different cast of characters. Some drugs are legal, and their manufacturers are seen as respectable, pillars of their communities. Other drugs are illegal, and their sellers are designated as villains, denounced in the media by politicians and other upstanding citizens. Some drugs are produced from plants that grow naturally in the wild or in an agricultural setting: Marijuana is made up of the leaves and flowering tops of the cannabis plant; opium is exuded when the mature pod of a type of poppy is lanced; peyote is the dried, sliced "buttons" of species of desert cactus; psilocybin is the active ingredient in several species of a mushroom, *Psilocybe mexicana* among them, which grow in the southwest. Other drugs are referred to as semisynthetics, and were derived from natural substances that were chemically transformed—cocaine's ultimate origin was the coca plant, heroin's was the opium poppy—while still others are completely synthetic chemicals, manufactured from other chemicals in a laboratory. A particular source will necessitate a particular type of distribution, as well as a distinct economic activity.

Perhaps one of the most painful ironies of the drug scene is the toleration and even encouragement the legal drug trade receives, and the aggressiveness with which they pursue their business. Although some restraints have been placed on the tobacco and alcohol industries—in the United States, cigarettes cannot be advertised on television; warning labels must be placed on all packs of cigarettes sold; advertisements cannot depict alcoholic beverages being drunk on television; still-active athletes cannot advertise alcohol or cigarettes—they are relatively moderate measures. (In some countries, alcohol and tobacco products cannot be advertised at all.) The legal drug industry lobbies forcefully against restrictions of any kind, and is often successful in blocking legislation that would cut into its profits or impede business in any way. For instance, the tobacco industry is waging a (in the long run, losing) campaign to convince the public and legislators that smoking in public is a basic right, comparable to the right of free speech, guaranteed by the Bill of Rights. And so far, the alcoholic beverage industry has been successful in blocking legislation to require that the contents of alcoholic beverages be listed on bottles sold to the public.

The economic activities of the illegal drug trade impact upon society in somewhat different ways. Dealers and smugglers are less likely to attempt to influence legislation or win the hearts and minds of the general public. In contrast, their methods tend to be cruder and more direct. Colombian cocaine kingpins offer the police and judges in their jurisdiction the choice of "plata o plomo"—silver or lead, that is, money or a bullet, a bribe in exchange for not arresting, prosecuting, or convicting them for their crimes, or death for doing so. In the United States, drug dealers have less unopposed powers, but they often dominate certain neighborhoods through intimidation and violence.

In short, those who sell drugs, whether legal or illegal, generally take steps to protect their profits. The economic character of the drug trade translates into power, or, at least, attempts to wield power. While this power is often struggled against and often overcome, it is a fixture of the drug scene and determines many crucial aspects of drug use and abuse specifically, and the structure and dynamics of the society generally. The economic dimension in the world of drug use is so important that it is ignored only at the risk of serious distortion.

Looking Ahead: Challenge Questions

Does the profit earned by the legal drug industry justify its acceptance? Can the same be said of the drug trade? Should drug dealers and smugglers pay taxes? Are the taxes paid by the cigarette and alcohol industries enough to cover the damage their use does to the society?

Should the alcohol and tobacco industries be more tightly regulated than they are? Should alcohol and cigarette ads be banned altogether? Must the contents of alcoholic beverages be listed on bottles sold to the public? Do we have the right to know what we are drinking? Should the tobacco industry be forced to pay for anti-smoking ads to counter their own commercials?

Is the right to smoke in public a basic right equivalent to free speech, guaranteed by the Bill of Rights? What about the right of the person near the smoker who finds cigarette smoke irritating?

Given the fact that drug dealers enforce their will through violence, how can their activities ever be eliminated?

Does the economic character of the drug trade influence drug use and abuse? How? If there were no profits in drugs, would anyone ever use them?

ADVERTISING ADDICTION: THE ALCOHOL INDUSTRY'S HARD SELL

Jean Kilbourne, Ed. D.

Jean Kilbourne, Ed.D., is the Chair of the Council on Alcohol Policy and is on the Board of Directors of the National Council on Alcoholism. Two award-winning films, "Still Killing Us Softly: Advertising's Image of Women" and "Calling the Shots: The Advertising of Alcohol," are based on her lectures.

Alcohol is the most commonly used drug in the United States. It is also one of the most heavily advertised products in the United States. The alcohol industry generates more than $65 billion a year in revenue and spends more than $1 billion a year on advertising. The advertising budget for one beer — Budweiser — is more than the entire federal budget for research on alcoholism and alcohol abuse. Unfortunately, young people and heavy drinkers are the primary targets of the advertisers.

What does advertising do?

There is no conclusive proof that advertising increases alcohol consumption. Research does indicate, however, that alcohol advertising contributes to increases in consumption by young people and serves as a significant source of negative socialization for young people. Those who argue that peer pressure is the major influence on young people strangely overlook the role of advertising.

The alcoholic beverage companies claim that they are not trying to create more or heavier drinkers. They say that they only want people who already drink to switch to another brand and to drink it in moderation. But this industry-wide claim does not hold up under scrutiny. An editorial in Advertising Age concluded: "A strange world it is, in which people spending millions on advertising must do their best to prove that advertising doesn't do very much!"

About a third of all Americans choose not to drink at all, a third drink moderately, and about a third drink regularly. Ten percent of the drinking-age population consumes over 60 percent of the alcohol. This figure corresponds closely to the percentage of alcoholics in society. If alcoholics were to recover (i.e. to stop drinking entirely), the alcohol industry's gross revenues would be cut in half. Recognizing this important marketing fact, alcohol companies deliberately devise ads designed to appeal to heavy drinkers. Advertising is usually directed toward promoting loyalty and increasing usage, and heavy users of any product are the best customers but, in the case of alcohol, the heavy user is usually an addict.

Another perspective on the industry's claim that it encourages only moderate drinking is provided by Robert Hammond, director of the Alcohol Research Information Service. He estimates that if all 105 million drinkers of legal age consumed the official maximum "moderate" amount of alcohol — .99 ounces per day, the equivalent of about two drinks — the industry would suffer "a whopping 40 percent decrease in the sale of beer, wine and distilled spirits, based on 1981 sales figures."

Such statistics show the role heavy drinkers play in maintaining the large profit margins of the alcohol industry. Modern research techniques allow the producers of print and electronic media to provide advertisers with detailed information about their readers, listeners and viewers. Target audiences are sold to the alcohol industry on a cost per drinker basis.

One example of how magazines sell target audiences appeared recently in Advertising Age: Good Housekeeping advertised itself to the alcohol industry as a good place to reach women drinkers, proclaiming, "You'll catch more women with wine than with vinegar. She's a tougher customer than ever. You never needed Good Housekeeping more."

The young audience is also worth a great deal to the alcohol industry. Sport magazine promoted itself to the alcohol industry as a conduit to young drinkers with an ad in Advertising Age stating, "What young money spends on drinks is a real eye-opener." Budweiser's Spuds MacKenzie campaign is clearly designed to appeal to young people. Miller has a new television commercial featuring animated clay figures of a monkey, an elephant and a lion with a voice that says "three out of four party animals preferred the taste of Miller Lite." Wine coolers are often marketed as soft drinks with ads featuring puppets, animated characters, Santa Claus and other figures that appeal especially to young people. Even in supposedly commercial-free movies, showing in theaters, viewers are targeted. Many films, especially those appealing to young people, include paid placements of cigarettes and alcohol.

The college market is particularly important to the alcohol industry not only because of the money the students will spend on beer today, but because they will develop drinking habits and brand allegiances that may be

From *Multinational Monitor,* June 1989, pp. 13-16. Reprinted with permission of *Multinational Monitor,* P.O. Box 19405, Washington, D.C. 20036, $22/individual.

with them for life. As one marketing executive said, "Let's not forget that getting a freshman to choose a certain brand of beer may mean that he will maintain his brand loyalty for the next 20 to 35 years. If he turns out to be a big drinker, the beer company has bought itself an annuity." This statement undercuts the industry's claim that it does not target advertising campaigns at underage drinkers since today almost every state prohibits the sale of alcohol to people under 21 years old and the vast majority of college freshman are below that age.

The alcohol industry's efforts to promote responsible drinking must also be evaluated carefully. Much of its advertising promotes irresponsible and dangerous drinking. For example, a poster for Pabst Blue Ribbon features a young woman speeding along on a bicycle with a bottle of beer where the water bottle is supposed to be. Obviously biking and drinking beer are not safely complementary activities.

Even some of the programs designed by the alcohol industry to educate students about responsible drinking subtly promote myths and damaging attitudes. Budweiser has a program called "The Buddy System" designed to encourage young people not to let their friends drive drunk. Although this is a laudable goal, it is interesting to note that none of the alcohol industry programs discourage or even question drunkenness per se. The implicit message is that it is alright to get drunk as long as you don't drive; abuse is acceptable, even encouraged.

Myth making

The industry often targets relatively disempowered groups in society, primarily women and minority groups, and associates alcohol with power. For example, a Cutty Sark Whiskey ad features a retired Black baseball player, Curt Flood, promoting its drink. The ad shows Flood holding forth a glass of whiskey with the text "Some people think you can't beat the system. Here's to those who show the way." This ad associates Flood and his successful athletic performance with his drinking Cutty Sark whiskey.

The link between advertising and alcoholism is unproven. Alcoholism is a complex illness and its etiology is uncertain. But alcohol advertising does create a climate in which abusive attitudes toward alcohol are presented as normal, appropriate and innocuous. One of the chief symptoms of alcoholism is denial that there is a problem. It is often not only the alcoholic who denies the illness but also his or her family, employer, doctor, etc. Alcohol advertising often encourages denial be creating a world in which myths about alcohol are presented as true and in which signs of trouble are erased or transformed into positive attributes.

One of the primary means of creating this distortion is through advertising. Most advertising is essentially myth-making. Instead of providing information about a product, such as its taste or quality, advertisements create an image of the product, linking the item with a particular lifestyle which may have little or nothing to do with the product itself. According to an article on beer marketing in Advertising Age, "Advertising is as important to selling beer as the bottle opener is to drinking it. . . . Beer advertising is mainly an exercise in building images." Another article a few months later on liquor marketing stated that "product image is probably the most important element in selling liquor. The trick for marketers is to project the right

message in their advertisements to motivate those motionless consumers to march down to the liquor store or bar and exchange their money for a sip of image."

The links are generally false and arbitrary but we are so surrounded by them that we come to accept them: the jeans will make you look sexy, the car will give you confidence, the detergent will save your marriage. Advertising spuriously links alcohol with precisely those attributes and qualities — happiness, wealth, prestige, sophistication, success, maturity, athletic ability, virility, creativity, sexual satisfaction and others — that the misuse of alcohol destroys. For example, alcohol is often linked with romance and sexual fulfillment, yet it is common knowledge that alcohol misuse often leads to sexual dysfunction. Less well known is the fact that people with drinking problems are seven times more likely than the general population to be separated or divorced.

Image advertising is especially appealing to young people who are more likely than adults to be insecure about the image they are projecting. Sexual and athletic prowess are two of the themes that dominate advertising aimed at young people. A recent television commercial for Miller beer featured Danny Sullivan, the race car driver, speeding around a track with the Miller logo emblazoned everywhere. The ad implies that Miller beer and fast driving go hand in hand. A study of beer commercials funded by the American Automobile Association found that they often linked beer with images of speed, including speeding cars.

The magic transformation

"It separates the exceptional from the merely ordinary." This advertising slogan for Piper champagne illustrates the major premise of the mythology that alcohol is magic. It is a magic potion that can make you successful, sophisticated and sexy; without it, you are dull, mediocre and ordinary. The people who are not drinking champagne are lifeless replicas of the happy couple who are imbibing. The alcohol has rescued the couple, resurrected them, restored them to life. At the heart of the alcoholic's dilemma and denial is this belief, this certainty, that alcohol is essential for life, that without it he or she will literally die — or at best suffer. This ad and many others like it present the nightmare as true, thus affirming and even glorifying one of the symptoms of the illness.

Glorifying alcoholism

Such glorification of the symptoms is common in alcohol advertising. "Your own special island," proclaims an ad for St. Croix rum. Another ad offers Busch beer as "Your mountain hide-a-way." Almost all alcoholics experience intense feelings of isolation, alienation and loneliness. Most make the tragic mistake of believing that the alcohol alleviates these feelings rather than exacerbating them. The two examples above distort reality in much the same way as the alcoholic does. Instead of being isolated and alienated, the people in the ad are in their own special places.

The rum ad also seems to be encouraging solitary drinking, a sign of trouble with alcohol. There is one drink on the tray and no room for another. Although it is unusual for solitary drinking to be shown (most alcohol ads feature groups or happy couples), it is not unusual for unhealthy attitudes toward alcohol to be presented as normal and acceptable.

The most obvious example is obsession with alcohol.

7. THE ECONOMY OF DRUG USE

Alcohol is at the center of the ads just as it is at the center of the alcoholic's life. The ads imply that alcohol is an appropriate adjunct to almost every activity from love-making to white-water canoeing. An ad for Puerto Rican rums says, "You know how to make every day special. You're a white rum drinker." In fact, less than 10 percent of the adult population makes drinking a part of their daily routine.

There is also an emphasis on quantity in the ads. A Johnnie Walker ad features 16 bottles of scotch and the copy, "Bob really knows how to throw a party. He never runs out of Johnnie Walker Red." Light beer has been developed and heavily promoted not for the dieter but for the heavy drinker. The ads imply that because it is less filling, one can drink more of it.

Thus the ads tell the alcoholic and everyone around him that it is all right to consume large quantities of alcohol on a daily basis and to have it be a part of all of one's activities. At the same time, all signs of trouble and any hint of addiction are conspicuously avoided. The daily drinking takes place in glorious and unique settings, such as yachts at sunset, not at the more mundane but realistic kitchen tables in the morning. There is no unpleasant drunkenness, only high spirits. There are never any negative consequences. Of course, one would not expect there to be. The advertisers are selling their product and it is their job to erase any negative aspects as well as to enhance the positive ones. When the product is a drug that is addictive to one out of 10 users, however, there are consequences that go far beyond product sales.

The U.S. culture as a whole, not just the advertising and alcohol industry, tends to glorify alcohol and dismiss the problems associated with it. The "war on drugs," as covered by newspapers and magazines in this country, rarely includes the two major killers, alcohol and nicotine. It is no coincidence that these are two of the most heavily advertised products. In 1987, the use of all illegal drugs combined accounted for about 3,400 deaths. Alcohol is linked with over 100,000 deaths annually. Cigarettes kill a thousand people every day.

A comprehensive effort is needed to prevent alcohol-related problems. Such an effort must include education, media campaigns, increased availability of treatment programs and more effective deterrence policies. It must also include public policy changes that would include raising taxes on alcohol, putting clearly legible warning labels on the bottles and regulating the advertising.

THE TEFLON COATING OF CIGARETTE COMPANIES

Larry C. White

Larry C. White, a lawyer, is the author of Merchants of Death, The American Tobacco Industry, *William Morrow & Co., 1988. Mr. White is a guest columnist invited by Dr. Whelan who regularly writes Top Priority.*

Americans have always loved to hate corporations. From the days of the muckrakers and the great trusts to the consumer movement and the corporate bad guys of the last few decades, it's been great fun and morally uplifting to pillory certain companies. In the 1960s, Dow Chemical was assailed for manufacturing napalm, in the 1970s Nestle was dragged through the mud for aggressively marketing infant formula in the Third World. Then came Johns Manville, the asbestos ogre, and A. H. Robins, whose Dalkon Shield made it the corporate despoiler of women. Some of these companies have undergone the equivalent of capital punishment for their crimes, others have been forced to great lengths to apologize.

The harm that these businesses have inflicted pales when compared to the havoc wreaked by the companies that manufacture cigarettes. Smoking has long been the number one preventable cause of premature death and disease in our society. At least 390,000 Americans die each year of smoking-related illness; and the cigarette companies are unrepentant. Refusing against overwhelming evidence to admit that cigarettes are harmful, cigarette companies gear their advertising towards young people, particularly young blacks, Hispanics and females to encourage smoking.

If the cigarette companies were held to the same standards of conduct as other companies, we would see mass demonstrations in front of the Park Avenue headquarters of Philip Morris, thundering denunciations from media pundits, and heavy pressure for stricter legislation. People who profit from the cigarette trade would be social pariahs.

But none of this has happened. Indeed, cigarette people are quite as respectable as those who don't make a living pushing addictive dangerous drugs. Laurence Tisch, who earns the bulk of his money from Lorillard cigarettes, gave New York University $30 million, in return for which the name of University Hospital was changed to Tisch Hospital. This happened despite the fact that Lorillard's Kents, Newports, and Trues kill about 32,000 Americans each year. When New York's former Speaker of the Assembly Stanley Steingut died in Tisch Hospital of lung cancer recently, the media failed to note the irony. Is it possible to imagine that New York University officials would accept money from a large asbestos manufacturer and rename it, say, the Johns Manville Hospital?

Mr. Tisch's wife Joan sent out a letter soliciting money for the Gay Men's Health Crisis (GMHC) to help in its fight against AIDS. The address on the return envelope was the Loew's Corporation, parent company of Lorillard. Mrs. Tisch's moving description of a man wasting away from AIDS bore an eerie resemblance to death from lung cancer. But GMHC did not notice the irony. Its director said that he was very proud to have Mrs. Tisch associated with GMHC. Would GMHC have been proud to be supported by A. H. Robins?

The nation's leading cigarette company, Philip Morris, which has approximately a 39 percent share of the cigarette market in U.S. sales, is known to many not as a merchant of death, but as a great corporate philanthropist. The company enticed the National Archives to allow it to use the Bill of Rights as part of a sophisticated advertising campaign to burnish the company's reputation. Never mind that its Marlboro cigarette is the number one cigarette brand in the world, or that it is by far the biggest starter brand for young people. The fact that Philip Morris products have killed far more Americans than all the drug dealers of the twentieth century put together will be politely forgotten when the National Archives allows itself to be used for a reception hosted by Philip Morris.

Not only is Philip Morris not in the media doghouse; it is positively adored by some publications. *FORTUNE* magazine recently singled it out as one of the best run companies in the country.

What makes cigarette company respectability all the more surprising is that smoking itself has become very unfashionable. Smoking on flights within the U.S. has been banned, and smoking is now restricted in many public places. We seem to be moving toward widespread acceptance of the idea that people should not smoke in public except in designated smoking areas. Smoking has lost its glamour; it's become declasse. Most Americans, including smokers, now know that smoking is harmful (although most do not know just how dangerous it is). The increasingly bad image of smoking has not rubbed off on the industry itself, however. The cigarette makers have long been noted for their ability to "make lemonade from lemons." The decline in smoking, instead of hurting the industry's image, has helped defuse criticism. Many opponents of smoking believe that the industry is on its last legs and that cigarettes will go the way of the dodo bird without any further effort. Unfortunately, this is not necessarily true. Cigarette profits are higher than ever and there is no guarantee that the downward trends in smoking prevalence will continue. Cigarettes are still the most heavily advertised product in America.

The news that cigarettes are addictive, announced by Surgeon General C. Everett Koop in 1986, should have shaken the cigarette companies. But, as usual, this teflon industry took the news in stride. After all, smoking has traditionally been seen (by non-smokers who do not know any better) as a matter of free individual choice like choosing to go for a walk or eat an orange. It would take more than an official announcement and a few news stories to change public opinion on this.

The Surgeon General's pronouncements can hardly compete with the more than $2 billion worth of cigarette ads to which Americans are subject. The reason people smoke, the ads say, is really simple—for pleasure, for the sheer fun of it. According to this logic, the cigarette companies have not victimized smokers, but are merely supplying them with what they demand. This contrasts starkly with the victim-perpetrator image of the A. H. Robins and the Johns Manvilles.

Probably the best thing the cigarette makers have going for them is simply

that cigarettes and cigarette advertising are ubiquitous—just a normal part of life. Media expert Tony Schwartz points out, "We see the brand logos on door pulls. The ads are everywhere." Cigarettes seem as though they've been around forever (actually they didn't become a mass phenomenon until World War I).

Tragically, cigarette-induced illness and death have become so familiar that we no longer really notice it. Lung cancer, emphysema, and heart attacks are familiar killers and when they appear, seem almost inevitable. One of the greatest ironies of the past several decades is that there are many Americans who will passionately oppose pesticides, which have had no adverse affect on their lives, while patiently tolerating an industry that has literally killed their nearest and dearest.

The lack of media attention to the issue of smoking and cigarettes has two main causes. One is the general feeling among newspeople that these particular stories have been told too many times already. The media in this country are obsessed with novelty. Recently a man in Oregon had brought back from Africa several giant frogs (up to twelve pounds each). This drew coverage on the network news and countless newspaper stories. In terms of what is accepted as "newsworthy," the routine death of hundreds of thousands from a preventable cause doesn't compare with the frogs.

Then there is the effect of cigarette advertising. Cigarette companies do not like anti-smoking stories and they do not hesitate to pull advertising away from media that present it. Now that Philip Morris is highly diversified, it can use its giant food subsidiaries such as Kraft and General Foods to punish publications and broadcast media who dare to publish anti-smoking, or even worse, anti-tobacco company stories. Media self-

censorship is rife; most editors and producers think of the potential loss of advertising revenue before they commission a cigarette story.

Unlike other industries which have had very little time to plan strategies to deal with bad news about their products, the tobacco industry has had thirty years to refine its defenses. We are all familiar with denial, but an equally effective defense of the industry's image is through camouflage. Bad news about other products has been turned into protective covering for cigarettes.

A favorite Tobacco Institute defense goes something like this: 'so what if there may be a risk in smoking, there's a risk in driving a car or eating too many eggs.' The unspoken implication is that General Motors and your local butter and egg man are complicit in supplying risky products in exactly the same way as cigarette companies.

It takes some understanding of the risk-benefit balance to unravel this argument. Cars and eggs are very high on the benefit index, and relatively low on the risk index. Thus, the primary function of those who supply them is positive—in general their products are useful and make life better for most people. Cigarettes on the other hand are very high on the risk scale, and are nil on the benefit index. So the primary function of the cigarette makers is negative—to sell a useless risk to their customers.

But the public hears only the tobacco industry point of view. Neither government nor major voluntary health organizations nor consumer education organizations have been able to counter effectively tobacco industry advertising and public relations. The tobacco industry has escaped the public wrath visited on other companies less damaging because the industry itself largely controls what is written and broadcast about it.

COKE INC.

INSIDE THE BIG BUSINESS OF DRUGS

MICHAEL STONE

ACTING ON A TIP FROM THE BROOKLYN DISTRICT ATTORney, federal Customs agents raided a warehouse on 44th Drive in Long Island City early last November. They were looking for cocaine, and they found it— 400 pounds stuffed in cardboard boxes lying in plain view. But that was only the start. Against a wall, the agents found hundreds of twenty-gallon cans filled with bricks of cocaine packed in lye so corrosive it had begun to eat through the metal containers. It took a police unit seven days to move out the drugs. By then, the agents had uncovered nearly 5,000 bricks: 4,840 kilograms—5.3 tons—of cocaine.

Richard Mercier, the agent in charge of the operation, says that in 1973, he put a dealer away for 34 years for possession of three ounces of cocaine. In those days, the seizure of a kilogram of drugs—2.2 pounds—was a major bust. After the Long Island City raid, Mercier recalls, he surveyed a 24-foot truck piled four feet high with cocaine. "How much more is out there?" he wondered.

Three months after that bust, in the early-morning hours of February 3, a police anti-crime unit rounded the corner at Lenox Avenue and 128th Street in Harlem and saw a young man we'll call Willie waving a .357 Magnum at a group of youths across the street. Someone yelled, "Yo, burgundy!"—the code name for the officers' red Chevy—and Willie darted into a nearby tenement. The cops cornered him in a second-floor apartment, and Willie dropped a brown bag containing almost 300 vials of crack. On a bench next to him, police found a plastic bag containing 2,900 more vials of crack. In a wastebasket they discovered more than $12,000 in small bills. It was Willie's second arrest. He was fifteen.

These events evoke the images New Yorkers most commonly associate with the city's drug trade: mountains of white powder smuggled by a faceless international cartel, and the dead-end kid hawking crack in the ghetto. But the smuggler and the street dealer are only the most obvious players in the city's bustling drug business. Between them, an army of unseen workers— middlemen, money counters, couriers, chemists, money launderers, labelers, and arm-breakers—tend the vast machinery of New York's dope trade. Seven days a week, 24 hours a day, they process, package, and distribute the hundreds of kilos of heroin and cocaine required to feed the city's habit.

A legion of entrepreneurs also supply New Yorkers with tons of marijuana, as well as a dazzling assortment of pharmaceuticals: barbiturates, amphetamines, LSD, ecstasy. You can still buy PCP on West 127th Street, and officials have run across "ice," a potent new methamphetamine derivative, in East New York. But today, the huge heroin and cocaine/crack markets are the focus of law-enforcement efforts, for these are the drugs that are corroding city life.

During the past decade, New York's drug business has undergone a revolution. Ten years ago, cocaine was still exotic, a drug popular with celebrities and people trying to be hip. Crack wasn't even an idea. Though heroin was plentiful, users tended to be older and more discreet about their habits. A *Times* survey in December 1981 asked New Yorkers to rate the most important problems facing the city, and drugs didn't make the top ten. The appetite for drugs that's since sprung up has developed together with a business that aggressively marketed its products and worked feverishly to keep pace with the demand it was creating. At times, dealer and user seemed locked in a fatal embrace, each egging the other on to new and dangerous highs.

The breakneck expansion in sales and revenues destabilized New York's entrenched distribution networks, ushered in an era of intense competition, and sparked episodes of unprecedented violence. Thousands of organizations—from mom-and-pop candy-store operations to vast criminal conspiracies—sprouted to meet the demand. The drug trade also became an equal-opportunity employer: As the Mafia pulled back from—or was muscled out of—the business, blacks and other minority-group members who'd previously been relegated to the lower levels of distribution were drafted into key roles. And with cocaine and heroin selling at several times the price of gold, street-smart young men suddenly found themselves awash in cash.

At the same time, these dealers influenced the type, price, availability, and quality of drugs in the city. Crack was an immediate success here, though in Boston and Chicago the drug is relatively rare. The taboo on selling dangerous drugs to minors, observed a generation ago, was breached, and now teenagers and even younger children play important roles in the trade.

Despite the efforts of the authorities and the opposition of community groups, the city's drug lords—many of them unedu-

The city's drug lords—many of them uneducated and seemingly unemployable—have built and managed amazingly efficient markets.

cated and seemingly unemployable—have developed and managed remarkably efficient markets. Gone are the periodic shortages that hit the city when organized crime ran the drug supply. The new traffickers not only increased profits but lowered prices and raised product quality. One wonders what might have been accomplished if all that energy, innovation, and daring had been harnessed to a worthy enterprise.

EVERYONE AGREES THAT THE DRUG BUSINESS IS BIG BUSIness, but there's wide disagreement over its exact size. The most quoted estimate—which comes from the House Narcotics Committee—is that retail drug sales nationally for 1987 amounted to $150 billion, a figure that one committee aide claims has grown substantially since then. There are no official figures for New York, but Sterling Johnson Jr., the city's special narcotics prosecutor, thinks the city's share may be as much as $80 billion.

Other experts argue that these numbers are grossly inflated. "If New Yorkers were spending $80 billion a year on drugs," says Peter Reuter, a researcher at the Rand Corporation, "then every man, woman, and child in the city would have a habit." Reuter calls the government's estimates "mythical numbers," created by agencies whose budgets and influence grow with the perceived size of the problem.

In fact, there simply isn't enough information to get an accurate reading of the size of the drug trade, although there are ways to make rough guesses. The most common method estimates the amount of drugs smuggled into the area and then multiplies that figure by the street value of the drugs to get a total price. For example, on the basis of figures from several law-enforcement agencies, it's estimated that officials intercepted around 14,000 kilograms of cocaine in the metropolitan area in the past twelve months, an amount experts assume to be around 10 percent of all the cocaine shipped here. Since the street value of a kilogram of cocaine runs from $80,000 to $190,000, cocaine sales in the city, according to the formula, ranged between $11.2 billion and $26.6 billion.

There are several problems with this method, however. For one thing, different government agencies often take credit for the same bust, thus inflating the overall figure for the amount seized. What's more, recent studies indicate that a substantial portion—perhaps 40 percent—of the cocaine and heroin brought into the country never reaches the street. Instead, it's consumed by dealers and their cronies or used as payments for services like prostitution. Finally, there's no good reason to believe that there's a fixed ratio between seizures and imports.

A second method for computing the size of the drug business focuses on heroin and is based on the number of users and the average cost of their daily habit. The state Division of Substance Abuse Services estimates that there are 200,000 heroin addicts (as opposed to recreational users) living in the city. If they spend an average of $50 a day to satisfy their habits, then addicts alone account for $3.6 billion in heroin sales each year.

Once again, however, the experts disagree on the data. Working from studies of the criminal activities of narcotics addicts, Reuter calculates that the common estimate of the number of heroin addicts and the cost of their addiction is far too high. "If there were 200,000 addicts in New York, each spending $50 a day, the city would have ceased to exist," he says. "The junkies would have stolen it long ago."

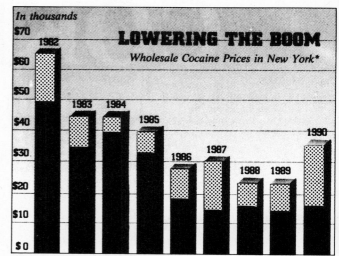

LOWERING THE BOOM
Wholesale Cocaine Prices in New York*

* Per kilogram. Prices vary depending on the location of the deal and the status of the buyer. The annual range is indicated in dots. By way of comparison, the consumer price index has risen 58 percent in the past decade.

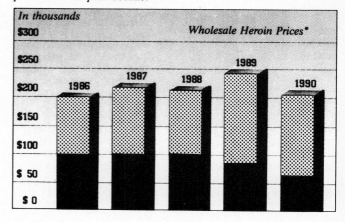

Wholesale Heroin Prices*

The average cost of a heroin habit is anybody's guess. "It might be $150 to $200 per day," says Paul Dinella, a former addict who until recently worked for the Division of Substance Abuse. "All I know is that a junkie will spend whatever he can get." Dinella also points out that most addicts vary their drug use over time. Some "dry out" periodically; around 40,000 heroin users entered treatment facilities around the state last year. Thousands more were jailed. When surveyed, though, addicts tend to exaggerate their habits, citing what they spend when they're binging. One study found that a group of addicts overstated the amount they spent on drugs by a factor of four.

A third approach attempts to place drug sales within the context of the economy as a whole. New York's gross economic product is about $180 billion. Given Sterling Johnson's drug-trade figure—$80 billion—that would mean that New Yorkers spend nearly half of what they produce on drugs. Many experts think that's impossible. Rather, they estimate that the city's underground economy is around $18 billion and that drug revenues are some fraction of that.

The wild card here is out-of-town sales. New York is a shipping point for many drugs, one of three or four main distribution centers in the United States. Revenues from these wholesale deals add billions to the total drug trade here and go some ways toward reconciling the difference between estimates based on interception and consumption.

Inevitably, the experts view the size of the drug problem through their personal lenses. The cop and the prosecutor see the crack crews on every corner and think the world has gone crazy. The economists and academicians look for the paper trail that tens of billions of dollars should leave and can't find it. Still, even moderate estimates place drug sales in New York at around $12 billion; by contrast, restaurant and bar revenues in the metropolitan area total around $7 billion.

In any case, the business has grown explosively in the past decade. Even heroin use is on the rise after declining for years. There are a few small positive signs: a recent reduction in casual cocaine use among high-school seniors, a decline in cocaine-related emergency-room visits after a dramatic rise, and a flattening out of the growth rate of crack consumption. But these developments may simply show that the market is saturated. "So we've stabilized crack use at record levels of consumption," says a House Narcotics Committee aide. "Is that something to be proud of?"

ALMOST EVERY COCAINE DEAL THAT takes place in New York begins in Colombia. Although the coca plant grows mainly in Peru and Bolivia, Colombians process about 80 percent of the region's crop and export it around the world. Of the estimated 450 tons of cocaine produced last year, as much as 75 tons may have passed through New York, says Arthur Stiffel, top Customs agent at Kennedy airport.

The Colombians smuggle cocaine in ways limited only by the imagination. Government agents have found the drug concealed in the cages of poisonous snakes and in blocks of chocolate. Every year, they intercept hundreds of human "mules" who swallow cocaine-filled condoms to sneak the stuff past Customs. Typically, Colombia's cartels smuggle boat- or planeloads of cocaine into a southern border state, then truck the drug up to New York. Recently, according to Stiffel, the smugglers have also been flying shipments directly into local airports. In June 1988, a Customs unit in Miami seized 1,200 kilos of cocaine that were en route to Suffolk County Airport in Westhampton, the first installment of a 15-ton load targeted for Long Island's East End summer population. The huge cargo ships that visit New York-area ports are another favorite vehicle for traffickers. "Not even counting what's hidden in the merchandise, a one-inch dropped ceiling in a standard container could hold thousands of pounds of cocaine," says Customs agent Richard Mercier. "But we only have the resources to inspect 3 percent of the containers that come in."

ON THE TRAIL
Kilograms of Cocaine Seized by the DEA in New York State.

Fiscal Year		Fiscal Year	
1990	8,715*	1985	332
1989	4,468	1984	1,119
1988	8,817	1983	229
1987	1,430	1982	335
1986	1,960	1981	149
	*To date	1980	160

Mercier's arithmetic explains the government's dilemma. Because the markup on cocaine is so high—a kilo that costs $4,000 to produce in Colombia sells in New York at wholesale for $14,000 to $23,000 and recently even as high as $35,000—the cartels would make a hefty profit even if Mercier's colleagues beat the odds and intercepted half the illegal drugs entering the city. The Colombians, of course, aren't indifferent to government seizures, but it costs them more to lose customers and sales to competitors than to lose an occasional shipment.

Some officials attribute a recent rise in the wholesale price of cocaine to the effectiveness of the war on drugs here and in Latin America. Others say it's too soon to tell if the war is helping, and in any case, drug prices vary widely depending on the location of the deal and the status of the buyer.

MOST OF THE COCAINE BROUGHT INTO NEW YORK—80 to 90 percent, says the DEA—is imported by the Cali cartel, an association of traffickers from Colombia's third-largest city. Headed by the two Rodriguez-Orjuela brothers and José Santa Cruz–Londoño, the group was formed in the early eighties to set drug policy and coordinate smuggling.

Before the cartel took over, most traffickers shipped their drugs to Miami, then sold them to middlemen with connections around the country. This arrangement worked fine as long as the market remained small and import prices stayed high. But as more and more traffickers got into the act and production levels jumped, import prices in Miami plummeted. As a result, the demand for cocaine rocketed, and local distributors racked up huge profits.

Today, the DEA maintains that the Cali cartel controls the first line of distribution in New York. Operating through teams, or "cells," of salaried employees, the cartel sells to the legions of mid-level dealers who ultimately supply the city's street dealers and retail organizations. Kenneth Robinson, one of the DEA's Cali experts, says that each cell typically includes a supervisor, or underboss, six to eight managers, and assorted workers. The supervisor takes possession of the drug shipments and stores them in safe houses—generally, private homes or warehouses. The managers place their orders through coded phone calls directly to the cartel in Colombia, which relays them to the supervisor. The supervisor then contacts the managers and arranges delivery at a safe house or at some public place, such as a mall, where the proliferation of shopping bags can help hide the transfer of drugs and money.

The cartel managers are the bureaucrats of the drug business. Contrary to the popular image of cocaine cowboys with flashy life-styles and flamboyant personalities, typical managers live modestly, blending into the suburbs where they often live. Overall, the cartel's operations are disciplined and difficult to trace. Money and drugs are kept separately, beepers are leased from legitimate businesses, written records are limited, and workers are trained in countersurveillance. When FBI undercover agents posing as money launderers recently met with cartel members, the Colombians brought along their lawyers.

But beneath the corporate veneer, the Colombians operate according to a code of violence and intimidation. Stiffel speculates that many of the cartel leaders came of age during Colombia's civil wars, when killing was a way of life. "They're not like the Mafia," says Robinson. "The Mafia isn't going to touch your family. But the Colombians will kill you, your wife, your children, and your dog. They're not going to leave anyone to take revenge later on."

Their methods are effective. Robinson points out that of the 400 or so cartel members arrested in the United States, only a handful have cooperated with the police. And in a business often disrupted by ripoffs and blunders, the Colombian operation seems to run smoothly. "I've busted dozens of Colombians over the years—peasants guarding rooms with tens, twenties, fifties piled floor to ceiling,'' Stiffel says. "But I've never yet found one of them with more than a few dollars in his pocket.''

Government officials don't know how much money the cartel actually makes from its New York operations. DEA agents busted a Cali money-laundering outfit in Great Neck and found records that indicated revenues of $44 million in less than two months. The 5.3-ton load in Long Island City—also identified as part of a Cali operation, though no one has been arrested in connection with the raid—would have brought around $200-million at wholesale prices. Robinson thinks that the Cali cartel has three or four cells operating independently of one another in the New York area and that, on average, it takes two or three months to distribute a major delivery.

One drug ring busted in Manorville, Long Island, is thought to have generated revenues of $200 million to $250 million a year.

New York's huge market has attracted other importers as well. In fact, Stiffel disputes the view that the Cali cartel controls New York's cocaine hierarchy. Rather, he argues that New York's traffickers are caught up in a kind of feeding frenzy, with all of Colombia's major cartels, as well as other groups and individual importers, competing for coca dollars. Two years ago, an apparent turf dispute between Cali and the Medellín cartel, the world's largest cocaine producer, sparked a rash of murders in Queens.

Last May, FBI agents busted a Medellín-operated ring based in Manorville, Long Island, that supplied cocaine to Jackson Heights, Flushing, and Jamaica, Queens. Agents say the group handled 6,400 kilos of cocaine during one five-month period in 1988. Jules Bonavolonta, the agent in charge of the investigation, estimates conservatively that the ring was generating revenues of $200 million to $250 million a year.

The Mafia has also continued to bring cocaine into the city. Law-enforcement officials speculate that at the time former Bonanno-family soldier Costabile "Gus" Farace murdered DEA undercover agent Everett Hatcher in February 1989 ("Death of a Hood," *New York*, January 29, 1990), he was building a cocaine-distribution ring in South Brooklyn and Staten Island. Farace was allegedly supplied from Miami by Gerard Chilli, his former prison mate and a reputed capo in the Bonanno family. Farace was gunned down last November because his actions had brought too much heat on the mob, investigators say.

After cocaine leaves the cartel's cell, it generally passes through a series of middlemen before reaching the street. Along the way, a dealer—who generally works on consignment—has three ways to make money. He can broker his supply intact and tack on a commission. He can divide it into smaller units and mark up the price. Or he can "cut" (dilute) the cocaine with harmless adulterants like milk sugar—in effect, increasing the amount of cocaine he has to sell.

In one typical sequence, using low-end prices, a high-level broker buys 100 kilos of pure cocaine at $17,000 per kilo and sells them in ten-kilo lots at an average price of $19,000 per kilo, earning $200,000. The second dealer sells the ten kilos for $23,000 a kilo, earning $40,000. His customers cut the cocaine by a third, producing, in all, 133 kilos, which they break into around 4,700 one-ounce units and sell to dealers for $800 each, for a total profit of about $1,460,000. Finally, these dealers add another one-half cut, creating in all 200 kilos, or about 7,050 ounces, of adulterated cocaine. That cocaine is converted into

crack at a rate of about 350 vials per ounce of cocaine. The crack vials are sold on the street for, say, $5 each, earning the dealers $8,577,500, of which around 20 percent goes to the street sellers.

This pyramid form of distribution has two main virtues: It maximizes the dealer's access to his market while minimizing his involvement in potentially dangerous transactions. No one at an intermediate level deals with more than a handful of contacts. Yet, after just five transfers, the system has supplied hundreds of street sellers who are reaching tens of thousands of customers. And the original 100 kilos of cocaine valued at $1.7-million have produced more than $12 million in revenues—a markup of around 700 percent.

SHARING IN THESE PROFITS ARE LITERALLY THOUSANDS of new, ethnically diverse mid-level dealers. Until the cartels arrived, cocaine distribution had been a closed shop, largely controlled by Cubans. But when the Colombians opened up the market in the early eighties, they created what one dealer at the time called the "ethnicization" of cocaine. Saddled with an oversupply of drugs, the cartels fronted "trusted friends" and associates, who sold to anyone—Latinos, blacks, Italians, even cops—who could deliver the cash. "Our undercover guys were always being told by dealers, 'I think you're "the man," ' " says Joseph Lisi, a New York police captain. "They'd say, 'Right, I'm the man. But I've got $80,000 in this briefcase, and if you don't want to deal with me, I'm out of here right now.' They'd never make it to the door."

Meanwhile, as prices began to fall, demand surged, and small-time street sellers suddenly found business soaring. If the Colombians were looking for dealers who could move "weight"—large quantities—those dealers were looking for high-level suppliers who could help them expand. All over the city, small cocaine retail outfits began cropping up—Dominicans in Washington Heights, blacks in Harlem and South Jamaica, Jamaicans in Brownsville, Bedford-Stuyvesant, and East New York.

The appearance of crack in late 1984 accelerated the process. No one group could control its spread. An ounce of cocaine that could be bought on the street for $1,000 yielded 320 to 360 vials of crack—more if cut—that sold for $10 each in hot locations. (The price is lower in poor neighborhoods that don't get suburban traffic.) Anyone with a few hundred dollars and a hot plate could go into business and triple his money overnight. Thousands of people did, and the old order—already shaken—crumbled completely. Crack turned the lower level of the cocaine trade into a freewheeling, decentralized business, with new outfits springing up and established groups growing into multi-million-dollar, citywide organizations.

DEA agents discovered just how sophisticated some of these groups had become when they started investigating the Basedballs organization in 1985. The brainchild of Santiago Polanco, now 29, Basedballs started out in 1982 as an outfit selling grams and half-grams of cocaine along Audubon Avenue, east of the George Washington Bridge—a prime drug location because of its suburban traffic from New Jersey. The operation was small, but profitable enough to enable Polanco to walk into an Englewood Cliffs car dealership in 1984 and plunk down $43,000 in cash for a Mercedes-Benz.

When crack appeared on the scene, Polanco was one of the first dealers to recognize its potential and aggressively market the drug. He packaged his product in red-topped vials, calling the stuff Basedballs—a play on the term "free-basing"—and took pains to ensure brand quality. He hired "cooks" to process the cocaine, and when one dealer was caught tampering with the product, Polanco had him beaten with a baseball bat. Among the customers driving over from New Jersey, Basedballs quickly became one of the most sought-after brands.

Though they often handle substantial sums, most street dealers make only modest profits for the roughest work in the business.

Basedballs employees were the only dealers on Audubon Avenue around 173rd, 174th, and 175th Streets. Organization members later told DEA agents that they had bought the territory from its former owners, but, just in case, Polanco imported a team of hit men from his family's village in the Dominican Republic to protect Basedballs's turf and ease its expansion. By 1986, the organization had wrested control of the intersection of Edgecombe Avenue and 145th Street—a prime spot, easily accessible to the Bronx across the 145th Street Bridge—from a group of black dealers and opened a string of new spots in Harlem and the South Bronx.

As Basedballs's business expanded, so did its organization. Polanco secured a major supplier, a Dominican who dealt directly with the cartels in Colombia. Polanco also centralized Basedballs's operations in a headquarters at 2400 Webb Avenue in the Bronx. There, his workers cooked, packaged, and stockpiled crack in separate apartments. And he arranged with one of the dozens of money-changing companies along upper Broadway to launder Basedballs's revenues through an investment company he set up in the Dominican Republic.

Meanwhile, Polanco began distancing himself from Basedballs's day-to-day operations, adding layers of bureaucracy and spending more and more time in the Dominican Republic. By the summer of 1986, Basedballs employed as many as nine mid-level managers to deal with street-level managers at a score of locations around the city. Each location manager, in turn, supervised teams of dealers, none of whom were supposed to know the people more than one level above them.

It took law-enforcement agents and their informants nearly two years to penetrate the highest levels of Basedballs's organization. They can only guess how much money the operation made, but by one estimate, Polanco may have been clearing $20-million a year. One DEA agent saw the fruits of Polanco's activities in the Dominican Republic: two nightclubs, a jeans company, a 30-unit condominium complex, an office building, a palatial home, and a gold-plated gull-wing Mercedes. Today, Polanco is believed to be serving a 30-year sentence in a Dominican prison for homicide, and U.S. law-enforcement officials have dismantled his organization and locked up more than 30 of his associates. But agents estimate that there may be dozens of organizations as large as, or larger than, Basedballs operating in New York.

AT THE BOTTOM OF THE distribution pyramid stands the street seller, subject to arrest, to ripoffs, to calculated violence by competitors. This is especially true for crack dealers. Over the past five years, law enforcement has focused on the cocaine trade, with street dealers the most visible target. They are also the first to get shot when a fight breaks out over turf, which is far more common in the cocaine trade than in the older, more established heroin business. Even the crack dealer's clients present special risks. "I wouldn't deal that crack s—-," says Reuben, a former heroin dealer in the South Bronx. "Once a [heroin addict] gets his fix, he's cool. But when those crackheads start bugging out, you don't know what they're going to do."

In contrast to the myth, most street dealers make only modest profits. The stories about their vast incomes probably arise in part because they generally don't point out the distinction between the large sums of cash they handle and the relatively small commissions they earn. "After factoring in the long hours, they

may come out a couple of dollars an hour ahead of the minimum wage," says Philippe Bourgois, an anthropologist studying East Harlem's drug culture.

Willie, the fifteen-year-old caught on gun- and drug-possession charges in Harlem last February, was probably earning about $300 to $350 per week, according to his arresting officer, Terry McGhee. "We see these kids out there in the cold, not moving from one spot, selling for ten hours at a stretch with nothing but a space heater. Maybe at the end of the night, they'll get paid $50," McGhee says. "I'll tell you one thing: You couldn't get a cop to do that."

But to compare dealing to a mainstream job may miss the point. Many youngsters drift in and out of the drug trade as a way of making pocket money or supporting their own drug habits. Part-time work is hard to find in the slum neighborhoods where most dealers live, and a full-time job often means a long commute and menial work. What's more, though a dealer's hours are long, they are often spent with friends on the streets. Willie, for example, belonged to a group called Boogie-Down Productions—the BDP—a gang of up to twenty teenagers that still pushes drugs on 128th Street and Lenox Avenue. "A lot of these young kids who become dealers are joining a crew," says McGhee. "It gives them access to power. Access to guns. It means no one can push them around anymore."

Crews like these are not simple throwbacks to the gangs of the fifties. They're richer and far better armed, and they're manipulated by adult criminals for profit. But their gang structure ensures discipline and loyalty. The graffiti on the walls of an abandoned BDP hangout—THIS BLOCK BELONGS TO THE BDP— indicate that Willie and his pals were protecting their turf, not just a business enterprise.

In even the poorest markets, however, some dealers make out well. "Everyone who goes into the crack business perceives that he's going to get rich," Bourgois says. "And some of them will. Kids who are responsible or street-smart or especially tough can still get promoted very quickly to manager and get a cut of the profits." Also, street dealing is the entry point into the trade, a way to make contacts or amass enough capital to go into business for oneself. Some street dealers get regular salaries or per diems, but many work on commission—usually between 10 and 20 percent. One of Basedballs's dealers boasted to DEA agents that he cleared $1,4000 in commissions during one eight-hour shift on Audubon Avenue.

BEFORE CRACK, HEROIN WAS THE DRUG OF CHOICE IN THE slums, and its popularity is said to be rebounding. According to Division of Substance Abuse data, roughly one in every sixteen working-age men in New York is a heroin addict. The ratio has remained constant over the past five years, but the high mortality rate associated with heroin—especially since the outbreak of AIDS among IV-drug users—may conceal an increase in new addicts. Meanwhile, heroin use among twenty-year-olds—a better indicator of trends in demand—has been rising.

Some experts think the change comes as a reaction to crack, as former crack users switch to a relatively milder drug. Others attribute the comeback to an improvement in the quality of heroin. Greater purity not only gives users a better high but enables them to snort the drug instead of shooting it. At least two factors account for heroin's better quality. For one, Southeast Asia—noted for its pure heroin—now supplies about 70 percent of the New York market. For another, the recent decentralization of heroin distribution in the city has increased the supply and fostered competition among dealers.

THROUGHOUT THE SIXTIES AND SEVENTIES, THE MAFIA dominated the heroin market as the major importer and distributor. In the early eighties, however, the so-called Pizza Connection prosecutions weakened the mob's hold and cut the flow of heroin from Sicily into the United States. Law-enforcement officials say that the ethnic Chinese took over as the industry's new leaders.

In fact, New York's Chinese have been smuggling heroin into the city for years, but until recently, they distrusted the distributors—most of them black—who supplied the street networks; as a result, Chinese smugglers delegated a few of their elders to broker the drug through the Mafia. But around the time that the Mafia began pulling out of the trade, Chinatown began to change.

"Thirty to 40 years ago, Chinatown was very provincial," says Michael Shum, an agent in the DEA's New York Southeast Asian Heroin Task Force. "People from different regions spoke different dialects. In my grandmother's day, if you were Fukienese and you went into a store owned by Toy Shanese, they wouldn't sell you groceries. Forget about drugs—if you didn't speak their language, you couldn't buy a tomato."

Today, Shum says, the old rivalries have broken down and cash has become a universal language. In one recent case, DEA agents turned up a connection between Puerto Rican heroin dealers and members of a Chinese youth gang; the young men had met in school and later "married up" in jail.

The big Chinese move into heroin has had two profound effects on the market. By stepping up their smuggling activities, the Chinese have flooded the city with Southeast Asian heroin. And by dealing directly with minority distributors, they have bypassed the Mafia middlemen who were notorious for heavily cutting their product. As a result, the average drug sold on the street has gone from being as low as 2 percent pure heroin in the early eighties to around 40 percent today.

Still, the heroin trade remains highly profitable. A kilo of pure heroin that costs around $11,000 in Bangkok can be sold for between $85,000 and $125,000 to an Asian broker in the United States or for $150,000 to $240,000 to a mid-level dealer acting as an intermediary between the importer and the street. Markups like these have attracted a grab bag of international trafficking organizations in addition to the Chinese, and even diplomats and businessmen have joined the trade. "We map out ten to twenty major trafficking routes and find out there are ten to twenty more," says DEA agent Dwight Rabb. "We're being inundated with dope."

Because of the huge markup, the drug cartels can afford to lose an occasional shipment to a bust.

Government agents have seized heroin hidden in imported cars, wheelbarrow tires, and the caskets of servicemen killed overseas. The "condom eaters" have also been busy. "Last year, we arrested 123 Nigerians alone at JFK, most of them carrying internally," says Arthur Stiffel, whose Customs agents use X-ray machines to search suspects. "This year, they're running at double the rate."

Though the Chinese dominate the heroin trade in the city, no single group controls the supply. Various foreign nationals—including Nigerians, Ghanaians, Pakistanis, Indians, Thais, and Vietnamese—and assorted American organized-crime groups all smuggle heroin independently of one another. What's more, the Chinese in the trade often operate separately. Unlike the Mafia, Chinatown's criminal organizations—descended from Hong Kong's ruthless triads—do not require their members to pay tribute or even, in many cases, to get permission to deal. Indeed, the new generation of Chinese traffickers may have broken into the violent American market at the expense of their ties to traditional criminal hierarchies. "When the young American Chinese go to Hong Kong now, the guys over there don't want to have anything to do with them," says Dwight Rabb. "The Hong Kong Chinese call them 'bananas'—yellow on the outside, white on the inside."

From the mid-level to the street, heroin distribution has mainly been controlled by black organizations. However, law-enforcement officials report that lately Chinese gangs have been selling in northern Queens and that Hispanic groups—often backed by cocaine money—have broken into the business. But the big heroin markets are found in the predominantly black slums, and dealers from outside are unwelcome.

Older and more established than their crack counterparts, these networks give the heroin business a stability unique in the drug trade. Many of them were Mafia franchises and developed along the same organizational lines as the mob. Until their recent bust, a handful of powerful dealers in southeastern Queens divided the lucrative market there into territories. In Harlem where several groups often run outlets on the same street or even in the same building, agreements over turf are strictly regulated.

WHAT'S MORE, HEROIN'S HIGH PRICE AND NARROW DIStribution make the business easier to control than the crack trade. For one thing, there's simply less heroin around. For another, top distributors are especially guarded about the people with whom they deal. Even if an enterprising young street dealer could find a connection, a kilo of heroin might cost him $200,000 or more wholesale—about six times as much as a similar amount of cocaine.

Heroin's high prices are reflected in the dealer's huge profit margins. While cocaine is rarely cut more than once, heroin can be "stepped on" two or three times. Mid-level transactions are based entirely on relationships; a trusted broker need never touch the product and only rarely the cash. From 1985 until recently, Lorenzo "Fat Cat" Nichols, the legendary Queens drug trafficker, ran a multi-million-dollar operation from prison. In 1988, according to the FBI, he was moving an average of 25 kilos of cocaine and 3 kilos of heroin a month. He bought the heroin from Chinese broker "John" Man Sing Eng—whom he'd met in prison—and, using two lieutenants as go-betweens, sold them to more than a dozen customers.

The big heroin money, however, is made by the dealers who process the drug and market it through networks of street sellers. Take the case of Earl Gibson, a veteran black dealer whose operation included a heroin mill in Queens and selling locations in Brooklyn, in the Bronx, and on the Lower East Side. Before his conviction on drug charges two years ago, Gibson cut, packaged, and sold about a kilo of heroin every four days, earning $150,000 to $200,000 a week. Gibson's occasional partner, Raymond Sanchez "Shorty" Rivera, a Puerto Rican dealer based on the Lower East Side, generated that kind of revenue every day. Based on the testimony of workers for Rivera—who has also been convicted—the FBI estimates that he was grossing more than $60 million a year.

WITH MONEY LIKE THAT TO BE MADE, THE DRUG BUSIness is a powerful lure. In 1987, when he was seventeen, a young Dominican we'll call Pedro had already tried several times to get into the drug business, passing his requests through an acquaintance who worked as a courier for one of the leading distributors in the Bushwick–East New York section of Brooklyn. The distributor, a fellow Dominican in his mid-twenties who knew Pedro and his family, eventually agreed to front him a small supply of heroin.

Pedro took in a partner who knew a location for selling—a spot on his East New York block that had opened up when the previous dealer was nabbed by police. Since neither youth had any extensive experience, they hired a seller recently out of jail. In those days, two distributors in the area were selling different brands, one called Goodyear and the other Airborne; Pedro handled Airborne.

The distributor supplied Pedro with heroin already cut and packaged in units called packs, each of which contained 100 $10 bags. Pedro took the packs on consignment and eventually returned 80 percent of the proceeds to the wholesaler. He paid a further 10 percent to his seller and split the remaining 10 percent with his partner—leaving him just $50 profit per pack sold.

Nevertheless, business was solid—on a good day, he could sell fifteen packs. Most clients were local addicts who could afford only a bag or two at a time, but, Pedro recalls, some were middle-class men in business suits. Others were out-of-town dealers who bought in bulk and who got discounts from Pedro.

Over the next two years, Pedro was able to open five locations, including spots on Knickerbocker Avenue and in Bushwick Park—prime areas that are restricted to well-connected dealers. At the height of his operation, he was personally clearing $600 a day.

Over time, though, competition picked up and cut into Pedro's revenues. By the time he got out last year, he was making $200 a day; now, he says, most dealers are just trying to survive.

"They're making $1,000 a week, if they're lucky," he says. "That may seem like a lot, but to a dealer, that's nothing." In Pedro's world, a successful dealer must project a certain image: He's got to be tough and free-spending. Fancy cars, gold jewelry, and designer warm-up gear are only the most obvious marks of his position. He's also got to pay for trips to Florida (stressed-out street dealers like to relax at theme parks) and pick up the tab at restaurants and clubs.

Beyond all that, a high-flying life-style can be especially expensive in the slums. Pedro's Cutlass Supreme was stolen right after he'd sunk $3,000 into customizing the tires and sound system. At a party, his $1,500 gold chain and medallion were lifted at gunpoint. And several times, he says, he was ripped off for the drugs he was carrying.

Meanwhile, Pedro's risks were high. Once, early on, some competing dealers tried to move in on one of his locations. Under the terms of their agreement, Pedro's wholesaler was supposed to provide him with protection. Instead, he supplied him with guns—expecting Pedro and his cronies to take care of themselves.

"Like most young guys from the neighborhood, carrying a gun made me feel power," he recalls. "At the time, I only thought about shooting other people. I never thought about getting shot myself."

Over time, twelve of the young men he worked with were arrested and jailed. He says that since their release, two have been killed trying to re-enter the drug trade and another was killed because he owed money to Pedro's former supplier. In fact, the police have determined that more than quarter of New York City's record 1,905 homicides last year were drug related.

The demise of his associates and the decline of his business finally led Pedro to give up dealing. But he still recalls the many times he rebuffed his mother's tearful pleas to stop. "That really made me sad, to see my mother cry," he says. "But not my mother or any job was ever going to give me the money that drugs was bringing to me."

Tales of the Crank Trade

Anarchy sweeps the world of illegal synthetic drugs

JONATHAN BEATY

Big John, first at the rendezvous somewhere southeast of Los Angeles, sits patiently in the captain's chair of his motor home, parked on a promontory overlooking a panorama of backcountry hills green as spring in the afternoon sun. A full silver beard spreads over his chest, almost obscuring the picture of a Thompson submachine gun on his red T shirt. THE LAST GREAT AMERICAN FREEDOM MACHINE, reads the legend. A bird-skinning knife is holstered parallel to his belt. Big John is an original road warrior, a man whose history stretches back to the beginning of time as bikers measure it: 20 years riding the Harley express across the country delivering a variety of drugs—first methamphetamines (called crank by the bikers and speed by city users), then cocaine, and now crank again. "When the good German meth was taken off the market by those guys in San Diego with the Mexican connection in 1981 or so, I decided I was too old to learn to cook [manufacture synthetic drugs] myself, so I just shifted over to coke."

He hitches around to look back at his companion, Jeanette, who sits on the bed doing something with stacks of tiny Ziploc bags. "Wasn't that '81, hon?" Taking a mumble for confirmation, Big John peers beyond the cat stretched out in the sunlight on the dashboard. "There are 150 narcs running around out there, and

everybody is in a stampede to roll over. Everybody and his brother is distributing Product, and it's getting to be a dog-eat-dog world." His face assumes a mournful set: "I've been ripped off by my friends big time; they get down into the bag, on the pure stuff, and get paranoid, and right away they want to get you first." Too much crank can easily produce self-destructive paranoia.

Far below, a black Jeep starts up the dirt road leading to the hilltop. Three alchemists, led by the inestimable Bernard, have come for a meeting. "At least there's one cook that ain't wired to the max," Big John concedes. "He never touches the Product." It shows: most illegal drug chemists, awash in dollars but their brains stewed by fumes, seldom pay attention to the little touches that transform banal consumer goods into personal statements of good taste. Bernard has 14-karat-gold-plated wheels on his favorite Corvette, and he gave a designer team jacket to the fellow who jockeys his offshore-racing boat. But Bernard is not some Johnny-come-lately cook with a jailhouse recipe in his jeans. He is a second-generation

outlaw who at 16 learned how to extract pure methamphetamine from common industrial chemical solutions in a laboratory hidden on an Indian reservation. He was tutored by two German chemists flown in by his father. Bernard can't pronounce methylmethamphetamine, but he knows how to make something very like it and how much to charge. "I've worked hard for everything I have," Bernard says, proudly citing the enduring American ethic.

Bernard's skills are much in demand these days. Crank sales in the revitalized industry pushed past the $3 billion mark last year. And because the 25-ton annual demand exceeds manufacturing capacity, there has been a scramble to increase production. Here in the heartland of the meth outlaws, a territory beginning roughly at the southerly edges of the great Los Angeles metropolitan sprawl, anarchy has replaced the discipline of a monopoly maintained for decades under the mailed fist of the renegade motorcycle clubs. Southern California, a nose ahead of Texas, remains the manufacturing capital of the country, with scores, if not hun-

---

Here is the heartland of the meth outlaws, a territory beginning roughly at the southerly edges of the great Los Angeles metropolitan sprawl

---

dreds, of clandestine operations scattered south from Orange County to San Diego and eastward into the Mojave Desert. "The absolute lock the bikers held has been broken, and it's now a wide-open game, with every player for himself," says Larry Bruce, a lean, bearded Orange County criminal lawyer and former public defender celebrated by the biker fraternity for his courtroom skills.

To Big John's way of thinking, the sacrifice of the Bikers' Code to the realities of Big Business is serious, a matter of forsaking fraternity for individual enterprise. "New members join just to get in the trade: there are even Hell's Angels chapters out cooking for themselves. Look at that chapter over there; they cashed in their fraternal defense fund to buy chemicals. Now they're all riding new bikes—them that don't have limousines."

The three cooks, master and apprentices, sit expressionless at a table perched atop the highest granite boulder, talking with macho casualness of the consecutive days and nights they spend tied to the maze of mantle heaters, two-way retorts, pumps, air-scavenging systems, condensers and plastic piping during a "burn." Says Bernard: "If you set it up right, nobody knows where you are; it's no big thing." Bernard is a virtuoso of camouflage by misdirection, of hiding the obvious in plain sight. Once, this kitchen crew recalls delightedly, they cooked a batch on the shore of Lake Elsinore, a popular tourist spot near Los Angeles, tending the bubbling retorts in a round-the-clock paranoid marathon. "We came in four

---

"I'm second generation in this, you know, and I don't want my kids to be the third."

'Vettes, pulling ten jet skis, followed by the RV," recalls Bernard, stroking a mustache that adds only slightly to his years. He is not yet 21 years old.

The old motor home, stripped of furniture and crammed with glassware and supplies, was parked in the trees next to a friend's lake-side shack. "They skied and chased girls while I cooked," Bernard remembers. This was no home-kitchen production with towels stuffed under the door to contain the pungent odor of the process. This was a major manufacturing operation disguised as a beach party, using black-market chemicals to produce 100 lbs. of crank, presold to a buyer in Grants Pass, Ore., for $15,000 a lb. Almost a million net, even before the powder hit the streets, sold by the gram for nearly the same price as cocaine. A lesser cook chortles, "Those people in Oregon are taking everything we can make, and they pay a premium." Adds Big John with the believer's certitude: "Dollar for dollar, crank is better than coke: coke is just a little sexier, but crank goes eight times as far." It is obviously a more profitable line for American traffickers inclined to avoid exporting their earnings to Colombia.

Wary eyes have been watching cars below wind up the dirt road and turn off to a ramshackle pig farm in the next ravine. Finally a Cadillac with four men inside bumps along the track. The presence of guards at a pig farm, waving visitors through, confirms the group's suspicion that a batch was brewing, its odor lost in the waft from the barns. "Don't ask me; it's not mine," Big John says. "That's a bunch of Mexican nationals down there, and I'm not of a mind to visit."

Danger is integral to the booming crank business, especially in the retailing end, where double crosses are as much a threat as arrest. In a far different territory from the backcountry rendezvous, Surfer Jim, a jobber of the Product, sits in a car in his sales district near glossy Newport Beach, Calif. Just back from a cruise to Jamaica with his wife, the tanned 26-year-old has been thinking things over. "I'm second generation in this, you know, and I don't want my kids to be the third." He jiggles a foot and flops one go-ahead from his toes as he talks. "I'm out. I've never been arrested, and I've never used speed; you can't do that and survive what

I do. But you really get an adrenaline rush from doing this sort of thing, and I'm an adrenaline junkie. If I wanted to keep on, I could make it big; I could make a couple million dollars."

A sudden segue: "They shot my father, you know, some people that were going to rob us, and he died in my arms. My brothers got out of it then; they were scared. I was too, but it kind of made me a little crazier at the time. I used a gun more quickly; I wasn't as slow to think it out. I'd just react, which is the way you got to be in this business, you know what I mean?" The stare is direct. "That's one reason I'm getting out, because I've got my kids, and I think about things and don't react the way I used to, and that isn't good in this business. When you're doing it big, you've got to act crazy. A guy is not going to pay you if he don't think you're the kind of guy going to come and stick a gun in his head and say, 'Hey, mother, I'm going to kill you right now.' You understand? You got to act crazy so people don't get over on you, so they think you'll come and kill them and their mother and their kids."

The pale gray eyes ask for empathy. "See, I don't have that in me anymore. When my dad got killed, you know, I could stick a gun in somebody's head and not shake and think about it. I can't do that anymore, so I'm getting out. I've got money put aside. I'm out."

Larry Bruce, the extraordinary dope lawyer, believes few retire voluntarily. "Some make it out," he says, "but this crank business is getting bigger. It's no longer limited to the backwoods, bikers and interstate truckers. It seems to me that I'm seeing as many arrests for possession of meth as for cocaine, and my user clients caught with meth are frequently young professionals and students. The business may be terrible—it is terrible—but you're looking at capitalism in action here. I wonder if it may be building toward critical mass."

The Perilous Swim in Heroin's Stream

SUMMARY: Chinese crime syndicates are getting rich on a river of heroin that flows from the hills of Burma to secret refineries in Thailand and Laos, through shipping points in Bangkok and Hong Kong to thirsting drug markets around the world. Insurgent groups in Asia's Golden Triangle are killing each other for control of the market; in the United States, where the drug, like crack, is available and cheap, some fear that it will set off a similar flood of addiction.

Bangkok, Valentine's Day 1988: The winter rains drenching this sprawling, Southeast Asian city were the worst anyone had seen in years. For more than a week the rain had come down in torrents, flooding Bangkok's twisting, junk-clogged canals and turning its crowded slums into miserable swamps. Traffic in the city, awful at its best, ground to a halt, and the outdoor markets shut down. At least, residents told themselves, the rains were doing one good thing: Layers of grime were washing off the magnificent mirror-clad temples, revealing again just how beautiful they were.

But on the docks at Klong Toey port on the southern edge of the city, the rains were uncovering something else entirely. Workers loading a freighter bound for the United States noticed that, among hundreds of bales of sheet rubber that had been standing in the rain, whitish puddles were starting to form. Dockworkers alerted police, who ripped the bales apart and dug down to the source of the pale ooze: almost 2,400 pounds of pure China White heroin.

What the Thai police stumbled over that afternoon became the largest seizure of heroin yet uncovered anywhere in the world, and it launched investigators on a path that led to the arrests of more than a dozen people and the discovery of a multi-billion-dollar syndicate that stretched from the remote hills of northern Thailand to the

money centers of Hong Kong and on to the streets of New York. The deeper investigators dug, the more they found. The smugglers had managed, it was discovered, to bring almost 2 tons of heroin into the United States the year before and had been arranging yet another huge shipment as soon as the Klong Toey delivery reached its New York destination. The network of operatives involved was so vast and so intricate that two years later several of its leaders are still being hunted down; the latest two came into the net in December.

The bust in Bangkok was only one of many signs in the past three years that massive amounts of heroin have been coming into the United States from Southeast Asia. As big as the Klong Toey gang was, say investigators, it was only one of dozens of complex, well-organized and hugely profitable heroin syndicates now in operation. Together with thousands of small-time smugglers, they control a river of heroin that runs from the remote opium fields of Burma to secret heroin refineries along the Thai and Laotian borders, down back roads through Thailand to Bangkok, up to Hong Kong by ship and then on to the streets of Australia, Europe and North America.

Huge amounts of highly refined Southeast Asian heroin, of far better quality than the impure, brownish heroin that comes from Mexico, Pakistan and Afghanistan, have been pouring into the drug markets of New York and Los Angeles since 1987, and more crosses the border every day. It arrives

in thousands of ways: hidden in crates of radios and tape recorders from Hong Kong factories; packaged inside lawn mower tires; "body-packed" by couriers who hide it under their clothes; even, in a case now coming to trial, sewn inside dead goldfish. Supply has skyrocketed — heroin seizures have more than tripled since 1985 — and so has quality: What is sold on the street now is more than 40 percent pure, up from only about 8 percent just a few years ago.

So far, Washington's war on drugs has been aimed at the epidemic of crack cocaine that has swept the country since the mid-1980s. But a growing number of doctors, drug officials and politicians warn that an even greater threat from heroin is closing in fast. Significant heroin busts are made almost every week, with little evident effect on either price or supply. Last February, for example, the FBI was shocked to discover that the seizure of a $1 billion, 800-pound shipment — enough to supply every addict in New York for a year — had only a "negligible" effect on prices. "It told us that there's a lot more heroin out there than we know about," said Dave Binney, the head of FBI drug investigations.

What has many drug enforcement and medical authorities worried is that the same factors that fueled the spread of crack — easy availability and low price — could set off a similar explosion in heroin use. And there is another factor: Unlike traditional addicts, few new users inject the drug. Instead they combine heroin with crack and

By Stephen Brookes. From *Insight*, February 5, 1990, pp. 8-17. Reprinted by permission. All rights reserved.

smoke the mixture to get the effects of both drugs simultaneously, which leads, many fear, to a double addiction.

William Hopkins, director of Street Research in the New York state Division of Substance Abuse Services, has seen the future firsthand, and he's scared. He and his team of researchers go undercover for weeks at a time on the streets of New York, keeping track of which drugs are popular and how they are sold. "We see more people selling heroin than ever before," Hopkins told a hearing of the Senate Judiciary Committee last August. "Smoking heroin with crack has widely spread, and we believe it is growing. And growing rapidly."

Smoking heroin is not a new phenomenon. It has been a favored method in Asia since the 1920s and appears to be coming back in fashion because of the fear of spreading AIDS through shared needles. Instead of injecting the drug, a user simply spoons some onto a piece of tinfoil, holds a lighted match under it, and inhales the upward-curling smoke through a rolled-up bill. It's known as "chasing the dragon."

Mixing heroin with cocaine has been around for a long time, too. Older addicts call it "speedballing" and say it smooths the sometimes edgy cocaine high. A crack high can be more of a roller coaster than highs from most drugs. Smoked in small, hard pellets called rocks, crack produces an intense but short-lived euphoria, followed by a depression so severe that it sometimes leads to suicide.

Therein lies the key to heroin's growing popularity. Sprinkling a bit onto crack can extend its effects for as much as an hour and can soften the crash that follows. Hopkins and others report that dealers, always on the lookout for new products, are now selling souped-up sandwiches of heroin and crack called "moon rock," "parachute rock" or "speedball rock" in small capsules for less than $15 each, a little more than the price of a similar amount of regular crack.

Buying heroin in America's biggest cities is almost as easy as buying aspirin. It is available in glassine envelopes, in short heat-sealed sections of ordinary drinking straws (known as HIS: heroin in a straw) or in vials. Business goes on around the clock, seven days a week, and is often better organized than many legal operations. Some dealers even pass out business cards, printed up with a street corner address and part of a phone number (to be filled in at the last minute). There are sale days and bargains and shopping malls, where a buyer can select whatever drug he wants. If that is too much trouble, home delivery can be arranged, the drugs brought by children on bicycles.

Dealers are said to be targeting users under the age of 22. Already hooked on crack, eager to try something new but unwilling to start using needles, younger users have few compunctions about starting in on heroin — especially as the price comes down. No studies have been done on how long it takes to become addicted to heroin this way, but addiction appears to be inevitable. And that has enforcement officials concerned that a whole new generation of young, poor, poly-addicted users is emerging.

The people growing rich on this trade belong to international Chinese organized crime syndicates, many based in Hong Kong, which maintain connections in Chinese communities in cities from Bangkok to Los Angeles to Amsterdam. The highly refined heroin they supply, says the Drug Enforcement Administration, now accounts for more than 40 percent of the American market, up from 14 percent in 1985. And the profits they make are huge. In its final form, adulterated and having been passed through many hands, a kilo can bring $1 million to $5 million on the streets of New York. The opium from which it was made, meanwhile, had been bought for just a few hundred dollars from a farmer in the highlands of Southeast Asia.

The emergence of the so-called Chinese connection has been partly due to the prosecutions in recent years of leaders of the big Italian organized crime syndicates, which traditionally ran the heroin trade from Southwest Asia into the United States. Chinese networks, which had previously supplied relatively small amounts of heroin, were quick to step into the void.

But the trade also has blossomed from nearly a full decade of bumper opium crops in the fertile regions of Burma, Laos and Thailand, the countries of Asia's Golden Triangle. Burma has emerged as the world's biggest supplier, and the amounts being grown there are staggering: Drug enforcement experts in Bangkok estimate the 1990 opium poppy crop to be about 2,600 metric tons, up from about 1,300 in 1989. An additional 350 tons are being produced in Laos, and as many as 50 tons will be grown this year in Thailand.

The heroin trail starts in thousands of small fields in the remote mountains where the opium poppy, *Papaver somniferum*, thrives in the alkaline soil. Poppies are by far the largest crop for most of the Burmese hill people. By some estimates, as much as 90 percent of the cultivated land in the northeastern part of the country is given over to them, and some 290,000 acres are thought to be under cultivation.

Tens of thousands of people are involved in growing, refining and transporting the drug, and tens of thousands more profit indirectly from the money that the opium trade brings in. In many areas, it is the only crop that makes economic sense. It takes about 2,000 poppies to produce a kilo of opium, but once grown, the valuable crop is inexpensively transported by mule through the hills.

The crop is sown in the late fall and is usually harvested about three months later, soon after the plants' white and purple petals have fallen off. The small, green seed capsule that remains is slit several times with a sharp, curved knife, and almost immediately a whitish sap begins to ooze out of the wound. Overnight, the sap dries into a dark brown gum, opium.

Some of the harvest is smoked by the villagers themselves, mostly older people, who roll a bit into a small ball and put it on a pin, holding it over a flame until it starts to smoke, then dropping it into an opium pipe. But most of the crop is wrapped in banana leaves and carried by mule to hillside refineries in the border areas, to be turned first into morphine, then into heroin.

The processing is done in small, makeshift labs, often manned just by a chemist, a few assistants and a contingent of guards; all that is really needed is a water source. In some areas, established refineries have been running for years, hidden under a cloak of camouflage netting and often surrounded by mine fields. All are well-protected, both from authorities and from competing traffickers; in Burma, a few are even reputed to have antiaircraft guns.

The initial refining step is quite simple, even crude: The opium is dissolved in hot water and mixed with lime fertilizer, which separates the morphine from the rest of the opium chemicals. Filtered, solidified with ammonia and then dried, the resulting powdered morphine has been reduced to one-tenth the weight of the opium.

But then the process gets much more delicate. Equal portions of morphine and acetic acid must be heated together for six hours at a precise temperature, binding the two chemicals into an impure form of heroin that is more than twice as strong as the original morphine. The brownish powder, when dried, is purified several more times with ether and hydrochloric acid. The final product — a fine, almost fluffy powder known as diacetyl morphine — is China White.

Once dried, the heroin is measured into 700-gram units and wrapped in paper or put into plastic bags, each stamped with an identifying logo. Brand names are important: One of the most famous is called Double UO Globe, made in Laos, which pictures two lions holding a globe in their paws. There are dozens of others, mostly from Burmese refineries; Crouching Lion, Lucky Strike, Panda and Dragon are a few. Each has its own reputation for quality.

With dozens of refineries now in operation, the stream of heroin out of Burma has turned into a flood, and the government in Rangoon appears unable, or unwilling, to do anything about it. That has partly been due to the political instability that has dominated the capital since the riots and subsequent military takeover in 1988. With a restless population and some 20 insurgency movements in the border regions, the military has been hard-pressed to devote the few resources it has to fighting a drug war.

For most of the past four decades, in fact, Rangoon has been trying to get full control of the northern and eastern provinces where the traffic flourishes. Ethnic minorities make up about 30 percent of Burma's population, and groups like the Kachin, the Karen, the Arakanese, the Shan and others have long insisted on regional autonomy, even independence. Most of them maintain their own armies, sometimes numbering thousands of troops. Heavily armed and fiercely independent, often under the leadership of a charismatic warlord, groups such as the Kachin Independence Army, the Wa National Army, the Pa-O National Liberation Army, the Karen National Liberation Army and dozens of others roam with little interference from the government.

The funding to keep the regional armies going comes almost entirely from smuggling, say Thai authorities. Teak, gold, jade and antiquities are all taken over the border into Thailand. But the big money-maker for all of them (with the exception of the Karen, a uniquely antidrug group) is heroin. "They all claim they're fighting for their independence," scoffs Lt. Gen. Chavolit Yodmani, head of Thailand's Office of the Narcotics Control Board and the director of his country's war against drugs. "I don't believe it. Many of them are just drug trafficking organizations."

As much as 90 percent of the heroin from Burma is said to be under the control of a single opium warlord: an enigmatic, notorious figure who operates under the nom de guerre of Khun Sa. Born Chang Chi-fu in 1934, Khun Sa heads the Shan United Army, a heavily armed force of 5,000-6,000 that controls a 200-kilometer stretch of the Burmese-Thai border where most of the refineries are located. Kicked out of Thailand in 1982, he now operates out of a fortified headquarters in the Doi Lang mountain range only a few kilometers inside Burma.

While Khun Sa admits to being involved in the drug trade — and has even boasted about it in the Asian press — he insists that he is the leader of a nationalist movement and the recognized chief of the 8 million Shan people. Claiming only to tax the opium that passes through his territory so that he can feed his people, Khun Sa has offered several times to abandon the drug trade if the United States will pay him $100 million a year for six years.

He has found an unusual defender in Abbot Phra Chamrdon Parnchant, a Buddhist who heads a drug rehabilitation program near Bangkok. "Khun Sa does not want to be recognized as a drug dealer," he says. "He says he only collects taxes, and I believe him." A heavyset man with a penetrating stare, tinted glasses and two gold Cross pens tucked into the folds of his brown robes, the abbot was asked by Khun Sa several years ago to serve as his spokesman. After meeting briefly with Henry Kissinger in 1987, he has been trying, without success, to get the White House to discuss a deal with Khun Sa.

For their part, both Washington and Bangkok continue to regard Khun Sa as a criminal and the Shan United Army as his personal bodyguard and trafficking force. "The guy's a drug dealer," says a Western drug official in Bangkok. "And he's stronger now than he's been in a long, long time. He's just sitting up there in his own little fiefdom." The Thai government has put a $25,000 price on his head, but there is little that Bangkok can do as long as he stays in Burma. "If he comes into Thailand," vows Chavolit, "we'll grab him."

Unless, that is, his enemies get him first. Some of the armed groups in northern Burma, such as the Kachin Independence Army and the Shan State Army, are occupied with smuggling heroin north into India and rarely clash with Khun Sa. But there is almost constant skirmishing in the hotly contested areas along the eastern border with Thailand, where a half-dozen groups are vying for the heroin trade. "It's a kaleidoscope up there," says the Western drug official. "Alliances are constantly shifting among the groups. Some that used to fight now are working together. It's a business. And business is business."

Among Khun Sa's most bitter competitors, Thai observers say, is the Wa National Army, another self-styled independence movement heavily involved in drugs. It has become stronger in recent months since teaming up with the Burmese Communist

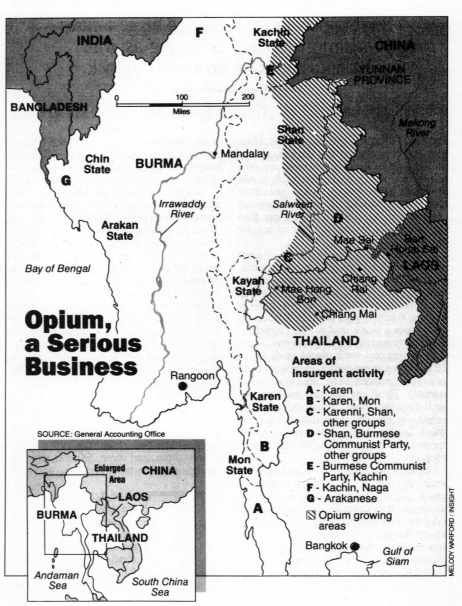

Opium, a Serious Business

SOURCE: General Accounting Office

INDIA
F
Kachin State
CHINA
YUNNAN PROVINCE
BANGLADESH
0   100   200
Miles
Shan State
Mekong River
Chin State
BURMA
Mandalay
Salween River
Irrawaddy River
D
Mae Sai
Hong Sai
LAOS
Arakan State
C
Chiang Rai
Bay of Bengal
Kayah State
Mae Hong Son
Chiang Mai
THAILAND
Areas of insurgent activity
Rangoon
Karen State
A - Karen
B - Karen, Mon
C - Karenni, Shan, other groups
D - Shan, Burmese Communist Party, other groups
E - Burmese Communist Party, Kachin
F - Kachin, Naga
G - Arakanese

Mon State
B

A
Opium growing areas
Bangkok
Gulf of Siam

Enlarged Area
CHINA
LAOS
BURMA
THAILAND
Andaman Sea
South China Sea

MELODY WARFORD / INSIGHT

Party, which under the leadership of Taik Aun is thought to control many of the opium growing areas. (The party has also reportedly enjoyed close ties with China, which it has used as a source for heroin-refining chemicals.) Conflicts between the WNA and the Shan United Army have been heating up since fall, often spilling violently over the border into Thailand. (Bangkok sent police reinforcements into the village of Ban Arunothai in early December after fighting broke out between the two groups, each of which accused the townspeople of helping the other.)

While Khun Sa and his army appear to have a firm grip on refining and trafficking opium, Thai authorities say much of the cultivation is under the control of the 3rd and 5th Chinese Irregular Force, headed by Gen. Lee Wan Huan. Numbering fewer than 2,000 troops, the CIF is a descendant of a force of nationalist Kuomintang troops driven out of China and into the Burmese border area after the communist takeover in 1949. Turning to the heroin trade to finance several aborted invasions of China in the early 1950s, the Kuomintang troops gradually degenerated into full-time traffickers. They were the ones who centralized the opium marketing structure (forcing hill tribes to pay an annual opium tax), set up trading routes over the border into northern Thailand and imported chemists from Hong Kong to set up refineries. By the late 1960s, they were producing heroin in the jungle that was almost 99 percent pure.

Perhaps Khun Sa's most dangerous enemy — and a major player in the complex and delicate politics of northeastern Burma — is the 5,000-man Karen National Union, led by Gen. Bo Mya. A genuine independence movement, the KNU is fiercely opposed to drug trafficking — any of its soldiers who get involved with drugs face a death penalty — in part because it depends for much of its funding on outside Christian organizations.

But the group also taxes shipments of jade, tungsten and tin that pass through the 800-kilometer-long region it controls, and its troops are heavily armed. Six Karen were arrested on the Thai border in December with hundreds of AK-47s, M-16s, mortar shells and grenade launchers, as well as more than 20,000 rounds of ammunition.

Unable to deal with both narcotics traffickers and antigovernment insurgents like the Karen and the Burmese Communists, Rangoon has been focusing on the insurgents — to the point that many believe it is now in bed with Khun Sa. In 1988, the Bangkok press reported that Rangoon had cut a deal with the drug lord, giving him free rein along the border in exchange for protection for teak exports (on which the

government depends for foreign currency). Since then, government checkpoints have been relaxed and troops withdrawn from many of the drug trafficking areas. And in March 1984, the Thai press reported that a secret meeting had taken place between Khun Sa and Brig. Gen. Aye San, the head of Burma's Eastern Military Command. The Burmese official agreed to leave Khun Sa alone if he would use his forces against the Karen insurgents and the Burmese Communists. "It's become live and let live with Khun Sa, so the Burmese government can concentrate on the fight with the Karen," says the Western official in Bangkok.

Washington also has long suspected that much of the equipment it has provided to fight opium production, notably helicopters and transport aircraft, has been diverted to the military's anti-insurgency drive. Because of these concerns and in protest against the military's brutal suppression of the 1988 uprising, in which hundreds died, Washington cut $14 million in annual aid last year and refused to recertify Burma as cooperating with antidrug activities. (Decertification means a country is automatically disqualified from receiving direct bilateral aid and requires the United States to vote against it in such multilateral organizations as the World Bank.)

The aid was not doing much good anyway. Many top Burmese police officials, including the head of the narcotics suppression unit, lost their jobs after the military takeover in 1988, and the few antidrug forces left in the country are understaffed, poorly trained and badly equipped. At the height of its efforts a few years ago, the government had five aircraft in its opium eradication squadron: slow, prop-driven Thrushes that could not go into insurgent-controlled areas without risking being shot down. In their best year, the planes sprayed 31,000 acres, about 10 percent of those under cultivation, and there was no eradication effort at all last year. Each year from 1984 to 1987, according to a recent U.S. General Accounting Office report, the Burmese seized an average of 1.5 metric tons of opium, less than 1 percent of the crop. The effect on traffic was "negligible."

Rangoon has tried halfheartedly to defend itself; the state organ Working People's Daily claimed in August that Burma had kept $16.5 billion in heroin from reaching world markets. But the government's usual attitude has been benign neglect; the Working People's Daily observed in 1988 that "opium from the Golden Triangle will spread throughout the world. For Burma, it is not our business what happens once it gets out. We can only look on with folded arms." With that kind of attitude among top brass, the country's opium problem is likely to become increasingly intractable.

Bad as it is there, Burma is not the only source of high-grade heroin. Some 300 metric tons of opium has been coming out of the arid plateaus of northern Laos at least

since 1987, aided, Thai and Western officials say, by top figures in the Marxist government of Prime Minister Kaysone Phomivane. Bangkok officially accused Vientiane of being involved in trafficking in 1987, and the State Department says dryly that the United States "continues to receive reports of the involvement of senior Lao officials in the narcotics trade."

Khun Sa himself is widely reported to enjoy close personal and professional ties with the prime minister and to have moved a number of his refineries into Laos's northern Sayaboury province near some of his Burmese operations. "Two years ago, Khun Sa formed an alliance with Kaysone in Laos," says Francis W. Belanger, the author of "Drugs, the United States, and Khun Sa." Belanger, who met with Khun Sa early in 1989, says flatly that the Burmese drug lord "now has refineries in Laos and can produce his heroin without any outside interference. And if things go to hell in Burma in the next year or two, he can move into Laos and continue his operations there."

Laos would be difficult to patrol even if the government were really trying. Like Burma, vast stretches of it are virtually inaccessible. Narrow mule trails and waterways take the place of roads. The economy is in a semipermanent shambles, making the opium and marijuana trade often the only way for poor villagers to survive. Provincial officials, who rule with a fair degree of autonomy from Vientiane, also depend on the trade: Two Laotian smugglers arrested in Bangkok last May told police they had paid local Lao officials about $2,000 per kilo to ensure safe passage out of the country.

Much of the Laotian heroin is simply ferried across the Mekong River into Thailand late at night at dozens of anonymous crossing points, then funneled into the town of Ban Houai Sai, long notorious to Thai police as a major trading center. But as surveillance has picked up all over Thailand, a new route has reportedly opened up out of central Laos: Multikilo shipments are said to be going east down Highway 13 out the Vietnamese port of Da Nang.

Washington has had little luck enlisting Vientiane in the war on drugs. It offered to fund a crop substitution and narcotics control program in 1987 but was met with mostly blank looks, and Laos was taken off the U.S. aid list last year. Things may or may not be changing: Laos has reportedly started a $5.8 million U.N. plan to eradicate the poppy, though the State Department reports "no known poppy eradication" in the 1988-89 growing season. Vientiane is said by Western officials to be eager to get back on the aid list.

The third corner of the Golden Triangle, Thailand, has been much more successful in attacking trafficking. About 50 tons of opium are still being produced each year in the highlands around Chiang Mai and

Chiang Rai, in the remote northern stretches of the country.

Bangkok has been aggressive in trying to wipe out the remaining poppy fields and in getting its hill tribes out of the business. Nine different "crop cultivation control" programs have been started in more than 600 villages, and a slow but apparently steady transition is being made away from the poppy crop and into the less lucrative but much safer ones of coffee, lettuce and kidney beans.

Thai authorities have also been trying to crack down on the refineries still operating along the borders. The surge in opium production in Burma, says the State Department, has led to a corresponding rise in refineries in Thailand. And while Thai authorities have managed to smash dozens in the past decade — nine last year — and claim to have cut production by 70 percent, the country still harbors a substantial refining and smuggling network.

Even if it can wipe out its remaining poppy fields and refineries, Thailand faces a struggle against smugglers from Burma and Laos. "Thailand is a natural funnel for both heroin and marijuana," says the Western official. "And it's growing. We used to see shipments of 30 or 40 kilos that we thought were big. Now, with the booming economy and the growth in exports, we're seeing shipments of hundreds of kilos."

Getting the heroin into Thailand is no big trick. Most of it is brought over on narrow mule trails at dozens of points in the hills, then gets trucked into small western towns like Mae Hong Son to be sold to middlemen. Some comes over the bridge farther north at Mae Sai, a dusty, beat-up border town that was sacked a decade ago by Khun Sa in one of the city's periodic drug shoot-outs. Mae Sai is the northernmost point of Thailand, and you can pick up Highway 1 there way down to Chiang Mai, Bangkok and the coast. But even here the border barely exists: Thais and Burmese can cross freely 5 kilometers into each other's country to trade (there is a thriving black market in gold and jade, as well), and the bridge is always jammed with trucks, foot traffic, overloaded bicycles and motorcycles. A handful of border guards, machine guns slung casually under their arms, watch the crowd without much interest. After all, anyone with anything to hide would merely wade across the shallow river a mile or two downstream.

There is an array of Thai forces on the border, including the Border Patrol Police, the Thai 3rd Army, the provincial police and agents from the Office of the Narcotics Control Board. They are supplemented by DEA agents, who have three offices in Thailand, and Interpol. "We've got thousands of people up there," says Chavolit.

Nevertheless, the border remains porous, and efforts to control the trade sometimes backfire. A strategic road built by the Thais on the Burmese border near Mae Hong Son in the early 1980s was quickly appropriated by Khun Sa, who established three refineries just over the border and used the road to move heroin into Thailand. When Thai officials responded by destroying a 5-kilometer section of the road, the trafficker brought in tractors and earthmoving machinery and rebuilt it. And when one of his men was killed by a mine planted by the Thai border police last April, Khun Sa reportedly moved in 100 men to guard the road. At last report, they were still in the area.

Once inside Thailand, the heroin usually makes its way to either Chiang Mai or Chiang Rai, where officials say the big deals are made, then down to Bangkok or one of the port cities farther down the coast for shipment out of the country. In these towns, a 700-gram bag of quality heroin will run $3,000 to $4,000, and there are big profits for the middlemen who arrange to transport it to Bangkok, where it will fetch 50 percent more than in the north.

These middlemen tend to be Chinese Haw: Thais of Chinese descent who are known by Thai names but maintain close contacts with other Chinese in Yunnan province in the People's Republic and in Hong Kong. Some are involved in production: Police in Mae Sai reported in October that Haw merchants were known to be running refineries just over the border in Burma. But most are in the transit business, recruiting couriers to move the drugs south.

The couriers could be anyone. Some are Haw themselves, and others are drivers who never know what they are carrying. Some are just people who need a little quick cash: Four women were arrested last June near Chiang Mai when a spot police check uncovered 9.2 kilos of high-grade heroin hidden in girdles designed to make them look pregnant. Profits, in a poor country like Thailand, can be huge. A Haw arrested with 34 kilos as he approached Bangkok in December said he was paid about $8,000 to transport the drug, apparently destined for the Netherlands.

Once in Bangkok, some of the heroin passes into the hands of the city's underworld distribution network. There are about 300,000 addicts in Thailand, more than half of them in the sprawling slums of Bangkok, where heroin is sold a gram at a time in brightly colored paper packages.

But most of what comes into the capital city is quickly exported: mostly to the United States, followed by Hong Kong, Malaysia, the Netherlands and Singapore. Huge amounts leave the country in tiny shipments, either mailed — more than 32 kilos was intercepted in the Bangkok postal system in 1988 — or body-packed out by individual couriers (known to Asians as "ant traffickers") on commercial airlines.

Most large shipments go by freighter. Heroin has been found in plaster Buddhas, in crates of fake jade, even dissolved in fish sauce. While Bangkok's Klong Toey port is still the most important exit point, says the Office of the Narcotics Control Board, increased police surveillance there has pushed some of the smuggling down to little-watched port towns in the southern and eastern provinces. Officials in Bangkok say increasing amounts are being transshipped through Laos to Da Nang, then over to Canada.

As frequently as not, the smugglers are foreigners. About 500 foreigners are in jail in Bangkok on drug charges, most of them Burmese, Chinese, Laotian or Malaysian. Fifteen Hong Kong smugglers were caught in 1988 (with more than half of all the heroin that authorities seized that year), as were 15 Americans and a handful of Middle Easterners and Europeans.

A more recent phenomenon has been the emergence of the so-called African connection. European traffickers have been recruiting couriers in poor Sub-Saharan countries, especially Nigeria, and using them to transport heroin out of both Bang-

Grisly Tonnage in the Triangle

Estimated opium production (in metric tons) in Southeast Asia

■ Burma (left)
□ Laos (center)
□ Thailand (right)

SOURCE: State Department

kok and the Southwest Asian producing countries, routing them via India, Sri Lanka, Kenya, Nigeria or other countries before going on to New York or European capitals. Some 236 Africans were arrested worldwide in 1988 for heroin smuggling, and Bangkok experienced a miniepidemic this fall: A Nigerian woman was arrested with 58 kilos of heroin at Bangkok's Don Muang International Airport Oct. 16; two were arrested the next week trying to ship out five televisions packed with more than 20 kilos; another was busted Nov. 23 with about 40 kilos.

For those who get caught, the penalties are tough: Anyone convicted of producing or exporting heroin faces a potential death sentence. Thailand seems to be getting increasingly serious about the drug problem. More than 51,000 were arrested in 1988, up from slightly more than 33,000 in 1986, and police crackdowns are ordered periodically; the most recent was in June. But Thailand lacks any kind of conspiracy law, so it can convict only traffickers it catches with drugs. That means that mostly little fish get caught. "We need to go a step beyond getting the couriers, who aren't so important," says Chavolit. "The big guys won't do it themselves."

To close the net around the kingpins, Bangkok is considering a bill that would allow authorities to seize traffickers' assets and to triple penalties if the trafficking is done by government officials. If passed, that provision could make a crucial difference. Corruption is almost a way of life in Thailand, say those who live and work there; it extends from the local cop to the highest levels of the military.

Things are changing, slowly. On Dec. 12, a Thai police investigatory committee accused former police Maj. Gen. Veth Petbarom of being involved in shipping heroin to five countries, including the United States. Veth, indicted in New York on trafficking charges last July, reportedly used his influence to get the drugs through customs checks at Don Muang. "We have to be careful," says Chavolit. "Cases of corruption can take place anywhere."

Much of the heroin leaving the Golden Triangle goes to Hong Kong, which has emerged as a key base of operations for financiers and traffickers. Situated along China's southeastern coast, Hong Kong has the biggest container port in the world and is one of Asia's foremost banking centers, handling some $50 billion a day. Most of the "Chinese Mafia" organized crime groups involved in the drug trade run the actual smuggling networks and launder profits from there, according to the DEA.

The trade has been going on since the 1920s, and the networks have become deeply entrenched. "The proximity to the source countries, the historical connections to Chinese communities elsewhere and the fact that we have very advanced communications and transport links with the rest of the world have given Hong Kong a long history of drug trafficking," says Tsang Yam-pui, chief staff officer of the Royal Hong Kong Police's Narcotics Bureau.

With 200 islands, most of them uninhabited, and hundreds of miles of coastline, it is easy for a trawler to anchor, bury a shipment on the beach and return to Thailand. Sometimes heroin will be dropped off the boat with a floating marker ar a prearranged spot, and another boat will zip out from the shore to pick it up. Others drag it underwater in sealed drums; if intercepted by Hong Kong police, they simply cut the cables and let the evidence sink.

That route is still strong, but Hong Kong police say that an increasing amount is coming in through routes that have opened up in recent years. Opium addiction, once a massive problem in China, was wiped out after the communists took power and began executing traffickers. But as the country's economy opened up to the outside world during the 1980s, the heroin trade came back to life. "All the previously used drug trafficking routes from the Golden Triangle through China to Hong Kong have been reestablished," says Tsang.

From refineries in Burma and Laos, the usual China route extends to K'un-ming, the capital of Yunnan, where a healthy black market exists, then goes overland to coastal cities like Canton (Guangzhou) and Shanghai. "I estimate that between 30 percent and 50 percent of the heroin is coming in from China," says David Tong, director of narcotics investigations for the Hong Kong Customs Service. "Hong Kong traffickers go down to Yunnan to buy the heroin or to the black markets right over the border in Guangzhou or Shenzhen."

They appear to be setting up networks within the People's Republic: Last year a Hong Kong resident was executed after being convicted of recruiting three Chinese couriers.

With the enormous volume of commerce across the border, intercepting the traffic is almost impossible. Some 12,000 vehicles cross every day, and thousands of commercial and fishing boats sail in and out of Hong Kong every day. "Look at this coastline," says Tong, running his hand over the huge, minutely detailed map of the colony that covers an entire wall of his office. "They could come in here or over here or down here. Almost anywhere."

Officials in the colony say the market has been changing as well. Most of the heroin entering the local market for the past few decades has been a rough, brownish, impure form known as No. 3, which Hong Kong addicts smoke. Now, the purer form known as No. 4 or China White, favored by American and European addicts, has apparently taken over, and the price has dropped as well, from $20,000 a kilo in 1987 to about $11,000 today. "In the last 18 months, the market has changed completely," says James Harris, a DEA agent in Hong Kong. "It's all No. 4 heroin now. So everybody who's in the drug business is potentially an exporter. And we're seeing a lot more local dealers crossing over and going into the international market."

Can the heroin tide out of Asia be stopped? So much has been produced that Asian drug officials say huge amounts are now just being warehoused. Even if every poppy plant in the world were chopped down tomorrow, they say, the market could still be fed for more than a year. That kind of oversupply, they say, will inevitably push prices down, and once that happens a real heroin epidemic could spread.

Sometimes even the people fighting the war wonder if it can ever be won. "What are you going to do?" asks Harris, looking out over Hong Kong's teeming streets and the harbor beyond. "Every time you take out somebody big, there's somebody else ready to step right in."

— Stephen Brookes in Thailand, Hong Kong and Washington

Fighting the Drug War

Everyone agrees that the United States has a drug problem; in fact, more Americans named drugs as the nation's number one problem than any other. But what should be done about drugs? How should we fight the drug war? Is there an answer to these questions—or is it a hopeless, unwinable battle? Of all drug-related issues, perhaps this one is the most controversial.

There are at least three currently-argued perspectives or models on the drug war. The first can be called the *punitive* model. The reasons why we are losing the war against drugs, the punitive model argues, is that we are not tough enough on users and dealers. The solution to the drug problem is tougher laws, more arrests, longer jail and prison terms for drug offenders, more police, more lethal police weapons, more interception of drugs smuggled into the country from abroad, more surveillance, fewer constitutional rights for dealers, users, and suspects, more planes, faster boats, more and bigger seizures of drug dealers' assets, more pressure on the governments of countries from which drugs originate, perhaps even the assistance of the armed forces.

The second model might be called the *maintenance* or the *medical* model. Addicts and drug abusers are not criminals, this model argues. Just as alcoholics are not committing any crime when they get drunk in the privacy of their own homes, abusers of the currently illegal drugs should not be arrested or imprisoned for their compulsive, self-destructive behavior. They are sick and in need of medical and psychiatric care, including, as a last resort, maintenance on an addictive drug, such as methadone. Maintenance is typically proposed only for the narcotics; for the other illegal drugs, some alternative form of therapy, which includes, eventually, abstinence, is called for by this model.

The third perspective is the *decriminalization* or *legalization* model. This model proposes that the problem with the use of the currently illegal drugs is the profit motive. Eliminate the laws against the possession, sale, and use of drugs, and they will no longer be profitable to sell, and most of the problems associated with their use—the violence, corruption, and medical problems that sellers and users cause or experience—will disappear. Some proponents of legalization even argue that the use of drugs will actually decline when criminal penalties are removed.

Some proponents of one model argue for that model only for certain drugs and another one for different drugs, while other proponents argue that their model applies to currently illegal drugs across the board. Hardly anyone argues that currently legal drugs, such as tobacco and alcohol, be criminalized. However, some observers do argue that legal penalties against marijuana should be removed, but that they stay in place for drugs such as heroin and cocaine. In fact, in 11 U.S. states, making up a third of the country's population, small-quantity marijuana possession has already been decriminalized: The possessor cannot be arrested, prosecuted, or jailed, and may receive only a citation equivalent to a traffic ticket. Nonetheless, most supporters of a strong version of the punitive model favor strictly enforced laws against all currently illegal drugs, and many supporters of legalization favor removing criminal penalties against all currently illegal drugs.

Much of the debate over the question of legalization hinges on whether national alcohol prohibition actually worked. In 1919, legislation banning the sale of all alcoholic beverages in the United States was passed, and in 1920, the law took effect; it was replaced in 1933, and Prohibition was regarded as a failure. After all, the legalization model argues, if it is not possible to legislate against the sale of alcohol, how can the criminalization of the other drugs work any better? In fact, as historical research shows, Prohibition actually did reduce the consumption of alcohol: Rates of cirrhosis of the liver, traffic accidents, and arrests for drunken driving and public drunkenness all declined sharply. In addition, when alcohol was re-legalized, sales in 1933, the first "wet" year after Prohibition, were far lower than in 1919, the last "wet" year before Prohibition, indicating that many drinkers had given up the alcohol habit during that period. Of course, many other problems accompanied Prohibition, including the rise of organized crime and a number of medical maladies associated with drinking alcohol substitutes—but use did decline.

It is entirely possible that the argument over drug legalization is little more than cocktail party chatter. Very, very few politicians can publicly support legalization and hope to get reelected. Public opinion polls show that 9 out of 10 Americans oppose the legalization of currently illegal drugs, over half believe that legalization would lead to

increased use, and, by a margin of 2-1, believe that legalization would lead to an increase in the crime rate. Only a quarter support the legalization of marijuana, considered the least dangerous of the illegal drugs; only slightly more than 1 in 20 supports the legalization of heroin and cocaine. Given this sort of opposition, legalization is, for all practical purposes, not a viable political option at this time.

Looking Ahead: Challenge Questions

What is the best way to fight the drug war? Should it be fought at all?

Would legalization take the profit motive out of drug selling? Would it result in diminished use? Or would use increase, as others have argued? Given the fact that decriminalization has not increased the rate of marijuana in the states that have decriminalized small-quantity possession, why shouldn't this also be the case for heroin and cocaine?

If Prohibition actually did decrease the use of alcohol, why was it discontinued? Is Prohibition an acceptable and workable model for the currently illegal drugs? Does arresting the drug user work?

Experts generally agree that interdiction—stopping drugs at the supply side—is not possible, and that demand should be reduced; how can we reduce the demand for drugs?

Is the Dutch model applicable to the United States? Why or why not?

DRUGS:

Searching for an Answer

". . . We need to understand that law enforcement is merely a holding operation. We must address the underlying causes of drug-selling and addiction in our society before we can hope for a solution."

Jerome H. Skolnick

Dr. Skolnick is Claire Clements Dean's Professor of Law, Jurisprudence and Social Policy Program, University of California, Berkeley.

PUBLIC anger about drug dealers, street crime, and violence is justifiable. However, the Bush-Bennett War on Drugs—which calls for an "unprecedented" expansion of police, prosecutors, courts, and prisons, in addition to military force and interdiction—seems more an expression of outrage than a sound appreciation of the limits of law enforcement. Drug czar William Bennett and the President seem to believe that we have been losing that war because of a lack of resolve, but I believe the reasons are more fundamental.

It is not fair to ask law enforcement to take responsibility for solving society's drug problem. In thinking about what might work and what won't, we need to appreciate the conundrums they face in trying to combat crimes involving the sale of an illegal and highly addictive product. *The National Drug Control Strategy* (the red book the President held up in his address to the nation on drug policy, along with the now famous bag of crack) acknowledges that, "Despite interdiction's successful disruptions of trafficking patterns, the supply of illegal drugs entering the United States has, by all estimates, continued to grow." Why should that have happened? No matter how hard Federal, state and local police officers try, they encounter frustrating dilemmas and paradoxes.

The Demand-Supply Dilemma. For any product, demand generates supply. U.S. and European demand for drugs has contributed to a rise in the number of suppliers from a variety of producing countries. Some of these are political allies; others are not. The key fact is that demand has resulted in multiple drug producers, followed by a rise in output, with a subsequent drop in price. As Edmundo Morales has observed in *Cocaine: White Gold Rush in Peru*, "Unquestionably, drug production and traffic in Peru have addicted thousands of people to illegal sources

of hard cash." Price reduction, in turn, further invigorates demand—once again stimulating the entire cycle.

The Darwinian Trafficker Dilemma. Bennett and the President acknowledge that, "As we have expanded our interdiction efforts, we have seized increasing amounts of illegal drugs. Stepped up interdiction has also forced drug traffickers to make significant operational changes. . . . Every time we disrupt or close a particular trafficking route, we have found that traffickers resort to other smuggling tactics that are even more difficult to detect."

This is undoubtedly true, but it seems to argue against, rather than for, the stepped-up interdiction advocated by *The National Drug Control Strategy*. As we develop increasingly sophisticated tactics for reducing both narcotic production and smuggling, only the stronger and more efficient producers and smugglers survive. This, in turn, heightens supply and lowers cost. As this occurs, suppliers seek wider markets, particularly in distressed populations, just as segments of the alcohol and tobacco industries do.

The Borders Are a Sieve Dilemma. The borders can not be sealed, according to Rand Corporation economist Peter Reuter, who studied the question for the Department of Defense. The Mexican border is especially permeable. There are few barriers from the south to transporting drugs into that country, and they can be "brought across by small plane, private vehicle, or even by boat." A Mexican-American California narcotics agent made a similar observation to me in an interview in 1989: "Four hundred thousand of my people cross the border every year. How can you stop a much smaller number who are carrying a kilo or two of cocaine on their back?"

The Irrelevance of Smuggling Costs Dilemma. Interdiction is supposed to reduce street sales by increasing production and smuggling costs, thus raising the street price. This assumes that production and smuggling costs constitute a significant percentage of street price, but that is not true. It is relatively cheap to produce and refine a kilo of cocaine—about $1,000 for a kilo that eventually, when broken down into quarter- or even eighth-gram units, might retail for $250,000.

Smuggling costs might amount to an additional few percent of the retail price. Most of that price is divided among those who distribute it on this side of the border. As Reuter explains, "Fully 99% of the price of the drug when sold on the streets in the United States is accounted for by payments to people who distribute it." Thus, a doubling or tripling of smuggling costs would have a negligible impact. Street prices of cocaine have dropped dramatically, by 60 to 75%, since the Reagan Administration introduced its War on Drugs in 1982, headed by then-Vice Pres. Bush. The evidence suggests that interdiction has had little, if any, positive effects, and that even these can be outweighed by unanticipated side effects.

The Drug Hardening Paradox. When the Nixon Administration succeeded in reducing the supply of low-potency Mexican marijuana to California in the early 1970's, agriculturally skilled drug entrepreneurs developed a high-potency marijuana (sensimilla) industry in northern California, generating a market for a drug five or more times as potent. The paradox is this: the more successful law enforcement is at cutting off supply, the more incentive drug dealers have for hardening drugs, for developing varieties that are more potent, portable, and dangerous.

Contemporary interdiction policy—and its expansion, as advocated by the Bush/Bennett strategy—is grounded in an assumption concerning the stability of drug preference among those who enjoy faster living through chemistry. We know from history that demand for a specific drug is less related to its intrinsic properties than to the social definition of a particular substance as the drug of choice. Twenty years ago, heroin was the "problem" drug in American society. Today, it is crack cocaine.

Reprinted from *USA Today Magazine* (Society for the Advancement of Education,) July 1990, pp. 16-18. Copyright © 1990 by the Society for the Advancement of Education.

Suppose we actually could destroy the Peruvian, Bolivian, and Colombian cocaine fields. Lurking in the background are a variety of manufactured drugs. It is likely that underground chemists could design and manufacture what addicts would consider the ideal drug—one with the kick of crack and the longevity of crank (methamphetamine). Indeed, a powerful new drug, a colorless and odorless form of crystal methamphetamine—street name "ice"—is said to be sweeping Hawaii and is threatening to invade the West Coast ports of San Francisco, Los Angeles, and Portland. Should that happen, it would be just a matter of time before ice found its way across the country to replace crack as the drug of choice during the 1990's. The only good news ice will bring is its economic challenge to the Medallin Cartel. Moreover, it is doubtful that the distributors of the new drug will prove more concerned for public health than the cocaine producers.

Corruption

The Official Greed Dilemma. Whatever the latest fashion on drug use, manufacturers, smugglers, and distributors can operate more efficiently by corrupting public officials. As we attempt to put pressure on foreign producers, we will have to work with authorities in such countries as Colombia, Bolivia, Panama, and Peru. The bribe is a familiar part of law enforcement in these countries. Thus, the State Department's Bureau of International Narcotics Matters finds that Jorge Luis Ochoa, a major Colombian drug trafficker, "was able to buy his freedom through the intimidated and vulnerable Colombian judicial system."

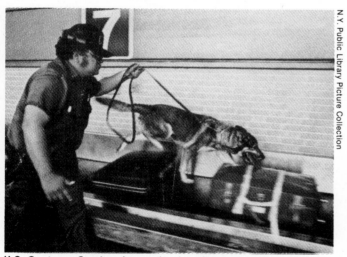

N.Y. Public Library Picture Collection

U.S. Customs Service dog, trained to detect the odor of heroin, cocaine, and marijuana, sniffs luggage at New York's John F. Kennedy International Airport.

What of our urban police? We are all too familiar with the narcotics scandals that have bedeviled the police in various cities, especially New York. Such corruption is not confined to the East Coast. Deputies in the Los Angeles County Sheriff's Department were involved in what *The Los Angeles Times* called "one of the worst corruption cases" in the department's history. Although the possibilities of official misconduct exist in any form of vice investigation, only in drug enforcement do we encounter large sums of cash and drugs held by perpetrators who are in no position to complain about being ripped off by cops.

By no means am I suggesting that all narcotics police are corrupt. The Los Angeles deputies were caught in a sting operation conducted by Sheriff Sherman Block. I *am* suggesting that it is difficult to uncover narcotics corruption, particularly when a small number of individuals are involved; that whatever amount is discovered has to be the tip of the iceberg; and that such mis-

conduct must be counted as one of the anticipated costs of an unprecedented expansion of drug law enforcement.

The Lock 'Em Up Dilemma. State and Federal prison populations virtually doubled in the 1980's and have tripled since the 1960's. Overcrowded jails and prisons are bulging with newly convicted criminals, as well as those whose probation and parole were revoked, largely because they failed their drug tests when released to the community. California, for example, had a 3,200% increase in parole violators returned to prison between 1978 and 1988. By the end of 1989, more than 1,000,000 Americans were behind bars.

As our advanced drug-testing technology consigns more parolees and probationers to prison, however, we find we can not continue to convict them and impose longer sentences without building new penal institutions. Bennett and the President recognize the critical lack of prison space as we expand law enforcement. They acknowledge that "most state prisons are already operating far above their designed capacity." They also recognize that "many states have been forced under court order to release prisoners before their terms have been served whenever a court-established prison population limit has been exceeded." Their solution is for state governments to persuade their citizens to support new facilities. "The task of building [prisons]," they write, "remains with state governments, who poorly serve their constituents when prison construction is stalled or resisted."

Yet, there is not a word in *The National Drug Control Strategy* about how to finance, staff, and pay for the continuing and rising expense of maintaining prisons. Evidently, the slogan "No New Taxes" applies only to the Federal government. If the states are to serve their citizens as Bush and Bennett exhort, *they* will have to raise taxes.

Even those citizens who demand longer and more certain sentences are reluctant to pay for penal institutions and understandably even more reluctant to live next door to them. Highly publicized plans for a 700-bed facility to house convicted Washington, D.C., drug dealers at Fort Meade, Md., were withdrawn—with embarrassment—the day after they were announced, *The New York Times* reported, because "there was too much public resistance."

The Prison Networking Dilemma. Even if we could build new facilities, imprisonment is not necessarily stigmatic or entirely foreboding for those who sell drugs. For the past two years, my students and I have been interviewing jailed California drug dealers. Imprisonment may offer a kind of "homeboy" status, especially for gang youth, for whom the institution can become an alternative neighborhood. Moreover, imprisonment often motivates prisoners in their illicit ways. Consigned to the margins of society anyhow, in jail they join gangs, use drugs, and make useful connections for buying and selling illegal substances. The penitentiary was perhaps once a place for experiencing penance. Today's correctional institutions, overcrowded as they are with short-term parole violators (many of whom have failed their court-mandated drug tests), often serve functions similar to those conventions perform for academics and business people—as an opportunity for networking.

The Felix Mitchell Paradox. In the mid 1980's, a Federal strike force, with considerable assistance and dogged investigation by the Oakland Police Department vice squad, succeeded in convicting and imprisoning the East Bay's three leading drug dealers. Among these was the legendary Felix Mitchell, who later was killed in Leavenworth Federal Prison and was regarded as a hero by the thousands who turned out for his funeral. Theoretically, Oakland's streets should have been cleansed of drugs. Did that happen? Hardly. The main result was a drop in price and a rise in street homicides and felonious assaults by gang members as they challenged each other for market share. As territorial arrangements have stabilized, so has the homicide rate—but the street price of crack has remained about the same or declined.

8. FIGHTING THE DRUG WAR

Police strategies

Is there *anything* law enforcement can do to impair the crack cocaine trade? There is little evidence to support the effectiveness of the law enforcement initiatives the Bush Administration proposes. Several colleagues at the Center for the Study of Law and Society and I recently evaluated such an initiative in Alameda County (Oakland), Calif. The sharp rise in drug selling and violence there persuaded the legislature and the Governor to provide $4,000,000 from 1985 to 1987 to bolster and expand prosecution, probation, and the courts—just the sort of expansion advocated by *The National Drug Control Strategy*. Following an ethnographic and statistical evaluation, we concluded that all of the law enforcement agencies carried out their mandate thoroughly and professionally, and that the intermediate goals of more prosecutions, convictions, and probation violations were met. That was the good news. The bad news was that it didn't seem to matter much. Crime—and narcotics felonies in particular—continued to increase. We concluded that, contrary to popular mythology, "The rise in narcotics crime in Alameda County can not be attributed to inefficient courts, prosecutors, probation officers, or police."

Of all the enforcement initiatives, the least effective will be those aimed at military interdiction; the most satisfying—at least initially—will be those that involve the community and local police. The Bush/Bennett strategy argues that "The first challenge facing our criminal justice system is to help reclaim neighborhoods that have been rendered unsafe by drugs." In a National Institute of Justice publication, Mark Kleiman, a proponent of street-level drug enforcement, points to two special threats that street drug dealing poses: that children may become users and that street dealing may become disruptive or violent.

At the same time, some law enforcement officials are skeptical about the positive effects of crackdowns. According to Minneapolis Police Chief Anthony Bouza, "Focused, saturation street enforcement will clean up an area, but it is costly and inefficient. It robs other areas of their fair share of scarce resources and it does not eliminate the intractable problem of drug dealing, merely displaces it. It also focuses, inefficiently, on the lowest level of the criminal chain and is sure to lead to abuses and repression, with sweeps and round-ups."

So, it is not clear how to repair the damage drug dealing imposes on local communities or what the costs would be of an expanded police effort in this direction. Still, so long as demand remains, local law enforcement initiatives are at least responsive to the complaints of law-abiding residents whose neighborhoods are undercut by street dealers and crack houses. Since public safety and civility should be law enforcement's highest priority, that's where I would recommend allocating restricted law enforcement funds. At the same time, we need to understand that law enforcement is merely a holding operation. We must address the underlying causes of drug-selling and addiction in our society before we can hope for a solution.

HOW TO WIN THE WAR ON DRUGS

Victory begins and ends at home. Washington should stop focusing on curbing the supply from abroad and put more money into programs that reduce demand in the U.S.

Louis Kraar

AMERICA'S so-called war on drugs is looking more and more like the real thing. Troops invade Panama in part to bring Manuel Noriega to justice for his alleged crimes as a drug trafficker. On the Mexican front, U.S. Marines, deployed for the first time in border patrols, engage marijuana smugglers in a firefight. And in mid-February, President Bush flies to Cartagena, Colombia, for an unprecedented antidrug summit aimed at rallying the governments of Colombia, Bolivia, and Peru to escalate their military struggle with the powerful cocaine cartels.

Will all this saber rattling make much of a difference? Don't bet on it. Despite record seizures, the supply of cocaine on America's mean streets—as well as the many not-so-mean ones—has never been more available or less expensive. In a persuasive study conducted for the Defense Department, Peter Reuter of Rand Corp. concludes that even a vastly more stringent interdiction program would at best reduce U.S. cocaine consumption by a mere 5%. Admits Jack Lawn, chief of the federal government's Drug Enforcement Administration (DEA): "Our enforcement efforts will continue to build statistics and fill prisons, but they won't turn around America's love affair with drugs."

Is the answer, then, to raise the white flag and legalize the stuff? Yes, say a small but influential number of professors and politicians, and at least one big-city judge. They argue that legalization would reduce violent crime and divert money from crooks to the government.

But they're probably wrong. The drugs popular today are so cheap to produce—a vial of crack cocaine selling for as little as $3 costs just 35 cents to import and manufacture—that a black market would continue to thrive alongside the legal one. Nor would legalization stop addicts from stealing to support their habits. What it would surely do is

REPORTER ASSOCIATE *Laurie Kretchmar*

swell the use of substances far more dangerous than alcohol. While 10% of drinkers become alcohol abusers, 20% to 30% of cocaine users wind up addicted. Since 1986 at least 100,000 infants have been born to drug abusers. The intensive care they require is costing several billion dollars a year.

Moreover, not all the battles in the drug war have been losing ones. Heroin use, which in the early 1970s threatened to become epidemic, has stabilized at roughly half a million addicts and attracts relatively few new recruits. Casual use of marijuana and cocaine also seems to be declining. The number of Americans who acknowledge using illicit drugs declined 37% between 1985 and 1988, according to household surveys conducted by the government's National Institute on Drug Abuse. The main reason the U.S. is experiencing what federal drug czar William Bennett describes as "the worst epidemic of illegal drug use in its history" is crack, the new plague.

The U.S. *can* gain further ground in the 1990s—but only by waging a more effective fight against illegal drugs at home. That doesn't mean policymakers ought to abandon longstanding efforts to curb the supply from abroad. But it does mean acknowledging that any new fiscal firepower should be targeted at reducing demand in the U.S.

Under President Bush, annual federal spending on the antidrug fight will have climbed 68%, to $10.6 billion, in two years. In a welcome reversal from the Reagan era cutbacks, Bush is increasing spending on prevention and treatment. But he still devotes only 30% of the budget to attacking the demand side of the problem. Instead, Bush is pouring $2.4 billion—a billion dollars more than Reagan—into the effort to interdict drugs before or as they enter the U.S., mainly by relying more on the armed forces.

FORTUNE would reverse those priorities. We would also invest a few billion dollars more in the struggle than the White House

has proposed, though most of that new money will have to come from states and cities on the front line. Treating every one of the country's drug abusers, for instance, would cost $5.6 billion a year—more than half Washington's total spending on the drug war. Happily, much can also be achieved by simply spending and reacting smarter. Here's what we suggest:

TREATMENT

■ **Provide more medical help for addicts.** The toughest challenge is curing the roughly four million Americans who are serious substance abusers. Only about 20% currently get medical help. Many shun it, but most cannot find it. While expensive private treatment centers have plenty of room, public centers—the only ones most addicts can afford—typically have long waiting lists. Says Robert Stutman, a veteran DEA agent in New York: "Imagine if I had cholera and walked into a city hospital and the doctor said, 'Come back in seven months.' It would be a scandal, but that's exactly what happens every day to addicts seeking help."

Though it has increased spending in this area, the Bush Administration is hardly acting like a government faced with an epidemic. Bennett's strategy, shaped more by budgetary constraints than hard evidence, is to focus on the half of the four million addicts whom he deems most capable of being helped. Another million, he argues, can help themselves. The remaining million are "hard-core addicts or career criminals" whom existing methods of treatment can't change much.

Doing better requires new medical techniques as well as more money. Only about half of cocaine addicts stay drug free for up to two years after treatment. Part of the problem is that some 70% of drug users also have an alcohol or mental disorder. Says Dr. Frederick Goodwin, head of the federal government's Alcohol, Drug Abuse, and Mental Health Administration: "We need more effective matching of individuals with particular treatments." A centralized registry of programs and openings in them would be an inexpensive first step.

Drug addiction can be cured, as successful treatment centers such as Phoenix House demonstrate (see box). Says Frank Gough, a former heroin addict and director of an adult treatment center for Daytop Village in New York State: "We return to society productive, responsible people." The big problem is getting those whose judgment has been spiked by drugs to enter and stay in treatment. Most are pushed into it by their family or the threat of imprisonment.

■ **Use local laws to allow courts to commit hard-core addicts to treatment.** Few states do this now. But California courts, for instance, can send convicted drug offenders to a special prison that includes a rehabilitation center. This so-called civil commitment program entails frequent drug testing after release and recommitment for those who resume the habit. Says Dr. Mitch Rosenthal of Phoenix House: "If the country wants to get serious, like a good family it has to demand that drug users stay in treatment."

■ **Convert surplus military bases to drug treatment sites.** As Nancy Reagan learned in trying to set up a rehabilitation center for adolescent drug abusers in Los Angeles, many communities object to having one in their midst. The Pentagon is supposed to identify surplus facilities but has not acted yet. With a glut of unneeded bases about to hit the market, this is an opportunity not to be missed.

■ **Expand research on medical treatments for addiction.** The idea is to treat brain dysfunctions caused by habitual drug use and, by reducing cravings, make patients more receptive to therapy. Medication is already used to treat many of the nation's 500,000 heroin addicts. Democratic Senator Joseph Biden of Delaware proposes spending $1 billion on research over the next ten years, a realistic target. This is a clear-cut case where Washington must take the lead: Pharmaceutical companies are uncertain whether such products would make money and fret they would hurt the companies' image.

PREVENTION
■ **Do more to equip children to resist drugs.** Surprisingly, only about half the nation's public schools provide comprehensive substance-abuse education. Less surprisingly, since the key is building character, it's a struggle to find methods that work. Merely providing information in a classroom does

THE TOP DRUG WARRIOR TALKS TOUGH

■ Like the Pope in Stalin's famous put-down, William J. Bennett, the President's designated drug czar, is a general with no divisions at his disposal. Because the war on drugs is run by a host of independent agencies and Cabinet departments, Bennett's primary weapon is thunderous rhetoric.

Since taking office, this Ph.D. in philosophy and former Secretary of Education has commanded headlines with his tough talk. He wishes the military could shoot down small planes carrying narcotics into the U.S. He'd like to execute drug kingpins and once observed that "beheading" them wasn't a bad idea. What about legalizing drugs, at least less dangerous ones like marijuana? "Moral surrender," roars the thunderer. "Why in God's name foster the use of a drug that makes you stupid?"

From his platform at the Office of National Drug Control Policy, Bennett recently outlined his views for FORTUNE:

■ **On the legal limits to the drug war:** "It's a funny war when the 'enemy' is entitled to due process of law and a fair trial. By the way, I'm in favor of due process. But that kind of slows things down."

■ **On destroying the drug cartels:** "We would go after them even if it didn't make prudent public-policy sense, because these are the enemies of America and of our children. But it also makes sense."

■ **On reducing the supply of drugs:** "We grossly underestimated how much is coming in." Still, record seizures and increased interdiction of drugs before they enter the U.S., he claims, "will make a difference in the long run by increasing the price of doing business."

■ **On tougher law enforcement:** "There's no way to win when the dealer on the streets looks out and says, 'The odds of my going to jail are one in five.' The odds have got to be better."

■ **On his claim that one million addicts are beyond treatment:** "It's not my triage. They've done it to themselves. You can stand up and say that everybody who has had a serious bout with cocaine is going to recover. But you're lying."

■ **On the hazards of drugs:** "This stuff does something to the brain, to the mind, to the soul, from which many people cannot recover. If this were something you could get into and get a shot or take a couple of aspirin and be okay, it wouldn't be the calamity it is."

■ **On the limits to Washington's role:** "There are things the federal government can't do. Restore the moral authority of families, churches, and schools, and you get rid of 85% of this problem. Meanwhile, we have a hell of a short-term problem."

little to curb demand and may even stimulate curiosity to try drugs.

Kansas City has proved that mobilizing parents and the community can make drug education more effective. Starting with sixth- and seventh-graders, schools discourage the use of cigarettes, alcohol, and marijuana, widely considered the path to more dangerous substances. Students get classroom training in skills for resisting drug use, involve parents in discussion sessions, and see their efforts covered in the local media. The result: These youngsters show only half the drug use typical among their age group.

Bringing local police into the classroom helps too. The Drug Abuse Resistance Education program that Los Angeles started in 1983 uses specially trained officers as instructors for fifth- and sixth-graders. By appearing in full uniform, the teachers in blue immediately command attention. They

maintain it by dealing with the real world of adolescents, presenting a course that aims at building self-esteem and teaches how to say no without losing friends. The L.A. cops' promising technique has spread to some 2,000 communities in 49 states.

■ **Do more to spot drug use early.** Many public schools require a health examination for new students, an ideal checkpoint. The Los Angeles County district attorney's office focuses heavily on truancy, an early sign of drug use, and gets families into fighting it.

■ **Shout louder from the most bully pulpit around.** The nonprofit Partnership for a Drug-Free America has created a starkly emotional series of ads now showing on TV all across the U.S. In one, a young woman snorts cocaine in the privacy of her home, while an offstage voice notes that one out of five users gets hooked, then asks, "But that's not your problem. Or is it?" In the last scene, she reappears driving a school bus. Space for this $150-million-a-year campaign is donated by newspapers, magazines, and TV. Surveys suggest that the ads do reduce consumption of marijuana and cocaine, particularly in markets that run them frequently. By slightly more than doubling the reach of its ads, the Partnership hopes to expose every American to an antidrug message at least once a day.

■ **Companies should join the drug war.** Already, federal law requires those in fields such as transportation, nuclear power, and defense to maintain a drug-free workplace. With good reason. In 1987 a Conrail train ran through a restricted switch into the path of a high-speed Amtrak train, killing 16 people and injuring 174. The "probable cause," according to the National Transportation Safety Board's report: The Conrail engineer was suffering from marijuana "impairment."

Now other corporations are getting interested in drug testing as a way to cut health insurance costs and productivity losses. According to a study by the Bureau of Labor Statistics, some 9% of corporate America's employees show up for work with illegal substances in their systems. The cost to the economy: an estimated $60 billion a year.

IBM has a model program that protects both the company and its employees from drug abuse. Since 1984 every job applicant has had to undergo a urine test for illegal drugs. Any employee caught bringing drugs into IBM, including its parking lots, gets fired. Employees who act strangely or perform erratically can be referred to the company's medical department, but are not required to take a drug test unless their job is safety sensitive. Those who admit to having a drug problem, however, get counseling and medical attention. Says Dr. Glenn E. Haughie, the company's director of corporate health and safety: "IBM considers drug use a treatable disease." Among his success stories is a manager who ran up big bills on a company credit card before admitting to a decade-long cocaine habit. After treatment the manager is back at work and drug free.

ENFORCEMENT
■ **Unclog the criminal justice system.** Crowded courts have taken much of the risk out of the drug business. Arrestees have a 15% chance of going to jail in New York City and face only slightly worse odds in Washington, D.C. Genuine deterrence requires not only more police but also more prosecutors, judges, and jails. The Administration is expanding the federal prisons, which house over 50,000 people, at a cost of $1.5 billion.

But 85% of drug offenders are in state and local prisons. Many are so jammed that

courts won't allow them to take in newcomers unless someone already there is released. As a result, drug traffickers convicted in state courts serve only 22 months on average, less time than for robbery or aggravated assault. State and local governments will just have to spend more on jails: $5 billion to $10 billion over the next few years. That's about half the costs of the jails they built in the past decade.

■ **Try alternative forms of punishment.** Drug czar Bennett wants swift, sure penalties, but he's willing to see them take forms other than long prison terms. Punishment for recreational drug users, who are more influential than addicts in popularizing drugs, should fit their crime. Says Dr. Herbert Kleber, a Yale psychiatrist who is serving as Bennett's deputy for demand reduction: "The casual user is saying, in effect, that you can enjoy drugs, keep your health and job, have it all."

In Phoenix that kind of attitude can get the casual drug user a heavy fine and a night

in jail. In Philadelphia a yuppie shopping at the local cocaine market risks having his BMW auctioned off if he is convicted. Denying teenage offenders a driver's license for a year is another promising deterrent. In Toledo the juvenile court can make parents answer for their children's mistakes by imposing fines or even a few days in jail.

■ **Get communities involved in policing troubled neighborhoods.** Operation Clean in Dallas has enabled residents to regain control of areas once overrun by drug dealers. In a six-week operation, the city first pours in cops to put the heat on dealers. It then brings in the full range of services literally to clean up the neighborhood, and finally stations police foot patrols in the community. So far four such cleanups of inner-city areas have reduced violent crimes significantly. Says assistant police chief Sam Gonzales: "We're displacing drug dealers. We can't allow them to take a foothold in part of the city and say, 'It's mine.'"

In Kansas City, the Ad Hoc Group

UP FROM THE ASHES AT PHOENIX HOUSE

■ New York psychiatrist Mitch Rosenthal, 54, has spent his career disproving what he was taught in medical school about drug abusers: "Once an addict, always an addict." Of the roughly 100 private, nonprofit agencies that offer residential and outpatient treatment programs in the U.S., his Phoenix House is the largest, with six sites in New York and four in California. In the view of many experts, including drug czar William Bennett, it also may be the best.

Rosenthal's guiding principle is that addicts must take responsibility for their actions. In his main program adult abusers voluntarily live together in a drug-free residential community for 18 to 24 months. From 6 A.M. until 10:30 P.M., they are kept on a regimented schedule, ranging from household chores to group therapy sessions. Every privilege, from wearing a tie to making a phone call, must be earned. Punishment for breaking house rules is swift.

Even Phoenix House's biggest fans admit it won't work for everyone. Indeed, half who start quit within the first year. But most of the 30,000 who have stuck with the residential program since its beginning in 1967 have turned their lives around. They remain off drugs, hold down jobs, and stay out of jail.

Salvation doesn't come cheap. Treating adults at Phoenix House costs about

$40 a day; $60 for adolescents. That's considerably more than outpatient programs. But compared with the alternatives—treating an addict in federal prison ($68 a day) or in profit-making clinics ($175 to $1,000 a day for 30 days)—taxpayers, who pick up one-third of the tab, are getting a good deal.

Rosenthal's most innovative venture is Phoenix Academy, a residential high school. Some 225 adolescents have earned diplomas since it opened a New York campus in 1981 and a San Diego site in 1986. The students are the kind of troublemakers most principals brag about expelling. Arturo Wong, 18, an ex-angel dust user who was caught driving a stolen car, came to the academy to beat jail time. Says Wong: "In the long run I know it's helping me out."

Wong is among a privileged lot: New York State has only 500 beds for adolescents needing long-term residential care; San Diego County has just 40. Phoenix Academy accounts for about half the slots in New York—and all of them in San Diego. Before opening, each academy, like other such centers, had to overcome protests from people living nearby. But if Americans are serious about getting kids off drugs, they will have to see such programs not as evidence of the disease but as part of its cure.

– Laurie Kretchmar

Against Crime runs a hotline that people can use to report suspected drug dealers to police. The organization also provides $1,000 rewards for information leading to convictions. Says Mary Weathers, director of the citizens' group: "The police cannot always get there, so we try to give visible community support." An offshoot of Ad Hoc called Black Men Together, formed to provide virtuous role models for youth, holds frequent antidrug rallies where citizens (backed by police) use bullhorns to shout suspected dealers off the streets.

Seattle is reclaiming drug-infested neighborhoods with bicycle patrols by pairs of officers who befriend local residents and sneak up on drug dealers. Officer Tony Little, who patrols a low-income housing project, says the technique definitely helps cut down drug trafficking. Riding a 21-speed mountain bike "makes you more approachable than if you're driving a patrol car," he argues. Often acting on tips from residents, the bike cops surprise dealers, put them in handcuffs, and radio for a patrol car. The bikes cost around $500 each.

The Drug Enforcement Administration has 2,800 agents, roughly the number of musicians in the U.S. Army. The Federal Bureau of Investigation has assigned 1,100 agents to drug cases. Given those limits, creative efforts by local police are crucial.

■ **Seize even more drug profits.** The most vulnerable commodity in the narcotics trade is money. Drug sales in the U.S. generate more than $80 billion in tax-free profits a year. But traffickers must find ways to get their proceeds into bank accounts and legitimate businesses to disguise the source. Tracing and confiscating cash and assets deal drugsters a double blow: Money is much harder for them to replace than drugs, and the government can use it to help pay for the war against them. Says Charles O. Simonsen, chief of the currency investigations branch at U.S. Customs: "We're having a bigger impact taking their money than their drugs. If we can attack the financial infrastructure of a drug organization, we can terminally damage it."

Over the past four years the federal government has seized more than $1 billion in assets. To do more than skim the surface, states should strengthen asset forfeiture laws for drug proceeds. The Treasury, which acquires an enormous amount of data from banks on cash transactions of $10,000 or more, as well as on "suspicious transactions," often still lacks the paper trail needed for convictions. Requiring more information on international wire transfers of money would help. Under prodding from Senator John Kerry of Massachusetts, the Treasury is also negotiating to get key foreign bank centers to maintain their own paper trails—and make them available to criminal investigations.

INTERNATIONAL

■ **Recognize that the long-term solution is to attack the economic roots of the supply problem.** Sure, there's always room for more military cooperation. But remember that farmers in Peru and Bolivia are hooked on coca as a cash crop, while in Colombia, which processes and exports the stuff, cocaine is one of the main earners of foreign exchange. Rensselaer Lee, a business consultant who has studied the South American cocaine trade, warns, "Trying to eradicate the problem quickly may create worse problems by throwing people out of work and destabilizing governments."

To help those economies go straight, the Bush Administration has promised $2.2 billion in military and economic aid over the next five years. That's not a bad start. But Washington could still show more sensitivity to the legitimate economic needs of drug-supplying countries. Recently the U.S. alienated Colombia by allowing the collapse of an international pact for stabilizing coffee prices. The cost to the Bogotá government: several hundred million dollars a year in legal export earnings.

In the struggle against drugs, what can we expect to achieve by the year 2000? Drug czar Bennett's goal is to reduce drug use in the U.S. by 55% in ten years. Sounds terrific, until you realize that's about what the U.S. has done since 1985. And who feels better off today? Moreover, who knows what cheap, new designer drug could come along to fuel the epidemic? Use of a smokable form of methamphetamine called ice, which gets users high for up to eight hours vs. 20 minutes for crack, could spread rapidly. Says Robert W. Burgreen, police chief in San Diego: "Anyone with a chemistry book and the ability to experiment can make meth."

Still, that's no reason to despair, as some do, that this fight is destined to prove another Vietnam. To the extent that it implies the U.S. can win a reasonably swift and clear-cut victory, as it did in World War II, today's drug war rhetoric is misleading. Think instead of another struggle that offered no quick fix but instead required patience, vast resources, bipartisan and international cooperation, but which America saw through successfully—the cold war. Policies based on containment may not stir the blood. Pursued long enough, though, they can ultimately prevail.

FACING UP TO Drugs

IS LEGALIZATION THE SOLUTION?

PETE HAMILL

H ARD DRUGS ARE NOW THE SCARIEST FACT
of New York life. They have spread
genuine fear among ordinary citizens.
They have stained every neighborhood in
every borough, respecting no boundaries
of class or color or geography. They have
destroyed marriages, corrupted cops and banks, diminished
productivity, fed the wild spiral of rents and condominium
prices, overwhelmed the public hospitals, and filled the
prisons to bursting.

The price of the drug scourge increases by the day. Hard
drugs have injured thousands of families, some named
Zaccaro and Kennedy, many others less well known. They
have ruined uncountable numbers of careers and distorted
others. Last year, when Dwight Gooden was sent off to the
Smithers clinic, hard drugs almost certainly cost the Mets a
championship. Gooden's friend, the brilliant pitcher Floyd
Youmans of the Montreal Expos, learned no lesson from this;
he was recently suspended indefinitely after once more failing
a drug test. But Gooden and Youmans are not isolated cases,
young men ensnared by the life-style of the poor
neighborhoods of Tampa. Hard drugs have damaged the
lives of pitcher Steve Howe, prizefighter Aaron Pryor, and
football players Mercury Morris, Hollywood Henderson, and
Don Reese, to mention only a few. Many other talented
Americans, with no excuses to make about poverty or
environment, have been hurt by hard drugs. And they cost
Len Bias, Janis Joplin, Jimi Hendrix, Jim Morrison, and John
Belushi their lives.

These terrible examples seem to make no difference; for the
druggies, there are no cautionary tales. All over New York
today, thousands of people are playing with drugs as if
nothing will happen to *them*. And in this dense and dangerous
city, such a taste for folly usually results in corpses.

New York, of course, is not unique. With the drug plague
spreading all over the United States, the Feds now estimate
that the country's cocaine-user population is now at 5.8-
million. These new druggies include prep-school students,
bankers, policemen, railroad workers, pilots, factory hands,
stockbrokers, journalists, and—with the arrival of crack—
vast numbers of the urban poor. According to the
National Institute on Drug Abuse, the average age of
first-time drug-users in the United States is now
thirteen.

The drug trade is one of the most successful of all multinational capitalist enterprises, brilliantly functioning on the
ancient rules of supply and demand. The demand is insatiable, the supply apparently limitless. In a business estimated
by the president's South Florida Task Force to gross more
than $100 billion a year, there are fortunes, large and small,
to be made. And the art of the drug deal always contains the
gun. As the authority of the old mob faded in the seventies
(with the breakup of the Istanbul-Marseilles-New York
pipeline), new bad guys moved in: Cubans and Colombians
first; then, as the cocaine business flourished, Bolivians and
Dominicans. Israeli hoodlums out of Brighton Beach took a
big hunk of the heroin trade. And 30 to 40 Jamaican
"posses" began operating in the United States, starting with
marijuana and hashish, then moving hard into the cocaine
trade. The Shower Posse works out of the Bronx, the Span-
gler Posse in Brooklyn, the Dunkirk Boys in Harlem.
Experts say the posses killed about 350 people last year, and
the number could be much higher (more than 200 homicides
here last year involved Jamaicans). Now the word on the

street is that the Pakistanis are moving into town, with an endless supply of heroin from home.

BUT THE ADVENT OF CRACK HAS LED TO THE true decentralization of the drug trade. The old days of iron control by the Gambino or Bonanno families are clearly over. Small groups of violent entrepreneurs now run the trade in individual housing projects, on specific streets, in the vicinity of valued high schools. Men have been killed in disputes over control of a single street corner. Such drug gangs as the Vigilantes in Harlem, the Wild Bunch in Bed-Stuy, and the Valley Boys in the northeast Bronx are young and deadly. And unless something is done, they are here to stay.

They all have guns, including automatic weapons, and they have a gift for slaughter that makes some people nostalgic for the old Mafia. Nearly every morning, the newspapers carry fresh bulletins from the drug wars, full of multiple homicides and the killing of women and children. The old hoodlums were sinister bums who often killed one another, but they had some respect for the innocence of children. Not this set. The first indication that the rules of the game had changed dawned on us in 1982. In February of that year, on the Grand Central Parkway, the eighteen-month-old daughter and the four-month-old son of a Colombian drug-dealer were destroyed by shotgun blasts and automatic weapons, after their parents had been blown away. One Dominican dealer was forced to watch the disembowelment of his wife before being shotgunned to death. In Jackson Heights, according to New York *Newsday*, the favored method of execution is now the "Colombian necktie": The throat is cut and the tongue pulled through the slit to hang down upon the chest. The drug gangs are not misunderstood little boys. Their violence is at once specific and general: When they get rid of a suspected informer, they send chilling lessons to many others. Yet most of us read about their mayhem as if it were taking place in some barbarous and distant country and not the city that also contains the Metropolitan Museum.

It isn't as if these people are simply breaking the law; in some place, the law doesn't even exist. Whole neighborhoods in Brooklyn and Queens have been abandoned to the rule of the men with the Uzis, the MAC-10s, and the 9-mm. pistols. When police officer Edward Byrne was stationed outside the South Jamaica home of a witness in a drug case, the bad guys just walked up and killed him. When police officer George Scheu started crusading last year against drug-dealers in his Flushing neighborhood, he was shot down and killed outside his home. These actions remind us of the criminal anarchy in Colombia, where scores of police officers, judges, and public officials (including the minister of justice) have been assassinated by the drug caudillos. The new drug gangs enforce their power with violence, demonstrating that they can successfully murder witnesses and cops who might get in the way. When the first prosecutor is killed, there may be outrage in New York, but there will be no surprise.

Officers of the law are not the only casualties. Every weekend, discos erupt in gunfire as drug gangs fight over money or women or the ambiguous intentions of a smile. Every other week, innocent bystanders are shot down, provided a day of tabloid mourning, swiftly forgotten.

These killers are servicing a huge number of New Yorkers. The population of the stupefied can no longer be accurately counted. It is estimated that New York heroin addicts number about 200,000, or ten full-strength army divisions. But nobody knows how many people are using cocaine or crack. Some cops say it is more than a million. This might be hyperbole, the result of what some perceive to be anti-drug hysteria. But

FACING UP TO DRUGS

Most of us read about the drug mayhem as if it were taking place in some barbarous and distant country.

nobody who lives in New York can deny the daily evidence of the drug plague.

You see blurred-out young men panhandling for crack money from Columbus Avenue to Wall Street. Every night, wide-eyed, gold-bedecked teenage crackheads do 75 miles an hour on the Henry Hudson Parkway, racing one another in BMWs. In the age of AIDS, schoolgirls are hooking on street corners. Thousands of other young New Yorkers, whacked on drugs, are now incapable of holding jobs or acquiring the basic skills that might make a decent life possible. They amble around the ghettos. They fill the welfare hotels. They mill about the Port Authority bus terminal. They career through subway cars, sometimes whipping out knives or pistols. The eyes of the heroin-users are glazed, their bodies filthy. The shooters among them often share "works," knowing that dirty needles can give them AIDS; they choose to risk an agonizing death in order to get high. The crackheads are wilder—eyes pinwheeling, speed-rapping away, or practicing various menacing styles. Smack or crack: They'd rather do either than go to a ball game, love someone, raise a child, listen to music, read a book, or master a difficult craft.

ALL OF US ARE PAYING FOR THIS SICK AND disastrous binge. Crime in New York, after tailing off for a few years, has risen drastically. The reason is simple: Most junkies don't work. To feed their habits, addicts must either deal or steal. A Justice Department study released last winter showed that 79 percent of men arrested in New York for serious crimes tested positive for recent use of illegal drugs, 63 percent for cocaine. In 1977, there were 505 cops in this city's Narcotics Division; today, there are nearly 1,200. They made 35,774 drug-related arrests last year and estimate that 40 percent of the city's murders (there were 1,672 in 1987) were drug-related. In the first three months of this year, murder was up 10 percent in the city; car theft, 18.2 percent; assault, 9.4 percent; larceny, 5 percent; robbery, 4 percent. New Yorkers must come up with billions of tax dollars to pay for the police work involved, along with the cost of the druggies' hospital treatment, the operation of various clinics, and welfare payments to those who are so blitzed they can't support themselves.

With the pervasive use of hard drugs, and the enormous profits involved, it is no surprise that policemen all over the country have been dirtied, most sickeningly in Miami. But there is evidence that the corruption goes beyond cases of underpaid street cops looking the other way for their kids' tuition. A few years ago, a veteran agent became the first FBI man to plead guilty to cocaine-trafficking. Assistant U.S. Attorney Daniel N. Perlmutter, a rising star in Rudolph Giuliani's office, went to jail for stealing cocaine and heroin from a safe where evidence was stored.

No wonder Jesse Jackson was able to make drugs a major part of this year's presidential campaign. No wonder a New York *Times*/CBS News poll in March showed that Americans were far more concerned with drug-trafficking than with Central America, arms control, terrorism, or the West Bank. Americans have learned one big thing in the past few years: There has been a war on drugs, all right, and we have lost. Nobody knows this better than New Yorkers.

The ancient question is posed: What is to be done? The drug culture is now so pervasive, the drug trade so huge, powerful, and complex, that there are no simple answers. But the attack on the problem must deal with the leading actors in this squalid drama: dealers and users. That is, any true war on drugs must grapple with the problems of supply and demand.

SUPPLY

IT IS ONE OF THE MORE DELICIOUS IRONIES OF THE Cold War era that the bulk of the cocaine and heroin supply comes from countries that used to be called part of the free world. While trillions have been spent on national security, the security of ordinary citizens has been destroyed by countries that are on our side. The cocaine cartel is headquartered in Medellín, Colombia. Most coca leaves are produced in Bolivia and Peru, where they are turned into coca paste for processing in Colombia. Most heroin is coming from Pakistan, Thailand, Turkey, and Mexico. The Colombians and Mexicans also produce much of the marijuana crop that is grown outside the United States.

The big supply-side coke-dealers control processing and distribution, leaving the grungy details of retailing to thousands of Americans. Many Caribbean islands are crucial to distribution, as was Panama until the indictment of Noriega. Mexico also is used as a transshipment point for huge supplies of cocaine and heroin that it does not produce. In all these countries, the governments themselves have been corrupted by the trade. The government of Colombia has virtually surrendered to the violence of the drug barons, while the governments of Panama and Bolivia are flat-out drug rings. Some Caribbean nations—the Bahamas in particular—have been accused of the same partnership with traffickers. The civilian government of Haiti was recently overthrown by the military in a dispute over the drug trade. In Mexico, the corruption is low-level in many places but is said to involve higher-ups in various state governments. In Thailand and Pakistan, drug-traffickers ply their trade with little interference from their governments; Thailand is more worried about Vietnam than about 110th Street, and Pakistan is making too much money off the war in Afghanistan to care about junkies in the United States.

Frustrated Americans have demanded that something drastic be done about the drug traffic. And over the past few years, the following measures have been advocated:

1. *War*. This is one of the most frequently voiced demands, what Maxwell Smart would have called the old let's-go-in-and-bomb-the-bejesus-out-of-them plan. Massachusetts senator John Kerry and Los Angeles police chief Daryl Gates

FACING UP TO DRUGS

It is hard to imagine a declaration of war against Panama, Colombia, Bolivia, Mexico, and Pakistan.

are among those who have suggested military action. After all, if the United States is truly the most powerful nation on earth, why can't it *go to the source?*

From 1839 to 1842, the British actually did fight a war in China over drugs. But in the case of the Opium War, the British were the drug-pushers. They went ashore in China and killed a lot of Chinese in the name of their holy cause (opium was produced in British India, sold in China), the equivalent of Colombia's attacking the United States for the right to sell cocaine.

But a United States war against the drug-producing countries would be a forbiddingly expensive enterprise. You can't do it with one or two Grenada-style public-relations spectacles. And a war against one country—say, Colombia—would have no effect; the bad guys would just move next door. To use military force effectively to stop the production of poppies and coca leaves, the United States would have to attack all of the offending countries *at the same time.*

But it is hard to imagine a simultaneous declaration of war against Panama, Colombia, Peru, Bolivia, Mexico, Turkey, Thailand, and Pakistan, with a smaller expedition against the Bahamas. We have had some comical adventurers in the National Security Council lately, but none *that* comical. There are 80 million people in Mexico alone, with rugged, mountainous terrain through the center of the country and dense jungles in the southern regions. Bolivia is twice the size of France and also mountainous. In Pakistan, American troops would face all the guns the CIA has been supplying to the anti-Communist Afghans, many of whom have been ripped off by Pakistani gangsters. Another war in Southeast Asia (to cut off the Thai supply) would be no fun, but it would carry its own ironies, since much of the current mass stupefaction in America can be traced to the Vietnam era.

The logistics of Drug War One would be staggering; planes, ships, and rockets would be sent on their way to three continents. In every country from Turkey to Thailand, an American invasion would unite most of the local population on nationalist grounds. (We had a mild sample of that recently in the wholly owned CIA subsidiary of Honduras when the arrest of a drug-dealer by U.S. agents led to the burning down of one of the embassy buildings, along with several nights of anti-U.S. rioting.) Various international agreements would get in the way (the Organization of American States is unlikely to authorize a mass invasion of its own most important member states). U.S. casualties in such a worldwide operation would be very heavy as local armies and nationalist guerrilla bands descended upon the invaders, prepared to die, as they say, for their country. In the event that the Americans won all of these simultaneous wars, they would then have to occupy those countries for a generation if they truly hoped to wipe out the sources of drugs. The cost of a dozen huge garrisons would finish off the already precarious U.S. economy.

2. *Economic pressure.* On paper, this sounds like a more rational means of eradicating drugs. The United States (and the other leading industrial countries) would cut off credits, foreign aid, and all legitimate trade with the drug-producing countries. Presumably, the governments of those countries would then realize swiftly that they must get rid of the drug barons and would dispatch their own soldiers to wipe them out. While wielding the economic Big Stick, the United States would hold out the carrots of crop replacement, expanded foreign aid, guaranteed purchase of legitimate crops. (Bolivia, for example, went heavily into coca-leaf production in the seventies after its cotton industry collapsed with the fall of worldwide cotton prices. This followed the sharp decline of its tin industry.) The idea would be to create as much domestic pain as possible, so the local governments would get out of the drug racket—or crush it.

Unfortunately, the recent fiasco in Panama showed us on a small scale that this probably wouldn't work. Again, nationalism would be a major factor (in Panama, most people blamed the U.S. for their plight, not Noriega). And in using economic sanctions, the U.S. could not make distinctions among drug-dealers; Washington would have to be as tough on NATO ally Turkey as it is on Bolivia, as ferocious against Thailand and Pakistan as against Colombia and Mexico.

But U.S. companies also need most of these countries as markets. Economic sanctions work both ways; all American goods would be stopped at other nations' borders, thus closing plants all over our own country. Mexico would stop paying its multi-billion-dollar debt to U.S. banks, which would then collapse—perhaps pulling the entire country into a major depression.

3. *Moral persuasion.* Don't even bother.

4. *The sealing of the borders.* Again, this would cost uncountable billions. We have a 5,426-mile undefended border with Canada. It was crossed without problem by Prohibition rumrunners, vaulted for decades by Mafia drug-peddlers, and is easily traversed these days by the cocaine-runners. The 1,942-mile border with Mexico is a sieve. In spite of tough immigration laws, several million illegal aliens are expected to cross it this year; well-financed drug-runners with their fleets of small aircraft and trucks are unlikely to be stopped.

Enlisting the Armed Forces as border guards almost certainly would only complicate matters—as the Israelis have learned on the West Bank, soldiers are not policemen. Chasing druggies back home to Mexico or Canada (in "hot pursuit") could lead to an international incident every other day. The first time a private plane flown by some orthodontist with a defective radio was shot down over Toronto, the plan would be abandoned.

America's miles of coastline are guarded by an underfinanced, undermanned Coast Guard. Florida alone has 580 miles of coast, and there are more than 120,000 pleasure boats registered in southern Florida. Smugglers have become very sophisticated about penetrating our feeble defenses. The South Florida Task Force—headed by Vice-President George Bush and supported by the Drug Enforcement Administration, the FBI, the Customs Service, the U.S. Army (which supplied Cobra helicopters), the Bureau of Alcohol, Tobacco & Firearms, the Internal Revenue Service, the Coast Guard, the U.S. Navy (whose warships gave the Coast Guard support), the U.S. Border Patrol, the U.S. Marshals, and the Treasury Department—has been a colossal flop. After more than six years of this effort, there are more drugs on the streets than ever before, and their lower prices (down from $47,000 a kilo for cocaine six years ago to about $12,000 now) indicate that all those well-photographed record-setting busts haven't stopped the flow.

The reason is simple. The demand and the profits are enormous. So it's no surprise that when the government concentrates its efforts in one spot (as it did in southern Florida), the druggies simply go elsewhere: to the Florida panhandle, the bayous of Louisiana, the shores of Mississippi. Many even follow the old rumrunner trails, dropping anchor off Montauk and using small boats to make runs against the unguarded shores of Long Island. One unexpected consequence of the patchwork War on Drugs has been the spread of the trade to places that once were free of it. Brilliant.

6. *Draconian measures, including the death penalty.* Mayor Koch and others have called for the death penalty for big-time drug-dealers. The problem is that most of them don't live here. For every Carlos Lehder, convicted recently after a long trial in Florida, there are thousands of others whose immunity is guaranteed by use of violence.

But if the death penalty is to be employed to solve the drug problem, why should it be limited to the few foreign wholesalers who are extradited and tried here? To be fair, you would have to attack every participant in the production and distribution systems. That is, you would have to do more than fry a few thousand pushers; you would have to execute every crooked cop, every corrupt banker who launders drug money, every politician who is on the take. You would also have to lock up all members of the CIA involved in the *contra* drug-running scheme (persuasively described in Leslie Cockburn's *Out of Control*) and strap them into the electric chair, along with their bosses and whoever in the White House collaborated in these operations. The death penalty for drug-dealing is a slogan, not a solution. Even if exceptions were made for ideological zealots, the state would have to kill several hundred thousand people. And the drugs would continue to flow.

DEMAND

ONE NIGHT A YEAR AGO, I HAD DINNER WITH A Mexican diplomat and asked him about the drug problem in Mexico. He said, "You have to understand something: If thousands of North American yuppies suddenly decided tomorrow to get high by shoving bananas up their noses—and they were willing to pay $10 a banana—Mexico would bloom in bananas."

His point was a simple one: The drug problem in the United States is one of demand, not of production. Poor countries are like poor people—in order to survive, they will sell whatever the market demands. In our time, in this country and this city, the market demands hard drugs.

There have been a variety of suggestions about dealing with the insatiable appetite that Americans have developed for cocaine and heroin.

1. *Willpower.* This is the Nancy Reagan plan, beautifully described by a recent beauty contestant as "Just Say Don't." It is primarily directed at teenagers, imploring them to resist the peer pressure that could lead to using drugs. A few weeks ago, I asked some New York street kids about this program. They just laughed and laughed.

2. *Education.* This is getting better. In the past, the country paid a heavy price for lies told in the name of education

(marijuana will lead to heroin, etc.). Television has been playing a more responsible role lately, with a variety of series and programs about the cost and consequences of drugs (*48 Hours on Crack Street;* the two Peter Jennings specials on ABC). If this effort is sustained, we may begin to see a slow, steady decline in drug use (the way cigarette-smoking began to wane after the truth was told about its connection to lung cancer and heart disease). The great risk is that education about drugs will merely provoke curiosity and lead to wider use. Kids always think they are immortal.

3. *Treatment.* I visited a drug-treatment center in Suffern a few weeks ago. The facilities were secure, the 28-day program tough, the staff dedicated. There were exactly 28 beds for junkies. There are 250,000 smack addicts in New York State alone. Around the state, there are about 5,000 beds available to treat heroin addicts. Obviously, not everyone who wants treatment can get it. Those who have summoned all the desiccated vestiges of their pride and hope in order to enter a treatment program should be able to do so. But this, too, will cost many billions if all the country's addicts are to be handled by such programs.

4. *More Draconian measures.* This would follow examples set in China, Singapore, and a few other places. It would attack both dealer and user, supply and demand. All would be subject to heavy prison sentences (or the electric chair, if the death-penalty advocates had their way). The user would be considered as guilty as the seller.

Again, those good old Draconian measures make better rhetoric than reality. In New York, the Rockefeller drug law was one such measure. Put into effect in 1973, this was the "nation's toughest" drug legislation: For possession of two ounces of heroin, the minimum sentence was 15 to 25 years in prison; the maximum was life. A repeat conviction for possessing any stimulant or hallucinogen "with intent to sell" sent a felon to jail for one to eight and a half, again with a maximum of life. Probation, alternate sentences, and plea bargaining were forbidden. Yes, a lot of bad guys did go to jail, and by 1975, 91 percent of convicted drug felons were serving maximum prison sentences.

But these measures also helped cause the current crisis. The courts were soon jammed with accused drug felons demanding jury trials. The spending of many additional millions on judges and new courtrooms didn't ease the problem. And it was also now worth killing cops to avoid doing life in Attica. The old mob *did* respond to the new laws. Many of them got out of the smack racket (with the usual exceptions), but that only opened the way for the Cubans and Colombians. Judges began releasing first offenders and low-level dealers for the simple reason that there was no room in our prisons: They were already packed with druggies. And as cops became more cynical about the justice system, corruption became more possible.

New Yorkers are already the most heavily taxed Americans. It's unlikely that they would agree to billions of dollars in additional taxes to pay for another 30 prisons or an additional 500 judges to deal with all the users and pushers in the state. Nor would anybody be happy paying even more for welfare to handle the women and children left behind by the imprisoned druggies.

WHAT IS TO BE DONE?

AFTER WATCHING THE RESULTS OF THE PLAGUE since heroin first came to Brooklyn in the early fifties, after visiting the courtrooms and the morgues, after wandering New York's neighborhoods to see for myself, and after consuming much of the literature on drugs,

I've reluctantly come to a terrible conclusion: The only solution is the complete legalization of these drugs.

I did not originate this idea, of course. In the past year, the mayors of Baltimore, Washington, and Minneapolis have urged that legalization be looked into. Various shapers of public opinion, including such conservatives as William F. Buckley Jr. and Milton Friedman, have done the same. Many have cited articles in such publications as *The Economist, Foreign Policy,* and the British medical journal *The Lancet,* all suggesting that the only solution is legalization.

Legalization doesn't mean endorsement. Cigarettes, liquor, and prescription drugs such as Valium are now legal, though neither government nor society endorses their use. Any citizen can now endanger his health with cigarettes (and 300,000 people die each year from smoking-related illnesses). Or make a mess of his life with whiskey (alcohol abuse costs us more than $100 billion a year). Or take too many Valiums and die. These drugs, however, have become respectable over the years. State banquets are often marked by the drinking of toasts, in which the drug called liquor is offered in honor of the distinguished visitor. Business, politics, and love affairs are often conducted with the lubricant of alcohol. I have no patience anymore for drunks, and I can't abide the company of cokeheads and junkies. But every sensible citizen must recognize that the current system under which some drugs are legal and others are not is hypocritical.

I think a ten-year experiment with legalization is worth the risk. If it doesn't accomplish its goals, legislators could always go back to the present disastrous system. And we might learn that we can live without hypocrisy.

The strongest argument for legalization is economic. We simply don't have the money to deal with eliminating supply or demand. Too many Americans want this stuff, and we are again falling into the trap created by Prohibition: We try to keep people from buying things they want, we cite moral reasons as our motives, and we create a criminal organization that will poison all of our lives for decades. The old mob was the child of Prohibition. A new mob, infinitely more ruthless, is certain to come out of the present crisis. That can be prevented by eliminating the illegal profits that fund and expand the power of the drug gangs.

HOW WOULD LEGALIZATION WORK? A FEW possibilities:
1. Marijuana—not a hard drug, of course, but described as one in the debate—could be the first to be legalized. About 20 million Americans smoke grass on a regular basis and about 400,000 are arrested every year for possession. Mark Kleiman, former director of policy analysis for the Criminal Division of the Justice Department, estimates that legalizing the sale of marijuana would save about $500 million in law-enforcement costs and produce about $7 billion in revenues. Those numbers alone should settle this part of the argument.

Pot could be sold openly in licensed liquor stores all over the country (legalization must be national; if it were limited to New York, every pothead, cokehead, and junkie in the country would soon arrive here). All laws now applicable to selling liquor (used legally by 100 million Americans) would apply to marijuana. Citizens would be arrested for driving under the influence. The weed could not be sold to minors. Advertising would be restricted. All taxes—including those on domestic farmers and importers—would be applied to drug treatment, education, and research for the duration of the ten-year experiment.

2. Heroin could be legalized a year later, dispensed through a network of neighborhood health stations and drugstores. While the old British system of registering addicts was in effect, the number of those receiving daily maintenance doses was low (about 500 in London). In the late sixties, the system was changed. The number of dispensing doctors was reduced nationwide to a few hundred (from thousands), and new registered addicts were required to enter methadone programs. The number of addicts soared. Obviously, the old system was better.

After legalization, this vile drug would be banned from commercial sale. The price would be very low (25 cents a dose), perhaps even free. All current addicts would have to register within six months of the passage of the enabling legislation. They would be supplied with identity cards resembling driver's licenses, showing their faces. They would also be given the opportunity to go drug-free through a greatly expanded system of treatment centers (funded by the marijuana tax and import fees). Their records would be kept confidential, but they would have to register.

Presumably, this would accomplish two things: (1) take the profits out of heroin sales and (2) contain the present addict population. Most junkies support their habits by dealing; they create new addicts to have more customers. There would be no economic point to creating new junkies. The street junkie also would gain relief from the degrading process of making his day's connection. He would stop stealing from old ladies, his family, and strangers. He would no longer have to risk AIDS infection by sharing works.

The mechanics would be difficult; some junkies need five or six doses a day, and if you hand them the supply all at once, they are likely to sell some of it to others. The cost of six separate needles a day for 200,000 junkies would be very high. New junkies would be a different problem. Certainly, there would be a continuing, if diminished, supply of young addicts, for a variety of reasons. Some would get heroin from family members who are junkies, the way young alcoholics have been known to raid the family liquor cabinet. There will always be sick old junkies ready to corrupt the young and others who may want to spread their personal misery to as many as possible. But new junkies would be able to enter the system only by telling the authorities how they got turned on. And this would be a point where one of those good old

Draconian measures would be useful. Part of the law could mandate life sentences for anyone who created a new junkie.

3. Cocaine could be legalized soon after heroin and sold in its conventional forms through liquor stores. The same regulations that govern the sale and use of liquor and marijuana would apply. The drug barons of the world could then go legitimate. The drug-user would have a regulated supply of cocaine that was not cut with Ajax or speed. He would pay a variety of prices depending on quality, as the drinker does for various wines, liquors, and champagnes. Even the crack-users, at the bottom of the social scale of coke-users, would be able to buy cocaine legally, thus putting the hoodlums out of business. If the customers wanted to go home, then, and cook up some crack in a microwave (all they would need is cocaine hydrochloride, baking soda, and water or ammonia), they could do so. If they then sold it to kids, they would end up doing life.

I SAY ALL OF THIS WITH ENORMOUS RELUCTANCE. I hate the idea of living in a country that is drowning in drugs. I know that if drugs were freely available, some of the most damaged people in society could fall into degradation, as many of the poor have across the years in countries where alcohol is legal. There would be casualties everywhere, and the big-city ghettos might suffer terribly (although the assumption that blacks and Hispanics automatically would fall into addiction faster than others is a kind of racism). I know that it would be strange to travel around the world and be an automatic drug suspect, my luggage searched, my body frisked, a citizen of a drug country. Alas, while researching this article, I realized that I live in that country now.

There are good and decent arguments against legalization that go beyond the minor problems of embarrassment and humiliation. The most obvious is that the number of addicts might increase dramatically as legalization and easy access tempted millions of citizens to experiment. History suggests that this is likely to happen, at least for a while. One study shows that the number of drinkers in this country increased by more than 60 percent after the end of Prohibition, returning to the level reached before the noble experiment. Forty years after the British drug-dealers won the Opium War, the number of opium addicts in China had risen to 90 million. In laboratory experiments with cocaine, animals keep taking larger and larger amounts of the drug, until they die. Dr. Frank H. Gawin, director of stimulant abuse, treatment, and research at Yale University, said recently, "I would be terrified to live in a cocaine-legalized society."

Another objection is that nobody knows whether legalization would work—and if it drastically increased the number of addicts over a ten-year period, reversing the process might be impossible. So I'm not suggesting that legalization would transform this violent city into Pericles' Athens. But all of us know that the present system doesn't work. And if the tax revenues from sales of legal drugs could fund real treatment programs, if we treated drug addiction the way we treat alcoholism (as a health problem instead of a crime problem), if education more powerfully stressed that all drug abuse is the pastime of idiots, an experiment with legalization might be worth the attendant risks.

Some of those risks could be covered by specific proposals in the new laws. Congress could insist, for example, that all law-enforcement money freed by legalization be used to attack the deeper problems of poverty, housing, family disintegration, and illiteracy, which make life in the ghettos so hopeless and drugs so tempting. With any luck, we then might see the number of drug-users decline as more citizens realized drugs' heavy costs and as the young realized that it

FACING UP TO DRUGS

A ten-year experiment with legalization is worth the risk. We might learn that we can live without hypocrisy.

isn't very hip to make yourself stupid. Certainly, as the huge illicit profits vanished, the level of urban violence would be swiftly reduced.

The police who have been diverted to the drug wars could be employed against more terrible crimes. The strain on the courts and prisons would ease, leading to a criminal-justice system that guarantees more thoughtful prosecutions, fairer trials, and certain punishment for malefactors.

Legalization wouldn't be a license to go wild. Drug use would continue to be regulated, perhaps in a tougher way, with heavy penalties for doctors, nurses, pilots, train engineers, and others who have heavy social responsibilities. The Armed Forces could continue to forbid the use of drugs. Employers could insist that they don't want drug-users

working for them any more than they want drunks. There would be sad and tragic examples of people fallen into the gutter, as there have always been with alcohol. A few hustlers would work the margins of the legal-drug business, trying to avoid taxes and duties. But we would rid ourselves of a lot of hypocrisy. We would be forced to face some truths about ourselves, deprived at last of the comforting figures of those foreign ogres who are supposed to be corrupting all these poor innocent Americans.

Perhaps, along the way, we might even discover why so many millions of Americans insist on spending their days and nights in a state of self-induced mental impairment. Perhaps. For now, we just have to discover a way to get home alive.

Against the Legalization of Drugs

James Q. Wilson

JAMES Q. WILSON, Collins Professor of Management and Public Policy at UCLA, is the author of *Thinking About Crime* and co-author (with Richard Herrnstein) of *Crime and Human Nature*. His latest book is *Bureaucracy,* published by Basic Books.

IN 1972, the President appointed me chairman of the National Advisory Council for Drug Abuse Prevention. Created by Congress, the Council was charged with providing guidance on how best to coordinate the national war on drugs. (Yes, we called it a war then, too.) In those days, the drug we were chiefly concerned with was heroin. When I took office, heroin use had been increasing dramatically. Everybody was worried that this increase would continue. Such phrases as "heroin epidemic" were commonplace.

That same year, the eminent economist Milton Friedman published an essay in *Newsweek* in which he called for legalizing heroin. His argument was on two grounds: as a matter of ethics, the government has no right to tell people not to use heroin (or to drink or to commit suicide); as a matter of economics, the prohibition of drug use imposes costs on society that far exceed the benefits. Others, such as the psychoanalyst Thomas Szasz, made the same argument.

We did not take Friedman's advice. (Government commissions rarely do.) I do not recall that we even discussed legalizing heroin, though we did discuss (but did not take action on) legalizing a drug, cocaine, that many people then argued was benign. Our marching orders were to figure out how to win the war on heroin, not to run up the white flag of surrender.

That was 1972. Today, we have the same number of heroin addicts that we had then—half a million, give or take a few thousand. Having that many heroin addicts is no trivial matter; these people deserve our attention. But not having had an increase in that number for over fifteen years is also something that deserves our attention. What happened to the "heroin epidemic" that many people once thought would overwhelm us?

The facts are clear: a more or less stable pool of heroin addicts has been getting older, with relatively few new recruits. In 1976 the average age of heroin users who appeared in hospital emer-

gency rooms was about twenty-seven; ten years later it was thirty-two. More than two-thirds of all heroin users appearing in emergency rooms are now over the age of thirty. Back in the early 1970's, when heroin got onto the national political agenda, the typical heroin addict was much younger, often a teenager. Household surveys show the same thing—the rate of opiate use (which includes heroin) has been flat for the better part of two decades. More fine-grained studies of inner-city neighborhoods confirm this. John Boyle and Ann Brunswick found that the percentage of young blacks in Harlem who used heroin fell from 8 percent in 1970-71 to about 3 percent in 1975-76.

Why did heroin lose its appeal for young people? When the young blacks in Harlem were asked why they stopped, more than half mentioned "trouble with the law" or "high cost" (and high cost is, of course, directly the result of law enforcement). Two-thirds said that heroin hurt their health; nearly all said they had had a bad experience with it. We need not rely, however, simply on what they said. In New York City in 1973-75, the street price of heroin rose dramatically and its purity sharply declined, probably as a result of the heroin shortage caused by the success of the Turkish government in reducing the supply of opium base and of the French government in closing down heroin-processing laboratories located in and around Marseilles. These were short-lived gains for, just as Friedman predicted, alternative sources of supply—mostly in Mexico—quickly emerged. But the three-year heroin shortage interrupted the easy recruitment of new users.

Health and related problems were no doubt part of the reason for the reduced flow of recruits. Over the preceding years, Harlem youth had watched as more and more heroin users died of overdoses, were poisoned by adulterated doses, or acquired hepatitis from dirty needles. The word got around: heroin can kill you. By 1974 new hepatitis cases and drug-overdose deaths had dropped to a fraction of what they had been in 1970.

Alas, treatment did not seem to explain much of the cessation in drug use. Treatment programs can and do help heroin addicts, but treatment did not explain the drop in the number of *new* users

From *Commentary*, February 1990, pp. 21-28. Copyright © 1990 by James Q. Wilson. Reprinted by permission of *Commentary* and the author.

(who by definition had never been in treatment) nor even much of the reduction in the number of experienced users.

No one knows how much of the decline to attribute to personal observation as opposed to high prices or reduced supply. But other evidence suggests strongly that price and supply played a large role. In 1972 the National Advisory Council was especially worried by the prospect that U.S. servicemen returning to this country from Vietnam would bring their heroin habits with them. Fortunately, a brilliant study by Lee Robins of Washington University in St. Louis put that fear to rest. She measured drug use of Vietnam veterans shortly after they had returned home. Though many had used heroin regularly while in Southeast Asia, most gave up the habit when back in the United States. The reason: here, heroin was less available and sanctions on its use were more pronounced. Of course, if a veteran had been willing to pay enough—which might have meant traveling to another city and would certainly have meant making an illegal contact with a disreputable dealer in a threatening neighborhood in order to acquire a (possibly) dangerous dose—he could have sustained his drug habit. Most veterans were unwilling to pay this price, and so their drug use declined or disappeared.

Reliving the Past

Suppose we had taken Friedman's advice in 1972. What would have happened? We cannot be entirely certain, but at a minimum we would have placed the young heroin addicts (and, above all, the prospective addicts) in a very different position from the one in which they actually found themselves. Heroin would have been legal. Its price would have been reduced by 95 percent (minus whatever we chose to recover in taxes.) Now that it could be sold by the same people who make aspirin, its quality would have been assured—no poisons, no adulterants. Sterile hypodermic needles would have been readily available at the neighborhood drugstore, probably at the same counter where the heroin was sold. No need to travel to big cities or unfamiliar neighborhoods—heroin could have been purchased anywhere, perhaps by mail order.

There would no longer have been any financial or medical reason to avoid heroin use. Anybody could have afforded it. We might have tried to prevent children from buying it, but as we have learned from our efforts to prevent minors from buying alcohol and tobacco, young people have a way of penetrating markets theoretically reserved for adults. Returning Vietnam veterans would have discovered that Omaha and Raleigh had been converted into the pharmaceutical equivalent of Saigon.

Under these circumstances, can we doubt for a moment that heroin use would have grown ex-

ponentially? Or that a vastly larger supply of new users would have been recruited? Professor Friedman is a Nobel Prize-winning economist whose understanding of market forces is profound. What did he think would happen to consumption under his legalized regime? Here are his words: "Legalizing drugs might increase the number of addicts, but it is not clear that it would. Forbidden fruit is attractive, particularly to the young."

Really? I suppose that we should expect no increase in Porsche sales if we cut the price by 95 percent, no increase in whiskey sales if we cut the price by a comparable amount—because young people only want fast cars and strong liquor when they are "forbidden." Perhaps Friedman's uncharacteristic lapse from the obvious implications of price theory can be explained by a misunderstanding of how drug users are recruited. In his 1972 essay he said that "drug addicts are deliberately made by pushers, who give likely prospects their first few doses free." If drugs were legal it would not pay anybody to produce addicts, because everybody would buy from the cheapest source. But as every drug expert knows, pushers do not produce addicts. Friends or acquaintances do. In fact, pushers are usually reluctant to deal with non-users because a non-user could be an undercover cop. Drug use spreads in the same way any fad or fashion spreads: somebody who is already a user urges his friends to try, or simply shows already-eager friends how to do it.

But we need not rely on speculation, however plausible, that lowered prices and more abundant supplies would have increased heroin usage. Great Britain once followed such a policy and with almost exactly those results. Until the mid-1960's, British physicians were allowed to prescribe heroin to certain classes of addicts. (Possessing these drugs without a doctor's prescription remained a criminal offense.) For many years this policy worked well enough because the addict patients were typically middle-class people who had become dependent on opiate painkillers while undergoing hospital treatment. There was no drug culture. The British system worked for many years, not because it prevented drug abuse, but because there was no problem of drug abuse that would test the system.

All that changed in the 1960's. A few unscrupulous doctors began passing out heroin in wholesale amounts. One doctor prescribed almost 600,000 heroin tablets—that is, over thirteen pounds—in just one year. A youthful drug culture emerged with a demand for drugs far different from that of the older addicts. As a result, the British government required doctors to refer users to government-run clinics to receive their heroin.

But the shift to clinics did not curtail the growth in heroin use. Throughout the 1960's the number of addicts increased—the late John Kaplan of Stanford estimated by fivefold—in part as a result of the diversion of heroin from clinic patients to new users on the streets. An addict would bargain with the clinic doctor over how big a dose he would receive. The patient wanted as much as he could get, the doctor wanted to give as little as was needed. The patient had an advantage in this conflict because the doctor could not be certain how much was really needed. Many patients would use some of their "maintenance" dose and sell the remaining part to friends, thereby recruiting new addicts. As the clinics learned of this, they began to shift their treatment away from heroin and toward methadone, an addictive drug that, when taken orally, does not produce a "high" but will block the withdrawal pains associated with heroin abstinence.

Whether what happened in England in the 1960's was a mini-epidemic or an epidemic depends on whether one looks at numbers or at rates of change. Compared to the United States, the numbers were small. In 1960 there were 68 heroin addicts known to the British government; by 1968 there were 2,000 in treatment and many more who refused treatment. (They would refuse in part because they did not want to get methadone at a clinic if they could get heroin on the street.) Richard Hartnoll estimates that the actual number of addicts in England is five times the number officially registered. At a minimum, the number of British addicts increased by thirtyfold in ten years; the actual increase may have been much larger.

In the early 1980's the numbers began to rise again, and this time nobody doubted that a real epidemic was at hand. The increase was estimated to be 40 percent a year. By 1982 there were thought to be 20,000 heroin users in London alone. Geoffrey Pearson reports that many cities—Glasgow, Liverpool, Manchester, and Sheffield among them—were now experiencing a drug problem that once had been largely confined to London. The problem, again, was supply. The country was being flooded with cheap, high-quality heroin, first from Iran and then from Southeast Asia.

The United States began the 1960's with a much larger number of heroin addicts and probably a bigger at-risk population than was the case in Great Britain. Even though it would be foolhardy to suppose that the British system, if installed here, would have worked the same way or with the same results, it would be equally foolhardy to suppose that a combination of heroin available from leaky clinics and from street dealers who faced only minimal law-enforcement risks would not have produced a much greater increase in heroin use than we actually experienced. My guess is that if we had allowed either doctors or clinics to prescribe heroin, we would have had far worse results than were produced in Britain, if for no other reason than the vastly larger number of addicts with which we began. We would have had

to find some way to police thousands (not scores) of physicians and hundreds (not dozens) of clinics. If the British civil service found it difficult to keep heroin in the hands of addicts and out of the hands of recruits when it was dealing with a few hundred people, how well would the American civil service have accomplished the same tasks when dealing with tens of thousands of people?

Back to the Future

Now cocaine, especially in its potent form, crack, is the focus of attention. Now as in 1972 the government is trying to reduce its use. Now as then some people are advocating legalization. Is there any more reason to yield to those arguments today than there was almost two decades ago?*

I think not. If we had yielded in 1972 we almost certainly would have had today a permanent population of several million, not several hundred thousand, heroin addicts. If we yield now we will have a far more serious problem with cocaine.

Crack is worse than heroin by almost any measure. Heroin produces a pleasant drowsiness and, if hygienically administered, has only the physical side effects of constipation and sexual impotence. Regular heroin use incapacitates many users, especially poor ones, for any productive work or social responsibility. They will sit nodding on a street corner, helpless but at least harmless. By contrast, regular cocaine use leaves the user neither helpless nor harmless. When smoked (as with crack) or injected, cocaine produces instant, intense, and short-lived euphoria. The experience generates a powerful desire to repeat it. If the drug is readily available, repeat use will occur. Those people who progress to "bingeing" on cocaine become devoted to the drug and its effects to the exclusion of almost all other considerations—job, family, children, sleep, food, even sex. Dr. Frank Gawin at Yale and Dr. Everett Ellinwood at Duke report that a substantial percentage of all high-dose, binge users become uninhibited, impulsive, hypersexual, compulsive, irritable, and hyperactive. Their moods vacillate dramatically, leading at times to violence and homicide.

Women are much more likely to use crack than heroin, and if they are pregnant, the effects on their babies are tragic. Douglas Besharov, who has been following the effects of drugs on infants for twenty years, writes that nothing he learned about heroin prepared him for the devastation of cocaine. Cocaine harms the fetus and can lead to physical deformities or neurological damage.

---

* I do not here take up the question of marijuana. For a variety of reasons—its widespread use and its lesser tendency to addict—it presents a different problem from cocaine or heroin. For a penetrating analysis, see Mark Kleiman, *Marijuana: Costs of Abuse, Costs of Control* (Greenwood Press, 217 pp., $37.95).

Some crack babies have for all practical purposes suffered a disabling stroke while still in the womb. The long-term consequences of this brain damage are lowered cognitive ability and the onset of mood disorders. Besharov estimates that about 30,000 to 50,000 such babies are born every year, about 7,000 in New York City alone. There may be ways to treat such infants, but from everything we now know the treatment will be long, difficult, and expensive. Worse, the mothers who are most likely to produce crack babies are precisely the ones who, because of poverty or temperament, are least able and willing to obtain such treatment. In fact, anecdotal evidence suggests that crack mothers are likely to abuse their infants.

The notion that abusing drugs such as cocaine is a "victimless crime" is not only absurd but dangerous. Even ignoring the fetal drug syndrome, crack-dependent people are, like heroin addicts, individuals who regularly victimize their children by neglect, their spouses by improvidence, their employers by lethargy, and their co-workers by carelessness. Society is not and could never be a collection of autonomous individuals. We all have a stake in ensuring that each of us displays a minimal level of dignity, responsibility, and empathy. We cannot, of course, coerce people into goodness, but we can and should insist that some standards must be met if society itself—on which the very existence of the human personality depends—is to persist. Drawing the line that defines those standards is difficult and contentious, but if crack and heroin use do not fall below it, what does?

The advocates of legalization will respond by suggesting that my picture is overdrawn. Ethan Nadelmann of Princeton argues that the risk of legalization is less than most people suppose. Over 20 million Americans between the ages of eighteen and twenty-five have tried cocaine (according to a government survey), but only a quarter million use it daily. From this Nadelmann concludes that at most 3 percent of all young people who try cocaine develop a problem with it. The implication is clear: make the drug legal and we only have to worry about 3 percent of our youth.

The implication rests on a logical fallacy and a factual error. The fallacy is this: the percentage of occasional cocaine users who become binge users *when the drug is illegal* (and thus expensive and hard to find) tells us nothing about the percentage who will become dependent when the drug is legal (and thus cheap and abundant). Drs. Gawin and Ellinwood report, in common with several other researchers, that controlled or occasional use of cocaine changes to compulsive and frequent use "when access to the drug increases" or when the user switches from snorting to smoking. More cocaine more potently administered alters, perhaps sharply, the proportion of "controlled" users who become heavy users.

The factual error is this: the federal survey Nadelmann quotes was done in 1985, *before* crack had become common. Thus the probability of becoming dependent on cocaine was derived from the responses of users who snorted the drug. The speed and potency of cocaine's action increases dramatically when it is smoked. We do not yet know how greatly the advent of crack increases the risk of dependency, but all the clinical evidence suggests that the increase is likely to be large.

It is possible that some people will not become heavy users even when the drug is readily available in its most potent form. So far there are no scientific grounds for predicting who will and who will not become dependent. Neither socioeconomic background nor personality traits differentiate between casual and intensive users. Thus, the only way to settle the question of who is correct about the effect of easy availability on drug use, Nadelmann or Gawin and Ellinwood, is to try it and see. But that social experiment is so risky as to be no experiment at all, for if cocaine is legalized and if the rate of its abusive use increases dramatically, there is no way to put the genie back in the bottle, and it is not a kindly genie.

Have We Lost?

MANY people who agree that there are risks in legalizing cocaine or heroin still favor it because, they think, we have lost the war on drugs. "Nothing we have done has worked" and the current federal policy is just "more of the same." Whatever the costs of greater drug use, surely they would be less than the costs of our present, failed efforts.

That is exactly what I was told in 1972—and heroin is not quite as bad a drug as cocaine. We did not surrender and we did not lose. We did not win, either. What the nation accomplished then was what most efforts to save people from themselves accomplish: the problem was contained and the number of victims minimized, all at a considerable cost in law enforcement and increased crime. Was the cost worth it? I think so, but others may disagree. What are the lives of would-be addicts worth? I recall some people saying to me then, "Let them kill themselves." I was appalled. Happily, such views did not prevail.

Have we lost today? Not at all. High-rate cocaine use is not commonplace. The National Institute of Drug Abuse (NIDA) reports that less than 5 percent of high-school seniors used cocaine within the last thirty days. Of course this survey misses young people who have dropped out of school and miscounts those who lie on the questionnaire, but even if we inflate the NIDA estimate by some plausible percentage, it is still not much above 5 percent. Medical examiners reported in 1987 that about 1,500 died from cocaine use;

hospital emergency rooms reported about 30,000 admissions related to cocaine abuse.

These are not small numbers, but neither are they evidence of a nationwide plague that threatens to engulf us all. Moreover, cities vary greatly in the proportion of people who are involved with cocaine. To get city-level data we need to turn to drug tests carried out on arrested persons, who obviously are more likely to be drug users than the average citizen. The National Institute of Justice, through its Drug Use Forecasting (DUF) project, collects urinalysis data on arrestees in 22 cities. As we have already seen, opiate (chiefly heroin) use has been flat or declining in most of these cities over the last decade. Cocaine use has gone up sharply, but with great variation among cities. New York, Philadelphia, and Washington, D.C., all report that two-thirds or more of their arrestees tested positive for cocaine, but in Portland, San Antonio, and Indianapolis the percentage was one-third or less.

In some neighborhoods, of course, matters have reached crisis proportions. Gangs control the streets, shootings terrorize residents, and drug-dealing occurs in plain view. The police seem barely able to contain matters. But in these neighborhoods—unlike at Palo Alto cocktail parties—the people are not calling for legalization, they are calling for help. And often not much help has come. Many cities are willing to do almost anything about the drug problem except spend more money on it. The federal government cannot change that; only local voters and politicians can. It is not clear that they will.

It took about ten years to contain heroin. We have had experience with crack for only about three or four years. Each year we spend perhaps $11 billion on law enforcement (and some of that goes to deal with marijuana) and perhaps $2 billion on treatment. Large sums, but not sums that should lead anyone to say, "We just can't afford this any more."

The illegality of drugs increases crime, partly because some users turn to crime to pay for their habits, partly because some users are stimulated by certain drugs (such as crack or PCP) to act more violently or ruthlessly than they otherwise would, and partly because criminal organizations seeking to control drug supplies use force to manage their markets. These also are serious costs, but no one knows how much they would be reduced if drugs were legalized. Addicts would no longer steal to pay black-market prices for drugs, a real gain. But some, perhaps a great deal, of that gain would be offset by the great increase in the number of addicts. These people, nodding on heroin or living in the delusion-ridden high of cocaine, would hardly be ideal employees. Many would steal simply to support themselves, since snatch-and-grab, opportunistic crime can be managed even by people unable to hold a regular job or plan an elaborate crime. Those British addicts who get their supplies from government clinics are not models of law-abiding decency. Most are in crime, and though their per-capita rate of criminality may be lower thanks to the cheapness of their drugs, the total volume of crime they produce may be quite large. Of course, society could decide to support all unemployable addicts on welfare, but that would mean that gains from lowered rates of crime would have to be offset by large increases in welfare budgets.

Proponents of legalization claim that the costs of having more addicts around would be largely if not entirely offset by having more money available with which to treat and care for them. The money would come from taxes levied on the sale of heroin and cocaine.

To obtain this fiscal dividend, however, legalization's supporters must first solve an economic dilemma. If they want to raise a lot of money to pay for welfare and treatment, the tax rate on the drugs will have to be quite high. Even if they themselves do not want a high rate, the politicians' love of "sin taxes" would probably guarantee that it would be high anyway. But the higher the tax, the higher the price of the drug, and the higher the price the greater the likelihood that addicts will turn to crime to find the money for it and that criminal organizations will be formed to sell tax-free drugs at below-market rates. If we managed to keep taxes (and thus prices) low, we would get that much less money to pay for welfare and treatment and more people could afford to become addicts. There may be an optimal tax rate for drugs that maximizes revenue while minimizing crime, bootlegging, and the recruitment of new addicts, but our experience with alcohol does not suggest that we know how to find it.

The Benefits of Illegality

THE advocates of legalization find nothing to be said in favor of the current system except, possibly, that it keeps the number of addicts smaller than it would otherwise be. In fact, the benefits are more substantial than that.

First, treatment. All the talk about providing "treatment on demand" implies that there is a demand for treatment. That is not quite right. There are some drug-dependent people who genuinely want treatment and will remain in it if offered; they should receive it. But there are far more who want only short-term help after a bad crash; once stabilized and bathed, they are back on the street again, hustling. And even many of the addicts who enroll in a program honestly wanting help drop out after a short while when they discover that help takes time and commitment. Drug-dependent people have very short time horizons and a weak capacity for commitment. These two groups—those looking for a quick fix and those unable to stick with a long-term fix—

are not easily helped. Even if we increase the number of treatment slots—as we should—we would have to do something to make treatment more effective.

One thing that can often make it more effective is compulsion. Douglas Anglin of UCLA, in common with many other researchers, has found that the longer one stays in a treatment program, the better the chances of a reduction in drug dependency. But he, again like most other researchers, has found that drop-out rates are high. He has also found, however, that patients who enter treatment under legal compulsion stay in the program longer than those not subject to such pressure. His research on the California civil-commitment program, for example, found that heroin users involved with its required drug-testing program had over the long term a lower rate of heroin use than similar addicts who were free of such constraints. If for many addicts compulsion is a useful component of treatment, it is not clear how compulsion could be achieved in a society in which purchasing, possessing, and using the drug were legal. It could be managed, I suppose, but I would not want to have to answer the challenge from the American Civil Liberties Union that it is wrong to compel a person to undergo treatment for consuming a legal commodity.

Next, education. We are now investing substantially in drug-education programs in the schools. Though we do not yet know for certain what will work, there are some promising leads. But I wonder how credible such programs would be if they were aimed at dissuading children from doing something perfectly legal. We could, of course, treat drug education like smoking education: inhaling crack and inhaling tobacco are both legal, but you should not do it because it is bad for you. That tobacco is bad for you is easily shown; the Surgeon General has seen to that. But what do we say about crack? It is pleasurable, but devoting yourself to so much pleasure is not a good idea (though perfectly legal)? Unlike tobacco, cocaine will not give you cancer or emphysema, but it will lead you to neglect your duties to family, job, and neighborhood? Everybody is doing cocaine, but you should not?

Again, it might be possible under a legalized regime to have effective drug-prevention programs, but their effectiveness would depend heavily, I think, on first having decided that cocaine use, like tobacco use, is purely a matter of practical consequences; no fundamental moral significance attaches to either. But if we believe—as I do—that dependency on certain mind-altering drugs *is* a moral issue and that their illegality rests in part on their immorality, then legalizing them undercuts, if it does not eliminate altogether, the moral message.

That message is at the root of the distinction we now make between nicotine and cocaine. Both

are highly addictive; both have harmful physical effects. But we treat the two drugs differently, not simply because nicotine is so widely used as to be beyond the reach of effective prohibition, but because its use does not destroy the user's essential humanity. Tobacco shortens one's life, cocaine debases it. Nicotine alters one's habits, cocaine alters one's soul. The heavy use of crack, unlike the heavy use of tobacco, corrodes those natural sentiments of sympathy and duty that constitute our human nature and make possible our social life. To say, as does Nadelmann, that distinguishing morally between tobacco and cocaine is "little more than a transient prejudice" is close to saying that morality itself is but a prejudice.

The Alcohol Problem

Now we have arrived where many arguments about legalizing drugs begin: is there any reason to treat heroin and cocaine differently from the way we treat alcohol?

There is no easy answer to that question because, as with so many human problems, one cannot decide simply on the basis either of moral principles or of individual consequences; one has to temper any policy by a common-sense judgment of what is possible. Alcohol, like heroin, cocaine, PCP, and marijuana, is a drug—that is, a mood-altering substance—and consumed to excess it certainly has harmful consequences: auto accidents, barroom fights, bedroom shootings. It is also, for some people, addictive. We cannot confidently compare the addictive powers of these drugs, but the best evidence suggests that crack and heroin are much more addictive than alcohol.

Many people, Nadelmann included, argue that since the health and financial costs of alcohol abuse are so much higher than those of cocaine or heroin abuse, it is hypocritical folly to devote our efforts to preventing cocaine or drug use. But as Mark Kleiman of Harvard has pointed out, this comparison is quite misleading. What Nadelmann is doing is showing that a *legalized* drug (alcohol) produces greater social harm than *illegal* ones (cocaine and heroin). But of course. Suppose that in the 1920's we had made heroin and cocaine legal and alcohol illegal. Can anyone doubt that Nadelmann would now be writing that it is folly to continue our ban on alcohol because cocaine and heroin are so much more harmful?

And let there be no doubt about it—widespread heroin and cocaine use are associated with all manner of ills. Thomas Bewley found that the mortality rate of British heroin addicts in 1968 was 28 times as high as the death rate of the same age group of non-addicts, even though in England at the time an addict could obtain free or low-cost heroin and clean needles from British clinics. Perform the following mental experiment: suppose we legalized heroin and cocaine in this country. In what proportion of auto fatalities would the state police report that the driver was nodding off on heroin or recklessly driving on a coke high? In what proportion of spouse-assault and child-abuse cases would the local police report that crack was involved? In what proportion of industrial accidents would safety investigators report that the forklift or drill-press operator was in a drug-induced stupor or frenzy? We do not know exactly what the proportion would be, but anyone who asserts that it would not be much higher than it is now would have to believe that these drugs have little appeal except when they are illegal. And that is nonsense.

An advocate of legalization might concede that social harm—perhaps harm equivalent to that already produced by alcohol—would follow from making cocaine and heroin generally available. But at least, he might add, we would have the problem "out in the open" where it could be treated as a matter of "public health." That is well and good, *if* we knew how to treat—that is, cure—heroin and cocaine abuse. But we do not know how to do it for all the people who would need such help. We are having only limited success in coping with chronic alcoholics. Addictive behavior is immensely difficult to change, and the best methods for changing it—living in drug-free therapeutic communities, becoming faithful members of Alcoholics Anonymous or Narcotics Anonymous—require great personal commitment, a quality that is, alas, in short supply among the very persons—young people, disadvantaged people—who are often most at risk for addiction.

Suppose that today we had, not 15 million alcohol abusers, but half a million. Suppose that we already knew what we have learned from our long experience with the widespread use of alcohol. Would we make whiskey legal? I do not know, but I suspect there would be a lively debate. The Surgeon General would remind us of the risks alcohol poses to pregnant women. The National Highway Traffic Safety Administration would point to the likelihood of more highway fatalities caused by drunk drivers. The Food and Drug Administration might find that there is a nontrivial increase in cancer associated with alcohol consumption. At the same time the police would report great difficulty in keeping illegal whiskey out of our cities, officers being corrupted by bootleggers, and alcohol addicts often resorting to crime to feed their habit. Libertarians, for their part, would argue that every citizen has a right to drink anything he wishes and that drinking is, in any event, a "victimless crime."

However the debate might turn out, the central fact would be that the problem was still, at that point, a small one. The government cannot legislate away the addictive tendencies in all of us, nor can it remove completely even the most dangerous addictive substances. But it can cope with harms when the harms are still manageable.

Science and Addiction

ONE advantage of containing a problem while it is still containable is that it buys time for science to learn more about it and perhaps to discover a cure. Almost unnoticed in the current debate over legalizing drugs is that basic science has made rapid strides in identifying the underlying neurological processes involved in some forms of addiction. Stimulants such as cocaine and amphetamines alter the way certain brain cells communicate with one another. That alteration is complex and not entirely understood, but in simplified form it involves modifying the way in which a neurotransmitter called dopamine sends signals from one cell to another.

When dopamine crosses the synapse between two cells, it is in effect carrying a message from the first cell to activate the second one. In certain parts of the brain that message is experienced as pleasure. After the message is delivered, the dopamine returns to the first cell. Cocaine apparently blocks this return, or "reuptake," so that the excited cell and others nearby continue to send pleasure messages. When the exaggerated high produced by cocaine-influenced dopamine finally ends, the brain cells may (in ways that are still a matter of dispute) suffer from an extreme lack of dopamine, thereby making the individual unable to experience any pleasure at all. This would explain why cocaine users often feel so depressed after enjoying the drug. Stimulants may also affect the way in which other neurotransmitters, such as serotonin and noradrenaline, operate.

Whatever the exact mechanism may be, once it is identified it becomes possible to use drugs to block either the effect of cocaine or its tendency to produce dependency. There have already been experiments using desipramine, imipramine, bromocriptine, carbamazepine, and other chemicals. There are some promising results.

Tragically, we spend very little on such research, and the agencies funding it have not in the past occupied very influential or visible posts in the federal bureaucracy. If there is one aspect of the "war on drugs" metaphor that I dislike, it is its tendency to focus attention almost exclusively on the troops in the trenches, whether engaged in enforcement or treatment, and away from the research-and-development efforts back on the home front where the war may ultimately be decided.

I believe that the prospects of scientists in controlling addiction will be strongly influenced by the size and character of the problem they face. If the problem is a few hundred thousand chronic, high-dose users of an illegal product, the chances of making a difference at a reasonable cost will be much greater than if the problem is a few million chronic users of legal substances. Once a drug is legal, not only will its use increase but many of those who then use it will prefer the drug to the treatment: they will want the pleasure, whatever the cost to themselves or their families, and they will resist—probably successfully—any effort to wean them away from experiencing the high that comes from inhaling a legal substance.

If I Am Wrong . . .

No one can know what our society would be like if we changed the law to make access to cocaine, heroin, and PCP easier. I believe, for reasons given, that the result would be a sharp increase in use, a more widespread degradation of the human personality, and a greater rate of accidents and violence.

I may be wrong. If I am, then we will needlessly have incurred heavy costs in law enforcement and some forms of criminality. But if I am right, and the legalizers prevail anyway, then we will have consigned millions of people, hundreds of thousands of infants, and hundreds of neighborhoods to a life of oblivion and disease. To the lives and families destroyed by alcohol we will have added countless more destroyed by cocaine, heroin, PCP, and whatever else a basement scientist can invent.

Human character is formed by society; indeed, human character is inconceivable without society, and good character is less likely in a bad society. Will we, in the name of an abstract doctrine of radical individualism, and with the false comfort of suspect predictions, decide to take the chance that somehow individual decency can survive amid a more general level of degradation?

I think not. The American people are too wise for that, whatever the academic essayists and cocktail-party pundits may say. But if Americans today are less wise than I suppose, then Americans at some future time will look back on us now and wonder, what kind of people were they that they could have done such a thing?

The Dutch Model

Eddy Engelsman

The Netherlands is the only country to have decriminalized drugs such as marijuana and hashish, although its punishment for traffickers is severe. Eddy Engelsman is the Dutch drug czar, in charge of drug policy in the ministry of Welfare, Public Health and Cultural Affairs. We talked to him recently about the Dutch model.

In 1982, the Netherlands amended the 1928 Opium Act and gave the new drug policy the name "normalization." Under this policy, drug use, even heroin and cocaine use, is not prohibited by law. Only possession is prohibited.

Drug normalization should not be misinterpreted as a lenient policy. It is, on the contrary, a well-considered and very practical policy that neither hides the drug problems of our society nor allows them to get out of control.

We never use the words "hard" and "soft" drugs in our legislation. Instead, we refer to Schedule One drugs – cocaine, heroin, amphetamines, LSD – as those with an "unacceptable risk." The other schedule refers only to what we call "traditional cannabis products," including marijuana and hashish.

Possession of these drugs, both Schedule One and the cannabis products, is prohibited, but possession of up to 30 grams of the cannabis products is only a misdemeanor – it is punishable by law, but our pragmatic prosecution policy allows for discretion.

Every country has this kind of prioritized drug policy, though probably not as overt as in the Netherlands. Indeed, if one asks a policeman in any American city what he would do, whether he would choose to catch the dealer of one

> Normalization is a well-considered and very practical policy that neither hides the drug problems of Dutch society nor allows them to get out of control.

kilogram of heroin or cocaine, or the dealer of 10 kilograms of marijuana, he would inevitably choose to put his energy into catching the cocaine or heroin dealer. In the Netherlands, this process is just more formalized.

Normalization does not mean everything is legal. If someone traffics in drugs, or if they steal for drugs, they will be punished. In the Netherlands, 30 percent of the prison population is incarcerated for drug-related reasons. In Amsterdam and Rotterdam, the number is 50 percent.

Avoiding A Cure Worse Than Disease | The Dutch drug policy of *de facto* decriminalization of cannabis products has not encouraged more drug use. In fact, the prevalence of cannabis use in the Netherlands is low. In the age bracket between 10 and 18 years, 4.2 percent has ever used cannabis in their lifetime. Among this group, less than two percent are still using occasionally. The number of daily cannabis users appears to be one in 1,000.

The Dutch have been pragmatic and have tried to avoid a situation in which consumers of cannabis products suffer more damage from criminal proceedings than from the use of the drug itself. This same principle accounts for the sale of limited quantities of hashish in youth centers and coffee shops, a policy that aims at separating markets in which hard drugs and soft drugs circulate. According to the Minister of Justice, this policy has succeeded in keeping the sale of hashish out of the realm of hard crime.

Compound Drug-Related Problems | Due to the mind-altering effect of drugs, most governments have tried to discourage their use through law enforcement and health education.

Today, however, we see that in addition to

By Eddy Engelsman. From *New Perspectives Quarterly*, Summer 1989, pp. 44-45. Reprinted by permission.

the mind-altering component of drug use, addicts are also affected by secondary problems – ones that are perhaps more serious than the original medical and social problems caused by addiction.

For the most part, initial medical problems have been compounded by risks of infectious disease, violence and social ostracism – complications that inevitably arise when drugs are pushed into the illegal sphere. On the societal level, additional problems have arisen from an intensified approach toward drug traffickers and the adoption of new, far-reaching legal measures that have led to an increasing corruption of the police, judiciary and government authorities.

These additional consequences – increased criminality and health problems – are the secondary problems, the unintended side-effects of conventional drug policy.

Harm Reduction Policy | The Dutch drug treatment philosophy addresses the socially backward position of most addicts and attempts to focus policy on the primary problems involved in drug abuse. The government encourages forms of treatment that are not intended to end addiction as such, but to improve addicts' physical and social well-being, and to help them function in society.

This kind of assistance may be defined as harm-reduction, or, more traditionally, secondary and tertiary prevention. The effort takes the form of fieldwork in the street, hospitals, jails and open door clinics for prostitutes.

This treatment effort also supplies medically prescribed methadone, material support and social rehabilitation opportunities. In Amsterdam, the conditions for participation in methadone treatment are regular contact with a medical doctor, registration with the methadone clinic, and a prohibition on take-home dosages of methadone.

In spite of the wide availability of medically prescribed methadone, there have never been so many addicts asking for detoxification and drug-free treatment. In Amsterdam, such requests doubled between 1981 and 1986.

The fact that the government has this policy toward addicts who are not able or do not, at least for the time being, want to establish a drug-free lifestyle is indicative of the realistic and pragmatic Dutch approach. It also shows the

The Dutch have been pragmatic and have tried to avoid a situation in which consumers of cannabis products suffer more damage from criminal proceedings than from the use of the drug itself.

determination not to leave drug addicts in the lurch. Failure to provide care of this type would simply increase the risk to the individual and to our society.

The result of Dutch health policy is that it is able to reach a very large segment of the total population of drug addicts. In Amsterdam, about 60-80 percent are being reached by some kind of assistance.

Needle exchange programs have also been instituted, since it is an established fact that many drug users are using intravenously and share needles. The effects of this approach: Only eight percent of the 605 Dutch AIDS patients are intravenous drug users, whereas this figure in Europe generally is 23 percent and is 26 percent in the United States. We have seen no negative side-effects, such as an increasing number of intravenous drug users, nor have we seen reduced interest in drug-free treatment.

Some other data: Reliable estimates on the number of drug addicts in the Netherlands, with a population of 14.5 million, vary between 15,000 and 20,000. Drug use appears to be stabilizing, even decreasing in some cities. Estimates on the number of addicts in Amsterdam, the largest city, vary from 4,000 to 7,000. The prevalence of heroin use in Amsterdam is estimated at 0.4 percent. The use of cocaine has stabilized at 0.6 percent, while crack use is still a virtual rarity. Finally, and perhaps most importantly, between 1981 and 1987 the average age of heroin and cocaine users in Amsterdam rose from 26 to 36 years.

The Dutch drug policy, which is administered by the Minister of Welfare, Health and Cultural Affairs, should not be seen as different from policies toward other areas of our society. Dutch measures for controlling drug abuse can only be understood in the context of history, and, perhaps, geography: The most striking feature of the Netherlands has always been the abundance of water – water that has historically constituted both a threat and a means of livelihood. The Dutch have never conquered the sea, but have succeeded in controlling this enemy. That sort of realistic relationship with the natural world has provided an important stimulus for a realistic and pragmatic approach to life in general for the Dutch, and has now come to typify our national drug policy approach.

Drug Prevention and Treatment

How do we convince nonusers not to become involved with drugs in the first place? How do we get abusers who are involved off drugs—and convince them to stay off drugs? Regardless of the legal question, we are still faced with the twin problems of prevention and treatment.

What is the best way of making sure that young people do not experiment with and become seriously involved with illegal drugs. In the 1980s, the then-First Lady Nancy Reagan's "Just Say No" slogan became the most well-known statement on the drug scene. But did it work? Did the slogan deter many, or any, young people from the path of drug abuse? This issue is still being debated. Ads appear on television and in magazines and local newspapers claiming that one's brain on drugs is roughly the same as an egg frying in a hot skillet. Does this campaign—its truth value aside—actually dissuade youngsters from using drugs? Again, the evidence is not conclusive. Celebrities appear regularly in the media denouncing drug use and urging that young people not try any drug. Again, is this effort effective? And once again, the answer has to be, it is not clear. Nonetheless, the issue of prevention is a much-discussed, hotly debated question.

Once someone does become ensnared in a compulsive, destructive pattern of drug abuse, what is to be done? What works? What treatment is most successful—or successful at all—in getting abusers off drugs—permanently?

Some treatment programs entail the addict living in a community, a *therapeutic community*, for a period of time, usually with strict supervision by ex-addict supervisors, eventually emerging back into society a changed person, purged of the impulses that causes him or her to abuse drugs in the first place. Therapeutic communities are a controversial mode of treatment, since they require a sizeable investment of resources, the "split" rate—addicts leaving the program prematurely, against the advice of the staff, to return to the streets—tends to be very high, and proponents often develop a dogmatic, sectarian attitude toward other treatment modalities. Still, for a minority of drug abusers, the therapeutic community clearly works.

Some experts believe that programs based on the Alcoholics Anonymous (AA) model will work for most, or some, drug abusers. Here, addicts living in the community meet on a regular basis, sharing testimony about their lives with one another. Still other observers believe that drug abusers need to be threatened with a jail or prison term in order to force them into a mandatory treatment program. Others argue that, at least for the long-term, hard-core heroin addict, methadone maintenance is the only viable program. Some insist that the environment in which abusers live—including friends, family, and employment—has to be changed before their drug use can be addressed. Others opt for a multimodality approach; they feel that abusers of each drug or drug type, as well as different kinds of drug abusers, are sufficiently distinct as to require a variety of programs, each tailored to each drug and drug abuser.

Regardless of which approach to drug abuse treatment is correct, three facts remain widely agreed-upon. First, there are not enough spaces in treatment programs to handle all the drug abusers who wish treatment. Second, there are not enough financial resources currently allocated to drug treatment to make a serious dent in the problem of abuse and addiction. And third, not enough is known about the outcome of the various treatment programs that are used to say definitively which one works best, or even which one works best for which type of drug abuser.

Looking Ahead: Challenge Questions

What is the best drug treatment program?

Will an AA-type program work for drug addicts?

Why shouldn't the therapeutic communities work for all addicts?

Does the threat of incarceration work as a way of focusing addicts toward treatment?

Why hasn't the government allocated sufficient resources to drug treatment programs?

Judgment Replaces Fear in Drug Lessons

Joseph Berger
Special to *The New York Times*

KANSAS CITY, Kan.—Once confined to a class session or to reciting horror stories and statistics, drug education in America is undergoing radical changes as the crack epidemic touches the lives of younger children across the country.

Rather than frightening students, as teachers often found themselves trying to do following the drug curriculum of the past, schools are now seeking to help students develop personal traits that make them resist drugs: strengthening their ability to make sound judgments, to handle the stressful times of life, to resist pressure from friends and to resolve confusing signals at home and in the community.

Visits to classrooms from the heart of Brooklyn to the heart of America here indicated that drug classes are now being introduced a great deal earlier than ever before and they are laced through a child's school career.

Preliminary indications are that the newer courses may have a beneficial effect on the students who take them. But critics of drug education programs, old and new, contend that far too little scientific evaluation has been done to know for certain. And they say the Bush Administration's new anti-drug policy does not provide enough money for such research.

In the schools in this area, where stores stock dolls of Dorothy of Kansas innocently skipping through Oz, teachers now give 15 lessons a year coaching sixth, seventh and eighth graders on how to refuse drugs. A skit illustrates how.

In the improvisation by eighth graders, Monica Navarro warned Danita Conway that she would tell their friends that Danita is a wimp for declining marijuana. Danita, using the ploy of "reverse pressure" she has just learned, snapped back that she will tell their friends "your momma still tucks you in at night."

Or, in the crack-ravaged Bushwick neighborhood of Brooklyn, Sharon Fleish-

man may never mention the drug to her kindergarten pupils, but she helps the 5-year-olds understand the importance of caring for their health. In a 20-minute class about prescription drugs that she enlivens with cartoons of an intoxicated raccoon, she tries to convey a simple lifelong lesson: "Only sick people should be taking drugs."

The scare tactics implicit in earlier programs, particularly those of the 60's and early 70's, were based on the notion that stark facts and figures about intoxicating effects and health perils of drugs would speak for themselves and send the message. But the thinking now is that the presentation of simple facts without helping a child deal with them has sometimes had the opposite effect. Particularly among the children of poor neighborhoods, the facts often seemed to make drugs more enticing.

"Children don't learn by scare tactics," said Anne Garfinkel, a drug education teacher in the Gowanus section of Brooklyn. Even experts who say such tactics can be effective for some children acknowledge that other approaches are needed in inner cities.

Paul J. Brounstein, senior research associate at the Urban Institute, said these tactics work best with people who have something to lose. But, he added, "if you're dealing with older, inner-city kids, kids with an experience of failure, with few perceived opportunities, you've got to overcome a major hurdle, which says drugs are an alternative to economic success."

The fact is that most students already know a good deal about the legal and health perils of crack and other drugs. What they often do not know, particularly if they come from chaotic or broken homes, is how to make important personal decisions and how to defend their values, says Ginay Marks, the drug coordinator of School District 15 in southern Brooklyn, which has one of New York's most ambitious programs.

Teachers who lead anti-drug classes are also trying to get across the idea that when

children feel hopeless, as almost everyone does from time to time, there are solutions other than drugs.

Gauging the Success

Positive Indications, But With Cautions

One persuasive study of the effects of drug education, published this year, focused on the Kansas City metropolitan area's experimental Refusal Skills program, the one taken by Danita and Monica. Researchers found that a year after taking the class, 3 percent of the students reported they smoked cigarettes, 4 percent drank alcohol, and 4 percent used marijuana. Figures for the schools where the program was not taught were higher: 13 percent smoked tobacco, 9 percent drank and 7 percent used marijuana.

But Dr. Joel Moskowitz, a research psychologist at the University of California at Berkeley, is quick to caution that schools chosen for the Kansas City experiment were not, strictly speaking, randomly picked. They were selected because their schedules were most flexible. Nevertheless, it turned out that the students given the drug instruction and those who were not were roughly identical in economic and racial backgrounds.

Dr. Moskowitz, who reviews applications for Federal grants for drug programs, notes that other studies that seem to show favorable results are not fully conclusive. They are usually do-neat well-functioning schools for middle-class children, he said. Even when they are conducted at schools with diverse populations, the researchers often lose track of the most troubled students, and these are the ones most likely to use drugs eventually.

"Nationally and locally there are no well-evaluated effective models for 'what works' in prevention and education," said a June report by Interface, a private Manhattan research group.

Still, teachers say they must try something, even if it is based only on their hunches about what will work. "We're the only agency that can make a difference on children," said Cathy L. Sillman, supervisor of drug education for the Kansas City, Kan., schools.

Selecting a Program

A Call for 25 Hours of Class in a Year

About 70 percent of the nation's schoolchildren get at least one class in drug education during their school years, said Zili Amsel, acting director of prevention research for the National Institute of Drug Abuse. But Robert M. Stutman, special agent in charge of the New York office of the Federal Drug Enforcement Administration, said more than 25 hours of classes a year that are led by teachers are needed to bring about "attitudinal changes." Most programs, he said, offer six to eight hours a year, do not start until junior high school and many use outsiders unfamiliar with classic teaching techniques.

School systems battling complaints that students cannot read and write well enough are finding it difficult to pack 25 hours of drug education into a school year. Nevertheless, many have bolstered their programs. After complaints last year from Mayor Edward I. Koch that too few elementary school children were receiving drug instruction, Richard R. Green, then the New York City School Chancellor, mandated that every student receive at least eight hours. The city now spends $34.5 billion a year on drug education.

Increasingly, instruction is starting in kindergarten. Experts have persuaded many parents that because children begin using illegal drugs in elementary school, they need to be alerted early. The average user's initiation age, said Ginay Marks, is 12.6 years old.

Most school systems cannot afford the time to invent their own drug programs, so they have adopted programs tried other places. These programs, complete with tapes, models and manuals, bear catchy titles like "Here's Looking at You, 2000," "Growing Healthy" and "Project Star." Building self-worth and rehearsing strategies to resist pressure from others are part of all the programs, along with a focus on health habits and drug information.

Reaching the Youngest

Drugs' Effects As a Health Matter

"Growing Healthy," sponsored in part by the New York Academy of Medicine, has been adopted by schools in 41 states. It tries to subtly steer children in kindergarten through seventh grade away from drugs, alcohol and tobacco.

Children learn about nutritious foods, brushing their teeth and caring for their eyes. Only occasionally are drugs mentioned. In the fifth grade, students will dissect a calf's lung and inflate the air sacs with straws. This vivid illustration, teachers hope, will buttress lessons about the harms of smoking tobacco and marijuana.

Mr. Fleishman's kindergartners in Brooklyn get a "Growing Healthy" lesson three times a week. Showing cartoons from a book, Ms. Fleishman told them that only parents should be giving them drugs.

Walking a Fine Line

"If you see your brother and sister taking some medicine, what are you going to do?" she asked.

"Call my mother," one boy shouted.

"Throw it in the toilet," another said.

"My cat was playing with it," said 6-year-old Jason Mungen, "and I went to my mommy and she told my brother to put it back in the cabinet."

Such lessons, teachers believe, are essential in a neighborhood like Bushwick where children with drug-addicted mothers are often being reared by grandmothers. Ms. Fleishman recalls that several years ago, when she first mentioned cocaine, a 5-year-old said: "My mother takes that white stuff and puts it up her nose."

"I have to walk a fine line between teaching children not to take drugs and not condemning their parents," said Ms. Fleishman. "I try to explain that sometimes adults do things that aren't good for them."

For Kansas City second graders, who receive 30 lessons a year from the "Here's Looking at You" program, the message is more overt. Seven children in Katie Mathews's class at the M. E. Pearson School arranged themselves like the organs of a human body by standing on chairs of varying heights.

In Exhaustion, a Lesson

Walter Dobbins played the brain, his fingers pecking away in the air like someone at a computer. Mark Reyes was the heart, pumping his arms like someone inflating a bicycle tire. Nicole Rodriguez and Camila Martinez played the lungs, taking deep breaths. Crystal Stafford and Linda Davis were the kidneys, making broomlike motions to sweep away poisons.

First, Mrs. Mathews had these organs go about their jobs at an easy rhythm, just as a healthy body would. Then she asked how they might respond if a drug were injected into this imaginary body. The actors speeded up and giggled. "Don't stop, keep going," Mrs. Mathews urged. When they seemed really fatigued, she let them stop.

"Imagine what would happen to a human body if it never stopped and you just keep putting drugs in and the organs would keep going faster and faster and faster," she gently said.

Middle School Approaches

How 'Just Say No' Can Be Practice

Children in more than 50 middle schools in Kansas City, Kan., and across the Missouri River in Kansas City, Mo., are learning from "Project Star," a 15-lesson program that teaches "resistance skills." It was begun by the local Ewing Marion Kauffman Foundation after disclosures of cocaine use by four Kansas City Royals baseball players.

"A lot of kids want to say no, but they don't know how," said Glenn Schoenfish, principal of the Argentine Middle School, on the Kansas side.

In Sally Welter's physical education class, children talked about ways their friends might entice, threaten or tease them to use drugs. Then, with prodding from Ms. Welter, they figured out ploys to combat the pressure. They decided on these methods: the Cold Shoulder, the Broken Record (constantly repeating refusals), the Good Excuse and Strength in Numbers (allying with friends who will not try drugs).

'O.K. to Be One of a Kind'

At Public School 32 in the drug-ridden Gowanus neighborhood of Brooklyn, Anne Garfinkel, known to her students as "the drug lady," commands the classroom like a conductor, squeezing just the right shadings of meaning from students.

"I'm going to give you a $25 word," she told a sixth-grade class and wrote "unique" on the blackboard. "What does it mean?"

After students ventured some definitions, she had them compose a three-column chart of how the class members were like all other people, like some other people and like no other people.

All people are alike, the students agreed, in needing food, clothing and shelter. Some are alike in tastes, opinions and talents. Nobody is alike in the way they look, their voices, even their fingerprints.

"What have you learned?" Ms. Garfinkel asked.

"It's O.K. to be one of a kind," a boy in the front volunteered.

Ms. Garfinkel smiled.

In older grades, the drug question is addressed more explicitly. But individuality and clear thinking are discussed as well.

Mark Sherman told his class of ninth graders in Sunset Park, Brooklyn, the news story of a 16-year-old Long Island girl whose boyfriend, after drinking several beers, was killed trying to beat a train across the tracks.

"Those people who ran across the railroad track—did they think they were doing to die?" the teacher asked.

He wrote the word "omnipotent" on the board and suggested that the boyfriend might have been thinking: "I'm quick and strong and I've got good reflexes."

Leaving the class, Israel Guzman, a student, said: "It makes you think. If I do this, then this is going to happen. If I don't do this, then this is going to happen."

High School Challenges

An Emphasis On Social Skills

By high school, students are given much more detailed information, but the emphasis remains on social skills.

Gregory Faulkner, an instructor at Phoenix House, a Manhattan drug treatment organization, visits a health class at Washington Irving High School in the Gramercy Park area for a series of three lessons and informs them that the euphoria of crack lasts 20 to 40 minutes and is followed by a long depression. But his main focus is on getting students to talk about what they most value and how drugs may affect those values.

"Can a drug user really say he's valuing his health?" he asked a class.

In an exercise, Reheim Moye, 17, acted the part of a senior class president who is being urged by the vice president, played by Jacqueline Moran, 17, to allow a keg of beer and marijuana on the annual class trip. The class evaluated Reheim's predicament.

"People will lose respect for him if he turns around and does the same thing she wants him to do," said one girl in the front row. But another added: "If you don't do it, you could lose friends."

For the most part, the students gave answers that adults would hope for. Reheim said he found the class valuable. "It puts you in a situation where you have to deal with your emotions."

In Making Drug Strategy, No Accord on Treatment

Andrew H. Malcolm

Even though drug experts cannot agree on how to define "treatment on demand" for addicts, there are widespread complaints that neither President Bush's proposed program nor any existing state approach provides nearly enough capacity to treat drug addicts who want to break the habit.

But how much more treatment, and, indeed, what kind of treatment should be provided are issues that bring no consensus.

Nor is there anything near unanimity over calls for required treatment or civil commitment that would force addicts who do not want treatment to get it. Forcing treatment is now illegal in a majority of states unless the addict has been convicted of a criminal charge.

There does appear to be agreement on the urgent need for a system of local coordination to steer those of the nation's estimated four million addicts who seek treatment into the 5,000 existing treatment centers.

Recent Federal and academic reports and interviews with Federal and state officials and private experts, reveal stark differences between those in hard-hit drug cities like New York who urge large-scale treatment expansion immediately, and others in the Bush Administration who advocate a more measured growth in treatment coupled with more thorough evaluation.

"There's a fire going on right now killing people and our communities," said Dr. Robert G. Newman, president of Beth Israel Medical Center in Manhattan, which runs the country's largest methadone program for heroin addicts. "Sure, I agree we need eval-

uation. But what are we going to do immediately for hundreds of thousands who need help this minute?"

Dr. Herbert Kleber, a Yale University professor who ran his own drug treatment clinic until becoming deputy director in the Bush Administration's Office of National Drug Control Policy last summer, replies: "Unless we improve the treatment system, simply increasing capacity will only increase the speed of the revolving door. We need to increase and improve at the same time."

Actually, no one knows precisely how many American drug addicts exist, there being no standard definition of addiction and no accurate census. Nor does anyone know how many addicts might actually benefit from treatment.

But President Bush's September speech announcing his anti-drug plan used a National Institute on Drug Abuse estimate of four million addicts, based on a 1988 household survey defining serious drug users as those who used drugs at least 200 times in the preceding 12 months.

50 Percent Need Treatment

The President's report estimated that 25 percent of those addicts could stop drug use with support from friends, family and clergy; that another 25 percent were hardcore users unable or unwilling to stop, and that two million users would benefit from well-designed professional treatment.

But there is not enough such treatment to go around. According to Salvatore di Menza, special assistant to

the director of the National Institute on Drug Abuse, statistics for 1987, the latest available, showed 338,365 drug treatment slots in the United States—60 percent in private nonprofit centers, 25 percent state and local, about 11 percent in profit-making centers and approximately 3 percent in Federal centers like Veterans Administration hospitals.

With graduates, dropouts and repeaters, that means there are centers where about 800,000 addicts can undergo treatment each year. That suggests that more than a million addicts want treatment that is not available.

To reduce that gap, the Bush Administration and Congress have agreed to spend nearly $700 million on drug treatment in fiscal 1990. States and local governments plan additional appropriations, and the Senate has approved a measure introduced by Senator Daniel Patrick Moynihan, Democrat of New York, to allow Medicaid to reimburse states for the cost of substance abuse treatment.

House and Senate negotiators proposed 1990 Federal drug treatment spending at a level 77 percent higher than the 1989 figure. But no national plans exist about how to spend the money or how to evaluate the results.

One stumbling block is disagreement over the advisability, affordability or efficiency of treatment on demand, that is, creating enough surplus treatment slots to have beds always available for walk-ins.

New York, which probably has the nation's most serious urban drug problems, is in the forefront of those demanding dramatic, immediate action. "Drug addiction is the greatest threat to our civilization and Government since the Civil War," said Stan Lundine, Lieutenant Governor of New York. "We believe in treatment for every addicted person who asks for help. We will have a very ambitious strategy and move every quickly."

Few centers treat the most urgent need: cocaine addiction.

He said the state soon plans to announce proposals for two massive drug treatment compounds or campuses on state or Federal land, each treating perhaps 1,000 addicts, where a variety of strategies would be implemented and simultaneously evaluated.

Treatment on Demand

Bush Administration officials said treatment on demand implies that somehow there should always be a vacancy available at every center, a system they said would be overwhelmingly expensive and inefficient. It also implies, Dr. Kleber said, "that people should get treatment from behind the same door they happen to knock on. But that treatment may not match their needs best."

The very existence of waiting lists can be an emotional issue. "Busy emergency rooms don't tell the seriously ill to come back another time," said Hector Maldonado, a Beth Israel drug counselor. "So how can we tell addicts looking for help to come back in a few weeks?"

Dr. Newman said that methadone treatment could be rapidly expanded, and that his center's five-month waiting list of 800 patients could be quickly reduced, simply by altering Government regulations to allow staff members to treat more patients.

"It's a scandal," he said. "Waiting lists are grossly understated because many programs are so full they don't even bother keeping a list and addicts, knowing this, don't even bother to apply."

Others disagree. "I'm always suspicious of walk-ins," said Bob Gilhooly, director of substance abuse technical services for the Roanoke Valley Mental Health Services. "I could

use 50 more residential beds tomorrow. But very few walk-ins want residential drug treatment. They're just looking to get detoxed for a couple days and go back out."

"Waiting lists are soft," says Dr. Mitchell S. Rosenthal, head of Phoenix House, which has 1,500 residential patients in New York and California and a 21-day waiting list. You've got one guy on four lists for two weeks and he's not waiting anymore anyway. Addicts by nature call for help one moment, and an hour later they're far away, emotionally or geographically. It's a motivation built on sand."

And even when accepted, many patients quit. Fully half the patients in therapeutic communities drop out. In Phoenix House's 18-month program, for instance, the average stay is only 11 months. "Yes, absolutely, we need more treatment slots," Dr. Rosenthal added. "And we know enough to expand and evaluate at the same time. Treatment on demand? Sure, but we also need demanding treatment, which requires learning another mode of behavior so when life gets tough, they don't mindlessly go off and take drugs again."

Not Enough Cocaine Treatment

A majority of the spaces for drug-addiction treatment in the United States are still designed for treating heroin users, who are now far outnumbered by cocaine addicts.

Cocaine addicts, who typically abuse several substances simultaneously, are treated differently from heroin addicts.

One result is that many of the available treatment slots do not match the addiction needing treatment. On any given day, according to the President's report, 20 percent of total treatment spaces in this country may be empty while many centers have waiting lists months long.

This is why most experts maintain that major metropolitan areas, at least, must get better information and referral services. One example is a drug counseling office in Kansas City, Mo.

Cecile van Thullenar, who is coordinator of the Assessment and Referral Center there, said it receives about a thousand calls a month from addicts seeking help. The center provides initial evaluations and steers addicts toward appropriate treatment; in many

cases, professional services are donated—$1 million worth in the past two years, she said.

Involuntary Programs

In recent years, an individual's decision to seek drug treatment in the United States has generally been voluntary. But that is expected to change as treatment programs expand to meet toughened sanctions. And treatment on demand may come to mean treatment on the demand of someone other than the addict.

Should addicts be able to get treatment upon demand?

"There's going to be a long, hard debate next year about civil commitment," said Dr. Joseph Autry, associate administrator for policy coordination in the Federal Government's Alcohol, Drug Abuse and Mental Health division, the Department of Health and Human Services.

Now courts can mandate drug treatment as part of punishment, although enforcement of treatment for convicts is often lax.

Nineteen states including California already have civil commitment laws, Dr. Autry said. These enable parents, for example, to commit troubled children for mandatory drug treatment. But in other states, including New York, this is illegal before a conviction.

"It's going to be a hot potato," Dr. Rosenthal said. "But the nature of addiction and its denial requires some method of humane coercion."

"There's no doubt," Mr. Lundine agreed, "we are moving toward the reality of coerced treatment. The problem is too serious. And the early evaluation of shock incarceration, for instance, is surprisingly positive."

Mr. di Menza foresees central urban treatment registries and a variety of drug treatment programs evolving in coming years as research shows which work best for which kinds of addicts. Research also continues on chemicals to block cocaine's high, as methadone does for heroin; buprenorphine, for example, has shown some preliminary effectiveness in blocking cocaine craving.

"It may be more satisfying to think mainly of residential programs," Mr. di Menza said, "because the addict is put away somewhere safe. But we're going to need a range of strategies. For many addicts, for instance, it's not rehabilitation; it's habilitation. They don't know how to read or look for work, let alone beat their addiction."

Research has shown, for example, no difference in effectiveness in similar cases between expensive inpatient programs, which can cost $1,000 or more a day, and less expensive outpatient treatment, increasingly popular with insurers, which allow addicts to remain at work while practicing recovery and staying under daily supervision including urine testing.

"Instead of making inpatient the first line of defense," Dr. Arnold Washton said, "let's reserve expensive residential treatment for those addicts with serious psychiatric problems who really need it."

Dr. Washton's New York City institute, which bears his name, handles 450 outpatients a year, charging $4,800 for an 18-week daily course of treatment. "It's no panacea," Dr. Washton said, "but outpatient care is grossly underutilized."

"There's no question," Mr. Lundine added, "that the country, and especially New York, has a colossal drug problem. We need five times the existing 50,000 treatment slots in this state alone. And we're just in the infancy of finding a solution."

GETTING CLEAN:

A NEW GENERATION FIGHTS ADDICTION

Phoebe Hoban

"You know that ad 'The Night Belongs to Michelob'?" asks Marissa,* a 21-year-old gamine in a chartreuse sweater, torn jeans, and cowboy boots. "All my nights used to be like that." She stops in front of a liquor-store window plastered with holiday displays about love, cheer, and tradition—amorous, glamorous couples toasting; neighbors swapping scotch. "It's everywhere. And the message is that drinking is fun, sexy, romantic."

I met Marissa in front of St. Monica's church on East 79th Street one Sunday before Christmas, when everyone else was out shopping. She and her "sponsor," a vivacious blonde named Tracy, were emerging from an Alcoholics Anonymous meeting in the basement. The 79th Street Workshop is one of the most popular meetings in the city. More than 100 well-heeled people congregate here on weekends at 12:30, and many of them are very young. According to a 1986 AA survey, 21 percent of AA members are under 30; 38 percent are also addicted to drugs.

Marissa and Tracy, 26, used to be party girls. They were good-looking and had money. They both had divorced parents, went to private schools, and were using drugs and alcohol by the time they were twelve years old. By the time they were sixteen, their lives revolved around getting high and going to clubs. Marissa drank, did coke, and free-based; Tracy free-based and did speedballs. She hung out with a group of artists and actors, including the late John Belushi. Her boyfriend was a doctor/dealer who eventually went to prison. She bounced checks, stole money from her boss, and ran up $50,000 in debts.

Now the nights at Area, Save the Robots, The World, and Nell's are over. Marissa and Tracy don't go to clubs much anymore. They go to meetings—Alcoholics Anonymous meetings, Narcotics Anonymous meetings, Cocaine Anonymous meetings. And so do most of their friends. "There are so many people in recovery," says Tracy, "there's a joke that when Dalton has its next class reunion, it's going to be at Haselden."

But they're not kidding about cleaning up. Marissa's been sober for eighteen months. Tracy's a three-and-a-half-year veteran. On New Year's Eve, Marissa and Tracy and several hundred other people went to a dance organized by Cocaine Anonymous in a loft on West 17th Street. There was music and dancing, but when the Times Square ball fell, everyone toasted with soda. "The party was absolutely packed," says Tracy.

Names of recovering addicts and some identifying details have been changed, since anonymity is the founding principle of AA and all other twelve-step programs.

Last year's movie version was *Clean and Sober,* starring Michael Keaton. This year, it's *The Boost,* with James Woods and Sean Young. In 1988, Margaux Hemingway admitted to alcoholism on the cover of *People:* this year, it's thirteen-year-old Drew Barrymore. "AA has lost the image of unshaven bums slugging down coffee in smoke-filled rooms," says Matthew, a 28-year-old actor who's been attending meetings for eight months. "Everybody's into it."

"Getting high is no longer hip," says Candy, a long-term pill popper who's been sober for seventeen months. "Now it's hip to be in recovery. The program is the best-kept secret in Manhattan."

Why the rush to "the rooms," as members call the meetings? Hipness has nothing to do with it; nobody hangs out in church basements for fun. While alcoholism takes its toll over the course of years, coke, free-basing, and crack are causing people to bottom out within months. "It's very simple," says Paul, a 45-year-old real-estate broker with a large investment firm, who became a born-again Christian when he kicked his coke habit. "There's a line you cross where it becomes impossible. It usually takes twenty years with alcohol, ten to fifteen years with pot, five years for snorting cocaine, six months for shooting it, and a matter of weeks for crack."

"Alcohol is a much slower route to addiction," says Nancy Dombrowski, a private therapist who is affiliated with the Alcoholism Council of Greater New York. "But when you mix alcohol with cocaine, you can get there on the express train." In the past four years, the number of CA groups nationwide has gone from 169 to 1,043. In New York, the number of NA groups has doubled to 266.

ON THE FRIDAY BEFORE NEW YEAR'S EVE, MARISSA and Tracy are at an NA meeting in a church basement in the East Eighties, where their friend Max is celebrating his fourth year of sobriety or, as he prefers to call it, "being clean." The 75 people are mostly under 40 and range from yuppies to obvious junkies. Marissa runs up to Max and gives him a stuffed dog. He gives her a big hug. One attractive couple has brought a new baby.

This is an anniversary meeting. The five speakers in the front of the room have been sober anywhere from a year to nine years.

Over the past four years, the number of Cocaine Anonymous groups has grown dramatically, from 169 to 1,043.

There's a chocolate cake to celebrate. A thin girl dressed in black is passing out slices. People help themselves to coffee from an urn in the back of the room. Others light up cigarettes in the smoking section.

"Don't compare drug stories," cautions Candy, the pixieish woman in leopard-skin boots who is leading the meeting. "Just relax and identify. One of the best things about this program is the idea of a day at a time. Otherwise, things look so big. All these days add up. What you see tonight are all these 'just for todays' adding up to one, four, nine years."

The speakers—two women and three men, ranging from 24 to 40—take turns. They introduce themselves as addicts and say how long they've been clean. Everyone applauds, and then their stories begin: burnout tales from hell that all end on a note of hope. This NA meeting seems raunchier than the AA meetings, a little more out of control. The word "death" comes up often. There's a sense of mortality that isn't dispelled by the Georgette Klinger bag passed around for donations. But there's also a feeling of victory and solidarity here. It's like a locker room full of athletes primed for the same goal: winning the game.

Max, 30, is one of the last to speak. "Hi, everybody. I'm Max, and I'm an addict, and today is four years." The room bursts into applause. Max's story is both banal and sad. With a little editing, his narrative could be another *Bright Lights, Big City*. Max, a middle-class kid from Long Island, worked at a club in the city where drugs flowed as freely as Rolling Rock. Max indulged with the best of them. "Everyone at work did coke," he says. "People were always giving it to me to get in free. But I didn't know where to draw the line. I would end up in court every three months because I hadn't paid my rent. I had no phone or electricity. My girlfriend broke up with me. One of the guys I worked with died. I remember people used to leave NA stationery on my desk and it was like, 'How dare you think I have a problem?' " People laugh in recognition.

"Then I hit rock bottom. I was taking money from my family. I forged a check to my father, who's an accountant. One day, I was sitting over this drawing board. My nose was stuffed and caked from doing blow, and then it started bleeding. It was like the beginning of the end. The next night, it was my birthday. I had an eighth of an ounce of coke, and I was with some girl whose name I didn't even know. The next morning, I called my parents and made them fly me down to Florida to get clean. My first meeting was in Florida."

Max winds up his story: "I always felt less than other people; I never felt like I fit in. I've learned how to be human in four years of recovery. I didn't do this alone. My recovery is about people; we have unity here. That's how all the healing is done. Now I have a beautiful midtown office. I laugh about it sometimes."

When the meeting ends, people join hands and recite a prayer: "God grant me the serenity to accept the things I cannot change, the courage to change the things I can, and the wisdom to know the difference. Keep coming back; it works if you work it." The ring breaks up, and people stand around chatting, exchanging phone numbers.

"The key to the rooms," says Marissa, "is that there are guidelines; there are rules. And there's unconditional love. Nobody ever says, 'Don't come back.' No matter how sick you are, no matter what you've done. No one leaves you or abandons you. When I first started the program, I used to think it was a cult thing. But it's not. It's just a better way of living."

ALL OVER MANHATTAN, THERE ARE SIMILAR MEETings around the clock. During lunch, midtown professionals flock to an AA group called Foglifters, at Fifth Avenue and 55th Street. On Sunday evenings, in a dimly lit, tiny room on Perry Street, there is a smaller, more intimate meeting. Every midnight in a building off Times Square, dozens of people climb the stairs to a *film noir*–ish room with a tin ceiling and slow-moving fan. At St. Bart's, an Adult Children of Alcoholics group fills a classroom decorated with elementary-school drawings. And actors gravitate to the Studio Group at a church on the Upper East Side.

AA meetings and their various spinoffs are based on a twelve-step program that hasn't changed since it was created in 1935 by two "hopeless" drunks, Dr. Bob Smith and Bill Wilson, who had a heart-to-heart talk about their mutual problem. Wilson, a broker from New York who had made several fortunes and lost them to alcohol, was in Akron, Ohio, on business. He had been sober for three months, but when the proxy takeover he had come to town for failed, he wanted a drink. Wilson, who had been hospitalized for his last binge, learned two important things: that alcoholism is a disease, "an allergy of the body and an obsession of the mind," and that relief would come only after he surrendered himself to God. (Wilson and his wife were members of the Oxford Group, an international organization that practiced the faith of the early Christians.) He called a local minister for advice, who in turn contacted a woman from the local Oxford Group. She introduced him to Dr. Bob Smith (known just as Dr. Bob), a surgeon who was also an incorrigible alcoholic. What he and Wilson came up with was powerful but simple: AA is based on both abstinence and the concept that talking about their addiction with fellow recovering alcoholics—real-life experts on the problem—is a potent form of reciprocal therapy. As Dr. Bob wrote about Wilson, "He was the first living human who knew what he was talking about in regard to alcoholism from actual experience. In other words, he talked my language."

By June 10, 1935, Dr. Bob was stone-cold sober. He and Wilson began to spread the word, drunk by drunk. By 1939, the group had developed a guidebook. A *New Yorker* writer came up with the title *Alcoholics Anonymous*. Popularly referred to as "the big book," it lists the twelve basic steps for recovery.

It's these steps that give AA its "religious" reputation. After admitting that they are powerless over their problem and that their lives are unmanageable, alcoholics are exhorted to believe in a "higher power" and to turn their will to the care and direction of God.

But between the pious-sounding lines is a pragmatic program: AA forces alcoholics to admit they have a problem and provides them with a structured solution and support group. Arnold Washton, who runs Washton Institute, an outpatient rehab center for addicts, says, "Twelve-step programs help define the problem in a meaningful way and enforce honesty with oneself and others. They maintain a focus on realistic goals. And they provide the support of a community of friends and peers with special understanding and empathy. The rewards can be extraordinary."

Dr. Anne Geller, director of the Smithers Alcoholism Treatment and Training Center, says, "Going to these groups also gives people some activity to fill up the time when they are struggling to come off an addiction. It fills the void."

The program is free. The only requirement is a desire to stop drinking and drugging. This is especially important for those without insurance. Members are asked only to make voluntary donations to help rent the rooms and pay for literature and refreshments.

For many, however, AA still seems like some kind of religious order. First, there are all the references to God, and then there are the slogans. Talk to a member for more than fifteen minutes and a lot of homilies inevitably pop up: "First things first." "One day at a time." "Easy does it." "Keep it simple." "You're only as sick as your secrets." "One [drink] is too much and a thousand isn't enough." "Progress, not perfection." "Life on life's terms." "God is good, orderly direction."

Some people are so turned off by the "God part" that they never return for a second meeting. Others solve the problem by thinking of this higher power as the collective strength and wisdom of the people in the rooms. And then there are those who become truly religious.

"My sponsor said, 'Get on your knees before you go to bed, and talk things through,'" remembers Max. "And I said, 'Jewish guys don't get down on their knees.' He said, 'Did you ever get down on your knees to do a line of blow?' I said I would have gotten on my belly. I call the higher power my spirit. There's nothing more spiritual than one person helping another."

"I hesitate to talk about a higher power because I am a very skeptical person to begin with," says Matthew. "For years, I thought of myself as an agnostic with no real ties to any kind of organized religion. But as the big book says, 'The hoop AA asks you to jump through is plenty wide.'"

Jay, 25, went from being agnostic to being fervently religious. "I remember going to my first meeting and seeing all these people that weren't religious fanatics. They weren't nuts, they weren't losers. They were hip people," he says. "They were happy, and they were talking about incredible things. If you go to these meetings for a year and you see somebody on their first day and then after six months, that's proof."

Just having lived long enough to get into the rooms can be proof of a higher power. "It wasn't hard for me to make that leap," says Anne, a 31-year-old sales representative. "Since I was fifteen, I can't tell you how many times I've been in a car with a drunk driver, and it always turned out okay."

BUT PEOPLE ARE PEOPLE, AND THE SACRED SOMETIMES becomes the profane. One step the founders didn't have in mind was the "Thirteenth Step"—when a member who's been in the program for a while picks up a newcomer. "A person is so vulnerable when they first come in. To hit on someone is just awful," says Paula. "Once a new girl raised her hand and said she'd been clean 50 days, and I heard this guy say, 'Good. Get them while they are still shaking.' This is not a social club. This is really a place to get better. It's medicine."

Max admits, "There are a lot of people who develop relationships in the rooms. But I'm sick enough on my own. The last thing I need is to find someone who is a similar thinker. Still, I know when I first came around, a pretty girl made it easier. Everybody's motives aren't that pure. Some people are looking for a lover. Some people are looking for a job."

"I remember people telling me that AA was 'in.' That it was the new scene," says Marissa. "That's not what it's about at all. Anyone who comes in thinking that loses so much. It's not a sex club or singles club of the eighties. People are terrified of endangering the safety of the rooms. And anyway, everybody knows, it's so incestuous."

There's an unwritten rule that members should avoid major changes in their lives—including relationships—for the first year of recovery. But the social aspects of the twelve-step programs are important, especially since members are told to try to avoid the "people, places, and things" associated with their habit. "These people are going to have to eliminate large parts of their life-style," says Dr. Washton. "Having new people to socialize with is very important."

"I have had to cut off so many people I used to see," says Dan, a cocaine addict who hasn't used the drug for nine days. "I really need the people in AA." Some members even begin finding it difficult, if not impossible, to deal with people outside the program. This can be a real problem for nonmembers who have intimate relationships with members.

One 33-year-old woman who recently separated from her husband says, "AA kept him alive but stole him from me. You expect problems to be solved, but they are replaced by a whole new set of problems. The irony is that if I could scrape him off the pavement when his heart was palpitating and his face was gray and his tongue was hanging out, you'd think I could deal with a healthy, sober person. But AA became a rival in the marriage. If he doesn't go to a meeting, he gets hypercritical, antsy, negative. He goes to a meeting and comes floating out. It's almost like a fix. But I still wouldn't trade his being in the program for anything in the world, because I know without it he would be dead."

The meetings can also bring people together. Jim, 31, is engaged to a woman he met in AA, and he knows at least six other couples who met through the program. Most people find a healthy medium in handling relationships: The dealer has to go; friends who aren't only drugging or drinking pals can stay.

Until recently, drug addicts were not always welcome at AA. Max remembers "going to a meeting in Florida and saying I was an addict and being asked not to share." Says Candy, "Eight years ago, I was thrown out of an AA meeting because I was a drug addict, and they said I had no right to be there. You still hear some resentment." But today, many young members identify themselves as cross-addicted: Most cocaine users are also alcoholics. "My husband used to say, 'I have a coke habit, not an alcohol problem.' Then he'd drink," says one woman. "But as soon as he had a drink, he'd lose control over his urge to do coke. Then he'd disappear." Fellowships like AA recommend complete abstinence from addictive substances. "Once you start getting high, it brings you back to your drug of choice," says one member.

Some addicts prefer meetings, such as CA or NA, that focus on their particular problem. Others are drawn to AA because its members tend to have longer histories of sobriety than those at the more recently founded fellowships. Many members rotate among several types of meetings to get the support they need.

New members try to do 90 meetings in 90 days. They are encouraged to call other members when they get cravings or urges, and there's a sponsorship program that provides one-on-one guidance. There are 1,800 AA meetings a week in Manhattan, varying in size and ambience.

This 54-year-old form of free therapy may have become a burgeoning subculture, but it's far from an instant panacea. It means a lifetime of hard work. Members know they can never drink or take drugs again: The "pink-cloud" high most newcomers get when they enter the program soon gives way to the realization that staying sober is just the beginning. Working the twelve steps means transforming yourself. Like psychotherapy, it's a process that involves peeling back layers of personality.

It's easy for an outsider to parody the program. Often, it seems like a New Age Salvation Army or seventies-style group therapy run amok. There are meetings that are overly social, and some people become as addicted to the meetings as they once were to a substance. Others take on the fervent tone and jargon of the born-again.

That's because those who've gotten sober feel that they've been saved. For many, private therapy didn't work; dividing their stashes into cute little packets didn't work; rationing drinks didn't work. The alternatives were a totally dysfunctional life, or death.

I T'S A TUESDAY EVENING, AND THE AA MEETING IN THE basement of a church on Park Avenue in the Sixties is bustling. The crowd is a mostly upscale mix of about 60 men and women. One woman seated in the front of the room has just finished "qualifying," or telling her story. She's obviously struck a chord. Hands shoot up all over the room. The first person to share is a pretty blonde. "Hi. I'm Paula, and I'm an addict and an alcoholic."

"Hi, Paula," the room booms back.

"Hi, everyone. I've seen you here a lot, but I never heard your story before," she says to the attractive brunette in her thirties who's just finished her own tale of drug abuse, abusive relationships, arrest, recovery, and professional success. "I really identified with you. I graduated from an Ivy League school, and I'd be sitting in a crack den saying, 'But I've got a Ph.D.,' and they'd be saying, 'Pass the pipe.'"

The meeting breaks up into small coed clusters. It's easy to pick up on some flirtation among members. "Sure, I go to meetings where I have crushes on some of the guys," says Paula. "They say that whatever gets you here doesn't matter. People do date people in the program. But there's an old-timers' saying that there's a slip under every skirt. It's true that most people slip up because of relationships too early on. It takes the focus off yourself and your recovery."

A WEEK LATER, IN HER OFFICE, PAULA TELLS A wild but typical story. Paula, 32, works in the entertainment business. Posters of celebrities cover the walls, and the conversation is constantly interrupted by the phone and fax machine. Like many in the program, Paula chain-smokes. "Basically, I'm a nice girl from the suburbs," she begins. "All I can say is that for my whole life, I felt something was just off. I always felt I was never good enough, and you'll hear this a lot from people in the program. From the minute I started getting high and drinking, I knew that's how I wanted to feel. They say that we have a disease, and the word is 'dis-ease,' you know. I knew that when I drank and did drugs I felt more comfortable. And if you go to enough meetings, you'll hear every alcoholic and drug addict say this. But once we take a drug or drink, it's like we have no stop button."

Paula did well in high school, went to college and then to graduate school. She moved to New York when she was 24. "I felt really lost, and that's when all the trouble started," she says. "I began by doing little teeny bits of coke. I felt so empty. And somebody turned me on to free-basing. I did one hit, and I thought, This is what normal people must feel like. I absolutely loved it. It rapidly started ruining my life."

She missed work and spent all her time hanging out with a dealer. "He was a disgusting sleazeball hairdresser," she says. "And there was this whole scene of washing your hair, cutting it, and free-basing and drinking champagne. I hated him, but the minute you free-base, you love everybody. Then there'd be these huge fights where he'd say everyone was using him and smash the free-base pipe. And I'd say, 'I'm never going to come back.' But then the craving would start."

Paula was fired from one job after another but always managed to scrounge up enough money for drugs. "I got money from my parents. I didn't pay bills. I charged roommates more rent than they should have been paying. I used money I was supposed to pay my shrink with. And I got a new boyfriend, another dealer. We were like little hustlers down at Washington Square Park. By the end, we were cooking crack for rich people. I stole from him constantly." By now, Paula was a physical wreck.

"I weighed 95 pounds," she says. "My apartment was full of mice. My eyes were bulging out. I looked like Don Knotts. But I kept going. I was fired from my final job. I was going to be thrown out of my apartment. I had no lights or electricity. I would look outside, and it would always be this beautiful sunny day. You'd miss work, and it would be ten in the morning, and you'd want to die. You'd wish you were anybody but who you were. That was the worst feeling. Just hating yourself so much."

Eventually, Paula's parents sent her to a rehab clinic, where she stayed for five months. She moved back to New York and started going to CA meetings. "In the beginning, the fellowship of people is more important than the actual steps," she says. "I mean, all you really have to do is remember that you are powerless over drugs and alcohol. But eventually the steps help you change. When it comes down to it, if you remain the same person, you're going to end up doing drugs and alcohol again. Basically, you're a sick person getting better. They say that whatever age you started drinking or drugging is when you really stopped growing emotionally. I've heard the program called 'growing up in public.'" Paula has now been sober two and a half years.

S ARAH AND MATTHEW ARE A RICH, GOOD-LOOKING YOUNG couple. They could be out on a date, but this Wednesday night, they are at one of their favorite AA meetings, in a church in the East Sixties. The elevator man is used to the activity and cheerfully takes the hordes up and down. The members are affluent, slinging their fur coats and leather jackets over the folding chairs, stashing their briefcases and shopping bags underneath. There are about 50 people in the room, and only five could be called skid-row types. Sarah and Matthew look perfectly at home.

Sarah, an investment broker, has been sober two years; Matthew, an actor, has been sober eight months. Both are trust-fund kids who went to prep schools. But somehow, their upbringing let them down. "You're enabled by your looks and your money," says Sarah, 24, who looks a little like Amy Irving. "But you are not given any foundation, any building blocks for living."

Sarah grew up in a "very high-society, party atmosphere." At ten, she was sampling the drinks she mixed for her parents. Her parents were divorced when she was twelve, and her mother, then in her late thirties, dated, partied, and hung out with her three daughters, all of whom are now in AA. "She tried to play mother and best friend. I partied, drank, and did coke with her a lot," Sarah says. Sarah and her sisters were popular, athletic, seemingly together. The truth wasn't quite so pretty.

It wasn't until Sarah's older brother tried to commit suicide that anyone in the family was willing to take a closer look. Sarah's father stopped "enabling" his children with money. But Sarah continued to play the party girl. "I still looked good. I had money in the bank and lived in a beautiful apartment," she says. "I would go on binges. Then I would try to go to meetings. Finally, I was able to get sober for a year, but I didn't work the first step at all. I didn't admit I was powerless over alcohol, and I thought I could control my drinking. Then I drank for three straight weeks, and I knew it was over. My life was a mess."

WHERE TO CALL

FOR INFORMATION ON MEETINGS, CONTACT:
INTERGROUP ASSOCIATION OF ALCOHOLICS ANONYMOUS OF GREATER NEW YORK: 473-6200
NARCOTICS ANONYMOUS: (718) 805-9835
COCAINE ANONYMOUS: 496-4266
CHILDREN OF ALCOHOLICS FOUNDATION: 351-2680
GREATER NEW YORK AREA AL-ANON FAMILY INTERGROUP: 254-7230

For many, private therapy and rationing drinks didn't work. The alternatives were a dysfunctional life, or death.

By now, Sarah's two sisters were sober, and Sarah began to take the program seriously. "Before, I didn't want to meet any of the people in the program," she says. "I thought I was different, better. This time, I embraced it in a totally different way. I was so relieved. I felt like this is where I belong. I'm an alcoholic. I felt safe. The program gives you tools to learn to function in the world, to learn to deal emotionally with things that used to baffle you, because you used alcohol to deal with emotions. It's a bridge back to life, but it's not life."

Pot smoking brought Matthew to the meetings. "I got through school on a combination of wit and charm," he says. "I thought it was a great joke to show up in class high. After a while, I could barely function. When I graduated, I wasn't getting any acting jobs. My life started to fall apart."

Matthew went to a rehab center on the West Coast. When he returned to the East Coast, he started going to meetings. "I knew I had a problem with pot for a long time," he says. "But I thought AA was a group of weaklings. The twelve steps are simple, not complicated, mystical, or cultish in any way. I have new friends, a new girlfriend, and my professional life has improved. I am hooking up with an agent as a result of taking some action I never would have taken if I weren't sober."

THE SATURDAY-NIGHT CA MEETING IN AN AUDITORIUM in a hospital uptown is packed. Tonight, the guy qualifying is a blue-collar worker with the timing and delivery of a stand-up comic. Before long, everyone is laughing at his descriptions of life under the influence of coke: the hours he spent glued to the window, convinced that his car was being stolen or that the Feds were in the street. The times he ripped up the carpet looking for coke. The way he terrorized the family cat, or spent all his time in the bathroom pretending to shower or to slug Pepto Bismol for his ulcer. His transparent attempts to explain missing paychecks to his wife or get credit from his dealer, who lived, conveniently, on the first floor.

"They say the difference between an addict and an alcoholic is that the alcoholic will steal your money and the addict will steal it and help you look for it," he says, remembering how he rolled back his sleeve to show off his watch at the first meeting so nobody would think he was an out-of-work bum. He also remembers how his wife threatened to leave him. He's now the proud father of a newborn daughter.

From the comments in the room, it's clear that he's touched a lot of people. "I can't believe your growth," says one woman. "When I look at you, I see that I must have grown, too."

Dan, a sweet-faced 26-year-old, looks very nervous. This is his fourth meeting. His drinking and drug problem, which started in high school, has escalated into a full-scale coke and beer addiction. He used to consider himself a "literary druggie." Now he can't even get through a day at the small publishing house where he works without taking drug and drink breaks. An eight ball (three and a half grams of coke) barely lasts him several days. Everything in his life is in jeopardy. "The physical urges are hell," he says. "But the program has given me a center, a way to get out all the urges and talk about it. I don't have to isolate myself or worry about shocking people. Recovery is subsuming my life, in some ways, more than the drugs and alcohol. If I didn't have the program to take me one day at a time, I'd be overwhelmed. But the little applause you get makes you come back." For Dan, the program is a slender thread between his present and future that could snap at any minute.

'WE ARE IN THE MIDST OF AN ANSWERED prayer," says Tommy, 29, who's just completed four months of recovery. "I think the program is pretty miraculous. I see people who would just be totally trashed become really decent members of society." But the people in the rooms are only a tiny fraction of addicts, and there are far more "slips" than long-term recoveries.

Marissa's ex-boyfriend is still doing drugs. "He thinks the program is full of s--- and that the people are fake. How can someone just hug you and not even know you? He thinks the people talk a lot of bulls--- and they don't really feel it. There are people who never grasp it, who miss something, and it's sad. It just doesn't work for them. My ex has been in and out of the rooms for six years. The program is not for him right now. He needs something more."

Recently, an NA member whom Max was sponsoring died. "I'd wait for him at St. Mark's Place and he wouldn't show up. He stopped coming to meetings. He stopped calling me. I saw it coming, but I didn't see him dying. People die from this." At some NA and CA meetings, a moment of silence is observed for those still out there.

Marissa, for one, counts herself lucky. Eighteen months ago, she was a burned-out club kid. Now she has a new apartment, is back in school, and has started a line of greeting cards that she says is being picked up by a major company. She's got a life of her own.

"When I first came in, I had no sense of self," Marissa says. "I felt I was a nonperson. For the first time, I'm honest with myself. I don't have to hide. There are people who go in and out of these rooms for years and never make it. It's an action program; nothing is delivered to you. If you don't work, the program doesn't work for you.

Out in the Open

Changing attitudes and new research give fresh hope to alcoholics

Just before the Betty Ford Center opened in the affluent desert town of Rancho Mirage, Calif., in 1982, neighbors ventured out across their well-manicured lawns to ask the staff a few questions. "Will there be bars on the windows?" they wanted to know. "Will they get out and go drinking in the neighborhood?" The answer in each case was of course no, but the questions reveal a familiar attitude toward alcoholics: many people thought of them as hardly better than criminals or at the very least disturbed and bothersome people. But at the same time the fact that a sanatorium for alcoholics had been started by a former First Lady who openly admitted to a drinking problem signaled that a hopeful change was in the air. Since then, a stream of recovering alcoholics, among them such celebrities as Elizabeth Taylor, Jason Robards and Liza Minnelli, have stepped forward to tell their stories with bracing candor—of being caught in the vortex of alcoholism, of taking the strenuous route to sobriety offered in therapy and of regaining their health and self-respect. The long process of recovering from alcohol abuse, which experts insist never ends, suddenly began to get favorable notices.

Today, in treatment centers nationwide, patients are getting a message of openness and hope. In his therapy sessions, John Wallace, director of treatment at Edgehill Newport, a center in Newport, R.I., explains that alcoholism is a disease with a genetic basis, and nothing to be ashamed of. "I ask how many had a close alcoholic relative," he says, "and 95% raise their hands. That astonishes them." He describes the latest theories about neurochemical imbalances that make an alcoholic incapable of drinking normally. "They are really fascinated," he says. "It takes away a lot of their guilt and makes them less defensive."

In ways unimagined ten years ago, the shadow that has obscured the truth about alcohol has begun to lift. There is encouraging news, and it is substantial. "Silence is each day giving way to courage," Otis Bowen, Secretary of Health and Human Services, said recently, "and shame to strength." Evident all around is a busy sense of awakening. Children are learning about the perils of alcohol in school through slogans like "Get Smart, Don't Start—Just Say No." The accumulated scientific findings of the past decade are having a major impact on the public. Recently a Gallup poll found that a great majority of American adults are convinced that alcoholism is indeed an illness rather than a sign of moral backsliding. In that, they have the support of the American Medical Association, which 21 years ago formally declared alcoholism a disease. At that time, only a handful of programs, such as Hazelden in Minnesota, offered treatment for alcoholics. Since then medical centers and treatment programs have proliferated across the country. There are more than 7,000 treatment programs, a 65% increase in the past six years alone. Partly because of the new spotlight on the dangers of alcohol, Americans are beginning to moderate their drinking habits: consumption of alcohol peaked in 1981 and has since declined by 5%. In many social circles today, the big drinker stands out like W.C. Fields at a temperance meeting.

The most exciting developments in the battle against alcoholism are taking place in the nation's laboratories, where scientists and medical researchers are probing its neurochemical roots and hunting for genes that may influence its development. Next month researchers from six national laboratories will meet in New York City to coordinate their search through human DNA for the genes that may underlie alcoholism. If they are successful, doctors may one day be able to test young people for certain genetic markers, the chromosomal quirks that predispose some individuals to alcoholism, and warn those who are at risk of developing the disease. Says Henri Begleiter, professor of psychiatry at the State University of New York Health Science Center and president of the Research Society on Alcoholism: "Never in the history of alcoholism have we made as much progress as we have in recent years."

For the 18 million Americans with serious drinking problems, life is a runaway roller coaster that, left untended, inevitably leads to disaster. "It ruins everything that matters to you," says *New York Times* Reporter Nan Robertson, a recovered alcoholic. "In the end, the bottle is your only friend. Alcoholics would rather do anything than stop drinking." For the vast majority of Americans, the occasional social drink is a harmless affair. For the afflicted, however, the most innocent gathering of family or friends—a wedding at a suburban country club, a casual gathering on an urban sidewalk—can turn into a nightmare of temptation, indulgence and worse. Recalls a youthful recovering alcoholic: "My biggest fear was getting through life without a drink. Today it is that I might pick up that one sucker drink."

The stakes are high. Alcoholism claims tens of thousands of lives each year, ruins untold numbers of families and costs $117 billion a year in everything from medical bills to lost workdays. The magnitude of the problem has been overshadowed in recent years by the national preoccupation with the new threat of AIDS and the widespread use of drugs such as heroin, cocaine, marijuana and crack. "Take the deaths from every other abused drug," says Loran Archer, deputy director of the National Institute on Alcohol Abuse and Alcoholism (NIAAA) in Washington. "Add them together, and they still don't equal the deaths or the cost to society of alcohol alone."

Alcoholism's toll is frightening. Cirrhosis of the liver kills at least 14,000 alcoholics a year. Drunk drivers were responsible for approximately half the 46,000 driving fatalities in the U.S. in 1986. Alcohol was implicated in up to 70% of the 4,000 drowning deaths last year and in about 30% of the nearly 30,000 suicides. A Department of Justice survey estimates that nearly a third of the nation's 523,000 state-prison inmates drank heavily before committing rapes, burglaries and assaults. As many as 45% of the country's more than 250,000 homeless are alcoholics.

Despite all the advances in knowledge and attitudes, plus the deluge of books, movies and television programs on alcoholism, the cartoon image of the cross-eyed drunk slumped in the gutter or staggering through the front door still lingers in the minds of some Americans. Not long ago many believed, as two researchers put it in the 1950s, that "alcoholism is no more a disease than thieving or lynching." Such attitudes are fading fast, to be sure, but not without leaving a residue of ambivalence. Says LeClair Bissell, 59, a recovered alcoholic and physician: "At the same time we say through our lips that alcoholism is a chronic disease, many of us feel in our guts that it's a moral or self-inflicted problem."

From *Time*, November 30, 1987, pp. 42-50. Copyright 1987, The Time Inc. Magazine Company. Reprinted by permission.

Yet it is a disease, and it can be a ruinously expensive one. A four-week drying-out regimen can cost anywhere from $4,000 to $20,000 for in-patient care; today medical insurance covers the tab for 70% of American workers in companies with more than 100 employees. In the early 1970s, the Kemper Group of Long Grove, Ill., was the first national insurance company to include coverage for alcoholism in all its group policies. The firm's hunch: the bill for helping an alcoholic quit today would be cheaper than nursing him through afflictions like cirrhosis of the liver and strokes later in life. The logic of acting sooner rather than later has since spread throughout corporate America. Some 10,000 firms and public agencies, including 70% of the FORTUNE 500 companies, now have employee-assistance programs to help alcohol and drug abusers pull their lives together and get back to work. "Before this," says William Durkin, employee assistant manager at ARCO, "the normal handling was to tolerate the alcoholic employee until he became intolerable and then to fire him."

Progress in the actual treatment of alcoholism is disappointing. Most facilities still rely on basic therapies worked out in the 1940s. Though some centers advertise grossly exaggerated success rates of 70% after four years, the best estimates are that only 12% to 25% of patients manage to stay on the wagon for three years. Alcoholics Anonymous, the tremendously popular association of an estimated 1 million recovering alcoholics, remains the single biggest source of support for chronic drinkers. But its record is hard to assess because of members' anonymity. Even so, only 15% to 20% of alcoholics get any treatment at all. Says Enoch Gordis, director of the NIAAA: "Something very important is still missing here."

Simultaneously, another shadowy fact of life about alcoholics has been dragged into the light: the severe emotional scars they leave on their spouses and especially on their children. "Years ago the focus fell solely on the alcoholic," says Carol, a mother of four and wife of an alcoholic. "Nobody identified the needs of the family." Indeed, alcohol abuse accounts for more family troubles than any other single factor. A Gallup poll this year found that one in four families reported a problem with liquor at home, the highest reported rate since 1950 and twice the 1974 rate. According to Health Secretary Bowen, alcohol is the culprit in 40% of family-court cases and accounts for between 25% and 50% of violence between spouses and a third of child-molestation incidents.

Though awareness of alcoholism's destructiveness is growing, the sheer number of alcoholics shows no sign of abating. Young people are especially vulnerable. Bowen states that nearly 5 million adolescents, or three in every ten, have drinking problems. Several studies show that children are beginning to drink earlier than ever before, and a *Weekly Reader* study earlier this year reported that 36% of fourth-graders were pressured by peers to drink. "Kids are making decisions about alcohol and drugs when they are 12 to 14, whereas in the preceding generation they made those decisions at ages 16 to 18," says Lee Dogoloff, executive director of the American Council for Drug Education. "The younger a person starts drinking, the more likely he is to develop problems later in life."

Who, exactly, is an alcoholic? The question is a tricky one: symptoms are not always clear cut, and even doctors do not agree on a definition of the disease. The extreme cases are obvious. A person in the grip of alcoholism blacks out from drinking too much, suffers memory loss, and wakes up trembling with craving for another drink. But most cases show fewer dramatic symptoms. Also, the behavior of alcoholics fluctuates wildly. Some drink heavily every day, while others can stop for brief periods, only to go off on binges. This past year the American Psychiatric Association settled on three basic criteria to define and diagnose alcoholism: physiological symptoms, such as hand tremors and blackouts; psychological difficulties, which include an obsessive desire to drink; and behavioral problems that disrupt social or work life.

The search for alcoholism's genetic underpinnings began in earnest in the early 1970s with a simple question: Why does the disease seem to run in families? Dr. Donald Goodwin, chairman of the psychiatry department at the University of Kansas School of Medicine, set about seeking an answer by studying 133 Danish men who were all adopted as small children and raised by nonalcoholics. Goodwin divided his subjects into two categories: those with nonalcoholic biological parents and those with at least one alcoholic parent. Then he interviewed each of the adopted men in depth and examined health records to see which of them developed alcoholism in adulthood. If the disease had a genetic basis, Goodwin reasoned, then the children who had an alcoholic biological parent would wind up with drinking problems more often than the others.

His findings were startling. The sons of alcoholics turned up with drinking problems four times as often as the sons of nonalcoholics. That result helped put to rest the popular assumption that alcoholics took up drinking simply because they learned it at home or turned to it because of abuse suffered at the hands of an alcoholic parent. The study, however, did not rule out environmental factors. Indeed, scientists now estimate that fully 30% of alcoholics have no family history of the disease. But Goodwin showed that some inherited attribute was involved. "What we learned from the adoption studies," says Dr. C. Robert Cloninger, a professor of psychiatry at Washington University in St. Louis, "is not that nature was important or nurture was important but that both are important."

But it was still far from clear how hereditary and environmental factors combine to create an alcoholic. In the early 1980s, Cloninger joined a team of Swedish investigators led by Michael Bohman, a psychiatrist at the University of Umeå, to study an even larger group of adoptees. Since Sweden's extensive welfare system keeps thorough records on each citizen, Bohman was able to compile detailed sketches of 1,775 adopted men and women, more than a third of whom had an alcoholic biological parent. As Cloninger studied the health, insurance, work and police records of his subjects, two distinct categories seemed to emerge—and with them new evidence that alcoholism may have more than one form.

Cloninger's first group of alcoholics, about 25% of the total, tended to drink heavily before the age of 25, had bad work and police records and met with little success in treatment programs. Drinking was a habit they seemed to pick up on their own, with little encouragement from friends or other influences. When Cloninger checked how often alcoholism appeared in the sons of men who fit this description, he found it surfaced nine times as often as in the general population. This variation of the disease, Cloninger concludes, is heavily influenced by heredity. Because it appears primarily in men, he calls this form "male limited" alcoholism.

The second type included both men and women and made up about 75% of the study's alcoholics. They started chronic drinking usually well after the age of 25, rarely had trouble with the law, and often successfully kicked the habit. Their children were only twice as likely to have trouble with alcohol compared with the general population. Cloninger labeled this category of alcoholism "milieu limited," indicating a genetic predisposition to the disease that is triggered by extended heavy drinking.

Cloninger's work added key pieces to the puzzle of alcoholism by suggesting traits that certain types of alcoholics have in common. For example, Cloninger found that his male-limited alcoholics tended to be aggressive, even violent types. He hypothesizes that the nervous system underlying such behavior may react to alcohol in a way that quickly leads to dependence. "It's not proved," says Cloninger. "It's testable." Says Boris Tabakoff of the NIAAA: "For those of us looking for biological markers, Dr. Cloninger's work gives us a road map we can follow to link genetic traits to behavior."

If researchers could develop medical tests that identify biochemical signposts indicating a predisposition to alcoholism, they could warn potential alcoholics before trouble started. SUNY's Begleiter found just such a potential marker in the brain. By using an electroencephalograph to measure the brain waves on nondrinking sons of alcoholic fathers, Begleiter discovered that a particular brain wave called the P₃ showed a dampened response. In each instance the sons' brain waves closely duplicated those of their fathers, while other subjects with no family history of alcoholism showed strong P_3 waves. In addition, Dr. Marc Schuckit, a researcher at the San Diego Veterans Administration, has found that after several drinks some men whose fathers are alcoholics show fewer changes in the levels of two hormones, prolactin and cortisol, than men who fathers are nonalcoholics. Eventually, such findings may provide important clues in the search for the genes involved in alcoholism.

Scientists acknowledge that work on the effects of alcohol on individual brain cells is still in its infancy. Part of the problem is that ethanol, the active ingredient in alcoholic drinks, easily penetrates the membranes of all cells and disrupts their normal function. Unlike other psychoactive drugs, ethanol does not target specific parts of nerve cells, or neurons, but seems to enter cell membranes indiscriminately.

Steven Paul, chief of the clinical neuroscience branch at the National Institute of Mental Health, is studying how ethanol affects certain cells in the brain to induce sedative effects. He is looking at a group of receptors, sites on the membranes of brain cells, that link with a molecule called gamma-aminobutyric acid (GABA), a neurotransmitter that moves across the synapses between neurons. GABA homes in on a complex known as the GABA-benzodiazepine receptor. If there are a sufficient number of GABA molecules present in certain areas of the brain, anxiety diminishes. Tranquilizers such as Valium and Librium work by attaching themselves to the receptor and increasing GABA's effectiveness.

Paul believes ethanol also reduces anxiety by acting on those GABA-sensitive neurons. Altering the amount of GABA in the brain could theoretically neutralize the effects of intoxication. To that end, Paul is currently experimenting with a drug, Ro15-4513, that blocks ethanol's ability to activate the GABA receptor, thus sharply reducing alcohol's sedative effects in rats. Although the drug is toxic to humans, variants could one day be useful in treatment. Other scientists are studying a new class of drugs that seem to block the alcoholic's craving for a drink. These compounds boost the amount of another neurotransmitter, serotonin, in the brain, thus encouraging a sense of well-being— and bolstering abstinence.

Ethanol has a harmful effect on nearly every organ in the body. Chronic heavy drinking increases the risk of myocardial disease and high blood pressure. Alcohol eats away at the stomach and intestines, causing bleeding in some drinkers. Alcoholic males may experience shrunken testes, reduced testosterone levels, and even impotence. Sustained drinking sometimes disrupts women's menstrual cycles and can render them infertile. Among expectant mothers, drinking can produce birth defects and is a major cause of mental retardation in American children. Even the immune system's efficiency is reduced by alcohol. Studies are under way to determine whether heavy drinking might cause AIDS to surface more quickly in infected carriers.

But alcohol takes the worst toll on the liver, where most of the ethanol in the bloodstream is broken down. Because alcohol is so high in calories (there are 110 calories per jigger of 90-proof liquor), the liver metabolizes it instead of important nutrients, a phenomenon that can lead to severe malnutrition. The high caloric content of ethanol also causes fat to build up in the liver, one of the earliest stages of alcoholic liver disease. This is frequently followed by scarring of the liver tissue, which interferes with the organ's task of filtering toxins from the blood. The slow poisoning leads to other complications, including cirrhosis, an often fatal degeneration of the liver that affects at least 10% of all alcoholics and is especially hard on women. "They die of cirrhosis earlier than men, even though they consume less alcohol," says Judith Gavaler, an epidemiologist at the University of Pittsburgh Medical School.

This year studies at the Harvard Medical School and the National Cancer Institute reported that even women who drink moderately may have a 30% to 50% greater chance than nondrinkers of developing breast cancer. Heavy drinking among men and women alike has been linked to cancer of the liver, lung, pancreas, colon and rectum. In October a team led by Dr. Charles Lieber, a leading alcoholism researcher at the Bronx Veterans Administration Medical Center in New York City, reported that it had isolated a possible link between alcohol and cancer in humans. The culprit appears to be a member of the family of enzymes called cytochrome P-450s. In the presence of alcohol, the cytochrome can turn certain chemicals in the body into carcinogens.

Despite the medical recognition of alcoholism as a disease 21 years ago, there is still uncertainty over its legal status as an illness. Michael Deaver, the former aide to President Reagan who is on trial for lying to a grand jury about his lobbying activities, is arguing that he was not responsible because he is an alcoholic and his drinking at the time impaired his memory of events and facts. In the past the so-called alcoholism defense generally has not been very successful, but it has worked on occasion in perjury cases.

Next month the Supreme Court will hear a case that is likely to hinge on the Justices' decision as to whether alcoholism is a disease. Two former soldiers, now recovered alcoholics, are seeking to overturn a 56-year-old Veterans Administration policy that classifies alcoholism as "willful misconduct" rather than a sickness. The VA's definition prevents alcoholics from receiving benefit extensions awarded to veterans with illnesses. In seeking to make their case, the plaintiffs' lawyers are expected to bring up the new evidence that alcoholism may have a genetic basis. Says Kirk Johnson, general counsel for the A.M.A., which filed an amicus brief in the case: "We want a medical judgment, not a ruling based on fear, misunderstanding and prejudice."

For alcoholics, the only way to stop the havoc alcohol causes is, of course, to quit drinking. That is easier said than done. The main barrier to ending the torment is the alcoholic's characteristic, and usually adamant, denial that any problem exists. Mary, 61, who has not taken a drink for 14 years, remembers blacking out and waking up with her hands trembling so badly that she could not hold a cup of coffee. "I had reasons for all those things happening to me," she says, "and none of them had to do with my drinking."

How, then, to break the psychological impasse? One way is to follow a strategy called intervention, which was pioneered in the early 1960s by Vernon Johnson, an Episcopal priest in a Minneapolis suburb. In intervention, family members, friends and co-workers directly confront the alcoholic to shatter his carefully nurtured self-delusions. Beforehand they meet with a specially trained counselor (the fee: $500 to $750) to rehearse. In the actual confrontation, the alcoholic is presented with a tough but sympathetic portrayal of the mess he is in and is urged to accept prearranged admission to a treatment center, often on the same day. Says Carol Remboldt, publications director at Johnson's institute in Minnesota: "Intervention allows a tiny aperture to be poked in the wall of an alcoholic."

The process can be painful. A 31-year-old daughter read her alcoholic parents a letter in which she described how she had seen her mother change "from the best friend I ever had" to an unhappy and unreliable woman. "The good parts of your character," she said, "are being stolen away by alcohol. Don't let the bottle overtake your life." Indeed, children often provide the most persuasive statements. One alcoholic's resistance crumbled when his son said, "Daddy, when you read me the funnies on Sunday morning, you smell." Peggi, a former schoolteacher and recovered alcoholic, remembers the day seven years ago when she was faced down by her husband, sister and three sons. "It was awful," she recalls. "But it was crucial for me to see how my drinking affected their lives."

As Poet Robert Bly, the son of an alcoholic, puts it in a book called *Family Secrets,* edited by Rachel V. (Harper & Row, 1987): "Every child of an alcoholic receives the knowledge that the bottle is more important to the parent than he or she is." To mend the damage from those year-in, year-out traumas, hundreds of thousands of Americans have turned to Al-Anon and other family-therapy organizations. An offshoot of A.A. that was formed in 1951 for relatives and friends of alcoholics, Al-Anon has more than doubled in size since 1975 and now boasts some 26,000 regional groups. But the real comer is the children-of-alcoholics movement, aimed at the nearly 30 million offspring of chronic drinkers in the U.S. Made up of a variety of organizations, the movement took off four years ago with the best-selling book *Adult Children of Alcoholics,* a guide to the dilemmas C.O.A.s face, by Janet Geringer Woititz, a human-relations counselor in Verona, N.J.

At a typical C.O.A. meeting, participants sit in a circle and offer reflections on their own experiences, from a paralyzing fear of intimacy to acute conditions like bulimia, a disorder marked by episodes of excessive eating. At the heart of their pain and confusion is a childhood fraught with anxiety. "When we were kids and our parents were drunk, it was our problem," a 21-year-old daughter of an alcoholic told TIME's Scott Brown. "Somehow it seemed that we should be super people and make our family healthy." Reliving painful childhood experiences among sympathetic listeners enables the C.O.A.s to feel emotions they had suppressed. Recalls Rokelle Lerner, a pioneer in the movement: "I had to learn to re-parent myself, to comfort the little girl inside."

For both family members and chronic drinkers, the greatest frustration is the absence of a surefire treatment for alcoholism. The truth is that success rates often depend more on the individual makeup of the alcoholic than on the treatment. Alcoholics fitting Cloninger's male-limited type are less likely to remain sober after treatment, along with those with unstable work and family backgrounds. "The best predictor of patient outcome is the patient," says Thomas Seessel, executive director of the National Council on Alcoholism. "Those who are steadily employed, married and in the upper middle class are more likely to succeed. They have more to lose." In response to allegations that some centers have exaggerated how well their patients do after treatment, Congress has ordered the NIAAA to investigate treatment programs.

Today about 95% of in-patient treatment centers in the U.S. use a 28-day drying-out program developed in 1949 at Hazelden. For the first few days, staff help patients through the tremors and anxiety of withdrawal. From that point on, the emphasis is on counseling. The aims: dispel the alcoholic's self-delusions about drinking, drive home an understanding of alcohol's destructive properties, and make it clear that the only reasonable course is to stop drinking—permanently. Some centers use Antabuse, a drug that induces vomiting and other symptoms if the patient has a drink. Schick Shadel, a program with hospitals in California, Texas and Washington, employs aversion therapy to condition alcoholics to recoil at the smell, taste and even sight of a drink. Most programs, however, rely on A.A. or other counseling programs to help reinforce the message of abstinence.

"Everyone knows how to get sober," says Michael Baar, an Albany, Calif., psychologist. "The problem is keeping them in that state." Relapse prevention is the latest attempt to help reduce the number of recovering alcoholics who fall off the wagon. Terence Gorski, president of the Center for Applied Sciences in Hazel Crest, Ill., has studied thousands of relapse cases and found that on their way to recovery, alcoholics go through specific stages, each with its dangerous temptation to return to drinking. Early on, it may be hard to cope with withdrawal. Later, the patient may falter in developing a normal family and social life. Finally, there is a period of complacency, when the recovering alcoholic no longer fears drinking as he once did. At each point, says Gorski, "the person is out of control before he actually starts to drink." His solution: counselors who meet regularly with recovering alcoholics to help them identify and face problems before they get out of hand. Says Gorski: "It is compatible with A.A. and self-help groups. The only difference is that we go beyond what A.A. has to offer."

Will there ever be a simple cure for alcoholism? Probably not. Even so, the next decade or so holds dramatic promise for advances in understanding and effectively treating the disease. Researchers hope eventually to sort out alcoholics according to the neurochemical bases of their addiction and treat them accordingly. "We are still trying to map out these neurochemical systems," says Edgehill Newport's Wallace. "If we succeed, then it is likely that we will be able to design treatments." A.A. and other groups may always be necessary to help alcoholics assess the psychological and emotional damage of chronic drinking, but there is hope that medicine may make the course to sobriety less perilous.

Medical and scientific promise, however, should not eclipse the importance of public policy efforts to curb heavy drinking among adults—and stop it altogether among youngsters and adolescents. Education is one approach. The Government's "Be Smart" campaign, aimed at eight-to-twelve-year-olds, has had some success. Mothers Against Drunk Driving has been a primary factor in the fight that has raised drinking ages from 18 to 21 in 34 states plus the District of Columbia since 1982. Despite strong opposition from the alcohol industry, which lobbies vigorously against higher excise taxes for alcohol and warning labels on beer, wine and liquor bottles, groups like MADD and the National Council on Alcoholism continue to push initiatives that will further discourage consumption of alcohol.

In his speech two weeks ago, Health Secretary Bowen complained that brewers and beer distributors spend $15 million to $20 million a year marketing their products on college campuses, encouraging heavy drinking and "contributing to poor grades, excessive vandalism, many injuries, and not so infrequently, death." Bowen asked Education Secretary William Bennett to encourage university presidents to restrict alcohol promotions on campus. Spuds MacKenzie, the canine star of Anheuser-Busch's advertising campaign for Bud Light beer, is also in the doghouse. This fall the National Association of State Alcohol and Drug Abuse Directors filed complaints with several federal agencies charging that the campaign encouraged kids to drink.

For those who know what British Novelist Malcolm Lowry described as the alcoholic's "fine balance between the shakes of too little and the abyss of too much," sobriety cannot come too soon. That is the challenge for medical researchers. But just as much energy should go into the job of preventing the disease. That means not only finding genetic markers to warn those susceptible but also changing attitudes in a society that still glorifies drinking. As Bowen remarked recently, "To do anything less than all this would be a disservice to ourselves, our society and to the many future generations whose lives and livelihoods are at stake." For millions of American alcoholics, there is no time to lose. —*By Edward W. Desmond. Reported by Barbara Dolan/St. Louis, Andrea Dorfman/New York and Melissa Ludtke/Boston*

Binding Together Addicts' Lives

Cynthia B. Hanson

Staff writer of The Christian Science Monitor

ELIZABETH BARBOSA had never held a job – except as an addicted, streetwise heroin dealer. So when she finally decided to check into a 17-month-long residential drug treatment program to kick her seven-year habit, she was dubious about her job prospects.

"I thought I could never work. I thought I wasn't part of society," says the soft-spoken high school dropout who grew up in the South Bronx. Yet for the last two years, this 25-year-old mother of two has held a full-time job and says she has been free of heroin use.

Ms. Barbosa attributes much of her success to the job training she received from Binding Together, Inc. (BTI), a not-for-profit printing and binding corporation that offers training in the printing industry for recovering addicts. During a six-month program, she learned how to set up, operate, service, and maintain high-tech office and copying equipment while she received regular counseling and treatment at a live-in drug treatment center.

Barbosa is one of 82 recovering addicts who have graduated from this two-year-old, one-of-a-kind program. Last spring, BTI was selected by the US Department of Labor for a presidential award for its "outstanding program for serving those with multiple barriers to employment."

"Everybody says that to place people who are homeless and addicted to drugs is impossible," says Ted Small, president of Small & Associates, a private consulting firm here that conceived the program five years ago. "It is not impossible, but it requires a complex partnership of a lot of different groups working together," Mr. Small continues. His company specializes in developing employment programs for people with drug and alcohol problems, as well as those with physical, mental, and emotional disabilities.

BTI participants are carefully selected by drug-rehabilitation agencies and BTI counselors.

Every aspect of a person's problem needs to be addressed – from rehabilitation to homelessness to job training, Small says. Even if you solve every problem but one, "you may have thrown your money away" if you can't solve the last one, says the Yale Law School graduate who was one of the first Peace Corps volunteers. What's unusual about BTI is that it combines the business community, counseling, residential drug treatment, and a job training program, he says.

Drugs, homeless link

Small & Associates first began working on the BTI program in 1985 at the request of New York's Division of Substance Abuse Service (DSAS). "They said they had a real problem in providing vocational services to people who were not only on drugs, but had been on drugs to such an extent that they'd become homeless," says Small in an interview at his office near Wall Street.

Drug abuse and homelessness often go hand in hand, he says. And recovering addicts seldom have enough money even for the security deposit on an apartment when they leave treatment programs. The problem is more acute in expensive cities like New York, he says.

Recovering addicts may find themselves at "the reentry phase," says Small: off drugs, but unsure of "what they are going to do with their lives." How do such people get themselves out of the circumstances that got them into drugs in the first place? Small asks. Too often, they return to the streets – and to drugs – because they have little money or means.

Recidivism can be reduced, Small claims, by giving recovering addicts job training and housing in a residential treatment center, and temporary housing while they look for jobs.

The most current statistics in an ongoing DSAS study show that of the 125 BTI participants enrolled since the program began in 1988, 30 were in training, 13 had dropped out, and 82 had graduated. Of the graduates, 76 got jobs. Six months later, 83 percent of them were still employed. Some had been promoted.

"Those outcomes are fabulous for any group in an employment and training program," says Joan Randell, assistant deputy director of DSAS. "To have 83 percent still working after six months is unheard-of . . . considering these people are among the hardest to be served."

DSAS is one of five state and city agencies funneling federal funds from the Job Training Partnership Act to provide half of BTI's $1 million annual budget. The rest comes from sales and private-sector grants.

"Binding Together stands for a commitment by the private sector and government agencies working for a common cause," says Phil Caldarella, the program's director. A former New York City police officer, Mr. Caldarella covered the Times Square beat before he retired on disability. He also worked in the printing industry for five years.

Firms such as Kodak, Xerox, Morgan Stanley Group, and Merrill Lynch are represented on BTI's board. Graduates have been placed in board-member companies. The com- panies also are clients of BTI.

"We're looking for ways to do collaborative efforts between business and government," says Mary Quigley, assistant commissioner for the Department of Employment in New York City, which also provides funding for BTI. "If you can identify an industry need . . . you've reduced the cost to the government," she says. And as BTI's business picks up, she adds, less and less money from government agencies will be needed until the program is self-sufficient.

'I felt like somebody'

When Barbosa first entered the Binding Together program, she thought it was going to be "nothing but time lost. But I learned a lot," she says. "When I started this training, I felt like somebody; I felt real good about me. You have to come dressed up every day. You know, little things that I never had before that made me feel better. . . . I got into it. I really enjoyed this work, and I kept coming."

Barbosa is still working for the same employer she started with a year ago, after she finished her training at BTI. "They tell me that I'm one of their best workers, and I feel good," she says.

Ted Small attributes part of the success of the program to the level of skill and expertise the trainees gain. "This is state-of-the-art stuff," he says of the office machinery that is becoming increasingly complex with computerization and redesign. "Part of the thing in any training program is to give people the sense that they can manipulate their environment – they can, in a real way, make something happen, make the machine do something," he adds. "Coming to work on time every day, doing a job – all of that increases their sense of self-respect, discipline, and control over their lives."

The printing industry is the fourth-largest in the United States, and workers are in short

---

ONE MAN'S ROAD BACK TO SOCIETY

■ Sammy Harkless says he starting using marijuana for fun and peer acceptance while in junior high. But 13 years later he found himself trading his coat and shoes for vials of crack cocaine.

"The last drug I did was crack. And that's the drug that really brought me to my knees, brought me down emotionally, spiritually, everything," he says with visible discomfort during an interview at the Binding Together offices.

"I would go home and I would take things. I would take my mother's camera. I was even taking from my nieces and my nephews – and they looked up to me at one time. It was sad, but I didn't care. I didn't have any pity. . . ."

Kicked out of the house by his family, Mr. Harkless eventually ended up living on the streets.

What prompted him to seek help? "I just woke up [one] day and I said to myself, 'I need help.' I was down to my last ounce of sanity. Maybe God," he concludes. "I guess He was watching over me at the time."

The next day, Harkless checked into a 18-24 month-long residential drug treatment program, one that had a short waiting list.

A former Marine, Harkless had once held a job in a bindery. When he was offered training through Binding Together during his rehabilitation, "I jumped on it quick – not because of the money, but because it was something that I knew about and I knew that I could gain more experience from it."

Today Harkless attends support groups, and has worked as a supervisor in the printing department of an investment firm for two years. His wife recently gave birth to their first child, a girl. Decked out in a sleek gray suit and polished shoes, he exudes an air of satisfied success.

Without Binding Together, "I think things would have been a lot different," he says. "I don't think I would have gotten this far."

– C. B. H.

supply, says Caldarella: Most graduates have landed jobs, and their average starting salary is about $14,000-15,000.

As an incentive, and as a way to satisfy welfare department requirements (benefits cannot be collected while working), each participant has a "deferred compensation" account set up at a local bank. A portion of BTI's sales goes into the accounts.

For graduates, a nest egg

Graduates continue to live at the treatment center while looking for jobs. Once they find one, the money that has accumulated in their accounts is handed over – about $2,000, enough for a security deposit and the first month's rent on an apartment.

"We thought that it would be very important to empower them to become consumers," says Small. "The way you do that is by giving them counseling, which is cheap, and money," he adds.

Including the deferred compensation money, the per-participant cost to the taxpayer for the six-month program is about $7,000, according to DSAS.

"Rehabilitating people long term takes a lot of money," says DSAS's Randell. "There are no quick fixes, really." The expense is "more than saved by the initial investment over time," she says, because it addresses the problem long term: "If these people be-

come workers in mainstream society, . . . you're changing not only their lives, but you're changing the lives of their children."

The possibility of replicating the program in other cities is being explored. And Caldarella has been contacted by numerous organizations in the New York area interested in setting up similar programs: a Vietnam veterans group, an organization for people with AIDS, a program for runaway children, and a program for recently released prison inmates.

"We're exploring possibilities of opening up a second shift with an entirely new population with additional staff," he says.

Healing Scars of Parental Drinking

SUMMARY: Long after they have left their drink-dominated childhood homes, many people find that the alcoholism of their parents still disrupts their lives. Banding together in self-help sessions enables such adults to confront the damage and recover.

Lillian began going to weekly Adult Children of Alcoholics meetings a year ago. For three months all she could do was listen and fight back tears.

Like most of the nation's 22 million men and women raised in homes where one or both parents abused alcohol, Lillian grew up believing she was somehow responsible for her family's problems. It was a heavy burden for a little girl.

When Dad passed out at dinner and fell into his fried chicken, Mom, desperate to cover up "the problem," kept eating and insisted that everything was OK. Lillian thus learned to distrust and ignore even what her eyes and ears told her.

She felt anger toward her parents. But knowing such feelings were "bad," she instead turned the anger inward, blaming herself. Her spontaneous, expressive impulses died, and she became like a small, serious grown-up, stifling her feelings. She came to have only one priority: survival.

Despite their shared background of frequent conflict and tension, adult children of alcoholics — ACOAs they are called by those who work closely with them — usually look healthy and often perform well. But the survival techniques they developed as children persist. They frequently have low self-esteem, guilt and depression. They are at high risk to marry alcoholics and are four times more likely than others to become alcoholics themselves.

In recent years, however, more and more such adults have banded together to confront the effects of parental alcoholism. There is even a telephone referral service for such meetings, at (213) 651-1710. In meetings modeled after Alcoholics Anonymous sessions, borrowing from AA's 12-step recovery program, the adults focus on a different topic each week. For most,

the pain of their chaotic upbringing has been buried under years of shame.

Partly as a result of therapist Janet Woititz's best-selling book "Adult Children of Alcoholics" and Claudia Black's "It Will Never Happen to Me," attendance at these self-help meetings nationwide is exploding. "People have started to pay attention the past few years. It was a lot harder 10 years ago for people to identify themselves" as children of alcoholics, says Woititz, who also heads the Institute for Counseling and Training in Verona, N.J.

The therapist initially came into contact with children from alcoholic families as an elementary school teacher in the early 1970s. "I noticed that about 25 percent of my students were different from the rest and I was real concerned. They were different in that there were skills they didn't have. They knew how to be compliant, but not how to cooperate. They knew how to handle a crisis or do something at the last minute, but not how to do anything systematically. They were worried and concerned most of the time. They didn't know how to relate to their peers, even though their peers liked them. They didn't know how to be friends."

Her 2-year-old clinic, which handles about 300 patients per week and has a long waiting list, also has therapy groups to work on deeper issues, including past sexual and physical abuse. In up to 90 percent of child abuse cases, alcohol is a significant factor, according to the National Association for Children of Alcoholics.

"It used to be that ACOAs didn't start to seek help until their late 20s," she says. "They really functioned quite well up to that point and were able to deny the things that were getting in their way. But as people become more aware, we are seeing younger and younger people."

Before discovering the self-help meetings, Lillian, a university professor in Washington, went through years of psychotherapy for bouts of depression. "I have a history of repressing anger and turning it against myself. In the program, I am learning tools that I never learned because my family life was so unhealthy. One of the

things I have to learn is how to recognize when I'm angry and then how to express it: how to say things to the people I'm angry at and not be waylaid into expressing it indirectly to somebody else."

According to the Children of Alcoholics Foundation in New York City, the children commonly adopt one of four roles that persist into adulthood. The responsible child is a high achiever who always does what's right, is successful and puts everyone else first. The problem child gets attention by being a troublemaker. He is strongly attracted to a peer group outside the home and is likely to be involved with alcohol and drugs. The silent child is a loner, quiet and withdrawn, who survives by retreating inward, not rocking the boat. The clown is a charmer who works hard to be the center of attention and uses humor to distract family members from a painful situation.

Woititz estimates that 70 percent of those seen at her clinic have a past or current drinking problem. "There is no way that an ACOA ever takes a drink without being conscious of it; it means something."

Recent research indicates that many recovering alcoholics who relapse into drinking after two to five years of sobriety often have not dealt with issues resulting from growing up in an alcoholic family, she says.

While her work concentrates on children of alcoholics, she emphasizes that many of their experiences and symptoms are also valid for others whose homes were "different": families where there was other compulsive behavior such as gambling or drug abuse, or even chronic illness or unbearably rigid religious attitudes.

One year after discovering the Adult Children of Alcoholics organization, Lillian is decidedly upbeat about the future. "At this stage, the most important thing in my life is this program of recovery. Recovery is learning new tools, learning how to live. I let nothing interfere with it. When people come around who are real unhealthy and I think that my program of recovery is threatened, I tell them good-bye. Right now, I'm just committed to getting better, to healing. And it's happening."

— *Charles Wheeler*

From *Insight*, February 23, 1987, p. 64. Originally from *The Washington Times*.

This glossary of 185 drug terms is included to provide you with a convenient and ready reference as you encounter general terms in your study of drugs and drug and alcohol abuse that are unfamiliar, technical, or require a review. It is not intended to be comprehensive, but, taken together with the many definitions included in the articles themselves, it should prove to be useful.

Absorption   The passage of chemical compounds, such as drugs or nutrients, into the bloodstream through the skin, intestinal lining, or other bodily membranes.

Acetylcholine   A cholinergic transmitter that forms salts used to lower blood pressure and increases peristalsis, and thought to be involved in the inhibition of behavior.

Addiction   Chronic, compulsive, or uncontrollable behavior.

Adrenergic System   The group of transmitters, including epinephrine, norepinephrine, and dopamine, that activates the sympathetic nervous system.

Alcohol Abuse   *See* Alcoholism.

Alcoholics Anonymous (AA)   A voluntary fellowship founded in 1935 and concerned with the recovery and continued sobriety of the alcoholic members who turn to the organization for help. The AA program consists basically of "Twelve Suggested Steps" designed for the personal recovery from alcoholism, and AA is the major proponent of the disease model of alcoholism.

Alcoholism   Any use of alcoholic beverages that causes damage to the individual or to society. *See also* Disease Model.

Amphetamines   A class of drugs, similar in some ways to the body's own adrenaline (epinephrine), that act as stimulants to the central nervous system.

Analgesics   Drugs that relieve pain.

Anesthetics   Drugs that abolish the sensation of pain, often used during surgery.

Angel Dust   Slang term for phencyclidine.

Anorectic   A drug that decreases appetite.

Antagonist Programs   Drug treatment programs that use antagonist agents, like naltrexone (antagonist of heroin) or antabuse (used in treating alcoholism), to block the effect of drugs on the body.

Antianxiety Tranquilizers   Tranquilizers, like Valium and Librium, used to relieve anxiety and tension, sometimes called minor tranquilizers.

Anticholinergics   Drugs that block the transmission of impulses in the parasympathetic nerves.

Antidepressants   Drugs that relieve mental depression. *See also* Depression, Mental

Antihistamines   Drugs that relieve allergy or cold symptoms by blocking the effects of histamine production.

Antipsychotic Tranquilizers   Drugs used to treat psychosis; include Thorazine (chlorpromazine). Also called major tranquilizers or neuroleptics. *See also* Tranquilizers.

Atropine   An alkaloid derivative of the belladonna and related plants that blocks responses to parasympathetic stimulation.

Autonomic Nervous System (ANS)   That part of the nervous system that regulates involuntary action, such as heartbeat; consists of the sympathetic and parasympathetic nervous systems.

Axon   The core of the nerve fiber that conducts impulses away from the nerve cell to the neurons and other tissue.

Barbiturates   Drugs used for sedation and to relieve tension and anxiety.

Binding   The attachment of a transmitter to its appropriate receptor site.

Blood Level   The concentration of alcohol in the blood, usually expressed in percent by weight.

Caffeine   An alkaloid found in coffee, tea, and kola nuts, that acts as a stimulant.

Caffeinism   Dependence on caffeine.

Cannabis   *See* Marijuana.

Capsule   A container, usually of gelatin, that encloses a dose of an oral medicine.

Central Nervous System (CNS)   The brain and spinal cord.

Chewing Tobacco   A form of tobacco leaves, sometimes mixed with molasses, that is chewed.

Chlorpromazine   An antianxiety tranquilizer, manufactured under the name of Thorazine, used for treating severe psychoses. Also used as an antagonist to LSD panic reactions.

Choline   A transmitter, part of the cholinergic system.

Cholinergic System   Group of transmitters that activate the parasympathetic nervous system.

Cocaine   A white crystaline narcotic alkaloid derived from the coca plant and used as a surface anesthetic and a stimulant.

Codeine   A narcotic alkaloid found in opium, most often used as an analgesic or cough suppressant.

Coke   Slang term for cocaine.

Cold Turkey   Slang expression for abrupt and complete withdrawal from drugs or alcohol without medication.

Compulsive Drug Use   Drug use that is frequent, with intensive levels of long duration, producing physiological or psychological dependence.

Constriction   Narrowing or shrinking.

Contraindication   A condition that makes it inadvisable or hazardous to use a particular drug or medicine.

Controlled Drinking   Moderate drinking by recovered alcoholics, discouraged by AA.

Controlled Drug Use   Use of drugs over a period of time without abusing them.

Controlled Substances   All psychoactive substances covered by laws regulating their sale and possession.

Controlled Substances Act of 1970   Federal act that classifies controlled substances into five categories and regulates their use. Schedule I drugs are those most strictly controlled, and include heroin, marijuana, LSD, and other drugs believed to have high abuse potential. Schedule II drugs are also strictly controlled but have some medicinal uses. These drugs include morphine, methadone, and amphetamines. Schedule III, IV, and V substances include drugs that have increasingly less abuse potential. Over-the-counter medicines not subject to any refill regulations fall into Schedule V.

Craving   Refers to both physical and psychological dependence; a strong desire or need for a substance.

Crisis Intervention   The process of diagnosing a drug crisis situation and acting immediately to arrest the condition.

Decriminalization   The legal process by which the possession of a certain drug would become a civil penalty instead of a criminal penalty. *See also* Legalization.

Deliriants   Substances, like some inhalants, that produce delirium.

Delirium   State of temporary mental confusion and diminished consciousness, characterized by anxiety, hallucinations, and delusions.

Dendrite   The part of the nerve cell that transmits impulses to the cell body.

Dependence, Drug A physical or psychological dependence on a particular drug resulting from continued use of that drug.

Dependence, Physical The physical need of the body for a particular substance such that abstinence from the substance leads to physical withdrawal symptoms. *See also* Addiction; Withdrawal Syndrome.

Dependence, Psychological A psychological or emotional reliance on a particular substance; a strong and continued craving.

Depression, Mental The state of mind that ranges from mild sadness to deep despair, often accompanied by a general feeling of hopelessness.

Detoxification Removal of a poisonous substance, such as a drug or alcohol, from the body.

Dilation Widening or enlargement.

Disease Model A theory of alcoholism, endorsed by AA, in which the alcoholism is seen as a disease rather than a psychological or social problem.

DMT Dimethyltryptamine, a psychedelic drug.

DNA Deoxyribonucleic acid, the carrier of chromosomes in the cell.

Dopamine An indoleaminergic transmitter necessary for normal nerve activity.

Downers Slang term for drugs that act to depress the central nervous system.

Drug Any substance that alters the structure or function of a living organism.

Drug Abuse Use of a drug to the extent that it is excessive, hazardous, or undesirable to the individual or the community.

Drug Misuse Use of a drug for any purpose other than that for which it is medically prescribed.

Drug Paraphernalia Materials, like hypodermic syringes, that are used for the preparation or administration of illicit drugs.

Drunkenness The state of being under the influence of alcohol such that mental and physical faculties are impaired; severe intoxication.

DWI Driving while intoxicated.

Dysphoria Emotional state characterized by anxiety, depression, and restlessness, as opposed to euphoria.

Ecstasy A derivative of nutmeg or sassafras, causing euphoria and sometimes hallucinations; also known as XTC, Adam, or MDMA.

Endorphins Any group of hormones released by the brain that have painkilling and tranquilizing abilities.

Epinephrine An adrenal hormone that acts as a transmitter and stimulates autonomic nerve action.

Ethical Drugs Drugs dispensed by prescription only.

Euphoria Exaggerated sense of happiness or well-being.

Experimental Drug Use According to the U.S. National Commission on Marijuana and Drug Abuse, the short-term non-patterned trial of one or more drugs, either concurrently or consecutively, with variable intensity but maximum frequency of ten times per drug.

Fetal Alcohol Syndrome (FAS) A pattern of birth defects, cardiac abnormalities, and developmental retardation seen in babies of alcoholic mothers.

Flashback A spontaneous and involuntary recurrence of psychedelic drug effects after the initial drug experience.

Food and Drug Administration (FDA) Agency of the U.S. Department of Health and Human Services that administers federal laws regarding the purity of food, the safety and effectiveness of drugs, and the safety of cosmetics.

Habituation Chronic or continuous use of a drug, with an attachment less severe than addiction.

Hallucination A sensory perception without external stimuli.

Hallucinogen Or, hallucinogenic drugs. Drugs that cause hallucinations. Also known as psychedelic drugs.

Harrison Narcotics Act Federal act passed in 1914 that controlled the sale and possession of prescription drugs, heroin, opium, and cocaine.

Hash Oil An oily extract of the marijuana plant, containing high levels of THC.

Hashish The dried resin of the marijuana plant, often smoked in water pipes.

Herb Commonly, any one of various aromatic plants used for medical or other purposes.

Heroin Diacetylmorphine hydrochloride, an opiate derivative of morphine.

High Intoxicated by a drug or alcohol; the state of being high.

Illicit Drugs Drugs whose use, possession, or sale is illegal.

Illusion A distorted or mistaken perception.

Indole An indoleaminergic transmitter.

Indoleaminergic System A system of neurotransmitters, including indole and serotonin.

Inebriation The state of being drunk or habitually drunk.

Intoxication Medically, the state of being poisoned. Usually refers to the state of being drunk, falling between drunkenness and a mild high.

Involuntary Smoking Involuntary inhalation of the cigarette smoke of others.

Ketamin A general anesthetic, also used as a deliriant.

Legalization The movement to have the sale or possession of certain illicit drugs made legal.

LSD Lysergic acid diethylamide-25, a hallucinogen.

Maintenance Treatment Treatment of drug dependence by a small dosage of the drug or another drug, such as methadone, that will prevent withdrawal symptoms.

Marijuana The dried leaves of the cannabis plant, usually smoked and resulting in feelings of well-being, relaxation, or euphoria. Also spelled: Marihuana.

MDMA *See* Ecstasy.

Medical Model A theory of drug abuse or addiction in which the addiction is seen as a medical, rather than a social, problem.

Medicine A drug used to treat disease or injury; medication.

Mescaline A hallucinogenic alkaloid drug, either derived from the peyote plant or made synthetically.

Metabolism The set of physical and chemical processes involved in the maintenance of life; or, the functioning of a particular substance in the body.

Methadone A synthetic opiate sometimes used to treat heroin or morphine addiction. *See also* Maintenance Treatment.

Methaqualone A non-barbiturate sedative/hypnotic drug, used to bring on feelings of muscular relaxation, contentment, and passivity. Also known as Quaaludes.

Morphine An organic compound extracted from opium, a light anesthetic or sedative.

Multimodality Programs Programs for the treatment of drug abuse or alcoholism involving several simultaneous treatment methods.

Multiprescribing   The situation in which a person is taking more than one prescription or over-the-counter drug simultaneously.

Narcotic   Any drug that dulls a person's senses and produces a sense of well-being in smaller doses, and insensibility, sometimes even death, in larger doses.

Nervous System   In human beings, the brain, spinal cord, and nerves. *See also* Somatic Nervous System; Autonomic Nervous System.

Neuroleptic   Any major, or antipsychotic, tranquilizer.

Neuron   The basic element responsible for the reception, transmission, and processing of sensory, motor, and other information of physiological or psychological importance to the individual.

Neurotransmitter   *See* Transmitter.

Nicotine   The main active ingredient of tobacco, extremely toxic and causing irritation of lung tissues, constriction of blood vessels, increased blood pressure and heart rate, and, in general, central nervous system stimulation.

Norepinephrine   Hormone found in the sympathetic nerve endings that acts as an adrenergic transmitter and is a vasoconstrictor.

Opiate Narcotics   A major subclass of drugs that act as pain relievers as well as central nervous system depressants; includes opium, morphine, codeine, and methadone.

Opiates   The drugs derived from opium—morphine and codeine—as well as those derived from them, such as heroin.

Opium   Narcotic derivative of the poppy plant that acts as an analgesic.

Opoids   The group of synthetic drugs, including Demerol and Darvon, that resemble the opiates in action and effect.

Overmedication   The prescription and use of more medication than necessary to treat a specific illness or condition.

Over-the-Counter Drugs   Drugs legally sold without a prescription.

Parasympathetic Nervous System   The part of the autonomic nervous system that inhibits or opposes the actions of the sympathetic nerves.

Parasympathomimetics   Drugs that produce effects similar to those of the parasympathetic nervous system.

Parkinson's Disease   A progressive disease of the nervous system characterized by muscular tremor, slowing of movement, partial facial paralysis, and general weakness.

Patent Medicines   Drugs or other medications protected by a patent and sold over the counter.

Peristalsis   Wave-like muscular contractions that help move matter through the tubular organs (e.g., intestines).

Phencyclidine (PCP)   A synthetic depressant drug used as a veterinary anesthetic and illegally as a hallucinogen. Also known as angel dust.

Placebo   An inactive substance used as a control in an experiment.

Placenta   The membranous organ that develops in the uterus of a pregnant female mammal to nourish the fetus. Though the fetus and mother are thus separated, drugs and alcohol are often still able to reach the developing fetus.

Polyabuse   Abuse of various drugs simultaneously.

Pot   Slang term for marijuana.

Potency   Term used to compare the relative strength of two or more drugs used to produce a given effect.

Prescription Drugs   Drugs dispensed only by a physician's prescription.

Primary Prevention   Efforts designed to prevent a person from starting to use drugs.

Proprietary Drugs   Patent medicines.

Psilocybin   A hallucinogenic alkaloid, found in various types of mushrooms, chemically related to LSD.

Psychedelic Drugs   Hallucinogens.

Psychoactive   Any drug that can cause alterations in the user's mood or behavior.

Psychopharmacology   The study of the effects of drugs on mood, sensation, or consciousness, or other psychological or behavioral functions.

Psychosis   Severe mental disorder, characterized by withdrawal from reality and deterioration of normal intellectual and social functioning.

Psychotherapeutic Drugs   Drugs that are used as medicines to alleviate psychological disorders.

Psychotomimetics   Drugs that produce psychosis-like effects.

Receptors   The input organs for the nervous system.

Recidivism   Return to former behavior.

Recombinant DNA   DNA prepared in the laboratory by the transfer or exchange of individual genes from one organism to another.

Recreational Drug Use   Drug use that takes place in social settings among friends who want to share a pleasant experience; characterized by less frequency and intensity than addictive drug use. Also called social-recreational drug use.

Rehabilitation   Restoration of a person's ability to function normally.

Reinforcement   A stimulus that increases the probability that a desired response will occur.

Rush   Slang term for an immediate feeling of physical well-being and euphoria after the administration of a drug.

Schedules   Categories of drugs as defined in the Controlled Substances Act of 1970.

Schizophrenia   A psychosis characterized by withdrawal from reality accompanied by affective, behavioral, and intellectual disturbances.

Scopolamine   Poisonous alkaloid found in the roots of various plants, used as a truth serum or with morphine as a sedative.

Secondary Prevention   Early treatment of drug abuse to prevent it from becoming more severe.

Sedative/Hypnotics   Class of non-narcotic depressant drugs that calm, sedate, or induce hypnosis or sleep. Sedative/hypnotics are divided into four categories: barbiturates, alcohol, antianxiety tranquilizers (minor tranquilizers), and nonbarbiturate proprietary drugs.

Serotonin   An indoleaminergic transmitter found in the blood serum, cells, and central nervous system, that acts as a vasoconstrictor.

Set   The combination of physical, mental, and emotional characteristics of an individual at the time a drug is administered.

Setting   The external environment of an individual at the time a drug is administered.

Side Effects   Secondary effects, usually undesirable, of a drug or therapy.

Snuff   A preparation of pulverized tobacco that is inhaled into the nostrils.

Sobriety   The quality of being free from alcohol intoxication.

Social-Recreational Drug Use   *See* Recreational Drug Use.

Socioeconomic   Both social and economic.

Somatic Nervous System   That part of the nervous system that deals with the senses and voluntary muscles.

Somatic Nervous System   That part of the nervous system that deals with the senses and voluntary muscles.

Speed   Slang term for methamphetamine, a central nervous system stimulant.

Stereospecificity   The matching of both electrical and chemical characteristics of the transmitter and receptor site so that binding can take place.

Stimulants   A major class of drugs that stimulate the central nervous system, causing mood elevation, increased mental and physical activity, alertness, and appetite suppression. Primary stimulants include the amphetamines and cocaine. Secondary stimulants include nicotine and caffeine.

STP   Early slang term for phencyclidine.

Subcutaneous   Beneath the skin.

Substance Abuse   Refers to overeating, cigarette smoking, alcohol abuse, or drug abuse.

Sympathetic Nervous System   That part of the autonomic nervous system that acts to release sugars from the liver, slow digestion, and increase heart and breathing rates.

Sympathomimetic   Any drug that produces effects like those resulting from stimulation of the sympathetic nervous system.

Synapse   The space, or gap, between two neurons.

Tars   The dark, oily, viscid substances created by burning tobacco, known to contain carcinogenic agents.

Temperance   The practice of moderation, especially with regard to alcohol consumption. The Temperance Movement was a popular movement in the nineteenth and twentieth centuries to restrict or prohibit the use of alcoholic beverages.

Tertiary Prevention   Treatment to prevent the permanent disability or death of a drug abuser.

THC   Tetrahydrocannabinol, a psychoactive derivative of the cannabis plant.

Therapeutic Community   Setting in which persons with similar problems meet and provide mutual support to help overcome those problems.

Titration   The ability to determine desired drug dosage.

Tolerance   The capacity to absorb a drug continuously or in large doses with no adverse effect.

Trance   Dazed or hypnotic state.

Tranquilizers   Drugs that depress the central nervous system, thus relieving anxiety and tension and sometimes relaxing the muscles, divided into the major tranquilizers, or antipsychotics, and minor tranquilizers, or antianxiety tranquilizers. *See also* Antianxiety Tranquilizers; Antipsychotic Tranquilizers.

Transmitters   Also known as neurotransmitters. Any substance that aids in transmitting impulses between a nerve and a muscle. Three known categories of transmitters are the cholinergic system, adrenergic system, and indoleaminergic system.

Treatment   Drug treatment programs can be drug-free or maintenance, residential or ambulatory, medical or nonmedical, voluntary or involuntary, or some combination of these.

Uppers   Slang term for amphetamines, and, sometimes, cocaine.

Withdrawal Syndrome   The group of reactions or behavior that follows abrupt cessation of the use of a drug upon which the body has become dependent. May include anxiety, insomnia, perspiration, hot flashes, nausea, dehydration, tremor, weakness, dizziness, convulsions, and psychotic behavior.

Credits/ Acknowledgments

Cover design by Charles Vitelli

1. Thinking About Drugs
Facing overview—EPA Documerica.

2. Use, Addiction, and Dependence
Facing overview—United Nations photo by Jane Schreibman.

3. Why Drugs?
Facing overview—WHO photo by E. Mandelmann and S. Bojar.

4. Patterns and Trends in Drug Use
Facing overview—United Nations photo.

5. The Major Drugs of Use and Abuse
Facing overview—United Nations photo by John Robaton.

6. The Impact of Drug Use on Society
Facing overview—American Cancer Society

7. The Economy of Drug Use
Facing overview—The Dushkin Publishing Group photo by Pamela Carley Petersen. 186—Map by Melody Warford/Insight. 188—Chart by George Tuggle, Jr./Insight.

8. Fighting the Drug War
Facing overview—U.S. Customs photo.

9. Drug Prevention and Treatment
Facing overview—WHO photo by Jean Mohr.

ANNUAL EDITIONS ARTICLE REVIEW FORM

■ NAME: _____ DATE: _____

■ TITLE AND NUMBER OF ARTICLE: _____

■ BRIEFLY STATE THE MAIN IDEA OF THIS ARTICLE: _____

_____

_____

_____

_____

■ LIST THREE IMPORTANT FACTS THAT THE AUTHOR USES TO SUPPORT THE MAIN IDEA:

_____

_____

_____

_____

_____

_____

■ WHAT INFORMATION OR IDEAS DISCUSSED IN THIS ARTICLE ARE ALSO DISCUSSED IN YOUR TEXTBOOK OR OTHER READING YOU HAVE DONE? LIST THE TEXTBOOK CHAPTERS AND PAGE NUMBERS:

_____

_____

_____

_____

_____

_____

_____

■ LIST ANY EXAMPLES OF BIAS OR FAULTY REASONING THAT YOU FOUND IN THE ARTICLE:

_____

_____

_____

_____

_____

■ LIST ANY NEW TERMS/CONCEPTS THAT WERE DISCUSSED IN THE ARTICLE AND WRITE A SHORT DEFINITION:

_____

_____

_____

_____

_____

ANNUAL EDITIONS:
DRUGS, SOCIETY, AND BEHAVIOR 91/92
Article Rating Form

Here is an opportunity for you to have direct input into the next revision of this volume. We would like you to rate each of the 55 articles listed below, using the following scale:

1. Excellent: should definitely be retained
2. Above average: should probably be retained
3. Below average: should probably be deleted
4. Poor: should definitely be deleted

Your ratings will play a vital part in the next revision. So please mail this prepaid form to us just as soon as you complete it.
Thanks for your help!

Rating	Article
	1. Drugs 'R' Us
	2. Getting Real About Getting High
	3. Grandma Was a Junkie
	4. Illicit Price of Cocaine in Two Eras
	5. Cycles of Craving
	6. Drugs: The World Picture
	7. Interview With James Schaefer
	8. Addiction and Dependence
	9. Drugs of Choice
	10. A Dirty Drug Secret
	11. The Biological Tangle of Drug Addiction
	12. Recognizing Everyday Addictions
	13. Alcoholism: The Mythical Disease
	14. Nicotine Becomes Addictive
	15. Street-Wise Crack Research
	16. High Times in the Wild Kingdom
	17. The Lure of Drugs: They 'Organize' An Addict's Life
	18. Intoxicating Habits
	19. Roots of Addiction
	20. Second Thoughts About a Gene for Alcoholism
	21. A Pleasurable Chemistry
	22. Drug Use, Drinking, and Smoking: National Survey Results from High School, College, and Young Adults Population
	23. Epidemiology of Alcohol Consumption, National Institute on Alcohol Abuse and Alcoholism, Alcohol and Health
	24. Smoking Becomes 'Deviant Behavior'
	25. Rich vs. Poor: Drug Patterns Are Diverging
	26. The Streets Are Filled With Coke
	27. The How and Why of a Cocaine High
	28. What Crack Is Like

Rating	Article
	29. The Fire of 'Ice'
	30. The New Drug They Call 'Ecstasy'
	31. Marijuana
	32. Hooked on Over-the-Counter Drugs
	33. Understanding Alcohol, There's More to This Than Just Saying No
	34. Using Heroin: Two Accounts
	35. Alcohol and the Family
	36. How Smoking Kills You
	37. The Crack Children
	38. In Cities, Poor Families Are Dying of Crack
	39. Is Coffee Harmful?
	40. Advertising Addiction: The Alcohol Industry's Hard Sell
	41. The Teflon Coating of Cigarette Companies
	42. Coke Inc.: Inside the Big Business of Drugs
	43. Tales of the Crank Trade
	44. The Perilous Swim in Heroin's Stream
	45. Drugs: Searching for an Answer
	46. How to Win the War on Drugs
	47. Facing Up to Drugs: Is Legalization the Solution?
	48. Against the Legalization of Drugs
	49. The Dutch Model
	50. Judgment Replaces Fear in Drug Lessons
	51. In Making Drug Strategy, No Accord on Treatment
	52. Getting Clean: A New Generation Fights Addiction
	53. Out in the Open
	54. Binding Together Addicts' Lives
	55. Healing Scars of Parental Drinking

(Continued on next page)

ABOUT YOU

Name_____ Date_____

Are you a teacher? ☐ Or student? ☐

Your School Name _____

Department _____

Address _____

City _____ State _____ Zip _____

School Telephone # _____

YOUR COMMENTS ARE IMPORTANT TO US!

Please fill in the following information:

For which course did you use this book? _____

Did you use a text with this Annual Edition? ☐ yes ☐ no

The title of the text? _____

What are your general reactions to the Annual Editions concept?

Have you read any particular articles recently that you think should be included in the next edition?

Are there any articles you feel should be replaced in the next edition? Why?

Are there other areas that you feel would utilize an Annual Edition?

May we contact you for editorial input?

May we quote you from above?